MW01195696

The United States-Mexico-Canada Agreement (USMCA)

The United States-Mexico-Canada Agreement (USMCA)

Legal and Business Implications

Leslie Alan Glick

Published by:
Kluwer Law International B.V.
PO Box 316
2400 AH Alphen aan den Rijn
The Netherlands
E-mail: international-sales@wolterskluwer.com
Website: lrus.wolterskluwer.com

Sold and distributed by:
Wolters Kluwer Legal & Regulatory U.S.
7201 McKinney Circle
Frederick, MD 21704
United States of America
Email: customer.service@wolterskluwer.com

Printed on acid-free paper.

ISBN 978-94-035-1475-8

e-Book: ISBN 978-94-035-1485-7
web-PDF: ISBN 978-94-035-1495-6

Printed and bound by CPI Group (UK) Ltd, Croydon, CR0 4YY

About the Author

Leslie Alan Glick received a B.S. degree from Cornell University, New York, and Juris Doctor Degree from Cornell Law School. After a judicial clerkship, he entered private law practice in Washington, D.C., where he has served as a partner/shareholder in several law firms. He also served as counsel to a Congressional committee and Special Assistant Attorney General of the State of Maryland, where he resides. He has been active in the American Bar Association as co-chair of two different committees: the Mexico Committee and The Customs Committee.

He is the author of several books, including "Understanding the North American Free Trade Agreement" and "Guide to U.S. Customs and Trade Laws," both of which were published in 3 editions by Kluwer Law International and are still available.

Table of Contents

Table of Contents

Preface

After much expectation and delays, July 1, 2020 was the official date of the new United States-Mexico-Canada Agreement ("USMCA"). Some groups, particularly within the automotive industry that faces newly revised and stricter rules of origin, wanted to see a later implementation date to provide more time for adjustment. However, the fact that an agreement was reached was a significant achievement given the politically charged atmosphere and polarization of the two major U.S. Political Parties on most issues, including a bruising impeachment battle.

Much of the credit for approval of USMCA by the U.S. Congress is due to Ambassador Robert Lighthizer, who managed to create a strong relationship with the U.S. Congress and Majority leader, Pelosi. There were major issues that, in the later stages of Congressional debate and approval, proved difficult. U.S. labor unions whose support is traditionally given to the Democratic Parties insisted on major reforms in the Mexican labor laws, and in the later days of discussion, focused on the enforceability of those laws by Mexico. This was a sensitive issue but was addressed in Mexico by their President, Andres Manuel Lopez Obredor (often referred to as AMLO), who was at earlier stages viewed by some in the United States as anti-North American Free Trade Agreement (NAFTA), but later proved to give important support. He shepherded the labor reforms through the Mexican Congress controlled by his own party. He was able to convince U.S. labor leaders who visited Mexico to trust the Mexican government with the enforcement of these laws. At the time of preparing this introduction, there appeared to be some internal challenges to these labor reform in the Mexican Supreme Court. Elections in Canada involved USMCA issues as Canada opened its very protected agricultural and particularly dairy sector to more U.S. competition. However, in the end, the agreement was praised by the three countries as a positive achievement. For President Trump, who campaigned against NAFTA, he kept his promise of replacing NAFTA. It was carefully given a new name, and the word trade was not included in its title to distance it from NAFTA.

Most American business groups, such as the National Association of Manufacturers and the Business Roundtable, supported it as a new modernized NAFTA pointing out that NAFTA was agreed to before the digital. The USMCA has a chapter on digital trade, which was entirely new. On the other hand, most business groups in the U.S. supported the NAFTA dispute mechanisms that were considerably diminished in the USMCA. One of the most significant changes, the stricter rules of origin for the automotive sectors, was eventually accepted by all concerned and recognized by at least some in Mexico as actually protecting them from competition from Asia. Probably one of the most controversial provisions was the new labor value content requirement requiring an average USD 16 minimum wage in auto plants to qualify for NAFTA benefits, much higher than the existing minimum wage in Mexico. This was considered a victory for the U.S. labor unions that traditionally had been concerned about the loss of jobs to lower-wage plants in Mexico.

There are many hopes and expectations for USMCA as the only multilateral trade agreement currently supported by the Trump Administration as negotiations with the European Union, United Kingdom, Brazil, and Kenya are being pursued.

Acknowledgments

I wish to thank all the people that assisted with work on this book. Three law students from the Columbus School of Law at Catholic University were of invaluable assistance through various stages of writing, editing and proofreading this manuscript: Tierny Walls, Morgan Willard, and Kennedy Davis, as well as two promising pre-law students, Daniel Sarfaraz, a student at Indiana University, and Darian Sarfaraz, a student at the University of Colorado, Boulder, both of whom made significant contributions to this book.

I also thank the people at Kluwer who shepherded me through this, my seventh individual book for Kluwer, three editions of Understanding NAFTA, and three editions of Guide to U.S. Customs and Trade Laws, not including a book for which I was a co-editor. These include Kiran N. Gore, here in Washington, and Simon Bellamy in London, and Mrs. Sudha and her staff in India that did the final editing.

I am privileged to have this long relationship with Kluwer, whose reputation in the international law field is well recognized throughout the world.

CHAPTER 1

Introduction: Summary of the Previous NAFTA Agreement

The North American Free Trade Agreement ("NAFTA") was a trade agreement between the United States, Canada, and Mexico. It became effective January 1, 1994. Modifications and the addition of new countries to the Agreement were to be approved by all member countries. The implementation of NAFTA came with many changes. All tariffs between the three countries were gradually eliminated, depending on the sensitivity of the product; and industrial and agricultural products became eligible for duty-free treatment. NAFTA adopted a rules of origin test, requiring for goods to undergo a change in the tariff classification (tariff shift), they must be sufficiently transformed in a NAFTA country. In addition, in most cases, there was also a regional value content requirement. For instance, in the automotive industry, tariffs were eliminated on cars where at least 62.5% of the content of the car is from one of or in part from one, two or three-member countries. Another set of rules of origin test applies to the textile industry. NAFTA also created protections for investors, financial services, telecommunications, advertising agencies, service industries, service providers, and intellectual property. Some of the protections include national treatment and most-favored nation (MFN) treatment. Additionally, NAFTA incorporated mechanisms to resolve disputes between the countries, settle investment disputes, regulate financial services by financial institutions, and enforce sanitation. There were also supplemental agreements to NAFTA; these included the Environmental Side Agreement and the Labor Side Agreement. Finally, in 2005 there was an effort to expand cooperation between the countries; this was known as the Security and Prosperity Partnership ("SPP"). However, very little was done with the SPP, and it never saw fruition. Some critics in the U.S. feared it would weaken U.S. sovereignty by creating a multinational government.

The North American Free Trade Agreement ("NAFTA") was a trade agreement between the United States, Canada, and Mexico. It became effective on January 1, 1994, after being adopted by all three countries independently.[1] It expired on the effective date of its successor agreement, the United States-Mexico-Canada Agreement

---

1. *See* Leslie Alan Glick, Understanding the North American Free Trade Agreement (Kluwer L. Int'l) (3d ed. 2010).

("USMCA"), which took effect on July 1, 2020, which is the main focus of this book. Some (although not in the Trump Administration) refer to the USMCA as NAFTA 2.0. While it is hoped that many of you have read my previous book on NAFTA referred to in footnote 1, since many of you may not have, I am beginning this book with a discussion of NAFTA as it is difficult to truly understand the USMCA without some understanding of its predecessor, NAFTA. Also, the third and last edition of the book was in 2010, so there are some new developments to discuss. Since later chapters point out changes in the USMCA from NAFTA, it is hoped that these introductory sections, which in large part summarize the contents of the third and last edition of the book, will be beneficial in understanding USMCA, which proponents call "a modernized NAFTA."

§1.1   CHAPTER 1: THE NORTH AMERICAN FREE TRADE AGREEMENT—WHAT IT IS AND WHAT IT ISN'T

The United States extended the use of "Fast Track"[2] legislation for NAFTA in 1991, which allowed the legislation to be approved within ninety legislative days.[3] Mexico and Canada passed the legislation through their respective legislative processes with little opposition.[4] NAFTA was never meant to be an economic union; it was only meant to be a trade agreement to increase economic growth in all three countries.[5] While many critics of NAFTA contend that it has hurt the U.S. economy, most economists agree that it has actually helped the U.S. economy because it has kept many manufacturing companies from going out of business, and while there have been some low-skill jobs moving from the U.S. to Mexico, there have been many additional high-skill jobs created in the U.S. as sales increase.[6] NAFTA itself did not impose any environmental standards, which could cause more companies to move jobs to Mexico since the environmental standards were, at least initially, lower there than in the U.S. or Canada.[7] However, in order to obtain the passage of NAFTA, there was a separate environmental side agreement.[8] U.S. President Bush and Mexican President Salinas created an environmental plan for the border concerning waste management and pollution issues.[9] The NAFTA members are also bound by international agreements, such as the Montreal Protocol on Substances that Deplete the Ozone Layer and the

---

2. "Fast Track" refers to a law,, that was intended to give greater authority to the president to negotiate trade agreements that would not be subject to amendment by Congress. It initially expired in 2007. *See* Free Trade Act of 1974 § 151. It was renewed again on Jun. 29, 2015 when President Obama signed the Bipartisan Congressional Trade Priorities and Accountability Act of 2015 (PL 114-26). Fast track allows congress to vote only yes or no but not to amend.
3. *See* Leslie Alan Glick, Understanding the North American Free Trade Agreement 6 (2010).
4. *See* Leslie Alan Glick, Understanding the North American Free Trade Agreement 6 (2010).
5. *See* Leslie Alan Glick, Understanding the North American Free Trade Agreement 3 (2010).
6. *See* Leslie Alan Glick, Understanding the North American Free Trade Agreement 4 (2010).
7. *See* Leslie Alan Glick, Understanding the North American Free Trade Agreement 5 (2010).
8. *See* Leslie Alan Glick, Understanding the North American Free Trade Agreement 4 (2010).
9. *See* Leslie Alan Glick, Understanding the North American Free Trade Agreement 4 (2010).

Basel Convention on the Control of Trans-boundary Movements of Hazardous Wastes and Their Disposal.[10]

There are also amendments in NAFTA that allow for modification or additions to the Agreement when approved by all member countries.[11] A member of NAFTA could withdraw six months after providing written notice.[12] Notably, President Trump has threatened such action on several occasions as a negotiation strategy.[13] Additionally, with member approval, a country or group of countries could join NAFTA, subject to terms and conditions agreed to by the countries involved.[14]

U.S. labor unions have always been critical of NAFTA.[15] However, the initial negotiators of NAFTA did not address labor standards.[16] The Labor Side agreement establishes its own commission relating to labor disputes.[17] It was known as the North American Agreement on Labor Cooperation ("NAALC") and allowed a Mexican civil society group to bring a complaint to the Department of Labor in Canada or in the U.S. regarding Mexican non-compliance.[18] However, only three of the eleven labor principles mentioned in the agreement give rise to potential trade-suspension sanctions.[19] Critics further noted that the agreement did not include "widely recognized" International Labor Organization rights.[20] One of the major changes labor unions promoted in the USMCA is an increase in wages. (Id.) Union leaders believed an increase in wages would ensure a "level playing field."[21]

Lastly, NAFTA created a method of resolving disputes between the member countries.[22] NAFTA's dispute resolution mechanisms were similar to the provisions in the U.S.-Canada Free Trade Agreement ("USCFTA"), which was a predecessor of NAFTA, but several changes were made.[23] NAFTA created a Free Trade Commission composed of cabinet-level officials or their designees.[24] The Commission oversaw the implementation and operation of NAFTA and supervised all committees and working

---

10. *See* Leslie Alan Glick, Understanding the North American Free Trade Agreement 4 (2010).
11. *See* Leslie Alan Glick, Understanding the North American Free Trade Agreement 7 (2010).
12. *See* Leslie Alan Glick, Understanding the North American Free Trade Agreement 7 (2010).
13. *See* Trump, Donald (@realDonaldTrump) "There is no political necessity to keep Canada in the new NAFTA deal. If we don't make a fair deal for the U.S. after decades of abuse, Canada will be out. Congress should not interfere w/ these negotiations or I will simply terminate NAFTA entirely & we will be far better off…" (Sep. 1, 2018); *see also* Remarks by President Trump in Press Gaggle Aboard Air Force One, White House (Dec. 2, 2018) https://www.whitehouse.gov /briefings-statements/remarks-president-trump-press-gaggle-aboard-air-force-one-2/.
14. *See* Leslie Alan Glick, Understanding the North American Free Trade Agreement 7 (2010).
15. *See* Leslie Alan Glick, Understanding the North American Free Trade Agreement 4 (2010).
16. *See* Leslie Alan Glick, Understanding the North American Free Trade Agreement 97 (2010).
17. Leslie Alan Glick, Understanding the North American Free Trade Agreement 8 (2010).
18. *See* Mark Aspinwall, Learning From The Experience of NAFTA Labor And Environmental Governance, Forbes (Aug. 10, 2017).
19. *See* Mark Aspinwall, Learning From The Experience of NAFTA Labor And Environmental Governance (Aug. 10, 2017).
20. *See* Mark Aspinwall, Learning From The Experience of NAFTA Labor And Environmental Governance (Aug. 10, 2017).
21. *See* Eduardo Porter, Labor Wants to Make Nafta Its Friend. Here's the Problem, The New York Times (Aug. 22, 2017).
22. *See* Leslie Alan Glick, Understanding the North American Free Trade Agreement 8 (2010).
23. *See* Leslie Alan Glick, Understanding the North American Free Trade Agreement 8 (2010).
24. *See* Leslie Alan Glick, Understanding the North American Free Trade Agreement 8 (2010).

groups created under the Agreement, including resolution of disputes.[25] There was also a permanent Trilateral Secretariat to assist the Commission.[26] Cooperation to resolve disputes was strongly encouraged, as the first step in a resolution required the Parties to proceed through a period of consultation and negotiation.[27] If consultation does not work, the Parties could request a meeting of the Free Trade Commission to use its expert advice.[28]

If the Parties could not resolve their differences through the Commission or through consultations, a Party could request that the matter be referred to an arbitration panel composed of legal, trade, and other experts, including nationals from non-Parties.[29] The arbitration results were non-binding, as the Parties had fourteen days after receiving the decision to submit comments to the panel.[30] Then, after a final report is written, the Parties were free to continue negotiating.[31]

§1.2   CHAPTER 2: "NAFTA—WHAT CHANGES WERE MADE"

All tariffs between the three NAFTA countries were gradually eliminated over the course of fifteen years, depending on the sensitivity of the product.[32] About 65% of U.S. industrial and agricultural exports to Mexico were eligible for duty-free treatment either immediately or within five years.[33] Mexican products that entered the U.S. duty-free under the Generalized System of Preferences ("GSP") obtained immediate duty-free treatment under NAFTA.[34] The GSP program was terminated for Mexico when NAFTA was implemented in 1994.[35]

The automotive industry was one of the more sensitive areas that NAFTA addressed.[36] Even before NAFTA, there has been considerable integration between the three countries in automotive parts and vehicles.[37] The U.S. already had an automotive agreement with Canada allowing duty-free importation of Canadian-manufactured vehicles, and NAFTA incorporates that agreement.[38] NAFTA eliminated restrictions on importations of U.S. vehicles to Mexico, and all three countries slowly eliminated tariffs on new and used cars where at least 62.5% of the content of the car is made from parts and labor from the U.S., Canada, or Mexico.[39] This is greater than the 50% content requirement under prior agreement with Canada, USCFTA.[40] These rules made it more

25. *See* Leslie Alan Glick, Understanding the North American Free Trade Agreement 8 (2010).
26. *See* Leslie Alan Glick, Understanding the North American Free Trade Agreement 8 (2010).
27. *See* Leslie Alan Glick, Understanding the North American Free Trade Agreement 9 (2010).
28. *See* Leslie Alan Glick, Understanding the North American Free Trade Agreement 9 (2010).
29. *See* Leslie Alan Glick, Understanding the North American Free Trade Agreement 9 (2010).
30. *See* Leslie Alan Glick, Understanding the North American Free Trade Agreement 9 (2010).
31. *See* Leslie Alan Glick, Understanding the North American Free Trade Agreement 9 (2010).
32. *See* Leslie Alan Glick, Understanding the North American Free Trade Agreement 11 (2010).
33. *See* Leslie Alan Glick, Understanding the North American Free Trade Agreement 11 (2010).
34. *See* Leslie Alan Glick, Understanding the North American Free Trade Agreement 11 (2010).
35. *See* Leslie Alan Glick, Understanding the North American Free Trade Agreement 12 (2010).
36. *See* Leslie Alan Glick, Understanding the North American Free Trade Agreement 13 (2010).
37. *See* Leslie Alan Glick, Understanding the North American Free Trade Agreement 13 (2010).
38. *See* Leslie Alan Glick, Understanding the North American Free Trade Agreement 13 (2010).
39. *See* Leslie Alan Glick, Understanding the North American Free Trade Agreement 14 (2010).
40. *See* Leslie Alan Glick, Understanding the North American Free Trade Agreement 14 (2010).

difficult for European and Japanese cars to produce products in Mexico to export to the United States and Canada unless they use parts that are made in North America.[41] The rules of origin are one of the major areas revised in the new USMCA. A more comprehensive discussion of the USMCA rules of origin for autos is in Chapter 5.

For the textile industry, customs duties were slowly phased out, and quotas were removed immediately on products that met a more stringent rules of origin test.[42] Under the NAFTA test, for garments to qualify for duty-free treatment as NAFTA products, they had to meet a double rules of origin test.[43] First, the yarn must be made in one of the NAFTA countries, and second, the cutting and sewing must be done in one of the NAFTA countries.[44] This essentially limited foreign textile interests from receiving NAFTA benefits.[45] This test is called the "Yarn Forward" requirement.[46] If garments did not meet the requirements of this test, they were subject to tariff-rate quotas.[47]

NAFTA included specific Bilateral Emergency Actions with regard to Tariff Actions and Quantitative Restrictions.[48] Under Quantitative Restrictions, one Party may request consultations with another Party to review the allegedly damaging imported goods.[49] If an agreement cannot be reached within ninety days, the complaining Party may impose annual quantitative restrictions on imports within certain guidelines.[50]

NAFTA was probably the first agreement of its kind that included significant protections for investors.[51] Investment covers many types of ownership and interest in a business enterprise, tangible and intangible property, and contracted investment interests.[52] The Agreement contained nondiscrimination clauses that required nationals of each of the three signatory countries to be treated equally in terms of a country's investment laws and regulations—this is called national treatment.[53] Additionally, the Parties have agreed to a most-favored-nation (MFN) treatment policy.[54] MFN provides that each Party shall accord to investors of any other Party treatment no less favorable than it accords to investors of another Party or non-Party.[55]

MFN and national treatment do not prevent a Party from adopting or maintaining special formalities in connection with the establishment of investments by another Party, nor is a Party precluded from requiring that an investor of another Party provide

---

41. *See* Leslie Alan Glick, Understanding the North American Free Trade Agreement 14 (2010).
42. *See* Leslie Alan Glick, Understanding the North American Free Trade Agreement 17 (2010).
43. *See* Leslie Alan Glick, Understanding the North American Free Trade Agreement 16 (2010).
44. *See* Leslie Alan Glick, Understanding the North American Free Trade Agreement 16 (2010).
45. *See* Leslie Alan Glick, Understanding the North American Free Trade Agreement 16 (2010).
46. *See* Leslie Alan Glick, Understanding the North American Free Trade Agreement 16 (2010).
47. *See* Leslie Alan Glick, Understanding the North American Free Trade Agreement 17 (2010).
48. *See* Leslie Alan Glick, Understanding the North American Free Trade Agreement 17 (2010).
49. *See* Leslie Alan Glick, Understanding the North American Free Trade Agreement 17 (2010).
50. *See* Leslie Alan Glick, Understanding the North American Free Trade Agreement 17 (2010).
51. *See* Leslie Alan Glick, Understanding the North American Free Trade Agreement 18 (2010).
52. *See* Leslie Alan Glick, Understanding the North American Free Trade Agreement 18 (2010).
53. *See* Leslie Alan Glick, Understanding the North American Free Trade Agreement 18 (2010).
54. *See* Leslie Alan Glick, Understanding the North American Free Trade Agreement 18 (2010).
55. *See* Leslie Alan Glick, Understanding the North American Free Trade Agreement 18 (2010).

business information to be used solely for informational or statistical purposes.[56] However, all matters must not be such as to impair or hinder the substance of the benefits accorded to the Parties under the Agreement.[57] NAFTA eliminated all performance requirements, including exporting a given level or percentage of goods or services.[58] The investment and free convertibility of currency were also guaranteed under NAFTA.[59]

There was also a mechanism under NAFTA to settle investment disputes before an impartial tribunal, giving Parties equal treatment and due process of law.[60] Basically, an investor could submit to arbitration a claim that another Party has breached, the agreement as it pertains to investments, and the loss or damages that the investor had incurred because of the breach.[61] Before submitting a claim, the Parties had to attempt to resolve their situation through consultations and negotiation.[62] If it went to arbitration, then it is heard by an impartial tribunal.[63] This investment chapter was changed considerably in the new USMCA.

NAFTA established a comprehensive approach to government disciplinary measures regulating the provision of financial services by financial institutions in the banking, insurance, and securities sectors.[64] Each Party was obligated to provide national treatment and MFN treatment to other NAFTA financial service providers operating within its borders.[65] Essentially, financial service providers of a NAFTA country could designate and establish financial services in any other NAFTA country.[66] These service providers could own the established financial institutions without the application of ownership requirements specific to foreign financial institutions.[67] This provision enabled U.S. banks and securities firms to establish wholly owned Mexican subsidiaries for the first time in fifty years.[68] Many of the same provisions apply to insurance providers.[69]

Under NAFTA, the Mexican telecommunications service and equipment industry was opened to competition.[70] Each Party to the Agreement agreed to ensure that persons of another Party have access to and use of any public telecommunications network or service offered in its territory or across its borders for the conduct of their business under reasonable and nondiscriminatory terms and conditions.[71] This does

---

56. *See* Leslie Alan Glick, Understanding the North American Free Trade Agreement 18 (2010).
57. *See* Leslie Alan Glick, Understanding the North American Free Trade Agreement 18-19 (2010).
58. *See* Leslie Alan Glick, Understanding the North American Free Trade Agreement 19 (2010).
59. *See* Leslie Alan Glick, Understanding the North American Free Trade Agreement 19 (2010).
60. *See* Leslie Alan Glick, Understanding the North American Free Trade Agreement 20 (2010).
61. *See* Leslie Alan Glick, Understanding the North American Free Trade Agreement 20 (2010).
62. *See* Leslie Alan Glick, Understanding the North American Free Trade Agreement 21 (2010).
63. *See* Leslie Alan Glick, Understanding the North American Free Trade Agreement 21 (2010).
64. *See* Leslie Alan Glick, Understanding the North American Free Trade Agreement 34 (2010).
65. *See* Leslie Alan Glick, Understanding the North American Free Trade Agreement 35 (2010).
66. *See* Leslie Alan Glick, Understanding the North American Free Trade Agreement 35 (2010).
67. *See* Leslie Alan Glick, Understanding the North American Free Trade Agreement 35 (2010).
68. *See* Leslie Alan Glick, Understanding the North American Free Trade Agreement 36 (2010).
69. *See* Leslie Alan Glick, Understanding the North American Free Trade Agreement 37 (2010).
70. *See* Leslie Alan Glick, Understanding the North American Free Trade Agreement 37 (2010).
71. *See* Leslie Alan Glick, Understanding the North American Free Trade Agreement 38 (2010).

not mean that a Party could not designate a monopoly to provide public telecommunications networks or services; however, such a monopoly may not abuse its power by engaging in anticompetitive behavior that adversely affects persons of another Party.[72]

With regard to energy, NAFTA respected the Mexican constitution, which limited foreign investment into its energy sector.[73] The provisions on energy are based upon World Trade Organization ("WTO") principles, including quantitative restrictions on energy and petrochemical imports and exports.[74] A country may develop import and export licensing requirements in accordance with the Agreement.[75] Imported goods may not be taxed or given a duty unless a domestic good is treated the same way.[76]

Advertising agencies and service industries from NAFTA countries received no less favorable treatment than domestic companies.[77] NAFTA also eliminated local presence laws, so an industry does not have to have any presence in the foreign state to receive benefits.[78]

Under NAFTA, there had been a liberalization of trade in services.[79] The service providers of one NAFTA country were required to accord to service providers of another NAFTA country treatment no less favorable than it accorded to its own service providers.[80] Each Party was also obligated under the Agreement to liberalize quantitative restrictions, licensing requirements, performance requirements, or other nondiscriminatory measures relating to the cross-border provision of a service.[81]

The automotive industry experienced big changes under NAFTA.[82] Before NAFTA, the U.S. and Canadian truck drivers were not permitted to carry cargo into Mexico.[83] Instead, trailers had to be switched to Mexican cabs with Mexican drivers at the border.[84]

This applied to Mexican trucks crossing into the U.S. as well. Each party had exclusive rights to strictly internal transportation in its own country.[85] This new provision was the source of considerable concern for the U.S. truck drivers' unions and some owner-operators who brought legal challenges to it based on the alleged lack of safety standards for Mexican trucks and their drivers. They had support from some members of the House of Representatives Transportation and Infrastructure Committee who, at times, blocked funds for the U.S. to determine Mexican truck and driver safety to implement the NAFTA provision. This battle that continued for years, with various court appeals, represented one of the lower points in NAFTA cooperation. There is access between all three countries for busses, and there is a set of integrated

---

72. *See* Leslie Alan Glick, Understanding the North American Free Trade Agreement 39 (2010).
73. *See* Leslie Alan Glick, Understanding the North American Free Trade Agreement 39 (2010).
74. *See* Leslie Alan Glick, Understanding the North American Free Trade Agreement 39 (2010).
75. *See* Leslie Alan Glick, Understanding the North American Free Trade Agreement 39 (2010).
76. *See* Leslie Alan Glick, Understanding the North American Free Trade Agreement 40 (2010).
77. *See* Leslie Alan Glick, Understanding the North American Free Trade Agreement 40 (2010).
78. *See* Leslie Alan Glick, Understanding the North American Free Trade Agreement 40 (2010).
79. *See* Leslie Alan Glick, Understanding the North American Free Trade Agreement 40 (2010).
80. *See* Leslie Alan Glick, Understanding the North American Free Trade Agreement 41 (2010).
81. *See* Leslie Alan Glick, Understanding the North American Free Trade Agreement 41 (2010).
82. *See* Leslie Alan Glick, Understanding the North American Free Trade Agreement 42 (2010).
83. *See* Leslie Alan Glick, Understanding the North American Free Trade Agreement 43 (2010).
84. *See* Leslie Alan Glick, Understanding the North American Free Trade Agreement 43 (2010).
85. *See* Leslie Alan Glick, Understanding the North American Free Trade Agreement 44 (2010).

safety standards and an oversight committee to make sure that all countries are conforming to a certain safety threshold.[86]

For Intellectual Property ("IP"), NAFTA established a high level of obligations for IP protection.[87] Each country was required to provide adequate and effective protection, treating foreign applicants the same as their nationals, and providing effective enforcement of their rights.[88]

NAFTA also established measures relating to the enforcement of sanitary and phytosanitary measures to protect humans, animals, and plants.[89] Each country uses international standards, such as the Codex Alimentarius Commission and the North American Plant Protection Organization.[90] A Committee on Sanitary and Phytosanitary Measures will oversee the facilitation of the use of international standards and equivalence, technical cooperation, and food and sanitary and phytosanitary conditions.[91]

Lastly, under NAFTA, there was an increased ability for companies from NAFTA countries to bid on each other's government projects.[92] However, there was also an attempt to limit European and Asian producers from benefitting from this agreement by making defined rules of origin requirements.[93] For a car to qualify for NAFTA benefits, 62.5% of the car had to be made from NAFTA content.[94] There were also tracing rules and rules that required manufacturers to maintain certificates of origins.[95]

§1.3   CHAPTER 3: RULES OF ORIGIN, VALUATION, AND CUSTOMS DUTIES—WHAT YOU NEED TO KNOW TO UNDERSTAND THE RULES OF ORIGIN

Chapter three focuses on the rules of origin requirements. There were different tests for the rules of origin under NAFTA and the prior GSP.[96] GSP, established under the Trade Act of 1974, sets out a list of products eligible for duty-free treatment for developing countries that included Mexico prior to NAFTA.[97] To be on the list, the product must be made from a Beneficiary Developing Country ("BDC"), meaning it must be a product of that country, and it must be directly imported to the U.S. from that country.[98] The President has the authority to decide which countries qualify as a BDC country.[99] If the product is not clearly produced in that country, it is presumed not to be from the

---

86. *See* Leslie Alan Glick, Understanding the North American Free Trade Agreement 45 (2010).
87. *See* Leslie Alan Glick, Understanding the North American Free Trade Agreement 48 (2010).
88. *See* Leslie Alan Glick, Understanding the North American Free Trade Agreement 48 (2010).
89. *See* Leslie Alan Glick, Understanding the North American Free Trade Agreement 49 (2010).
90. *See* Leslie Alan Glick, Understanding the North American Free Trade Agreement 50 (2010).
91. *See* Leslie Alan Glick, Understanding the North American Free Trade Agreement 50 (2010).
92. *See* Leslie Alan Glick, Understanding the North American Free Trade Agreement 50 (2010).
93. *See* Leslie Alan Glick, Understanding the North American Free Trade Agreement 53 (2010).
94. *See* Leslie Alan Glick, Understanding the North American Free Trade Agreement 54 (2010).
95. *See* Leslie Alan Glick, Understanding the North American Free Trade Agreement 55 (2010).
96. *See* Leslie Alan Glick, Understanding the North American Free Trade Agreement 58 (2010).
97. *See* Leslie Alan Glick, Understanding the North American Free Trade Agreement 58 (2010).
98. *See* Leslie Alan Glick, Understanding the North American Free Trade Agreement 59 (2010).
99. *See* Leslie Alan Glick, Understanding the North American Free Trade Agreement 59 (2010).

country.[100] Manufacturers under NAFTA were required to trace their North American content, thereby ensuring that the real North American content level is accurately calculated.[101]

NAFTA had different rules of origin than GSP for which Mexico was considered a designated beneficiary country prior to NAFTA.[102] Goods must be sufficiently transformed in a NAFTA country so as to undergo a sufficient change in the tariff classification.[103] In certain cases, the good must include a specific percentage of North American content.[104] For instance, in the automotive industry, NAFTA required 62.5% of the automobile to be made from North America for passenger automobiles and light trucks.[105]

For textiles, NAFTA required that for a textile to receive preferential tariff treatment, it must be "yarn forward".[106] This means that textiles and apparel goods must be produced from yarn made in a NAFTA country.[107] There was also a Fiber Forward requirement that applies to cotton and man-made fiber yarns.[108]

To receive preferential treatment under NAFTA, the importer was required to make a written declaration upon entry about the country of origination of the merchandise.[109] At the time of importation, the importer should have a valid certificate of origin.[110] If the exporter is not the producer of the merchandise, it may complete the certificate of origin based on its knowledge about the origination of the good, and its reasonable reliance on the producer's written representation about the origination of the good.[111]

NAFTA allowed the Parties to continue applying their own domestic law in antidumping and countervailing duty determinations.[112] However, Parties were to notify each other in advance of any statutory changes to significant trade laws.[113] Also, under NAFTA, binational panels were formed that substituted for domestic judicial review where either the importing or exporting country seeks a panel review of a determination.[114] The binational panels applied the same standard of review and general legal principles as the domestic law of the importing country, except in Canada.[115]

---

100. *See* Leslie Alan Glick, Understanding the North American Free Trade Agreement 59 (2010).
101. *See* Leslie Alan Glick, Understanding the North American Free Trade Agreement 63 (2010).
102. *See* Leslie Alan Glick, Understanding the North American Free Trade Agreement 62 (2010).
103. *See* Leslie Alan Glick, Understanding the North American Free Trade Agreement 62 (2010).
104. *See* Leslie Alan Glick, Understanding the North American Free Trade Agreement 62 (2010).
105. *See* Leslie Alan Glick, Understanding the North American Free Trade Agreement 62 (2010).
106. *See* Leslie Alan Glick, Understanding the North American Free Trade Agreement 63 (2010).
107. *See* Leslie Alan Glick, Understanding the North American Free Trade Agreement 63 (2010).
108. *See* Leslie Alan Glick, Understanding the North American Free Trade Agreement 63 (2010).
109. *See* Leslie Alan Glick, Understanding the North American Free Trade Agreement 63 (2010).
110. *See* Leslie Alan Glick, Understanding the North American Free Trade Agreement 63 (2010).
111. *See* Leslie Alan Glick, Understanding the North American Free Trade Agreement 63 (2010).
112. *See* Leslie Alan Glick, Understanding the North American Free Trade Agreement 67 (2010).
113. *See* Leslie Alan Glick, Understanding the North American Free Trade Agreement 67 (2010).
114. *See* Leslie Alan Glick, Understanding the North American Free Trade Agreement 67 (2010).
115. *See* Leslie Alan Glick, Understanding the North American Free Trade Agreement 67 (2010).

For agriculture, Mexico and the United States eliminated all non-tariff barriers.[116] Between Mexico and Canada, all non-tariff barriers were eliminated except for dairy, egg, poultry, and sugar.[117] NAFTA did not address agriculture between the United States and Canada, and instead, the USCFTA still applied.[118] This was a major area of reform in the USMCA, allowing increased access into Canada for U.S. agricultural, and particularly dairy products. It was a source of considerable internal political opposition in Canada due to the historically protected dairy sector concerns.

NAFTA required the countries to have antitrust laws but did not specify what they had to be.[119] NAFTA still allowed any country to designate a monopoly as long as it does not hurt the interests of the other countries.[120] NAFTA also allowed temporary entry for business persons.[121] However, there are certain requirements that had to be satisfied so that it does not interfere with the country's immigration laws.[122]

§1.4   CHAPTER 4: THE SUPPLEMENTAL AGREEMENTS

NAFTA did not encompass every agreement made between the countries. There were side agreements, including the Environmental Side Agreement and the Labor Side Agreement. The Environmental Side Agreement, signed in 1993, affirmed the commitment of the Parties to sustainable development.[123] The Environmental Side Agreement established a commission for environmental cooperation and enforceable compliance.[124] The commission included a Council, a Secretariat, and a Joint Public Advisory Committee.[125] The Council is the governing body of the Commission.[126] It also included a way to resolve disputes and arbitration requirements. Each Party agreed to equally fund the commission.[127]

The labor side agreement established safeguards enforced by the commission for labor cooperation, governed by a ministerial council.[128] The Agreement addressed issues, such as child labor, health and safety, minimum wage, and industrial relations.[129] In order to complete the goals, the Labor Agreement was centered around three principles: enhancing the collaboration, cooperation, and information exchange among the three countries.[130] Additionally, the Agreement increased efforts to make each country's labor laws and their implementation explicit and transparent.[131] A Party

116. *See* Leslie Alan Glick, Understanding the North American Free Trade Agreement 69 (2010).
117. *See* Leslie Alan Glick, Understanding the North American Free Trade Agreement 70 (2010).
118. *See* Leslie Alan Glick, Understanding the North American Free Trade Agreement 69 (2010).
119. *See* Leslie Alan Glick, Understanding the North American Free Trade Agreement 71 (2010).
120. *See* Leslie Alan Glick, Understanding the North American Free Trade Agreement 71 (2010).
121. *See* Leslie Alan Glick, Understanding the North American Free Trade Agreement 72 (2010).
122. *See* Leslie Alan Glick, Understanding the North American Free Trade Agreement 73 (2010).
123. *See* Leslie Alan Glick, Understanding the North American Free Trade Agreement 87 (2010).
124. *See* Leslie Alan Glick, Understanding the North American Free Trade Agreement 87 (2010).
125. *See* Leslie Alan Glick, Understanding the North American Free Trade Agreement 87 (2010).
126. *See* Leslie Alan Glick, Understanding the North American Free Trade Agreement 87 (2010).
127. *See* Leslie Alan Glick, Understanding the North American Free Trade Agreement 87 (2010).
128. *See* Leslie Alan Glick, Understanding the North American Free Trade Agreement 100 (2010).
129. *See* Leslie Alan Glick, Understanding the North American Free Trade Agreement 99 (2010).
130. *See* Leslie Alan Glick, Understanding the North American Free Trade Agreement 99 (2010).
131. *See* Leslie Alan Glick, Understanding the North American Free Trade Agreement 99 (2010).

could withdraw from the Labor Agreement six months after it provided written notice of the withdrawal to other Parties.[132]

A big concern in the U.S. with NAFTA was because of the lower tariffs and duties. However, NAFTA had built-in safeguards to combat this fear. NAFTA set up bilateral safeguards, where a country may suspend further reduction of duty rate or exceed duties up to the MFN rate. There are also global safeguards that apply to all countries. Additionally, NAFTA allowed the countries to have their own antidumping laws. However, NAFTA did establish its own binational panels in case a NAFTA country sought judicial review.

§1.5   CHAPTER 5: POST-NAFTA DEVELOPMENTS

When Senator Obama was running for President in 2008, his position was that NAFTA needed to be renegotiated.[133] However, once he became President, he retreated from this position, most likely because of the economic downturn and financial crisis.[134] He still believed in strengthening NAFTA but did not re-open the Agreement.[135]

In 2005, there was a post-NAFTA effort to expand cooperation between the three countries.[136] This was called the Security and Prosperity Partnership ("SPP").[137] Many believed that this was a precursor to a North American agreement similar to the European Union ("EU").[138] While it lacked formal structure, there were various working groups that developed various recommendations.[139] However, after 2008 very little was done with SPP, and it is was never consummated.[140]

Many groups opposed it, spreading fears of the U.S. losing sovereignty to an EU type arrangement.

---

132. *See* Leslie Alan Glick, Understanding the North American Free Trade Agreement 103 (2010).
133. *See* Leslie Alan Glick, Understanding the North American Free Trade Agreement 117 (2010).
134. *See* Leslie Alan Glick, Understanding the North American Free Trade Agreement 117 (2010).
135. *See* Leslie Alan Glick, Understanding the North American Free Trade Agreement 117 (2010).
136. *See* Leslie Alan Glick, Understanding the North American Free Trade Agreement 118 (2010).
137. *See* Leslie Alan Glick, Understanding the North American Free Trade Agreement 118 (2010).
138. *See* Leslie Alan Glick, Understanding the North American Free Trade Agreement 118 (2010).
139. *See* Leslie Alan Glick, Understanding the North American Free Trade Agreement 118 (2010).
140. *See* Leslie Alan Glick, Understanding the North American Free Trade Agreement 118 (2010).

CHAPTER 2

Summary of NAFTA From 2010 to July 2020

NAFTA had become increasingly unpopular across both political aisles. While economists believe that it had benefited the U.S. economy and strengthened North American competitiveness, some believe that NAFTA caused outsourcing and lower wages for U.S. workers due to Mexico's lower wages and fewer regulations. During the 2016 Presidential campaign, all candidates argued that NAFTA needed to be changed. A major decline in support for NAFTA was caused by an announcement by Carrier, a manufacturing company, that they would close two major factories and move them to Mexico. President Trump revealed a plan to punish Carrier by imposing a 35% tariff on all products that Carrier made from the new plants in Mexico. This overwhelming call to renegotiate, on both sides of the aisle, is what led to the USMCA.

This chapter picks up where the third edition of our previous book left off concerning the developments of NAFTA from 2010 to the present day, and how public sentiment has changed over the course of the past ten years. Overall, NAFTA had become increasingly unpopular and has been the subject of attacks from politicians across both political aisles.

NAFTA has been a controversial agreement since its enactment and continued to be up until its replacement by the USMCA. While many supporters called the USMCA NAFTA 2.0, its opponents wanted no legacy of the NAFTA name. In 2012, presidential candidates spent $68 million attacking NAFTA style trade deals.[141] A May 2012 poll found that 53% of people wanted to renegotiate or leave NAFTA, and only 15% wanted to continue the way it was.[142] Only 1 in 3 people believed NAFTA had benefited the

---

141. *See* NAFTA's Broken Promises 1994-2013: Outcomes of the North American Free Trade Agreement, Public Citizen, https://www.citizen.org/wp-content/uploads/migration/naftas-broken-promises.pdf.
142. *See* NAFTA's Broken Promises 1994-2013: Outcomes of the North American Free Trade Agreement, Public Citizen, https://www.citizen.org/wp-content/uploads/migration/naftas-broken-promises.pdf.

economy as a whole, and only 1 in 4 believed it had benefited U.S. workers.[143] In 1999, 30% of people thought FTAs were bad for the economy, but in 2010 that number increased to 53% of people believing FTAs were bad for the economy.[144]

NAFTA was continuously still a source of tension because, while economists believed that it benefitted the economy, many believed that NAFTA caused outsourcing and lower wages for U.S. workers.[145] This was primarily because of Mexico's lower wages and accusations of lesser environmental and labor standards in comparison to the U.S. People who believed that NAFTA had been a success believed that NAFTA was never meant to alleviate every problem in the economy; instead, they believed that they were better off with NAFTA than without.[146]

During the 2016 Presidential campaign, all of the candidates argued that NAFTA needed to be changed. Donald Trump called NAFTA the worst trade deal the U.S. ever signed.[147] Hillary Clinton, despite the fact that President Bill Clinton presided over NAFTA during his administration, said she would like to renegotiate the agreement, and that there were parts of it that did not work as hoped for.[148] A major decline in support for NAFTA during the campaign was caused by an announcement by Carrier, a manufacturing company, that they would close two major factories and move them to Mexico.[149] Donald Trump quickly revealed a plan to punish the Carrier for this decision by levying a 35% tariff on all products that Carrier made from the new plants in Mexico. The overwhelming call to renegotiate, on both sides of the aisle, was what led to the USMCA.

---

143. *See* NAFTA's Broken Promises 1994-2013: Outcomes of the North American Free Trade Agreement, Public Citizen, https://www.citizen.org/wp-content/uploads/migration/naftas-broken-promises.pdf.

144. *See* NAFTA's Broken Promises 1994-2013: Outcomes of the North American Free Trade Agreement, Public Citizen, https://www.citizen.org/wp-content/uploads/migration/naftas-broken-promises.pdf.

145. *See* Twenty Years Later, Nafta Remains a Source of Tension, New York Times (Dec. 2012), https://www.nytimes.com/2012/12/07/us/twenty-years-later-nafta-remains-a-source-of-tension.html.

146. *See* Twenty Years Later, Nafta Remains a Source of Tension, New York Times (Dec. 2012), https://www.nytimes.com/2012/12/07/us/twenty-years-later-nafta-remains-a-source-of-tension.html.

147. *See* Stephen Gandel, Donald Trump Says NAFTA Was the Worst Trade Deal the U.S. Ever Signed, Fortune (Sep. 27, 2016, 1:02 AM EDT), https://fortune.com/2016/09/27/presidential-debate-nafta-agreement/.

148. *See* Xenia V. Wilkinson, Though it is not the first U.S. election that has really mattered to Mexico, there may be more at stake this time than ever before, (Oct. 2016), https://www.afsa.org/mexico-nafta-and-election-2016.

149. *See* Carl M. Cannon, NAFTA and the Angry Middle-Class Voter, RealClear Politics (Jun. 9, 2016), https://www.realclearpolitics.com/articles/2016/06/09/nafta_and_the_angry_middle-class_voter_130832.html.

CHAPTER 3
NAFTA Economic Impact Summaries

Multiple organizations have published reports on the true economic impact of NAFTA. The Center for Automotive Research ("CAR") argues that even though jobs left for Mexico, the U.S. auto industry benefits because many of the parts are produced in the U.S. and sent to Mexico to be installed. The Congressional Research Service (CRS) concluded that the true effects of NAFTA are hard to determine because of external events that happened during this time; these include the devaluation in the peso and the 2008 financial crisis. The Peterson Institute for International Economics argues that many criticisms of NAFTA are misguided, including the criticism that NAFTA caused a bilateral trade deficit with Mexico. Additionally, it argues that even though 200,000 jobs were lost due to the trade with Mexico, over 180,000 higher-paying jobs were gained. However, the International Monetary Fund argues that the macroeconomic effects of the new USMCA are essentially negligible. It argues that the rules of origin test will result in the price of automobiles to increase. It also indicates that the U.S. will see a drop of USD 85 million due to the new agriculture rules. Finally, it argues that it will cause a small depreciation of the Canadian dollar, no change to the U.S. dollar, and a small depreciation of the Mexican peso. Overall, the data shows a small positive impact on three-member countries.

§3.1   INTRODUCTION

NAFTA was passed in 1994, and since then, multiple organizations have published reports on the true economic impact of the agreement. This chapter introduces the relevant reports on the overall impact of NAFTA on the three-member countries. Overall, the data shows a small positive impact on three-member countries. The U.S. had a slight impact mainly because manufacturing moved to Mexico instead of China, which increased production of U.S. parts and because of lower prices due to increased production in Mexico.

§3.2   NAFTA BRIEFING: TRADE BENEFITS TO THE AUTOMOTIVE INDUSTRY AND POTENTIAL CONSEQUENCES OF WITHDRAWAL FROM THE AGREEMENT—CENTER FOR AUTOMOTIVE RESEARCH JANUARY 2017

The Center for Automotive Research (CAR) published a report in January 2017, analyzing the trade benefits NAFTA had on the U.S. economy.[150] Overall, CAR believed that NAFTA had been a net benefit for the U.S. The argument's main premise was that without NAFTA, automotive jobs would still have left the U.S.—they would have left to other parts of the world like East Asia. However, with NAFTA, the jobs left to Mexico, and the U.S. auto industry benefited because many of the parts were produced in the U.S. and sent to Mexico to be installed. If the automobile was produced in East Asia, the U.S. would not benefit at all due to high shipping costs.

Rising international automotive production in Mexico was viewed as a net gain for U.S. employment since many of the parts were produced in the U.S. and then shipped to Mexico for final assembly.[151] This was the traditional maquiladora concept. Before NAFTA, U.S. content in a vehicle made in Mexico was 5%; after NAFTA, that number had jumped to 40%.[152] Therefore, U.S. suppliers had benefited from increased capacity throughout North America.[153] Additionally, research indicated that a 10% increase in employment at a Mexican affiliate operation led to a 1.3% increase in U.S. employment, a 1.7% increase in U.S. exports, and a 4.1% increase in research and development spending.[154]

Lastly, CAR believed that most of the U.S. jobs lost in the automotive sector were due to increases in technology.[155] This included the use of more robotics that would

---

150. *See* Kristin Dziczek et. al, NAFTA Briefing: Trade benefits to the automotive industry and potential consequences of withdrawal from the agreement, Center for Automotive Research (Jun. 2017), https://www.cargroup.org/wp-content/uploads/2017/01/nafta_briefing_january_2017_public_version-final.pdf.

151. *See* Kristin Dziczek et. al, NAFTA Briefing: Trade benefits to the automotive industry and potential consequences of withdrawal from the agreement, Center for Automotive Research (Jun. 2017) at 7, https://www.cargroup.org/wp-content/uploads/2017/01/nafta_briefing_january_2017_public_version-final.pdf.

152. *See* Kristin Dziczek et. al, NAFTA Briefing: Trade benefits to the automotive industry and potential consequences of withdrawal from the agreement, Center for Automotive Research (Jun. 2017) at 7, https://www.cargroup.org/wp-content/uploads/2017/01/nafta_briefing_january_2017_public_version-final.pdf.

153. *See* Kristin Dziczek et. al, NAFTA Briefing: Trade benefits to the automotive industry and potential consequences of withdrawal from the agreement, Center for Automotive Research (Jun. 2017) at 8, https://www.cargroup.org/wp-content/uploads/2017/01/nafta_briefing_january_2017_public_version-final.pdf.

154. *See* Kristin Dziczek et. al, NAFTA Briefing: Trade benefits to the automotive industry and potential consequences of withdrawal from the agreement, Center for Automotive Research (Jun. 2017) at 8, https://www.cargroup.org/wp-content/uploads/2017/01/nafta_briefing_january_2017_public_version-final.pdf.

155. *See* Kristin Dziczek et. al, NAFTA Briefing: Trade benefits to the automotive industry and potential consequences of withdrawal from the agreement, Center for Automotive Research (Jun. 2017) at 8, https://www.cargroup.org/wp-content/uploads/2017/01/nafta_briefing_january_2017_public_version-final.pdf.

have occurred whether NAFTA was passed or not. They found that 87% of manufacturing jobs were lost due to technology.[156] Also, the jobs in the U.S. had shifted toward more highly-skilled workers.[157]

§3.3   THE NAFTA: CONGRESSIONAL RESEARCH SERVICE REPORT

The Congressional Research Service (CRS) was a legislative branch within the Library of Congress that serviced the U.S. Congress. The CRS published a report about the effect of NAFTA on the three economies in May 2017.[158] It concluded that the true effects of NAFTA were hard to determine because of external events that happened during its time.[159] The biggest events were the sharp devaluation in the peso at the end of the 1990s and the 2008 financial crisis.[160] Trade between the NAFTA countries more than tripled since the agreement took effect.[161] However, the overall net effect on the U.S. economy had been relatively small, mainly because total trade with both Mexico and Canada was less than 5% of the overall U.S. Gross Domestic Product ("GDP").[162] Several reports suggested that NAFTA had led to an increase in U.S. GDP of 0.1%-0.5%, with a small increase in U.S. welfare, and little to no change in aggregate employment.[163]

In Mexico, NAFTA brought economic and social benefits to the country as a whole, but the benefits had not been evenly distributed throughout the country.[164] While NAFTA brought benefits to Mexico, it was not enough to narrow the disparities

---

156. *See* Kristin Dziczek et. al, NAFTA Briefing: Trade benefits to the automotive industry and potential consequences of withdrawal from the agreement, Center for Automotive Research (Jun. 2017) at 8, https://www.cargroup.org/wp-content/uploads/2017/01/nafta_briefing_january_2017_public_version-final.pdf.

157. *See* Kristin Dziczek et. al, NAFTA Briefing: Trade benefits to the automotive industry and potential consequences of withdrawal from the agreement, Center for Automotive Research (Jun. 2017) at 8, https://www.cargroup.org/wp-content/uploads/2017/01/nafta_briefing_january_2017_public_version-final.pdf.

158. *See* M. Angeles Villareal and Ian F. Fergusson, The North American Free Trade Agreement (NAFTA), Congressional Research Service (May 24, 2017), https://fas.org/sgp/crs/row/R42965.pdf.

159. *See* M. Angeles Villareal and Ian F. Fergusson, The North American Free Trade Agreement (NAFTA), Congressional Research Service (May 24, 2017) at 11, https://fas.org/sgp/crs/row/R42965.pdf.

160. *See* M. Angeles Villareal and Ian F. Fergusson, The North American Free Trade Agreement (NAFTA), Congressional Research Service (May 24, 2017) at 11, https://fas.org/sgp/crs/row/R42965.pdf.

161. *See* M. Angeles Villareal and Ian F. Fergusson, The North American Free Trade Agreement (NAFTA), Congressional Research Service (May 24, 2017) at 11, https://fas.org/sgp/crs/row/R42965.pdf.

162. *See* M. Angeles Villareal and Ian F. Fergusson, The North American Free Trade Agreement (NAFTA), Congressional Research Service (May 24, 2017) at 15, https://fas.org/sgp/crs/row/R42965.pdf.

163. *See* M. Angeles Villareal and Ian F. Fergusson, The North American Free Trade Agreement (NAFTA), Congressional Research Service (May 24, 2017) at 15, https://fas.org/sgp/crs/row/R42965.pdf.

164. *See* M. Angeles Villareal and Ian F. Fergusson, The North American Free Trade Agreement (NAFTA), Congressional Research Service (May 24, 2017) at 18, https://fas.org/sgp/crs/row/R42965.pdf.

in economic conditions between Mexico and the U.S.[165] This was because Mexico needed to do more, such as investing in education, innovation, and infrastructure.[166]

§3.4 NAFTA AT 20: MISLEADING CHARGES AND POSITIVE ACHIEVEMENTS PETERSON—INSTITUTE FOR INTERNATIONAL ECONOMICS MAY 2014

The Peterson Institute for International Economics published a paper that tried to respond to potentially misleading statements frequently made about NAFTA.[167] Published in May 2014, this paper explained that overall, NAFTA had been good for the U.S. economy.[168] While there were job losses due to increased imports, many criticisms of NAFTA were misguided. First, the argument that NAFTA caused a bilateral trade deficit with Mexico was misguided.[169] While it was important to note that having a bilateral trade deficit was not necessarily bad, it was a reflection that the U.S. had an overall trade deficit with the rest of the world.[170] The trade deficits were actually caused by a growing imbalance between income and spending in the U.S.[171] Since the U.S. was a large net borrower, due to budget deficits and falling household savings, the money had to be spent on goods produced outside of the U.S.[172]

Additionally, there were other factors unrelated to NAFTA that led to the increased trade deficit. The first was the peso devaluation in the 1990s.[173] This happened because the Mexican government and businesses held billions of debts

---

165. *See* M. Angeles Villareeal and Ian F. Fergusson, The North American Free Trade Agreement (NAFTA), Congressional Research Service (May 24, 2017) at 18, https://fas.org/sgp/crs/row/R42965.pdf.

166. *See* M. Angeles Villareeal and Ian F. Fergusson, The North American Free Trade Agreement (NAFTA), Congressional Research Service (May 24, 2017) at 21, https://fas.org/sgp/crs/row/R42965.pdf.

167. *See* Gary Clyde Hufbauer, Cathleen Cimino, and Tyler Moran, NAFTA at 20: Misleading Charges and Positive Achievements. Peterson Institute for International Economics (May 2014), https://www.piie.com/sites/default/files/publications/pb/pb14-13.pdf.

168. *See* Gary Clyde Hufbauer, Cathleen Cimino, and Tyler Moran, NAFTA at 20: Misleading Charges and Positive Achievements. Peterson Institute for International Economics (May 2014), https://www.piie.com/sites/default/files/publications/pb/pb14-13.pdf.

169. *See* Gary Clyde Hufbauer, Cathleen Cimino, and Tyler Moran, NAFTA at 20: Misleading Charges and Positive Achievements. Peterson Institute for International Economics (May 2014) at 3, https://www.piie.com/sites/default/files/publications/pb/pb14-13.pdf.

170. *See* Gary Clyde Hufbauer, Cathleen Cimino, and Tyler Moran, NAFTA at 20: Misleading Charges and Positive Achievements. Peterson Institute for International Economics (May 2014) at 4, https://www.piie.com/sites/default/files/publications/pb/pb14-13.pdf.

171. *See* Gary Clyde Hufbauer, Cathleen Cimino, and Tyler Moran, NAFTA at 20: Misleading Charges and Positive Achievements. Peterson Institute for International Economics (May 2014) at 4, https://www.piie.com/sites/default/files/publications/pb/pb14-13.pdf.

172. *See* Gary Clyde Hufbauer, Cathleen Cimino, and Tyler Moran, NAFTA at 20: Misleading Charges and Positive Achievements. Peterson Institute for International Economics (May 2014) at 5, https://www.piie.com/sites/default/files/publications/pb/pb14-13.pdf.

173. *See* Gary Clyde Hufbauer, Cathleen Cimino, and Tyler Moran, NAFTA at 20: Misleading Charges and Positive Achievements. Peterson Institute for International Economics (May 2014) at 5, https://www.piie.com/sites/default/files/publications/pb/pb14-13.pdf.

denominated in U.S. dollars.[174] Seeing this as unsustainable, investors cashed out on their held debt, depleting the central bank's holdings they used to keep a fixed exchange rate.[175] Suddenly, they abandoned the exchange rate fixed valuation, which led to a collapse of imports and a surge in exports because the peso was very weak compared to the dollar.[176] Since the peso was so cheap, it was very cheap to import goods from Mexico and very expensive for Mexico to import goods from the U.S.

Increased trade with other countries generally created changes in employment where some jobs are lost, and others were gained. Each year, 4 million jobs were lost, even when the U.S. was adding jobs overall.[177] However, only 5% of jobs lost (200,000) could be explained due to increased trade with Mexico.[178] Additionally, for these 200,000 jobs lost, there were over 180,000 jobs gained due to increased trade with Mexico.[179] These jobs created pay of 7-15% more than the jobs that were lost, and the new workers were + oblivious to the fact their job was created because of NAFTA.[180]

§3.5 NAFTA TO USMCA: WHAT IS GAINED? IMF WORKING PAPER MARCH 2019

The International Monetary Fund (IMF) published a paper arguing the macroeconomic effects of the USMCA are essentially negligible.[181] Instead of real GDP gains, the GDP in the United States was predicted to actually fall.[182] The effects varied by the specific sector. For instance, the IMF argued that the rules of origin requirements contributed a USD 700 million loss for the member countries because the new rules would increase

---

174. *See* Gary Clyde Hufbauer, Cathleen Cimino, and Tyler Moran, NAFTA at 20: Misleading Charges and Positive Achievements. Peterson Institute for International Economics (May 2014) at 5, https://www.piie.com/sites/default/files/publications/pb/pb14-13.pdf.

175. *See* Gary Clyde Hufbauer, Cathleen Cimino, and Tyler Moran, NAFTA at 20: Misleading Charges and Positive Achievements. Peterson Institute for International Economics (May 2014) at 5, https://www.piie.com/sites/default/files/publications/pb/pb14-13.pdf.

176. *See* Gary Clyde Hufbauer, Cathleen Cimino, and Tyler Moran, NAFTA at 20: Misleading Charges and Positive Achievements. Peterson Institute for International Economics (May 2014) at 5, https://www.piie.com/sites/default/files/publications/pb/pb14-13.pdf.

177. *See* Gary Clyde Hufbauer, Cathleen Cimino, and Tyler Moran, NAFTA at 20: Misleading Charges and Positive Achievements. Peterson Institute for International Economics (May 2014) at 5, https://www.piie.com/sites/default/files/publications/pb/pb14-13.pdf.

178. *See* Gary Clyde Hufbauer, Cathleen Cimino, and Tyler Moran, NAFTA at 20: Misleading Charges and Positive Achievements. Peterson Institute for International Economics (May 2014) at 5, https://www.piie.com/sites/default/files/publications/pb/pb14-13.pdf.

179. *See* Gary Clyde Hufbauer, Cathleen Cimino, and Tyler Moran, NAFTA at 20: Misleading Charges and Positive Achievements. Peterson Institute for International Economics (May 2014) at 7, https://www.piie.com/sites/default/files/publications/pb/pb14-13.pdf.

180. *See* Gary Clyde Hufbauer, Cathleen Cimino, and Tyler Moran, NAFTA at 20: Misleading Charges and Positive Achievements. Peterson Institute for International Economics (May 2014) at 7, https://www.piie.com/sites/default/files/publications/pb/pb14-13.pdf.

181. *See* Mary E. Burfisher et. al., NAFTA to USMCA: What is Gained? International Monetary Fund (Mar. 26, 2019) at 12, https://www.imf.org/en/Publications/WP/Issues/2019/03/26/NAFTA-to-USMCA-What-is-Gained-46680.

182. *See* Mary E. Burfisher et. al., NAFTA to USMCA: What is Gained? International Monetary Fund (Mar. 26, 2019) at 12, https://www.imf.org/en/Publications/WP/Issues/2019/03/26/NAFTA-to-USMCA-What-is-Gained-46680.

the price of automobiles.[183] In the agricultural sector, there was an overall gain in GDP, but the U.S. actually saw a drop of USD 85 million due to the new agriculture rules.[184]

The authors also argued that the USMCA would cause a small depreciation of the Canadian dollar, no change in the U.S. dollar, and a small depreciation of the Mexican peso.[185] Lastly, they argued that wages would remain unchanged in the United States.[186]

183. *See* Mary E. Burfisher et. al., NAFTA to USMCA: What is Gained? International Monetary Fund (Mar. 26, 2019) at 12, https://www.imf.org/en/Publications/WP/Issues/2019/03/26/NAFTA -to-USMCA-What-is-Gained-46680.
184. *See* Mary E. Burfisher et. al., NAFTA to USMCA: What is Gained? International Monetary Fund (Mar. 26, 2019) at 12, https://www.imf.org/en/Publications/WP/Issues/2019/03/26/NAFTA -to-USMCA-What-is-Gained-46680.
185. *See* Mary E. Burfisher et. al., NAFTA to USMCA: What is Gained? International Monetary Fund (Mar. 26, 2019) at 15, https://www.imf.org/en/Publications/WP/Issues/2019/03/26/NAFTA -to-USMCA-What-is-Gained-46680.
186. *See* Mary E. Burfisher et. al., NAFTA to USMCA: What is Gained? International Monetary Fund (Mar. 26, 2019) at 19, https://www.imf.org/en/Publications/WP/Issues/2019/03/26/NAFTA -to-USMCA-What-is-Gained-46680.

CHAPTER 4

Summary of the U.S. INTERNATIONAL TRADE COMMISSION Report

The U.S. International Trade Commission (Commission) was tasked to assess the likely impact of the United States-Mexico-Canada Agreement (USMCA) on the U.S. economy and on specific industry standards. It reports, in terms of six years, the effects of the U.S. economy are as follows: real GDP increases by 0.35% (USD 68 billion), and output increases in agriculture, manufacturing, and services. Additionally, overall employment in the U.S. will increase by 0.12% (175,700 jobs). The report also analyzes the effects on U.S. trade. It reports that U.S. exports will increase by 2.4%; imports will increase by 2%. USMCA will also impact the automotive industry. It reports that the new rules of origin requirement will increase the cost of automobiles; however, this will be offset by the increase in manufacturing jobs and wages. It also reports on agriculture, indicating that both dairy, poultry, and egg exports from the U.S. to Canada will increase. The USMCA is unlikely to increase output in the U.S. service industry; however, the trade between the countries will increase due to changes in financial systems and the audiovisual service industry. Additionally, the report estimates that the new provisions regarding digital trade will have a significant positive impact on industries that rely on digitally enabled trade. A similar trend is estimated for intellectual property. Finally, USMCA contains new provisions that expand on NAFTA's requirement for Parties to adopt and maintain laws against anticompetitive business conduct, ensuring that persons of another member country are treated no less favorably than persons of that country in like circumstances.

§4.1   INTRODUCTION

The U.S. International Trade Commission ("the Commission" or "USITC") is an independent, bipartisan federal agency that provides guidance on policy matters relating to international trade and adjudicates various trade cases such as antidumping and countervailing duties where it is charged with determining the existence of injury or threat of injury caused by imports. On August 31, 2018, the Commission received a letter from the U.S. Trade Representative requesting that the Commission provide a report assessing the likely impact of the USMCA on the U.S. economy under 19 U.S.C. § 4204(c).[187] The statute requires the Commission to assess the likely impact of the USMCA as a whole and on specific industry sectors, and its impact on U.S. GDP, exports and imports, and aggregate employment.[188]

§4.2   CHAPTER 1

Chapter one of the International Trade Commission Report (the Report) on the USMCA introduced the purpose of the report, the scope of the analysis, and current characteristics of the trade between the U.S., Mexico, and Canada.[189] The purpose of the Report was to assess the likely impact of the USMCA on the U.S. economy and on specific industry standards.[190] The Report analyzed over 20 sectors, including the agricultural industry, manufacturing, textiles, services, and digital trade.[191]

The chapter ends by discussing general information about trade between the U.S., Mexico, and Canada. These three countries make up 26% of the global economy (24% U.S. and 2% for both Canada and Mexico).[192] All three countries are operating under a trade deficit for goods and services. (*Id.* at 32.) Thirty-four percent of all the goods the U.S. exports go to Canada and Mexico, and 26% of all goods the U.S. imports comes from Mexico and Canada.[193]

§4.3   CHAPTER 2

Chapter two explains the Report's methodology and then analyzes the economy as a whole if the USMCA is passed.[194] The results cover six years after USCMA has been enacted since there are many provisions that will not be fully in effect until six years

---

187. *See* U.S.-Mexico-Canada Trade Agreement: Likely Impact on the U.S. Economy and on Specific Industry Sectors, United Stated International Trade Commission (Apr. 2019), https://www.usitc.gov/publications/332/pub4889.pdf.
188. *See* U.S.-Mexico-Canada Trade Agreement: Likely Impact on the U.S. Economy and on Specific Industry Sectors, United Stated International Trade Commission (Apr. 2019) at 27, https://www.usitc.gov/publications/332/pub4889.pdf.
189. *See* U.S.-Mexico-Canada Trade Agreement: Likely Impact on the U.S. Economy and on Specific Industry Sectors, United Stated International Trade Commission (Apr. 2019) at 27, https://www.usitc.gov/publications/332/pub4889.pdf.
190. *See* U.S.-Mexico-Canada Trade Agreement: Likely Impact on the U.S. Economy and on Specific Industry Sectors, United Stated International Trade Commission (Apr. 2019) at 27, https://www.usitc.gov/publications/332/pub4889.pdf.
191. *See* U.S.-Mexico-Canada Trade Agreement: Likely Impact on the U.S. Economy and on Specific Industry Sectors, United Stated International Trade Commission (Apr. 2019) at 27, https://www.usitc.gov/publications/332/pub4889.pdf.
192. *See* U.S.-Mexico-Canada Trade Agreement: Likely Impact on the U.S. Economy and on Specific Industry Sectors, United Stated International Trade Commission (Apr. 2019) at 31, https://www.usitc.gov/publications/332/pub4889.pdf.
193. *See* U.S.-Mexico-Canada Trade Agreement: Likely Impact on the U.S. Economy and on Specific Industry Sectors, United Stated International Trade Commission (Apr. 2019) at 33, https://www.usitc.gov/publications/332/pub4889.pdf.
194. *See* U.S.-Mexico-Canada Trade Agreement: Likely Impact on the U.S. Economy and on Specific Industry Sectors, United Stated International Trade Commission (Apr. 2019) at 37, https://www.usitc.gov/publications/332/pub4889.pdf.

after its enactment, and the Report does not analyze the transition.[195] The effects on the U.S. economy are as follows: real GDP increases by 0.35% (USD 68 billion), output increases 0.18% in agriculture, output increases by 0.57% in manufacturing, output increases by 0.17% in services.[196] Overall employment in the U.S. will increase by 0.12% (175,700 jobs).[197] There will be an increase of 0.12% in agriculture (1,700 jobs), 0.37% in manufacturing (49,700 jobs), and an increase of 0.09% in services (124,300 jobs).[198] The Report concludes that the provisions which produce the most impact are the ones that reduce uncertainty, and the rules of origin requirements.[199]

The Report also analyzes the effects on U.S. trade. The Report finds that U.S. exports will increase by 2.4%, with a 1.1% increase in agriculture, a 3.3% increase in manufacturing, and a 1.2% increase in services. U.S. imports will increase by 2%, with a 1.8% increase in agriculture, a 1.3% increase in manufacturing, and a 5.4% increase in services.[200]

The Report predicted that USMCA would also have an effect on wages. On average, all wages will increase an average of 0.27% ($150/year).[201] There will be a 0.3% increase in wages of people with a graduate degree and a 0.27% increase for people with a bachelor's degree.[202] There is a 0.25% increase for people with a general college diploma, a 0.27% increase for people with a high school diploma, and a 0.23% increase for people without a high school diploma.[203] While all types of industries were forecast to have a rise in wages, manufacturing was predicted to have the greatest increase because of the new rules of origin requirements.[204]

---

195. *See* U.S.-Mexico-Canada Trade Agreement: Likely Impact on the U.S. Economy and on Specific Industry Sectors, United Stated International Trade Commission (Apr. 2019) at 43, https://www.usitc.gov/publications/332/pub4889.pdf.

196. *See* U.S.-Mexico-Canada Trade Agreement: Likely Impact on the U.S. Economy and on Specific Industry Sectors, United Stated International Trade Commission (Apr. 2019) at 44, https://www.usitc.gov/publications/332/pub4889.pdf.

197. *See* U.S.-Mexico-Canada Trade Agreement: Likely Impact on the U.S. Economy and on Specific Industry Sectors, United Stated International Trade Commission (Apr. 2019) at 44, https://www.usitc.gov/publications/332/pub4889.pdf.

198. *See* U.S.-Mexico-Canada Trade Agreement: Likely Impact on the U.S. Economy and on Specific Industry Sectors, United Stated International Trade Commission (Apr. 2019) at 44, https://www.usitc.gov/publications/332/pub4889.pdf.

199. *See* U.S.-Mexico-Canada Trade Agreement: Likely Impact on the U.S. Economy and on Specific Industry Sectors, United Stated International Trade Commission (Apr. 2019) at 43, https://www.usitc.gov/publications/332/pub4889.pdf.

200. *See* U.S.-Mexico-Canada Trade Agreement: Likely Impact on the U.S. Economy and on Specific Industry Sectors, United Stated International Trade Commission (Apr. 2019) at 45, https://www.usitc.gov/publications/332/pub4889.pdf.

201. *See* U.S.-Mexico-Canada Trade Agreement: Likely Impact on the U.S. Economy and on Specific Industry Sectors, United Stated International Trade Commission (Apr. 2019) at 46, https://www.usitc.gov/publications/332/pub4889.pdf.

202. *See* U.S.-Mexico-Canada Trade Agreement: Likely Impact on the U.S. Economy and on Specific Industry Sectors, United Stated International Trade Commission (Apr. 2019) at 46, https://www.usitc.gov/publications/332/pub4889.pdf.

203. *See* U.S.-Mexico-Canada Trade Agreement: Likely Impact on the U.S. Economy and on Specific Industry Sectors, United Stated International Trade Commission (Apr. 2019) at 46, https://www.usitc.gov/publications/332/pub4889.pdf.

204. *See* U.S.-Mexico-Canada Trade Agreement: Likely Impact on the U.S. Economy and on Specific Industry Sectors, United Stated International Trade Commission (Apr. 2019) at 46, https://www.usitc.gov/publications/332/pub4889.pdf.

The Report creates three different levels of potential impact—no impact, moderate impact, and high impact.[205] The above analysis is based on a moderate impact.[206] When assuming there is no impact, there are very few changes in the economy compared to NAFTA.[207] If we assume a high impact, then there is a very large positive change in the economy with the USMCA.[208]

The Report addresses concerns about the movement of the labor force.[209] Some believe that the labor force is not restricted, and people can move from one unskilled job to another.[210] Others believe that the labor force is somewhat restricted, and it is somewhat difficult to move to another unskilled job if they have been doing a different type of job for the last number of years.[211] To address this, the Report provides an analysis with both somewhat restrictive assumptions and no restrictive assumptions.[212] The above results are based on the somewhat restricted model, and the model with no labor restrictions produces even greater positive results.[213]

§4.4   CHAPTER 3

Chapter three analyzes the impact of the USMCA on automotive, steel, and aluminum products.[214] The Report believes that the new Rules of Origin requirements will

---

205. *See* U.S.-Mexico-Canada Trade Agreement: Likely Impact on the U.S. Economy and on Specific Industry Sectors, United Stated International Trade Commission (Apr. 2019) at 55, https://www.usitc.gov/publications/332/pub4889.pdf.

206. *See* U.S.-Mexico-Canada Trade Agreement: Likely Impact on the U.S. Economy and on Specific Industry Sectors, United Stated International Trade Commission (Apr. 2019) at 55, https://www.usitc.gov/publications/332/pub4889.pdf.

207. *See* U.S.-Mexico-Canada Trade Agreement: Likely Impact on the U.S. Economy and on Specific Industry Sectors, United Stated International Trade Commission (Apr. 2019) at 56, https://www.usitc.gov/publications/332/pub4889.pdf.

208. *See* U.S.-Mexico-Canada Trade Agreement: Likely Impact on the U.S. Economy and on Specific Industry Sectors, United Stated International Trade Commission (Apr. 2019) at 56, https://www.usitc.gov/publications/332/pub4889.pdf.

209. *See* U.S.-Mexico-Canada Trade Agreement: Likely Impact on the U.S. Economy and on Specific Industry Sectors, United Stated International Trade Commission (Apr. 2019) at 60, https://www.usitc.gov/publications/332/pub4889.pdf.

210. *See* U.S.-Mexico-Canada Trade Agreement: Likely Impact on the U.S. Economy and on Specific Industry Sectors, United Stated International Trade Commission (Apr. 2019) at 60, https://www.usitc.gov/publications/332/pub4889.pdf.

211. *See* U.S.-Mexico-Canada Trade Agreement: Likely Impact on the U.S. Economy and on Specific Industry Sectors, United Stated International Trade Commission (Apr. 2019) at 60, https://www.usitc.gov/publications/332/pub4889.pdf.

212. *See* U.S.-Mexico-Canada Trade Agreement: Likely Impact on the U.S. Economy and on Specific Industry Sectors, United Stated International Trade Commission (Apr. 2019) at 61, https://www.usitc.gov/publications/332/pub4889.pdf.

213. *See* U.S.-Mexico-Canada Trade Agreement: Likely Impact on the U.S. Economy and on Specific Industry Sectors, United Stated International Trade Commission (Apr. 2019) at 61, https://www.usitc.gov/publications/332/pub4889.pdf.

214. *See* U.S.-Mexico-Canada Trade Agreement: Likely Impact on the U.S. Economy and on Specific Industry Sectors, United Stated International Trade Commission (Apr. 2019) at 69, https://www.usitc.gov/publications/332/pub4889.pdf.

increase the cost of automobiles, which will result in lower demand.[215] This will be offset by the increase in manufacturing jobs and wages.[216]

The Report asserts that manufacturers who are already close to compliance with the new Rules of Origin laws will increase their North American content to comply when USMCA is enacted.[217] The Report also predicts that companies that are not close to compliance will not try to comply because it will be too expensive to do so.[218]

The Report finds that the average price increase for all cars will be between 0.37% and 1.61%.[219] The Report also finds that the total vehicles sold will decrease by 1.25% (140,219 vehicles).[220] U.S. vehicle exports and imports to Canada and Mexico will decrease, and imports to the U.S. from the rest of the world will increase.[221]

§4.5 CHAPTER 4

Chapter four analyzes the effect of the USMCA on other manufactured goods, natural resources, and energy products. For these specific goods, the USMCA makes some key changes. It revises the Rules of Origin requirements, it gives national treatment for Mexico's energy export license program, and it increases the "*de minimis*" allowance for non-originating fibers or yarns in textiles from 7%-10%.[222]

For chemical and pharmaceutical products, the Report predicts that there will be little impact, as over 95% of imports from Canada and Mexico were previously duty-free.[223] The Report estimates a small positive impact on the production and trade

215. *See* U.S.-Mexico-Canada Trade Agreement: Likely Impact on the U.S. Economy and on Specific Industry Sectors, United Stated International Trade Commission (Apr. 2019) at 85, https://www.usitc.gov/publications/332/pub4889.pdf.

216. *See* U.S.-Mexico-Canada Trade Agreement: Likely Impact on the U.S. Economy and on Specific Industry Sectors, United Stated International Trade Commission (Apr. 2019) at 85, https://www.usitc.gov/publications/332/pub4889.pdf.

217. *See* U.S.-Mexico-Canada Trade Agreement: Likely Impact on the U.S. Economy and on Specific Industry Sectors, United Stated International Trade Commission (Apr. 2019) at 84, https://www.usitc.gov/publications/332/pub4889.pdf.

218. *See* U.S.-Mexico-Canada Trade Agreement: Likely Impact on the U.S. Economy and on Specific Industry Sectors, United Stated International Trade Commission (Apr. 2019) at 84, https://www.usitc.gov/publications/332/pub4889.pdf.

219. *See* U.S.-Mexico-Canada Trade Agreement: Likely Impact on the U.S. Economy and on Specific Industry Sectors, United Stated International Trade Commission (Apr. 2019) at 85, https://www.usitc.gov/publications/332/pub4889.pdf.

220. *See* U.S.-Mexico-Canada Trade Agreement: Likely Impact on the U.S. Economy and on Specific Industry Sectors, United Stated International Trade Commission (Apr. 2019) at 85, https://www.usitc.gov/publications/332/pub4889.pdf.

221. *See* U.S.-Mexico-Canada Trade Agreement: Likely Impact on the U.S. Economy and on Specific Industry Sectors, United Stated International Trade Commission (Apr. 2019) at 86, https://www.usitc.gov/publications/332/pub4889.pdf.

222. *See* U.S.-Mexico-Canada Trade Agreement: Likely Impact on the U.S. Economy and on Specific Industry Sectors, United Stated International Trade Commission (Apr. 2019) at 95, https://www.usitc.gov/publications/332/pub4889.pdf.

223. *See* U.S.-Mexico-Canada Trade Agreement: Likely Impact on the U.S. Economy and on Specific Industry Sectors, United Stated International Trade Commission (Apr. 2019) at 100, https://www.usitc.gov/publications/332/pub4889.pdf.

of electronics because of the new Rules of Origin ("ROO") requirements.[224] The new ROO requirements include reducing regional value content requirements on and adjusting tariff shifts on other items from the Harmonized Tariff System heading level.[225]

The USMCA will have little impact on energy trade.[226] Since Canada and Mexico already give MFN duty-free treatment to imports of crude petroleum, few U.S. exports will qualify for a lower tariff by demonstrating origin.[227] The updates to the textile industry from the USMCA will also have little effect on trade.[228] This is because there are some new provisions that make the textile industry more restrictive, and some that will make it less restrictive.[229]

§4.6   CHAPTER 5

Chapter five analyzes the effects of the USMCA on agriculture. Under the USMCA, Canada will gain additional access to the U.S. market for sugar and dairy.[230] Canada also eliminated class 6 and 7 quotas on milk so the U.S. can increase its access to the dairy industry in Canada. This was probably one of the most contentious issues in the USMCA negotiations between the U.S. and Canada, and the source of internal political debate within Canada.[231] The USMCA will not have an effect on the trade of agricultural products between the U.S. and Mexico because the USMCA did not change the relationship between the two countries within this industry.[232]

---

224. *See* U.S.-Mexico-Canada Trade Agreement: Likely Impact on the U.S. Economy and on Specific Industry Sectors, United Stated International Trade Commission (Apr. 2019) at 102, https://www.usitc.gov/publications/332/pub4889.pdf.
225. *See* U.S.-Mexico-Canada Trade Agreement: Likely Impact on the U.S. Economy and on Specific Industry Sectors, United Stated International Trade Commission (Apr. 2019) at 102, https://www.usitc.gov/publications/332/pub4889.pdf.
226. *See* U.S.-Mexico-Canada Trade Agreement: Likely Impact on the U.S. Economy and on Specific Industry Sectors, United Stated International Trade Commission (Apr. 2019) at 107, https://www.usitc.gov/publications/332/pub4889.pdf.
227. *See* U.S.-Mexico-Canada Trade Agreement: Likely Impact on the U.S. Economy and on Specific Industry Sectors, United Stated International Trade Commission (Apr. 2019) at 107, https://www.usitc.gov/publications/332/pub4889.pdf.
228. *See* U.S.-Mexico-Canada Trade Agreement: Likely Impact on the U.S. Economy and on Specific Industry Sectors, United Stated International Trade Commission (Apr. 2019) at 111, https://www.usitc.gov/publications/332/pub4889.pdf.
229. *See* U.S.-Mexico-Canada Trade Agreement: Likely Impact on the U.S. Economy and on Specific Industry Sectors, United Stated International Trade Commission (Apr. 2019) at 112, https://www.usitc.gov/publications/332/pub4889.pdf.
230. *See* U.S.-Mexico-Canada Trade Agreement: Likely Impact on the U.S. Economy and on Specific Industry Sectors, United Stated International Trade Commission (Apr. 2019) at 118, https://www.usitc.gov/publications/332/pub4889.pdf.
231. *See* U.S.-Mexico-Canada Trade Agreement: Likely Impact on the U.S. Economy and on Specific Industry Sectors, United Stated International Trade Commission (Apr. 2019) at 118, https://www.usitc.gov/publications/332/pub4889.pdf.
232. *See* U.S.-Mexico-Canada Trade Agreement: Likely Impact on the U.S. Economy and on Specific Industry Sectors, United Stated International Trade Commission (Apr. 2019) at 118, https://www.usitc.gov/publications/332/pub4889.pdf.

The Report predicts a 0.1% increase in dairy output in the U.S. ($226.8 million).[233] Dairy exports will increase by 7.1% ($314.5 million), with a 9% increase in exports to Canada ($227 million).[234] For poultry and eggs, there is again no change between the U.S. and Mexico.[235] For poultry and eggs, the report estimates U.S. exports to Canada will increase by 49% ($183 million), and there will be a decrease in imports.[236] For sugar, U.S. imports from Canada will increase by 1.4% ($16 million), exports to Canada will increase by 2.1% ($21.1 million), and sugar output will increase by $34 million.[237] The Report also believes that there will be increased access to U.S. alcohol in other member countries.[238]

For U.S. imports into Canada, the USCMA requires U.S. wheat to be treated like Canadian wheat.[239] This will likely lead to a small increase in market access of wheat into the Canadian market.[240] New Sanitary and Phytosanitary provisions will increase trade because of equivalent sanitary measures between the member countries.[241] Lastly, the USMCA will have a small positive impact on biotechnology because of greater transparency between the Party members.[242]

§4.7 CHAPTER 6

The USMCA is unlikely to increase output in the U.S. service industry, but trade between the countries will increase because of the elimination of certain barriers to

---

233. *See* U.S.-Mexico-Canada Trade Agreement: Likely Impact on the U.S. Economy and on Specific Industry Sectors, United Stated International Trade Commission (Apr. 2019) at 124, https://www.usitc.gov/publications/332/pub4889.pdf.
234. *See* U.S.-Mexico-Canada Trade Agreement: Likely Impact on the U.S. Economy and on Specific Industry Sectors, United Stated International Trade Commission (Apr. 2019) at 124, https://www.usitc.gov/publications/332/pub4889.pdf.
235. *See* U.S.-Mexico-Canada Trade Agreement: Likely Impact on the U.S. Economy and on Specific Industry Sectors, United Stated International Trade Commission (Apr. 2019) at 127, https://www.usitc.gov/publications/332/pub4889.pdf.
236. *See* U.S.-Mexico-Canada Trade Agreement: Likely Impact on the U.S. Economy and on Specific Industry Sectors, United Stated International Trade Commission (Apr. 2019) at 128, https://www.usitc.gov/publications/332/pub4889.pdf.
237. *See* U.S.-Mexico-Canada Trade Agreement: Likely Impact on the U.S. Economy and on Specific Industry Sectors, United Stated International Trade Commission (Apr. 2019) at 130, https://www.usitc.gov/publications/332/pub4889.pdf.
238. *See* U.S.-Mexico-Canada Trade Agreement: Likely Impact on the U.S. Economy and on Specific Industry Sectors, United Stated International Trade Commission (Apr. 2019) at 130, https://www.usitc.gov/publications/332/pub4889.pdf.
239. *See* U.S.-Mexico-Canada Trade Agreement: Likely Impact on the U.S. Economy and on Specific Industry Sectors, United Stated International Trade Commission (Apr. 2019) at 131, https://www.usitc.gov/publications/332/pub4889.pdf.
240. *See* U.S.-Mexico-Canada Trade Agreement: Likely Impact on the U.S. Economy and on Specific Industry Sectors, United Stated International Trade Commission (Apr. 2019) at 131, https://www.usitc.gov/publications/332/pub4889.pdf.
241. *See* U.S.-Mexico-Canada Trade Agreement: Likely Impact on the U.S. Economy and on Specific Industry Sectors, United Stated International Trade Commission (Apr. 2019) at 132, https://www.usitc.gov/publications/332/pub4889.pdf.
242. *See* U.S.-Mexico-Canada Trade Agreement: Likely Impact on the U.S. Economy and on Specific Industry Sectors, United Stated International Trade Commission (Apr. 2019) at 135, https://www.usitc.gov/publications/332/pub4889.pdf.

entry.[243] There will be no changes in the audiovisual services industry.[244] There will be a change in financial systems because the USMCA prevents member countries from restricting cross-border flows of financial data.[245] The Report estimates that sales by foreign commercial banks will increase by 7.1% in Mexico.[246] The Report estimates a small positive impact on U.S. providers of professional services due to increased market access.[247]

§4.8   CHAPTER 7

Under the NAFTA, there were no provisions dealing with digital trade and electronic commerce because the digital age had not started in 1994 when NAFTA was enacted.[248] This chapter includes several provisions that will affect owners of digital products as they attempt to further their digital footprint in the United States, Mexico, and Canada.[249] The first provision is that no country party to the USCMA will enact customs fees, duties, or other charges for imports and exports of digital products between member countries.[250] Under the USMCA, electronic signatures must be valid between the member countries.[251] Each member country has also agreed not to require that a Party in a USMCA country have a computing facility (e.g., servers) in that country as a condition for conducting business in that country.[252]

---

243. *See* U.S.-Mexico-Canada Trade Agreement: Likely Impact on the U.S. Economy and on Specific Industry Sectors, United Stated International Trade Commission (Apr. 2019) at 141, https://www.usitc.gov/publications/332/pub4889.pdf.
244. *See* U.S.-Mexico-Canada Trade Agreement: Likely Impact on the U.S. Economy and on Specific Industry Sectors, United Stated International Trade Commission (Apr. 2019) at 156, https://www.usitc.gov/publications/332/pub4889.pdf.
245. *See* U.S.-Mexico-Canada Trade Agreement: Likely Impact on the U.S. Economy and on Specific Industry Sectors, United Stated International Trade Commission (Apr. 2019) at 159, https://www.usitc.gov/publications/332/pub4889.pdf.
246. *See* U.S.-Mexico-Canada Trade Agreement: Likely Impact on the U.S. Economy and on Specific Industry Sectors, United Stated International Trade Commission (Apr. 2019) at 159, https://www.usitc.gov/publications/332/pub4889.pdf.
247. *See* U.S.-Mexico-Canada Trade Agreement: Likely Impact on the U.S. Economy and on Specific Industry Sectors, United Stated International Trade Commission (Apr. 2019) at 160, https://www.usitc.gov/publications/332/pub4889.pdf.
248. *See* U.S.-Mexico-Canada Trade Agreement: Likely Impact on the U.S. Economy and on Specific Industry Sectors, United Stated International Trade Commission (Apr. 2019) at 172, https://www.usitc.gov/publications/332/pub4889.pdf.
249. *See* U.S.-Mexico-Canada Trade Agreement: Likely Impact on the U.S. Economy and on Specific Industry Sectors, United Stated International Trade Commission (Apr. 2019) at 172, https://www.usitc.gov/publications/332/pub4889.pdf.
250. *See* U.S.-Mexico-Canada Trade Agreement: Likely Impact on the U.S. Economy and on Specific Industry Sectors, United Stated International Trade Commission (Apr. 2019) at 174, https://www.usitc.gov/publications/332/pub4889.pdf.
251. *See* U.S.-Mexico-Canada Trade Agreement: Likely Impact on the U.S. Economy and on Specific Industry Sectors, United Stated International Trade Commission (Apr. 2019) at 174, https://www.usitc.gov/publications/332/pub4889.pdf.
252. *See* U.S.-Mexico-Canada Trade Agreement: Likely Impact on the U.S. Economy and on Specific Industry Sectors, United Stated International Trade Commission (Apr. 2019) at 174, https://www.usitc.gov/publications/332/pub4889.pdf.

The Report estimates that the provisions on digital trade will have a significant positive impact on many industries that rely on digitally enabled trade.[253] There is an estimated reduction in trade costs stemming from the international data transfer provisions that range between 0.5-5%.[254] The new provisions will also positively impact telecommunications by improving the business and regulatory climate within which USMCA members negotiate with their foreign counterparts to assemble and operate domestic networks and data centers.[255]

§4.9   CHAPTER 8

Chapter eight assesses the likely impact of changes to "crosscutting" provisions, such as investor-state dispute settlement (ISDS), intellectual property rights, and labor.[256] New ISDS provisions provide arbitration options for investors who allege that host governments have violated investment terms.[257] However, the USCMA limits the scope of ISDS generally.[258] The Report estimates that there will be a decrease in foreign affiliate sales in Mexico, part of which will be redirected to the U.S, though it will likely be a small amount.[259]

The new provisions on IP rights will benefit U.S. industries that rely on IP protection.[260] The Report notes a statistically significant positive relationship between trade flows and IP protection.[261] So, higher domestic IP protections are associated with

---

253. *See* U.S.-Mexico-Canada Trade Agreement: Likely Impact on the U.S. Economy and on Specific Industry Sectors, United Stated International Trade Commission (Apr. 2019) at 171, https://www.usitc.gov/publications/332/pub4889.pdf.

254. *See* U.S.-Mexico-Canada Trade Agreement: Likely Impact on the U.S. Economy and on Specific Industry Sectors, United Stated International Trade Commission (Apr. 2019) at 178, https://www.usitc.gov/publications/332/pub4889.pdf.

255. *See* U.S.-Mexico-Canada Trade Agreement: Likely Impact on the U.S. Economy and on Specific Industry Sectors, United Stated International Trade Commission (Apr. 2019) at 180, https://www.usitc.gov/publications/332/pub4889.pdf.

256. *See* U.S.-Mexico-Canada Trade Agreement: Likely Impact on the U.S. Economy and on Specific Industry Sectors, United Stated International Trade Commission (Apr. 2019) at 193, https://www.usitc.gov/publications/332/pub4889.pdf.

257. *See* U.S.-Mexico-Canada Trade Agreement: Likely Impact on the U.S. Economy and on Specific Industry Sectors, United Stated International Trade Commission (Apr. 2019) at 193, https://www.usitc.gov/publications/332/pub4889.pdf.

258. *See* U.S.-Mexico-Canada Trade Agreement: Likely Impact on the U.S. Economy and on Specific Industry Sectors, United Stated International Trade Commission (Apr. 2019) at 194, https://www.usitc.gov/publications/332/pub4889.pdf.

259. *See* U.S.-Mexico-Canada Trade Agreement: Likely Impact on the U.S. Economy and on Specific Industry Sectors, United Stated International Trade Commission (Apr. 2019) at 194, https://www.usitc.gov/publications/332/pub4889.pdf.

260. *See* U.S.-Mexico-Canada Trade Agreement: Likely Impact on the U.S. Economy and on Specific Industry Sectors, United Stated International Trade Commission (Apr. 2019) at 203, https://www.usitc.gov/publications/332/pub4889.pdf.

261. *See* U.S.-Mexico-Canada Trade Agreement: Likely Impact on the U.S. Economy and on Specific Industry Sectors, United Stated International Trade Commission (Apr. 2019) at 213, https://www.usitc.gov/publications/332/pub4889.pdf.

greater import activity.[262] The Report further estimates that the new labor provisions to protect labor rights will increase unionization rates and wages in Mexico, and will also increase Mexican output.[263] This would lead to an increase in U.S. output and employment, resulting in a small wage increase for U.S. workers.[264]

§4.10   CHAPTER 9

Chapter nine assesses other broad crosscutting provisions, such as rules of origin, temporary entry, antitrust, environmental standards, small- and medium-sized enterprises ("SMEs"), and exchange rates.[265] The Report provides little assessment because the impacts will be limited.[266]

The USCMA changes the ROO requirements and continues a regional value content approach.[267] It includes a lengthy transitional period, and there are mixed opinions about the effectiveness of this long transition period.[268] Another crosscutting provision is the removal of trade barriers and small changes in customs requirements.[269]

New customs provisions in the USCMA allow importers to voluntarily report and correct clerical errors on customs forms with no penalty.[270] Currently, penalties are

---

262. *See* U.S.-Mexico-Canada Trade Agreement: Likely Impact on the U.S. Economy and on Specific Industry Sectors, United Stated International Trade Commission (Apr. 2019) at 213, https://www.usitc.gov/publications/332/pub4889.pdf.
263. *See* U.S.-Mexico-Canada Trade Agreement: Likely Impact on the U.S. Economy and on Specific Industry Sectors, United Stated International Trade Commission (Apr. 2019) at 215, https://www.usitc.gov/publications/332/pub4889.pdf.
264. *See* U.S.-Mexico-Canada Trade Agreement: Likely Impact on the U.S. Economy and on Specific Industry Sectors, United Stated International Trade Commission (Apr. 2019) at 215, https://www.usitc.gov/publications/332/pub4889.pdf.
265. *See* U.S.-Mexico-Canada Trade Agreement: Likely Impact on the U.S. Economy and on Specific Industry Sectors, United Stated International Trade Commission (Apr. 2019) at 233, https://www.usitc.gov/publications/332/pub4889.pdf.
266. *See* U.S.-Mexico-Canada Trade Agreement: Likely Impact on the U.S. Economy and on Specific Industry Sectors, United Stated International Trade Commission (Apr. 2019) at 233, https://www.usitc.gov/publications/332/pub4889.pdf.
267. *See* U.S.-Mexico-Canada Trade Agreement: Likely Impact on the U.S. Economy and on Specific Industry Sectors, United Stated International Trade Commission (Apr. 2019) at 235, https://www.usitc.gov/publications/332/pub4889.pdf.
268. *See* U.S.-Mexico-Canada Trade Agreement: Likely Impact on the U.S. Economy and on Specific Industry Sectors, United Stated International Trade Commission (Apr. 2019) at 235, https://www.usitc.gov/publications/332/pub4889.pdf.
269. *See* U.S.-Mexico-Canada Trade Agreement: Likely Impact on the U.S. Economy and on Specific Industry Sectors, United Stated International Trade Commission (Apr. 2019) at 236, https://www.usitc.gov/publications/332/pub4889.pdf.
270. *See* U.S.-Mexico-Canada Trade Agreement: Likely Impact on the U.S. Economy and on Specific Industry Sectors, United Stated International Trade Commission (Apr. 2019) at 238, https://www.usitc.gov/publications/332/pub4889.pdf.

only for serious infractions.[271] Importers can now file customs documents without a customs broker.[272] Technical barriers to trade ("TBT") provisions would eliminate cross-border trade frictions by ensuring that voluntary and mandatory product standards do not create unnecessary obstacles to trade between the member countries.[273] The USMCA's provisions on temporary entry are very similar to the provisions in NAFTA, so there should be little to no impact.[274]

USMCA contains new provisions expanding on NAFTA's requirement for the Parties to adopt and maintain laws against anticompetitive business conduct.[275] The laws provide that the Parties must treat persons of another Party no less favorably than persons of that Party in like circumstances.[276] The laws and regulations must be transparent, and a country cannot disclose privileged information obtained during an investigation.[277] Each Party must also adopt consumer protection laws that proscribe fraudulent and deceptive commercial activities.[278] State-owned enterprises are to be regulated impartially and cannot benefit from any special treatment compared to private firms.[279] Since Canada has the greatest presence of State-owned enterprises, U.S. firms operating in Canada are expected to benefit.[280] Additionally, all Parties agree

---

271. *See* U.S.-Mexico-Canada Trade Agreement: Likely Impact on the U.S. Economy and on Specific Industry Sectors, United Stated International Trade Commission (Apr. 2019) at 238, https://www.usitc.gov/publications/332/pub4889.pdf.
272. *See* U.S.-Mexico-Canada Trade Agreement: Likely Impact on the U.S. Economy and on Specific Industry Sectors, United Stated International Trade Commission (Apr. 2019) at 238, https://www.usitc.gov/publications/332/pub4889.pdf.
273. *See* U.S.-Mexico-Canada Trade Agreement: Likely Impact on the U.S. Economy and on Specific Industry Sectors, United Stated International Trade Commission (Apr. 2019) at 242, https://www.usitc.gov/publications/332/pub4889.pdf.
274. *See* U.S.-Mexico-Canada Trade Agreement: Likely Impact on the U.S. Economy and on Specific Industry Sectors, United Stated International Trade Commission (Apr. 2019) at 245, https://www.usitc.gov/publications/332/pub4889.pdf.
275. *See* U.S.-Mexico-Canada Trade Agreement: Likely Impact on the U.S. Economy and on Specific Industry Sectors, United Stated International Trade Commission (Apr. 2019) at 247, https://www.usitc.gov/publications/332/pub4889.pdf.
276. *See* U.S.-Mexico-Canada Trade Agreement: Likely Impact on the U.S. Economy and on Specific Industry Sectors, United Stated International Trade Commission (Apr. 2019) at 248, https://www.usitc.gov/publications/332/pub4889.pdf.
277. *See* U.S.-Mexico-Canada Trade Agreement: Likely Impact on the U.S. Economy and on Specific Industry Sectors, United Stated International Trade Commission (Apr. 2019) at 248, https://www.usitc.gov/publications/332/pub4889.pdf.
278. *See* U.S.-Mexico-Canada Trade Agreement: Likely Impact on the U.S. Economy and on Specific Industry Sectors, United Stated International Trade Commission (Apr. 2019) at 249, https://www.usitc.gov/publications/332/pub4889.pdf.
279. *See* U.S.-Mexico-Canada Trade Agreement: Likely Impact on the U.S. Economy and on Specific Industry Sectors, United Stated International Trade Commission (Apr. 2019) at 249, https://www.usitc.gov/publications/332/pub4889.pdf.
280. *See* U.S.-Mexico-Canada Trade Agreement: Likely Impact on the U.S. Economy and on Specific Industry Sectors, United Stated International Trade Commission (Apr. 2019) at 249, https://www.usitc.gov/publications/332/pub4889.pdf.

to let the market determine exchange rates.[281] This provision will not be impactful because all USMCA countries already do this; however, it could have an impact on future trade agreements.[282] The last provision is a sunset provision where the USMCA will expire in sixteen years unless it is renewed.[283]

281. *See* U.S.-Mexico-Canada Trade Agreement: Likely Impact on the U.S. Economy and on Specific Industry Sectors, United Stated International Trade Commission (Apr. 2019) at 263, https://www.usitc.gov/publications/332/pub4889.pdf.
282. *See* U.S.-Mexico-Canada Trade Agreement: Likely Impact on the U.S. Economy and on Specific Industry Sectors, United Stated International Trade Commission (Apr. 2019) at 263, https://www.usitc.gov/publications/332/pub4889.pdf.
283. *See* U.S.-Mexico-Canada Trade Agreement: Likely Impact on the U.S. Economy and on Specific Industry Sectors, United Stated International Trade Commission (Apr. 2019) at 265, https://www.usitc.gov/publications/332/pub4889.pdf.

CHAPTER 5
Origin Procedures

Unlike NAFTA's uniform Certificate of Origin that certified preferentially treated goods, the USMCA allows Parties to use invoices or other commercial documents that have no prescribed format. The USMCA allows for both exporters and importers to complete a certificate of origin; however, there are additional requirements for importing Parties. Additionally, the USMCA has different requirements for producers and exporters when demonstrating origin. It also allows one certificate of origin to apply to multiple shipments. In any case, Parties must keep all information provided by another Party private. The USMCA also has specific provisions regarding errors and discrepancies for certificates of origin. Parties cannot reject certifications due to minor errors or discrepancies that do not affect the correctness of the import documents; and importers have at least five days to correct such errors. Additionally, importers must maintain records for at least five years after the date of importation; exporters must maintain records for at least five years after the certificate of origin is final. There are criminal, civil, or administrative penalties for violations of each party's laws/regulations related to origin procedures. To avoid penalties, the USMCA mandates that a Party may obtain the issuance of a written advance ruling on whether a good qualifies as originating. Parties must notify the others of determinations of origin. Finally, the USMCA establishes a Committee on Rules of Origin and Origin Procedure to consult the interpretation, application, and administration of these rules.

§5.1   CERTIFICATES OF ORIGIN FOR PREFERENTIAL TREATMENT

NAFTA created a uniform Certificate of Origin that certified preferentially eligible goods.[284] The USMCA does away with that requirement, *allowing* Parties to use invoices or other commercial documents that have no prescribed format *but must* contain minimum data elements set forth in Annex 5-A.[285] As a part of the USMCA emphasis on digital trade, the USMCA states that each Party *must* allow a certificate of

---

284. *See* North American Free Trade Agreement, § 501.1, Jan. 1, 1994.
285. *See* United States-Mexico-Canada Agreement, Annex 5-A, Jan. 29, 2020.

origin to be completed and submitted electronically with a digital signature.[286] NAFTA did not make this mandatory.

A Party must meet the chapter's other requirements, including describing the originating material in great detail in order for it to be properly identified, and the form must be provided in the language of the requesting party. Under NAFTA, only an exporter could complete and sign the Certificate of Origin[287]; *whereas*, the USMCA allows importers to complete a certificate of origin subject to certain requirements and thus obtain preferential tariff treatment for originating goods.[288] Canada and the U.S. will allow importers to complete new certification of origin requirements immediately upon the USMCA's effective date.[289] Mexico will have up to three years and six months after the USMCA's effective date to implement this requirement.[290]

Potential requirements for importing Parties include: requiring the importer who completes the certification to provide documents and information to support the certification; establishing laws that prohibit the importer from providing its own certificate if it fails to meet those conditions for certification; or prohibiting the importer from issuing a certification based on a certification or a written representation completed by the exporter or producer and making a subsequent claim for preferential tariff treatment based on a certification of origin completed by the exporter/producer.[291]

In any case, Parties must keep all information provided by another Party in accordance with this chapter private.[292] If a Party fails to do so, another *Party* may decline to provide the information requested.[293] The private information may only be disclosed for administration or enforcement of customs laws.[294]

§5.2   CERTIFICATE OF ORIGIN BASIS AND OBLIGATIONS REGARDING IMPORTS

The USMCA has different requirements for producers and exporters for demonstrating origin.[295] Producers should have information and documents that demonstrate the good's *origin*.[296] Exporters who are not the producer must have the knowledge or reasonable reliance on the producer's written representation (e.g., Certificate of Origin) *of the good's origin*.[297] NAFTA also allowed exporters to complete a Certificate of Origin on the same basis.[298] Similar to NAFTA, the USMCA allows one Certificate of

---

286. *See* United States-Mexico-Canada Agreement, Section 5.2.5, Jan. 29, 2020.
287. *See* North American Free Trade Agreement, § 501.3, Jan. 1, 1994.
288. *See* United States-Mexico-Canada Agreement, Section 5.2.1, Jan. 29, 2020.
289. *See* United States-Mexico-Canada Agreement, Section 5.2.1, Jan. 29, 2020.
290. *See* United States-Mexico-Canada Agreement, Section 5.2.1, Jan. 29, 2020.
291. *See* United States-Mexico-Canada Agreement, Section 5.2.1, Jan. 29, 2020.
292. *See* United States-Mexico-Canada Agreement, Section 5.1.2, Jan. 29, 2020.
293. *See* United States-Mexico-Canada Agreement, Section 5.1.2, Jan. 29, 2020.
294. *See* United States-Mexico-Canada Agreement, Section 5.1.2, Jan. 29, 2020.
295. *See* United States-Mexico-Canada Agreement, Section 5.3, Jan. 29, 2020.
296. *See* United States-Mexico-Canada Agreement, Section 5.3.2, Jan. 29, 2020.
297. *See* United States-Mexico-Canada Agreement, Section 5.3.2, Jan. 29, 2020.
298. *See* North American Free Trade Agreement, § 501.3(b), Jan. 1, 1994.

Origin to apply to a single shipment or to multiple shipments of identical goods within a twelve-month period and must be accepted by a Party's customs administration for four years after its completion.[299] Furthermore, most of the obligations regarding importations are carried over from NAFTA.[300] Importers must *state in their import documents* that the good qualifies as originating; they must have a valid certification of origin in possession at the time that statement is made; and they must provide a copy of the certificate at request.[301]

Under the USMCA, Parties may request that importers demonstrate that goods have been shipped in accordance with § 4.17 (Rules of Origin—Transit and Transshipment) by providing information regarding the shipping route, all points of shipment and transshipment prior to import, and documents demonstrating that the *goods* remained under customs control.[302] No such requirement is listed in the respective NAFTA provision.[303] Additionally, since the USMCA allows an importer to submit certificates of origin if the importer claims preferential tariff treatment, based on a certification of origin completed by a producer, they must demonstrate that the good did not undergo operation afterward.[304] Despite these differences, the USMCA keeps the same threshold (USD USD 1,000) *for* which a certificate of origin is not required and continues to allow exceptions when an importing Party territory has waived the requirement.[305]

§5.3 OBLIGATIONS REGARDING EXPORTS

The USMCA *also creates* special obligations for exports.[306] Exporters or producers must provide a copy of the documentation of origin to the customs administration on request.[307] If the exporter/producer has reason to believe that the certificate is based on or contains false information, they must notify every Party to whom they've provided the certificate of any change.[308] As a result, of such notification, the Party may not be penalized.[309]

---

299. *See* North American Free Trade Agreement, § 501.5, Jan. 1, 1994; *see also* United States-Mexico-Canada Agreement, Section 5.3.5, Jan. 29, 2020.
300. *See* North American Free Trade Agreement, § 502, Jan. 1, 1994; *see also* United States-Mexico-Canada Agreement, Section 5.4, Jan. 29, 2020.
301. *See* North American Free Trade Agreement, § 502, Jan. 1, 1994; *see also* United States-Mexico-Canada Agreement, Section 5.4, Jan. 29, 2020.
302. *See* United States-Mexico-Canada Agreement, Section 5.4.3, Jan. 29, 2020.
303. *See* North American Free Trade Agreement, § 502, Jan. 1, 1994.
304. *See* United States-Mexico-Canada Agreement, Section 5.4.2(e), Jan. 29, 2020.
305. *See* North American Free Trade Agreement, § 503, Jan. 1, 1994; *see also* United States-Mexico-Canada Agreement, Section 5.5, Jan. 29, 2020.
306. *See* United States-Mexico-Canada Agreement, Section 5.6, Jan. 29, 2020.
307. *See* United States-Mexico-Canada Agreement, Section 5.6.1, Jan. 29, 2020.
308. *See* United States-Mexico-Canada Agreement, Section 5.6.2, Jan. 29, 2020.
309. *See* United States-Mexico-Canada Agreement, Section 5.6.2, Jan. 29, 2020.

§5.4   ERRORS, DISCREPANCIES, AND RECORDS

Unlike NAFTA, the USMCA has specific provisions regarding errors and discrepancies for certificates of origin.[310] Under these provisions, Parties cannot reject certifications due to minor errors or discrepancies that do not affect the correctness of the import documents.[311] In fact, Parties must give importers *at least five working days to correct illegible, defective, or incomplete certificates.*[312] The USMCA also imposes recordkeeping requirements for importers.[313] These requirements, however, are very similar to NAFTA. Under NAFTA and the USMCA, importers claiming preferential tariff treatment must maintain import-related records for at least five years after the date of importation.[314] Exporters or producers must maintain records for at least five years after the certificate of origin is final.[315]

§5.5   ORIGIN VERIFICATION AND DETERMINATIONS OF ORIGIN

With respect to verification, the USMCA is consistent with NAFTA, especially because they both authorize an importing Party's customs authorities to verify whether goods qualify as originating as stated on the Certificate of Origin.[316] However, the USMCA *allows* Customs to direct written requests and questionnaires to the importer.[317] NAFTA did not include *this* provision; furthermore, *the* USMCA *requires* that the verifying Party give *a* written determination on whether a good is originating within 120 days after it has received all necessary information.[318] Extensions of ninety days are available in exceptional circumstances.[319]

Like NAFTA, Parties may deny a preferential tariff treatment claim if importers do not comply with the requirements in the *agreement's* respective chapters. Under the USMCA specifically, a Party may deny preferential treatment if: (1) it determines the good does not qualify; (2) it has not received sufficient information to make the determination; (3) the exporter, producer, *or* importer fails to respond to a written request or questionnaire; (4) the exporter or producer fails to provide written consent for a verification visit; (5) an exporter, producer, or importer fails to comply with other requirements of the chapter; or (6) it fails to maintain records for the time period specified or *deny* access to those records.[320]

---

310. *See* United States-Mexico-Canada Agreement, Section 5.8, Jan. 29, 2020.
311. *See* United States-Mexico-Canada Agreement, Section 5.8.1, Jan. 29, 2020.
312. *See* United States-Mexico-Canada Agreement, Section 5.8.2, Jan. 29, 2020.
313. *See* United States-Mexico-Canada Agreement, Section 5.9, Jan. 29, 2020.
314. *See* North American Free Trade Agreement, § 505(b), Jan. 1, 1994; *see also* United States-Mexico-Canada Agreement, Section 5.9.1, Jan. 29, 2020.
315. *See* North American Free Trade Agreement, § 505(a), Jan. 1, 1994; *see also* United States-Mexico-Canada Agreement, Section 5.9.2, Jan. 29, 2020.
316. *See* North American Free Trade Agreement, § 506, Jan. 1, 1994; *see also* United States-Mexico-Canada Agreement, Section 5.10, Jan. 29, 2020.
317. *See* United States-Mexico-Canada Agreement, Section 5.10.1(a), Jan. 29, 2020.
318. *See* United States-Mexico-Canada Agreement, Section 5.10.14, Jan. 29, 2020.
319. *See* United States-Mexico-Canada Agreement, Section 5.10.14, Jan. 29, 2020.
320. *See* United States-Mexico-Canada Agreement, Section 5.11, Jan. 29, 2020.

§5.6 REFUNDS AND POST-IMPORTATION CLAIMS

Like NAFTA, Parties must allow importers to apply for preferential tariff treatment and a refund of any excess duties if the importer did not make a claim for preferential tariff treatment at the time of importation, *and* the goods would have qualified when it was imported.[321] Both trade agreements allow importing Parties to request that the importer making a claim provide a statement that the good was originating, and provide a certificate of origin copy or any other related documentation.[322] Under both agreements, the statute of limitations for the refund is one year.[323]

§5.7 PENALTIES, ADVANCE RULINGS, NOTICE, REVIEW, AND APPEAL

There are criminal, civil, or administrative penalties for violations of each Party's laws/regulations related to origin procedures.[324] In order to avoid penalties, the USMCA, like NAFTA, mandates that a Party must, on request, provide for the issuance of a written advance ruling on whether a good qualifies as originating.[325] Under the USMCA, Parties must notify the others of determinations of origin issued as a result of origin verification and notify regarding a determination of origin that is contrary to the ruling of another Party or consistent treatment given by the customs administration of another.[326] They must *also* notify of measures establishing or modifying administrative policies that will likely affect determination.[327] They must *further* notify of advance rulings or a rule modifying or revoking an advance ruling.[328] Like NAFTA, the USMCA requires Parties to grant substantially the same rights of review and appeal of determinations of origin and advance rulings as it provides to importers in its territory to an exporter or producer: (1) who completes a certification of origin for a good that has been the subject of a determination of origin under the Agreement; or (2) who has received an advance ruling on origin under the Agreement.[329]

---

321. *See* North American Free Trade Agreement, § 502.3, Jan. 1, 1994; *see also* United States-Mexico-Canada Agreement, Section 5.12, Jan. 29, 2020.
322. *See* North American Free Trade Agreement, § 502.3, Jan. 1, 1994; *see also* United States-Mexico-Canada Agreement, Section 5.12, Jan. 29, 2020.
323. *See* North American Free Trade Agreement, § 502.3, Jan. 1, 1994; *see also* United States-Mexico-Canada Agreement, Section 5.12, Jan. 29, 2020.
324. *See* United States-Mexico-Canada Agreement, Section 5.14, Jan. 29, 2020.
325. *See* North American Free Trade Agreement, § 509, Jan. 1, 1994; *see also* United States-Mexico-Canada Agreement, Section 5.15, Jan. 29, 2020.
326. *See* United States-Mexico-Canada Agreement, Section 5.17(a)-(b), Jan. 29, 2020.
327. *See* United States-Mexico-Canada Agreement, Section 5.17.1(c), Jan. 29, 2020.
328. *See* United States-Mexico-Canada Agreement, Section 5.17.1(d), Jan. 29, 2020.
329. *See* North American Free Trade Agreement, § 510, Jan. 1, 1994; *see also* United States-Mexico-Canada Agreement, Section 5.16, Jan. 29, 2020.

§5.8   ORIGIN COMMITTEE AND SUBCOMMITTEE

The USMCA establishes a Committee on Rules of Origin and Origin Procedure ("Origin Committee").[330] The Origin Committee must consult to discuss Uniform Regulations regarding the interpretation, application, and administration of these rules.[331] The Committee must notify the Commission of any modification or addition to its Uniform Regulations.[332] The USMCA also establishes a subcommittee on Origin Verification.[333] The subcommittee will discuss and develop technical papers related to Chapters 4 and 5.[334] They will develop and improve the NAFTA 1994 Audit Manual and recommend verification procedures, write and update verification forms and questionnaires.[335] They will provide a forum for Parties to consult for issues regarding origin verification.[336]

---

330. *See* United States-Mexico-Canada Agreement, Section 5.18, Jan. 29, 2020.
331. *See* United States-Mexico-Canada Agreement, Section 5.16.1, Jan. 29, 2020.
332. *See* United States-Mexico-Canada Agreement, Section 5.16.4, Jan. 29, 2020.
333. *See* United States-Mexico-Canada Agreement, Section 5.19, Jan. 29, 2020.
334. *See* United States-Mexico-Canada Agreement, Section 5.19.3(a), Jan. 29, 2020.
335. *See* United States-Mexico-Canada Agreement, Section 5.19.3(b)-(c), Jan. 29, 2020.
336. *See* United States-Mexico-Canada Agreement, Section 5.19.3(d), Jan. 29, 2020.

CHAPTER 6
Textile and Apparel Goods

The USMCA has different requirements for a textile or apparel good to qualify for preferential tariff treatment. Under the USMCA, there is more flexibility in the rules of origin because they allow manufacturers to use textile inputs not generally available for use in North America. If a textile or apparel originates in a USMCA country, and contains non-USMCA materials, those non-origination fibers and goods cannot exceed 10% of the total weight of that component. This differs under NAFTA, where it capped the entire weight of non-originating fibers at 7%. Further, the USMCA introduces special provisions for handmade, folkloric, or indigenous goods. Under the USMCA, Parties can request a meeting to determine which goods should be subject to different rules of origin or to address supply issues in the free trade area; these assessments should be made within ninety days of the consultation. Additionally, under the USMCA, textile and apparel enforcement is stronger than under NAFTA. A Party may also deny a claim for preferential tariff treatment for a textile or apparel good for a reason listed in 5.10 (Determination of Origin). Finally, the USMCA establishes a committee to update textile and apparel matters.

§6.1   DE MINIMIS THRESHOLD FOR TEXTILE AND APPAREL GOODS AND TARIFF PREFERENCE LEVELS

This chapter restructures Tariff Preference Levels ("TPLs") in a way that limits the exception to the rules of origin to ensure it is not overused.[337] While TPLs will be reduced for some U.S. imports from Canada and Mexico, TPLs are likely to substantially increase for U.S. exports to Canada for apparel and other finished textile goods.[338] This will provide a new opportunity for U.S. textile manufacturers.[339] Under the

---

337. *See* Arkansas World Trade Center, The United States-Mexico-Canada Agreement Fact Sheet, http://arwtc.org/wp-content/uploads/2019/05/USMCA-Textiles-1-Pager.pdf.
338. *See* Arkansas World Trade Center, The United States-Mexico-Canada Agreement Fact Sheet, http://arwtc.org/wp-content/uploads/2019/05/USMCA-Textiles-1-Pager.pdf.
339. *See* Arkansas World Trade Center, The United States-Mexico-Canada Agreement Fact Sheet, http://arwtc.org/wp-content/uploads/2019/05/USMCA-Textiles-1-Pager.pdf.

USMCA, there is more flexibility in the rules of origin because they allow manufacturers to use textile inputs not generally available for use in North America (e.g., rayon fibers and visible lining fabric).[340]

If a textile or apparel originates in a USMCA country and contains non-USMCA materials, it must meet the rules of origin for its specific HTSU designation (Annex-B).[341] Non-originating fibers cannot exceed 10% of the total weight of that component, of which the total weight of elastomeric content may not exceed 7%.[342] Compared to NAFTA, the *de minimis* level is more generous *as it* caps the entire weight of non-originating fibers at 10% instead of 7%.[343] The USMCA adopts the yarn forward approach.[344] Furthermore, sets of textile and apparel goods must not contain non-originating goods that exceed 10% of the value of the set.[345] The USMCA introduces special provisions for handmade, folkloric, or indigenous goods.[346] Under § 6.2, countries must give duty-free treatment to these goods that come from another USMCA country provided that any requirements agreed by the importing and exporting Parties are met.[347]

§6.2   REVIEW AND REVISION OF RULES OF ORIGIN

Parties can request a meeting to determine which goods should be subject to different rules of origin or to address supply issues in the free trade area.[348] Assessments should be made within ninety days of the consultation.[349] If the Parties agree that fibers, yarns, or fabrics are commercially unavailable, then they must try to resolve the issue within sixty days after the initial assessment.[350] Any agreement will supersede any prior rule of origin when approved by each Party.[351]

§6.3   VERIFICATION AND DETERMINATIONS

Under the USMCA, textile and apparel ROO enforcement is stronger than the NAFTA apparel provisions.[352] Parties may request a site visit from an exporter or producer of

---

340. *See* Arkansas World Trade Center, The United States-Mexico-Canada Agreement Fact Sheet, http://arwtc.org/wp-content/uploads/2019/05/USMCA-Textiles-1-Pager.pdf.
341. *See* Arkansas World Trade Center, The United States-Mexico-Canada Agreement Fact Sheet, http://arwtc.org/wp-content/uploads/2019/05/USMCA-Textiles-1-Pager.pdf.
342. *See* Arkansas World Trade Center, The United States-Mexico-Canada Agreement Fact Sheet, http://arwtc.org/wp-content/uploads/2019/05/USMCA-Textiles-1-Pager.pdf.
343. *See* Arkansas World Trade Center, The United States-Mexico-Canada Agreement Fact Sheet, http://arwtc.org/wp-content/uploads/2019/05/USMCA-Textiles-1-Pager.pdf.
344. *See* United States-Mexico-Canada Agreement, Section 6, Jan. 29, 2020.
345. *See* Arkansas World Trade Center, The United States-Mexico-Canada Agreement Fact Sheet, http://arwtc.org/wp-content/uploads/2019/05/USMCA-Textiles-1-Pager.pdf.
346. *See* United States-Mexico-Canada Agreement, Section 6.2, Jan. 29, 2020.
347. *See* United States-Mexico-Canada Agreement, Section 6.2, Jan. 29, 2020.
348. *See* United States-Mexico-Canada Agreement, Section 6.4.1, Jan. 29, 2020.
349. *See* United States-Mexico-Canada Agreement, Section 6.4.2, Jan. 29, 2020.
350. *See* United States-Mexico-Canada Agreement, Section 6.4.3, Jan. 29, 2020.
351. *See* United States-Mexico-Canada Agreement, Section 6.4.3, Jan. 29, 2020.
352. *See* United States-Mexico-Canada Agreement, Section 6.6, Jan. 29, 2020.

textile or apparel goods to verify whether they qualify for preferential tariff treatment or to verify whether customs offenses have occurred.[353] During the visit, they may ask for access to records and facilities relevant to the claim for preferential tariff treatment or to the customs offenses being verified.[354] Parties must provide notice at least twenty days prior to the proposed dates, the number and general location of exporters or producers to be visited, whether they request assistance by the host party, the suspected customs to be verified, and whether the importer claimed preferential treatment.[355] However, the importer does not have to divulge which exporters or producers it may visit.[356]

A Party may deny a claim for preferential tariff treatment for a textile or apparel good for a reason listed in section 5.10 (Determination of Origin).[357] They may also deny a claim if they have not received sufficient information to determine whether the good qualifies.[358] They may further deny a claim if they are unable to conduct a site visit due to a denial or prevention of access.[359]

§6.4 COMMITTEE AND CONFIDENTIALITY

The USMCA establishes a committee that will be used to update the textile and apparel rules if needed.[360] They will meet at least once a year and contain government representatives from each USMCA country.[361] They must review the impact of removing trade restrictions between the Parties.[362] The same confidentiality provisions apply as those under the general rules of origin, set out in Article 5.12.[363]

---

353. *See* United States-Mexico-Canada Agreement, Section 6.6.1, Jan. 29, 2020.
354. *See* United States-Mexico-Canada Agreement, Section 6.6.2-6.6.3, Jan. 29, 2020.
355. *See* United States-Mexico-Canada Agreement, Section 6.6.4, Jan. 29, 2020.
356. *See* United States-Mexico-Canada Agreement, Section 6.6.5, Jan. 29, 2020.
357. *See* United States-Mexico-Canada Agreement, Section 5.10, Jan. 29, 2020.
358. *See* United States-Mexico-Canada Agreement, Section 6.6.2, Jan. 29, 2020.
359. *See* United States-Mexico-Canada Agreement, Section 6.6.2, Jan. 29, 2020.
360. *See* United States-Mexico-Canada Agreement, Section 6.8, Jan. 29, 2020.
361. *See* United States-Mexico-Canada Agreement, Section 6.8, Jan. 29, 2020.
362. *See* United States-Mexico-Canada Agreement, Section 6.8, Jan. 29, 2020.
363. *See* United States-Mexico-Canada Agreement, Section 6.9, Jan. 29, 2020.

CHAPTER 7

Customs Administration and Trade Facilitation

The USMCA creates a new system for customs documentation and data. The USMCA contains many new requirements for the Parties. Parties must issue written advance rulings prior to importation, adopt procedures that provide for immediate release of goods, use information technology and maintain a single window to allow electronic submissions. Additionally, the Parties must review their procedural and document/data requirement. They must also maintain risk management systems and post-clearance audits. The USCMA also imposes a new requirement that Parties must maintain a trade facilitation partnership program for operators who meet specified security criteria. It also requires Parties to ensure persons with customs administrative issues have access to an appeal or judicial review of the determination. Additionally, the USCMA adopts penalties and standards of conduct; it introduces an Anti-Corruption clause. With respect to border inspections, Parties are required to coordinate to develop procedures or facilities at adjacent ports for efficiency purposes. The USMCA also establishes cooperation and enforcement mechanisms that ensure the confidentiality and the accuracy of claims for preferential tariff treatment. Under these provisions, Parties must take appropriate legislative, administrative, or judicial actions to enforce its laws and address custom issues. Additionally, under USCMA, if one Party claims information is confidential, another Party must keep that information confidential

Chapter 7 of the USMCA is similar to Chapter 5 of NAFTA, Customs Procedures. This chapter addresses increased modernization through the use of information technology. It creates a new system for customs documentation and data.[364] The chapter also focuses on cooperation and enforcement mechanisms that ensure the confidentiality and the accuracy of claims for preferential tariff treatment.[365]

First, the Parties affirm their rights and obligations under the WTO Agreement on Trade Facilitation.[366] Second, this chapter sets provisions which require that Parties

---

364. *See* generally United States-Mexico-Canada Agreement, Section 7, Jan. 29, 2020.
365. *See* generally United States-Mexico-Canada Agreement, Section 7, Jan. 29, 2020.
366. *See* United States-Mexico-Canada Agreement, Section 7.1, Jan. 29, 2020.

make information free on a publicly accessible website and continually update that information.[367] This covers procedures, forms, laws, regulations, duties, taxes, fees, and contact information for inquiry points that relate to imports, exports, and transit.[368]

Furthermore, where NAFTA merely suggested it, the USMCA requires Parties to maintain a mechanism to regularly communicate with traders within its territory and allow them to bring attention to emerging issues.[369] Under the USMCA, Parties must maintain at least one inquiry point where people can inquire about imports, exports, and transits.[370] No fee can be charged for answering inquiries, and Parties must respond within a reasonable time period.[371] This mechanism is for issue-specific matters and financial services—not for general customs matters.[372]

§7.1   ADVANCE RULINGS AND ADVICE

Parties, through their custom administrations, must issue written advance ruling, prior to the importation of a good into its territory that sets forth the treatment the Party shall provide to the good at import.[373] Any person with a justifiable cause may request a written advance ruling without needing to establish or maintain a contractual or other relationship with a person located in the importing party territory.[374] Parties must give advice regarding drawbacks and deferral within a reasonable time frame upon request.[375]

§7.2   RELEASE OF GOODS

The USMCA requires Parties to adopt/maintain procedures that provide for the immediate release of goods upon receipt of the customs declaration and fulfillment of all applicable requirements and procedures.[376] This includes electronic submission and processing.[377] They must adopt procedures providing for the pre-processing of goods and for goods to be released at the point of arrival without requiring temporary warehousing.[378] Furthermore, goods must be released prior to final determination and payment of duties, on the condition that the duties had not been determined prior to or on arrival.[379] This will reduce the amount of time that imported goods are left in warehouses and reduce barriers to trade.

---

367. *See* United States-Mexico-Canada Agreement, Section 7.2, Jan. 29, 2020.
368. *See* United States-Mexico-Canada Agreement, Section 7.2, Jan. 29, 2020.
369. *See* United States-Mexico-Canada Agreement, Section 7.2, Jan. 29, 2020.
370. *See* United States-Mexico-Canada Agreement, Section 7.3, Jan. 29, 2020.
371. *See* United States-Mexico-Canada Agreement, Section 7.3, Jan. 29, 2020.
372. *See* United States-Mexico-Canada Agreement, Section 7.3, Jan. 29, 2020.
373. *See* United States-Mexico-Canada Agreement, Section 7.4, Jan. 29, 2020.
374. *See* United States-Mexico-Canada Agreement, Section 7.4, Jan. 29, 2020.
375. *See* United States-Mexico-Canada Agreement, Section 7.6, Jan. 29, 2020.
376. *See* United States-Mexico-Canada Agreement, Section 7.7, Jan. 29, 2020.
377. *See* United States-Mexico-Canada Agreement, Section 7.7, Jan. 29, 2020.
378. *See* United States-Mexico-Canada Agreement, Section 7.7, Jan. 29, 2020.
379. *See* United States-Mexico-Canada Agreement, Section 7.7, Jan. 29, 2020.

[A]   Article 7.8. Express Shipments

The USMCA contains new provisions related to express shipments.[380] The Agreement allows Parties to submit and process information prior to the goods' arrival.[381] It allows a single submission to cover all the goods in one shipment.[382] It expedites the release immediately after arrival, so long as all relevant documents and data are submitted.[383] No customs duties or taxes will be assessed at the time or point of importation, and formal entry procedures will not be required.[384] However, fixed costs will be imposed for express shipments of particular values.[385] Additionally, there is a threshold above which customs duties and taxes are levied, and formal entry is required.[386]

For the United States, the threshold is USD 800 for customs duties and taxes.[387] For Mexico, the threshold is USD 117 for customs duties and USD 50 for taxes.[388] Lastly, Canada's threshold is CAD 150 for customs and CAD 40 for taxes.[389] However, "Notwithstanding [these amounts], a Party may impose a reciprocal amount that is lower for shipments from another Party if the amount provided for under that other Party's law is lower than that of the Party." Some argue that this clause suggests that the United States could lower its *de minimis* threshold to match Canada or the United States.[390] In such a situation, the United States would be able to lower its *de minimis* level to USD 117 or CAD 150, an amount even below the 2016 limit of USD 200 (which Congress raised to USD 800).[391] Such an action was characterized by one commentator that it would be regarded as "an attack on economic liberty for American citizens, but it would be an enormous step backward on a policy where the United States has been a leader for liberalization."[392] However, there were threats of such action by the U.S. during the later stages of the USMCA negotiations and discussions on this point could continue.

§7.3   USE OF INFORMATION TECHNOLOGY (IT)

In addition to those new reciprocity provisions, the USMCA requires Parties to use *IT* to: (a) expedite the release of goods; (b) make available declarations and other forms;

---

380. Dean Barclay, & Francisco de Rosenzweig, et. al., Overview of Chapter 7 (Customs Administration and Trade Facilitation) of the US-Mexico-Canada Agreement, JD Supra (Nov. 1, 2018) https://www.jdsupra.com/legalnews/overview-of-chapter-7-customs-28828/.
381. *See* United States-Mexico-Canada Agreement, Section 7.8, Jan. 29, 2020.
382. *See* United States-Mexico-Canada Agreement, Section 7.8, Jan. 29, 2020.
383. *See* United States-Mexico-Canada Agreement, Section 7.8, Jan. 29, 2020.
384. *See* United States-Mexico-Canada Agreement, Section 7.8, Jan. 29, 2020.
385. *See* United States-Mexico-Canada Agreement, Section 7.8, Jan. 29, 2020.
386. *See* United States-Mexico-Canada Agreement, Section 7.8, Jan. 29, 2020.
387. *See* United States-Mexico-Canada Agreement, Section 7.8, Jan. 29, 2020.
388. *See* United States-Mexico-Canada Agreement, Section 7.8, Jan. 29, 2020.
389. *See* United States-Mexico-Canada Agreement, Section 7.8, Jan. 29, 2020.
390. *See* Inu Manak, How a Footnote in the USMCA Undermines Economic Liberty, CATO Institute (Aug. 30, 2019), https://www.cato.org/blog/how-footnote-usmca-undermines-economic-liberty.
391. *See* United States-Mexico-Canada Agreement, Section 7.8, Jan. 29, 2020.
392. *See* United States-Mexico-Canada Agreement, Section 7.8, Jan. 29, 2020.

(c) allow a declaration and other forms to be submitted; (d) make it easier for persons engaged in trade or transit to submit and receive information; (e) facilitate communication between traders and customs; (f) permit electronic payment of duties, taxes, and fees; (g) run electronic risk management systems; and (h) endeavor to allow importers to correct multiple import declarations through a single form.[393] Parties must maintain a single window that allows electronic submission through a single-entry point of the documentation and data required for importation.[394] Parties should review and endeavor to expand the single window functionality to cover all import, export, and transit transactions.[395]

§7.4   PROCEDURAL ASPECTS OF CUSTOMS ADMINISTRATION

Under the USMCA, Parties must review their procedures and document/data requirements to ensure that they are adopted and applied: (a) with a view to a rapid release of goods; (b) in a manner that aims at reducing time, burden and cost of compliance; and (c) that is least restrictive to trade.[396] Additionally, Parties must maintain risk management systems that allow customs and other agencies to inspect high-risk goods and simplify the release of low-risk goods.[397] The USMCA also requires Parties to maintain post-clearance audits to ensure compliance with customs and related laws.[398] It requires Parties to inform the traders with respect to laws.[399]

The USMCA imposes a new requirement that Parties must maintain a trade facilitation partnership program for operators who meet specified security criteria.[400] This is consistent with the *Framework of Standard to Secure and Facilitate Global Trade of the World Customs Organization.*[401] The USMCA also requires Parties to ensure persons with customs administration issues have access to an appeal or review of the determination by a higher or independent authority in a quasi-judicial or judicial review manner.[402] In addition, the USMCA creates a mechanism where a customs office can request guidance from the appropriate authority to ensure they are properly applying the regulations and procedures to the transaction.[403]

---

393. *See* United States-Mexico-Canada Agreement, Section 7.9, Jan. 29, 2020.
394. *See* United States-Mexico-Canada Agreement, Section 7.10, Jan. 29, 2020.
395. *See* United States-Mexico-Canada Agreement, Section 7.10, Jan. 29, 2020.
396. *See* United States-Mexico-Canada Agreement, Section 7.11, Jan. 29, 2020.
397. *See* United States-Mexico-Canada Agreement, Section 7.12, Jan. 29, 2020.
398. *See* United States-Mexico-Canada Agreement, Section 7.12, Jan. 29, 2020.
399. *See* United States-Mexico-Canada Agreement, Section 7.13, Jan. 29, 2020.
400. *See* United States-Mexico-Canada Agreement, Section 7.14, Jan. 29, 2020.
401. *See* generally World Customs Organization, SAFE Framework of Standards to Secure and Facilitate Global Trade (Jun. 2005).
402. *See* United States-Mexico-Canada Agreement, Section 7.15, Jan. 29, 2020.
403. *See* United States-Mexico-Canada Agreement, Section 7.16, Jan. 29, 2020.

§7.5 TRANSIT

The USMCA provides that transit through a Party's territory must occur freely if the transit begins and terminates beyond the frontier of the Party across whose territory the traffic passes (traffic in transit).[404]

§7.6 PENALTIES AND STANDARDS OF CONDUCT

Parties must adopt penalty procedures for breach of customs laws.[405] Clerical or minor errors in a customs transaction do not constitute a breach.[406] The USMCA introduces an Anti-Corruption clause, not present in NAFTA, which provides that "[n]o portion of the remuneration of a government official shall be calculated as a fixed portion or percentage of any penalties or duties assessed or collected."[407] To this end, the USMCA requires Parties to establish measures to deter customs officials from improper or corrupt behavior.[408] This includes using the position for private gain, including monetary benefits.[409]

§7.7 CUSTOMS BROKERS

The USMCA contains new provisions that put self-filers and customs brokers on equal footing.[410] Importers are able to self-file electronically, without needing a custom broker to do so on their behalf.[411] Parties may require licensing, registration, or other qualifications for customs brokers.[412] However, if licenses are required, Parties cannot impose limits on the number of ports/locations that the broker can operate in.[413]

§7.8 BORDER INSPECTIONS

With respect to inspections at the border, Parties must coordinate to carry out examinations "to the extent practicable simultaneously within a single location" in order to promote the efficient and effective release of goods.[414] To this end, Parties must coordinate to develop procedures or facilities at adjacent ports for efficiency purposes.[415]

---

404. *See* United States-Mexico-Canada Agreement, Section 7.17, Jan. 29, 2020.
405. *See* United States-Mexico-Canada Agreement, Section 7.18, Jan. 29, 2020.
406. *See* United States-Mexico-Canada Agreement, Section 7.18, Jan. 29, 2020.
407. *See* United States-Mexico-Canada Agreement, Section 7.18, Jan. 29, 2020.
408. *See* United States-Mexico-Canada Agreement, Section 7.19, Jan. 29, 2020.
409. *See* United States-Mexico-Canada Agreement, Section 7.19, Jan. 29, 2020.
410. *See* United States-Mexico-Canada Agreement, Section 7.20, Jan. 29, 2020.
411. *See* United States-Mexico-Canada Agreement, Section 7.20, Jan. 29, 2020.
412. *See* United States-Mexico-Canada Agreement, Section 7.20, Jan. 29, 2020.
413. *See* United States-Mexico-Canada Agreement, Section 7.20, Jan. 29, 2020.
414. *See* United States-Mexico-Canada Agreement, Section 7.21, Jan. 29, 2020.
415. *See* United States-Mexico-Canada Agreement, Section 7.21, Jan. 29, 2020.

§7.9   CONFIDENTIALITY, COOPERATION, AND COMMITTEES

The USMCA explicitly states that confidential information must be protected from use or disclosure that could jeopardize the competitive position of traders.[416] Parties must cooperate on developing and implementing customs initiatives that promote free trade. Under this provision, the Committee on Trade Facilitation is established.[417] This Committee is comparable to the NAFTA Committee on Trade in Goods; however, the new Committee has a more specific mandate that includes AEO programs, technical assistance, and single windows.[418]

§7.10   COOPERATION AND ENFORCEMENT

Section B of Chapter 7 contains cooperation and enforcement provisions that are standard and left largely unchanged from NAFTA. Generally, where a customs offense takes place, the rule of the territory where it occurred applies.[419] Thus, it is unlikely that this section will have a significant impact on international trade. Under these provisions, Parties must take measures to provide other Parties with notice of administrative, regulatory, or legal changes that are likely to substantially affect the operation of the Agreement or the effective implementation and enforcement of trade laws.[420] USMCA requires Parties to take appropriate legislative, administrative, or judicial actions to enforce its laws and address custom issues.[421]

When comparing the two agreements, NAFTA is similar in its limited disclosure of confidential information, but USMCA goes into greater detail.[422] If one Party says the information is confidential, another Party must keep that information confidential.[423] If they fail to do so, a Party may decline to provide information to that other Party.[424] NAFTA also had procedures in place for origin verifications. The USMCA is slightly different in that the verification visit will be conducted by the requesting Party.[425] The USMCA also establishes a new subcommittee that addresses issues related to potential or real customs offenses, which is comparable to NAFTA's Customs Subgroup under the Working Group on Rules of Origin.

---

416. *See* United States-Mexico-Canada Agreement, Section 7.22, Jan. 29, 2020.
417. *See* United States-Mexico-Canada Agreement, Section 7.24, Jan. 29, 2020.
418. *See* United States-Mexico-Canada Agreement, Section 7.24, Jan. 29, 2020.
419. *See* United States-Mexico-Canada Agreement, Section 7.25, Jan. 29, 2020.
420. *See* United States-Mexico-Canada Agreement, Section 7.25, Jan. 29, 2020.
421. *See* United States-Mexico-Canada Agreement, Section 7.25, Jan. 29, 2020.
422. *See* United States-Mexico-Canada Agreement, Section 7.26, Jan. 29, 2020.
423. *See* United States-Mexico-Canada Agreement, Section 7.28, Jan. 29, 2020.
424. *See* United States-Mexico-Canada Agreement, Section 7.28, Jan. 29, 2020.
425. *See* United States-Mexico-Canada Agreement, Section 7.27, Jan. 29, 2020.

CHAPTER 8

Recognition of the United Mexican States' Direct, Inalienable, and Imprescriptible Ownership of Hydrocarbons

The USMCA recognizes Mexico's ownership of Hydrocarbons in the subsoil of their national territory, including the continental shelf. Additionally, Mexico reserves its sovereign right to reform its Constitution and domestic legislation, and all Parties must confirm their respect of this right.

There is only one article in this chapter, and it recognizes Mexico's Direct, Invaluable and Imprescriptible Ownership of Hydrocarbons in the subsoil of their national territory, including the continental shelf.[426] Mexico reserved its sovereign right to reform its Constitution and domestic legislation, and all Parties to this agreement must confirm their respect of this right.[427]

This was one of the most important accomplishments for Mexico in the USMCA, which preserved its unilateral ownership of its oil and gas reserves but, at the same time, opened the economy for the first time to the possibility of greater exploration of its vast reserves and licenses for foreign participation in exploration.

---

426. *See* United States-Mexico-Canada Agreement, Section 8.1, Jan. 29, 2020.
427. *See* United States-Mexico-Canada Agreement, Section 8.1, Jan. 29, 2020.

CHAPTER 9

Sanitary and Phytosanitary Measures

The USMCA has a chapter on sanitary and phytosanitary measures; its main objectives are related to ensuring the implementation of these measures in order to protect human, animal, or plant life or health. It allows Parties to adopt any measure to achieve the objectives. In doing so, it must base these measures on relevant international guidelines and they must provide information related to the scientific basis. When making adjustments, Parties should consider relevant measures of the other Parties and strive to make their measures identical to those of other Parties. In doing so, Parties will use WTO SPS Committee guidelines for making determinations regarding regional conditions and equivalence assessments. Additionally, under the USMCA Parties have a right to audit the exporting Party's competent authorities; however, prior to audit all involved Parties must discuss the scope of the audit. Parties may also use import checks to assess compliance; and they may use certificates to assure compliance. Furthermore, Parties agree to be transparent and share information about their measures. Here, the WTO SOS notification submission system applies; and Parties must allow at least sixty days for the other Parties to provide written comments on a proposed measure. Finally, Parties may request information on any matter related to this chapter; the other Parties should provide the available information within a reasonable time.

NAFTA had a chapter on sanitary and phytosanitary measures.[428] In the USMCA, the status quo is maintained on food safety provisions. There is no joint food safety risk assessment. The main objectives of the USMCA chapter are to: (a) protect human, animal, or plant life or health; (b) reinforce and build upon the WTO Agreement on the Application of Sanitary and Phytosanitary Measures (SPS Agreement); (c) strengthen communication between the relevant authorities; (d) ensure implementation of each Party's sanitary and phytosanitary; (e) ensure transparency in understanding each Party's measures; (f) encourage science-based international standards; (g) enhance the compatibility of each Party's measures; and (h) advance science-based decision-making.[429] To this end, the Parties affirm their rights and obligations under the SPS

---

428. *See* North American Free Trade Agreement, § 709, Jan. 1, 1994.
429. *See* United States-Mexico-Canada Agreement, Section 9.3, Jan. 29, 2020.

Agreement.[430] Measures that conform to relevant international standards are deemed to be necessary and presumed to be consistent with this chapter.[431]

The USMCA allows Parties to adopt any measure to achieve the objectives provided that they are consistent with the chapter.[432] In doing so, Parties must base these measures on relevant international guidelines or an assessment of the risk to human, animal, or plant life or health.[433] Parties must also provide information related to the scientific basis for its measures because they are to be applied only to the extent necessary to protect human, animal, or plant life or health.[434] The main concern here is that Parties might engage in a protectionist scheme under the guise of sanitary or phytosanitary measures.[435] In the past, there were issues concerning U.S. restrictions on imports from Mexico of avocados and mangoes.

Parties will enhance the compatibility of Sanitary and Phytosanitary Measures provided that it does not reduce each Party's appropriate level of protection.[436] When making adjustments, Parties should consider relevant measures of the other Parties and strive to make their measures identical to those of the other Parties.[437]

§9.1   ADAPTION TO REGIONAL CONDITIONS AND EQUIVALENCE

In order to achieve the objective of acquiring confidence in the procedures followed by each Party, Parties will use WTO SPS Committee guidelines for making determinations regarding regional conditions.[438] If an importing Party receives a request from an exporting Party for the determination of conditions and determines that they have provided sufficient information, the importing Party must initiate an assessment without undue delay.[439] Determinations must include explanations if an area is not a pest-or disease-free area.[440] Parties must maintain risk management measures in anticipation of a change in the status.[441]

Parties must recognize the importance of equivalence and apply it to a specific sanitary or phytosanitary measure and must take into account WTO SPS Committee guidelines to do so.[442] On request, and without undue delay, importing Parties must explain the objective and rationale of its measures and identify the risk it is intended to address.[443] When the importing Party initiates an equivalence assessment, they must

---

430. *See* United States-Mexico-Canada Agreement, Section 9.4, Jan. 29, 2020.
431. *See* United States-Mexico-Canada Agreement, Section 9.4, Jan. 29, 2020.
432. *See* United States-Mexico-Canada Agreement, Section 9.6, Jan. 29, 2020.
433. *See* United States-Mexico-Canada Agreement, Section 9.6, Jan. 29, 2020.
434. *See* United States-Mexico-Canada Agreement, Section 9.6, Jan. 29, 2020.
435. Understanding the WTO Agreement on Sanitary and Phytosanitary Measures, World Trade Organization (last visited Apr. 2, 2020) https://www.wto.org/english/tratop_e/sps_e/spsund _e.htm.
436. *See* United States-Mexico-Canada Agreement, Section 9.7, Jan. 29, 2020.
437. *See* United States-Mexico-Canada Agreement, Section 9.7, Jan. 29, 2020.
438. *See* United States-Mexico-Canada Agreement, Section 9.8, Jan. 29, 2020.
439. *See* United States-Mexico-Canada Agreement, Section 9.8, Jan. 29, 2020.
440. *See* United States-Mexico-Canada Agreement, Section 9.8, Jan. 29, 2020.
441. *See* United States-Mexico-Canada Agreement, Section 9.8, Jan. 29, 2020.
442. *See* United States-Mexico-Canada Agreement, Section 9.9, Jan. 29, 2020.
443. *See* United States-Mexico-Canada Agreement, Section 9.8, Jan. 29, 2020.

explain, on request, without undue delay, how it made the equivalence determination.[444] Any results should be reported to the SPS Committee.[445]

§9.2 AUDITS, IMPORT CHECKS FOR COMPLIANCE, AND CERTIFICATIONS

Importing Parties shall have the right to audit the exporting Party's competent authorities, including inspection systems.[446] Audits may include assessing control programs, such as on-site inspections; however, they must be systems-based and designed to check the effectiveness of the regulatory controls.[447] Prior to an audit, all involved Parties must discuss the rationale, objectives, and scope of the audit and the criteria it must meet.[448] Parties may decide to collaborate on audits of non-Parties or share the results of audits of non-Parties.[449]

In addition, Parties must use import checks to assess compliance with its measures and to conduct a risk assessment.[450] These checks must be associated with importation risks and carried out without undue delay.[451] Parties must make available, upon request, their import procedures and the basis for determining the nature and frequency of import checks.[452] Responses to non-conformities must be limited to what is reasonable and necessary to respond to each non-conformity.[453]

Parties can use certificates to assure compliance provided that the requirement is based on the relevant international standard or is appropriate to the circumstances of risk.[454] (Certification). If certification is required from a Party, they must provide, on request, the rationale for any attestations or information that the Party requires to be included on the certificate.[455]

§9.3 TRANSPARENCY AND EMERGENCY MEASURES

Parties agree to be transparent and share information about their sanitary and phytosanitary measures on an ongoing basis.[456] Parties should use the WTO SOS notification submission system as a means of notifying the other Parties.[457] Parties must allow at least sixty days for the other Parties to provide written comments on a

---

444. *See* United States-Mexico-Canada Agreement, Section 9.9, Jan. 29, 2020.
445. *See* United States-Mexico-Canada Agreement, Section 9.9, Jan. 29, 2020.
446. *See* United States-Mexico-Canada Agreement, Section 9.9, Jan. 29, 2020.
447. *See* United States-Mexico-Canada Agreement, Section 9.9, Jan. 29, 2020.
448. *See* United States-Mexico-Canada Agreement, Section 9.9, Jan. 29, 2020.
449. *See* United States-Mexico-Canada Agreement, Section 9.9, Jan. 29, 2020.
450. *See* United States-Mexico-Canada Agreement, Section 9.10, Jan. 29, 2020.
451. *See* United States-Mexico-Canada Agreement, Section 9.10, Jan. 29, 2020.
452. *See* United States-Mexico-Canada Agreement, Section 9.10, Jan. 29, 2020.
453. *See* United States-Mexico-Canada Agreement, Section 9.10, Jan. 29, 2020.
454. *See* United States-Mexico-Canada Agreement, Section 9.12, Jan. 29, 2020.
455. *See* United States-Mexico-Canada Agreement, Section 9.12, Jan. 29, 2020.
456. *See* United States-Mexico-Canada Agreement, Section 9.13, Jan. 29, 2020.
457. *See* United States-Mexico-Canada Agreement, Section 9.13, Jan. 29, 2020.

proposed measure unless urgent problems arise or threaten to arise.[458] The Party must include the proposed measure and a legal basis for it and publish any final measures online.[459]

An importer must promptly notify the exporter, in writing, of each affected Party if a measure is put in place for emergencies.[460] The Party must review the scientific basis of that measure within six months and make the results available to any Party upon request.[461] After that, the Party should review the measure periodically.[462]

[A]   Article 9.15. Information Exchange

[1]   *Cooperation*

Parties may request information on any matter of this chapter.[463] The other Parties should provide the available information within a reasonable time—if possible, by electronic means.[464] Parties agree to collaborate and exchange information on sanitary and phytosanitary matters of mutual interest.[465] The USMCA establishes the SPS Committee as a forum to consider any matter related to this chapter.[466] The Committee will meet annually and report to the Commission.[467] The USMCA allows any ongoing technical working groups to meet annually unless otherwise decided.[468] Any ad hoc tactical working group must meet as frequently as decided by the Parties.[469] If a Party wants to consult on technical considerations, they may initiate consultations by delivering a written request to the Contact Point of the Responding Party.[470] The request must identify the reason for the request, including a description of the concern.[471] The Parties must meet within thirty days of the request's receipt and aim to resolve the matter within one hundred and eighty days of the request.[472] If a dispute arises where the issue is scientific or technical in nature, a panel should seek expert advice and may establish an advisory technical experts' group.[473]

---

458. *See* United States-Mexico-Canada Agreement, Section 9.13, Jan. 29, 2020.
459. *See* United States-Mexico-Canada Agreement, Section 9.13, Jan. 29, 2020.
460. *See* United States-Mexico-Canada Agreement, Section 9.14, Jan. 29, 2020.
461. *See* United States-Mexico-Canada Agreement, Section 9.14, Jan. 29, 2020.
462. *See* United States-Mexico-Canada Agreement, Section 9.14, Jan. 29, 2020.
463. *See* United States-Mexico-Canada Agreement, Section 9.15, Jan. 29, 2020.
464. *See* United States-Mexico-Canada Agreement, Section 9.15, Jan. 29, 2020.
465. *See* United States-Mexico-Canada Agreement, Section 9.16, Jan. 29, 2020.
466. *See* United States-Mexico-Canada Agreement, Section 9.17, Jan. 29, 2020.
467. *See* United States-Mexico-Canada Agreement, Section 9.17, Jan. 29, 2020.
468. *See* United States-Mexico-Canada Agreement, Section 9.18, Jan. 29, 2020.
469. *See* United States-Mexico-Canada Agreement, Section 9.18, Jan. 29, 2020.
470. *See* United States-Mexico-Canada Agreement, Section 9.19, Jan. 29, 2020.
471. *See* United States-Mexico-Canada Agreement, Section 9.19, Jan. 29, 2020.
472. *See* United States-Mexico-Canada Agreement, Section 9.19, Jan. 29, 2020.
473. *See* United States-Mexico-Canada Agreement, Section 9.20, Jan. 29, 2020.

CHAPTER 10
Trade Remedies

The USMCA keeps trade remedy dispute settlement in place with a few changes. However, it adds a section aimed at preventing "duty evasion of antidumping, countervailing, and safeguard duties." Under the USMCA, Parties maintain their rights and obligations under Article XIX of the General Agreement on Tariffs Trade (GATT) 1994 and the Safeguards Agreement. However, any Party taking an emergency action under these must exclude goods imported by the Parties, unless the imports individually account for a substantial share of total imports. Additionally, when implementing safeguards, determinations must be made by a competent investigating authority that are subject to review by judicial or administrative tribunals. With regards to antidumping and countervailing duties, the USMCA introduces a section that provides for cooperation on preventing duty evasion of trade remedy laws. The USMCA also establishes panels for Review of Statutory Amendments and Review of Final Antidumping Law and Countervailing Duty Law. For reviews of amendments, Parties may request to be referred to a binational panel. For reviews of antidumping and countervailing duty laws, determinations that were published by a Party before the entry into force of the USMCA, Chapter 19 of NAFTA still applies. However, for determinations published thereafter, judicial review is replaced with binational panel review. Finally, regarding administrative matters, Parties have a duty to establish a code of conduct for panelists and members of committees, consult annually, designate officials in their respective country to ensure consultations occur, and maintain a Secretariat to facilitate the operation of this section.

USMCA Chapter 10 covers trade remedies, including safeguard measures, which were in Chapter 8 of NAFTA, and the application of antidumping and countervailing duties that were in Chapter 19 of NAFTA.[474] The USMCA keeps trade remedy dispute settlement in place with a few changes. However, it adds a section aimed at preventing "duty evasion of antidumping, countervailing, and safeguard duties."

---

474. *See* United States-Mexico-Canada Agreement, Section 10, Jan. 29, 2020.

§10.1   SAFEGUARDS

Regarding the safeguard provision of the USMCA, little has changed between NAFTA and now. Under the USMCA, Parties maintain their rights and obligations under Article XIX of the General Agreement on Tariffs Trade (GATT) 1994 and the Safeguards Agreement, except those regarding compensation or retaliation and exclusion.[475] Any Party taking an emergency action under Article XIX and the Safeguards Agreement must exclude goods imported by the Parties unless imports from a Party individually account for a substantial share of total imports, or in exceptional circumstances, collectively, contribute to the serious injury or threat caused by imports.[476] Under the USMCA, a share of imports is not considered substantial if it is not among the top five suppliers.[477] When implementing safeguards, determinations must be made by a competent investigating authority that are subject to review by judicial or administrative tribunals.[478] This would relate to actions under section 201 of the Trade Act of 1974 at the U.S. International Trade Commission, often referred to as the "escape clause".

§10.2   ANTIDUMPING AND COUNTERVAILING DUTIES

With regards to antidumping and countervailing duties, Parties retain their rights and obligations under Article VI of GATT 1994, the Anti-Dumping Agreement, and the Subsidies and Countervailing Measures Agreement.[479] However, with the exception of Annex 10-A, nothing in the Agreement confers any rights or imposes any obligations with respect to the measures taken pursuant to these agreements.[480]

The USMCA introduces a section that provides for cooperation on preventing duty evasion of trade remedy laws.[481] No such provisions were included in NAFTA. While the USMCA does not specify how evasion is identified, the Parties agree to share information that can lead to the discovery of evasion.[482] To this end, Parties agree to strengthen and expand their customs and trade enforcement efforts in matters related to duty evasion.[483]

§10.3   DUTY EVASION COOPERATION

In order to prevent duty evasion, Parties should cooperate, share customs information, maintain mechanisms for sharing, and collect information that will help enable Parties to determine whether entry into its territory is subject to antidumping, countervailing,

---

475. *See* United States-Mexico-Canada Agreement, Section 10.2, Jan. 29, 2020.
476. *See* United States-Mexico-Canada Agreement, Section 10.2, Jan. 29, 2020.
477. *See* United States-Mexico-Canada Agreement, Section 10.2, Jan. 29, 2020.
478. *See* United States-Mexico-Canada Agreement, Section 10.3, Jan. 29, 2020.
479. *See* United States-Mexico-Canada Agreement, Section 10.5, Jan. 29, 2020.
480. *See* United States-Mexico-Canada Agreement, Section 10.5, Jan. 29, 2020.
481. *See* United States-Mexico-Canada Agreement, Section 10.7, Jan. 29, 2020.
482. *See* United States-Mexico-Canada Agreement, Section 10.7, Jan. 29, 2020.
483. *See* United States-Mexico-Canada Agreement, Section 10.6, Jan. 29, 2020.

or safeguard duties.[484] The USMCA allows requests for duty evasion verifications to be made in writing by the customs administrations by electronic or other means and includes sufficient information.[485] The responding Party must reply within thirty days of receiving the request.[486] After the verification is conducted, the responding Party must provide the requesting Party with a report of verification.[487] Verifications may be conducted in the territory of the responding party, so long as there is mutual agreement, reasonable notice, and consent.[488]

§10.4 REVIEW AND SETTLEMENT DISPUTE

The USMCA establishes panels for Review of Statutory Amendments and *Review* of Final Antidumping Law and Countervailing Duty Law.[489] Notwithstanding review, each country can apply its antidumping law and countervailing duty law to goods imported from the territory of another Party.[490] Parties can change and modify these laws; however, modifications apply to other Party's goods only if the amendment specifies that it applies to goods from that Party.[491] Additionally, written notification must be made as soon as possible prior to the enactment, and, on request, Parties must consult with affected Parties prior to the amendment's enactment.[492] Any amendment must be consistent with GATT 1994, the SCM Agreement, or any successor agreement and the USMCA.[493]

§10.5 REVIEW OF STATUTORY AMENDMENTS AND FINAL ANTIDUMPING AND COUNTERVAILING DUTY DETERMINATIONS

Parties may request that amendments be referred to a binational panel for a declaratory opinion on whether it conforms to the provisions of this Article or whether the amendment overturns a prior decision of a panel and does not conform to this Article.[494] In the event that the panel recommends modifications to the amendment, the two Parties shall begin consultations and seek to achieve a solution within ninety days, including corrective legislation.[495] If corrective legislation is not enacted within nine months from the end of those ninety days, and no other solution is reached, the Party that requests a panel may take comparable legislative or equivalent executive

484. *See* United States-Mexico-Canada Agreement, Section 10.7, Jan. 29, 2020.
485. *See* United States-Mexico-Canada Agreement, Section 10.7, Jan. 29, 2020.
486. *See* United States-Mexico-Canada Agreement, Section 10.7, Jan. 29, 2020.
487. *See* United States-Mexico-Canada Agreement, Section 10.7, Jan. 29, 2020.
488. *See* United States-Mexico-Canada Agreement, Section 10.7, Jan. 29, 2020.
489. *See* United States-Mexico-Canada Agreement, Section 10.9, Jan. 29, 2020.
490. *See* United States-Mexico-Canada Agreement, Section 10.10, Jan. 29, 2020.
491. *See* United States-Mexico-Canada Agreement, Section 10.10, Jan. 29, 2020.
492. *See* United States-Mexico-Canada Agreement, Section 10.10, Jan. 29, 2020.
493. *See* United States-Mexico-Canada Agreement, Section 10.10, Jan. 29, 2020.
494. *See* United States-Mexico-Canada Agreement, Section 10.11, Jan. 29, 2020.
495. *See* United States-Mexico-Canada Agreement, Section 10.11, Jan. 29, 2020.

action or terminate this Agreement with regard to the amending Party on a sixty-day written notice to that party.[496]

Chapter 19 of NAFTA, which provided for binational panel reviews of antidumping and countervailing duty determinations made by the governments of the NAFTA Parties,[497] will continue to apply to binational panel reviews related to final determinations published by a Party before the entry into force of the USMCA. NAFTA Chapter 19 will not apply to determinations published thereafter. Furthermore, Chapter 19 of NAFTA contained an investor-state dispute settlement mechanism which allowed aggrieved investors or companies to appeal to a NAFTA arbitration tribunal.[498] The USMCA eliminates this mechanism for Canada within three years of implementation and will likely eliminate it for Mexico, excluding certain key exceptions, such as energy and telecommunications.[499]

For a review of Final Antidumping and Countervailing Duty Determinations, judicial review is replaced with a binational panel review.[500] Requests for a panel must be made in writing to the other Party involved within thirty days following the date of publication of the final determination in question in the official journal of the importing party.[501] The investigating authority that issued the final determination has the right to appear and be represented by counsel before the panel.[502] The panel my uphold a decision or remand for action so long as it remains consistent with the panel's decision.[503] Afterward, a reasonable time must be given for the implementation of compliance measures with the remand.[504] Decisions are binding on the involved Parties with respect to that particular *matter*.[505] This should not affect decisions other than final determinations.[506] Parties may not permit appeals of the panel decision to be heard in their domestic courts.[507] However, there is an extraordinary challenge procedure set out in Annex 10-B.3, which Parties may utilize if there is an abuse of discretion or other major concerns the Party believes materially affected the panel's decision.[508] This article further sets out the rules on timing for the judicial appellate procedure.[509]

If a situation arises where the opportunity for review by a binational panel is unavailable, then a Party may make a written request to the other Party regarding the allegations.[510] If it is not resolved within forty-five days thereof, the complaining Party

---

496. *See* United States-Mexico-Canada Agreement, Section 10.11, Jan. 29, 2020.
497. *See* North American Free Trade Agreement, Chapter 19, Jan. 1, 1994.
498. *See* North American Free Trade Agreement, § 501.1, Jan. 1, 1994.
499. *See* United States-Mexico-Canada Agreement, Section 10, Jan. 29, 2020.
500. *See* United States-Mexico-Canada Agreement, Section 10.12, Jan. 29, 2020.
501. *See* United States-Mexico-Canada Agreement, Section 10.12, Jan. 29, 2020.
502. *See* United States-Mexico-Canada Agreement, Section 10.12, Jan. 29, 2020.
503. *See* United States-Mexico-Canada Agreement, Section 10.12, Jan. 29, 2020.
504. *See* United States-Mexico-Canada Agreement, Section 10.12, Jan. 29, 2020.
505. *See* United States-Mexico-Canada Agreement, Section 10.12, Jan. 29, 2020.
506. *See* United States-Mexico-Canada Agreement, Section 10.12, Jan. 29, 2020.
507. *See* United States-Mexico-Canada Agreement, Section 10.12, Jan. 29, 2020.
508. *See* United States-Mexico-Canada Agreement, Section 10.12, Jan. 29, 2020.
509. *See* United States-Mexico-Canada Agreement, Section 10.12, Jan. 29, 2020.
510. *See* United States-Mexico-Canada Agreement, Section 10.13, Jan. 29, 2020.

may request that a special committee be established.[511] This must occur within fifteen days pursuant to § 10.13. The procedural rules for this committee are established in Annex 10B-3 (Extraordinary Challenge Procedure).[512] In such a case, reports must be made at every level of the appellate process.[513]

§10.6   PROSPECTIVE APPLICATION

Final determinations of a competent investigating authority can impose prospective applications when made after the USMCA's effective date.[514] Prospective application also applies to declaratory opinions under the Review of Statutory Amendments and amendments to antidumping or countervailing duty statutes enacted after the date of the Agreement's effective date.[515]

§10.7   ADMINISTRATIVE MATTERS

Parties must establish a code of conduct for panelists and members of committees.[516] On request of another Party, the competent investigating authority must provide to the other Party copies of all public information submitted to it, for purposes of an antidumping or countervailing duty investigation, with respect to the goods of that other Party.[517] Additionally, Parties must consult annually or upon request of any Party to consider problems that may arise with respect to the implementation of this section.[518] Parties must designate officials in their respective country to ensure consultations occurs.[519]

Furthermore, each Party must maintain a Secretariat to facilitate the operation of this section, including the work of panels or committees.[520] The Secretaries must act jointly to provide administrative assistance to all panels or committees.[521] They must maintain records of the proceedings and preserve an original copy in the Party's section office.[522] They shall file all requests, briefs, and other papers.[523] They must provide copies to the other Secretaries when requested.[524]

---

511. *See* United States-Mexico-Canada Agreement, Section 10.13, Jan. 29, 2020.
512. *See* United States-Mexico-Canada Agreement, Section 10.13, Jan. 29, 2020.
513. *See* United States-Mexico-Canada Agreement, Section 10.13, Jan. 29, 2020.
514. *See* United States-Mexico-Canada Agreement, Section 10.14, Jan. 29, 2020.
515. *See* United States-Mexico-Canada Agreement, Section 10.14, Jan. 29, 2020.
516. *See* United States-Mexico-Canada Agreement, Section 10.17, Jan. 29, 2020.
517. *See* United States-Mexico-Canada Agreement, Section 10.18, Jan. 29, 2020.
518. *See* United States-Mexico-Canada Agreement, Section 10.15, Jan. 29, 2020.
519. *See* United States-Mexico-Canada Agreement, Section 10.15, Jan. 29, 2020.
520. *See* United States-Mexico-Canada Agreement, Section 10.16, Jan. 29, 2020.
521. *See* United States-Mexico-Canada Agreement, Section 10.16, Jan. 29, 2020.
522. *See* United States-Mexico-Canada Agreement, Section 10.16, Jan. 29, 2020.
523. *See* United States-Mexico-Canada Agreement, Section 10.16, Jan. 29, 2020.
524. *See* United States-Mexico-Canada Agreement, Section 10.16, Jan. 29, 2020.

§10.8 ANTIDUMPING AND COUNTERVAILING DUTY PRACTICES AND PROCEDURES

Parties must minimize the number of webpages used in providing guidance on antidumping and countervailing proceedings, their laws and regulations, and sample questionnaires.[525] After a proceeding, each investigating authority must maintain and make available online a file that contains all non-confidential documents that are part of its administrative record for each segment of a proceeding and non-confidential summaries of confidential information contained in the administrative record.[526] They must also make their docket available in a manner that enables any interested Party to identify and locate particular documents in the file.[527] Parties must maintain a system for submitting documents electronically in these proceedings.[528] However, they may require manual submission of a petition or of other documents in exceptional circumstances. These electronic access points must be established no later than five days after the USMCA's effective date.[529]

---

525. *See* United States-Mexico-Canada Agreement, Annex 10-A, Jan. 29, 2020.
526. *See* United States-Mexico-Canada Agreement, Annex 10-A, Jan. 29, 2020.
527. *See* United States-Mexico-Canada Agreement, Annex 10-A, Jan. 29, 2020.
528. *See* United States-Mexico-Canada Agreement, Annex 10-A, Jan. 29, 2020.
529. *See* United States-Mexico-Canada Agreement, Annex 10-A, Jan. 29, 2020.

CHAPTER 11
Technical Barriers to Trade

The USMCA incorporates many articles of the WTO TBT Agreement; however, Parties cannot use Chapter 31 (Dispute Settlement) for matters brought under this Chapter. Additionally, Parties should use the TBT Committee Decision on International Standards to determine if a standard, guide, or recommendation exists on the subject. Each Party must also assess any technical regulations it proposes to adopt; they must also periodically review these regulations to ensure they align with relevant international standards. When a Party rejects an international standard, it should issue a written explanation whenever practicable. There are requirements for these written explanations. Additionally, conformity assessments and requests for such assessments have their own requirements. In terms of transparency, Parties must allow other USMCA members to participate in the development of technical regulations, standards, and conformity assessment procedures. For regulations/procedures that conform to international standards, Parties must notify each other of proposed regulations or procedures that may have a significant effect on trade. For emergency regulations, Parties shall notify each other of a regulation/ conformity that is in accordance with relevant international standards. Proposed and final technical regulations and mandatory conformity assessment procedures must be published by the Parties. Furthermore, all notifications have requirements. Finally, the USMCA requires cooperation between the Parties. To further cooperation, the USCMA establishes the TBT committee to monitor, discuss, and resolve issues regarding the issues in this Chapter.

§11.1   INCORPORATION OF THE TBT AGREEMENT

The USMCA incorporates Articles 2.2-2.5, 2.9-2.12, 3.1, 4.1, 5.1-5.4, 5.6-5.9, 7.1 and Annex 3 Paragraphs D, E, F, and J of the TBT Agreement.[530] However, Parties cannot use Chapter 31 (Dispute Settlement) for matters brought under this chapter if the dispute concerns claims that arise out of TBT provisions or concern a measure that was referred to a WTO dispute settlement panel, taken to comply in response to the

---

530. *See* United States-Mexico-Canada Agreement, Section 11.3, Jan. 29, 2020.

recommendation/rulings from the WTO or bears a close nexus with respect to WTO recommendations.[531] The Parties should use the TBT Committee Decision on International Standards to determine if a standard, guide, or recommendation exists on the subject.[532] They cannot apply any additional principles or criteria to recognize a standard as an international standard.[533] Parties are also restricted from according preference to standards that are inconsistent with the TBT Committee or that treat any Party less favorably than persons whose domicile is in the same as the standardization body.[534] Any obligations that a Party has with a non-Party state must not facilitate or require the withdrawal or limitation of these standards.[535]

§11.2   TECHNICAL REGULATIONS

Each Party must assess any technical regulations it proposes to adopt.[536] The assessment can include a regulatory impact analysis or an analysis of alternative measures.[537] Parties must periodically review these regulations, examine if they align with relevant international standards, and consider less trade-restrictive approaches, or they must maintain a process where a person of another Party may directly petition the Party's regulatory authorities to review regulations.[538] If multiple international standards are found to be effective, the Party should endeavor to use the one that fulfills the legitimate objectives of its technical regulations; or when rejecting an international standard, Parties should issue a written explanation whenever practicable.[539] Under NAFTA, Parties were not required to make a written statement when rejecting an international standard.[540]

Conformity assessments should include an evaluation of risks involved, the need to address said risks, relevant scientific and technical information, incidence of non-compliant products, and possible alternative approaches for establishing that the standard has been met.[541] Conformity assessment bodies in another Party's territory must receive national treatment, including procedures, criteria, fees, etc.[542] If assessments or tests are required, a Party must not require the conformity assessment body to be located within its territory.[543] They should not effectively require the body to operate an office within its territory.[544] They should, however, permit conformity assessment bodies in other Parties' territories to apply to the Party for a compliance

---

531. *See* United States-Mexico-Canada Agreement, Section 11.3, Jan. 29, 2020.
532. *See* United States-Mexico-Canada Agreement, Section 11.4, Jan. 29, 2020.
533. *See* United States-Mexico-Canada Agreement, Section 11.4, Jan. 29, 2020.
534. *See* United States-Mexico-Canada Agreement, Section 11.4, Jan. 29, 2020.
535. *See* United States-Mexico-Canada Agreement, Section 11.4, Jan. 29, 2020.
536. *See* United States-Mexico-Canada Agreement, Section 11.5, Jan. 29, 2020.
537. *See* United States-Mexico-Canada Agreement, Section 11.5, Jan. 29, 2020.
538. *See* United States-Mexico-Canada Agreement, Section 11.5, Jan. 29, 2020.
539. *See* United States-Mexico-Canada Agreement, Section 11.5, Jan. 29, 2020.
540. *See* North American Free Trade Agreement, § 501.1, Jan. 1, 1994.
541. *See* United States-Mexico-Canada Agreement, Section 11.6, Jan. 29, 2020.
542. *See* United States-Mexico-Canada Agreement, Section 11.6, Jan. 29, 2020.
543. *See* United States-Mexico-Canada Agreement, Section 11.6, Jan. 29, 2020.
544. *See* United States-Mexico-Canada Agreement, Section 11.6, Jan. 29, 2020.

determination.[545] Additionally, Parties must be able to use subcontractors to perform a conformity assessment.

Requests for information must explain: how the information is necessary to assess conformity; what sequence is the assessment procedure taken in and completed; how the Party ensures that confidential information is protected; and the procedure to review complaints regarding this procedure.[546] Parties must explain any denials to accredit, approve licenses, or otherwise recognize a conformity assessment body.[547] They must explain when they decline to recognize the results from a body that is a signatory to a mutual recognition arrangement.[548] They must explain when they fail to accept the results of a conformity assessment procedure conducted in another Party's territory, or when they discontinue negotiations for a mutual recognition agreement.[549]

Parties cannot refuse to accept or take action because the accreditation body: (a) operates in the territory of a Party where there is more than one accreditation body; (b) is a non-governmental body (c) is domiciled in another Party's territory who does not maintain a procedure for recognized accreditation bodies; (d) does not operate an office in the Party's territory; or (e) is a for-profit entity.[550]

If fees are imposed for technical regulations, they must be made publicly available limited to the costs of services rendered.[551] New or modified fees may not be applied until they are published, and Parties must explain reassessment upon request.[552]

§11.3   TRANSPARENCY

Parties must allow other USMCA members to participate in the development of technical regulations, standards, and conformity assessment procedures.[553] Parties must publish proposed regulations, allow for comment, and revise after taking them into account.[554] Written comments must be publicly available and shall withhold personal identifying information or inappropriate content.[555] Parties must also publish and make free all proposed and final technical regulations and mandatory conformity assessment procedures except with respect to standards that are developed by NGOs and have been incorporated by reference into a technical regulation or conformity assessment procedure.[556]

---

545. *See* United States-Mexico-Canada Agreement, Section 11.6, Jan. 29, 2020.
546. *See* United States-Mexico-Canada Agreement, Section 11.6, Jan. 29, 2020.
547. *See* United States-Mexico-Canada Agreement, Section 11.6, Jan. 29, 2020.
548. *See* United States-Mexico-Canada Agreement, Section 11.6, Jan. 29, 2020.
549. *See* United States-Mexico-Canada Agreement, Section 11.6, Jan. 29, 2020.
550. *See* United States-Mexico-Canada Agreement, Section 11.6, Jan. 29, 2020.
551. *See* United States-Mexico-Canada Agreement, Section 11.6, Jan. 29, 2020.
552. *See* United States-Mexico-Canada Agreement, Section 11.6, Jan. 29, 2020.
553. *See* United States-Mexico-Canada Agreement, Section 11.7, Jan. 29, 2020.
554. *See* United States-Mexico-Canada Agreement, Section 11.7, Jan. 29, 2020.
555. *See* United States-Mexico-Canada Agreement, Section 11.7, Jan. 29, 2020.
556. *See* United States-Mexico-Canada Agreement, Section 11.7, Jan. 29, 2020.

For regulations/procedures that conform to international standards, Parties must notify proposed regulations or procedures that may have a significant effect on trade.[557] They must state the precise standards with which it is in accordance.[558] For emergency regulations, Parties shall provide notification of a regulation/conformity that is in accordance with relevant international standards.[559] They must state the precise standards with which it is in accordance.[560] Furthermore, where proposed regional level regulations/procedures may have effects on trade, Parties must be notified.[561] All notifications must: (1) be timely; (2) include objectives; (3) explain how the objectives are fulfilled; (4) provide a copy of the regulation or a web link; (5) sent electronically through Parties' inquiry points; and (6) provide sufficient comment time (usually sixty days).[562]

Parties must try to provide an interval of more than six months between publications of a final regulation of a procedure and its entry into force.[563] A reasonable period of time must be allotted to demonstrate the conformity of a supplier's products with the relevant requirements.[564] A reasonable time is normally a period of not less than six months.[565]

§11.4 COOPERATION AND TRADE FACILITATION

Under the USMCA, Parties must give consideration to requests made by other Parties with respect to sector-specific proposals for cooperation.[566] Parties must work together to develop common standards and procedures in sectors of mutual interest.[567] To this end, Parties may request that another engage in technical discussions or provide information regarding any proposed or final regulation/procedure.[568] Any requests must be in writing and identify the matter, the reasons for request, level of urgency, and the precise information requested (if applicable).[569]

To further cooperation, the USMCA establishes the TBT committee, which will monitor, discuss, and resolve issues regarding the issues in Chapter 11.[570] The USMCA requires contact points to be designated by each Party so that the others may notify it for matters arising under this chapter.[571]

---

557. *See* United States-Mexico-Canada Agreement, Section 11.7, Jan. 29, 2020.
558. *See* United States-Mexico-Canada Agreement, Section 11.7, Jan. 29, 2020.
559. *See* United States-Mexico-Canada Agreement, Section 11.7, Jan. 29, 2020.
560. *See* United States-Mexico-Canada Agreement, Section 11.7, Jan. 29, 2020.
561. *See* United States-Mexico-Canada Agreement, Section 11.7, Jan. 29, 2020.
562. *See* United States-Mexico-Canada Agreement, Section 11.7, Jan. 29, 2020.
563. *See* United States-Mexico-Canada Agreement, Section 11.7, Jan. 29, 2020.
564. *See* United States-Mexico-Canada Agreement, Section 11.7, Jan. 29, 2020.
565. *See* United States-Mexico-Canada Agreement, Section 11.7, Jan. 29, 2020.
566. *See* United States-Mexico-Canada Agreement, Section 11.9, Jan. 29, 2020.
567. *See* United States-Mexico-Canada Agreement, Section 11.9, Jan. 29, 2020.
568. *See* United States-Mexico-Canada Agreement, Section 11.10, Jan. 29, 2020.
569. *See* United States-Mexico-Canada Agreement, Section 11.10, Jan. 29, 2020.
570. *See* United States-Mexico-Canada Agreement, Section 11.11, Jan. 29, 2020.
571. *See* United States-Mexico-Canada Agreement, Section 11.12, Jan. 29, 2020.

CHAPTER 12
Sectoral Annexes

This chapter broadly addresses the preparation, adoption, and application of regulations and standards, as well as the procedures of communicating information on the use of chemicals in the workplace. Additionally, it addresses regulations on import and export permits for these chemicals. Parties will use risk management to assess specific chemicals; Parties shall also attempt to align their risk management assessment measures. However, protection, or improvement, is more important than alignment. Annex 12-B applies to cosmetic products; each Party retains their own definition of cosmetic. This annex addresses Parties' technical regulations, standards, conformity assessment procedures, and notification procedures that could affect trade in cosmetic products. Annex 12-C addresses information and Communication Technology (ICT); it applies to goods that use cryptography; however, exceptions apply. Annex 12-D applies to the Party's process of creating and applying regulations involving energy performance standards and related test procedures. Annex 12-E addresses the overall process, regulations, procedures, and marketing authorization of each Party's central government that could affect trade in medical devices. Finally, Annex 12-F addresses the scope, competent authorities' requirements, and how to best enhance regulatory compatibility for pharmaceuticals.

This Annex provides a wide scope, encompassing the preparation, adoption, and application of regulations and standards and assessing procedures and measures of communicating information on the use and response of chemicals in the workplace, as well as regulating import and export permits for chemical substances and mixtures by central level governments.[572]

Each Party shall publish a description online of each authority tasked with implementing and enforcing measures regulating chemical substances and chemical mixtures, including its "specific responsibilities," and provide a contact point within the said authority.[573] If any material changes occur, the Party must notify the other Parties and update the information promptly.[574]

---

572. *See* United States-Mexico-Canada Agreement, Article 12.A.1-2, Jan. 29, 2020.
573. *See* United States-Mexico-Canada Agreement, Article 12.A.3 (a-b), Jan. 29, 2020.
574. *See* United States-Mexico-Canada Agreement, Article 12.A.3 (a-b), Jan. 29, 2020.

The objective of this section is to protect human health and the environment by regulating chemical substances and chemical mixtures.[575] The Parties will use a risk-based methodology when assessing specific chemical substances and chemical mixtures both in international fora and between it and non-Party states.[576]

Parties shall attempt to align their risk management and assessment measures provided the alignment does not prevent one Party from achieving its full protection.[577] Protection or improvement of protection is more important than alignment. Parties will consider the changes adopted by the other members when developing and modifying their own measures.[578] To strengthen cooperation between the Parties, this section implements the respective Party's adoption of the United Nations Globally Harmonized System for Classification and Labeling of Chemicals (GHS), as well as other cooperation measures, including the use of safety data sheets and explanations of the scientific criteria used to develop new regulatory measures.[579]

A Party must share any available data or assessments, meaning full data studies or summaries, on particular substances when requested by another member.[580] Each Party shall develop its own procedures to maintain and ensure confidentiality of requested information.[581] The Parties may request the following kinds of information: (1) how the Party keeps its public informed on the safety of chemical substances; and (2) any new information or studies conducted by the Party on chemical substance management and data.[582]

§12.1   ANNEX 12-B: COSMETIC PRODUCTS

Each Party retains their own definition of cosmetics.[583] For Canada, section 2 of the Food and Drugs Act governs the definition; for Mexico, article 269 Ley General de Salud and article 187 Reglamento Control Sanitario de Productos y Servicios contains the definition; and for the U.S., the definition is found in 21 USC § 321(i).[584]

This Annex applies to the Party's technical regulations, standards, conformity assessment procedures, and notification procedures that could affect trade in cosmetic products.[585] However, sanitary or phytosanitary measures are excluded from this Annex.[586]

---

575. *See* United States-Mexico-Canada Agreement, Article 12.A.4, Jan. 29, 2020.
576. *See* United States-Mexico-Canada Agreement, Article 12.A.4, Jan. 29, 2020.
577. *See* United States-Mexico-Canada Agreement, Article 12.A.4, Jan. 29, 2020.
578. *See* United States-Mexico-Canada Agreement, Article 12.A.4, Jan. 29, 2020.
579. *See* United States-Mexico-Canada Agreement, Article 12.A.4, Jan. 29, 2020.
580. *See* United States-Mexico-Canada Agreement, Article 12.A.5, Jan. 29, 2020.
581. *See* United States-Mexico-Canada Agreement, Article 12.A.5, Jan. 29, 2020.
582. *See* United States-Mexico-Canada Agreement, Article 12.A.5, Jan. 29, 2020.
583. *See* United States-Mexico-Canada Agreement, Article 12.B.1, Jan. 29, 2020.
584. *See* United States-Mexico-Canada Agreement, Article 12.B.1, Jan. 29, 2020.
585. *See* United States-Mexico-Canada Agreement, Article 12.B.2, Jan. 29, 2020.
586. *See* United States-Mexico-Canada Agreement, Article 12.B.2, Jan. 29, 2020.

[A]   Annex 12.B.3: Competent Authorities

Parties must publish a description of each relevant authority, including its responsibilities and the point of contact.[587] If material changes are made to the authority or its responsibilities, then that Party must notify the other Parties and update the information online.[588] Furthermore, Parties shall avoid unnecessarily repetitive regulatory requirements in this sector, and will periodically examine their procedures to ensure compliance.[589]

The Parties shall work to align their individual regulations and regulatory activities through the application of international and regional harmonization initiatives.[590] When implementing regulations for cosmetic products, Parties shall take relevant scientific or technical guidance from international collaborative efforts into consideration.[591]

Parties are also required to share information regarding post-market surveillance of the cosmetic product, and any findings regarding the product ingredients and the effect that it might have on inter-Party trade.[592]

Parties must ensure that the safety, effectiveness, and quality of the product.[593] They must further ensure that products imported from another Party are treated no less favorably than like products of national origin or originating from any other country, "in a comparable situation."[594]

In developing its regulatory process, a Party should implement procedures that ensure the safety, effectiveness, and quality of cosmetic products, and it should avoid procedures that could lead to substantial delays in product availability.[595]

Parties shall work to meet the standards of the International Nomenclature Cosmetic Ingredient (INCI) agreement.[596] Parties must report their progress, in meeting this goal, to the INCI Commission no later than one year after the USMCA enters into force.[597]

This Appendix only applies to the U.S. and Canada and applies to toothpaste, mouthwashes, personal care use antiseptic skin cleansers, sunscreens, anti-dandruff shampoos, diaper rash creams, antiperspirants, medicated skin care products, and acne products.[598] If the importing Party authorizes the sale of one of the mentioned products, then the product may be shipped directly to retailers or wholesalers without re-testing or quarantine unless a specific shipment poses an identified human health concern or a Party establishes a risk-based inspection system with the intent of

---

587. *See* United States-Mexico-Canada Agreement, Article 12.B.3, Jan. 29, 2020.
588. *See* United States-Mexico-Canada Agreement, Article 12.B.3, Jan. 29, 2020.
589. *See* United States-Mexico-Canada Agreement, Article 12.B.3, Jan. 29, 2020.
590. *See* United States-Mexico-Canada Agreement, Article 12.B.4, Jan. 29, 2020.
591. *See* United States-Mexico-Canada Agreement, Article 12.B.4, Jan. 29, 2020.
592. *See* United States-Mexico-Canada Agreement, Article 12.B.4, Jan. 29, 2020.
593. *See* United States-Mexico-Canada Agreement, Article 12.B.5, Jan. 29, 2020.
594. *See* United States-Mexico-Canada Agreement, Article 12.B.5, Jan. 29, 2020.
595. *See* United States-Mexico-Canada Agreement, Article 12.B.4, Jan. 29, 2020.
596. *See* United States-Mexico-Canada Agreement, Article 12.B.6, Jan. 29, 2020.
597. *See* United States-Mexico-Canada Agreement, Article 12.B.6e, Jan. 29, 2020.
598. *See* United States-Mexico-Canada Agreement, Section 12 Appendix 1, Jan. 29, 2020.

protecting human health. Parties will work together to strengthen cooperating in regulating the products covered by this section.[599]

§12.2   ANNEX 12-C: INFORMATION AND COMMUNICATION TECHNOLOGY (ICT)

Article 12.C.1 sets out the definitions applicable to the technology covered under this article.[600] This article applies to goods that use cryptography but does not apply when individual Party's law enforcement authorities require service suppliers to provide unencrypted communications for legal purposes; when regulating financial instruments; Party's requirements for adopting and maintaining related access to networks; supervisory, investigatory, or examination measures taken in relation to financial institutions or financial markets; or the manufacture, sale, distribution, import or use of the good by or for an individual Party's government.[601]

No Party shall require a manufacturer or supplier of an ICT good that uses cryptography to transfer or provide access to any proprietary information relating to the cryptography; partner or cooperate with a person in the same country in the development, manufacture, sale, distribution, import, or use of the product; or require the use of a particular cryptographic algorithm or cipher.[602]

This article covers the requirements regarding the electromagnetic compatibility of ICT products.[603] It does not apply to products that are regulated as medical devices, medical device systems, or if it is a component of a medical device or medical device system; or products that a Party demonstrates have a high risk of causing harmful electromagnetic interference with a safety or radio transmission or reception device or system.[604]

If a Party requires assurance that an ICT product meets the above standard or technical regulation for electromagnetic compatibility, it shall accept a supplier's declaration of conformity, provided the declaration satisfies the Party's testing requirements.[605]

This article encourages Parties to implement the APEC Mutual Recognition Arrangement for Conformity Assessment of Telecommunications Equipment of May 8, 1998 (MRA-TEL), as well as the APEC Mutual Recognition Arrangement for Equivalence of Technical Requirements of October 31, 2010 (MRA-ETR), and any other arrangements that could facilitate trade in telecommunications equipment.[606]

---

599. *See* United States-Mexico-Canada Agreement, Section 12 Appendix 1, Jan. 29, 2020.
600. *See* United States-Mexico-Canada Agreement, Article 12.C.1-.2, Jan. 29, 2020.
601. *See* United States-Mexico-Canada Agreement, Article 12.C.1-.2, Jan. 29, 2020.
602. *See* United States-Mexico-Canada Agreement, Article 12.C.1-.2, Jan. 29, 2020.
603. *See* United States-Mexico-Canada Agreement, Article 12.C.3, Jan. 29, 2020.
604. *See* United States-Mexico-Canada Agreement, Article 12.C.3, Jan. 29, 2020.
605. *See* United States-Mexico-Canada Agreement, Article 12.C.3, Jan. 29, 2020.
606. *See* United States-Mexico-Canada Agreement, Article 12.C.4, Jan. 29, 2020.

The U.S. and Mexico will continue to act in accordance with the Mutual Recognition Agreement between the Government of the United States and the Government of the United Mexican States for the Conformity Assessment of Telecommunications Equipment.[607] This requires both Parties to accept test reports provided by a recognized testing laboratory of one Party no less favorably than it recognizes testing laboratories in its territory.[608] Similarly, Canada and Mexico will continue to act in accordance with the Mutual Recognition Agreement between the Government of Canada and the Government of the United Mexican States for the Conformity Assessment of Telecommunications Equipment.[609] It requires the same level of acceptance of laboratory tests as the agreement between the U.S. and Mexico.[610]

A Party may require a label containing compliance information for products subject to electromagnetic compatibility and radio frequency requirements, but the information should be provided through an electronic label.[611]

If terminal equipment is to be attached to the public communications network, then Parties must ensure that their technical regulations, standards, and conformity assessment procedures are adopted or maintained to the extent necessary to prevent damage to the networks; degradation of the services, electromagnetic interference, and ensure compatibility with other uses; billing equipment malfunction; or to ensure the safety of and access to public telecommunications or services.[612] Parties are required to ensure that network termination points are established on a "reasonable and transparent basis."[613] An approved conformity assessment body shall perform tests required under each Party's conformity procedures for attaching terminal equipment, subject to review by the Party.[614]

§12.3 ANNEX 12-D: ENERGY PERFORMANCE STANDARDS

This Annex applies to each Party's process of creating and applying regulations, involving energy performance standards and related test procedures.[615]

The competent authorities for each Party must publish online a description of each authority, its specific responsibilities, and the point of contact as it relates to the development, implementation, revision, and enforcement of energy performance standards or related test procedures.[616]

The Parties will cooperate with one another when defining performance standards and related test procedures.[617] The current energy performance and test procedures conducted by individual Parties on the date of entry of force shall be harmonized

---

607. *See* United States-Mexico-Canada Agreement, Article 12.C.4, Jan. 29, 2020.
608. *See* United States-Mexico-Canada Agreement, Article 12.C.4, Jan. 29, 2020.
609. *See* United States-Mexico-Canada Agreement, Article 12.C.4, Jan. 29, 2020.
610. *See* United States-Mexico-Canada Agreement, Article 12.C.4, Jan. 29, 2020.
611. *See* United States-Mexico-Canada Agreement, Article 12.C.4, Jan. 29, 2020.
612. *See* United States-Mexico-Canada Agreement, Article 12.C.5, Jan. 29, 2020.
613. *See* United States-Mexico-Canada Agreement, Article 12.C.5, Jan. 29, 2020.
614. *See* United States-Mexico-Canada Agreement, Article 12.C.5, Jan. 29, 2020.
615. *See* United States-Mexico-Canada Agreement, Article 12.D.1-.2, Jan. 29, 2020.
616. *See* United States-Mexico-Canada Agreement, Article 12.D.3, Jan. 29, 2020.
617. *See* United States-Mexico-Canada Agreement, Article 12.D.4, Jan. 29, 2020.

accordingly: no later than eight days for test procedures, and no longer than nine days for energy performance.[618]

If a Party wishes to develop or modify energy performance standards or test procedures, it must give due consideration when adopting either directly from another Party or adopting industry standards that have developed in the territory of another party, by an accredited organization.[619]

Due consideration will also be applied to the unique operating conditions of each Party in developing or modifying its test procedures.[620]

The Parties acknowledge the value of voluntary programs and mechanisms in improving energy efficiency.[621] These programs and mechanisms should be open, transparent, and designed to maximize benefits for both consumers and the environment, without creating unnecessary barriers to trade.[622] The Parties shall strive to cooperate with one another to facilitate greater transparency and compatibility between the programs and mechanisms.[623]

§12.4   ANNEX 12-E: MEDICAL DEVICES

This Annex addresses the overall process, regulations, procedures and marketing authorization of each Party's central government that could affect trade in medical devices.[624] It excludes sanitary or phytosanitary measures or technical specifications by an individual Party for the production or consumption requirements for these products.[625]

Parties must publish online a description of each responsible authority, including its responsibilities and contact information.[626] If any material changes to this information occur, then the Parties must promptly notify the other members and update the information online.[627] Parties must periodically examine their current regulatory requirements to ensure there are no unnecessarily duplicative regulatory requirements.[628]

Each Party should apply this Annex's definition of the medical device within their respective laws and regulations, and ensure it is consistent with the definition in the *Definition of the Terms 'Medical Device' and "In Vitro Diagnostic (IVD) Medical Device* endorsed by the Global Harmonized Task Force.[629]

---

618. *See* United States-Mexico-Canada Agreement, Article 12.D.4, Jan. 29, 2020.
619. *See* United States-Mexico-Canada Agreement, Article 12.D.4, Jan. 29, 2020.
620. *See* United States-Mexico-Canada Agreement, Article 12.D.4, Jan. 29, 2020.
621. *See* United States-Mexico-Canada Agreement, Article 12.D.5, Jan. 29, 2020.
622. *See* United States-Mexico-Canada Agreement, Article 12.D.5, Jan. 29, 2020.
623. *See* United States-Mexico-Canada Agreement, Article 12.D.5, Jan. 29, 2020.
624. *See* United States-Mexico-Canada Agreement, Article 12.E.1-.2, Jan. 29, 2020.
625. *See* United States-Mexico-Canada Agreement, Article 12.E.1-.2, Jan. 29, 2020.
626. *See* United States-Mexico-Canada Agreement, Article 12.E.3, Jan. 29, 2020.
627. *See* United States-Mexico-Canada Agreement, Article 12.E.3, Jan. 29, 2020.
628. *See* United States-Mexico-Canada Agreement, Article 12.E.3, Jan. 29, 2020.
629. *See* United States-Mexico-Canada Agreement, Article 12.E.4, Jan. 29, 2020.

Parties shall work to improve their respective regulations and regulatory activities by aligning them with relevant international initiatives, including the International Medical Device Regulators Forum.[630]

Parties must comply with the Medical Device Single Audit Program, thereby recognizing audits of device manufacturers' quality management systems.[631] Relevant scientific or technical guidance documents shall be considered by the Parties when developing or implementing regulations for the marketing authorization of medical devices. Parties should consider both international and regionally developed efforts.[632]

Medical devices will be classified based on risk.[633] All regulatory requirements implemented for the purpose of assuring the product's safety and effectiveness must be based on an assessment of the medical device's risks.[634] When developing regulatory requirements, Parties must assess, based on their available resources and technical capacity, how the regulation could "inhibit the efficacy of procedures for ensuring the safety, effectiveness, or quality of medical devices; or lead to substantial delays for medical devices becoming available in that Party's market."[635]

Parties shall evaluate information on the safety, effectiveness, and quality of the medical device when determining whether to grant marketing authorization.[636] Parties should consider the following information, but this list is not exhaustive: clinical data and information on safety and effectiveness, information on performance design and quality, labeling information.[637] Parties may not rely upon or require sales data, pricing data, or other financial data in making their determination.[638]

Marketing authorizations shall be reasonably, objectively, impartially, and transparently administered.[639] Parties must maintain review procedures for denied applications.[640] If a product requires periodic re-authorization, Parties will allow the product to remain on the market throughout the re-authorization process; unless the product is found to pose a significant safety, effectiveness, or quality concern.[641] Regulatory authorities may not use marketing authorization as a condition when the product is manufactured in that Party's country.[642] However, if the Party's regulatory resources are limited, then the Party may require, as a condition, marketing authorization from another reference country.[643] Parties may also accept prior marketing authorizations issues by one of the other regulatory authorities as evidence that the product meets its requirements.[644]

---

630. *See* United States-Mexico-Canada Agreement, Article 12.E.4, Jan. 29, 2020.
631. *See* United States-Mexico-Canada Agreement, Article 12.E.4, Jan. 29, 2020.
632. *See* United States-Mexico-Canada Agreement, Article 12.E.4, Jan. 29, 2020.
633. *See* United States-Mexico-Canada Agreement, Article 12.E.5, Jan. 29, 2020.
634. *See* United States-Mexico-Canada Agreement, Article 12.E.5, Jan. 29, 2020.
635. *See* United States-Mexico-Canada Agreement, Article 12.E.5, Jan. 29, 2020.
636. *See* United States-Mexico-Canada Agreement, Article 12.E.6, Jan. 29, 2020.
637. *See* United States-Mexico-Canada Agreement, Article 12.E.6, Jan. 29, 2020.
638. *See* United States-Mexico-Canada Agreement, Article 12.E.6, Jan. 29, 2020.
639. *See* United States-Mexico-Canada Agreement, Article 12.E.6, Jan. 29, 2020.
640. *See* United States-Mexico-Canada Agreement, Article 12.E.6, Jan. 29, 2020.
641. *See* United States-Mexico-Canada Agreement, Article 12.E.6, Jan. 29, 2020.
642. *See* United States-Mexico-Canada Agreement, Article 12.E.6, Jan. 29, 2020.
643. *See* United States-Mexico-Canada Agreement, Article 12.E.6, Jan. 29, 2020.
644. *See* United States-Mexico-Canada Agreement, Article 12.E.6, Jan. 29, 2020.

If upon importation, the product's label is insufficient, then the Party must allow the manufacturer or supplier the ability to relabel or provide supplementary labeling after importation but before offering for sale.[645]

§12.5   ANNEX 12-F: PHARMACEUTICALS

This article lays out the same scope, competent authorities' requirements, and how to best enhance regulatory compatibility as the preceding Annex.[646]

Parties shall collaborate, or work to collaborate, on pharmaceutical inspections.[647] For example, when a Party conducts a surveillance inspection of a manufacturing facility, for products within the territory of another Party, it must notify the other Party prior to inspection.[648] Notification is required unless there are reasonable grounds to believe that the effectiveness of the inspection will be compromised by it.[649] The Party must also allow representatives of the other Party to observe the inspection, if practicable.[650] Lastly, the Party must notify the other Party of its finding as soon as possible after the inspection, unless the information is subject to treatment as confidential information under the inspecting Party's laws.[651] If the finding is made to be made public, then the Party must provide the information in a reasonable time before release.[652]

Parties shall consider relevant scientific or technical guidance documents, both regionally and internationally developed, when developing and implementing regulations regarding the marketing authorization of pharmaceutical products.[653] In making its determination to grant marketing authorization, the Party shall evaluate the safety, effectiveness, and quality of the pharmaceutical product.[654] Sales data or financial marketing of the product may not be considered in the determination of granting marketing authorization.[655]

Parties will administer marketing authorizations reasonably, objectively, impartially, and transparently.[656] Reasonably includes avoiding duplicative and unnecessary information from the applicant, communicating deficiencies and the potential for prevention or delayed consideration of the application, and providing a determination within a reasonable time.[657] Parties must ensure there is a review process in place for

645. *See* United States-Mexico-Canada Agreement, Article 12.E.6, Jan. 29, 2020.
646. *See* United States-Mexico-Canada Agreement, Article 12.F.1-.4, Jan. 29, 2020.
647. *See* United States-Mexico-Canada Agreement, Article 12.F.5, Jan. 29, 2020.
648. *See* United States-Mexico-Canada Agreement, Article 12.F.5, Jan. 29, 2020.
649. *See* United States-Mexico-Canada Agreement, Article 12.F.5, Jan. 29, 2020.
650. *See* United States-Mexico-Canada Agreement, Article 12.F.5, Jan. 29, 2020.
651. *See* United States-Mexico-Canada Agreement, Article 12.F.5, Jan. 29, 2020.
652. *See* United States-Mexico-Canada Agreement, Article 12.F.5, Jan. 29, 2020.
653. *See* United States-Mexico-Canada Agreement, Article 12.F.6, Jan. 29, 2020.
654. *See* United States-Mexico-Canada Agreement, Article 12.F.6, Jan. 29, 2020.
655. *See* United States-Mexico-Canada Agreement, Article 12.F.6, Jan. 29, 2020.
656. *See* United States-Mexico-Canada Agreement, Article 12.F.6, Jan. 29, 2020.
657. *See* United States-Mexico-Canada Agreement, Article 12.F.6, Jan. 29, 2020.

denied applications, but this does not preclude a Party from setting a review dead-line.[658]

Periodic re-authorization and conditional marketing authorization require the same commitments from each Party as the preceding Annex.[659]

Parties must ensure compliance with the Common Technical Document (CTD) of the International Conference on Harmonization of Technical Requirements for Registration of Pharmaceuticals for Human Use.[660]

---

658. *See* United States-Mexico-Canada Agreement, Article 12.F.6, Jan. 29, 2020.
659. *See* United States-Mexico-Canada Agreement, Article 12.F.6, Jan. 29, 2020.
660. *See* United States-Mexico-Canada Agreement, Article 12.F.6, Jan. 29, 2020.

CHAPTER 13

Government Procurement

This chapter applies only as between Mexico and the United States. The USMCA government procurement provisions reflect international standards. Additionally, TSA textile purchases are excluded from the USMCA, whereas they were included under NAFTA. Under the USMCA, government procurement provisions, thresholds between the two are the same and the Government Procurement Committee is established in order to facilitate issues under this chapter. The USMCA adopts four exceptions to these provisions. Additionally, some general principles apply; including national treatment and using electronic means whenever possible. Parties must also publish any measure relating to procurement. However, Parties may not use limited tendering to avoid competition between suppliers, to protect domestic suppliers, or in a manner that discriminates against the other Parties' suppliers. Additionally, procuring entities may negotiate. In terms of technical specifications and tender documentation, entities cannot adopt specification in order to create an unnecessary obstacle to trade; additionally, tender documentation must be available to any interested supplier. Such documentation has requirements. Entities must provide sufficient time for suppliers to obtain the tender documentation and to prepare and submit a request. The USMCA requires entities to treat all tenders fairly and impartially. Transparency and disclosures apply the tenders; entities must promptly inform suppliers that submitted tender of the contract decision.

USMCA's government procurement chapter is compatible with Chapter 10 of NAFTA.[661] However, this chapter applies only between Mexico and the United States—whereas NAFTA included provisions between all three North American Parties. The World Trade Organization Government Procurement Agreement (WTO-GPA) will govern procurement between Canada and the United States. Under the WTO-GPA, the monetary threshold will increase from NAFTA's $25,000 to GPA's $180,000.[662] Without lower NAFTA thresholds, firms located in the United States will have reduced

---

661. *See* North American Free Trade Agreement, Chapter 10, Jan. 1, 1994; *see also* United States-Mexico-Canada Agreement, Section 13, Jan. 29, 2020.
662. U.S.-Mexico-Canada (USMCA) Trade Agreement, Congressional Research Service (Updated Jan. 30, 2020) https://crsreports.congress.gov/product/pdf/IF/IF10997.

access to Canadian procurement.[663] The USMCA government procurement provisions that apply between Mexico and the United States reflect international standards, whereas, in NAFTA, they did not.[664]

§13.1 ALSO NEW, TSA TEXTILE PURCHASES ARE EXCLUDED FROM THIS TRADE AGREEMENT (ALTHOUGH THEY WERE INCLUDED UNDER NAFTA)

Under the USMCA, government procurement provisions still cover the United States 52 federal entities and 6 government entities. The provisions still cover 23 Mexican federal entities and 36 Mexican government enterprises. In this case, thresholds between the two are the same and the Government Procurement Committee is established in order to facilitate issues under this chapter.[665]

USMCA adopts the four exceptions to the government procurement provisions, which include measures: (1) necessary to protect public morals, order, or safety; (2) necessary to protect human, animal, or plant life or health; (3) necessary to protect intellectual property; or (4) relating to goods/Services of a disabled person, a philanthropic or non-profit institution or of prison labor.[666] However, the USMCA's provisions on human, animal, or plant life also apply to environmental measures.[667] Additionally, National Treatment and Nondiscrimination paragraphs shall not apply to customs duties and similar charges in connection with importation.[668]

§13.2 GENERAL PRINCIPLES

A Party must give national treatment to the goods and services of the other Party.[669] For example, with regard to covered procurement, Parties cannot treat locally established suppliers less favorably than another locally established supplier on the basis of foreign affiliation or ownership.[670] They cannot discriminate against locally established suppliers because a good/service offered by that supplier for procurement is a good/service of the other party.[671] A Party must apply the same rules to the other Party that are applied in the normal course of trade to imports/supplies of the same goods/services from itself.[672] Parties must use an open tender procurement method

663. U.S.-Mexico-Canada (USMCA) Trade Agreement, Congressional Research Service (Updated Jan. 30, 2020) https://crsreports.congress.gov/product/pdf/IF/IF10997.
664. U.S.-Mexico-Canada (USMCA) Trade Agreement, Congressional Research Service (Updated Jan. 30, 2020) https://crsreports.congress.gov/product/pdf/IF/IF10997.
665. *See* United States-Mexico-Canada Agreement, Section 13.21, Jan. 29, 2020.
666. *See* North American Free Trade Agreement, Section 10.18, Jan. 1, 1994; *see also* United States-Mexico-Canada Agreement, Section 13.3, Jan. 29, 2020.
667. *See* United States-Mexico-Canada Agreement, Section 13.3, Jan. 29, 2020.
668. *See* United States-Mexico-Canada Agreement, Section 13.4, Jan. 29, 2020.
669. *See* United States-Mexico-Canada Agreement, Section 13.4, Jan. 29, 2020.
670. *See* United States-Mexico-Canada Agreement, Section 13.4, Jan. 29, 2020.
671. *See* United States-Mexico-Canada Agreement, Section 13.4, Jan. 29, 2020.
672. *See* United States-Mexico-Canada Agreement, Section 13.4, Jan. 29, 2020.

unless Qualification of Suppliers or Limited Tendering applies (Articles 13.8 & 13.9).[673] Additionally, no offsets should be imposed or enforced at any stage of a procurement.[674]

Parties must use electronic means whenever possible.[675] When conducting covered procurement electronically, a procuring entity should make sure the IT and software are generally available interoperable with other generally available IT systems and software.[676] Parties must also ensure the integrity of the information provided.[677]

§13.3 NOTICES

Parties must promptly publish any measure of general application relating to covered procurement.[678] Notice of intended procurement must be published through the appropriate paper or electronic means and remain accessible to the public until at least the expiration of the time period for responding to the notice or deadline for submission of tender.[679] A notice of future plans is published as early as possible in each fiscal year, which should include the subject matter and planned date of publication of the notice of intended procurement.[680] Electronic notices must be free of charge for centrally governed entities that are covered under Annex 13-A through a single point of access.[681] Electronic notices must be free of charge for other entities covered under Annex 13-A, through links in a single electronic portal.[682]

[A] Conditions of Participation

Conditions shall be limited to those that ensure the supplier has the legal and financial capacities and the commercial and technical abilities to fulfill the requirements.[683] Parties cannot require that a supplier previously be awarded a contract or have prior work experience in that territory.[684] However, they may require prior experience if it is essential to meet the requirements of the procurement.[685] Sufficient grounds for exclusion include bankruptcy; insolvency; false declarations; deficiencies and performance on prior contracts; final judgments in respect of serious crimes or offenses; professional misconduct that affect commercial integrity; and tax default.[686]

---

673. *See* United States-Mexico-Canada Agreement, Section 13.4, Jan. 29, 2020.
674. *See* United States-Mexico-Canada Agreement, Section 13.4, Jan. 29, 2020.
675. *See* United States-Mexico-Canada Agreement, Section 13.5, Jan. 29, 2020.
676. *See* United States-Mexico-Canada Agreement, Section 13.5, Jan. 29, 2020.
677. *See* United States-Mexico-Canada Agreement, Section 13.5, Jan. 29, 2020.
678. *See* United States-Mexico-Canada Agreement, Section 13.6, Jan. 29, 2020.
679. *See* United States-Mexico-Canada Agreement, Section 13.6, Jan. 29, 2020.
680. *See* United States-Mexico-Canada Agreement, Section 13.6, Jan. 29, 2020.
681. *See* United States-Mexico-Canada Agreement, Section 13.6, Jan. 29, 2020.
682. *See* United States-Mexico-Canada Agreement, Section 13.6, Jan. 29, 2020.
683. *See* United States-Mexico-Canada Agreement, Section 13.7, Jan. 29, 2020.
684. *See* United States-Mexico-Canada Agreement, Section 13.7, Jan. 29, 2020.
685. *See* United States-Mexico-Canada Agreement, Section 13.7, Jan. 29, 2020.
686. *See* United States-Mexico-Canada Agreement, Section 13.7, Jan. 29, 2020.

[B]   Qualification of Suppliers

Parties may maintain a supplier registration system but cannot do so in order to create unnecessary obstacles to the participation of suppliers or use it to prevent or delay the inclusion of suppliers of the other Party.[687] If Parties want to use selective tendering, they need to publish a notice that invites suppliers to submit a request for participation.[688] This must be published sufficiently and advance and provide a time period for tendering.[689] Parties must allow all Parties to submit a tender unless they state in the notice that there is a limitation on the number of submissions (must justify the limit as well).[690]

Parties may have multi-use lists as long as they publish annually, or make continuously available online, a notice inviting interested suppliers to apply for inclusion.[691] They must provide a reasonable time period for a list of suppliers that satisfy the conditions.[692] If a supplier is not included and submits all required documents, the procuring entity must examine the request.[693] The entity must promptly inform any supplier who submits a request for its decision and a reason for deciding.[694]

[C]   Limited Tendering

Parties may not use limited tendering to avoid competition between suppliers, to protect domestic suppliers, or in a manner that discriminates against the other Party's suppliers.[695] If they use limiting tender, it does not need to apply Article 13.6 (Notices of Intended Procurement), Article 13.7 (Conditions for Participation), Article 13.8 (Qualification of Suppliers), Article 13.10 (Negotiations), Article 13.11 (Technical Specifications), Article 13.12 (Tender Documentation), Article 13.13 (Time Periods), or Article 13.14 (Treatment of Tenders and Awarding of Contracts).[696] Procuring entities may use limited tendering only under these circumstances:

(a) No tenders submitted, no suppliers requested participation, no conforming tenders submitted, no suppliers satisfied condition, or tenders submitted were collusive.

(b) Goods/services can only be supplied by a particular supplier and no reasonable alternative. (e.g., work of art, IP rights, absence of competition)

---

687. *See* United States-Mexico-Canada Agreement, Section 13.8, Jan. 29, 2020.
688. *See* United States-Mexico-Canada Agreement, Section 13.8, Jan. 29, 2020.
689. *See* United States-Mexico-Canada Agreement, Section 13.8, Jan. 29, 2020.
690. *See* United States-Mexico-Canada Agreement, Section 13.8, Jan. 29, 2020.
691. *See* United States-Mexico-Canada Agreement, Section 13.8, Jan. 29, 2020.
692. *See* United States-Mexico-Canada Agreement, Section 13.8, Jan. 29, 2020.
693. *See* United States-Mexico-Canada Agreement, Section 13.8, Jan. 29, 2020.
694. *See* United States-Mexico-Canada Agreement, Section 13.8, Jan. 29, 2020.
695. *See* United States-Mexico-Canada Agreement, Section 13.7, Jan. 29, 2020.
696. *See* United States-Mexico-Canada Agreement, Section 13.9, Jan. 29, 2020.

(c) For additional deliveries by the original supplier that were not included in the procurement if a change of supplier cannot be made for technical reasons or would cause significant inconvenience or costs.

(d) The good is purchased on a commodity market or exchange.

(e) The good/service is a limited trial or developed at the procuring entity's request

(f) The purchase was made under exceptionally advantageous conditions that only arise in the short term (e.g., liquidation, bankruptcy, etc.)

(g) The contract was given to a design contest winner if the contest was organized in a manner consistent with the chapter, and the contest is judged by an independent jury.

(h) Extreme urgency that is brought on by unforeseeable events and the good/service cannot be obtained in times but means of open or selective tender.[697]

[D]   Negotiations

Procuring entities may negotiate if they indicated this in the notice, or it appears that no tender is obviously the most advantageous.[698] When negotiations are done, they must provide a deadline for the remaining suppliers to submit any new or revised tenders.[699]

§13.4   TECHNICAL SPECIFICATIONS AND TENDER DOCUMENTATION

Under the USMCA, entities cannot adopt specifications in order to create an unnecessary obstacle to trade.[700] The specifications must be set out in terms of performance and functional requirements and based on international standards (if possible).[701] If not, they must be based on national technical regulations.[702] Specifications cannot refer to a trademark or trade name, patent, copyright, design, type, origin, producer, or supplier unless there is no other way of describing the requirements.[703] If it has to say so, it must include the words "or equivalent."[704]

Tender documentation must be available to any interested supplier.[705] If not already in the notice of intended procurement, documentation must include a complete description of the procurement; any conditions; all criteria; date, time, and place for any public openings of tender; any other terms or conditions for evaluation; and any

---

697. *See* United States-Mexico-Canada Agreement, Section 13.9, Jan. 29, 2020.
698. *See* United States-Mexico-Canada Agreement, Section 13.10, Jan. 29, 2020.
699. *See* United States-Mexico-Canada Agreement, Section 13.10, Jan. 29, 2020.
700. *See* United States-Mexico-Canada Agreement, Section 13.11, Jan. 29, 2020.
701. *See* United States-Mexico-Canada Agreement, Section 13.11, Jan. 29, 2020.
702. *See* United States-Mexico-Canada Agreement, Section 13.11, Jan. 29, 2020.
703. *See* United States-Mexico-Canada Agreement, Section 13.11, Jan. 29, 2020.
704. *See* United States-Mexico-Canada Agreement, Section 13.11, Jan. 29, 2020.
705. *See* United States-Mexico-Canada Agreement, Section 13.12, Jan. 29, 2020.

date for delivery of a good or supply of a service.[706] If evaluation criteria or requirements are modified before a contract is awarded, the entity shall publish those
modifications or reissue notice to all suppliers that are participating at that time and do
some in adequate time to allow suppliers to modify and re-submit tender if appropriate.[707]

§13.5   TIME PERIODS

Consistent with its needs, entities must provide sufficient time for suppliers to obtain
the tender documentation and to prepare and submit a request.[708] For selective tender,
the date for submitting requests cannot be less than twenty-five days from the date of
the notice publication.[709] For urgent procurement, ten days is the earliest.[710] A
procuring entity must make the final date for tender submission no less than forty days
from the notice being published (open tendering) or when suppliers are notified that
they will be invited to submit tenders (selective tendering).[711] Exceptions to this are
allowed when the notice is published electronically, the documentation is made
available that day, and the procuring entity accepts tender electronically.[712]

§13.6   TREATMENT OF TENDERS AND AWARDING OF CONTRACTS

Tender must be submitted in writing, comply with requirements, and be submitted by
a supplier who satisfies the conditions for participation.[713] The USMCA requires
entities to treat all tenders fairly and impartially.[714] If the tender is received after the
deadline due to other mishandling of the procuring entity, they cannot penalize the
supplier.[715] If the entity allows a supplier to correct unintentional errors, they must
allow other suppliers to do so.[716] Unless the entity believes it is not in public interest to
award a contract, they should get it to the supplier that is fully capable of fulfilling the
contract terms, and based solely on evaluation criteria, submits the most advantageous
tender or the lowest price (if the price is the sole criterion).[717] If the price is abnormally
low, they may verify with the supplier that it satisfies the conditions and is capable of
fulfilling the contract.[718]

---

706. *See* United States-Mexico-Canada Agreement, Section 13.12, Jan. 29, 2020.
707. *See* United States-Mexico-Canada Agreement, Section 13.12, Jan. 29, 2020.
708. *See* United States-Mexico-Canada Agreement, Section 13.13, Jan. 29, 2020.
709. *See* United States-Mexico-Canada Agreement, Section 13.13, Jan. 29, 2020.
710. *See* United States-Mexico-Canada Agreement, Section 13.13, Jan. 29, 2020.
711. *See* United States-Mexico-Canada Agreement, Section 13.13, Jan. 29, 2020.
712. *See* United States-Mexico-Canada Agreement, Section 13.13, Jan. 29, 2020.
713. *See* United States-Mexico-Canada Agreement, Section 13.14, Jan. 29, 2020.
714. *See* United States-Mexico-Canada Agreement, Section 13.14, Jan. 29, 2020.
715. *See* United States-Mexico-Canada Agreement, Section 13.14, Jan. 29, 2020.
716. *See* United States-Mexico-Canada Agreement, Section 13.14, Jan. 29, 2020.
717. *See* United States-Mexico-Canada Agreement, Section 13.14, Jan. 29, 2020.
718. *See* United States-Mexico-Canada Agreement, Section 13.14, Jan. 29, 2020.

§13.7   TRANSPARENCY, POST-AWARD INFORMATION, AND DISCLOSURES

Entities must promptly inform suppliers about the submitted tenders of the contract decision.[719] They must publish a notice containing a description of the good or service procured, the name and address of the procuring entity, the name and address of the successful supplier, the value of the contract awarded, the date of award or the contract date, and the procurement method used.[720] In addition, procuring entities must maintain records for at least three years after the award of a contract.

Each Party must prepare a statistical report on its covered procurement, which must be available on an official website.[721] It must cover one year and be within two years of the end of the reporting period.[722] This will include the number and value of all government procurement contracts.[723] Then, they must break it down by categories of goods/services and by the entity.[724]

If requested, a Party must demonstrate to the other Party that a procurement was fairly conducted.[725] A receiving Party must not disclose this information to any supplier.[726] Notwithstanding disclosure requirements, Parties and their procuring entities, with the exception of legal restraints, may not disclose information that would prejudice the commercial interests of a supplier or fair competition.[727]

§13.8   ENSURING INTEGRITY VIA DOMESTIC REVIEW

The USMCA adds provisions to its procurement requirements that address corruption and are drawn from the TPP.[728] Under the USMCA, Parties must ensure that criminal, civil, or administrative measures exist that can address corruption, fraud, and other wrongful acts in its government procurement.[729] They must maintain procedures to address potential conflicts of interest.[730]

In addition, Parties must establish, maintain or designate at least one review authority that is independent of its procuring entities to review complaints by a supplier that there has been a breach of this chapter or failure of a procuring entity to comply with the Party's measures implementing this chapter.[731] The procuring entity and the supplier shall first seek resolution through consultations.[732] Any compensation

---

719. *See* United States-Mexico-Canada Agreement, Section 13.15, Jan. 29, 2020.
720. *See* United States-Mexico-Canada Agreement, Section 13.15, Jan. 29, 2020.
721. *See* United States-Mexico-Canada Agreement, Section 13.15, Jan. 29, 2020.
722. *See* United States-Mexico-Canada Agreement, Section 13.15, Jan. 29, 2020.
723. *See* United States-Mexico-Canada Agreement, Section 13.15, Jan. 29, 2020.
724. *See* United States-Mexico-Canada Agreement, Section 13.15, Jan. 29, 2020.
725. *See* United States-Mexico-Canada Agreement, Section 13.16, Jan. 29, 2020.
726. *See* United States-Mexico-Canada Agreement, Section 13.16, Jan. 29, 2020.
727. *See* United States-Mexico-Canada Agreement, Section 13.16, Jan. 29, 2020.
728. *See* United States-Mexico-Canada Agreement, Section 13.17, Jan. 29, 2020.
729. *See* United States-Mexico-Canada Agreement, Section 13.17, Jan. 29, 2020.
730. *See* United States-Mexico-Canada Agreement, Section 13.17, Jan. 29, 2020.
731. *See* United States-Mexico-Canada Agreement, Section 13.18, Jan. 29, 2020.
732. *See* United States-Mexico-Canada Agreement, Section 13.18, Jan. 29, 2020.

may be limited to the reasonable costs incurred in preparing a tender, bringing the complaint, or both.[733]

§13.9   MODIFICATIONS AND RECTIFICATIONS OF ANNEX

A Party must notify any proposed modification to its Annex by circulating a written notice to the other Party through the agreement coordinator.[734] Compensatory adjustments shall be provided if necessary.[735] However, Parties aren't required to provide compensatory adjustments if the modification concerns a procuring entity over which the Party has effectively eliminated its control or influence in respect of covered procurement or rectifications of a purely formal nature and minor modifications.[736] If a Party objects to a modification, they must notify the other Party within forty-five days of the notice.[737]

§13.10   FACILITATION OF PARTICIPATION BY SMEs

If a Party provides preferential treatment for SMEs, the Party must make that known in its notice.[738] Parties must provide information defining SMEs electronically, make tender documentation available free of charge, conduct procurement by electronic means, and consider the size, design, and structure of the procurement, including the use of subcontracting by SMEs.[739]

---

733. *See* United States-Mexico-Canada Agreement, Section 13.18, Jan. 29, 2020.
734. *See* United States-Mexico-Canada Agreement, Section 13.19, Jan. 29, 2020.
735. *See* United States-Mexico-Canada Agreement, Section 13.19, Jan. 29, 2020.
736. *See* United States-Mexico-Canada Agreement, Section 13.19, Jan. 29, 2020.
737. *See* United States-Mexico-Canada Agreement, Section 13.19, Jan. 29, 2020.
738. *See* United States-Mexico-Canada Agreement, Section 13.20, Jan. 29, 2020.
739. *See* United States-Mexico-Canada Agreement, Section 13.20, Jan. 29, 2020.

CHAPTER 14

Investments

This Chapter covers matters related to investments. These provisions do not apply to Canada. In terms of treatment standards, the minimum standard of treatment is one in accordance with the international standard, including fair and equitable treatment and full protection and security. Nondiscrimination treatment applies to specific measures. In terms of expropriation, Parties must not expropriate or nationalize a covered investment except for a public purpose, in a nondiscriminatory manner, on payment on just compensation, and in accordance with due process. Additionally, there are performance requirements that list when requirements cannot be imposed. However, the above requirements do not apply to any existing non-conforming measure that is in Annex I, or to sectors, subsectors, or activities set out in Annex II. Under the USCMA, National Treatment should not be used to prevent a Party from adopting special formalities in connection with covered investments. Additionally, a Party may deny the benefits of this Chapter to an investor and investment of another Party that is owned or controlled by a person of a non-Party or of the denying Party. Annex 14-B deals with expropriation and defines it as an action by a Party that interferes with a tangible or intangible property right or property interest in an investment. The USMCA incorporates the Investor-State Dispute Settlement (ISDS) process, but limits ISDS protections to certain sectors in Mexico. Finally, unlike NAFTA, the USMCA provides that claims related to this chapter should not be submitted to arbitration unless initial proceedings take place in court or tribunals.

The investment chapter of the USMCA defines an investment as "every asset that an investor owns or controls, directly or indirectly, that has the characteristics of an investment, including such characteristics as the commitment of capital or other resources, the expectation of gain or profit, or the assumption of risk."[740] NAFTA included examples that include "an enterprise," "real estate or other property, tangible or intangible," and certain kinds of contracts.[741] This chapter covers matters relating to

---

740. *See* United States-Mexico-Canada Agreement, Section 14.1, Jan. 29, 2020.
741. *See* Stephanie Forrest, Rachael Kent, & Danielle Morris, NAFTA 2.0: Investment Protection and Dispute Settlement Under Chapter 14 of the United States-Mexico-Canada Agreement, (Oct. 11, 2018), https://www.jdsupra.com/legalnews/nafta-2-0-investment-protection-and-21909/.

investors of another Party; covered investments; and investments in the territory a given Party with respect to performance requirements, environmental, health, safety and other regulatory objectives.[742] The investment provisions of the USMCA do not apply to Canada, and Canada has not signed on to Annexes 14-D and 14-E.[743] Canada's withdrawal is suspected to be due to its lack of success in bringing investor-state claims, as well as it being subject to more investor-state claims than either the U.S. or Mexico.[744] As a result of Canada's omission, the USMCA "reduce[s] the scope of relief available to American firms that are subject to Canadian environmental or other regulations, as well as to American firms operating in the non-covered sectors in Mexico."[745] These investment provisions prevail if there is any inconsistency with other chapters; however, these provisions do not apply to measures under Chapter 17 (Financial Services).[746] In addition, Parties may adopt any environmental, health, safety and regulatory measures that it considers appropriate if it is otherwise consistent with this chapter.[747] Many U.S. business groups had unsuccessfully pressed for a stronger investment dispute chapter. This is viewed by some as one of the important failures of the new USMCA. Since the U.S. had successfully used the investment dispute provisions under the prior NAFTA to the advantage of many U.S. companies, the lack of U.S. government support to maintain and strengthen these provisions was puzzling to many.

§14.1   TREATMENT STANDARDS

Parties must accord no less favorable treatment than it accords to its own investors.[748] Additionally, Parties may accord no less favorable treatments to investors of any other Party or non-Party with respect to investments in its territory.[749] The minimum standard of treatment required is one in accordance with international law, including fair and equitable treatment and full protection and security.[750] A determination of a breach of another provision of this Agreement or a separate agreement does not establish that there has been a breach of this Article.[751] The USMCA adds a provision from TPP stating that "the mere fact that a Party takes or fails to take an action that may

---

742. *See* United States-Mexico-Canada Agreement, Section 14.1, Jan. 29, 2020.
743. *See* Daniel Garcia, Alexandra Mitretodis & Andrew Tuck, The New NAFTA: Scaled-Back Arbitration in the USMCA, Journal of International Arbitration (2019), https://www.alston.com/-/media/files/insights/publications/2019/12/the-new-nafta.pdf.
744. *See* Daniel Garcia, Alexandra Mitretodis & Andrew Tuck, The New NAFTA: Scaled-Back Arbitration in the USMCA, Journal of International Arbitration (2019), https://www.alston.com/-/media/files/insights/publications/2019/12/the-new-nafta.pdf.
745. *See* Tori Smith & Gabriella Beaumont-Smith, An Analysis of the United States-Mexico-Canada Agreement, The Heritage Foundation (Jan. 28, 2019), https://www.heritage.org/trade/report/analysis-the-united-states-mexico-canada-agreement.
746. *See* United States-Mexico-Canada Agreement, Section 14.3, Jan. 29, 2020.
747. *See* United States-Mexico-Canada Agreement, Section 14.16, Jan. 29, 2020.
748. *See* United States-Mexico-Canada Agreement, Section 14.4, Jan. 29, 2020.
749. *See* United States-Mexico-Canada Agreement, Section 14.5, Jan. 29, 2020.
750. *See* United States-Mexico-Canada Agreement, Section 14.6, Jan. 29, 2020.
751. *See* United States-Mexico-Canada Agreement, Section 14.6, Jan. 29, 2020.

be inconsistent with an investor's expectations does not constitute a breach of this Article, even if there is loss or damage to the covered investment as a result."[752]

Notwithstanding Non-Conforming Measures (14.12.5(b)), Parties shall provide nondiscriminatory treatment to measures it adopts relating to losses suffered by investments in its territory owing to armed conflict or civil strife.[753] If an investor of a Party that is in conflict/strife suffers a loss resulting from requesting of its covered investment or destruction of its investment by authorities (that was not necessary), the Party whose territory it is in shall prove restitution, compensation or both.[754] The USMCA also requires Parties to encourage enterprises operating within its territory or subject to its jurisdiction to voluntarily incorporate into their internal policies internationally recognized standards of corporate social responsibility.[755]

§14.2 EXPROPRIATION, COMPENSATION, AND TRANSFERS

Parties must not expropriate or nationalize a covered investment except for a public purpose, in a nondiscriminatory manner, on payment on just compensation, and in accordance with due process.[756] Compensation cannot be delayed, must equal fair market value at the time of expropriation, must not reflect any change in value, and must be fully realizable and transferable.[757]

Transfers shall be permitted without delay, including capital contributions, profits, dividends, interest, capital gains, royalties, management fees, technical assistance and other fees.[758] It also includes proceeds from sale or liquidations, payments made under a contract entered into by the investor and payments made pursuant to matters of conflict/strife and expropriation/compensation.[759] However, Parties can prevent or delay transfer for bankruptcy, insolvency, creditor's rights, issuing, trading, and dealing in securities and derivatives, criminal/penal offenses, financial reporting or record keeping, assisting law enforcement or financial regulatory agencies, or ensuring compliance with orders or judgments in judicial or administrative proceedings.[760]

§14.3 PERFORMANCE REQUIREMENTS

Requirements cannot be imposed to:

(1) export a given level or percentage of goods or services;
(2) achieve a given level or percentage of domestic content;

---

752. *See* United States-Mexico-Canada Agreement, Section 14.6, Jan. 29, 2020.
753. *See* United States-Mexico-Canada Agreement, Section 14.7, Jan. 29, 2020.
754. *See* United States-Mexico-Canada Agreement, Section 14.7, Jan. 29, 2020.
755. *See* United States-Mexico-Canada Agreement, Section 14.17, Jan. 29, 2020.
756. *See* United States-Mexico-Canada Agreement, Section 14.8, Jan. 29, 2020.
757. *See* United States-Mexico-Canada Agreement, Section 14.8, Jan. 29, 2020.
758. *See* United States-Mexico-Canada Agreement, Section 14.9, Jan. 29, 2020.
759. *See* United States-Mexico-Canada Agreement, Section 14.9, Jan. 29, 2020.
760. *See* United States-Mexico-Canada Agreement, Section 14.9, Jan. 29, 2020.

(3) purchase, use, or accord a preference to a good produced or a service supplied in its territory, or to purchase a good or service from a person in its territory;

(4) relate in any way the volume or value of imports to the volume or value of exports or to the amount of foreign exchange inflows associated with the investment;

(5) restrict sales of a good or service in its territory that the investment produces or supplies by relating those sales in any way to the volume or value of its exports or foreign exchange earnings;

(6) transfer technology, a production process, or other proprietary knowledge to a person in its territory;

(7) supply exclusively from the territory of the Party a good that the investment produces or a service that it supplies to a specific regional market or to the world market;

(8) adopt a given rate or amount of royalties for a given duration of the term of a license contract. Sections (2)(3)(4) and(5) also cannot be conditions to the receipt or continued receipt of an advantage of an investment. [761]

§14.4   SENIOR MANAGEMENT AND BOARD OF DIRECTORS

Parties may not require that an enterprise that is a covered investment appoint to senior management positions a natural person of a particular nationality.[761] However, Parties may require that a majority of the board of directors, or any committee thereof, of an enterprise of that Party that is a covered investment, be of a particular nationality, or a resident in the territory of the Party, provided that the requirement does not materially impair the ability of the investor to exercise control over its investment.[762]

§14.5   NON-CONFORMING MEASURES

National Treatment, MFN Status, Performance Requirements, and Senior Management and Board of Directors Requirements do not apply to any existing non-conforming measure that is maintained by a Party at the central and regional government and is in Annex I, or any local level of government.[763] These exclusions apply to the continuation or renewal of any non-conforming measure or an amendment of those measures.[764] The exclusions apply to measures Parties adopt with respect to sectors, subsectors, or activities set out in Annex II.

---

761. *See* United States-Mexico-Canada Agreement, Section 14.11, Jan. 29, 2020.
762. *See* United States-Mexico-Canada Agreement, Section 14.11, Jan. 29, 2020.
763. *See* United States-Mexico-Canada Agreement, Section 14.12, Jan. 29, 2020.
764. *See* United States-Mexico-Canada Agreement, Section 14.12, Jan. 29, 2020.

[A] Special Formalities and Information Requirements

National Treatment should not be construed to prevent a Party from adopting or maintaining a measure that prescribes special formalities in connection with covered investments, such as a requirement that investors be residents or that covered investments be legally constituted under the laws or regulations of the Party.[765] In addition, National Treatment and MFN should not prevent Parties from requiring an investor of another Party or its covered investment to provide information concerning that investment solely for informational or statistical purposes.[766]

[B] Denial of Benefits

A Party may deny the benefits of this chapter to an investor and investments of another Party that is owned or controlled by a person of a non-Party or of the denying Party and has no substantial business activities in the territory of any Party other than the denying Party.[767] They may also deny benefits if persons of a non-Party own or control the enterprise, and the denying Party adopts or maintains measures with respect to the non-Party or a person of the non-Party that prohibit transactions with the enterprise.[768]

[C] Subrogation

If a Party, or an agency of a Party, makes a payment to an investor of the Party under guarantee, a contract of insurance or another form of indemnity that it has entered into with respect to a covered investment, the other Party in whose territory the covered investment was made shall recognize the subrogation or transfer of any right the investor would have possessed with respect to the covered investment but for the subrogation, and the investor shall be precluded from pursuing that right to the extent of the subrogation unless a Party or an agency of a Party authorizes the investor to act on its behalf.[769]

§14.6 CUSTOMARY INTERNATIONAL LAW

Customary international law results from a general and consistent practice of States that they follow from a sense of legal obligation.[770] The customary international law minimum standard of treatment of aliens refers to all customary international law principles that protect the investments of aliens.[771]

---

765. *See* United States-Mexico-Canada Agreement, Section 14.13, Jan. 29, 2020.
766. *See* United States-Mexico-Canada Agreement, Section 14.13, Jan. 29, 2020.
767. *See* United States-Mexico-Canada Agreement, Section 14.14, Jan. 29, 2020.
768. *See* United States-Mexico-Canada Agreement, Section 14.14, Jan. 29, 2020.
769. *See* United States-Mexico-Canada Agreement, Section 14.15, Jan. 29, 2020.
770. *See* United States-Mexico-Canada Agreement, Annex 14-A, Jan. 29, 2020.
771. *See* United States-Mexico-Canada Agreement, Annex 14-A, Jan. 29, 2020.

§14.7   EXPROPRIATION

[A]   Annex 14-B: Expropriation

Under the USMCA, an action or a series of actions by a Party cannot constitute an expropriation unless it interferes with a tangible or intangible property right or property interest in an investment.[772] Direct expropriation exists when an investment is nationalized or otherwise directly expropriated through formal transfer of title or outright seizure.[773] Indirect expropriation results when an action or series of actions by a Party has an effect equivalent to direct expropriation without formal transfer of title or outright seizure.[774] Indirect expropriation requires a case-by-case, fact-based inquiry that considers, among other factors: economic impact, the extent to which the action interferes with reasonable investment-backed expectations, and the character of the government action, including its object, context, and intent.[775]

§14.8   LEGACY INVESTMENT CLAIMS AND PENDING CLAIMS

The USMCA incorporates section B of Chapter 11 of NAFTA 1994 for arbitrations that are ongoing.[776] Under the USMCA, investors that have made investments covered by the NAFTA before it is terminated have three years from the date of termination of the NAFTA in which they can bring a claim under the provisions of the NAFTA.[777]

§14.9   MEXICO-UNITED STATES INVESTMENT DISPUTES

The USMCA incorporates the Investor-State Dispute Settlement (ISDS) process but limits ISDS protections to certain sectors in Mexico.[778] This section is similar to NAFTA Chapter 11 Section B, but it is limited to investments in oil and gas, power generation, telecommunications, transportation, infrastructure, and other listed sectors that have a contract with the central government of Mexico (Annex 14-E-6 (b) "covered sectors").[779] Some have described the new ISDS as "[a] neutral and independent ISDS arbitration process [that] ensures that American investors are guaranteed fair treatment, an especially important consideration for investments in developing countries."[780] Yet, it is more limited in scope than in the original NAFTA.

---

772. *See* United States-Mexico-Canada Agreement, Annex 14-B, Jan. 29, 2020.
773. *See* United States-Mexico-Canada Agreement, Annex 14-B, Jan. 29, 2020.
774. *See* United States-Mexico-Canada Agreement, Annex 14-B, Jan. 29, 2020.
775. *See* United States-Mexico-Canada Agreement, Annex 14-B, Jan. 29, 2020.
776. *See* United States-Mexico-Canada Agreement, Annex 14-C, Jan. 29, 2020; *see also* North American Free Trade Agreement, Chapter 11, Jan. 1, 1994.
777. *See* United States-Mexico-Canada Agreement, Annex 14-C, Jan. 29, 2020.
778. *See* United States-Mexico-Canada Agreement, Annex 14-D, Jan. 29, 2020.
779. *See* United States-Mexico-Canada Agreement, Annex 14-D, Jan. 29, 2020.
780. *See* Tori Smith & Gabriella Beaumont-Smith, An Analysis of the United States–Mexico–Canada Agreement, The Heritage Foundation (Jan. 28, 2019), https://www.heritage.org/trade/report/analysis-the-united-states-mexico-canada-agreement.

Under the ISDS provisions, a claimant can be "an investor of an Annex Party [i.e., the United States or Mexico], excluding an investor that is owned or controlled by a person of a non-Annex Party that the other Annex Party considers to be a non-market economy, that is a party to a qualifying investment dispute."[781] This definition of "Claimant" is new and seems to be directed at Chinese-owned or -controlled investments in the United States and Mexico.[782]

The USMCA goes on to limit substance by preventing investors from bringing a claim for breach of the minimum standard of treatment in or for indirect expropriation.[783] National Treatment and MFN claims related to the establishment or acquisition of investment are also excluded.[784] Claimants can only allege discrimination regarding "expansion, management, conduct, operation, and sale or other disposition of investments."[785] As a result, Parties will seek alternative dispute resolution.[786] Then, they may submit a claim to Arbitration if the respondent has breached National Treatment, MFN Treatment, or Direct Expropriation and Compensation.[787] Under Annex 14-D, each Party consents to the submission of a claim under this Annex and in accordance with this agreement.[788]

In contrast to NAFTA, the USMCA provides that claims should not be submitted to arbitration unless the claimant or the claimant and the enterprise first initiated a proceeding before a competent court or administrative tribunal of the respondent; they obtained a final decision or thirty months have elapsed since the proceeding was initiated; no more than four years have elapsed since the claimant should have known of the breach and damage; the claimant consents in writing to arbitration and the notice of arbitration contains clams of any right to initiate a trial.[789] This will diminish the value of these provisions for U.S. companies bringing claims. Many U.S. business groups had wanted to preserve or strengthen the NAFTA investor dispute provisions and even strengthen them, but the U.S. negotiators followed a different path.

781. *See* United States-Mexico-Canada Agreement, Annex 14-D, Jan. 29, 2020.
782. *See* Susan G. Esserman & Luke Tillman, et al., USMCA Unlocked: Working Under the New NAFTA, (Mar. 29, 2019) https://www.steptoe.com/en/news-publications/usmca-unlocked-working-under-the-new-nafta.html.
783. *See* United States-Mexico-Canada Agreement, Annex 14-D, Jan. 29, 2020; *see also* Stephanie Forrest, Rachael Kent, & Danielle Morris, NAFTA 2.0: Investment Protection and Dispute Settlement Under Chapter 14 of the United States-Mexico-Canada Agreement, (Oct. 11, 2018), https://www.jdsupra.com/legalnews/nafta-2-0-investment-protection-and-21909/.
784. *See* United States-Mexico-Canada Agreement, Annex 14-D, Jan. 29, 2020; *see also* Stephanie Forrest, Rachael Kent, & Danielle Morris, NAFTA 2.0: Investment Protection and Dispute Settlement Under Chapter 14 of the United States-Mexico-Canada Agreement, (Oct. 11, 2018), https://www.jdsupra.com/legalnews/nafta-2-0-investment-protection-and-21909/.
785. *See* United States-Mexico-Canada Agreement, Annex 14-D, Jan. 29, 2020; *see also* Stephanie Forrest, Rachael Kent, & Danielle Morris, NAFTA 2.0: Investment Protection and Dispute Settlement Under Chapter 14 of the United States-Mexico-Canada Agreement, (Oct. 11, 2018), https://www.jdsupra.com/legalnews/nafta-2-0-investment-protection-and-21909/.
786. *See* United States-Mexico-Canada Agreement, Annex 14-D, Jan. 29, 2020.
787. *See* United States-Mexico-Canada Agreement, Annex 14-D, Jan. 29, 2020.
788. *See* United States-Mexico-Canada Agreement, Annex 14-D, Jan. 29, 2020.
789. *See* United States-Mexico-Canada Agreement, Annex 14-D, Jan. 29, 2020.

§14.10   TRIBUNALS

Tribunals must have three arbitrators: one from each Party and a third appointed by agreement of the Parties.[790] The Secretary-General will serve as the third party under this annex.[791] The USMCA changes the location requirements of the tribunal, providing that if Parties cannot agree where to conduct an arbitration, the tribunal will decide a location that (must be in a State that is a party to the New York Convention).[792] This is a change from NAFTA, where Parties had to choose a forum within NAFTA states.[793]

§14.11   ADDITIONAL INFORMATION

More information is given on arbitration in this Annex 14-D, including governing law, interpretation of annexes, expert reports, claim consolidation, awards, service of documents, and public debt.[794] In particular, the USMCA requires that arbitration documents be published, and amicus participation be allowed.[795] The USMCA also requires arbiters to comply with the International Bar Association Guidelines on Conflicts of Interest in International Arbitration and refrain from taking instructions from any organization or government regarding the dispute.[796]

Further, Article 5 of Annex 14-D requires claimants to "initiate and maintain domestic litigation proceedings for thirty months (or to a final decision) before being able to initiate arbitration, with a limited exception if domestic recourse would be obviously futile."[797] National courts and USMCA tribunals will have the responsibility of determining how to navigate overlapping decisions.[798]

§14.12   MEXICO-UNITED STATES INVESTMENT DISPUTES RELATED TO COVERED GOVERNMENT CONTRACTS

The USMCA defines covered government contracts as written agreements between an investor or investment and a "national authority" of the respondent State related to certain sectors, which the investor relied upon in making its investment.[799] The covered sectors are oil and gas, power generation, telecommunications, transportation,

---

790. *See* United States-Mexico-Canada Agreement, Annex 14-D, Jan. 29, 2020.
791. *See* United States-Mexico-Canada Agreement, Annex 14-D, Jan. 29, 2020.
792. *See* United States-Mexico-Canada Agreement, Annex 14-D, Jan. 29, 2020.
793. *See* North American Free Trade Agreement, Chapter 11 Part 2, Jan. 1, 1994.
794. *See* United States-Mexico-Canada Agreement, Annex 14-D, Jan. 29, 2020.
795. *See* United States-Mexico-Canada Agreement, Annex 14-D, Jan. 29, 2020.
796. *See* United States-Mexico-Canada Agreement, Annex 14-D, Jan. 29, 2020.
797. *See* Daniel Garcia, Alexandra Mitretodis & Andrew Tuck, The New NAFTA: Scaled-Back Arbitration in the USMCA, Journal of International Arbitration (2019), https://www.alston.com/-/media/files/insights/publications/2019/12/the-new-nafta.pdf.
798. *See* Daniel Garcia, Alexandra Mitretodis & Andrew Tuck, The New NAFTA: Scaled-Back Arbitration in the USMCA, Journal of International Arbitration (2019), https://www.alston.com/-/media/files/insights/publications/2019/12/the-new-nafta.pdf.
799. *See* United States-Mexico-Canada Agreement, Annex 14-E, Jan. 29, 2020.

and ownership or management of infrastructure.[800] The USMCA allows Parties to bring their indirect expropriation and violation of the minimum standard treatment for disputes related to covered government contracts.[801] No pre-arbitration local litigation requirement is needed.[802] However, claimants must wait six months from the events giving rise to their claim before initiating the arbitration, and there is a three-year statute of limitations.[803] The respondent State must be a party to at least one other "international trade or investment agreement that permits investors to initiate dispute settlement procedures to resolve an investment dispute with a government."[804] Lastly, the U.S. and Mexico can modify or eliminate this Annex.[805]

---

800. *See* United States-Mexico-Canada Agreement, Annex 14-E, Jan. 29, 2020.
801. *See* Stephanie Forrest, Rachael Kent, & Danielle Morris, NAFTA 2.0: Investment Protection and Dispute Settlement Under Chapter 14 of the United States-Mexico-Canada Agreement, (Oct. 11, 2018), https://www.jdsupra.com/legalnews/nafta-2-0-investment-protection-and-21909/.
802. *See* United States-Mexico-Canada Agreement, Annex 14-E, Jan. 29, 2020.
803. *See* United States-Mexico-Canada Agreement, Annex 14-E, Jan. 29, 2020.
804. *See* United States-Mexico-Canada Agreement, Annex 14-E, Jan. 29, 2020.
805. *See* United States-Mexico-Canada Agreement, Annex 14-E, Jan. 29, 2020.

CHAPTER 15

Cross-Border Trade in Services

This Chapter discusses cross-border trade in services that was discussed in Chapter 12 of NAFTA. These provisions ensure that Parties accord national treatment to another Party and MFN treatment to another Party or non-Party. Unlike NAFTA, the USCMA has provisions relating to market access. However, none of these provisions apply to non-conforming measures listed in Annex I, nor do they apply to sectors, subsectors, or activities listed in Annex II. Under the USMCA, Parties must administer measures in a reasonable, objective, and impartial manner. However, under the USMCA, recognition of any education or experience obtained, requirements met, or licenses or certifications granted, in the territory of another Party or a non-Party is not mandatory. Parties may also deny benefits if the service supplier meets specific requirements. In terms of delivery under this Chapter, certain restrictions apply, including the notion that Parties cannot place a condition for an authorization or license related to the delivery. The USMCA also establishes two committees related to this chapter: Committee on Transportation Services and The Professional Services Working Group. Appendix I of this Chapter allows for Parties to work towards a Mutual Recognition Agreement (MRAs); however, these guidelines are non-binding. Under Annex 15-D, the Agreement rescinds the rule that barred Canadian cable companies from blocking U.S. television signals transmitting simultaneous programs. This will promote competition within Canada; Finally, Annex 15-E preserves and promotes the development of Mexican culture in broadcasting, cinema, and audiovisual services.

USMCA Chapter 15 discusses cross-border trade in services that was previously discussed in Chapter 12, Part 5 of NAFTA.[806] Similar to NAFTA, these provisions apply to production, distribution, marketing, sale or delivery of a service.[807] They also apply to purchase of, use of, or payment for services.[808] They apply to transportation, distribution, or telecommunications in connection with services.[809] They apply to the presence of a service supplier of another Party or the provision of financial security as

---

806. *See* United States-Mexico-Canada Agreement, Section 15, Jan. 29, 2020; *see also* North American Free Trade Agreement, Chapter 12 Part 5, Jan. 1, 1994.
807. *See* United States-Mexico-Canada Agreement, Section 15.2, Jan. 29, 2020.
808. *See* United States-Mexico-Canada Agreement, Section 15.2, Jan. 29, 2020.
809. *See* United States-Mexico-Canada Agreement, Section 15.2, Jan. 29, 2020.

a condition for service.[810] Under both the USMCA and NAFTA, Parties must accord national treatment to another Party and MFN treatment to another Party or non-Party.[811]

Exclusive to the USMCA are provisions relating to market access.[812] The USMCA uses wording similar to the General Agreement on Trade in Services (GATS) and states that Parties must not impose certain limitations on the basis or regional subdivision or its entire territory.[813] These limitations are limitations on the number of service suppliers, the total value of service transactions/assets, the total number of service operations or the total quantity of service output, or the total number of natural persons that may be employed in a particular service sector.[814] In addition, Parties may not require a specific type of legal entity/joint venture through which a service supplier may supply a service.[815] Nor can Parties require suppliers of another Party to reside or maintain an office in its territory.[816] However, none of these provisions apply to non-conforming measures listed in Annex I or maintained by local levels of government.[817] They also do not apply to sectors, subsectors or activities listed in Annex II.[818]

§15.1 DEVELOPMENT AND ADMINISTRATION OF MEASURES

Parties must administer measures in a reasonable, objective, and impartial manner.[819] If a Party uses licensing, procedures or criteria that affect trade in services, they must make sure it is based on objective and transparent criteria.[820] If authorization is required for the supply of services, Parties must permit applicants to submit an application at any time unless a specific time period exists—then they must allow a reasonable time.[821] Parties must endeavor to accept electronic applications.[822] Lastly, Parties must provide the person or supplier seeking to supply a service with all of the necessary information to comply, including fees, contact information, procedures, and technical standards.[823]

§15.2 RECOGNITION

Unlike NAFTA, the USMCA *allows* a Party to recognize any education or experience obtained, requirements met, or licenses or certifications granted, in the territory of

---

810. *See* United States-Mexico-Canada Agreement, Section 15.2, Jan. 29, 2020.
811. *See* United States-Mexico-Canada Agreement, Section 15.3-.4, Jan. 29, 2020.
812. *See* United States-Mexico-Canada Agreement, Section 15.5, Jan. 29, 2020.
813. *See* United States-Mexico-Canada Agreement, Section 15.5, Jan. 29, 2020.
814. *See* United States-Mexico-Canada Agreement, Section 15.5, Jan. 29, 2020.
815. *See* United States-Mexico-Canada Agreement, Section 15.5, Jan. 29, 2020.
816. *See* United States-Mexico-Canada Agreement, Section 15.6, Jan. 29, 2020.
817. *See* United States-Mexico-Canada Agreement, Section 15.7, Jan. 29, 2020.
818. *See* United States-Mexico-Canada Agreement, Section 15.7, Jan. 29, 2020.
819. *See* United States-Mexico-Canada Agreement, Section 15.8, Jan. 29, 2020.
820. *See* United States-Mexico-Canada Agreement, Section 15.8, Jan. 29, 2020.
821. *See* United States-Mexico-Canada Agreement, Section 15.8, Jan. 29, 2020.
822. *See* United States-Mexico-Canada Agreement, Section 15.8, Jan. 29, 2020.
823. *See* United States-Mexico-Canada Agreement, Section 15.8, Jan. 29, 2020.

another Party or a non-Party.[824] However, MFN Treatment does not *require* the Party to accord recognition to the education or experience obtained, requirements met, or licenses or certifications granted, in the territory of another Party.[825] In any case, a Party shall not accord recognition in a manner that would constitute a means of discrimination between Parties or between a Party and a non-Party.[826] Since recognition is not mandatory, the value of this is not clear; yet, the potential ease of movement could have a positive impact on professional services.[827]

§15.3   SMALL- AND MEDIUM-SIZED ENTERPRISES

Parties should support the development of SME trade in services and SME-enabling business models, such as direct selling services.[828] Parties should adopt measures to consider the effects of regulatory actions on SME service suppliers that enable small businesses to participate in regulatory policy development.[829]

§15.4   DENIAL OF BENEFITS

Parties can deny benefits if the service supplier is an enterprise owned or controlled by a person of a non-Party, and the denying Party adopts or maintains a measure with respect to the non-Party or a person of the non-Party that prohibits a transaction with that enterprise.[830]

§15.5   PAYMENTS AND TRANSFERS

The USMCA, unlike NAFTA, requires Parties to permit payments to be made freely and without delay.[831] For cross-border supply of services, Parties must have transfers and payments to be made in a freely usable currency at the market exchange rate.[832] The USMCA makes exceptions for bankruptcy, insolvency, protection of the rights of creditors; issuing, trading, or dealing in securities or derivatives; financial reporting or record keeping of transfers when necessary to assist law enforcement or financial regulatory authorities; criminal or penal offenses; or ensuring compliance with orders or judgments in judicial or administrative proceedings.[833]

---

824. *See* United States-Mexico-Canada Agreement, Section 15.9, Jan. 29, 2020.
825. *See* United States-Mexico-Canada Agreement, Section 15.9, Jan. 29, 2020.
826. *See* United States-Mexico-Canada Agreement, Section 15.9, Jan. 29, 2020.
827. *See* Tori Smith & Gabriella Beaumont-Smith, An Analysis of the United States–Mexico–Canada Agreement, The Heritage Foundation (Jan. 28, 2019), https://www.heritage.org/trade/report/analysis-the-united-states-mexico-canada-agreement.
828. *See* United States-Mexico-Canada Agreement, Section 15.10, Jan. 29, 2020.
829. *See* United States-Mexico-Canada Agreement, Section 15.10, Jan. 29, 2020.
830. *See* United States-Mexico-Canada Agreement, Section 15.11, Jan. 29, 2020.
831. *See* United States-Mexico-Canada Agreement, Section 15.12, Jan. 29, 2020.
832. *See* United States-Mexico-Canada Agreement, Section 15.12, Jan. 29, 2020.
833. *See* United States-Mexico-Canada Agreement, Section 15.12, Jan. 29, 2020.

§15.6   DELIVERY SERVICES

The USMCA provides specific provisions with respect to delivery in Annex 15-A.[834] These provisions do not apply to the maritime, internal waterway, air, rail, or road transportation, including cabotage, and focuses on postal delivery services. Instead, they apply to postal services and Parties that maintain a postal monopoly shall define the scope of the monopoly.[835] Under the USMCA, suppliers of a delivery service covered by a postal monopoly cannot use revenues derived from supply of these services to cross-subsidize the supply of a service not covered by a postal monopoly.[836] Parties cannot unjustifiably differentiate among mailers in like circumstances with respect to tariffs or other terms and conditions for the supply of a delivery service covered by a postal monopoly.[837]

No Party shall require the supply of a delivery service on a universal basis as a condition for an authorization or license to supply a delivery service not covered by a postal monopoly; or assess fees or other charges exclusively on the supply of any delivery service that is not a universal service for the purpose of funding the supply of a universal service.[838] Nor can a Party require a supplier of a delivery service not covered by a postal monopoly to contract or prevent such a supplier from contracting with another service supplier to supply a segment of the delivery service.[839]

§15.7   COMMITTEE ON TRANSPORTATION SERVICES

The USMCA establishes the Transportation Services Committee that will discuss issues that arise from the implication and operation of the Parties obligations related to transportation services in Chapter 14 (Investment) and Chapter 15 (Cross-Border Trade in Services).[840]

§15.8   PROFESSIONAL SERVICES

Much of the professional services provisions are similar to NAFTA. Parties must consult with bodies in their territories to identify professional service where at least two Parties can establish a dialogue on recognition of professional qualifications, licensing or registration.[841] They must encourage their respective relevant bodies, as appropriate, to consider undertaking related activity within a mutually agreed time.[842] The USMCA, unlike NAFTA, establishes the Professional Services Working Group

---

834. *See* United States-Mexico-Canada Agreement, Annex 15-A, Jan. 29, 2020.
835. *See* United States-Mexico-Canada Agreement, Annex 15-A, Jan. 29, 2020.
836. *See* United States-Mexico-Canada Agreement, Annex 15-A, Jan. 29, 2020.
837. *See* United States-Mexico-Canada Agreement, Annex 15-A, Jan. 29, 2020.
838. *See* United States-Mexico-Canada Agreement, Annex 15-A, Jan. 29, 2020.
839. *See* United States-Mexico-Canada Agreement, Annex 15-A, Jan. 29, 2020.
840. *See* United States-Mexico-Canada Agreement, Annex 15-B, Jan. 29, 2020.
841. *See* United States-Mexico-Canada Agreement, Annex 15-C, Jan. 29, 2020.
842. *See* United States-Mexico-Canada Agreement, Annex 15-C, Jan. 29, 2020.

(PSWG) composed of representatives of each Party that will work on the related activity.[843]

Appendix 1 Guidelines for Mutual Recognition Agreements or Arrangements for the Professional Services Sector

These guidelines are non-binding and are intended to be used by the Parties on a voluntary basis.[844] They do not modify or affect the rights and obligations of the Parties under this Agreement.[845] The objective of these guidelines is to facilitate the negotiation of mutual recognition agreements or arrangements (MRAs).[846]

Section A: Conduct of Negotiations and Relevant Obligations.

Parties should inform the PSWG if they intend to work towards an MRA.[847] Parties to an MRA should inform the PSWG of the content of a new MRA, significant modifications to an existing MRA, how the MRA complies with this chapter, implementation and monitoring measures, and that the text of the MRA is publicly available.[848] If no single negotiating entity exists, the Parties are encouraged to establish one.[849]

Section B: Form and Content of MRAs.

Clearly identifies the Parties, competent authorities, and the status and is of competence of each party.[850] Identifies purpose, scope, professional titles, qualifications, licensing requirements, and whether it covers temporary access, permanent access, or both, to the profession concerned.[851]

MRA must clearly specify the conditions to be met for recognition in the territories of each Party, and the level of equivalence agreed between the Parties to the MRA.[852] The Parties should seek to ensure that recognition does not require citizenship or any form of residency, or education, experience, or training in the territory of the host jurisdiction.[853]

If there are qualifications, they must state the minimum level of education and experience required, examinations passed, the extent to which home country qualifications are recognized in the host country and the qualifications which the Parties to the MRA are prepared to recognize.[854]

---

843. *See* United States-Mexico-Canada Agreement, Annex 15-C, Jan. 29, 2020.
844. *See* United States-Mexico-Canada Agreement, Annex 15-C Appendix 1, Jan. 29, 2020.
845. *See* United States-Mexico-Canada Agreement, Annex 15-C Appendix 1, Jan. 29, 2020.
846. *See* United States-Mexico-Canada Agreement, Annex 15-C Appendix 1, Jan. 29, 2020.
847. *See* United States-Mexico-Canada Agreement, Annex 15-C Appendix 1, Jan. 29, 2020.
848. *See* United States-Mexico-Canada Agreement, Annex 15-C Appendix 1, Jan. 29, 2020.
849. *See* United States-Mexico-Canada Agreement, Annex 15-C Appendix 1, Jan. 29, 2020.
850. *See* United States-Mexico-Canada Agreement, Annex 15-C Appendix 1, Jan. 29, 2020.
851. *See* United States-Mexico-Canada Agreement, Annex 15-C Appendix 1, Jan. 29, 2020.
852. *See* United States-Mexico-Canada Agreement, Annex 15-C Appendix 1, Jan. 29, 2020.
853. *See* United States-Mexico-Canada Agreement, Annex 15-C Appendix 1, Jan. 29, 2020.
854. *See* United States-Mexico-Canada Agreement, Annex 15-C Appendix 1, Jan. 29, 2020.

If the MRA is based on recognition or registration, it should specify the mechanism by which eligibility for recognition may be established. If additional requirements are deemed necessary, the MRA should set out in detail what they entail.[855]

Among other things, MRAs can include rules and procedures for monitoring and enforcement; mechanisms for dialogue and administrative cooperation; and arbitration.[856]

If applicable, the MRA could also set out the means by which and the conditions under which a license is actually obtained following the establishment of eligibility and what such license entails.[857] If the MRA includes terms under which it can be reviewed or revoked, the details of such terms should be clearly stated.[858]

Annex 15-D: Programming Services

Simultaneous Substitution

This Annex provided that Canada can distribute the signal of a local or regional over-the-air station in place of the signal of a foreign or non-local television station when the two stations are broadcasting the same program simultaneously.[859] Canada must rescind Broadcasting Regulatory Policy CRTC 2016-334 and Broadcasting Order CRTC 2016-335.[860] The rule barred Canadian cable and satellite companies from blocking U.S. television signals transmitting simultaneous programs, such as the Super Bowl.[861]

U.S. and Canada must provide in its copyright law that retransmission to the public of program signals not intended in the original transmission for free, over-the-air reception by the general public shall be permitted only with the authorization of the holder of the copyright in the program; and if the original transmission of the program is carried in signals intended for free, over-the-air reception by the general public, willful retransmission in altered form or non-simultaneous retransmission of signals carrying a copyright holder's program shall be permitted only with the authorization of the holder of the copyright in the program.[862]

While rescinding this rule will promote competition within Canada, it is unlikely to facilitate trade between Canada and the U.S.[863] For example, the license agreement between the NFL and Bell Media will allow the Superbowl to be shown on CTV, but

---

855. *See* United States-Mexico-Canada Agreement, Annex 15-C Appendix 1, Jan. 29, 2020.
856. *See* United States-Mexico-Canada Agreement, Annex 15-C Appendix 1, Jan. 29, 2020.
857. *See* United States-Mexico-Canada Agreement, Annex 15-C Appendix 1, Jan. 29, 2020.
858. *See* United States-Mexico-Canada Agreement, Annex 15-C Appendix 1, Jan. 29, 2020.
859. *See* United States-Mexico-Canada Agreement, Annex 15-D, Jan. 29, 2020.
860. *See* United States-Mexico-Canada Agreement, Annex 15-D, Jan. 29, 2020.
861. *See* Tori Smith & Gabriella Beaumont-Smith, An Analysis of the United States–Mexico–Canada Agreement, The Heritage Foundation (Jan. 28, 2019), https://www.heritage.org/trade/report/analysis-the-united-states-mexico-canada-agreement.
862. *See* United States-Mexico-Canada Agreement, Annex 15-D, Jan. 29, 2020.
863. *See* Tori Smith & Gabriella Beaumont-Smith, An Analysis of the United States–Mexico–Canada Agreement, The Heritage Foundation (Jan. 28, 2019), https://www.heritage.org/trade/report/analysis-the-united-states-mexico-canada-agreement.

local or regional advertisements will replace American ads.[864] Some argue that the U.S. and Canada need to readdress these rules so that U.S. companies can sell their advertisements in Canada more easily, thereby increasing the variety of goods and services in both countries.[865]

Home Shopping Programming Services

Canada will allow U.S. home shopping programs into the Canadian market and allow them to negotiate affiliation agreements with Canadian cable, satellite, and IPTV distributors.[866]

Annex 15-E Mexico's Cultural Exceptions

In order to preserve and promote the development of Mexican culture, Mexico has negotiated reservations in its schedules to Annex I and Annex II for certain obligations in Chapter 14 (Investment) and Chapter 15 (Cross-Border Trade in Services).[867]

Broadcasting

Reservations have been taken against National Treatment obligations for Investment, and Cross-Border Trade, as well as local presence obligation for Cross-Border Trade, are also located in the Services Chapter. Concessions have been granted to Mexican nationals or Mexican enterprises.[868] Sole concessions and frequency band concessions are reserved for Mexican nationals or enterprises only.[869] Investors of a Party may participate up to 49% in concessionaire enterprises providing broadcasting services.[870] Indigenous social concessions will be solely granted to Mexican indigenous communities.[871] These concessions may not be assigned, encumbered, pledged, mortgaged, or transferred to any foreign government or state.[872]

Reservations against National Treatment for Investment Chapter for Newspaper Publishing allow investors of another Party to own up to 49% "in an enterprise established or to be established in the territory of Mexico" engaged in either the printing or publication of daily newspapers directed at Mexican audiences or its territory.[873]

---

864. *See* Tori Smith & Gabriella Beaumont-Smith, An Analysis of the United States–Mexico–Canada Agreement, The Heritage Foundation (Jan. 28, 2019), https://www.heritage.org/trade/report /analysis-the-united-states-mexico-canada-agreement.
865. *See* Tori Smith & Gabriella Beaumont-Smith, An Analysis of the United States–Mexico–Canada Agreement, The Heritage Foundation (Jan. 28, 2019), https://www.heritage.org/trade/report /analysis-the-united-states-mexico-canada-agreement.
866. *See* United States-Mexico-Canada Agreement, Annex 15-D, Jan. 29, 2020.
867. *See* United States-Mexico-Canada Agreement, Annex 15-E, Jan. 29, 2020.
868. *See* United States-Mexico-Canada Agreement, Annex 15-E, Jan. 29, 2020.
869. *See* United States-Mexico-Canada Agreement, Annex 15-E, Jan. 29, 2020.
870. *See* United States-Mexico-Canada Agreement, Annex 15-E, Jan. 29, 2020.
871. *See* United States-Mexico-Canada Agreement, Annex 15-E, Jan. 29, 2020.
872. *See* United States-Mexico-Canada Agreement, Annex 15-E, Jan. 29, 2020.
873. *See* United States-Mexico-Canada Agreement, Annex 15-E, Jan. 29, 2020.

Cinema Services and Audiovisual Services

Reservations require that 10% of the total screen time must be allocated to national films.[874] Further, Mexico is taking limited commitments in the Market Access obligation with respect to the audiovisual services sector.[875]

There is a similar argument made against Mexico's exceptions as with Canada's. The limitations restrict businesses and investors from freely investing. It can be argued that not only does this burden the investor but also harms the economy by deterring investors from directly investing in that country.[876]

---

874. *See* United States-Mexico-Canada Agreement, Annex 15-E, Jan. 29, 2020.
875. *See* United States-Mexico-Canada Agreement, Annex 15-E, Jan. 29, 2020.
876. *See* Tori Smith & Gabriella Beaumont-Smith, An Analysis of the United States–Mexico–Canada Agreement, The Heritage Foundation (Jan. 28, 2019), https://www.heritage.org/trade/report /analysis-the-united-states-mexico-canada-agreement.

Chapter 16
Temporary Entry

This chapter is similar to NAFTA; the same professionals eligible under NAFTA will continue to be eligible to apply for a trade NAFTA nonimmigration classification. Such individuals may work in the U.S. for three years. Parties shall grant temporary entry to qualified business people as it relates to their public health, safety, and national security. Parties may refuse entry to such persons if entry could adversely affect the settlement of a labor dispute or intended place of business. Parties must make available materials explaining the requirements for temporary entry. There are requirements for a Party to qualify as a business person. A Party will afford temporary access to qualify persons upon proof of citizenship of a Party. Additionally, the business must demonstrate the purpose for entry and their engagement, demonstrate that the business activity is internal in scope, and that the business person is not seeking to enter the local market. This chapter also governs the temporary entry of traders and investors; business persons may qualify for temporary entry under this sector when they seek to carry on substantial trade in goods and services. Temporary entry of intra-company transferees also is covered in this chapter; the same requirements apply as listed above. However, professionals conducting business in another Party's country only need to present proof of citizenship of their Party country and documentation of the purpose of their entry.

Under the USMCA, no significant changes have been made to NAFTA rules on temporary entry. The sixty types of professionals eligible under NAFTA will continue to be eligible to apply for a "Trade NAFTA nonimmigrant classification."[877] Once a person is granted entry under this chapter, they may work in the U.S. for three years.[878] This article does not affect the immigration or naturalization process of nonbusiness persons.[879] It is beyond the scope of this book, but there have been various efforts by the Trump administration to limit nonbusiness immigration and to fortify the southern

---

877. *See* Tori Smith & Gabriella Beaumont-Smith, An Analysis of the United States–Mexico–Canada Agreement, The Heritage Foundation (Jan. 28, 2019), https://www.heritage.org/trade/report/analysis-the-united-states-mexico-canada-agreement.
878. *See* Tori Smith & Gabriella Beaumont-Smith, An Analysis of the United States–Mexico–Canada Agreement, The Heritage Foundation (Jan. 28, 2019), https://www.heritage.org/trade/report/analysis-the-united-states-mexico-canada-agreement.
879. *See* United States-Mexico-Canada Agreement, Article 16, Jan. 29, 2020.

U.S. border. The appearance of the COVID-19 pandemic in March 2020 resulted in further restrictions on non-commercial border crossings.

Parties shall grant temporary entry to qualified business persons as it relates to their public health, safety, and national security.[880] Parties may also refuse entry to a business person if the temporary entry could adversely affect the settlement of a labor dispute at their place or intended place, of business, or a Party may refuse to grant entry if the business person is involved in a current labor dispute.[881] If a Party does not grant temporary entry, it must provide written notice to the business person communicating the reasons for refusal.[882] The Party must also provide the same notice to the business person's Party.[883]

Parties are required to publish online, or make otherwise available, materials explaining the requirements for temporary entry.[884] Likewise, Parties will publish data and information regarding who has been issued immigration documentation based on their occupation, profession, or activity.[885]

This chapter establishes a Temporary Entry Working Group, which includes representatives of each Party.[886] The Working Group will meet yearly to discuss improvements to this chapter and any common developments or issues that arise within this area.[887]

If a Party wants to initiate proceedings regarding a refusal to grant temporary entry, it must demonstrate that "the matter involves a pattern of practice, and the business person has exhausted the available administrative remedies regarding the particular matter."[888] Remedies have been exhausted when "a final determination in the matter has not been issued by the competent authority within one year of the institution of an administrative proceeding, and the failure to issue a determination is not attributable to delay caused by the business person."[889]

Annex 16-A

This Annex includes the requirements for a Party to qualify as a business person.[890] Under each of the sections, there is a disclaimer that a Party has the power to require a business person, as defined by this section, to obtain a visa or its equivalent.[891] A Party will afford temporary access to qualify persons upon the presentation of: proof of citizenship of a Party; either orally or through documentation, the business person must demonstrate the purpose for entry and their engagement; as well as demonstrate that "the proposed business activity is international in scope and that the business

---

880. *See* United States-Mexico-Canada Agreement, Article 16.4, Jan. 29, 2020.
881. *See* United States-Mexico-Canada Agreement, Article 16.4, Jan. 29, 2020.
882. *See* United States-Mexico-Canada Agreement, Article 16.4, Jan. 29, 2020.
883. *See* United States-Mexico-Canada Agreement, Article 16.4, Jan. 29, 2020.
884. *See* United States-Mexico-Canada Agreement, Article 16.5, Jan. 29, 2020.
885. *See* United States-Mexico-Canada Agreement, Article 16.5, Jan. 29, 2020.
886. *See* United States-Mexico-Canada Agreement, Article 16.6, Jan. 29, 2020.
887. *See* United States-Mexico-Canada Agreement, Article 16.6, Jan. 29, 2020.
888. *See* United States-Mexico-Canada Agreement, Article 16.7, Jan. 29, 2020.
889. *See* United States-Mexico-Canada Agreement, Article 16.7, Jan. 29, 2020.
890. *See* United States-Mexico-Canada Agreement, Annex 16-A, Jan. 29, 2020.
891. *See* United States-Mexico-Canada Agreement, Annex 16-A, Jan. 29, 2020.

person is not seeking to enter the local labor market."[892] To satisfy the third criteria, Parties ask that the business person demonstrate that: "the primary source of remuneration for the proposed business activity is outside the territory of the Party granting temporary entry, and the business person's principal place of business and the actual place of accrual of profits."[893] If the Party requires further proof, a letter from the business person's employer will be sufficient. See Annex 16-A-2.

Section B of this Annex governs the temporary entry of traders and investors.[894] If a business person seeks to "carry on substantial trade in goods and services" between the territory and a Party or establishes, develops, administers, or provides "advice or key technical services to the operation of an investment," then they may qualify for temporary entry.[895] However, Parties may not require labor certification tests or other similar procedures, nor create numerical restrictions to the temporary entry of such business persons.[896]

Section C regulates the temporary entry of intra-company transferees.[897] Employees must meet the same requirements and be acting in either a managerial, executive or specialized employee capacity.[898] As in Section B, Parties may not place conditions or maintain numerical restrictions on the temporary entry of intra-company transferees.[899]

Section D applies to professionals conducting business in another Party's country.[900] Professionals are merely required to present proof of citizenship of their Party country and documentation of the purpose of their entry.[901] The same conditions and restrictions applied in Section B and C apply for this section.[902]

The Appendices in this chapter provide the definitions and applicable degrees for a person to be considered a "business person."[903]

---

892. *See* United States-Mexico-Canada Agreement, Annex 16-A-1, Jan. 29, 2020.
893. *See* United States-Mexico-Canada Agreement, Annex 16-A-2, Jan. 29, 2020.
894. *See* United States-Mexico-Canada Agreement, Annex 16-A-2, Jan. 29, 2020.
895. *See* United States-Mexico-Canada Agreement, Annex 16-A-2, Jan. 29, 2020.
896. *See* United States-Mexico-Canada Agreement, Annex 16-A-2, Jan. 29, 2020.
897. *See* United States-Mexico-Canada Agreement, Annex 16-A-3, Jan. 29, 2020.
898. *See* United States-Mexico-Canada Agreement, Annex 16-A-3, Jan. 29, 2020.
899. *See* United States-Mexico-Canada Agreement, Annex 16-A-3, Jan. 29, 2020.
900. *See* United States-Mexico-Canada Agreement, Annex 16-A-3, Jan. 29, 2020.
901. *See* United States-Mexico-Canada Agreement, Annex 16-A-3, Jan. 29, 2020.
902. *See* United States-Mexico-Canada Agreement, Annex 16-A-3, Jan. 29, 2020.
903. *See* United States-Mexico-Canada Agreement, Section 16 Appendix 1, Jan. 29, 2020.

CHAPTER 17

Financial Services

This chapter deals with how Parties may regulate financial institutions of other Parties, and invest in those institutions, and cross-border trade in financial services. However, unlike NAFTA, it does not include any assurance that domestic persons in one country be permitted to purchase cross-border services in another member country so long as the services are located elsewhere. Commentators has suggested that this creates a level of "government favoritism" and can lead to "a drag on innovation and cost efficiency." Other commentators have suggested that this will bolster U.S. financial service firms by granting them "wider access to financial service firms that are operating in each other's countries." Under this chapter, requirements apply, such as National Treatment, MFN Treatment, recognition, and transparency. Additionally, Parties cannot limit access to markets where cross-border financial providers or investors wish to enter. Parties must allow each other to supply a new financial service. Additional requirements apply. However, there are numerous exceptions to the requirements. This section establishes the Financial Services Committee. For financial service issues, Parties use the methods from the Dispute Settlement chapter (Chapter 31). Canada, Mexico, and the United States share similar provisions related to cross-border trade; these include insurance and insurance-related services and banking and other financial services. This section also indicates the property authorities for each Party that is responsible for Financial Services.

This chapter is similar to Chapter 14 of NAFTA.[904] It details how Parties may regulate financial institutions of other Parties, and investment in those institutions, and cross-border trade in financial services.[905] Unlike NAFTA, USMCA does not include any assurance that domestic persons in one country be permitted to purchase cross-border services in another member country so long as the services are located

---

904. *See* Tori Smith & Gabriella Beaumont-Smith, An Analysis of the United States–Mexico–Canada Agreement, The Heritage Foundation (Jan. 28, 2019), https://www.heritage.org/trade/report /analysis-the-united-states-mexico-canada-agreement.
905. *See* Tori Smith & Gabriella Beaumont-Smith, An Analysis of the United States–Mexico–Canada Agreement, The Heritage Foundation (Jan. 28, 2019), https://www.heritage.org/trade/report /analysis-the-united-states-mexico-canada-agreement.

elsewhere.[906] NAFTA stated that "[e]ach Party shall permit persons located in its territory, and its nationals wherever located, to purchase financial services from cross-border financial service providers of another Party located in the territory of that other Party or of another Party."[907] This obligation does not require a Party to permit such providers to do business or solicit in its territory."[908] Some commentators believe, overall, this chapter creates a level of "government favoritism" which could be considered a "drag on innovation and cost efficiency."[909] Other commentators have suggested that the USMCA will bolster U.S. Financial Service firms by granting them "wider access to financial service firms that are operating in each other's countries."[910]

Further, FinTech commentators recognize the importance of this chapter because the competing national regulatory frameworks created conflicts for non-banking FinTech companies.[911] Three such conflicts include forcing "Fintech firms into compliance with multiple inefficient regulatory frameworks"; harming competition by implementing different regulations for similar service providers; and working to create a "harmonized regulation for the data-driven concept of open banking[.]"[912] This chapter of the USMCA works to correct these conflicts and promote a stable regulatory environment for FinTech companies working in the Financial Services Industry.[913]

§17.1   ARTICLE 17.2. SCOPE

This chapter covers financial institutions, investors in financial institutions, investments in financial institutions, and cross-border trade in financial services investments.[914]

---

906. *See* Tori Smith & Gabriella Beaumont-Smith, An Analysis of the United States–Mexico–Canada Agreement, The Heritage Foundation (Jan. 28, 2019), https://www.heritage.org/trade/report /analysis-the-united-states-mexico-canada-agreement.

907. *See* Tori Smith & Gabriella Beaumont-Smith, An Analysis of the United States–Mexico–Canada Agreement, The Heritage Foundation (Jan. 28, 2019), https://www.heritage.org/trade/report /analysis-the-united-states-mexico-canada-agreement.

908. *See* Tori Smith & Gabriella Beaumont-Smith, An Analysis of the United States–Mexico–Canada Agreement, The Heritage Foundation (Jan. 28, 2019), https://www.heritage.org/trade/report /analysis-the-united-states-mexico-canada-agreement.

909. *See* Tori Smith & Gabriella Beaumont-Smith, An Analysis of the United States–Mexico–Canada Agreement, The Heritage Foundation (Jan. 28, 2019), https://www.heritage.org/trade/report /analysis-the-united-states-mexico-canada-agreement.

910. New NAFTA: implications on U.S. financial services industry, International Law Office (Dec. 7, 2018) https://www.internationallawoffice.com/Newsletters/International-Trade/USA/Arent-Fox-LLP/New-NAFTA-implications-on-US-financial-services-industry#.

911. Luis Alejandro Estoup, FinTech under the new United States-Mexico-Canada Agreement, Thomson Reuters (Jun. 1, 2019) https://uk.practicallaw.thomsonreuters.com/w-020-8365? transitionType = Default&contextData = (sc.Default)&firstPage = true&bhcp = 1.

912. Luis Alejandro Estoup, FinTech under the new United States-Mexico-Canada Agreement, Thomson Reuters (Jun. 1, 2019) https://uk.practicallaw.thomsonreuters.com/w-020-8365? transitionType = Default&contextData = (sc.Default)&firstPage = true&bhcp = 1.

913. Luis Alejandro Estoup, FinTech under the new United States-Mexico-Canada Agreement, Thomson Reuters (Jun. 1, 2019) https://uk.practicallaw.thomsonreuters.com/w-020-8365? transitionType = Default&contextData = (sc.Default)&firstPage = true&bhcp = 1.

914. *See* United States-Mexico-Canada Agreement, Section 17.2, Jan. 29, 2020.

The chapter does not cover public retirement plans, social security, or activates and services conducted for the account or with the guarantee of using the financial resources of the Party, including its public entities.[915] It does not apply to government procurement of financial institutions, subsidy or grants; this includes loans, guarantees, and insurance.[916]

NAFTA has no provisions related to the application of Chapter 14 (Financial Services) on government procurement and subsidies.[917]

§17.2 ARTICLE 17.3. NATIONAL TREATMENT

Parties must ensure that investors, investments, and financial institutions of each Party are treated no less favorable than the Parties' domestic counterparts in areas of financial services.[918]

For example, the Office of Comptroller of Currency (OCC) published a policy statement allowing Mexican and Canadian Fintech companies to apply for a bank charter as a special purpose national bank (SPNB), so long as the companies do not accept deposits.[919]

§17.3 ARTICLE 17.4. MFN TREATMENT

Parties' investors, investments, and financial institutions of another Party are to be treated no less favorably than investors, investments, and financial institutions of non-Party or another Party on issues of financial services.[920]

§17.4 ARTICLE 17.5. MARKET ACCESS

Parties cannot limit access to markets where cross-border financial providers or investors wish to enter.[921]

No Party shall require a cross-border financial service supplier of another Party to establish or maintain a representative office or an enterprise or to be resident in its territory as a condition for the cross-border supply of financial service.[922]

A Party may require the registration or authorization of a cross-border financial service supplier of another Party or of a financial instrument.[923]

---

915. *See* United States-Mexico-Canada Agreement, Section 17.2, Jan. 29, 2020.
916. *See* United States-Mexico-Canada Agreement, Section 17.2, Jan. 29, 2020.
917. *See* United States-Mexico-Canada Agreement, Section 17.2, Jan. 29, 2020.
918. *See* United States-Mexico-Canada Agreement, Section 17.3, Jan. 29, 2020.
919. Luis Alejandro Estoup, FinTech under the new United States-Mexico-Canada Agreement, Thomson Reuters (Jun. 1, 2019) https://uk.practicallaw.thomsonreuters.com/w-020-8365?transitionType = Default&contextData = (sc.Default)&firstPage = true&bhcp = 1.
920. *See* United States-Mexico-Canada Agreement, Section 17.4, Jan. 29, 2020.
921. *See* United States-Mexico-Canada Agreement, Section 17.5, Jan. 29, 2020.
922. *See* United States-Mexico-Canada Agreement, Section 17.5, Jan. 29, 2020.
923. *See* United States-Mexico-Canada Agreement, Section 17.5, Jan. 29, 2020.

Under NAFTA, countries had to permit other NAFTA financial service providers to establish financial institutions in their territory.[924] There are no similar quantitative market access provisions relating to financial services. However, Chapter 3 goes over general market access, and Article 1103 stated that Parties cannot require a minimum level of equity in an enterprise in the territory of the party.[925]

§17.5   ARTICLE 17.6. CROSS-BORDER TRADE STANDSTILL

Under the USMCA, no Party shall adopt a measure restricting any type of cross-border trade in financial services by cross-border financial service suppliers of another Party that the Party permitted on January 1, 1994, or that is inconsistent with Article 17.3.3 (National Treatment), with respect to the supply of those services.[926]

§17.6   ARTICLE 17.7. NEW FINANCIAL SERVICES

Parties must allow each other to supply a new financial service that the Party would permit its own financial institutions, in like circumstances, to supply without adopting a law or modifying an existing law.[927]

Parties may require authorization subject to the new financial services provisions (reasonable, objective and impartial).[928]

NAFTA contained similar requirements to the USMCA regarding proposing new measures.[929]

§17.7   ARTICLE 17.8. TREATMENT OF CUSTOMER INFORMATION

Parties are not required to disclose information related to the financial affairs or accounts of individual customers.[930]

§17.8   ARTICLE 17.9. SENIOR MANAGEMENT AND BOARDS OF DIRECTORS

Parties cannot require senior management to be of a particular nationality.[931]

No Party can require more than a simple majority of the board of directors of a financial institution of another Party to be composed of nationals of the Party, persons residing in the territory of the Party, or a combination thereof.[932]

---

924. *See* North American Free Trade Agreement, Chapter 3, Jan. 1, 1994.
925. *See* North American Free Trade Agreement, Article 1103, Jan. 1, 1994.
926. *See* United States-Mexico-Canada Agreement, Section 17.6, Jan. 29, 2020.
927. *See* United States-Mexico-Canada Agreement, Section 17.7, Jan. 29, 2020.
928. *See* United States-Mexico-Canada Agreement, Section 17.7, Jan. 29, 2020.
929. *See* North American Free Trade Agreement, Article 1401, Jan. 1, 1994.
930. *See* United States-Mexico-Canada Agreement, Section 17.8, Jan. 29, 2020.
931. *See* United States-Mexico-Canada Agreement, Section 17.9, Jan. 29, 2020.
932. *See* United States-Mexico-Canada Agreement, Section 17.9, Jan. 29, 2020.

§17.9   ARTICLE 17.10. NON-CONFORMING MEASURES

National Treatment, MFN Treatment, Market Access, and Senior Management and Board of Directors provisions do not apply to non-conformities in Annex III-A or non-conformities existing at a local level of government.[933]

§17.10   ARTICLE 17.11. EXCEPTIONS

A Party is not prevented from conducting measures for prudential reasons, including for the protection of investors, depositors, policyholders, or persons to whom a fiduciary duty is owed or to ensure the integrity and stability of the financial system.[934]

If the measure does not conform to the provisions of this Agreement to which this exception applies, the measure must not be used as a means of avoiding the Party's commitments or obligations under those provisions.[935]

Noting in this chapter applies to nondiscriminatory measures of general application taken by a public entity in pursuit of monetary and related credit policies or exchange rate policies.[936]

Parties may prevent or limit a transfer by a financial institution or a cross-border financial service supplier to, or for the benefit of, an affiliate of or person related to that institution or supplier, through the equitable, nondiscriminatory and good faith application of a measure relating to maintenance of the safety, soundness, integrity, or financial responsibility of financial institutions or cross-border financial service supplier.[937]

§17.11   ARTICLE 17.12 RECOGNITION

A Party may recognize prudential measures of another Party or a non-Party in the application of a measure covered by this chapter. That recognition may be: accorded autonomously; achieved through harmonization or other means; or based upon an agreement or arrangement with another Party or a non-Party.[938]

Parties must allow another Party to show that there should be an equivalent regulation between them.[939]

---

933. *See* United States-Mexico-Canada Agreement, Section 17.10, Jan. 29, 2020.
934. *See* United States-Mexico-Canada Agreement, Section 17.11, Jan. 29, 2020.
935. *See* United States-Mexico-Canada Agreement, Section 17.11, Jan. 29, 2020.
936. *See* United States-Mexico-Canada Agreement, Section 17.11, Jan. 29, 2020.
937. *See* United States-Mexico-Canada Agreement, Section 17.11, Jan. 29, 2020.
938. *See* United States-Mexico-Canada Agreement, Section 17.12, Jan. 29, 2020.
939. *See* United States-Mexico-Canada Agreement, Section 17.12, Jan. 29, 2020.

§17.12   ARTICLE 17.13. TRANSPARENCY AND ADMINISTRATION OF CERTAIN MEASURES

Parties shall publish in advance any regulation that it proposes and the regulation's purpose.[940] They must provide interested persons and other Parties with a reasonable opportunity to comment.[941] Parties must address the comments, if possible and publish the final regulation before it enters into effect.[942] Parties must be transportation about any authorizations needed and any associated fees.[943] Further, self-regulatory systems must observe the obligations contained in this chapter.[944]

§17.13   ARTICLE 17.15. PAYMENT AND CLEARING SYSTEMS

Parties must allow financial institutions of another Party established in its territory, access to payment and clearing systems operated by public entities, and to official funding and refinancing facilities available in the normal course of ordinary business.[945]

Parties are not required to provide access to the party's lender of last resort facilities.[946]

NAFTA did not have any comparable provisions relating to payment and clearing systems.

§17.14   ARTICLE 17.16. EXPEDITED AVAILABILITY OF INSURANCE SERVICES

If a Party maintains regulatory product approval procedures, that Party should try to maintain or improve those procedures to expedite the availability of insurance services by licensed suppliers.[947]

This includes allowing the introduction of products unless they are disapproved, not requiring product approval for certain types of insurance lines or not imposing limitations on the number of product introductions.[948]

NAFTA stated that Parties must consult on the possibility of allowing a wider range of insurance services to be provided on a cross-border basis and determine whether Mexico's limitation regarding insurance needs to be modified.[949]

---

940. *See* United States-Mexico-Canada Agreement, Section 17.13, Jan. 29, 2020.
941. *See* United States-Mexico-Canada Agreement, Section 17.13, Jan. 29, 2020.
942. *See* United States-Mexico-Canada Agreement, Section 17.13, Jan. 29, 2020.
943. *See* United States-Mexico-Canada Agreement, Section 17.13, Jan. 29, 2020.
944. *See* United States-Mexico-Canada Agreement, Section 17.14, Jan. 29, 2020.
945. *See* United States-Mexico-Canada Agreement, Section 17.15, Jan. 29, 2020.
946. *See* United States-Mexico-Canada Agreement, Section 17.15, Jan. 29, 2020.
947. *See* United States-Mexico-Canada Agreement, Section 17.16, Jan. 29, 2020.
948. *See* United States-Mexico-Canada Agreement, Section 17.16, Jan. 29, 2020.
949. *See* North American Free Trade Agreement, Annex 1404.4, Jan. 1, 1994.

§17.15 ARTICLE 17.17. TRANSFER OF INFORMATION

Parties cannot prevent a covered person from transferring information, including personal information, into and out of the Party's territory by electronic or other means when this activity is for the conduct of business within the scope of the license, authorization, or registration of that covered person.[950]

NAFTA allowed regulated financial institutions from other NAFTA countries to transfer information for data processing into and out of the host country's territory if the transfer is required for the ordinary course of business. Subject to the provisions in this chapter, Parties may still adopt actions to "protect personal data, personal privacy and confidentiality."[951]

§17.16 ARTICLE 17.18. LOCATION OF COMPUTING FACILITIES

No Party shall require a covered person to use or locate computing facilities (computer servers and storage devices) in the Party's territory; this is known as data localization, so long as the Party's financial regulatory authorities, for regulatory and supervisory purposes, have immediate, direct, complete, and ongoing access to information processed or stored on computing facilities that the covered person uses or locates outside the Party's territory.[952]

Parties must allow for a reasonable time to fix access issues before requiring covered persons to use facilities in their territory.[953]

NAFTA did not have any provisions creating specific rules related to the location of computing facilities. This is considered a key development for the financial services industry.[954] This provision is expected to enhance the sector through increased regulatory transparency by reducing the cost and complications of operating "redundant" facilities.[955] Chapter 17 does not apply to existing measures of Canada for one year after the entry into force of this Agreement.[956]

---

950. *See* United States-Mexico-Canada Agreement, Section 17.17, Jan. 29, 2020.
951. Daniel A. Leslie, The USMCA – Impact on the Financial Services Sector, Norton Rose Fulbright (Oct. 2018), https://www.nortonrosefulbright.com/en-us/knowledge/publications/5dde68a0/the-usmca--impact-on-the-financial-services-sector.
952. *See* United States-Mexico-Canada Agreement, Section 17.18, Jan. 29, 2020.
953. *See* United States-Mexico-Canada Agreement, Section 17.18, Jan. 29, 2020.
954. New NAFTA: implications on U.S. financial services industry, International Law Office (Dec. 7, 2018) https://www.internationallawoffice.com/Newsletters/International-Trade/USA/Arent-Fox-LLP/New-NAFTA-implications-on-US-financial-services-industry.
955. New NAFTA: implications on U.S. financial services industry, International Law Office (Dec. 7, 2018) https://www.internationallawoffice.com/Newsletters/International-Trade/USA/Arent-Fox-LLP/New-NAFTA-implications-on-US-financial-services-industry.
956. *See* United States-Mexico-Canada Agreement, Annex 17.19, Jan. 29, 2020.

§17.17   ARTICLE 17.19. COMMITTEE ON FINANCIAL SERVICES

This section establishes the Financial Services Committee, which implements this chapter.[957] The greatest hurdle this Committee will have to overcome, and the hope of many executives is to manage the various regulatory perspectives across the continent.[958]

§17.18   ARTICLE 17.20. CONSULTATIONS

Parties can request, in writing, consultations with each other, and results must be reported to the Financial Services Committee.[959] Parties may request information on existing non-conforming measures from financial authorities in Annex 17-B.[960]

§17.19   ARTICLE 17.21. DISPUTE SETTLEMENT

For financial services issues, Parties use the methods from Chapter 31 (Dispute Settlement) and select a chairperson that has expertise in financial services law or practice and meet the requirements of Chapter 31.[961] They must select panelists who at least meet the qualifications set out in Chapter 31.[962]

Annex 17-A: Cross-Border Trade

Canada

Insurance and Insurance-Related Services

National Treatment and Market access apply to insurance of risks related to maritime transport, commercial aviation, and space launching and freight (including satellites) and goods in international transit.[963] They also apply to reinsurance, retrocession, services auxiliary to insurance, and insurance intermediation, such as brokerage and agency.[964]

Banking and Other Financial Services (excluding insurance)

National Treatment and Market access apply to the provision and transfer of financial information and financial data processing.[965] It applies to advisory and other auxiliary financial services and credit reference and analysis, excluding intermediation, relating

---

957. *See* United States-Mexico-Canada Agreement, Section 17.15, Jan. 29, 2020.
958. Blake C. Goldring, Post-USMCA Business Conditions in North America, AGF (Oct. 23, 2018) https://perspectives.agf.com/post-usmca-business-conditions-in-north-america/.
959. *See* United States-Mexico-Canada Agreement, Section 17.20, Jan. 29, 2020.
960. *See* United States-Mexico-Canada Agreement, Annex 17-B, Jan. 29, 2020.
961. *See* United States-Mexico-Canada Agreement, Section 17.21, Jan. 29, 2020.
962. *See* United States-Mexico-Canada Agreement, Section 17.21, Jan. 29, 2020.
963. *See* United States-Mexico-Canada Agreement, Annex 17-A, Jan. 29, 2020.
964. *See* United States-Mexico-Canada Agreement, Annex 17-A, Jan. 29, 2020.
965. *See* United States-Mexico-Canada Agreement, Annex 17-A, Jan. 29, 2020.

to banking and other financial services.[966] These provisions also apply to electronic payment services for payment through card transactions (physical and electronic debit/credit/pre-paid cards).[967]

Specifically, they apply to investment advice and portfolio management services that are provided to a collective investment scheme (investment fund) located in Canada (except trustee and custodial/execution services unrelated to collective investment).[968]

Mexico

Insurance and insurance-related services

The Mexico provisions are almost identical to Canada's section.

National Treatment and Market access apply to insurance of risks related to maritime transport, commercial aviation, and space launching and freight (including satellites) and goods in international transit.[969] It also applies to reinsurance, retrocession, services auxiliary to insurance, and insurance intermediation such as brokerage and agency.[970]

Here, it will also cover insurance risks related to vehicle transporting of goods when such vehicles have foreign registration or are the property of persons domiciled abroad.[971]

Banking and other financial services (excluding insurance)

National Treatment and Market access apply to the provision and transfer of financial information and financial data processing.[972] These provisions apply to advisory and other auxiliary financial services, excluding intermediation and credit reference and analysis, relating to banking and other financial services.[973] These provisions also apply to electronic payment services for payment through card transactions (physical and electronic debit/credit/reloadable cards).[974]

E-Payment card transactions include only: receiving and sending messages for:

(i) authorization requests, responses (approvals or declines), stand-in authorizations, adjustments, refunds, returns, retrievals, chargebacks and related administrative messages,

(ii) calculation of fees and balances, and receiving and sending messages related to this process to acquirers and issuers, and their agents and representatives,

---

966. *See* United States-Mexico-Canada Agreement, Annex 17-A, Jan. 29, 2020.
967. *See* United States-Mexico-Canada Agreement, Annex 17-A, Jan. 29, 2020.
968. *See* United States-Mexico-Canada Agreement, Annex 17-A, Jan. 29, 2020.
969. *See* United States-Mexico-Canada Agreement, Annex 17-A, Jan. 29, 2020.
970. *See* United States-Mexico-Canada Agreement, Annex 17-A, Jan. 29, 2020.
971. *See* United States-Mexico-Canada Agreement, Annex 17-A, Jan. 29, 2020.
972. *See* United States-Mexico-Canada Agreement, Annex 17-A, Jan. 29, 2020.
973. *See* United States-Mexico-Canada Agreement, Annex 17-A, Jan. 29, 2020.
974. *See* United States-Mexico-Canada Agreement, Annex 17-A, Jan. 29, 2020.

(iii) provision of periodic reconciliation, summaries and instructions regarding the net financial position of acquirers and issuers, and their agents and representatives for approved transactions,

(iv) fraud prevention and mitigation activities, and administration of loyalty programs, and

(v) services on a business-to-business basis that use proprietary networks to process payment transactions[975]

Specifically, they apply to investment advice and portfolio Mexico services that are provided to a collective investment scheme (Managing Companies of Investment Funds) located in Mexico (except trustee and custodial/execution services unrelated to collective investment).[976]

A financial institution organized in the territory of another Party will only be authorized to provide portfolio management services to a collective investment scheme located in Mexico if it provides the same services in the territory of the Party where it is established.[977]

United States

Insurance and insurance-related services

This is identical to the Canada section.

National Treatment and Market access apply to insurance of risks related to maritime transport, commercial aviation, and space launching and freight (including satellites) and goods in international transit.[978] It also applies to reinsurance, retrocession, services auxiliary to insurance, and insurance intermediation, such as brokerage and agency.[979]

Banking and other financial services (excluding insurance)

National Treatment and Market access apply to the provision and transfer of financial information and financial data processing and related software.[980] It applies to advisory and other auxiliary financial services, excluding intermediation, relating to banking and other financial services.[981] The provisions apply to investment advice to a collective investment scheme located in the Party's territory.[982] These provisions also apply to electronic payment services for payment card transactions (physical and electronic debit/credit/charge/check/ ATM cards).[983]

---

975. *See* United States-Mexico-Canada Agreement, Annex 17-A, Jan. 29, 2020.
976. *See* United States-Mexico-Canada Agreement, Annex 17-A, Jan. 29, 2020.
977. *See* United States-Mexico-Canada Agreement, Annex 17-A, Jan. 29, 2020.
978. *See* United States-Mexico-Canada Agreement, Annex 17-A, Jan. 29, 2020.
979. *See* United States-Mexico-Canada Agreement, Annex 17-A, Jan. 29, 2020.
980. *See* United States-Mexico-Canada Agreement, Annex 17-A, Jan. 29, 2020.
981. *See* United States-Mexico-Canada Agreement, Annex 17-A, Jan. 29, 2020.
982. *See* United States-Mexico-Canada Agreement, Annex 17-A, Jan. 29, 2020.
983. *See* United States-Mexico-Canada Agreement, Annex 17-A, Jan. 29, 2020.

National Treatment and Market Access Provisions also apply to portfolio management services, excluding trustee services and custodial/execution services unrelated to a collective investment scheme (SEC-registered investment company).[984]

E-payment includes only:

> The processing of financial transactions such as verification of financial balances, authorization of transactions, notification of banks (or credit card issuers) of individual transactions and provision of daily summaries and instructions regarding the net financial position of relevant institutions for authorized transactions, and those services that are provided on a business-to-business basis and use proprietary networks to process payment transactions This does not include the transfer of funds to and from transactors' accounts.[985]

Annex 17-B Authorities Responsible for Financial Services

> Canada—Department of Finance of Canada
> Mexico—Ministry of Finance and Public Credit (Secretaría de Hacienda y Crédito Público)
> United States—Department of the Treasury—Annex 17-C (Mexico-United States Investment Disputes in Financial Services) and for all matters involving banking, securities, financial services other than insurance and the Department of the Treasury, in cooperation with the Office of the U.S. Trade Representative, for insurance matters.[986]

Annex 17-C: Mexico-United States Investment Disputes in Financial Services

This provision puts a system in place in the event that a qualifying investment dispute under this chapter cannot be settled by consultation and negotiation.[987]

If brought by a claimant on its own behalf: An allegation must allege that the respondent has breached National Treatment, MFN Treatment or Expropriation and Compensation sections of the Agreement and that the claimant has incurred loss or damage by reason of, or arising out of, that breach.[988]

If brought by a claimant, on behalf of a financial institution of the respondent that is a juridical person that the claimant owns or controls directly or indirectly: An allegation must allege that the respondent has breached National Treatment, MFN Treatment or Expropriation and Compensation sections of the Agreement and that the financial institution has incurred loss or damage by reason of, or arising out of, that breach.[989]

---

984. *See* United States-Mexico-Canada Agreement, Annex 17-A, Jan. 29, 2020.
985. *See* United States-Mexico-Canada Agreement, Annex 17-A, Jan. 29, 2020.
986. *See* United States-Mexico-Canada Agreement, Annex 17-A, Jan. 29, 2020.
987. *See* United States-Mexico-Canada Agreement, Annex 17-C, Jan. 29, 2020.
988. *See* United States-Mexico-Canada Agreement, Annex 17-C, Jan. 29, 2020.
989. *See* United States-Mexico-Canada Agreement, Annex 17-C, Jan. 29, 2020.

Arbitrators must be selected so that they have expertise and experience, and the respondent should consult its domestic financial regulatory authorities on the claim.[990]

Other procedural rules are set in place for arbitration between the two Parties.[991]

Annex 17-D: Location of Computing Facilities

Article 17.18 does not apply to existing measures of Canada for one year after the entry into force of this Agreement.[992]

---

990. *See* United States-Mexico-Canada Agreement, Annex 17-C, Jan. 29, 2020.
991. *See* United States-Mexico-Canada Agreement, Annex 17-C, Jan. 29, 2020.
992. *See* United States-Mexico-Canada Agreement, Annex 17-D, Jan. 29, 2020.

CHAPTER 18

Telecommunications

The USMCA updates certain provisions in this section and includes elements considered "WTO plus." One of the changes include provisions intended "to ensure that dominant telecommunications firms do not use their positions to keep international competitors out of their market." This section applies to measures relating to access to and use of public telecommunications networks or services; obligations of suppliers of public telecommunications services; supply of value-added services; and public telecommunications networks or services. Several requirements apply to this section; including, but not limited to, that Parties must have access to use of public telecommunications, provide number portability, ensure dialing parity have access to telephone numbers, practice transparency, and maintain measures to prevent anticompetitive practices. Additionally, Parties may not prohibit the sale of a public telecommunications services or prohibit a supplier of public telecommunications services from entering into an agreement to provide roaming services. Specific provisions apply relating to interconnection with major suppliers. In terms of regulation, Parties can regulate directly in anticipation of an issue or to resolve an issue; Parties can make an exception in a regulation that will not apply the law to a service that the Party classifies as a public telecommunication service if the enforcement is not necessary to prevent unreasonable practices or to protect consumers. Finally, the USMCA established the Telecommunications Committee to review and monitor the implementation of this Chapter.

While this chapter is akin to NAFTA, the USMCA updates certain provisions and includes elements considered "WTO plus."[993] The most contentious changes include provisions intended "to ensure that dominant telecommunications firms do not use their position to keep international competitors out of their market."[994]

---

993. United States-Mexico-Canada Agreement (USMCA) Chapter and Annex Fact Sheets, Office of the United States Trade Representative (Oct. 2018).

994. *See* Tori Smith & Gabriella Beaumont-Smith, An Analysis of the United States–Mexico–Canada Agreement, The Heritage Foundation (Jan. 28, 2019), https://www.heritage.org/trade/report /analysis-the-united-states-mexico-canada-agreement.

§18.1   ARTICLE 18.2. SCOPE

It applies to a measure relating to access to and use of public telecommunications networks or services; a measure relating to obligations of suppliers of public telecommunications services; a measure relating to the supply of value-added services; and any other measure relating to public telecommunications networks or services.[995]

It does not apply to broadcast or cable distribution of radio or TV programming, except to ensure that an enterprise operating a broadcast station or cable system has continued access to and use of public telecommunications networks and services.[996]

§18.2   ARTICLE 18.3. ACCESS AND USE

Enterprises of another Party must have access to the use of public telecommunications networks and services on reasonable and nondiscriminatory terms and conditions in a way that allows them to move information in the other's territory or across its borders.[997]

These enterprises must be able to purchase or lease, and attach terminal or other equipment that interfaces with a public telecommunications network; provide services to an individual or multiple end-users over leased or owned circuits; connect leased or owned circuits with public telecommunications networks and services or with circuits leased or owned by another enterprise; perform switching, signaling, processing, and conversion functions; use operating protocols of its choice.[998]

Party may take measures necessary to ensure the security and confidentiality of messages or to protect the privacy of personal data.[999]

No conditions can be imposed unless they are necessary for public safety or to protect the technical integrity of public telecommunications networks or services.[1000]

§18.3   ARTICLE 18.4. OBLIGATIONS RELATING TO SUPPLIERS OF PUBLIC TELECOMMUNICATIONS SERVICES

[A]   Interconnection

Suppliers of public telecommunications service must provide interconnection with those from another party, at reasonable rates, and with the confidentiality of commercially sensitive information protected.[1001]

---

995. *See* United States-Mexico-Canada Agreement, Section 18.2, Jan. 29, 2020.
996. *See* United States-Mexico-Canada Agreement, Section 18.2, Jan. 29, 2020.
997. *See* United States-Mexico-Canada Agreement, Section 18.3, Jan. 29, 2020.
998. *See* United States-Mexico-Canada Agreement, Section 18.3, Jan. 29, 2020.
999. *See* United States-Mexico-Canada Agreement, Section 18.3, Jan. 29, 2020.
1000. *See* United States-Mexico-Canada Agreement, Section 18.3, Jan. 29, 2020.
1001. *See* United States-Mexico-Canada Agreement, Section 18.4, Jan. 29, 2020.

[B]   Resale

No Party shall prohibit the resale of a public telecommunications service.[1002]

[C]   Roaming

"No Party shall prohibit a supplier of public telecommunications services from entering into an agreement to provide roaming services," nor shall a Party preclude provided roaming services from a permanent presence in a Party's territory.[1003]

[D]   Number Portability

Parties must provide number portability without impairment to quality and reliability.[1004] Regarding Mexico, it applies "only to end-users switching suppliers within the same category of service . . . until Mexico is economically and technically feasible to implement number portability without the restriction."[1005] Regarding the U.S. and Canada, it applies only to "the ability of end-users to retain at the same location the same telephone numbers . . . until they are economically and technically feasible to implement number portability without that restriction in its territory."[1006]

[E]   Dialing Parity

Parties must ensure dialing parity within the same category of service to suppliers of public telecommunications services of another Party.[1007]

[F]   Access to Numbers

A supplier of public telecommunications services of another Party established in its territory must have access to telephone numbers on a nondiscriminatory basis.[1008]

§18.4   ARTICLE 18.5. TREATMENT BY MAJOR SUPPLIERS OF PUBLIC TELECOMMUNICATIONS SERVICES

A major supplier in each territory must accord no less favorable treatment than they accord in like circumstances to its subsidiaries, its affiliates, or non-affiliated service

---

1002. *See* United States-Mexico-Canada Agreement, Section 18.4, Jan. 29, 2020.
1003. *See* United States-Mexico-Canada Agreement, Section 18.4, Jan. 29, 2020.
1004. *See* United States-Mexico-Canada Agreement, Section 18.4, Jan. 29, 2020.
1005. *See* United States-Mexico-Canada Agreement, Section 18.4, Jan. 29, 2020.
1006. *See* United States-Mexico-Canada Agreement, Section 18.4, Jan. 29, 2020.
1007. *See* United States-Mexico-Canada Agreement, Section 18.4, Jan. 29, 2020.
1008. *See* United States-Mexico-Canada Agreement, Section 18.4, Jan. 29, 2020.

regarding the availability, provisioning, rates, or quality of like public telecommunications services, and the availability of technical interfaces necessary for interconnection.[1009]

§18.5 ARTICLE 18.6. COMPETITIVE SAFEGUARDS

It requires each Party to maintain appropriate measures to prevent anticompetitive practices, such as cross-subsidization, using information obtained from competitors with anticompetitive results, and not making available timely technical information about essential facilities and commercially relevant information that are necessary for suppliers provide services.[1010] These requirements are tailored to telecommunications markets that enjoy government regulatory benefits and a large amount of market power due to this government favoritism.[1011]

§18.6 ARTICLE 18.7. RESALE

Each Party cannot impose unreasonable or discriminatory conditions on the resale of its public telecommunications services.[1012]

§18.7 ARTICLE 18.8. UNBUNDLING OF NETWORK ELEMENTS

Each Party shall grant authority to its telecommunications regulatory body to require major suppliers to offer public telecommunications service suppliers unbundled access to their network.[1013] Each Party may determine the compulsory network elements, in keeping with its laws and regulations, but the terms and conditions must be reasonable cost-oriented rates, nondiscriminatory, and transparent.[1014] This "piece-by-piece" offering was not included in NAFTA but was included in the U.S.' Telecommunications Act of 1996.[1015]

1009. *See* United States-Mexico-Canada Agreement, Section 18.5, Jan. 29, 2020.
1010. *See* United States-Mexico-Canada Agreement, Section 18.6, Jan. 29, 2020.
1011. *See* Tori Smith & Gabriella Beaumont-Smith, An Analysis of the United States–Mexico–Canada Agreement, The Heritage Foundation (Jan. 28, 2019), https://www.heritage.org/trade/report/analysis-the-united-states-mexico-canada-agreement.
1012. *See* United States-Mexico-Canada Agreement, Section 18.7, Jan. 29, 2020.
1013. *See* United States-Mexico-Canada Agreement, Section 18.8, Jan. 29, 2020.
1014. *See* United States-Mexico-Canada Agreement, Section 18.8, Jan. 29, 2020.
1015. *See* Tori Smith & Gabriella Beaumont-Smith, An Analysis of the United States–Mexico–Canada Agreement, The Heritage Foundation (Jan. 28, 2019), https://www.heritage.org/trade/report/analysis-the-united-states-mexico-canada-agreement.

§18.8 §18.9. INTERCONNECTION WITH MAJOR SUPPLIERS

[A] General Terms and Conditions

All providers must offer interconnection to their network at reasonable rates, under nondiscriminatory terms, of equal quality to its own, and in a timely manner.[1016]

[B] Options for Interconnecting with Major Suppliers

Telecommunications suppliers must be able to connect through a reference interconnection offer, or "the terms and conditions of an interconnection agreement in effect."[1017]

[C] Public Availability of Interconnection Offers and Agreements

Each Party shall have applicable procedures for interconnection are made publicly available.[1018] Means must be provided for suppliers to obtain the rates, terms, and conditions offered by a major supplier.[1019]

§18.9 ARTICLE 18.10. PROVISIONING AND PRICING OF LEASED CIRCUITS SERVICES

Leased circuit services must be provided to suppliers of another Party within a reasonable time, in a reasonable and nondiscriminatory manner and must be based on a generally available offer.[1020]

Regulatory bodies in each Party must be able to require major suppliers to do so at capacity-based and cost-oriented prices.[1021]

§18.10 ARTICLE 18.11. CO-LOCATION

Under the USMCA, major suppliers must now provide to suppliers of another Party in the Party's territory physical co-location of equipment necessary for interconnection or access to unbundled network elements.[1022]

Where physical co-location is not practical for technical reasons or because of space limitations, each major supplier must provide an alternative solution (e.g.,

---

1016. *See* United States-Mexico-Canada Agreement, Section 18.9, Jan. 29, 2020.
1017. *See* United States-Mexico-Canada Agreement, Section 18.9, Jan. 29, 2020.
1018. *See* United States-Mexico-Canada Agreement, Section 18.9, Jan. 29, 2020.
1019. *See* United States-Mexico-Canada Agreement, Section 18.9, Jan. 29, 2020.
1020. *See* United States-Mexico-Canada Agreement, Section 18.10, Jan. 29, 2020.
1021. *See* United States-Mexico-Canada Agreement, Section 18.10, Jan. 29, 2020.
1022. *See* United States-Mexico-Canada Agreement, Section 18.11, Jan. 29, 2020.

virtual co-location or some other arrangement that facilitates interconnection or access to unbundled network elements).[1023]

§18.11   ARTICLE 18.12. ACCESS TO POLES, DUCTS, CONDUITS, AND RIGHTS-OF-WAY

Unless technically infeasible, major suppliers must provide another Party's suppliers access to poles, ducts, conduits, rights-of-way, and any other structures.[1024]

§18.12   ARTICLE 18.13. SUBMARINE CABLE SYSTEMS

For a major supplier that controls international submarine cable landing stations in the Party's territory for which there are no economically or technically feasible alternatives, they must provide access to those landing stations to suppliers of another Party.[1025]

Mexico has not applied major supplier-related measures to submarine cable landing stations.[1026]

§18.13   ARTICLE 18.14. CONDITIONS FOR THE SUPPLY OF VALUE-ADDED SERVICES

Parties must consider public policy, technical feasibility, and the characteristics when imposing requirements on value-added services.[1027]

All procedures must be transparent and nondiscriminatory.[1028] They must process applications expeditiously and require only information necessary to demonstrate financial solvency or to assess conformity with technical standards.[1029]

§18.14   ARTICLE 18.15. FLEXIBILITY IN THE CHOICE OF TECHNOLOGY

Parties cannot limit the technologies a supplier wishes to use to supply its services, subject to public policy requirements.[1030] The manner in which it is supplied cannot create an unnecessary obstacle to trade.[1031]

1023. *See* United States-Mexico-Canada Agreement, Section 18.11, Jan. 29, 2020.
1024. *See* United States-Mexico-Canada Agreement, Section 18.12, Jan. 29, 2020.
1025. *See* United States-Mexico-Canada Agreement, Section 18.13, Jan. 29, 2020.
1026. *See* United States-Mexico-Canada Agreement, Section 18.13, Jan. 29, 2020.
1027. *See* United States-Mexico-Canada Agreement, Section 18.14, Jan. 29, 2020.
1028. *See* United States-Mexico-Canada Agreement, Section 18.14, Jan. 29, 2020.
1029. *See* United States-Mexico-Canada Agreement, Section 18.14, Jan. 29, 2020.
1030. *See* United States-Mexico-Canada Agreement, Section 18.15, Jan. 29, 2020.
1031. *See* United States-Mexico-Canada Agreement, Section 18.15, Jan. 29, 2020.

§18.15   ARTICLE 18.16. APPROACHES TO REGULATION

Parties can regulate directly in anticipation of an issue or to resolve and issue.[1032] Parties can make an exception in a regulation that will not apply the law to a service that the Party classifies as a public telecommunications service if the enforcement is not necessary to: prevent unreasonable and discriminatory practices or to protect consumers. It must also be consistent with the public interest.[1033]

Parties can rely on market forces or use other appropriate means that benefit the long-term interests of end-users.[1034]

§18.16   ARTICLE 18.17. TELECOMMUNICATIONS REGULATORY BODIES

Must be separate from a supplier of telecom services to ensure impartiality.[1035] Regulatory bodies cannot hold financial interests or manage any supplier.[1036] All regulatory decisions and procedures must be impartial. Regulatory bodies must have the authority to impose requirements on a major supplier that is additional to or different from those on other suppliers.[1037]

§18.17   ARTICLE 18.18. STATE ENTERPRISES

Government-owned suppliers cannot receive more favorable treatment than privately owned telecommunications service providers.[1038]

§18.18   ARTICLE 18.19. UNIVERSAL SERVICES

Each Party can define the universal service obligation it maintains in a nondiscriminatory, transparent, and competitively neutral manner. [1039]

§18.19   ARTICLE 18.20. LICENSING PROCESS

If a license is required, criteria, procedures, the normal time period for approval, and terms and conditions must be publicly available.[1040] If requested, Parties must give reasons for the denial, revocation, conditioning, or refusal to renew a license.[1041]

1032. *See* United States-Mexico-Canada Agreement, Section 18.16, Jan. 29, 2020.
1033. *See* United States-Mexico-Canada Agreement, Section 18.16, Jan. 29, 2020.
1034. *See* United States-Mexico-Canada Agreement, Section 18.16, Jan. 29, 2020.
1035. *See* United States-Mexico-Canada Agreement, Section 18.17, Jan. 29, 2020.
1036. *See* United States-Mexico-Canada Agreement, Section 18.17, Jan. 29, 2020.
1037. *See* United States-Mexico-Canada Agreement, Section 18.17, Jan. 29, 2020.
1038. *See* United States-Mexico-Canada Agreement, Section 18.18, Jan. 29, 2020.
1039. *See* United States-Mexico-Canada Agreement, Section 18.19, Jan. 29, 2020.
1040. *See* United States-Mexico-Canada Agreement, Section 18.20, Jan. 29, 2020.
1041. *See* United States-Mexico-Canada Agreement, Section 18.20, Jan. 29, 2020.

§18.20   ARTICLE 18.21. ALLOCATION AND USE OF SCARCE RESOURCES

Procedures for allocation must be objective, and Parties must publish the current state of frequency bands allocated and assigned to specific suppliers (exception for government uses).[1042] Parties should use market-based approaches in assigning spectrum for terrestrial commercial telecommunications services (can use auctions).[1043]

§18.21   ARTICLE 18.22. ENFORCEMENT

Regulatory bodies should be able to enforce the obligations of this chapter by imposing effective sanctions.[1044]

§18.22   ARTICLE 18.23. RESOLUTION OF DISPUTES

Enterprises have recourse to the telecommunications regulatory body of the Party to resolve disputes with a supplier of public telecommunications services regarding the Party's measure.[1045]

If a regulatory body declines to take action, they must explain why within a reasonable time.[1046]

An enterprise whose legally protected interests are adversely affected by a determination or decision of the Party's telecommunications regulatory body may appeal to or petition the body to reconsider that determination or decision.[1047]

A Party may limit the circumstances under which reconsideration is available, in accordance with its laws and regulations.[1048]

Parties cannot permit the making of an application for judicial review to constitute grounds for non-compliance with the determination of the telecommunications regulatory body unless the judicial body issues an order that the determination or decision not be enforced while the proceeding is pending.[1049]

§18.23   ARTICLE 18.24. TRANSPARENCY

Proposals for regulations must be public, state the purpose, provide for comments that will be public, and respond to relevant issues.[1050]

1042. *See* United States-Mexico-Canada Agreement, Section 18.21, Jan. 29, 2020.
1043. *See* United States-Mexico-Canada Agreement, Section 18.21, Jan. 29, 2020.
1044. *See* United States-Mexico-Canada Agreement, Section 18.22, Jan. 29, 2020.
1045. *See* United States-Mexico-Canada Agreement, Section 18.23, Jan. 29, 2020.
1046. *See* United States-Mexico-Canada Agreement, Section 18.23, Jan. 29, 2020.
1047. *See* United States-Mexico-Canada Agreement, Section 18.23, Jan. 29, 2020.
1048. *See* United States-Mexico-Canada Agreement, Section 18.23, Jan. 29, 2020.
1049. *See* United States-Mexico-Canada Agreement, Section 18.23, Jan. 29, 2020.
1050. *See* United States-Mexico-Canada Agreement, Section 18.24, Jan. 29, 2020.

Measures related to public telecommunications services must be available, including tariffs, technical specifications, conditions for equipment attachment, licensing requirements, dispute procedures, and any other measure of the telecommunications body.[1051]

§18.24 ARTICLE 18.25. INTERNATIONAL ROAMING SERVICES

Parties must try to cooperate on promoting transparent and reasonable rates for international mobile roaming services (making retail information available and minimizing impediments to technical alternatives to roaming).[1052]

§18.25 ARTICLE 18.26. RELATION TO OTHER CHAPTERS

If there is any inconsistency between this chapter and another chapter of this Agreement, this chapter shall prevail to the extent of the inconsistency.[1053]

§18.26 ARTICLE 18.27. TELECOMMUNICATIONS COMMITTEE

This section is new to the USMCA and established the Telecommunications Committee that will review and monitor the implementation of this chapter.[1054]

Annex 18-A: Rural Telephone Suppliers

United States

The United States may exempt rural local exchange carriers and rural telephone companies, as defined, amended, and obligated under this chapter.[1055]

1051. *See* United States-Mexico-Canada Agreement, Section 18.24, Jan. 29, 2020.
1052. *See* United States-Mexico-Canada Agreement, Section 18.25, Jan. 29, 2020.
1053. *See* United States-Mexico-Canada Agreement, Section 18.26, Jan. 29, 2020.
1054. *See* United States-Mexico-Canada Agreement, Section 18.27, Jan. 29, 2020.
1055. *See* United States-Mexico-Canada Agreement, Annex 18-A, Jan. 29, 2020.

CHAPTER 19

Digital Trade

This Chapter aims to modernize NAFTA since the establishment of the internet. It addresses electronic contracting, electronic signatures, nondiscriminatory treatment of digital services, data transfers, and much more. There are requirements for Parties in this section. These requirements relate to not imposing customs duties for digital products, practicing nondiscriminatory treatment, maintaining a legal framework that governs electronic transactions, accepting the validity of electronic signatures, adopting consumer and personal information protections, accepting paperless trading, practicing transparency, and cooperating. Additionally, Parties cannot restrict the cross-border transfer of information by electronic means, Parties cannot require transfers of, or access to, a source code, algorithm, or software owned by another Party's person. Additional restrictions apply relating to interactive computer services. Exceptions and exemptions apply to these requirements.

This chapter is new in the USMCA, and its aim is to modernize NAFTA since the internet did not exist when NAFTA was drafted. It addresses electronic contracting, electronic signatures, nondiscriminatory treatment of digital services, data transfers, and much more.[1056] NAFTA did not provide the necessary protection for businesses selling digital services or products throughout the continent. The USMCA goes beyond similar provisions in other free trade agreements, such as in the U.S.-South Korea ("KORUS") and the Transpacific Partnership ("TPP") free trade agreement.[1057]

§19.1   ARTICLE 19.2. SCOPE AND GENERAL PROVISIONS

This chapter does not apply to government procurement or to information held or processed by or on behalf of a Party.[1058] Information held or processed by Parties is not

---

1056. *See* generally United States-Mexico-Canada Agreement, Chapter 19, Jan. 29, 2020.
1057. Chairman Erik Paulsen, Digital Trade in the U.S.-Mexico-Canada Agreement, Joint Economic Committee (Dec. 21, 2018), https://www.jec.senate.gov/public/_cache/files/7ba61fd0-19c2 -42d3-b32c-960497f486dd/usmca-digital-trade-provisions-.pdf. (The U.S. is not currently a party to the TPP, although it participated in negotiations.)
1058. *See* United States-Mexico-Canada Agreement, Section, Jan. 29, 2020.

within the scope of this chapter unless the information is personal information of digital trade users. *See* Article 19.8.

§19.2   ARTICLE 19.3. CUSTOMS DUTIES

Parties cannot impose customs duties, fees, or other charges on or in connection with the importation or exportation of digital products transmitted electronically. This includes e-books, videos, music, software, and games.

Parties can still impose internal taxes, fees, or other charges on digital products transmitted electronically.

Countries outside of this agreement have taken steps to impose duties in connection with digital products or services. For example, on March 6, 2019, France released its proposal for the Digital Services Tax (DST). The DST levies a 3% tax on annual revenues generated by "some companies that provide certain digital services to, or aimed at, French users."[1059] The United States Trade Representative ("USTR") initiated an investigation into the French DST, claiming it violates section 301 of the Trade Act.[1060] Section 301 cases arise where "acts, policies, and practices of a foreign country [] are unreasonable or discriminatory and burden or restrict U.S. commerce."[1061]

USTR centered its investigation on potential discrimination, the retroactive aspects of the bill, and the tax as unreasonable tax policy.[1062] USTR argued that the DST amounts to "de facto discrimination against U.S. companies" because the revenue thresholds target U.S. firms and exempt smaller, particularly French, companies.[1063] USTR further questioned the fairness of the tax, based on its retroactive nature.[1064] Firms will need to assess their potential liability dating back to January 1, 2019.[1065] Lastly, USTR asserted that the tax deviates from traditional international and domestic tax systems. For example, the tax applies extraterritorially, it taxes revenue, and it

---

1059. Public Hearing on Proposed Action to France's Digital Services Tax, USTR (Jan. 1, 2020) https://ustr.gov/about-us/policy-offices/press-office/press-releases/2020/january/public-hearing-proposed-action-frances-digital-services-tax.

1060. Federal Register Vol. 84, No. 235 https://ustr.gov/sites/default/files/Notice_of_Determination_and_Request_for_Comments_Concerning_Action_Pursuant_to_Section_301_France%E2%80%99s_Digital_Services_Tax.pdf.

1061. Federal Register Vol. 84, No. 235 https://ustr.gov/sites/default/files/Notice_of_Determination_and_Request_for_Comments_Concerning_Action_Pursuant_to_Section_301_France%E2%80%99s_Digital_Services_Tax.pdf.

1062. Federal Register Vol. 84, No. 235 https://ustr.gov/sites/default/files/Notice_of_Determination_and_Request_for_Comments_Concerning_Action_Pursuant_to_Section_301_France%E2%80%99s_Digital_Services_Tax.pdf.

1063. Federal Register Vol. 84, No. 235 https://ustr.gov/sites/default/files/Notice_of_Determination_and_Request_for_Comments_Concerning_Action_Pursuant_to_Section_301_France%E2%80%99s_Digital_Services_Tax.pdf.

1064. Federal Register Vol. 84, No. 235 https://ustr.gov/sites/default/files/Notice_of_Determination_and_Request_for_Comments_Concerning_Action_Pursuant_to_Section_301_France%E2%80%99s_Digital_Services_Tax.pdf.

1065. Federal Register Vol. 84, No. 235 https://ustr.gov/sites/default/files/Notice_of_Determination_and_Request_for_Comments_Concerning_Action_Pursuant_to_Section_301_France%E2%80%99s_Digital_Services_Tax.pdf.

penalizes technology companies for their success.[1066] USTR collected public comments and conducted hearings on the subject,

The Organization for Economic Cooperation and Development ("OECD") has initiated discussions with government representatives regarding how and where large technology companies would be taxed.[1067] The OECD published a proposal on September 10, 2019, which highlighted the need for states to discuss the taxation of Multinational Enterprises "wherever they have significant consumer-facing activities and generate their profits."[1068] Negotiations between the representatives are moving quickly due to the potential ramifications of a failed agreement, such as a trade war.[1069] The EU has aggressively pursued taxing large tech firms but has faced backlash and failed to come to an agreement within its own coalition as to how to best tax tech groups in nations where they are not physically present.[1070]

The USTR eventually found the French digital services tax violated section 301 and imposed significant tariffs focused on French consumer products like wines and cheeses. However, these were suspended pending further OECD negotiations. However, subsequently, the U.S. has abandoned the OECD negotiation as not progressing. At the time of finalizing this book, the USTR had launched a new investigation against the entire EU and other countries, such as Turkey, concerning their digital taxes and had invited public comment.

§19.3 ARTICLE 19.4. NONDISCRIMINATORY TREATMENT OF DIGITAL PRODUCTS

Parties cannot discriminate or give less favorable treatment to a digital product created by another Party, produced, contracted for, commissioned, or first made available on commercial terms in another territory.[1071]

This article does not apply to subsidies or grants, which includes providing subsidies, grants, government-supported loans, guarantees, and insurance.[1072]

1066. Federal Register Vol. 84, No. 235 https://ustr.gov/sites/default/files/Notice_of_Deter mination_and_Request_for_Comments_Concerning_Action_Pursuant_to_Section_301_France %E2%80%99s_Digital_Services_Tax.pdf.

1067. Oscar Williams, OECD launches negotiations on new international tech tax regime, New Statesman Tech (Jan. 31, 2020) https://tech.newstatesman.com/policy/oecd-tech-tax.

1068. OECD leading multilateral efforts to address tax challenges from digitalisation of the economy, OECD (Sep. 10, 2019) https://www.oecd.org/tax/oecd-leading-multilateral-efforts-to-address-tax-challenges-from-digitalisation-of-the-economy.htm.

1069. Oscar Williams, OECD launches negotiations on new international tech tax regime, New Statesman Tech (Jan. 31, 2020) https://tech.newstatesman.com/policy/oecd-tech-tax.

1070. Oscar Williams, OECD launches negotiations on new international tech tax regime, New Statesman Tech (Jan. 31, 2020) https://tech.newstatesman.com/policy/oecd-tech-tax. *See also* USTR Initiation of Section 301 Investigation of Digital Services Taxes 85 Fed Reg. 34709, Jun. 5, 2020.

1071. United States-Mexico-Canada Agreement, Section 19.4, Jan. 29, 2020.

1072. United States-Mexico-Canada Agreement, Section 19.4, Jan. 29, 2020.

§19.4   ARTICLE 19.5. DOMESTIC ELECTRONIC TRANSACTIONS FRAMEWORK

Parties must maintain a legal framework governing electronic transactions consistent with the principles of the UNCITRAL Model Law on Electronic Commerce 1996.[1073] The framework should avoid unnecessary regulatory burdens and facilitate input concerning its development.[1074] The tax will be applied to companies with annual revenues of at least EUR 750 million globally and EUR 25 million in France.[1075]

§19.5   ARTICLE 19.6. ELECTRONIC AUTHENTICATION AND ELECTRONIC SIGNATURES

Parties must accept the legal validity of a signature in electronic form, except in the circumstances provided for under its law.[1076] Measures for electronic authentication cannot prohibit Parties to an electronic transaction from determining the appropriate authentication methods or preventing them from establishing that their transaction complies with any legal requirements.[1077]

§19.6   ARTICLE 19.7. ONLINE CONSUMER PROTECTION

Parties must adopt or maintain consumer protection laws to prohibit fraud and other deceptive commercial activities that harm consumers, as described in Articles 21.4.3 through 21.4.5 (Competition Policy—Consumer Protection).[1078]

§19.7   ARTICLE 19.8. PERSONAL INFORMATION PROTECTION

Each Party must adopt or maintain a legal framework that provides protection for the personal information of digital trade users.[1079] USMCA suggests that Parties should refer to the *APEC Privacy Framework and the OECD Recommendation of the Council concerning Guidelines governing the Protection of Privacy and Transborder Flows of Personal Data (2013)*.[1080]

Parties must promote compatibility between their legal frameworks and adopt nondiscriminatory practices.[1081] Parties shall publish how natural persons can pursue a remedy and how an enterprise can comply with legal requirements.[1082]

1073. United States-Mexico-Canada Agreement, Section 19.5, Jan. 29, 2020.
1074. United States-Mexico-Canada Agreement, Section 19.5, Jan. 29, 2020.
1075. United States-Mexico-Canada Agreement, Section 19.5, Jan. 29, 2020.
1076. United States-Mexico-Canada Agreement, Section 19.6, Jan. 29, 2020.
1077. United States-Mexico-Canada Agreement, Section 19.6, Jan. 29, 2020.
1078. United States-Mexico-Canada Agreement, Section 19.7, Jan. 29, 2020.
1079. United States-Mexico-Canada Agreement, Section 19.8, Jan. 29, 2020.
1080. United States-Mexico-Canada Agreement, Section 19.8, Jan. 29, 2020.
1081. United States-Mexico-Canada Agreement, Section 19.8, Jan. 29, 2020.
1082. United States-Mexico-Canada Agreement, Section 19.6, Jan. 29, 2020.

At the time of writing, the U.S. has a bill in the Senate directed to protecting personal data.[1083] The Data Protection Act of 2020 would establish an independent federal Data Protection Agency. This agency would have the power to regulate the processing of personal data through…the power to enforce defined Federal privacy laws.[1084] The bill states that "in order to protect the privacy of individuals, it is necessary and proper for Congress to regulate the collection, maintenance, use, processing, storage, and dissemination of information."[1085] This Agency would act as a referee, defining, arbitrating, and enforcing rules, through civil actions against violators.[1086]

The EU has already enacted legislation to ensure data privacy. On April 14, 2016, the European Parliament approved the General Data Protection Regulation ("GDPR").[1087] The GDPR builds off of the OECD's Guidelines on the Protection of Privacy and Transborder Flows of Personal Data.[1088] GDPR protection applies "to all corporate entities that process the person data of EU citizens, even if the processing of relevant data does not take place within the EU."[1089] The regulatory measures the GDPR puts in place is "to give citizens back control over their personal data."[1090]

§19.8 ARTICLE 19.9. PAPERLESS TRADING

Parties should accept a trade administration document submitted electronically as the legal equivalent of the paper version of that document.[1091]

§19.9 ARTICLE 19.10. PRINCIPLES ON ACCESS TO AND USE OF THE INTERNET FOR DIGITAL TRADE

Consumers benefit from access and use of services and applications available on the Internet.[1092] They further benefit from connecting their end-user devices of choice to the Internet.[1093] Consumers also benefit from accessing information using the network

---

1083. Fred J.M. Price, The Data Protection Act of 2020, Bond, Schoeneck, & King PLLC (Mar. 4, 2020) https://www.jdsupra.com/legalnews/the-data-protection-act-of-2020-33638/.
1084. Fred J.M. Price, The Data Protection Act of 2020, Bond, Schoeneck, & King PLLC (Mar. 4, 2020) https://www.jdsupra.com/legalnews/the-data-protection-act-of-2020-33638/.
1085. Fred J.M. Price, The Data Protection Act of 2020, Bond, Schoeneck, & King PLLC (Mar. 4, 2020) https://www.jdsupra.com/legalnews/the-data-protection-act-of-2020-33638/.
1086. Fred J.M. Price, The Data Protection Act of 2020, Bond, Schoeneck, & King PLLC (Mar. 4, 2020) https://www.jdsupra.com/legalnews/the-data-protection-act-of-2020-33638/.
1087. Chris Mirasola, Summary: The EU General Data Protection Regulation, LawFare (Mar. 1, 2018) https://www.lawfareblog.com/summary-eu-general-data-protection-regulation.
1088. Chris Mirasola, Summary: The EU General Data Protection Regulation, LawFare (Mar. 1, 2018) https://www.lawfareblog.com/summary-eu-general-data-protection-regulation.
1089. Chris Mirasola, Summary: The EU General Data Protection Regulation, LawFare (Mar. 1, 2018) https://www.lawfareblog.com/summary-eu-general-data-protection-regulation.
1090. Chris Mirasola, Summary: The EU General Data Protection Regulation, LawFare (Mar. 1, 2018) https://www.lawfareblog.com/summary-eu-general-data-protection-regulation.
1091. United States-Mexico-Canada Agreement, Section 19.9, Jan. 29, 2020.
1092. United States-Mexico-Canada Agreement, Section 19.10, Jan. 29, 2020.
1093. United States-Mexico-Canada Agreement, Section 19.10, Jan. 29, 2020.

management practices of their country's Internet supplier. This applies to devices that do not harm the network.[1094]

§19.10   ARTICLE 19.11. CROSS-BORDER TRANSFER OF INFORMATION BY ELECTRONIC MEANS

Parties cannot restrict the cross-border transfer of information by electronic means that is for business use of a covered person.[1095] Parties may adopt public policy measures that are inconsistent with this article so long as they are not arbitrary, discriminating, or overbroad.[1096]

§19.11   ARTICLE 19.12. LOCATION OF COMPUTING FACILITIES

No Party shall require a covered person to use or locate computing facilities in that Party's territory as a condition for conducting business in that territory.[1097]

§19.12   ARTICLE 19.13. UNSOLICITED COMMERCIAL ELECTRONIC COMMUNICATIONS

Parties must adopt or maintain measures for limiting unsolicited commercial electronic communications by requiring suppliers of these messages to allow recipients to prevent ongoing reception or require the consent of recipients to retrieve those messages.[1098]

§19.13   ARTICLE 19.14. COOPERATION

Parties shall endeavor to exchange information and experiences on regulations and enforcement related to digital trade.[1099] They will try to cooperate and maintain a dialogue on the promotion of mechanisms that further global interoperability of privacy regimes.[1100]

§19.14   ARTICLE 19.15. CYBERSECURITY

Parties recognize threats to digital trade created by issues of cybersecurity.[1101] Parties will endeavor to build cybersecurity incident response capabilities and strengthen

---

1094. United States-Mexico-Canada Agreement, Section 19.10, Jan. 29, 2020.
1095. United States-Mexico-Canada Agreement, Section 19.11, Jan. 29, 2020.
1096. United States-Mexico-Canada Agreement, Section 19.11, Jan. 29, 2020.
1097. United States-Mexico-Canada Agreement, Section 19.12, Jan. 29, 2020.
1098. United States-Mexico-Canada Agreement, Section 19.13, Jan. 29, 2020.
1099. United States-Mexico-Canada Agreement, Section 19.14, Jan. 29, 2020.
1100. United States-Mexico-Canada Agreement, Section 19.14, Jan. 29, 2020.
1101. United States-Mexico-Canada Agreement, Section 19.15, Jan. 29, 2020.

"risk-based" measures that favor "self-policing according to 'consensus-based standards' over more prescriptive regulations."[1102]

§19.15   ARTICLE 19.16. SOURCE CODE

Parties cannot require transfers of, or access to, a source code, algorithm, or software owned by another Party's person.[1103] There is an exception for a disclosure required by a regulatory body for a specific investigation, inspection, examination, enforcement action, or judicial proceeding.[1104]

§19.16   ARTICLE 19.17. INTERACTIVE COMPUTER SERVICES

Interactive Computer Services are any systems or services that provide or enable electronic access by multiple users to a computer server.[1105]

These services are vital to the growth of digital trade.[1106] Therefore, Parties cannot treat the supplier or user of an interactive computer service as an information content provider in determining liability for harms related to information present on the server, except to the extent they have created or developed the information.[1107]

The Parties cannot impose liability on a supplier or user of an interactive computer service on account of:

> (a) any action voluntarily taken in good faith by the supplier or user to restrict access to or availability of material that is accessible or available through its supply or use of the interactive computer services and that the supplier or user considers to be harmful or objectionable; or (b) any action taken to enable or make available the technical means that enable an information content provider or other persons to restrict access to material that it considers to be harmful or objectionable.[1108]

§19.17   ARTICLE 19.18. OPEN GOVERNMENT DATA

The Parties recognize that facilitating public access to and use of government information fosters economic and social development, competitiveness, and innovation. [1109]

Public data must be machine-readable and in an open format that can be searched, retrieved, used and redistributed.[1110]

1102. United States-Mexico-Canada Agreement, Section 19.15, Jan. 29, 2020.
1103. United States-Mexico-Canada Agreement, Section 19.16, Jan. 29, 2020.
1104. United States-Mexico-Canada Agreement, Section 19.16, Jan. 29, 2020.
1105. United States-Mexico-Canada Agreement, Section 19.17, Jan. 29, 2020.
1106. United States-Mexico-Canada Agreement, Section 19.17, Jan. 29, 2020.
1107. United States-Mexico-Canada Agreement, Section 19.17, Jan. 29, 2020.
1108. United States-Mexico-Canada Agreement, Section 19.17, Jan. 29, 2020.
1109. United States-Mexico-Canada Agreement, Section 19.18, Jan. 29, 2020.
1110. United States-Mexico-Canada Agreement, Section 19.18, Jan. 29, 2020.

Annex 19-A

Article 19.17 (Interactive Computer Services) shall not apply with respect to Mexico until the date of three years after entry into force of USMCA.[1111]

Mexico will comply with the obligations of Interactive Computer Services because they are required to enact legislation to do so.[1112]

Article 19.17 is "subject to Article 32.1 (General Exceptions), which, among other things, provides that, for purposes of Chapter 19, the exception for measures necessary to protect public morals pursuant to paragraph (a) of Article XIV of GATS is incorporated into and made part of this Agreement, *mutatis mutandis.*"[1113]

There are exemptions for measures necessary to protect public morals, including protection against online sex trafficking, sexual exploitation of children, and prostitution, such as Public Law 115-164, the "Allow States and Victims to Fight Online Sex Trafficking Act of 2017," which amends the Communications Act of 1934, and any relevant provisions of *Ley General para Prevenir, Sancionar y Erradicar los Delitos en Materia de Trata de Personas y para la Protección y Asistencia a las Víctimas de estos delitos*, are measures necessary to protect public morals."[1114]

1111. United States-Mexico-Canada Agreement, Annex 19-A, Jan. 29, 2020.
1112. United States-Mexico-Canada Agreement, Annex 19-A, Jan. 29, 2020.
1113. Digital Trade –USMCA Chapter 19, USMCA.com, https://usmca.com/digital-trade-usmca-chapter-19/ (last visited Feb. 28, 2020).
1114. Digital Trade–USMCA Chapter 19, USMCA.com, https://usmca.com/digital-trade-usmca-chapter-19/ (last visited Feb. 28, 2020).

CHAPTER 20
Intellectual Property Rights

The objective of this Chapter is to promote technological innovation, transfer and dissemination of technology, and competition in open and efficient markets. Parties may adopt measures to protect public health and nutrition, and to promote the public interest in sectors of importance to their socio-economic and technological development. Parties should protect the IP of nationals of other Parties in its territory. Parties must also practice National Treatment, transparency and cooperation on IP-related matters. This section established The Intellectual Property Rights Committee. In terms of trademarks, Parties cannot require a visually perceptible sign. Trademarks should include collective and certification marks. Trademark owners must have exclusive rights to prevent Parties that do not have consent from using similar marks in trade if it would result in a likelihood of confusion. Additional requirements and exceptions apply. In terms of geographical indications, such indications may be protected through a trademark or other legal means. Certain requirements apply. Patents, with limited exceptions, must be available for any invention. The patent must claim new uses of a known product, new methods of using a known product, or new processes of using a known product. Additional requirements and exceptions apply for measures relating to pharmaceutical products, industrial designs, copyright and related rights, and trade secrets. In terms of enforcement, Parties must have enforcement mechanisms in place to remedy and deter infringement. For violations of infringements on a commercial sale, criminal procedures and penalties must be applied.

§20.1   SECTION A: GENERAL PROVISIONS

[A]   Article 20.2. Objectives

The objectives are to promote technological innovation, transfer and dissemination of technology, and competition in open and efficient markets.[1115]

1115. *See* United States-Mexico-Canada Agreement, Section 20.2, Jan. 29, 2020.

[B]   Article 20.3. Principles

A Party may adopt measures necessary to protect public health and nutrition, and to promote the public interest in sectors of vital importance to their socio-economic and technological development, provided that those measures are consistent with the provisions of this chapter.[1116]

Appropriate measures may be needed to prevent the abuse of intellectual property rights by right holders or the resort to practices which unreasonably restrain trade or adversely affect the international transfer of technology.[1117]

[C]   Article 20.5. Nature and Scope of Obligations

Parties should protect the IP of nationals of another Party in its territory in a way that does not create barriers to trade.[1118]

Parties may provide more extensive protection than is required by the chapter so long as it doesn't contravene the chapter.[1119]

[D]   Article 20.6. Understandings Regarding Certain Public Health Measures

The Parties affirm their commitment to the Declaration on Trade-Related Aspects of Intellectual Property Rights (TRIPS) and Public Health.

The Parties are building on existing international agreements that address IP, such as the World Trade Organization Agreement on TRIPS and treaties administered by the World Intellectual Property Organization (WIPO).[1120]

Parties have the right to determine what constitutes a national emergency and may take measures to protect public health.[1121]

[E]   Article 20.7. International Agreements

Parties have already ratified: Patent Cooperation Treaty, as amended on September 28, 1979, and modified on February 3, 1984; Paris Convention; Berne Convention; WIPO Copyright Treaty (WCT); and WIPO Performance and Phonograms Treaty (WPPT).[1122]
Parties must ratify: Madrid Protocol; Budapest Treaty; Singapore Treaty; UPOV 1991; Hague Agreement; and Brussels Convention.[1123]

1116. *See* United States-Mexico-Canada Agreement, Section 20.3, Jan. 29, 2020.
1117. *See* United States-Mexico-Canada Agreement, Section 20.3, Jan. 29, 2020.
1118. *See* United States-Mexico-Canada Agreement, Section 20.5, Jan. 29, 2020.
1119. *See* United States-Mexico-Canada Agreement, Section 20.5, Jan. 29, 2020.
1120. *See* United States-Mexico-Canada Agreement, Section 20.6, Jan. 29, 2020.
1121. *See* United States-Mexico-Canada Agreement, Section 20.6, Jan. 29, 2020.
1122. *See* United States-Mexico-Canada Agreement, Section 20.7, Jan. 29, 2020.
1123. *See* United States-Mexico-Canada Agreement, Section 20.7, Jan. 29, 2020.

Parties must consider ratifying: PLT.[1124]

[F]   Article 20.8. National Treatment

In respect of all categories of IP covered, each Party shall accord to nationals of another Party treatment no less favorable than it accords to its own nationals with regard to the protection of IP rights.[1125] This does not apply to procedures provided in multilateral agreements concluded under the auspices of WIPO relating to the acquisition or maintenance of intellectual property rights.[1126]

[G]   Article 20.9. Transparency

Parties should make public its laws and regulations concerning the protection and enforcement of IP rights.[1127] They should also make public applications and confirmed registrations for trademarks, geographical indications, designs, patents and plant variety rights.[1128]

[H]   Article 20.10. Application of Chapter to Existing Subject Matter and Prior Acts

This chapter gives rise to obligations in respect of all subject matters existing on USMCA's effective date (unless provided in Article 20.64), and that is protected on that date or that meets or comes subsequently to meet the criteria for protection under this chapter.[1129]

Parties shall not be required to restore protection to subject matter that on USMCA's effective date has fallen into the public domain in its territory.[1130]

[I]   Article 20.11. Exhaustion of Intellectual Property Rights

Parties can determine whether or under what conditions the exhaustion of IP rights applies under its legal system.[1131]

1124. *See* United States-Mexico-Canada Agreement, Section 20.7, Jan. 29, 2020.
1125. *See* United States-Mexico-Canada Agreement, Section 20.8, Jan. 29, 2020.
1126. *See* United States-Mexico-Canada Agreement, Section 20.8, Jan. 29, 2020.
1127. *See* United States-Mexico-Canada Agreement, Section 20.9, Jan. 29, 2020.
1128. *See* United States-Mexico-Canada Agreement, Section 20.9, Jan. 29, 2020.
1129. *See* United States-Mexico-Canada Agreement, Section 20.10, Jan. 29, 2020.
1130. *See* United States-Mexico-Canada Agreement, Section 20.10, Jan. 29, 2020.
1131. *See* United States-Mexico-Canada Agreement, Section 20.11, Jan. 29, 2020.

§20.2   SECTION B: COOPERATION

Each Party may designate and notify the other Parties of one or more contact points for the purpose of cooperation.[1132] Parties shall endeavor to cooperate on the IP-related matters by coordinating and exchanging information.[1133]

Intellectual Property Rights Committee is established, which should work towards cooperation, strengthening border enforcement, procedural fairness in patent litigation, and/or exchanging information on trade secret-related matters, etc.[1134] The committee created under this section is unlike any other trade agreement; neither NAFTA nor TPP included or established a committee like this one.[1135]

[A]   Article 20.15. Patent Cooperation and Work Sharing

Parties will cooperate with their respective patent offices to facilitate the sharing and use of search and examination work in order to streamline and improve the quality of patent registration systems.[1136]

[B]   Article 20.16. Cooperation on Request

Cooperation activities undertaken under this chapter are subject to the availability of resources, on request, and on terms and conditions mutually decided upon between the Parties involved.[1137]

§20.3   SECTION C: TRADEMARKS

[A]   Article 20.17. Types of Signs Registrable as Trademarks

Parties cannot require a visually perceptible sign. Sounds are okay, and Parties should try to register scents too.[1138] Parties may require a concise and accurate description, or graphical representation, or both, as applicable, of the trademark.[1139]

1132. *See* United States-Mexico-Canada Agreement, Section 20.12, Jan. 29, 2020.

1133. *See* United States-Mexico-Canada Agreement, Section 20.13, Jan. 29, 2020.

1134. *See* United States-Mexico-Canada Agreement, Section 20.14, Jan. 29, 2020.

1135. United States Trade Alert Overview of Chapter 20 (Intellectual Property Rights) of the US-Mexico-Canada Agreement, White & Case (Oct. 24, 2018) https://www.whitecase.com/publications/alert/united-states-trade-alert-overview-chapter-20-intellectual-property-rights-us.

1136. *See* United States-Mexico-Canada Agreement, Section 20.15, Jan. 29, 2020.

1137. *See* United States-Mexico-Canada Agreement, Section 20.16, Jan. 29, 2020.

1138. *See* United States-Mexico-Canada Agreement, Section 20.17, Jan. 29, 2020.

1139. *See* United States-Mexico-Canada Agreement, Section 20.17, Jan. 29, 2020.

[B]   Article 20.18. Collective and Certification Marks

Trademarks should include collective and certification marks.[1140] Parties are not required to treat certification marks as a separate category if those marks are protected.[1141] Geographical indications must be eligible for protection.[1142]

[C]   Article 20.19. Use of Identical or Similar Signs

Trademark owners in each territory must have the exclusive right to prevent Parties that do not have consent from using similar signs in trade if it would result in a likelihood of confusion.[1143]

Likelihood of confusion is presumed when there are identical signs for identical goods and services.[1144]

[D]   Article 20.20. Exceptions

Limited exceptions, such as fair use of descriptive terms, are acceptable when they take into account the interests of the trademark owners and of third parties.[1145]

[E]   Article 20.21. Well-Known Trademarks

Parties cannot condition the "well-known" certification of a trademark on its registration in the Party or in another jurisdiction, inclusion on a list of well-known trademarks, or prior recognition as a well-known trademark.[1146]

Paris Convention Article 6*bis* applies, *mutatis mutandis*, to goods/services that are not identical or similar to those identified by a well-known trademark when the use of a particular trademark in relation to those goods/services would indicate a connection between them and the trademark owner, potentially damaging the owner's interest.[1147]

Parties recognize the importance of the Joint Recommendation Concerning Provisions on the Protection of Well-Known Marks.[1148]

Parties must allow registrations to be refused or canceled and prohibit the use of a trademark that is identical or similar to a well-known trademark for identical or similar goods/services when it is likely to cause confusion or likely to deceive.[1149]

1140. *See* United States-Mexico-Canada Agreement, Section 20.18, Jan. 29, 2020.
1141. *See* United States-Mexico-Canada Agreement, Section 20.18, Jan. 29, 2020.
1142. *See* United States-Mexico-Canada Agreement, Section 20.18, Jan. 29, 2020.
1143. *See* United States-Mexico-Canada Agreement, Section 20.19, Jan. 29, 2020.
1144. *See* United States-Mexico-Canada Agreement, Section 20.19, Jan. 29, 2020.
1145. *See* United States-Mexico-Canada Agreement, Section 20.20, Jan. 29, 2020.
1146. *See* United States-Mexico-Canada Agreement, Section 20.21, Jan. 29, 2020.
1147. *See* United States-Mexico-Canada Agreement, Section 20.21, Jan. 29, 2020.
1148. *See* United States-Mexico-Canada Agreement, Section 20.21, Jan. 29, 2020.
1149. *See* United States-Mexico-Canada Agreement, Section 20.21, Jan. 29, 2020.

[F]   Article 20.22. Procedural Aspects of Examination, Opposition, and Cancellation

Parties must have a system in place to examine registrations.[1150] Parties must communicate reasons for registration refusal, provide applicants with an opportunity to respond and appeal, provide an opportunity to oppose a registration, and require all decisions and proceedings to be reasoned and in writing.[1151]

[G]   Article 20.23. Electronic Trademarks System

Parties must provide an electronic application and maintenance system.[1152] They must provide access to an online database of applications and registrations.[1153]

[H]   Article 20.24. Classification of Goods and Services

Parties must have a trademark classification system consistent with the Nice Agreement Concerning the International Classification of Goods and Services for the Purposes of the Registration of Marks.[1154]

Registrations must indicate the classification of the goods and services.[1155] Goods or services may not be considered as being similar to each other on the grounds that they are classified in the same class of the Nice Classification or dissimilar because they are in different classes.[1156]

[I]   Article 20.25. Term of Protection for Trademarks

Protection must last for at least ten years after registration and each renewal.[1157]

[J]   Article 20.26. Non-Recordal of a License

Parties cannot require recordal to establish the validity of a license.[1158] Recordal cannot be a condition for the use of a trademark by a licensee to be deemed to constitute use by the holder in a proceeding that relates to the acquisition, maintenance, or enforcement of trademarks.[1159]

1150. *See* United States-Mexico-Canada Agreement, Section 20.22, Jan. 29, 2020.
1151. *See* United States-Mexico-Canada Agreement, Section 20.22, Jan. 29, 2020.
1152. *See* United States-Mexico-Canada Agreement, Section 20.23, Jan. 29, 2020.
1153. *See* United States-Mexico-Canada Agreement, Section 20.23, Jan. 29, 2020.
1154. *See* United States-Mexico-Canada Agreement, Section 20.24, Jan. 29, 2020.
1155. *See* United States-Mexico-Canada Agreement, Section 20.24, Jan. 29, 2020.
1156. *See* United States-Mexico-Canada Agreement, Section 20.24, Jan. 29, 2020.
1157. *See* United States-Mexico-Canada Agreement, Section 20.25, Jan. 29, 2020.
1158. *See* United States-Mexico-Canada Agreement, Section 20.26, Jan. 29, 2020.
1159. *See* United States-Mexico-Canada Agreement, Section 20.26, Jan. 29, 2020.

[K]   **Article 20.27. Domain Names**

Parties must have a system to settle disputes based on the principles established in the *Uniform Domain Name Dispute Resolution Policy,* or that resolves disputes at low cost, expeditiously, fairly, equitably, without burden, and in a way does not preclude resort to judicial proceeds.[1160]

Parties must maintain a public online database of contact information of domain name registrants.[1161]

§20.4   SECTION D: COUNTRY NAMES

[A]   **Article 20.28. Country Names**

Parties must provide legal means for the prevention of commercial use of a Party's country name in relation to a good in a manner that misleads consumers as to the origin of that good.[1162]

§20.5   SECTION E: GEOGRAPHICAL INDICATIONS

[A]   **Article 20.29. Recognition of Geographical Indications**

Geographical indications ("GI") may be protected through a trademark or other legal means.[1163]

[B]   **Article 20.30. Administrative Procedures for the Protection or Recognition of Geographical Indication**

Parties that have administrative proceedings must accept applications for protection or recognition without requiring intercession by a Party on behalf of its nationals or imposing overly burdensome formalities.[1164] The public shall have access to laws, regulations, and procedures that govern the filing of these applications.[1165]

Parties must allow applicants to specify a particular translation or transliteration for which protection is being sought.[1166] Any application must be published for opposition, and any decisions made on the opposition or cancellation must be reasoned and in writing.[1167]

1160. *See* United States-Mexico-Canada Agreement, Section 20.27, Jan. 29, 2020.
1161. *See* United States-Mexico-Canada Agreement, Section 20.27, Jan. 29, 2020.
1162. *See* United States-Mexico-Canada Agreement, Section 20.28, Jan. 29, 2020.
1163. *See* United States-Mexico-Canada Agreement, Section 20.29, Jan. 29, 2020.
1164. *See* United States-Mexico-Canada Agreement, Section 20.30, Jan. 29, 2020.
1165. *See* United States-Mexico-Canada Agreement, Section 20.30, Jan. 29, 2020.
1166. *See* United States-Mexico-Canada Agreement, Section 20.30, Jan. 29, 2020.
1167. *See* United States-Mexico-Canada Agreement, Section 20.30, Jan. 29, 2020.

[C]   Article 20.31. Grounds of Denial, Opposition, and Cancellation

These grounds include the likelihood of confusion with a trademark of a pre-existing good faith pending application or registration, the likelihood of confusion with a pre-existing trademark, and the use of a term customary in common language as the common name for the relevant good in the territory.[1168] In common words, Parties may withdraw refusal if the applicant or registrant disclaims any claim of exclusive rights to the particular individual term.[1169]

Parties cannot preclude cancellation of protection or recognition of a geographical indication because the term has ceased meeting the condition upon which protection or recognition was granted.[1170]

For the sui generis system, Parties must give its judicial authorities the power to deny the protection or recognition indicator for the reasons stated above (likelihood of confusion or customary term).[1171]

[D]   Article 20.32. Guidelines for Determining Whether a Term is the Term Customary in the Common Language

Relevant factors include: whether the term is used to refer to the type of good in question, as indicated by competent sources, such as dictionaries, newspapers, and relevant websites; how the good is marketed and used in trade in the Party's territory; whether the term is used in relevant international standards recognized by the Parties to refer to a type or class of good in the Party's territory (e.g., Codex Alimentarius); whether the good in question is imported into the Party's territory, in significant quantities, from a place other than the territory identified in the application or petition; and whether those imported goods are named by the term.[1172]

[E]   Article 20.33. Multi-Component Terms

An individual component of a multi-component term that is protected as a GI in a Party shall not be protected in that Party if that individual component is a customary term.[1173]

[F]   Article 20.34. Date of Protection of a Geographical Indication

Protection or recognition cannot commence earlier than the filing date or registration date.[1174]

1168. *See* United States-Mexico-Canada Agreement, Section 20.31, Jan. 29, 2020.
1169. *See* United States-Mexico-Canada Agreement, Section 20.31, Jan. 29, 2020.
1170. *See* United States-Mexico-Canada Agreement, Section 20.31, Jan. 29, 2020.
1171. *See* United States-Mexico-Canada Agreement, Section 20.31, Jan. 29, 2020.
1172. *See* United States-Mexico-Canada Agreement, Section 20.32, Jan. 29, 2020.
1173. *See* United States-Mexico-Canada Agreement, Section 20.33, Jan. 29, 2020.
1174. *See* United States-Mexico-Canada Agreement, Section 20.34, Jan. 29, 2020.

[G]   Article 20.35. International Agreements

If the protection or recognition of a GI is pursuant to an international agreement but is not protected through Administrative Procedures in Article 20.30. or 20.31,[1175] the Party should *at least* apply procedures and grounds that are equivalent to those in Article 20.30 (f)-(i).[1176]

They should also make sure the public can obtain guidance regarding the procedures and status of requests for recognition.[1177] They must publish online details regarding the terms that the Party is considering protecting or recognizing through an international agreement.[1178]

They must allow a reasonable time for the opposition and inform the other Parties of this opportunity no later than the commencement of the opposition period.[1179]

For international agreements, wine and spirits GIs are not obligated under Article 20.31 or similar obligations.[1180]

For GIs protected by international agreements, this article does not need to apply to them if the agreement was concluded prior to the USMCA, ratified prior to the ratification of the USMCA, or entered into force prior to USMCA's entry into force.[1181] For Mexico, protection of names, such as Tequila, under a GI and for the U.S. Bourbon, were important issues.

§20.6   SECTION F: PATENTS AND UNDISCLOSED TEST OR OTHER DATA

[A]   Subsection A: General Patents

[1]   Article 20.36. Patentable Subject Matter

With limited exceptions, patents in each nation must be available for any invention, in any field, provided that it is new, involves an inventive step (non-obvious), and is capable of industrial application (useful).[1182] The patent must claim new uses of a known product, new methods of using a known product, or new processes of using a known product.[1183]

Parties can exclude inventions when necessary to protect public order or morality, including protecting human, animal, or plant life or health or avoiding serious prejudice to nature or the environment.[1184]

1175. *See* United States-Mexico-Canada Agreement, Section 20.35, Jan. 29, 2020.
1176. *See* United States-Mexico-Canada Agreement, Section 20.35, Jan. 29, 2020.
1177. *See* United States-Mexico-Canada Agreement, Section 20.35, Jan. 29, 2020.
1178. *See* United States-Mexico-Canada Agreement, Section 20.35, Jan. 29, 2020.
1179. *See* United States-Mexico-Canada Agreement, Section 20.35, Jan. 29, 2020.
1180. *See* United States-Mexico-Canada Agreement, Section 20.35, Jan. 29, 2020.
1181. *See* United States-Mexico-Canada Agreement, Section 20.35, Jan. 29, 2020.
1182. *See* United States-Mexico-Canada Agreement, Section 20.36, Jan. 29, 2020.
1183. *See* United States-Mexico-Canada Agreement, Section 20.36, Jan. 29, 2020.
1184. *See* United States-Mexico-Canada Agreement, Section 20.36, Jan. 29, 2020.

Parties can exclude diagnostic, therapeutic, and surgical methods for the treatment of humans or animals and animals other than microorganisms, and essentially biological processes for the production of plants or animals, other than non-biological and microbiological processes.[1185] Parties may exclude plants other than microorganisms.[1186]

[2]   Article 20.37. Grace Period

Parties must disregard public disclosure information if the disclosure was made by the patent applicant or someone who obtained their information from the applicant, and the public disclosure occurred within twelve months prior to the filing date in the territory of the Party.[1187]

[3]   Article 20.38. Patent Revocation

Patents must be subject to cancellation, revocation or nullification only on the grounds that would have justified a refusal to grant the patent or for fraud, misrepresentation, or inequitable conduct.[1188]

   Parties can also revoke for reasons listed in Article 5A of the Paris Convention and the TRIPS Agreement.[1189]

[4]   Article 20.39. Exceptions

Exceptions cannot unreasonably conflict with a normal exploitation of the patent and cannot unreasonably prejudice the legitimate interests of the patent owner (weighed against those of third parties).[1190]

[5]   Article 20.40. Other Use Without Authorization of the Right Holder

Nothing in this chapter limits a Party's rights and obligations under Article 31 of the TRIPS Agreement, and any waiver of or amendment to that Article that the Parties accept.[1191]

1185. *See* United States-Mexico-Canada Agreement, Section 20.36, Jan. 29, 2020.
1186. *See* United States-Mexico-Canada Agreement, Section 20.36, Jan. 29, 2020.
1187. *See* United States-Mexico-Canada Agreement, Section 20.37, Jan. 29, 2020.
1188. *See* United States-Mexico-Canada Agreement, Section 20.38, Jan. 29, 2020.
1189. *See* United States-Mexico-Canada Agreement, Section 20.38, Jan. 29, 2020.
1190. *See* United States-Mexico-Canada Agreement, Section 20.39, Jan. 29, 2020.
1191. *See* United States-Mexico-Canada Agreement, Section 20.40, Jan. 29, 2020.

[6]   Article 20.41: Amendments, Corrections, and Observations

Patent applicants must have at least one opportunity to correct, amend, or make observations of its application.[1192]

[7]   Article 20.42: Publication of Patent Applications

Parties must try to publish unpublished pending patent applications promptly after the expiration of eighteen months from the filing date or if priority is claimed, from the earliest priority date.[1193]

If it does not do it by those deadlines, they must publish the application or corresponding patent it as soon as practicable.[1194] Applicants may request early publication.[1195]

[8]   Article 20.43. Information Relating to Published Patent Applications and Granted Patents

Parties must make public search and examination results; non-confidential communications from applicants (as appropriate); and patent and non-patent related literature citations submitted by applicants and relevant third parties.[1196]

[9]   Article 20.44. Patent Term Adjustment for Unreasonable Granting Authority Delays

Parties may provide expedition procedures but should make best efforts to process all applications in a timely and efficient manner.[1197] If there are unreasonable delays, a Party must provide means to adjust the term of the patent to compensate for those delays.[1198]

Unreasonable delay includes a delay of more than five years after filing or three years after a request for examination of the application (whichever is later).[1199]

Delay exclusions exist for periods of time that do not occur during the processing or examination of the application, those that are not directly attributable to the patent authority, and periods of time that are attributable to the patent applicant.[1200]

1192. *See* United States-Mexico-Canada Agreement, Section 20.41, Jan. 29, 2020.
1193. *See* United States-Mexico-Canada Agreement, Section 20.42, Jan. 29, 2020.
1194. *See* United States-Mexico-Canada Agreement, Section 20.42, Jan. 29, 2020.
1195. *See* United States-Mexico-Canada Agreement, Section 20.42, Jan. 29, 2020.
1196. *See* United States-Mexico-Canada Agreement, Section 20.43, Jan. 29, 2020.
1197. *See* United States-Mexico-Canada Agreement, Section 20.44, Jan. 29, 2020.
1198. *See* United States-Mexico-Canada Agreement, Section 20.44, Jan. 29, 2020.
1199. *See* United States-Mexico-Canada Agreement, Section 20.44, Jan. 29, 2020.
1200. *See* United States-Mexico-Canada Agreement, Section 20.44, Jan. 29, 2020.

**[10]   Article 20.45. Protection of Undisclosed Test or Other Data for
          Agricultural Chemical**

If testing or data is required for a new agricultural chemical product, Parties cannot
allow third parties without the consent of the person that previously submitted that
information to market the same or similar product on the basis of that information for
at least ten years from the date of marketing approval of the new agricultural chemical
product.[1201]

 The same ten-year period exists for when a person must submit evidence of prior
marketing approval in another territory.[1202]

 New agricultural chemical product: contains a chemical entity that has not
been previously approved in the territory of the Party for use in an agricultural
chemical product.[1203]

[B]   Subsection C: Measures Relating to Pharmaceutical Products

[1]   Article 20.46. Patent Term Adjustment for Unreasonable Curtailment

Parties must make best efforts to process applications for marketing approval of
pharmaceutical products in a timely and efficient manner.[1204] For pharmaceutical
products subject to patents, Parties must be able to adjust the patent term for
unreasonable delay caused by the marketing approval process.[1205]

[2]   Article 20.47. Regulatory Review Exception

Each Party must have a regulatory review exception for pharmaceutical products.[1206]

[3]   Article 20.48. Protection of Undisclosed Test or Other Data

For five years after marketing approval, third parties, without consent of the applicant,
cannot market the same or similar product on the basis of information of marketing
approval granted to the applicant as a result of undisclosed tests or other data.[1207]

 The same five-year period is in place for third parties when an original applicant
is required to submit evidence of prior marketing approval of the product in another
territory.[1208]

1201. *See* United States-Mexico-Canada Agreement, Section 20.45, Jan. 29, 2020.
1202. *See* United States-Mexico-Canada Agreement, Section 20.45, Jan. 29, 2020.
1203. *See* United States-Mexico-Canada Agreement, Section 20.45, Jan. 29, 2020.
1204. *See* United States-Mexico-Canada Agreement, Section 20.46, Jan. 29, 2020.
1205. *See* United States-Mexico-Canada Agreement, Section 20.46, Jan. 29, 2020.
1206. *See* United States-Mexico-Canada Agreement, Section 20.47, Jan. 29, 2020.
1207. *See* United States-Mexico-Canada Agreement, Section 20.48, Jan. 29, 2020.
1208. *See* United States-Mexico-Canada Agreement, Section 20.48, Jan. 29, 2020.

These periods should be applied for at least three years with respect to new clinical information submitted as required in support of marketing approval of a previously approved pharmaceutical product covering a new indication, new formulation, or new method of administration, or apply for five years to new pharmaceutical products that contain a chemical entity that has not been previously approved in that Party.[1209]

Parties can take measures to protect: (a) public health in accordance with the Declaration on TRIPS and Public Health; (b) any waiver of a provision of the TRIPS Agreement granted by WTO Members; or (c) any amendment of the TRIPS Agreement.[1210]

[4]   Article 20.49. Biologics

New pharmaceutical products that contain a biologic particle must provide effective market protection for at least ten years from the date of first marketing approval of that product in that Party.[1211]

This applies at a minimum to products that are made using biotechnology processes or contain a virus, therapeutic serum, toxin, antitoxin, vaccine, blood, blood component or derivative, allergenic product, protein, or an analogous product, for use in human beings for the prevention, treatment, or cure of a disease or condition.[1212]

[5]   Article 20.50. Definition of New Pharmaceutical Product

These are pharmaceutical products that do not contain a chemical entity that has been previously approved in that Party.[1213]

[6]   Article 20.51. Measures Relating to the Marketing of Certain
Pharmaceutical Products

If a Party allows persons other than the original submitter of safety and efficacy information to rely on the submitter's evidence, the Party must provide notice to the patent holder.[1214] The must provide time for the patent holder to seek remedies, and they must provide procedures (hearings, injunctions, etc.) for the timely resolution of disputes.[1215]

1209. *See* United States-Mexico-Canada Agreement, Section 20.48, Jan. 29, 2020.
1210. *See* United States-Mexico-Canada Agreement, Section 20.48, Jan. 29, 2020.
1211. *See* United States-Mexico-Canada Agreement, Section 20.49, Jan. 29, 2020.
1212. *See* United States-Mexico-Canada Agreement, Section 20.49, Jan. 29, 2020.
1213. *See* United States-Mexico-Canada Agreement, Section 20.50, Jan. 29, 2020.
1214. *See* United States-Mexico-Canada Agreement, Section 20.51, Jan. 29, 2020.
1215. *See* United States-Mexico-Canada Agreement, Section 20.51, Jan. 29, 2020.

As an alternative, Parties must instead have a system in place based on patent-related information that precludes the use of the patent holder's information by a third party unless by consent or acquiescence of the patent holder.[1216]

[7]   Article 20.52. Alteration of Period of Protection

Subject to Article 20.48.3 (Protection of Undisclosed Test or Other Data), if a product is subject to a system of marketing approval and is also covered by a patent in the territory of that Party, that Party shall not alter the period of protection that it provides.[1217]

§20.7   SECTION G: INDUSTRIAL DESIGNS

[A]   Article 20.53. Protection

Parties must ensure adequate and effective protection of industrial designs consistent with TRIPS Articles 25 and 26.[1218]

[B]   Article 20.54. Non-Prejudicial Disclosures/Grace Period

Parties must disregard public disclosure information if the disclosure was made by the design applicant or someone who obtained their information from the applicant, and the public disclosure occurred within twelve months prior to the filing date in the territory of the Party.[1219]

[C]   Article 20.55. Electronic Industrial Design System

Parties must have a system for people to electronically apply for industrial design rights and must maintain a public online database of protected industrial designs.[1220]

[D]   Article 20.56. Term of Protection

Must be at least ten years from either the date of filing or the date of grant or registration.[1221]

1216. *See* United States-Mexico-Canada Agreement, Section 20.51, Jan. 29, 2020.
1217. *See* United States-Mexico-Canada Agreement, Section 20.52, Jan. 29, 2020.
1218. *See* United States-Mexico-Canada Agreement, Section 20.53, Jan. 29, 2020.
1219. *See* United States-Mexico-Canada Agreement, Section 20.54, Jan. 29, 2020.
1220. *See* United States-Mexico-Canada Agreement, Section 20.55, Jan. 29, 2020.
1221. *See* United States-Mexico-Canada Agreement, Section 20.56, Jan. 29, 2020.

§20.8 SECTION H: COPYRIGHT AND RELATED RIGHTS

[A] Article 20.58. Right of Reproduction

Parties must give creators of phonograms the exclusive right to authorize or prohibit all reproduction of their works, performances, or phonograms in any manner or form, including in electronic form.[1222]

[B] Article 20.59. Right of Communication to the Public

Creators must create the exclusive right to authorize or prohibit communication to the public of their works, by wire or wireless means.[1223]

[C] Article 20.60. Right of Distribution

Creators must have the exclusive right to publication, copying, and distribution of their works through sales and transfers.[1224]

[D] Article 20.61. No Hierarchy

When authorization is needed from the author and a performer or producer that owns the rights of a phonogram, both authorizations are absolutely necessary.[1225]

[E] Article 20.62. Related Rights

In addition to National Treatment protection (Art. 20.8), Parties should accord the rights provided for in this chapter to performances and phonograms first published or first fixed (finalized) in the territory of another Party.[1226]
First published: published in the territory of that Party within thirty days of its original publication.[1227]
Performers can exclusively control the broadcasting and communication of their unfixed performances unless it is already a broadcast performance.[1228] Parties must allow performers the exclusive right to control the fixation of their unfixed performances.[1229]
Other than some limitations and exceptions (Art 20.65), the right referred to limit or make available communications to the public through analog transmissions and

---

1222. *See* United States-Mexico-Canada Agreement, Section 20.58, Jan. 29, 2020.
1223. *See* United States-Mexico-Canada Agreement, Section 20.59, Jan. 29, 2020.
1224. *See* United States-Mexico-Canada Agreement, Section 20.60, Jan. 29, 2020.
1225. *See* United States-Mexico-Canada Agreement, Section 20.61, Jan. 29, 2020.
1226. *See* United States-Mexico-Canada Agreement, Section 20.62, Jan. 29, 2020.
1227. *See* United States-Mexico-Canada Agreement, Section 20.62, Jan. 29, 2020.
1228. *See* United States-Mexico-Canada Agreement, Section 20.62, Jan. 29, 2020.
1229. *See* United States-Mexico-Canada Agreement, Section 20.62, Jan. 29, 2020.

non-interactive free over-the-air broadcasts, and exceptions or limitations to this right for those activities is a matter of each Party's law.[1230]

[F]   Article 20.63. Term of Protection for Copyright and Related Rights

The term must be for at least seventy years after the author's death or at least seventy-five years from the end of the calendar year of the first authorized publication or if the creation is not publicized with authorization within twenty-five years of its making, at least seventy years from the end of the calendar year of its making.[1231]

[G]   Article 20.64. Application of Article 18 of the Berne Convention and Article 14.6 of the TRIPS Agreement

These articles must be applied m*utatis mutandis* to works, performances, and phono-grams, and the rights and protections afforded to that subject matter as required by this section.[1232]

[H]   Article 20.65. Limitations and Exceptions

Limitations must be confined to certain special cases that do not conflict with a normal exploitation of creations and do not unreasonably prejudice the legitimate interests of the right holder.[1233]

    This Article does not reduce or extend the scope of applicability of the limitations and exceptions permitted by the Trade-Related Intellectual Property Rights (TRIPS) Agreement, the Berne Convention, the WCT, or the WPPT.[1234]

[I]   Article 20.66. Contractual Transfers

Copyright and related rights must be freely and separately transferable, and holders of these rights must be able to exercise that right in that person's own name and enjoy fully the benefits derived from that right.[1235]

    Parties can still provide reasonable limits to protect the interests of the original right holders. They can also establish which specific contractions result in the transfer of economic rights.[1236]

1230. *See* United States-Mexico-Canada Agreement, Section 20.62, Jan. 29, 2020.
1231. *See* United States-Mexico-Canada Agreement, Section 20.63, Jan. 29, 2020.
1232. *See* United States-Mexico-Canada Agreement, Section 20.64, Jan. 29, 2020.
1233. *See* United States-Mexico-Canada Agreement, Section 20.65, Jan. 29, 2020.
1234. *See* United States-Mexico-Canada Agreement, Section 20.65, Jan. 29, 2020.
1235. *See* United States-Mexico-Canada Agreement, Section 20.66, Jan. 29, 2020.
1236. *See* United States-Mexico-Canada Agreement, Section 20.66, Jan. 29, 2020.

[J] Article 20.67. Technological Protection Measures

Parties must hold liable people that knew or reasonably should have known, yet circumvented without authority an effective technological measure (technology, device, or component that, in the normal course of its operation, controls access to a protected work, performance, or phonogram, or protects copyright or rights related to copyright) that controls access to a protected work, performance, or phonogram.[1237] Liability must also be in place for those who manufactured, imported, distributed, offered for sale or rental to the public, or otherwise provided devices, products, or components, or offers to the public or provided services, that: (i) were promoted, advertised, or otherwise marketed by that person for the purpose of circumvention; (ii) had only a limited commercially significant purpose or use other than circumvention; or (iii) were primarily designed, produced, or performed for the purpose of circumvention.[1238]

Criminal procedures and penalties must be in place for willful circumvention for the purpose of commercial advantage or financial gain (exceptions for non-profit, libraries, archives, educational institutions, or public non-commercial broadcasting entities.).[1239]

Parties are not obligated to require that electronics or telecommunications products provide a response to any particular technological measure.[1240]

Any violation under this Article is a separate cause of action from any infringement action.[1241]

Exceptions to measures implementing liability are limited.[1242]

[K] Article 20.68. Rights Management Information (RMI)

RMI: information that identifies a work, performance, or phonogram, the author of the work, the performer of the performance, or the producer of the phonogram or the owner of a right in the work, performance, or phonogram or information about the terms and conditions of the use of the work, performance, or phonogram or any numbers or codes that represent this information.[1243]

Parties should hold liable any person who, without authority, knew or should have known that it would induce, enable, facilitate, or conceal an infringement of the copyright or related right of creators: removed or altered any RMI; distributed or imported for distribution RMI knowing that the RMI was altered without authority; or distributed, imported for distribution, broadcasted, communicated, or made available

---

1237. *See* United States-Mexico-Canada Agreement, Section 20.67, Jan. 29, 2020.
1238. *See* United States-Mexico-Canada Agreement, Section 20.67, Jan. 29, 2020.
1239. *See* United States-Mexico-Canada Agreement, Section 20.67, Jan. 29, 2020.
1240. *See* United States-Mexico-Canada Agreement, Section 20.67, Jan. 29, 2020.
1241. *See* United States-Mexico-Canada Agreement, Section 20.67, Jan. 29, 2020.
1242. *See* United States-Mexico-Canada Agreement, Section 20.67, Jan. 29, 2020.
1243. *See* United States-Mexico-Canada Agreement, Section 20.68, Jan. 29, 2020.

to the public copies of works, performances, or phonograms, knowing that RMI was removed or altered without authority.[1244]

If a person has done the above in order to gain commercial advantage or financial gain, they must be subject to criminal procedures and penalties.[1245] These procedures or penalties do not have to apply to a non-profit library, museum, archive, educational institution or public non-commercial broadcasting entity.[1246]

Right holders are not required to attach RMI to copies of their creations.[1247]

[L]   Article 20.69. Collective Management

Collective management societies are important for copyright and related rights in collecting and distributing royalties based on practices that are fair, efficient, transparent, and accountable.[1248]

§20.9   SECTION I: TRADE SECRETS

[A]   Article 20.70. Protection of Trade Secrets

In order to fight against unfair competition, Parties must instill legal means to prevent the non-consensual disclosure, acquisition, or use of others (including state-owned enterprises).[1249]

[B]   Article 20.71. Civil Protection and Enforcement

Parties must provide civil judicial procedures for people lawfully in control of a trade secret to hold liable those that misappropriate the trade secret.[1250] The duration of trade secret protection must be unlimited, so long as the conditions that define a trade secret exist.[1251]

[C]   Article 20.72. Criminal Enforcement

Parties must provide criminal procedures and penalties for unauthorized and willful misappropriations of trade secrets.[1252] However, these procedures or penalties may be limited to one or more cases where the act is: (a) for commercial purposes or financial

---

1244. *See* United States-Mexico-Canada Agreement, Section 20.68, Jan. 29, 2020.
1245. *See* United States-Mexico-Canada Agreement, Section 20.68, Jan. 29, 2020.
1246. *See* United States-Mexico-Canada Agreement, Section 20.68, Jan. 29, 2020.
1247. *See* United States-Mexico-Canada Agreement, Section 20.68, Jan. 29, 2020.
1248. *See* United States-Mexico-Canada Agreement, Section 20.69, Jan. 29, 2020.
1249. *See* United States-Mexico-Canada Agreement, Section 20.70, Jan. 29, 2020.
1250. *See* United States-Mexico-Canada Agreement, Section 20.71, Jan. 29, 2020.
1251. *See* United States-Mexico-Canada Agreement, Section 20.71, Jan. 29, 2020.
1252. *See* United States-Mexico-Canada Agreement, Section 20.72, Jan. 29, 2020.

gain; (b) related to a product or service in national or international commerce; or (c) intended to injure the trade secret owner.[1253]

[D]   Article 20.73. Definitions

Trade secret:

> (a) secret information in the sense that it is not generally known among or readily accessible to persons within the circles that normally deal with the kind of information in question; (b) has actual or potential commercial value because it is secret; and (c) has been subject to reasonable steps under the circumstances, by the person lawfully in control of the information, to keep it secret.[1254]

Misappropriation: the acquisition, use, or disclosure of a trade secret in a manner contrary to honest commercial practices—including by a third party that knew or had reason to know, that the trade secret was acquired in a manner contrary to honest commercial practices.[1255]

Not misappropriation: reverse engineering a lawfully obtained item, independently discovering information claimed as a trade secret; or acquiring the subject information from another person in a legitimate manner without an obligation of confidentiality or knowledge that the information was a trade secret.[1256]

Manner contrary to honest commercial practices: breach of contract, breach of confidence, inducement to breach, acquisition of undisclosed information by third parties that knew, or were grossly negligent in failing to know, that those practices were involved in the acquisition.[1257]

[E]   Article 20.74. Provisional Measures

Parties must provide its judicial authorities with the power to order prompt and effective provisional measures.[1258]

[F]   Article 20.75. Confidentiality

The judicial authority must have the power to order specific procedures to protect the confidentiality of an alleged or existing trade secret or any other asserted confidential information.[1259]

Parties must sanction those responsible for violations of orders concerning this information.[1260]

1253. *See* United States-Mexico-Canada Agreement, Section 20.72, Jan. 29, 2020.
1254. *See* United States-Mexico-Canada Agreement, Section 20.73, Jan. 29, 2020.
1255. *See* United States-Mexico-Canada Agreement, Section 20.73, Jan. 29, 2020.
1256. *See* United States-Mexico-Canada Agreement, Section 20.73, Jan. 29, 2020.
1257. *See* United States-Mexico-Canada Agreement, Section 20.73, Jan. 29, 2020.
1258. *See* United States-Mexico-Canada Agreement, Section 20.74, Jan. 29, 2020.
1259. *See* United States-Mexico-Canada Agreement, Section 20.75, Jan. 29, 2020.
1260. *See* United States-Mexico-Canada Agreement, Section 20.75, Jan. 29, 2020.

Parties must allow people to make a submission under seal describing the interest in keeping information confidential before judicial authorities can disclose a trade secret.[1261]

[G]   Article 20.76. Civil Remedies

Authorities in each territory must be able to order injunctive relief and/or damages that compensate the lawful holder of a trade secret for the injury suffered due to the misappropriation of that secret.[1262] They should be able to impose attorney fees as well.[1263]

[H]   Article 20.77. Licensing and Transfer of Trade Secrets

Parties cannot dilute the value of or impose excessive or discriminatory conditions on the voluntary licensing of trade secrets.[1264]

[I]   Article 20.78. Prohibition of Unauthorized Disclosure or Use of a Trade Secret by Government Officials Outside the Scope of Their Official Duties

Each Party must prohibit unauthorized exposure of trade secrets by central government officials that are not within the scope of the official's duties.[1265]

In order to deter this behavior, penalties must be imposed, such as fines, suspension, termination of employment, or imprisonment.[1266]

§20.10   SECTION J: ENFORCEMENT

[A]   Article 20.79. General Obligations

Generally, Parties need to have enforcement mechanisms in place to remedy and deter infringement.[1267] These mechanisms must be fair, equitable, and applied in a manner that creates barriers to trade.[1268] Parties must enforce this chapter in a way that takes into account the seriousness of the infringement, the applicable remedies, and third-party interests.[1269]

1261. *See* United States-Mexico-Canada Agreement, Section 20.75, Jan. 29, 2020.
1262. *See* United States-Mexico-Canada Agreement, Section 20.76, Jan. 29, 2020.
1263. *See* United States-Mexico-Canada Agreement, Section 20.76, Jan. 29, 2020.
1264. *See* United States-Mexico-Canada Agreement, Section 20.77, Jan. 29, 2020.
1265. *See* United States-Mexico-Canada Agreement, Section 20.78, Jan. 29, 2020.
1266. *See* United States-Mexico-Canada Agreement, Section 20.78, Jan. 29, 2020.
1267. *See* United States-Mexico-Canada Agreement, Section 20.79, Jan. 29, 2020.
1268. *See* United States-Mexico-Canada Agreement, Section 20.79, Jan. 29, 2020.
1269. *See* United States-Mexico-Canada Agreement, Section 20.79, Jan. 29, 2020.

The enforcement procedures set forth in this chapter (Articles 20.82, 20.83, and 20.85) must be available to the same extent with regard to trademark infringement, copyright infringement, or related rights infringement in the digital market.[1270]

Parties do not have to create a new judicial system for IP rights or change the distribution of resources allocated to the enforcement of the law in general and the enforcement of IP rights, separately.[1271]

[B]   Article 20.80. Presumptions

It is presumed that the designated right holder of a creation is the person whose name is indicated in the usual manner (defined by a Party) as the creator or, in some cases, publisher of the creation.[1272]

For the purpose of proceedings, trademarks and each claim in a patent are prima facie valid.[1273]

[C]   Article 20.81. Enforcement Practices with Respect to Intellectual Property Rights

Final decisions and rulings related to the general enforcement of IP rights must be in writing, state findings of fact and reasoning or the legal basis on which they are made.[1274] They must be published or made otherwise available.[1275]

[D]   Article 20.82. Civil and Administrative Procedures and Remedies

Civil judicial procedures concerning IP rights must be made available to right holders.[1276]

Parties must allow its judicial authorities to order injunctions—including those to prevent infringing goods from entering channels of commerce.[1277] They must also be able to order the infringer to pay damages to compensate for the infringement-related injury.[1278] They must be able to consider, among other things, any legitimate measure of value that a right holder submits (including lost profits and market or suggested retail price).[1279]

1270. *See* United States-Mexico-Canada Agreement, Section 20.79, Jan. 29, 2020.
1271. *See* United States-Mexico-Canada Agreement, Section 20.79, Jan. 29, 2020.
1272. *See* United States-Mexico-Canada Agreement, Section 20.80, Jan. 29, 2020.
1273. *See* United States-Mexico-Canada Agreement, Section 20.80, Jan. 29, 2020.
1274. *See* United States-Mexico-Canada Agreement, Section 20.81, Jan. 29, 2020.
1275. *See* United States-Mexico-Canada Agreement, Section 20.81, Jan. 29, 2020.
1276. *See* United States-Mexico-Canada Agreement, Section 20.82, Jan. 29, 2020.
1277. *See* United States-Mexico-Canada Agreement, Section 20.82, Jan. 29, 2020.
1278. *See* United States-Mexico-Canada Agreement, Section 20.82, Jan. 29, 2020.
1279. *See* United States-Mexico-Canada Agreement, Section 20.82, Jan. 29, 2020.

For copyright or related rights infringement and trademark counterfeiting, judicial authorities must be able to order the infringer to pay the right holder the infringer's profits that are attributable to the infringement.[1280]

For copyright or related rights infringement and trademark counterfeiting, Parties must have a system in place that provides pre-established damages and/or additional damages (e.g., exemplary/punitive damages).[1281]

Pre-established damages must be sufficient to deter future infringements and fully compensate the right holder.[1282]

Additional damages must be available when authorities consider appropriate—taking into account the nature of the infringement and the need to deter similar infringements.[1283]

Judicial authorities must have the authority to order payment of court and attorney's fees and expenses by the losing party.[1284]

If expert testimony is appointed and Parties must pay for the expert, Parties must ensure that the costs are reasonable and appropriate to the quantity and nature of the work performed.[1285]

At the request of a right holder, judicial authorities must be able to order that pirated and counterfeit goods be destroyed without compensation to the infringer.[1286] They can also order that materials and implements used to create the infringing goods be destroyed without compensation.[1287] Removal of a trademark unlawfully affixed is not sufficient, other than in exceptional circumstances, to permit the release of goods into the channels of commerce.[1288]

Judicial authorities must be able to order an (alleged) infringer to provide to them or the right holder, relevant information that the infringer possesses or controls.[1289] This includes information relating to any person involved in any aspect of the (alleged) infringement and the means of production or the channels of distribution.[1290] If refused without good reason, judicial authorities must be able to make determinations on the basis of the evidence presented.[1291]

Judicial authorities must be able to sanction a requesting Party that abused enforcement procedures by making that requesting Party compensate the Party wrongfully enjoyed or restrained.[1292] They may have to pay the defendant's expenses.[1293]

1280. *See* United States-Mexico-Canada Agreement, Section 20.82, Jan. 29, 2020.
1281. *See* United States-Mexico-Canada Agreement, Section 20.82, Jan. 29, 2020.
1282. *See* United States-Mexico-Canada Agreement, Section 20.82, Jan. 29, 2020.
1283. *See* United States-Mexico-Canada Agreement, Section 20.82, Jan. 29, 2020.
1284. *See* United States-Mexico-Canada Agreement, Section 20.82, Jan. 29, 2020.
1285. *See* United States-Mexico-Canada Agreement, Section 20.82, Jan. 29, 2020.
1286. *See* United States-Mexico-Canada Agreement, Section 20.82, Jan. 29, 2020.
1287. *See* United States-Mexico-Canada Agreement, Section 20.82, Jan. 29, 2020.
1288. *See* United States-Mexico-Canada Agreement, Section 20.82, Jan. 29, 2020.
1289. *See* United States-Mexico-Canada Agreement, Section 20.82, Jan. 29, 2020.
1290. *See* United States-Mexico-Canada Agreement, Section 20.82, Jan. 29, 2020.
1291. *See* United States-Mexico-Canada Agreement, Section 20.82, Jan. 29, 2020.
1292. *See* United States-Mexico-Canada Agreement, Section 20.82, Jan. 29, 2020.
1293. *See* United States-Mexico-Canada Agreement, Section 20.82, Jan. 29, 2020.

Sanctions must be available for violations of judicial orders by party, counsel, expert or other persons subject to the court's jurisdiction.[1294]

For Technological Protection Measure and RMI-related proceedings, Parties must allow their judicial authorities to seize devices and products suspected of being involved, order damages similar to those for copyright infringement, order court costs, fees or expenses, and order the destruction of devices and products *found* to be involved in the prohibited activity.[1295]

Again, Parties may make exceptions for a non-profit library, museum, archive, educational institution, or public non-commercial broadcasting entity if it sustains the burden of proving that it was not aware or had no reason to believe that its acts constituted a prohibited activity.[1296]

[E] Article 20.83. Provisional Measures

Parties must act on a request for relief, expeditiously and without notice to the other side, in accordance with the Party's judicial rules.[1297]

Parties must allow its authorities to require applicants for a provisional measure to provide reasonably available evidence that demonstrates with a sufficient degree of certainty that the applicant's right is being infringed upon or infringement is imminent.[1298] They must be able to order the applicant to provide security to protect the defendant and prevent abuse without deterring recourse to these proceedings.[1299]

Authorities must be able to seize suspected infringing, goods and materials, and trademark counterfeits, documentary evidence relevant to the infringement.[1300]

[F] Article 20.84. Special Requirements Related to Border Measures

Parties must allow applications to suspend the release of or to detain suspected counterfeits, confusingly similar trademarks, or pirated copyright goods that are imported.[1301] Right holders must, in its application, provide adequate evidence to prove that there is a prima facie infringement and give the authorities enough information to make the suspect goods recognizable.[1302]

Parties must allow its authorities to require an applicant to give reasonable security or assurance to protect the defendant and prevent abuse in a way that does not deter recourse.[1303] This can be a conditional bond to hold the defendant harmless from

---

1294. *See* United States-Mexico-Canada Agreement, Section 20.82, Jan. 29, 2020.
1295. *See* United States-Mexico-Canada Agreement, Section 20.82, Jan. 29, 2020.
1296. *See* United States-Mexico-Canada Agreement, Section 20.82, Jan. 29, 2020.
1297. *See* United States-Mexico-Canada Agreement, Section 20.83, Jan. 29, 2020.
1298. *See* United States-Mexico-Canada Agreement, Section 20.83, Jan. 29, 2020.
1299. *See* United States-Mexico-Canada Agreement, Section 20.83, Jan. 29, 2020.
1300. *See* United States-Mexico-Canada Agreement, Section 20.83, Jan. 29, 2020.
1301. *See* United States-Mexico-Canada Agreement, Section 20.84, Jan. 29, 2020.
1302. *See* United States-Mexico-Canada Agreement, Section 20.84, Jan. 29, 2020.
1303. *See* United States-Mexico-Canada Agreement, Section 20.84, Jan. 29, 2020.

the loss or damage resulting from the suspension of the release of goods in the event authorities determine the good is not infringing.[1304]

Parties may allow their authorities to immediately provide a right holder with the names and addresses of the consignor, exporter, consignee, or importer; a description of the goods; the quantity of the goods; and the country of origin of the goods.[1305] If Parties do not allow this, they must allow, at least with imported goods, the authorities to provide this information within thirty working days of seizure or determination that the goods are counterfeit or pirated.[1306]

These provisions apply to suspected infringing goods that are imported, destined for export, in transit and admitted into or exiting from a free trade zone or a bonded warehouse.[1307]

Parties may exchange information with other Parties about goods it has examined in order to help that other Party identify suspect goods.[1308]

When infringing goods are not destroyed, Parties must ensure that they are disposed of outside the channels of commerce in a manner that will avoid harm to the right holder.[1309]

Any application, storage or destruction fees shall not unreasonably deter recourse.[1310]

Small quantities of goods of a non-commercial nature in a traveler's personal luggage may be excluded from the application of this article.[1311]

[G]   Article 20.85. Criminal Procedures and Penalties

For violations or infringements on a commercial scale, criminal procedures and penalties must be applied.[1312] This includes acts carried out for commercial advantage or financial gain and significant acts that have a substantial prejudicial impact on the interests of the copyright or related rights holder in relation to the marketplace.[1313]

Willful importation or exportation of counterfeit or pirated goods on a commercial scale is grounds for a criminal penalty.[1314]

For labels and packaging to which a trademark has been applied without authorization or that is identical or indistinguishable from a registered trademark *and* is intended to be used in the course of trade in ways that are identical to the registered trademark, Parties must provide criminal procedures and penalties for those that willfully import or domestically use the goods on a commercial scale.[1315]

1304. *See* United States-Mexico-Canada Agreement, Section 20.84, Jan. 29, 2020.
1305. *See* United States-Mexico-Canada Agreement, Section 20.84, Jan. 29, 2020.
1306. *See* United States-Mexico-Canada Agreement, Section 20.84, Jan. 29, 2020.
1307. *See* United States-Mexico-Canada Agreement, Section 20.84, Jan. 29, 2020.
1308. *See* United States-Mexico-Canada Agreement, Section 20.84, Jan. 29, 2020.
1309. *See* United States-Mexico-Canada Agreement, Section 20.84, Jan. 29, 2020.
1310. *See* United States-Mexico-Canada Agreement, Section 20.84, Jan. 29, 2020.
1311. *See* United States-Mexico-Canada Agreement, Section 20.84, Jan. 29, 2020.
1312. *See* United States-Mexico-Canada Agreement, Section 20.85, Jan. 29, 2020.
1313. *See* United States-Mexico-Canada Agreement, Section 20.85, Jan. 29, 2020.
1314. *See* United States-Mexico-Canada Agreement, Section 20.85, Jan. 29, 2020.
1315. *See* United States-Mexico-Canada Agreement, Section 20.85, Jan. 29, 2020.

For cinematographic work, criminal procedures must be applied to those who willfully and without authorization knowingly use or attempt to use a recording device to transmit or make a copy in a movie theater or other venue used for the exhibition of a copyrighted motion picture.[1316]

There must be criminal liability for aiding and abetting any of these activities.[1317]

Penalties must include imprisonment and sufficiently deterrent monetary fines.[1318] Judicial authorities must be able to account for the seriousness of the circumstances when determining penalties.[1319] They must be able to order the seizure of goods, documentary evidence, and assets derived from the alleged infringing activity.[1320] They must be able to order forfeiture or destruction of all counterfeit or pirated goods and the materials used in their creation, as well as any other labels or packaging, to which counterfeit trademark is affixed and that have been used in the commission of the offense.[1321]

[H] Article 20.86. Protection of Encrypted Program-Carrying Satellite and Cable Signals

It must be a criminal offense in each territory to:

(a) manufacture, assemble, modify, import, export, sell, or otherwise distribute a device or system knowing or having reason to know that the device or system (i) it is intended to be used to assist, or (ii) it is primarily of assistance, in decoding an encrypted program-carrying satellite signal without the authorization of the lawful distributor of that signal; and (b) with respect to an encrypted program-carrying satellite signal, willfully: (i) receive that signal, or (ii) further distribute that signal, knowing that it has been decoded without the authorization of the lawful distributor of the signal.[1322]

Civil remedies must be in place for persons that hold an interest in an encrypted program-carrying satellite signal or its content, and that is injured by the above activity.[1323]

Criminal penalties and civil remedies must be available for willful manufacturing or distributing equipment knowing that the equipment is intended to be used in the unauthorized reception of any encrypted program-carrying cable signal; and receiving, or assisting another to receive, an encrypted program-carrying cable signal without authorization of the lawful distributor of the signal.[1324]

1316. *See* United States-Mexico-Canada Agreement, Section 20.85, Jan. 29, 2020.
1317. *See* United States-Mexico-Canada Agreement, Section 20.85, Jan. 29, 2020.
1318. *See* United States-Mexico-Canada Agreement, Section 20.85, Jan. 29, 2020.
1319. *See* United States-Mexico-Canada Agreement, Section 20.85, Jan. 29, 2020.
1320. *See* United States-Mexico-Canada Agreement, Section 20.85, Jan. 29, 2020.
1321. *See* United States-Mexico-Canada Agreement, Section 20.85, Jan. 29, 2020.
1322. *See* United States-Mexico-Canada Agreement, Section 20.86, Jan. 29, 2020.
1323. *See* United States-Mexico-Canada Agreement, Section 20.86, Jan. 29, 2020.
1324. *See* United States-Mexico-Canada Agreement, Section 20.86, Jan. 29, 2020.

[I] Article 20.87. Government Use of Software

Parties must have laws or guidelines in place that provide its central government agencies use only non-infringing computer software and, if applicable, only use that computer software in a manner authorized by the relevant license.[1325]

[J] Article 20.88. Internet Service Providers

These are providers of services for the transmission, routing, or providing of connections for digital online communications without modification of their content, between or among points specified by a user, of the material of the user's choosing, undertaking the function of transmitting, routing, or providing connections for material without modification of its content or the intermediate and transient storage of that material done automatically in the course of such a technical process.[1326]

They are also providers of online services that perform caching carried out through an automated process; store, at the direction of a user, of material residing on a system or network controlled or operated by or for the Internet Service Provider (ISPs); or refer or link users to an online location by using information location tools.[1327]

[K] Article 20.89. Legal Remedies and Safe Harbors

There must be safe harbors in respect of online services that are ISPs that include legal incentives for ISPs to cooperate with copyright owners or take other actions to deter the unauthorized storage and transmission of copyrighted materials.[1328]

There must be safe harbors that limit the effect of precluding monetary relief against ISPs for copyright infringements that they do not control, initiate or direct, and that take place through systems or networks controlled or operated by them or on their behalf.[1329]

Parties must require ISPs to expeditiously remove or disable access to material residing on their networks or systems upon obtaining actual knowledge of the copyright infringement or becoming aware of facts or circumstances from which the infringement is apparent.[1330] If they do so, they must be exempt from any liability for having done so, provided that it takes reasonable steps in advance or promptly after to notify the person whose material is removed or disabled.[1331]

Parties must provide a framework for effective notices of claimed infringement and effective counter-notices by those whose material is removed or disabled through

1325. *See* United States-Mexico-Canada Agreement, Section 20.87, Jan. 29, 2020.
1326. *See* United States-Mexico-Canada Agreement, Section 20.88, Jan. 29, 2020.
1327. *See* United States-Mexico-Canada Agreement, Section 20.88, Jan. 29, 2020.
1328. *See* United States-Mexico-Canada Agreement, Section 20.89, Jan. 29, 2020.
1329. *See* United States-Mexico-Canada Agreement, Section 20.89, Jan. 29, 2020.
1330. *See* United States-Mexico-Canada Agreement, Section 20.89, Jan. 29, 2020.
1331. *See* United States-Mexico-Canada Agreement, Section 20.89, Jan. 29, 2020.

mistake or misidentification.[1332] Material misrepresentations in any of these notices must be subject to monetary remedy.[1333]

Eligibility for limitations cannot be conditioned on the ISP monitoring its service or affirmatively seeking facts indicating infringing activity, except that ISPs cannot interfere with standard technical measures accepted in the Party's territory that protect and identify copyrighted material.[1334]

Failure to qualify for limitations precluding monetary relief for defendants does not itself result in liability.[1335]

§20.11   SECTION K: FINAL PROVISIONS

[A]   Article 20.90. Final Provisions

All provisions must be implemented on the USMCA's effective date—except those in Article 20.10 (Application of Chapter to Existing Subject Matter and Prior Acts) and in the charts below.[1336]

During transition periods, Parties cannot amend or adopt measures that are less consistent with their obligation under the USMCA.[1337]

Starting on the USMCA's effective date, **Mexico** must fully implement within:[1338]

Three years	Article 20.88 (Internet Service Providers)
	Article 20.89 (Legal Remedies and Safe Harbors),
Four years	Article 20.7 (International Agreements)
	UPOV 1991
Four and a half years	Article 20.46 (Patent Term Adjustment for Unreasonable Curtailment)
Five years	Article 20.45 (Protection of Undisclosed Test or Other Data for Agricultural Chemical Products)
	Article 20.48 (Protection of Undisclosed Test or Other Data
	Article 20.49 (Biologics)
	Article 20.71 (Civil Protection and Enforcement)
	Article 20.74 (Provisional Measures)
	Article 20.76 (Civil Remedies)

1332. *See* United States-Mexico-Canada Agreement, Section 20.89, Jan. 29, 2020.
1333. *See* United States-Mexico-Canada Agreement, Section 20.89, Jan. 29, 2020.
1334. *See* United States-Mexico-Canada Agreement, Section 20.89, Jan. 29, 2020.
1335. *See* United States-Mexico-Canada Agreement, Section 20.89, Jan. 29, 2020.
1336. *See* United States-Mexico-Canada Agreement, Section 20.90, Jan. 29, 2020.
1337. *See* United States-Mexico-Canada Agreement, Section 20.90, Jan. 29, 2020.
1338. *See* United States-Mexico-Canada Agreement, Section 20.90, Jan. 29, 2020.

Starting on the USMCA's effective date, **Canada** must fully implement within:[1339]

Two and a half years	Article 20.63(a) (Term of Protection for Copyright and Related Rights)
Four years	Article 20.7.2(f) (International Agreements)
Four and a half years	Article 20.44 (Patent Term Adjustment for Unreasonable Granting Authority Delays)
Five years	Article 20.49 (Biologics)

Annex 20-A Annex to Section J

Legal remedies and safe harbor do not apply to a Party that, from the effective date of the USMCA, prescribes in its law circumstances under which ISPs do not qualify for the limitations, provides statutory secondary liability for copyright infringement in cases in which a person, by means of the Internet or another digital network, provides a service primarily for the purpose of enabling acts of copyright infringement.[1340] The Party must also require ISPs to participate in a system for forwarding notices of alleged infringement and induce them to offer information location tools to remove within a specified period of time any reproductions.[1341] They must also induce ISPs to remove or disable access to material upon becoming aware of a decision of a court of that Party to the effect that the person storing the material infringes copyright in the material.[1342]

1339. *See* United States-Mexico-Canada Agreement, Section 20.90, Jan. 29, 2020.
1340. *See* United States-Mexico-Canada Agreement, Annex 20-A, Jan. 29, 2020.
1341. *See* United States-Mexico-Canada Agreement, Annex 20-A, Jan. 29, 2020.
1342. *See* United States-Mexico-Canada Agreement, Annex 20-A, Jan. 29, 2020.

CHAPTER 21
Competition Policy

The Parties in the NAFTA agreement, USA, Canada, and Mexico, have agreed to combat anticompetitive business behavior in its territories. However, Parties may allow exemptions based on public policy. To enforce these laws, the Parties must maintain that they will treat all persons equally. There are several new policies in the USMCA that aren't in NAFTA. The first policy is enforcement proceeding, in which judicial or administrative proceeding following an investigation into the alleged violation of the national competition laws. The next is timeliness, which states that national competition authorities must be transparent of competition laws and procedural rules in investigations and enforcement proceedings. The next policy is confidentiality, where Parties must ensure that its authorities do not disclose confidential or privileged information. Finally, there is the burden of proof policy, which states that the authorities have the burden of proof in establishing the legal and factual basis for an allegation, but the Parties can require that the alleged violator establish certain defenses. The Parties also recognize how important it is to cooperate to combat commercial practices that hinder market efficiency and reduce consumer welfare within the free trade area. Furthermore, the Parties must maintain and enforce consumer protection laws and other laws that forbid fraudulent and deceptive commercial activities. To increase transparency, Parties must agree to make available, when requested, its national competition law enforcement law and policy. If requested by another Party, a Party must enter into consultations and must give "full and sympathetic consideration to the concerns of the other Party."

Compare this chapter with Chapter 15 in NAFTA.[1343]

Chapter 15 of NAFTA address monopolies and state enterprises.[1344]

Here, monopolies and state enterprises are not mentioned by name.[1345]

1343. *See* North American Free Trade Agreement, Chapter 15, Jan. 1, 1994; *see also* United States-Mexico-Canada Agreement, Chapter 21, Jan. 29, 2020.

1344. *See* North American Free Trade Agreement, Chapter 15, Jan. 1, 1994.

1345. *See* United States-Mexico-Canada Agreement, Chapter 21, Jan. 29, 2020.

§21.1   ARTICLE 21.1. COMPETITION LAW AND AUTHORITIES

Parties agree to maintain law to combat anticompetitive business behavior in all commercial activities in its territory.[1346] They may still apply the law to commercial activities outside of its territory when there is an "appropriate nexus to its jurisdiction."[1347] "Appropriate nexus" is not defined and is, thus, open to interpretation.[1348] Parties may allow exemptions based on public interest or public policy.[1349]

In order to enforce these laws, Parties must maintain national competition authorities that will treat persons equally, consider the effects of their enforcement activities on other Parties and limit remedies relating to conduct or assets outside of the Party's territory to situations where there is a nexus to the harm that affects the Party's territory or commerce.[1350]

§21.2   ARTICLE 21.2. PROCEDURAL FAIRNESS IN COMPETITION LAW ENFORCEMENT

This concept is new to USMCA, and was not mentioned at all in NAFTA:

> *Enforcement proceeding*: judicial or administrative proceedings are provided for following an investigation into the alleged violation of the national competition laws (excludes: matters occurring before a grand jury).[1351]
> *Timeliness*: national competition authorities ("authorities") must be transparent with how they apply competition laws and procedural rules in investigations and enforcement proceedings. They must conduct the investigations subject to definitive deadlines or within a reasonable time.[1352]
> Authorities must allow representation by legal counsel and, in the case of mergers, must permit early consultations between the authority and the merging persons to provide their view and concerns before the authority alleges any violation.[1353]
> *Confidentiality*: Parties must ensure that its authorities do not disclose confidential or privileged information.[1354] They cannot state or imply in any public notice confirming or revealing the existence of a pending or ongoing investigation against a particular person that the person has, in fact, violated the Party's national competition laws.[1355]

1346. *See* United States-Mexico-Canada Agreement, Section 21.1, Jan. 29, 2020.
1347. *See* United States-Mexico-Canada Agreement, Section 21.1, Jan. 29, 2020.
1348. *See* United States-Mexico-Canada Agreement, Section 21.1, Jan. 29, 2020.
1349. *See* United States-Mexico-Canada Agreement, Section 21.1, Jan. 29, 2020.
1350. *See* United States-Mexico-Canada Agreement, Section 21.1, Jan. 29, 2020.
1351. *See* United States-Mexico-Canada Agreement, Section 21.2, Jan. 29, 2020.
1352. *See* United States-Mexico-Canada Agreement, Section 21.2, Jan. 29, 2020.
1353. *See* United States-Mexico-Canada Agreement, Section 21.2, Jan. 29, 2020.
1354. *See* United States-Mexico-Canada Agreement, Section 21.2, Jan. 29, 2020.
1355. *See* United States-Mexico-Canada Agreement, Section 21.2, Jan. 29, 2020.

Burden of Proof: The authorities have the burden of proof in establishing the legal and factual basis for an allegation, but Parties can require that the alleged violator establish certain defenses.[1356]

Final decisions must explain findings of fact, state the conclusions of law on which they are based, and be published with confidential material withheld.[1357]

Before sanctioning a person, Parties must allow the person to obtain information regarding their concerns, including the specific competition laws allegedly violated.[1358] People must be allowed to engage with authorities at key points on legal, factual and procedural issues.[1359] They must have access to information that is necessary to prepare an adequate defense.[1360] They must be able to present that evidence and cross-examine any testifying witnesses.[1361]

Alleged violators must be able to seek judicial review by a court or independent tribunal unless they voluntarily agreed to the imposition of the fine, sanction, or remedy.[1362]

Parties must be transparent about the criteria used for calculating a fine for a violation of national competition laws.[1363] If the fine relates to revenue or profit, that should be the revenue or profit relating to the Party's territory.[1364]

Authorities must attempt to preserve all relevant evidence that is collected until the review is finished.[1365]

§21.3   ARTICLE 21.3. COOPERATION

Parties recognize the importance of cooperating to combat commercial practices that hinder market efficiency and reduce consumer welfare within the free trade area.[1366] This includes the coordination of investigations that raise common law enforcement concerns and collaboration on training programs.[1367]

1356. *See* United States-Mexico-Canada Agreement, Section 21.2, Jan. 29, 2020.
1357. *See* United States-Mexico-Canada Agreement, Section 21.2, Jan. 29, 2020.
1358. *See* United States-Mexico-Canada Agreement, Section 21.2, Jan. 29, 2020.
1359. *See* United States-Mexico-Canada Agreement, Section 21.2, Jan. 29, 2020.
1360. *See* United States-Mexico-Canada Agreement, Section 21.2, Jan. 29, 2020.
1361. *See* United States-Mexico-Canada Agreement, Section 21.2, Jan. 29, 2020.
1362. *See* United States-Mexico-Canada Agreement, Section 21.2, Jan. 29, 2020.
1363. *See* United States-Mexico-Canada Agreement, Section 21.2, Jan. 29, 2020.
1364. *See* United States-Mexico-Canada Agreement, Section 21.2, Jan. 29, 2020.
1365. *See* United States-Mexico-Canada Agreement, Section 21.2, Jan. 29, 2020.
1366. *See* United States-Mexico-Canada Agreement, Section 21.3, Jan. 29, 2020.
1367. *See* United States-Mexico-Canada Agreement, Section 21.3, Jan. 29, 2020.

§21.4 ARTICLE 21.4. CONSUMER PROTECTION

Parties must maintain and enforce consumer protection laws or other laws that proscribe fraudulent and deceptive commercial activities.[1368] Parties agree to cooperate, including sharing complaints and other enforcement information.[1369]

§21.5 ARTICLE 21.5. TRANSPARENCY

In efforts to increase transparency, Parties agree to make available on request, its national competition law enforcement policies and practices and exemptions and immunities thereto—provided the request specifies the particular good/service and market and explains how the exemption/immunity may hinder trade/investment.[1370]

§21.6 ARTICLE 21.6. CONSULTATIONS

On request of another Party, a Party must enter into consultations.[1371] The request must indicate how the matter affects trade or investment between the Parties.[1372] To facilitate consultations, Parties must give "full and sympathetic consideration to the concerns of the other Party" and try to provide relevant non-confidential, non-privileged information.[1373] "Full and sympathetic consideration" is not defined and will need to be later defined.[1374]

§21.7 ARTICLE 21.7. NON-APPLICATION OF DISPUTE SETTLEMENT

Matters that arise under this chapter cannot be resolved under Chapter 14 (Investment) or Chapter 31 (Dispute Settlement).[1375]

1368. *See* United States-Mexico-Canada Agreement, Section 21.4, Jan. 29, 2020.
1369. *See* United States-Mexico-Canada Agreement, Section 21.4, Jan. 29, 2020.
1370. *See* United States-Mexico-Canada Agreement, Section 21.5, Jan. 29, 2020.
1371. *See* United States-Mexico-Canada Agreement, Section 21.6, Jan. 29, 2020.
1372. *See* United States-Mexico-Canada Agreement, Section 21.6, Jan. 29, 2020.
1373. *See* United States-Mexico-Canada Agreement, Section 21.6, Jan. 29, 2020.
1374. *See* United States-Mexico-Canada Agreement, Section 21.6, Jan. 29, 2020.
1375. *See* United States-Mexico-Canada Agreement, Section 21.7, Jan. 29, 2020.

CHAPTER 22

State-Owned Enterprises and Designated Monopolies

If Parties have control over state-owned enterprises (SOE), they must ensure that those enterprises follow the agreement. Each Party must give goods/services from its own enterprises no less favorable treatment than it gives a like good or a like service supplied by enterprises in the relevant market in the Party's territory that are investments of investors of the Party, of another Party or of a non-Party. Courts in each Party have jurisdiction over civil claims against an enterprise controlled through ownership interests by a foreign government based on a commercial activity in its territory. In regards to aid, the USMCA prohibits certain forms of non-commercial assistance, such as loans provided by state enterprises, or non-commercial assistance to state-owned enterprises. Injury is defined as material injury to a domestic industry or the threat thereof, or material retardation of the establishment of a domestic industry. This is the same definition used in the United States antidumping and countervailing duty laws. This can have an effect on both the volume of goods produced as well as the price of each good. However, Nondiscriminatory Treatment and Commercial Considerations and Non-Commercial Assistance do not apply to the non-conforming activities of SOEs or designated monopolies listed in its Schedule to Annex IV. For improved transparency, Parties must give to each other or publish a list of its SOEs within six months of the USMCA's effective date; and, if appropriate, Parties must exchange information regarding operation of SOEs. Exceptions to rules can be made in times of economic emergency, and further negotiations to the rules will be made within six months of implementation.

NAFTA does not contain a special chapter addressing these issues; some of the comparable text can be seen in Chapter 15 of NAFTA.[1376]

1376. *See* generally North American Free Trade Agreement, Chapter 15, Jan. 1, 1994.

§22.1   ARTICLE 22.2. SCOPE

Chapter 22 "applies to the activities of state-owned enterprises, state enterprises, or designated monopolies of a Party that affect or could affect trade or investment between Parties."[1377] It also applies to activities of a state-owned enterprise that cause adverse effects in non-Party markets.[1378]

§22.2   ARTICLE 22.3. DELEGATED AUTHORITY

If Parties have delegated authority to its state-owned enterprises, state enterprises, or designated monopolies ("entities"), the Party must ensure those entities act in a manner consistent with this Agreement.[1379]

§22.3   ARTICLE 22.4. NONDISCRIMINATORY TREATMENT AND COMMERCIAL CONSIDERATIONS

State-Owned Enterprises in their purchase of goods/services must give no less favorable treatment to a good/services supplied by another Party's enterprise than they give to a like supplied by an enterprise that is a covered investment in the Party's territory.[1380] Parties must give those goods/services no less favorable treatment than they give a like good or a like service supplied by enterprises in the relevant market in the Party's territory that are investments of investors of the Party, of another Party or of a non-Party.[1381]

Monopolies in their purchase of the monopoly goods/services must give to a good/service supplied by an enterprise of another Party no less favorable treatment than they give to a like good/services supplied by enterprises of the national Party, any other Party, or any non-Party.[1382]

For covered investments, they must accord good/services supplied by an enterprise that is a covered investment in the Party's territory treatment no less favorable than they accord to a like good or a like service supplied by enterprises in the relevant market in the Party's territory that are investments of investors of the Party, of another Party or of a non-Party.[1383]

1377. *See* United States-Mexico-Canada Agreement, Section 22.2, Jan. 29, 2020.
1378. *See* United States-Mexico-Canada Agreement, Section 22.2, Jan. 29, 2020.
1379. *See* United States-Mexico-Canada Agreement, Section 22.3, Jan. 29, 2020.
1380. *See* United States-Mexico-Canada Agreement, Section 22.4, Jan. 29, 2020.
1381. *See* United States-Mexico-Canada Agreement, Section 22.4, Jan. 29, 2020.
1382. *See* United States-Mexico-Canada Agreement, Section 22.4, Jan. 29, 2020.
1383. *See* United States-Mexico-Canada Agreement, Section 22.4, Jan. 29, 2020.

§22.4 ARTICLE 22.5. COURTS AND ADMINISTRATIVE BODIES

Courts in each Party must have jurisdiction over civil claims against an enterprise owned or controlled through ownership interests by a foreign government based on a commercial activity carried on in its territory.[1384]

There is an exception for claims in which a Party does not provide jurisdiction over similar claims against enterprises that are not owned or controlled through ownership interests by a foreign government.[1385]

In any case, the courts or administrative bodies must exercise impartial discretion with respect to all enterprises it regulates.[1386]

§22.5 ARTICLE 22.6 NON-COMMERCIAL ASSISTANCE

USMCA prohibits certain forms of non-commercial assistance provided to a state-owned enterprise primarily engaged in the production or sale of goods other than electricity.[1387]

This includes:

(a) loan or loan guarantees provided by a state enterprise or state-owned enterprise of a Party to a creditworthy state-owned enterprise of that Party; (b) non-commercial assistance to a state-owned enterprise of its own Party where the recipient is insolvent or on the brink of insolvency and there is no restructuring plan; and (c) conversion by a Party or a state enterprise or state-owned enterprise of a Party of the outstanding debt of a state-owned enterprise of that Party to equity, in circumstances where this would be inconsistent with the usual investment practice of a private investor.[1388]

Parties and their enterprises shall not cause adverse effects or injury to a domestic industry or enterprise of another Party through the use of non-commercial assistance.[1389]

§22.6 ARTICLE 22.7. ADVERSE EFFECTS

Adverse effects include displacing or impeding imports of a like good of another Party or sales of a like good produced by an enterprise that is a covered investment in another Party's territory.[1390]

Displacing or impeding of a good or service includes significant changes in relative shares of the market.[1391]

1384. *See* United States-Mexico-Canada Agreement, Section 22.5, Jan. 29, 2020.
1385. *See* United States-Mexico-Canada Agreement, Section 22.5, Jan. 29, 2020.
1386. *See* United States-Mexico-Canada Agreement, Section 22.5, Jan. 29, 2020.
1387. *See* United States-Mexico-Canada Agreement, Section 22.6, Jan. 29, 2020.
1388. *See* United States-Mexico-Canada Agreement, Section 22.6, Jan. 29, 2020.
1389. *See* United States-Mexico-Canada Agreement, Section 22.6, Jan. 29, 2020.
1390. *See* United States-Mexico-Canada Agreement, Section 22.7, Jan. 29, 2020.
1391. *See* United States-Mexico-Canada Agreement, Section 22.7, Jan. 29, 2020.

Adverse effects also include displacing or impeding the market of another Party's sales of a like good or imports of a like good of any other Party, or the market of non-Party imports of a like good of another Party.[1392]

Price undercutting creates adverse effects if it results in significant price suppression, price depression or lost sales to like goods of another Party in the same market.[1393]

Non-commercial assistance that a Party provides before the signing of the USMCA shall be deemed not to cause adverse effects.[1394]

§22.7   ARTICLE 22.8. INJURY

Injury means material injury to a domestic industry or the threat thereof, or material retardation of the establishment of a domestic industry.[1395]

Important factors are (a) volume of production by the covered investment that has received non-commercial assistance, (b) the effect of that production on prices for like goods, and the effect on the domestic industry producing like goods.[1396]

For volume, consideration will be given to significant increases in production or consumption in the Party claiming injury.[1397]

For effect on prices, consideration will be given to whether there has been a significant price undercutting by the goods produced and sold by the covered investment as compared with the price of like goods in the domestic industry.[1398] Parties will consider whether the effect of production by the covered investment, otherwise depresses prices or prevents price increases to a significant degree.[1399]

For effect on the industry, consideration will be given to macroeconomic as well as microeconomic factors.[1400]

A causal relationship must be shown in order to prove the non-commercial assistance is the cause of injury.[1401]

For a threat of material injury to be substantial, it must be clearly foreseen and imminent.[1402]

1392. *See* United States-Mexico-Canada Agreement, Section 22.7, Jan. 29, 2020.
1393. *See* United States-Mexico-Canada Agreement, Section 22.7, Jan. 29, 2020.
1394. *See* United States-Mexico-Canada Agreement, Section 22.7, Jan. 29, 2020.
1395. *See* United States-Mexico-Canada Agreement, Section 22.8, Jan. 29, 2020.
1396. *See* United States-Mexico-Canada Agreement, Section 22.8, Jan. 29, 2020.
1397. *See* United States-Mexico-Canada Agreement, Section 22.8, Jan. 29, 2020.
1398. *See* United States-Mexico-Canada Agreement, Section 22.8, Jan. 29, 2020.
1399. *See* United States-Mexico-Canada Agreement, Section 22.8, Jan. 29, 2020.
1400. *See* United States-Mexico-Canada Agreement, Section 22.8, Jan. 29, 2020.
1401. *See* United States-Mexico-Canada Agreement, Section 22.8, Jan. 29, 2020.
1402. *See* United States-Mexico-Canada Agreement, Section 22.8, Jan. 29, 2020.

§22.8 ARTICLE 22.9. PARTY-SPECIFIC ANNEXES

Nondiscriminatory Treatment and Commercial Considerations and Non-Commercial Assistance do not apply to the non-conforming activities of SOEs or designated monopolies listed in is Schedule to Annex IV.[1403]

Nondiscriminatory Treatment and Commercial Considerations, Courts and Administrative Bodies, Non-Commercial Assistance, and Transparency don't apply to Annex 22-D.[1404]

§22.9 ARTICLE 22.10. TRANSPARENCY

Parties must give to each other or publish a list of its SOEs within six months of the USMCA's effective date.[1405] For designated monopolies, the standard is "prompt notification" for new designations or expansions.[1406]

Parties may request in writing, information concerning SOEs or government monopolies, and the other Party must promptly respond in a way that is sufficiently specific to enable the requesting Party to understand the operation of an SOE/monopoly or the implementation of a policy.[1407]

§22.10 ARTICLE 22.11. TECHNICAL COOPERATION

If appropriate, Parties must exchange information regarding the improvement of corporate governance and the operation of SOEs. They must share best practices on policy approaches.[1408] They must organize international fora for sharing technical expertise related to the governances of SOEs.[1409]

§22.11 ARTICLE 22.12. COMMITTEE ON STATE-OWNED ENTERPRISES AND DESIGNATED MONOPOLIES

SOE Committee is established to review and consider the operation of this chapter and to consult on matters arising under the chapter. [1410]

1403. *See* United States-Mexico-Canada Agreement, Section 22.9, Jan. 29, 2020.
1404. *See* United States-Mexico-Canada Agreement, Section 22.9, Jan. 29, 2020.
1405. *See* United States-Mexico-Canada Agreement, Section 22.10, Jan. 29, 2020.
1406. *See* United States-Mexico-Canada Agreement, Section 22.10, Jan. 29, 2020.
1407. *See* United States-Mexico-Canada Agreement, Section 22.10, Jan. 29, 2020.
1408. *See* United States-Mexico-Canada Agreement, Section 22.11, Jan. 29, 2020.
1409. *See* United States-Mexico-Canada Agreement, Section 22.11, Jan. 29, 2020.
1410. *See* United States-Mexico-Canada Agreement, Section 22.12, Jan. 29, 2020.

§22.12   ARTICLE 22.13. EXCEPTIONS

Parties can still adopt or enforce measures to respond temporarily to economic emergencies without violating this chapter.[1411]

Nondiscriminatory Treatment and Commercial Considerations and Non-Commercial Assistance does not apply to the supply of financial services by an SOE pursuant to a government mandate if that supply of financial services supports exports, imports, or private investment outside of the territory of a Party.[1412] This is only the case if these measures are not intended to displace commercial financing or have terms no more favorable than comparable financial services in the commercial market.[1413]

The supply of financial services by an SOE pursuant to a government mandate does not to give rise to adverse effects if the Party in which the financial service is supplied requires a local presence in order to supply those services supports exports, imports, or private investment outside of the territory of a Party.[1414] This is only the case if these measures are not intended to displace commercial financing or have terms no more favorable than comparable financial services in the commercial market.[1415]

Non-Commercial Assistance does not apply with respect to an enterprise located outside the territory of a Party over which an SOE of that Party has assumed temporary ownership as a consequence of a foreclosure or a similar action, provided that any support the Party, a state enterprise, or SOE of the Party provides to the enterprise during the period of temporary ownership is provided in order to recoup the SOE's investment in accordance with a restructuring or liquidation plan.[1416]

Nondiscriminatory Treatment and Commercial Considerations, Non-Commercial Assistance, Transparency, and SOE Committee Articles don't apply to SOEs/designated monopolies when in any if in any one of the three previous consecutive fiscal years, the annual revenue derived from the commercial activities of the SOE or designated monopoly was less than a threshold amount in Annex 22-A.[1417]

§22.13   ARTICLE 22.14. FURTHER NEGOTIATIONS

Once USMCA is effective, Parties will begin to further negotiate this chapter within six months.[1418]

1411. *See* United States-Mexico-Canada Agreement, Section 22.13, Jan. 29, 2020.
1412. *See* United States-Mexico-Canada Agreement, Section 22.13, Jan. 29, 2020.
1413. *See* United States-Mexico-Canada Agreement, Section 22.13, Jan. 29, 2020.
1414. *See* United States-Mexico-Canada Agreement, Section 22.13, Jan. 29, 2020.
1415. *See* United States-Mexico-Canada Agreement, Section 22.13, Jan. 29, 2020.
1416. *See* United States-Mexico-Canada Agreement, Section 22.13, Jan. 29, 2020.
1417. *See* United States-Mexico-Canada Agreement, Section 22.13, Jan. 29, 2020.
1418. *See* United States-Mexico-Canada Agreement, Section 22.14, Jan. 29, 2020.

§22.14 ARTICLE 22.15. PROCESS FOR DEVELOPING INFORMATION

The process for developing information in Annex 220B applies in Chapter 31 dispute settlements if it is regarding a Party's conformity with Nondiscriminatory Treatment or Commercial Considerations.[1419]

Annex 22-A: Threshold Calculation

On USMCA's effective date, the exception threshold is 175 million Special Drawing Rights (SDRs).[1420] This is adjusted every three years, beginning January 1, following the USMCA's entry into force.[1421] The adjustment calculation uses data from the IMF's *International Financial Statistics* database.[1422] The adjustment calculation is below:[1423]

$$T_1 = \left(1 + \left(\sum_i w_i^{\text{SDR}} \times \prod_i {}^{\text{SDR}}_i\right)\right) T_0$$

T_0 = Threshold value at base period.
T_1 = New (adjusted) threshold value.

w_i^{SDR} = respective (fixed) weights of each currency, i, in the SDR (as at June 30 of the year prior to adjustment taking effect; and

$\prod_i^{\text{SDR}}$ = cumulative percent change in the GDP deflator of each currency, i, in the SDR over the three-year period ending June 30 of the year prior to adjustment taking effect.

Annex 22-B: Process for Developing Information Concerning State-Owned Enterprises and Designated Monopolies

Disputing Parties may exchange written questions and responses to obtain relevant information if a panel has been established pursuant to Chapter 31 (Dispute Settlement).[1424] A questioning Party may provide written questions within fifteen days of the panel's establishment.[1425] The answering Party must respond within thirty days of receipt. After the response, the questioning Party may ask follow-up questions within fifteen days.[1426] The answering Party has thirty days to answer the follow-up questions.[1427]

1419. *See* United States-Mexico-Canada Agreement, Section 22.15, Jan. 29, 2020.
1420. *See* United States-Mexico-Canada Agreement, Annex 22-A, Jan. 29, 2020.
1421. *See* United States-Mexico-Canada Agreement, Annex 22-A, Jan. 29, 2020.
1422. *See* United States-Mexico-Canada Agreement, Annex 22-A, Jan. 29, 2020.
1423. *See* United States-Mexico-Canada Agreement, Annex 22-A, Jan. 29, 2020.
1424. *See* United States-Mexico-Canada Agreement, Annex 22-B, Jan. 29, 2020.
1425. *See* United States-Mexico-Canada Agreement, Annex 22-B, Jan. 29, 2020.
1426. *See* United States-Mexico-Canada Agreement, Annex 22-B, Jan. 29, 2020.
1427. *See* United States-Mexico-Canada Agreement, Annex 22-B, Jan. 29, 2020.

When one Party questions or responds to another, it must also provide the panel with a copy of the questions or responses.[1428] If a Party does not cooperate, the panel should draw adverse inferences in its findings of fact.[1429]

Annex 22-C: Further Negotiation

Once USMCA is effective, Parties will begin to further negotiate this chapter within six months.[1430]

The negotiations will look at extending the obligations of this chapter to SOEs that are owned or controlled by a sub-central level of government and designated monopolies designated by those governments.[1431]

Parties will also negotiate on other matters that address adverse effects caused in a market of a non-Party as a result of an SOE.[1432]

Annex 22-D: Application to Sub-Central State-Owned Enterprises and Designated Monopolies

For Mexico and Canada, the following do not apply to the sub-central level of government or a designated monopoly designated by a sub-central level of government:[1433]

Nondiscriminatory Treatment and Commercial Considerations

This is covered in the following articles:

> Article 22.4.1(a)
> Article 22.4.1(b) with respect to purchases of a good or service
> Article 22.4.1(c)(i)
> Article 22.4.2 with respect to designated monopolies designated by a sub-central level of government

Courts and Administrative Bodies

Article 22.5.2 with respect to administrative regulatory bodies established or maintained by a sub-central level of government

Non-commercial Assistance

This is covered in the following articles:

> Article 22.6.1

1428. *See* United States-Mexico-Canada Agreement, Annex 22-B, Jan. 29, 2020.
1429. *See* United States-Mexico-Canada Agreement, Annex 22-B, Jan. 29, 2020.
1430. *See* United States-Mexico-Canada Agreement, Annex 22-C, Jan. 29, 2020.
1431. *See* United States-Mexico-Canada Agreement, Annex 22-C, Jan. 29, 2020.
1432. *See* United States-Mexico-Canada Agreement, Annex 22-C, Jan. 29, 2020.
1433. *See* United States-Mexico-Canada Agreement, Annex 22-D, Jan. 29, 2020.

> Article 22.6.2
> Article 22.6.3
> Article 22.6.4(b) and (c)
> Article 22.6.5(b) and (c)

Transparency

See Article 22.10.1

Canada Only[1434]

Non-commercial Assistance Is Covered in the Following Articles:

> Article 22.6.4(a) with respect to the production and sale of a good in competition with a like good produced and sold by a covered investment
> Article 22.6.5(a) with respect to the production and sale of a good in competition with a like good produced and sold by a covered investment
> Article 22.6.6
> Article 22.6.6

Transparency

Article 22.10.4 with respect to a policy or program adopted or maintained by a sub-central level of government

Mexico Only[1435]

Non-commercial Assistance is Covered in the Following Articles:

> Article 22.6.4(a) with respect to the production and sale of a good in competition with a like good produced and sold by a covered investment in the territory of Mexico
> Article 22.6.5(a) with respect to the production and sale of a good in competition with a like good produced and sold by a covered investment in the territory of Mexico

Annex 22-E: Special Purpose Vehicles of State Productive Enterprises

This chapter applies to State Productive Enterprises ("SPEs") referred to in the Decree amending the Political Constitution of the United Mexican States on December 20, 2013, as published in the Official Gazette ("the Decree"), and to the subsidiaries and affiliates of the SPEs.[1436]

It does not, however, apply to Special Purpose Vehicles ("SPVs"), which are private legal entities established by the SPEs, their subsidiaries and affiliates, as a result

---

1434. *See* United States-Mexico-Canada Agreement, Annex 22-D, Jan. 29, 2020.
1435. *See* United States-Mexico-Canada Agreement, Annex 22-D, Jan. 29, 2020.
1436. *See* United States-Mexico-Canada Agreement, Annex 22-E, Jan. 29, 2020.

of a venture with private investors, created to perform, develop, own, or operate a specific project.[1437]

Mexico must ensure SPVs are established in a competitive way that pursues the performance of commercial activities on a level playing field. SPVs must be aimed at generating economic value and profitability.[1438] They must follow generally accepted accounting principles and generally accepted international corporate governance.[1439] They must act in accordance with Article 22.4 (Nondiscriminatory Treatment and Commercial Considerations), Article 22.5 (Courts and Administrative Bodies), and Article 22.6 (Non-Commercial Assistance).[1440] Mexico must be transparent about SPVs and their provisions.[1441]

Annex 22-F: Non-commercial Assistance to Certain State Productive Enterprises

Mexico or its state enterprises or SOEs may provide non-commercial assistance to an SPE referred to in Annex 22-E (SPVs) that is primarily engaged in oil and gas activities, in circumstances that jeopardize the continued viability of the recipient enterprise, and for the sole purpose of enabling the enterprise to return to viability and fulfill its mandate under the Decree and Article 25 of Mexico's Constitution.[1442]

On request, Parties may consult regarding the duration, or elimination of this Annex, which should only be maintained in Mexico's circumstances continue to require the use of non-commercial assistance to ensure SPE viability.[1443]

1437. *See* United States-Mexico-Canada Agreement, Annex 22-E, Jan. 29, 2020.
1438. *See* United States-Mexico-Canada Agreement, Annex 22-E, Jan. 29, 2020.
1439. *See* United States-Mexico-Canada Agreement, Annex 22-E, Jan. 29, 2020.
1440. *See* United States-Mexico-Canada Agreement, Annex 22-E, Jan. 29, 2020.
1441. *See* United States-Mexico-Canada Agreement, Annex 22-E, Jan. 29, 2020.
1442. *See* United States-Mexico-Canada Agreement, Annex 22-F, Jan. 29, 2020.
1443. *See* United States-Mexico-Canada Agreement, Annex 22-F, Jan. 29, 2020.

Chapter 23
Labor

All Parties should affirm their obligations under the International Labor Organization ("ILO") and recognize the important role of workers' and employers' organizations in protecting internationally recognized labor rights. The Parties must ensure the following rights: freedom of association, including collective bargaining and the right to strike, the elimination of forced or compulsory labor, effective abolition of child labor and a prohibition on the worst forms of child labor, and freedom from employment and occupational discrimination. Parties should understand that they should not promote trade or investment by weakening labor laws. Parties cannot allow its enforcement of labor laws to become lax through sustained or recurring (in)action when the course of (in)action involves trade or investment between Parties. Each Party must prohibit imported goods produced with any sort of forced or compulsory labor. Labor workers and organizations must be able to exercise their labor rights without the use or threat of violence or intimidation.

Migrant workers are especially vulnerable, so Parties must protect them under labor laws regardless of their citizenship status. Parties must implement policies to protect workers against employment discrimination. Parties must promote public awareness of its labor laws by at least ensuring its laws and procedures are publicly available. Parties must maintain contact points that receive and consider submissions on labor matters. A Labor Council must be established and made up of senior officials from trade and labor ministers. Parties must maintain a national labor consultative or advisory body and must respond to requests to consult.

§23.1   ARTICLE 23.2. STATEMENT OF SHARED COMMITMENTS

Parties affirm their obligations under the International Labor Organization ("ILO") and recognize the important role of workers' and employers' organizations in protecting internationally recognized labor rights.[1444]

1444. *See* United States-Mexico-Canada Agreement, Section 23.2, Jan. 29, 2020.

§23.2   ARTICLE 23.3. LABOR RIGHTS

This was a new provision in USMCA. In NAFTA, there was a separate labor side agreement negotiated separately from NAFTA and became one of the conditions of passage. Labor issues were an important part of the USMCA and an important part of the agenda of the Democratic majority in the House of Representatives. Ultimately, organized labor in the U.S. was satisfied with these reforms and supported the USMCA, although there were concerns, even up to the time of preparing this book, about the willingness and ability of Mexico to enforce these provisions. Mexico did, in fact, make significant changes in its labor laws. Some of these were under court challenged at the time of this writing. The labor rights issues were mostly directed towards Mexico rather than Canada.

This chapter provides that the Parties must ensure these rights:

(a) freedom of association, including collective bargaining and the right to strike;
(b) elimination of forced or compulsory labor;
(c) effective abolition of child labor and a prohibition on the worst forms of child labor; and
(d) freedom from employment and occupational discrimination.[1445]

Parties must also adopt and maintain measures for acceptable work conditions with respect to minimum wages, work duration, safety and health.[1446]

§23.3   ARTICLE 23.4. NON-DEROGATION

Parties understand that they should not promote trade or investment by weakening labor laws.[1447] They cannot waive or otherwise derogate from its measures implementing the rights listed in Article 23.3.1 (Labor Rights) in a way that is inconsistent with those rights.[1448] They cannot waive or otherwise derogate from its measures implementing acceptable working conditions listed in Article 23.3.2 (Labor Rights) if it would weaken adherence to acceptable work conditions in special trade or customs area (e.g., export processing zone or foreign trade zone) in the Party's territory.[1449]

§23.4   ARTICLE 23.5. ENFORCEMENT OF LABOR LAWS

Parties cannot allow its enforcement of labor laws to become lax through sustained or recurring inaction when the course of inaction involves trade or investment between Parties.[1450]

1445. *See* United States-Mexico-Canada Agreement, Section 23.3, Jan. 29, 2020.
1446. *See* United States-Mexico-Canada Agreement, Section 23.3, Jan. 29, 2020.
1447. *See* United States-Mexico-Canada Agreement, Section 23.4, Jan. 29, 2020.
1448. *See* United States-Mexico-Canada Agreement, Section 23.4, Jan. 29, 2020.
1449. *See* United States-Mexico-Canada Agreement, Section 23.4, Jan. 29, 2020.
1450. *See* United States-Mexico-Canada Agreement, Section 23.5, Jan. 29, 2020.

Appropriate enforcement measures include:

(a) appointing and training inspectors;
(b) monitoring compliance and investigating suspected violations;
(c) seeking voluntary compliance;
(d) requiring recordkeeping and reporting;
(e) encouraging labor-management committees at worksites;
(f) providing or encouraging mediation, conciliation, and arbitration;
(g) conducting proceedings for sanctions or remedies for violations; and
(h) implementing those remedies and sanctions.[1451]

Failure to enforce is not excused on the grounds of lack of resources because parties must make bona fide decisions regarding the allocation of resources between labor enforcement activities.[1452]

This chapter does not empower a Party to enforce labor laws in another Party's territory.[1453] This became a sensitive issue since U.S. labor wanted to have American government personnel involved in enforcement in Mexico.

§23.5   ARTICLE 23.6. FORCED OR COMPULSORY LABOR

Each Party must prohibit imported goods produced with any sort of forced or compulsory labor. In order to enforce this provision, Parties must cooperate to identify and track the movement of these goods.[1454]

§23.6   ARTICLE 23.7. VIOLENCE AGAINST WORKERS

Labor workers and organizations must be able to exercise their labor rights without the use or threat of violence or intimidation.[1455] The Parties must effectively address incidents of threat of violence or intimidation without allowing enforcement to lax through sustained or recurring (in)action.[1456]

§23.7   ARTICLE 23.8. MIGRANT WORKERS

Migrant workers are especially vulnerable, so Parties must protect them under labor laws regardless of their citizenship status.[1457]

1451. *See* United States-Mexico-Canada Agreement, Section 23.5, Jan. 29, 2020.
1452. *See* United States-Mexico-Canada Agreement, Section 23.5, Jan. 29, 2020.
1453. *See* United States-Mexico-Canada Agreement, Section 23.5, Jan. 29, 2020.
1454. *See* United States-Mexico-Canada Agreement, Section 23.6, Jan. 29, 2020.
1455. *See* United States-Mexico-Canada Agreement, Section 23.7, Jan. 29, 2020.
1456. *See* United States-Mexico-Canada Agreement, Section 23.7, Jan. 29, 2020.
1457. *See* United States-Mexico-Canada Agreement, Section 23.8, Jan. 29, 2020.

§23.8   ARTICLE 23.9. DISCRIMINATION IN THE WORKPLACE

Parties must implement policies to protect workers against employment discrimination on the basis of sex (including harassment), pregnancy, sexual orientation, gender identity, and caregiving responsibilities.[1458] They must allow protected leave for birth or adoption of a child and care of family members and protect against wage discrimination.[1459]

§23.9   ARTICLE 23.10. PUBLIC AWARENESS AND PROCEDURAL GUARANTEES

Parties must promote public awareness of its labor laws by at least ensuring its laws and procedures are publicly available.[1460] Those with labor interests must have access to tribunals for labor law enforcement that are fair, equitable, and transparent.[1461] The tribunals must ensure due process and cannot entail unreasonable fees, time limits, or delay.[1462] All hearings must be open to the public unless the judicial administration otherwise requires.[1463]

Parties must be able to support or defend their positions with evidence.[1464] Final decisions must be based on that information or evidence and state the reasoning for the decision.[1465] All final decisions must be made available in writing to the Parties without undue delay, and consistent with the Parties law, to the public.[1466]

Parties to proceedings must be able to seek review from independent and impartial tribunals. Remedies must be available and executed in a timely manner.[1467]

§23.10   ARTICLE 23.11. PUBLIC SUBMISSIONS

Parties must maintain contact points that receive and consider submissions on labor matters.[1468] It must make publicly available and readily accessible procedures for the receipt and consideration.[1469] Responses must be made timely and in writing as appropriate.[1470] As appropriate, Parties must make the submission and the results timely available to the Parties and the public.[1471]

1458. *See* United States-Mexico-Canada Agreement, Section 23.9, Jan. 29, 2020.
1459. *See* United States-Mexico-Canada Agreement, Section 23.9, Jan. 29, 2020.
1460. *See* United States-Mexico-Canada Agreement, Section 23.10, Jan. 29, 2020.
1461. *See* United States-Mexico-Canada Agreement, Section 23.10, Jan. 29, 2020.
1462. *See* United States-Mexico-Canada Agreement, Section 23.10, Jan. 29, 2020.
1463. *See* United States-Mexico-Canada Agreement, Section 23.10, Jan. 29, 2020.
1464. *See* United States-Mexico-Canada Agreement, Section 23.10, Jan. 29, 2020.
1465. *See* United States-Mexico-Canada Agreement, Section 23.10, Jan. 29, 2020.
1466. *See* United States-Mexico-Canada Agreement, Section 23.10, Jan. 29, 2020.
1467. *See* United States-Mexico-Canada Agreement, Section 23.10, Jan. 29, 2020.
1468. *See* United States-Mexico-Canada Agreement, Section 23.11, Jan. 29, 2020.
1469. *See* United States-Mexico-Canada Agreement, Section 23.11, Jan. 29, 2020.
1470. *See* United States-Mexico-Canada Agreement, Section 23.11, Jan. 29, 2020.
1471. *See* United States-Mexico-Canada Agreement, Section 23.11, Jan. 29, 2020.

§23.11   ARTICLE 23.12. COOPERATION

Parties may cooperate to share and study best practices.[1472] They may collaborate to research and develop practices of mutual interests and exchange technical expertise.[1473]

The Parties may establish cooperative arrangements with the ILO or other international and regional organizations.[1474]

§23.12   ARTICLE 23.13. COOPERATIVE LABOR DIALOGUE

Parties may request dialogue by writing the contact point of the other Party and including specific and sufficient information that enables the receiving Party to respond.[1475] Unless otherwise decided, dialogue must begin within thirty days after the request is received.[1476] Dialogue may be electronic or in-person; it must address all issues raised in the request.[1477]

§23.13   ARTICLE 23.14. LABOR COUNCIL

A Labor Council is established and made up of senior officials from trade and labor ministries.[1478] The main part of their job will be to consider labor matters and to receive and review concerns of interested Parties.[1479]

§23.14   ARTICLE 23.15. CONTACT POINTS

Within sixty days of the USMCA effective date, Parties must designate and make known an office or official within its labor ministry or equivalent entity that will serve as a labor contact point.[1480] The contact points must communicate and coordinate between Parties, assist and report to the Labor Council, communicate with the public in their territory, and work together to address the needs of the Parties.[1481]

1472. *See* United States-Mexico-Canada Agreement, Section 23.12, Jan. 29, 2020.
1473. *See* United States-Mexico-Canada Agreement, Section 23.12, Jan. 29, 2020.
1474. *See* United States-Mexico-Canada Agreement, Section 23.12, Jan. 29, 2020.
1475. *See* United States-Mexico-Canada Agreement, Section 23.13, Jan. 29, 2020.
1476. *See* United States-Mexico-Canada Agreement, Section 23.13, Jan. 29, 2020.
1477. *See* United States-Mexico-Canada Agreement, Section 23.13, Jan. 29, 2020.
1478. *See* United States-Mexico-Canada Agreement, Section 23.14, Jan. 29, 2020.
1479. *See* United States-Mexico-Canada Agreement, Section 23.14, Jan. 29, 2020.
1480. *See* United States-Mexico-Canada Agreement, Section 23.15, Jan. 29, 2020.
1481. *See* United States-Mexico-Canada Agreement, Section 23.15, Jan. 29, 2020.

§23.15   ARTICLE 23.16. PUBLIC ENGAGEMENT

Parties must maintain a national labor consultative or advisory body or similar mechanism for members of its public to provide views on labor matters.[1482]

§23.16   ARTICLE 23.17. LABOR CONSULTATIONS

Parties must respond to requests to consult, and a third party that believes it has a substantial interest in the matter may participate if they notify the other Parties contact points no later than seven days after the date of delivery of the request for labor consultations.[1483]

If they can resolve the matter, they must document the outcome, and any specific steps and timelines decided upon.[1484] This should be available to the other Party and to the public unless they decide otherwise.[1485]

If Consulting Parties made every effort to resolve a matter but failed to do so, a consulting Party may request that the relevant Ministers (or their designees) of the consulting Parties convene to consider the matter at issue by delivering a written request to the other consulting Party through its contact point.[1486]

If the matter is still not resolved, Parties may request a meeting with the Commission in Chapter 31 (Dispute Settlement) Article 31.5 and request the establishment of a panel.[1487]

Annex 23-A: Worker Representation in Collective Bargaining in Mexico

Mexico must provide in its labor laws the right of workers to engage in collective bargaining and the organization, formation, and participation in the union of their choice.[1488]

Mexico must prohibit employers from dominating or interfering in union activities.[1489] Discrimination or coercion against workers for union activity is also prohibited.[1490] Mexico cannot allow employers to refuse to bargain collectively with the duly recognized union.[1491] Although unions have existed in Mexico for some time, the U.S. labor movement was concerned with so-called company unions that were not part of national unions and were often actually controlled by the employers.

Through legislation, Mexico must establish an independent entity for conciliation and registration of unions and collective bargaining agreements.[1492] This entity must

---

1482. *See* United States-Mexico-Canada Agreement, Section 23.16, Jan. 29, 2020.
1483. *See* United States-Mexico-Canada Agreement, Section 23.17, Jan. 29, 2020.
1484. *See* United States-Mexico-Canada Agreement, Section 23.17, Jan. 29, 2020.
1485. *See* United States-Mexico-Canada Agreement, Section 23.17, Jan. 29, 2020.
1486. *See* United States-Mexico-Canada Agreement, Section 23.17, Jan. 29, 2020.
1487. *See* United States-Mexico-Canada Agreement, Section 23.17, Jan. 29, 2020.
1488. *See* United States-Mexico-Canada Agreement, Annex 23-A, Jan. 29, 2020.
1489. *See* United States-Mexico-Canada Agreement, Annex 23-A, Jan. 29, 2020.
1490. *See* United States-Mexico-Canada Agreement, Annex 23-A, Jan. 29, 2020.
1491. *See* United States-Mexico-Canada Agreement, Annex 23-A, Jan. 29, 2020.
1492. *See* United States-Mexico-Canada Agreement, Annex 23-A, Jan. 29, 2020.

have the authority to issue sanctions for violations of its orders.[1493] However, Mexico must also allow persons to appeal these decisions to independent courts.[1494] Mexico must require the independent entity to verify that collective bargaining agreements meet legal worker support requirements in order for them to be registered and take legal effect.[1495]

Through legislation, Mexico must establish independent, impartial Labor Courts for the adjudication of labor disputes.[1496] The Courts must handle union representation challenges by providing a secret ballot vote and establishing clear time limits and procedures.[1497] Through legislation, Mexico must provide a verification system for the election of union leaders that allows personal, free, and secret votes for union members.[1498]

For the registration of an initial collective bargaining agreement, majority support and effective verification by the independent entity must be required.[1499] This may include documentary evidence, direct consultations with workers, or on-site inspections.[1500]

Mexico must require majority support for future revisions of collective bargaining agreements that address salary and work conditions.[1501] They must require that all existing collective bargaining agreements be revised at least once within four years of its effective date.[1502]

All revisions must be deposited with the independent entity, which must verify that a copy of the revised collective bargaining agreement was made readily accessible to the workers covered by the collective bargaining agreement, and they demonstrated support for the revision through a personal, free, and secret vote.[1503]

Any agreement or revision must be made readily accessible to all workers covered by the collective bargaining agreement.[1504] Mexico must establish a centralized website that provides public access to all collective bargaining agreements in force, and that is operated as an independent entity in charge of the registration of agreements.[1505]

Mexico must do all of this before January 1, 2019.[1506] Mexico did, in fact, pass the necessary laws. If they had not, the USMCA could have been delayed until the legislation described above becomes effective.[1507]

1493. *See* United States-Mexico-Canada Agreement, Annex 23-A, Jan. 29, 2020.
1494. *See* United States-Mexico-Canada Agreement, Annex 23-A, Jan. 29, 2020.
1495. *See* United States-Mexico-Canada Agreement, Annex 23-A, Jan. 29, 2020.
1496. *See* United States-Mexico-Canada Agreement, Annex 23-A, Jan. 29, 2020.
1497. *See* United States-Mexico-Canada Agreement, Annex 23-A, Jan. 29, 2020.
1498. *See* United States-Mexico-Canada Agreement, Annex 23-A, Jan. 29, 2020.
1499. *See* United States-Mexico-Canada Agreement, Annex 23-A, Jan. 29, 2020.
1500. *See* United States-Mexico-Canada Agreement, Annex 23-A, Jan. 29, 2020.
1501. *See* United States-Mexico-Canada Agreement, Annex 23-A, Jan. 29, 2020.
1502. *See* United States-Mexico-Canada Agreement, Annex 23-A, Jan. 29, 2020.
1503. *See* United States-Mexico-Canada Agreement, Annex 23-A, Jan. 29, 2020.
1504. *See* United States-Mexico-Canada Agreement, Annex 23-A, Jan. 29, 2020.
1505. *See* United States-Mexico-Canada Agreement, Annex 23-A, Jan. 29, 2020.
1506. *See* United States-Mexico-Canada Agreement, Annex 23-A, Jan. 29, 2020.
1507. *See* United States-Mexico-Canada Agreement, Annex 23-A, Jan. 29, 2020.

CHAPTER 24
Environment

Each Parties laws must strive for environmental protection. Parties cannot use sustained or recurring action or inaction that results in an effective failure to enforce environmental laws. Additionally, Parties must promote public awareness of its environmental laws by at least ensuring its laws and procedures are publicly available. Parties must also have measures in place to assess the environmental impact and must cooperate to find alternatives to ozone-depleting resources. Efforts must also be made in order to limit marine pollution and maintain air quality. Non-Government Organizations (NGOs) must establish voluntarily environmental measures that are truthful and relevant to international standards. The measures must also promote competition and innovation. Parties must also share and receive information from various groups regarding topics such as the entrance of invasive species that may harm the environment. Various Parties must also design and implement systems in order to prevent overfishing/illegal fishing and conserve marine life. Parties must also promote sustainable forest management practices. Parties must cooperate in order to achieve environmental goals and must maintain a contact point within ninety days of the implementation of the USMCA. A Party may submit an assertion that another Party is failing to effectively enforce its environmental laws. These assertions must be submitted to the Commission for Environmental Cooperation. Parties can agree to consult to address any aspect relating to environmental affairs that can be found in the USMCA. If matters are not resolved through the consultation process, the Environmental Committee can be called upon to resolve the issue. Additional dispute resolution measures can be found in other chapters.

§24.1 ARTICLE 24.2. SCOPE AND OBJECTIVES

This chapter exists to promote mutually supportive trade and environmental policies and practices, high levels of environmental protection, and effective enforcement of environmental laws.[1508] Similar to the labor chapter discussed above, NAFTA had no

---

1508. *See* United States-Mexico-Canada Agreement, Section 24.2, Jan. 29, 2020.

separate environmental chapter, but there was a side agreement negotiated on the environment that was important to obtain congressional passage.

§24.2   ARTICLE 24.3. LEVELS OF PROTECTION

Parties can establish their own level of environmental priorities, protection, and laws must they strive to reach high levels of protection.[1509]

§24.3   ARTICLE 24.4. ENFORCEMENT OF ENVIRONMENTAL LAWS

Once the USMCA is effective, Parties cannot use sustained or recurring action or inaction that results in an effective failure to enforce environmental laws.[1510] A Party is in compliance with this measure when a course of action or inaction reflects a reasonable exercise of discretion or from a bona fide decision regarding the allocation of environmental enforcement resources.[1511]

It is inappropriate for Parties to promote trade or investment by weakening environmental laws.[1512] They cannot waive or otherwise derogate from their measures implementing environmental laws in a way that weakens or reduces protection given under those laws.[1513]

This chapter does not empower a Party to enforce environmental laws in another Party's territory.[1514]

§24.4   ARTICLE 24.5. PUBLIC INFORMATION AND PARTICIPATION

Parties must promote public awareness of its environmental laws by at least ensuring that its laws and procedures are publicly available.[1515] They must receive and consider and timely respond to written questions and comments from persons of that Party regarding the implementation of this chapter.[1516] All questions, comments, and responses should be available to the public.[1517]

1509. *See* United States-Mexico-Canada Agreement, Section 24.3, Jan. 29, 2020.
1510. *See* United States-Mexico-Canada Agreement, Section 24.4, Jan. 29, 2020.
1511. *See* United States-Mexico-Canada Agreement, Section 24.4, Jan. 29, 2020.
1512. *See* United States-Mexico-Canada Agreement, Section 24.4, Jan. 29, 2020.
1513. *See* United States-Mexico-Canada Agreement, Section 24.4, Jan. 29, 2020.
1514. *See* United States-Mexico-Canada Agreement, Section 24.4, Jan. 29, 2020.
1515. *See* United States-Mexico-Canada Agreement, Section 24.5, Jan. 29, 2020.
1516. *See* United States-Mexico-Canada Agreement, Section 24.5, Jan. 29, 2020.
1517. *See* United States-Mexico-Canada Agreement, Section 24.5, Jan. 29, 2020.

§24.5 ARTICLE 24.6. PROCEDURAL MATTERS

Persons in each Party territory must be able to request investigations of alleged violations of the Party's environmental laws.[1518] The authorities must give requests due consideration.[1519]

Persons must have appropriate access to tribunals for the enforcement of the Party's environmental laws and the ability to seek recourse for those violations.[1520]

These proceedings must be fair, equitable, transparent, and compliant with due process.[1521] They cannot be unreasonably costly or time-constrained.[1522] All hearings must be open to the public unless the judicial administration otherwise requires.[1523]

Final decisions must be based on that information or evidence and state the reasoning for the decision.[1524] All final decisions must be made available in writing to the Parties without undue delay, and consistent with the Parties law, to the public.[1525]

As appropriate, Parties must provide Parties to the proceedings to seek judicial review and, if warranted, correction or redetermination.[1526]

§24.6 ARTICLE 24.7. ENVIRONMENTAL IMPACT ASSESSMENT

Parties must maintain suitable mechanisms for measuring the environmental impacts of proposed projects that may have significant effects on the environment.[1527] The procedures must allow public disclosure, and in some cases, public participation.[1528]

§24.7 ARTICLE 24.8. MULTILATERAL ENVIRONMENTAL AGREEMENTS

Parties affirm their commitments to implement their already existing multilateral agreements on the environment.[1529] They commit to exchange information on the implementation of these agreements, conduct ongoing negotiations of new agreements, and discuss their respective views on joining additional multilateral agreements.[1530]

1518. *See* United States-Mexico-Canada Agreement, Section 24.6, Jan. 29, 2020.
1519. *See* United States-Mexico-Canada Agreement, Section 24.6, Jan. 29, 2020.
1520. *See* United States-Mexico-Canada Agreement, Section 24.6, Jan. 29, 2020.
1521. *See* United States-Mexico-Canada Agreement, Section 24.6, Jan. 29, 2020.
1522. *See* United States-Mexico-Canada Agreement, Section 24.6, Jan. 29, 2020.
1523. *See* United States-Mexico-Canada Agreement, Section 24.6, Jan. 29, 2020.
1524. *See* United States-Mexico-Canada Agreement, Section 24.6, Jan. 29, 2020.
1525. *See* United States-Mexico-Canada Agreement, Section 24.6, Jan. 29, 2020.
1526. *See* United States-Mexico-Canada Agreement, Section 24.6, Jan. 29, 2020.
1527. *See* United States-Mexico-Canada Agreement, Section 24.7, Jan. 29, 2020.
1528. *See* United States-Mexico-Canada Agreement, Section 24.7, Jan. 29, 2020.
1529. *See* United States-Mexico-Canada Agreement, Section 24.8, Jan. 29, 2020.
1530. *See* United States-Mexico-Canada Agreement, Section 24.8, Jan. 29, 2020.

§24.8   ARTICLE 24.9. PROTECTION OF THE OZONE LAYER

In order to reduce emissions that deplete the Earth's ozone layer, Parties agree to cooperate in developing environmentally friendly alternatives to ozone-depleting substances; review refrigerant management practices, policies and programs; review methodologies for stratospheric ozone measurements; and combat illegal trade in ozone-depleting substances.[1531]

Because public participation is important, Parties must make its ozone protection programs and activities publicly available.[1532]

§24.9   ARTICLE 24.10. PROTECTION OF THE MARINE ENVIRONMENT FROM SHIP POLLUTION

Parties must take measures to prevent marine environmental pollution.[1533]

Because public participation is important, Parties must make their marine environmental pollution programs and activities publicly available.[1534]

Parties agree to cooperate on marine environmental pollution matters, including from accidental, routine, and deliberate pollution from ships and their emissions.[1535] They may also cooperate on the development of waste-minimizing technology for those ships and waste management at port waste reception facilities.[1536] Parties should increase protection in special geographic areas and cooperate on enforcement measures.[1537]

§24.10   ARTICLE 24.11. AIR QUALITY

Parties understand that air pollution is a serious threat to humanity and the ecosystem.[1538] They understand that it is important to reduce domestic and trans-boundary air pollution.[1539] Because public participation is important, Parties must make their air quality data, programs and activities publicly available.[1540]

The chapter address harmonization of air quality monitory methods and agree to cooperate to address air quality matters of mutual interest.[1541] This includes discussing ambient air quality planning; modeling and monitoring emissions; measuring and

---

1531. *See* United States-Mexico-Canada Agreement, Section 24.9, Jan. 29, 2020.
1532. *See* United States-Mexico-Canada Agreement, Section 24.9, Jan. 29, 2020.
1533. *See* United States-Mexico-Canada Agreement, Section 24.10, Jan. 29, 2020.
1534. *See* United States-Mexico-Canada Agreement, Section 24.10, Jan. 29, 2020.
1535. *See* United States-Mexico-Canada Agreement, Section 24.10, Jan. 29, 2020.
1536. *See* United States-Mexico-Canada Agreement, Section 24.10, Jan. 29, 2020.
1537. *See* United States-Mexico-Canada Agreement, Section 24.10, Jan. 29, 2020.
1538. *See* United States-Mexico-Canada Agreement, Section 24.11, Jan. 29, 2020.
1539. *See* United States-Mexico-Canada Agreement, Section 24.11, Jan. 29, 2020.
1540. *See* United States-Mexico-Canada Agreement, Section 24.11, Jan. 29, 2020.
1541. *See* United States-Mexico-Canada Agreement, Section 24.11, Jan. 29, 2020.

implementing inventory methodologies for air quality, and using reduction, control, and prevention technologies and practices.[1542]

§24.11   ARTICLE 24.12. MARINE LITTER

The Parties understand that they must take action to prevent and reduce marine litter, including plastic and microplastics.[1543] They must cooperate to address the issue of marine litter by addressing land- and sea-based pollution, waste management infrastructure, and reducing, abandoned lost, or otherwise discarded fishing gear.[1544]

§24.12   ARTICLE 24.13. CORPORATE SOCIAL RESPONSIBILITY AND RESPONSIBLE BUSINESS CONDUCT

Parties must encourage enterprises organized or operating in their respective territories to implement voluntary best practices of environment-related corporate social responsibility, such as international standards and guidelines.[1545]

§24.13   ARTICLE 24.14. VOLUNTARY MECHANISMS TO ENHANCE ENVIRONMENTAL PERFORMANCE

In accordance with their laws, Parties must encourage the use and development of flexible, voluntary mechanisms to protect the environment and the Earth.[1546] This includes encouraging conservation and sustainable use of natural resources.[1547]

Parties must encourage entities or Non-Governmental Organizations ("NGOs") to develop voluntary mechanisms that are truthful and based on relevant international standards.[1548] These mechanisms should promote competition and innovation.[1549] They should not treat a product less favorably on the basis of origin.[1550]

§24.14   ARTICLE 24.15. TRADE AND BIODIVERSITY

Parties must promote sustainable use of biodiversity, including respecting the "knowledge and practices of indigenous peoples and local communities embodying traditional lifestyles that contribute to the conservation and sustainable use of biological diversity."[1551]

1542. *See* United States-Mexico-Canada Agreement, Section 24.11, Jan. 29, 2020.
1543. *See* United States-Mexico-Canada Agreement, Section 24.12, Jan. 29, 2020.
1544. *See* United States-Mexico-Canada Agreement, Section 24.12, Jan. 29, 2020.
1545. *See* United States-Mexico-Canada Agreement, Section 24.13, Jan. 29, 2020.
1546. *See* United States-Mexico-Canada Agreement, Section 24.14, Jan. 29, 2020.
1547. *See* United States-Mexico-Canada Agreement, Section 24.14, Jan. 29, 2020.
1548. *See* United States-Mexico-Canada Agreement, Section 24.14, Jan. 29, 2020.
1549. *See* United States-Mexico-Canada Agreement, Section 24.14, Jan. 29, 2020.
1550. *See* United States-Mexico-Canada Agreement, Section 24.14, Jan. 29, 2020.
1551. *See* United States-Mexico-Canada Agreement, Section 24.15, Jan. 29, 2020.

Parties understand the importance of making it easier to access genetic re-sources.[1552] However, they are aware that prior informed consent and/or mutually agreed terms may be required to access these resources.[1553]

Because public participation is important, Parties must make their biodiversity data, programs and activities publicly available.[1554]

Parties must address issues of biodiversity, including conservation, sustainabil-ity, protection and maintenance of ecosystems and access to genetic resources.[1555]

§24.15   ARTICLE 24.16. INVASIVE ALIEN SPECIES

Parties must identify and share information regarding the "movement, prevention, detection, control, and eradication of invasive alien species" that adversely impact environmental, economic, and human health.[1556]

§24.16   ARTICLE 24.17. MARINE WILD CAPTURE FISHERIES

Parties understand that they need to take measures that conserve and sustain fisheries, such as promoting and facilitating trade in fish and fish products from legal and sustainably managed fisheries, without creating unnecessary barriers to trade.[1557]

Any measures need to be based on the best scientific evidence available, tailored to conserve, and only implemented after the importing Party has consulted with the exporting Party and allowed them to take measures to address any issues.[1558]

Parties must cooperate with or in Regional Fisheries Management Organizations ("RFMO") and Regional Fisheries Management Arrangements ("RFMA") if they are members, observers or cooperating Parties.[1559]

§24.17   ARTICLE 24.18. SUSTAINABLE FISHERIES MANAGEMENT

Parties should implement a system designed to prevent overfishing and overcapacity, reduce bycatch of non-target species and juveniles, promote the recovery of overfished stocks, and protect marine habitats.[1560] They must implement measures to prohibit shark finning and the use of poisons and explosives for commercial fishing.[1561] They must maintain measures to prohibit shark finning.[1562]

1552. *See* United States-Mexico-Canada Agreement, Section 24.15, Jan. 29, 2020.
1553. *See* United States-Mexico-Canada Agreement, Section 24.15, Jan. 29, 2020.
1554. *See* United States-Mexico-Canada Agreement, Section 24.15, Jan. 29, 2020.
1555. *See* United States-Mexico-Canada Agreement, Section 24.15, Jan. 29, 2020.
1556. *See* United States-Mexico-Canada Agreement, Section 24.16, Jan. 29, 2020.
1557. *See* United States-Mexico-Canada Agreement, Section 24.17, Jan. 29, 2020.
1558. *See* United States-Mexico-Canada Agreement, Section 24.17, Jan. 29, 2020.
1559. *See* United States-Mexico-Canada Agreement, Section 24.17, Jan. 29, 2020.
1560. *See* United States-Mexico-Canada Agreement, Section 24.18, Jan. 29, 2020.
1561. *See* United States-Mexico-Canada Agreement, Section 24.18, Jan. 29, 2020.
1562. *See* United States-Mexico-Canada Agreement, Section 24.18, Jan. 29, 2020.

§24.18   ARTICLE 24.19. CONSERVATION OF MARINE SPECIES

Parties must implement measures that promote the conservation of sharks, sea turtles, seabirds, and marine mammals. This includes studying fisheries, marine habitats, and the bycatch of non-target species.[1563] Parties must prohibit the killing of great whales for commercial purposes unless it is authorized to do so in a multilateral treaty.[1564] Furthermore, the whaling clause does not apply to indigenous people in accordance with a Party's laws.[1565] The U.S. and Mexico have had disputes concerning the protection of the Vaquita porpoise and banning imports from Mexico, whose netting endangered these porpoises.

§24.19   ARTICLE 24.20. FISHERIES SUBSIDIES

Parties understand that to prevent overfishing and recovery for overfished stocks, they must control, reduce, and terminate all subsidies that contribute to overfishing and overcapacity.[1566] To that end, Parties may not grant or maintain subsidies provided to a fishing vessel or operated while listed for Illegal, Unreported, and Unregulated (IUU) fishing by the flag state, the subsidizing party or a relevant RFMO or FMA.[1567] They cannot allow subsidies for fishing that negatively affect fish stocks that are in overfished condition (mortality from fishing needs to be restricted for the stock to rebuild).[1568]

Within one year of the USMCA's effective date, Parties must notify each other of any fishing-related subsidy they grant or maintain.[1569]

§24.20   ARTICLE 24.21. ILLEGAL, UNREPORTED, AND UNREGULATED (IUU) FISHING

Parties must endeavor to improve international cooperation to address IUU fishing by deterring trade in products from IUU fishing. This includes implementing port state measures; monitoring and enforcing IUU regulation; maintaining a vessel documentation system and registry; acting consistently with RFMOs/RFMAs; and exchanging information and best practices.[1570]

1563. *See* United States-Mexico-Canada Agreement, Section 24.19, Jan. 29, 2020.
1564. *See* United States-Mexico-Canada Agreement, Section 24.19, Jan. 29, 2020.
1565. *See* United States-Mexico-Canada Agreement, Section 24.19, Jan. 29, 2020.
1566. *See* United States-Mexico-Canada Agreement, Section 24.20, Jan. 29, 2020.
1567. *See* United States-Mexico-Canada Agreement, Section 24.20, Jan. 29, 2020.
1568. *See* United States-Mexico-Canada Agreement, Section 24.20, Jan. 29, 2020.
1569. *See* United States-Mexico-Canada Agreement, Section 24.20, Jan. 29, 2020.
1570. *See* United States-Mexico-Canada Agreement, Section 24.21, Jan. 29, 2020.

§24.21   ARTICLE 24.22. CONSERVATION AND TRADE

Parties will adopt and maintain laws or regulations to fulfill its obligations under the *Convention on International Trade in Endangered Species of Wild Fauna and Flora* (CITES).[1571] Parties will exchange information, work jointly on conservation issues, and implement CITES resolutions when appropriate.[1572] They will take measures to protect wild fauna and flora that are at risk in its territory (e.g., grasslands and wetlands).[1573] Parties must issue penalties, sanctions, and other measures to those that trade wild fauna and flora in violation of a Party's law, which was enacted to preserve wild fauna or flora.[1574]

§24.22   ARTICLE 24.23. SUSTAINABLE FOREST MANAGEMENT AND TRADE

Parties will "maintain or strengthen government capacity and institutional frameworks to promote sustainable forest management and promote trade in legally harvested forest products."[1575]

§24.23   ARTICLE 24.24. ENVIRONMENTAL GOODS AND SERVICES

Parties must "strive to promote trade and investment in environmental goods and services"—including clean technologies.[1576] They should encourage sustainable development and contribute to green growth and jobs.[1577]

The Environment committee must consider issues related to these matters, and the Parties must cooperate to further facilitate global trade in environmental goods and services.[1578]

§24.24   ARTICLE 24.25. ENVIRONMENTAL COOPERATION

Cooperation is a mechanism to implement this chapter and achieve shared environmental goals.[1579] Parties are committed to adopting shared environmental initiatives pursuant to the Agreement on Environmental Cooperation among the Governments of Canada, the United Mexican States, and the United States of America ("ECA").[1580]

1571. *See* United States-Mexico-Canada Agreement, Section 24.22, Jan. 29, 2020.
1572. *See* United States-Mexico-Canada Agreement, Section 24.22, Jan. 29, 2020.
1573. *See* United States-Mexico-Canada Agreement, Section 24.22, Jan. 29, 2020.
1574. *See* United States-Mexico-Canada Agreement, Section 24.22, Jan. 29, 2020.
1575. *See* United States-Mexico-Canada Agreement, Section 24.23, Jan. 29, 2020.
1576. *See* United States-Mexico-Canada Agreement, Section 24.24, Jan. 29, 2020.
1577. *See* United States-Mexico-Canada Agreement, Section 24.24, Jan. 29, 2020.
1578. *See* United States-Mexico-Canada Agreement, Section 24.24, Jan. 29, 2020.
1579. *See* United States-Mexico-Canada Agreement, Section 24.25, Jan. 29, 2020.
1580. *See* United States-Mexico-Canada Agreement, Section 24.25, Jan. 29, 2020.

§24.25 ARTICLE 24.26. ENVIRONMENT COMMITTEE AND CONTACT POINTS

Each Party must designate and maintain a contact point within ninety days of the USMCA's effective date.[1581] The Environment Committee is established to coordinate, discuss, and implement this chapter.[1582] The Environment Committee must make decisions by consensus unless they decide otherwise.[1583] The Environmental Committee must hold a public session at each meeting.[1584]

§24.26 ARTICLE 24.27. SUBMISSIONS ON ENFORCEMENT MATTERS

A Party may submit an assertion that another Party is failing to effectively enforce its environmental laws.[1585] Submissions must be made in writing, identify the submitter, provide sufficient evidence for review, be aimed at promoting enforcement, indicate whether the communication has been made to the relevant Party, and be made to the Secretariat of the Commission for Environmental Cooperation ("CEC Secretariat").[1586] The CEC Secretariat can request a response from the Party.[1587]

§24.27 ARTICLE 24.28. FACTUAL RECORDS AND RELATED COOPERATION

If the CEC Secretariat warrants a factual record, they must inform the Council and the Environmental Committee, prepare the record if the at least Council members instruct it to do so.[1588] It must submit a draft within 120 days to which Parties may provide comments.[1589] The final record with comments must be publicly available unless at least two Council members state otherwise.[1590]

§24.28 ARTICLE 24.29. ENVIRONMENT CONSULTATIONS

Parties agree to consult with one another to address any matter affecting this chapter.[1591] A Party may request consultations by notifying the contact point and providing specific and sufficient information regarding the matter to be addressed.[1592] A third party that wants to participate in consultations may notify the contact points of

---

1581. *See* United States-Mexico-Canada Agreement, Section 24.26, Jan. 29, 2020.
1582. *See* United States-Mexico-Canada Agreement, Section 24.26, Jan. 29, 2020.
1583. *See* United States-Mexico-Canada Agreement, Section 24.26, Jan. 29, 2020.
1584. *See* United States-Mexico-Canada Agreement, Section 24.26, Jan. 29, 2020.
1585. *See* United States-Mexico-Canada Agreement, Section 24.27, Jan. 29, 2020.
1586. *See* United States-Mexico-Canada Agreement, Section 24.27, Jan. 29, 2020.
1587. *See* United States-Mexico-Canada Agreement, Section 24.27, Jan. 29, 2020.
1588. *See* United States-Mexico-Canada Agreement, Section 24.28, Jan. 29, 2020.
1589. *See* United States-Mexico-Canada Agreement, Section 24.28, Jan. 29, 2020.
1590. *See* United States-Mexico-Canada Agreement, Section 24.28, Jan. 29, 2020.
1591. *See* United States-Mexico-Canada Agreement, Section 24.29, Jan. 29, 2020.
1592. *See* United States-Mexico-Canada Agreement, Section 24.29, Jan. 29, 2020.

the other Parties within seven days of the request for consultations and include an explanation of its substantial interest in the matter.[1593]

§24.29   ARTICLE 24.30. SENIOR REPRESENTATIVE CONSULTATIONS

If a matter is not resolved through consultations, a consulting Party may request Environment Committee representatives to convene to resolve the matter.[1594]

§24.30   ARTICLE 24.31. MINISTERIAL CONSULTATIONS

If the Senior Representatives cannot resolve the matter, a consulting Party may refer it to the Ministers of the consulting Parties who should attempt to resolve the matter.[1595]

§24.31   ARTICLE 24.32. DISPUTE RESOLUTION

If the matter is not resolved by Party, Senior Representative, or Ministerial Consultations, Parties may request a panel be established under the Dispute Resolution Chapter (Chapter 31).[1596] Such a panel, if appropriate, should seek technical advice from a CITES entity.[1597]

Annex 24-A

A Party is taking appropriate measures to control the production and consumption of, and trade in substances that deplete the Ozone layer when they act in compliance with the Montreal Protocol or measures equivalent to or higher than:

For Canada, the *Ozone-depleting Substances and Halocarbon Alternatives Regulations of the Canadian Environmental Protection Act, 1999* (CEPA).[1598]

For Mexico, the General Law on Ecological Equilibrium and Environmental Protection (*Ley General del Equilibrio Ecológico y la Protección al Ambiente – LGEEPA*), under Title IV Environmental.[1599]

Protection, Chapter I and II regarding federal enforcement of atmospheric provisions.

For the United States, 42 U.S.C. §§ 7671-7671q (*Stratospheric Ozone Protection*).[1600]

1593. *See* United States-Mexico-Canada Agreement, Section 24.29, Jan. 29, 2020.
1594. *See* United States-Mexico-Canada Agreement, Section 24.30, Jan. 29, 2020.
1595. *See* United States-Mexico-Canada Agreement, Section 24.31, Jan. 29, 2020.
1596. *See* United States-Mexico-Canada Agreement, Section 24.32, Jan. 29, 2020.
1597. *See* United States-Mexico-Canada Agreement, Section 24.32, Jan. 29, 2020.
1598. *See* United States-Mexico-Canada Agreement, Annex 24-A, Jan. 29, 2020.
1599. *See* United States-Mexico-Canada Agreement, Annex 24-A, Jan. 29, 2020.
1600. *See* United States-Mexico-Canada Agreement, Annex 24-A, Jan. 29, 2020.

Annex 24-B

A Party is taking appropriate measures to prevent the pollution of the marine environment for ships when they act in compliance with the MARPOL Convention or measures equivalent to or higher than:

For Canada, the *Canada Shipping Act, 2001* and its related regulations.[1601]

For Mexico, Article 132 of the *General Law on Ecological Equilibrium and Environmental Protection* (*Ley General del Equilibrio Ecológico y la Protección al Ambiente – LGEEPA*).[1602]

For the United States, the *Act to Prevent Pollution from Ships*, 33 U.S.C. §§ 1901-1915.[1603]

1601. *See* United States-Mexico-Canada Agreement, Annex 24-B, Jan. 29, 2020.
1602. *See* United States-Mexico-Canada Agreement, Annex 24-B, Jan. 29, 2020.
1603. *See* United States-Mexico-Canada Agreement, Annex 24-B, Jan. 29, 2020.

CHAPTER 25

Small- and Medium-Sized Enterprises

A Party must cooperate with SMEs of the other Parties and cooperate to promote jobs and growth within those enterprises. Parties must promote cooperation between their respective small business support infrastructures. They must collaborate more on activities to promote SMEs owned by underrepresented groups—including women, indigenous peoples, youth, minorities, start-ups, agricultural SMEs, and rural SMEs. Parties must exchange information and best practices for improving SME access to capital and credit and encourage the use of web-based platforms that help link SMEs with potential international business partners.

Parties involved must maintain a publicly accessible website that contains the text and a summary of the USMCA. The site must have a description of the SME-related provisions and any other information that would be useful to SMEs. The site must have links to the equivalent website of the other Parties and to each Party's own SME-related government agencies and entities. Additionally, the SME Committee is established to assist SMEs in the Parties' territories and to facilitate exchange and cooperation between Parties with respect to SMEs. The Small-and Medium-Enterprise committee must convene a trilateral SME dialogue annually, unless it decides otherwise. The Small- and Medium-Enterprise dialogue is very inclusive. Underrepresented groups may participate in the dialogue and provide information that is relevant to the committee. In addition to this Chapter there are provisions in other Chapters of the USMCA that are designed to enhance cooperation on SME issues.

§25.1   ARTICLE 25.1. GENERAL PRINCIPLES

A Party must cooperate with SMEs of the other Parties and cooperate to promoting jobs and growth in SMEs.[1604]

1604. *See* United States-Mexico-Canada Agreement, Section 25.1, Jan. 29, 2020.

§25.2   ARTICLE 25.2. COOPERATION TO INCREASE TRADE AND INVESTMENT OPPORTUNITIES FOR SMEs

Parties must promote cooperation between their respective small business support infrastructures.[1605] They must collaborate more on activities to promote SMEs owned by underrepresent groups—including women, indigenous peoples, youth, minorities, start-ups, agricultural SMEs, and rural SMEs.[1606] Parties must exchange information and best practices for improving SME access to capital and credit and encourage the use of web-based platforms that help link SMEs with potential international business partners.[1607]

§25.3   ARTICLE 25.3. INFORMATION SHARING

Parties must maintain a publicly accessible website that contains the text and a summary of the USMCA.[1608] The site must have a description of the SME-related provisions and any other information that would be useful to SMEs.[1609] The site must have links to the equivalent website of the other Parties and to each Party's own SME-related government agencies and entities.[1610]

§25.4   ARTICLE 25.4. COMMITTEE ON SME ISSUES

The SME Committee is established to assist SMEs in the Parties' territories and to facilitate exchange and cooperation between Parties with respect to SMEs.[1611]

§25.5   ARTICLE 25.5. SME DIALOGUE

The SME Committee must convene a Trilateral SME Dialogue (the "SME Dialogue") annually unless it decides otherwise.[1612] The SME Dialogue is very inclusive.[1613] The Private sector, employees, NGOs, academic experts, diverse and underrepresented groups, and other stakeholders may participate in the SME Dialogue and can provide relevant information to the Committee.[1614]

1605. *See* United States-Mexico-Canada Agreement, Section 25.2, Jan. 29, 2020.
1606. *See* United States-Mexico-Canada Agreement, Section 25.2, Jan. 29, 2020.
1607. *See* United States-Mexico-Canada Agreement, Section 25.2, Jan. 29, 2020.
1608. *See* United States-Mexico-Canada Agreement, Section 25.3, Jan. 29, 2020.
1609. *See* United States-Mexico-Canada Agreement, Section 25.3, Jan. 29, 2020.
1610. *See* United States-Mexico-Canada Agreement, Section 25.3, Jan. 29, 2020.
1611. *See* United States-Mexico-Canada Agreement, Section 25.4, Jan. 29, 2020.
1612. *See* United States-Mexico-Canada Agreement, Section 25.5, Jan. 29, 2020.
1613. *See* United States-Mexico-Canada Agreement, Section 25.5, Jan. 29, 2020.
1614. *See* United States-Mexico-Canada Agreement, Section 25.5, Jan. 29, 2020.

§25.6   ARTICLE 25.6. OBLIGATIONS IN THE AGREEMENT THAT BENEFIT SMEs

In addition to this chapter, there are provisions in other chapters of the USMCA that are designed to enhance cooperation on SME issues.[1615]

§25.7   ARTICLE 25.7. NON-APPLICATION OF DISPUTE SETTLEMENT

Chapter 31 (Dispute Settlement) is not applicable to this chapter.[1616]

1615. *See* United States-Mexico-Canada Agreement, Section 25.6, Jan. 29, 2020.
1616. *See* United States-Mexico-Canada Agreement, Section 25.7, Jan. 29, 2020.

CHAPTER 26
Competitiveness

The Parties have a shared interest in strengthening economic growth, prosperity, and competitiveness. The USMCA establishes The Competitiveness Committee and it is made up of government representatives of each party. They will discuss and develop measures to facilitate trade and investment in the region. They will work to enhance a transparent regulatory environment and encourage the swift movement of goods and provision of services. The Competitiveness Committee will submit a report to the Commission with results that have been achieved and recommendations on how to further increase regional competitiveness. Parties must designate a contact point for the Competitiveness Committee and notify the others of this appointment and any subsequent changes. In Article 26.2. Engagement with Interested Persons, Parties must maintain appropriate mechanisms to allow interested persons to provide comment on matters of competition.

§26.1   ARTICLE 26.1. NORTH AMERICAN COMPETITIVENESS COMMITTEE

[T]he Parties affirm their shared interest in strengthening regional economic growth, prosperity, and competitiveness.[1617]

The Competitiveness Committee is established and made up of government representatives of each party.[1618] They will discuss and develop measures to facilitate trade and investment in the region.[1619] They will work to enhance a transparent regulatory environment and encourage the swift movement of goods and provision of services.[1620] The Competitiveness Committee will submit a report to the Commission with results

---

1617. *See* United States-Mexico-Canada Agreement, Section 26.1, Jan. 29, 2020.
1618. *See* United States-Mexico-Canada Agreement, Section 26.1, Jan. 29, 2020.
1619. *See* United States-Mexico-Canada Agreement, Section 26.1, Jan. 29, 2020.
1620. *See* United States-Mexico-Canada Agreement, Section 26.1, Jan. 29, 2020.

that have been achieved and recommendations on how to further increase regional competitiveness.[1621]

Parties must designate a contact point for the Competitiveness Committee and notify the others of this appointment and any subsequent changes.[1622]

§26.2   ARTICLE 26.2. ENGAGEMENT WITH INTERESTED PERSONS

Parties must maintain appropriate mechanisms to allow interested persons to provide comments on matters of competition.[1623]

§26.3   ARTICLE 26.3. NON-APPLICATION OF DISPUTE SETTLEMENT

Chapter 31 (Dispute Settlement) is not applicable to this chapter.[1624]

1621. *See* United States-Mexico-Canada Agreement, Section 26.1, Jan. 29, 2020.
1622. *See* United States-Mexico-Canada Agreement, Section 26.1, Jan. 29, 2020.
1623. *See* United States-Mexico-Canada Agreement, Section 26.2, Jan. 29, 2020.
1624. *See* United States-Mexico-Canada Agreement, Section 26.3, Jan. 29, 2020.

CHAPTER 27

Anti-corruption

The Anti-corruption Chapter covers all measures "to prevent and combat bribery and corruption" related to any matter covered by the USMCA. For the U.S., it does not apply to conduct outside of federal criminal jurisdiction. Parties must implement measures to establish criminal offenses that cover a person subject to its jurisdiction when they intentionally promise, offer, or give a public official an undue advantage, in exchange for the official's action or inaction in relation to their official duties. Parties must promote "integrity, honesty and responsibility among its public officials.". They must maintain standards of conduct for the "correct, honorable and proper performance of public functions" and implement measures to discipline a public official who violates the standards. Parties must promote active participation of the private sector in preventing and combating corruption in international trade and investment matters. They must endeavor to encourage private enterprises to implement internal auditing methods for their employees, their accounts, and their financial statements. Parties cannot allow its enforcement of anti-corruption measures to lax through sustained or recurring (in)action when the course of (in)action involves trade or investment between Parties. Parties must work to further cooperation and coordination among their anti-corruption law enforcement agencies and share their expertise and best practices. Parties understand it is important to cooperate and coordinate on international anti-corruption matters and in international organizations. Nothing in this Agreement affects the rights and obligations of the Parties under the IACAC; the OECD Convention; the UNCAC; or the United Nations Convention against Transnational Organized Crime.

§27.1   ARTICLE 27.2. SCOPE

The Anti-corruption Chapter covers all measures "to prevent and combat bribery and corruption" related to any matter covered by the USMCA.[1625] For the U.S., it does not apply to conduct outside of federal criminal jurisdiction:[1626]

1625. *See* United States-Mexico-Canada Agreement, Section 27.2, Jan. 29, 2020.
1626. *See* United States-Mexico-Canada Agreement, Section 27.2, Jan. 29, 2020.

[T]he Parties affirm their adherence to the OECD Convention, with its Annex, the IACAC, and the UNCAC.[1627]

The Parties support the principles aimed at preventing and combatting corruption that were developed at APEC and G-20 anti-corruption fora.[1628] They also support and encourage awareness of available anti-corruption compliance guidelines available through APEC and G-20.[1629]

Parties reserve the right to define their applicable legal principles and defenses and how they will be prosecuted and punished within their territory.[1630]

§27.2   ARTICLE 27.3. MEASURES TO COMBAT CORRUPTION

Parties must implement measures to establish criminal offenses that cover a person subject to its jurisdiction when they intentionally promise, offer, or give a public official an undue advantage, in exchange for the official's action or inaction in relation to their official duties.[1631] There must be criminal offenses that cover the intentional solicita-tion or acceptance by a public official of such undue advantage.[1632] There must be criminal offenses that cover a similar promise, offer, or giving of an undue advantage to a foreign public official or an official of an international organization when it is intended to obtain or retain business or undue advantage in international business.[1633] Aiding, abetting, or conspiracy in any of these cases must also be a criminal offense.[1634] Intentional embezzlement, misappropriation, or diversion of a thing of value by a public official in the Parties' territory must be a criminal offense when the action is for the benefit of the official or another person/entity.[1635]

Parties must establish the liability of legal persons for those offenses and permit sanctions that take into account the gravity of the offense.[1636]

Parties may not allow tax deductions for bribes and other illegal expenses.[1637]

Parties must prohibit persons or entities from: (a) establishing off-the-books accounts; (b) making off-the-books or poorly identified transactions; (c) recording non-existent expenditure; (d) entering liabilities with incorrect information; (e) using false documents; and (f) intentionally destroying bookkeeping documents earlier than the law foresees.[1638]

1627. *See* United States-Mexico-Canada Agreement, Section 27.2, Jan. 29, 2020.
1628. *See* United States-Mexico-Canada Agreement, Section 27.2, Jan. 29, 2020.
1629. *See* United States-Mexico-Canada Agreement, Section 27.2, Jan. 29, 2020.
1630. *See* United States-Mexico-Canada Agreement, Section 27.2, Jan. 29, 2020.
1631. *See* United States-Mexico-Canada Agreement, Section 27.3, Jan. 29, 2020.
1632. *See* United States-Mexico-Canada Agreement, Section 27.3, Jan. 29, 2020.
1633. *See* United States-Mexico-Canada Agreement, Section 27.3, Jan. 29, 2020.
1634. *See* United States-Mexico-Canada Agreement, Section 27.3, Jan. 29, 2020.
1635. *See* United States-Mexico-Canada Agreement, Section 27.3, Jan. 29, 2020.
1636. *See* United States-Mexico-Canada Agreement, Section 27.3, Jan. 29, 2020.
1637. *See* United States-Mexico-Canada Agreement, Section 27.3, Jan. 29, 2020.
1638. *See* United States-Mexico-Canada Agreement, Section 27.3, Jan. 29, 2020.

The last prohibition is limited in the U.S. to "those who have a class of securities registered pursuant to 15 U.S.C. 78l or that are otherwise required to file reports pursuant to 15 U.S.C. 78o (d)."[1639]

Parties must implement measures to protect those who report offenses to the competent authorities.[1640]

§27.3 ARTICLE 27.4. PROMOTING INTEGRITY AMONG PUBLIC OFFICIALS

Parties must promote "integrity, honesty and responsibility among its public officials."[1641] This includes:

> (a) implementing measures to select and train persons in public positions suscep-
> tible to corruption; (b) promoting transparency in the behavior of public officials
> in their official capacity; establishing policies and procedures to identify and
> manage conflicts of interest; (d) requiring senior public officials to disclose their
> outside activities, employment, investments, assets, gifts, etc. from which a
> conflict of interest might result; and (e) facilitating reporting by public officials to
> the appropriate authorities when they notice facts concerning an offense.[1642]

Parties must maintain standards of conduct for the "correct, honorable and proper performance of public functions" and implement measures to discipline a public official who violates the standards.[1643] Parties may allow its authorities to remove, suspend or reassign a public official who is accused of a corruption offense keeping in mind the presumption of innocence.[1644]

§27.4 ARTICLE 27.5. PARTICIPATION OF PRIVATE SECTOR AND SOCIETY

Parties must promote active participation of the private sector in preventing and combatting corruption in international trade and investment matters.[1645] They must endeavor to encourage private enterprises to implement internal auditing methods for their employees, their accounts, and their financial statements.[1646]

Relevant anti-corruption bodies must be known and accessible to the public and should allow anonymous reporting.[1647] Parties must encourage enterprises to maintain internal compliance programs.[1648]

1639. *See* United States-Mexico-Canada Agreement, Section 27.3, Jan. 29, 2020.
1640. *See* United States-Mexico-Canada Agreement, Section 27.3, Jan. 29, 2020.
1641. *See* United States-Mexico-Canada Agreement, Section 27.4, Jan. 29, 2020.
1642. *See* United States-Mexico-Canada Agreement, Section 27.4, Jan. 29, 2020.
1643. *See* United States-Mexico-Canada Agreement, Section 27.4, Jan. 29, 2020.
1644. *See* United States-Mexico-Canada Agreement, Section 27.4, Jan. 29, 2020.
1645. *See* United States-Mexico-Canada Agreement, Section 27.5, Jan. 29, 2020.
1646. *See* United States-Mexico-Canada Agreement, Section 27.5, Jan. 29, 2020.
1647. *See* United States-Mexico-Canada Agreement, Section 27.5, Jan. 29, 2020.
1648. *See* United States-Mexico-Canada Agreement, Section 27.5, Jan. 29, 2020.

§27.5   ARTICLE 27.6. APPLICATION AND ENFORCEMENT OF ANTI-CORRUPTION LAWS

Parties cannot allow its enforcement of anti-corruption measures to lax through sustained or recurring (in)action when the course of (in)action involves trade or investment between Parties.[1649]

Each Party may make their bona fide decisions about allocating resources and providing discretion to authorities to enforce the anti-corruption laws.[1650]

§27.6   ARTICLE 27.7. RELATION TO OTHER AGREEMENTS

Nothing in this Agreement affects the rights and obligations of the Parties under the IACAC; the OECD Convention; the UNCAC; or the *United Nations Convention against Transnational Organized Crime*, done at New York on November 15, 2000.[1651]

§27.7   ARTICLE 27.8. DISPUTE SETTLEMENT

Chapter 31 (Dispute Settlement) applies to this chapter.[1652] However, Parties may only have recourse under Chapter 31 if it considers that another Party's measure is inconsistent within obligation under this chapter, or they have otherwise failed to carry out this chapter's obligation.

Chapter 31 does not apply to § 27.6 (Application and Enforcement of Anti-corruption Laws) or § 27.9 (Cooperation).[1653]

For Chapter 31 Consultations, each Consulting Party must include government authorities that cover the relevant anti-corruption issue.[1654]

If practicable, for Chapter 31 Commissions, any discussion held by the Free Trade Commission must include a Minister responsible for the relevant anti-corruption dispute or their designee.[1655]

For Chapter 31 Panels, the panel must be comprised of relevant anti-corruption experts.

1649. *See* United States-Mexico-Canada Agreement, Section 27.6, Jan. 29, 2020.
1650. *See* United States-Mexico-Canada Agreement, Section 27.6, Jan. 29, 2020.
1651. *See* United States-Mexico-Canada Agreement, Section 27.7, Jan. 29, 2020.
1652. *See* United States-Mexico-Canada Agreement, Section 27.8, Jan. 29, 2020.
1653. *See* United States-Mexico-Canada Agreement, Section 27.8, Jan. 29, 2020.
1654. *See* United States-Mexico-Canada Agreement, Section 27.8, Jan. 29, 2020.
1655. *See* United States-Mexico-Canada Agreement, Section 27.8, Jan. 29, 2020.

§27.8   ARTICLE 27.9. COOPERATION

Parties must work to further cooperation and coordination among their anti-corruption law enforcement agencies and share their expertise and best practices.[1656] Parties understand it is important to cooperate and coordinate on international anti-corruption matters and in international organizations.[1657]

1656. *See* United States-Mexico-Canada Agreement, Section 27.9, Jan. 29, 2020.
1657. *See* United States-Mexico-Canada Agreement, Section 27.9, Jan. 29, 2020.

Good Regulatory Practices

Chapter 28 sets out specific good regulatory practice requirements. It is important for the regulatory bodies of each Party to promote good regulatory practices, advice on key issues, review regulatory functions, and to develop regulatory improvements. Each Party must promote government-wide adherence to good regulatory practices, as well as improve current practices, as well as develop new ones. All of the regulations in each Party's territory must be based on reliable and high-quality information that was obtained in a reasonable manner and that is relevant to the regulatory practices. Based on information gathered and upcoming regulations, a Party must publish a list of regulations that it reasonably expects to adopt or propose in the following twelve months. Additionally, each Party must have a free and publicly available website that contains all information that it is required to publish for the sake of transparency. Regulations must use language that is easy to understand and must be transparent in their development. Expert advisory groups are established in order to give recommendations. Additionally, the cost and impact of assessments should be measured and regulations should be reviewed in order to determine the need for potential changes or improvements. Each Party must publish online descriptions of the regulatory mechanisms used to prepare, evaluate and review regulations. Each Party is required to publish an annual report on estimated costs/benefits. Parties must promote cooperation within regulatory agencies through the Committee on Good Regulatory Practices as well as establishing contact points.

§28.1   ARTICLE 28.2. SUBJECT MATTER AND GENERAL PROVISIONS

Chapter 28 sets out specific "good regulatory practice" requirements.[1658]

1658. *See* United States-Mexico-Canada Agreement, Section 28.2, Jan. 29, 2020.

§28.2   ARTICLE 28.3. CENTRAL REGULATORY COORDINATING BODY

Parties understand it is important for their central regulatory coordinating bodies to promote good regulatory practices, advise on key issues, review regulatory functions and develop regulatory improvements.[1659]

§28.3   ARTICLE 28.4. INTERNAL CONSULTATION, COORDINATION, AND REVIEW

Parties must promote government-wide adherence to good regulatory practices; identify and develop improvements; identify areas of potential overlap that may create inconsistent requirements; support compliance with international obligations; promote consideration of regulatory impacts of information collection and implementation; and encourage approaches that do not unnecessarily restrict competition.[1660] Any measures in furtherance of these requirements must be made public.[1661]

§28.4   ARTICLE 28.5. INFORMATION QUALITY

Regulations in each Party's territory must be based on reliable and high-quality information, so Parties must seek the best, reasonably obtainable information; rely on information that is relevant for the context of the matter; and transparently identify sources, assumptions, and limitations.[1662]

If a regulatory authority uses surveys, they must "use sound statistical methodologies before drawing generalized conclusions concerning the impact of the regulation on the population affected by the regulation; avoid unnecessary duplication; and otherwise minimize unnecessary burdens on those being surveyed."[1663]

§28.5   ARTICLE 28.6. EARLY PLANNING

Each year, Parties must publish a list of regulations that it reasonably expects to adopt or propose in the following twelve months.[1664] The publication must include a description of the regulation, a point of conduct for inquiry, an indication of sectors to be affected, and any expected significant effects on international trade or investment.[1665] They must include time tables if available.[1666]

1659. *See* United States-Mexico-Canada Agreement, Section 28.3, Jan. 29, 2020.
1660. *See* United States-Mexico-Canada Agreement, Section 28.4, Jan. 29, 2020.
1661. *See* United States-Mexico-Canada Agreement, Section 28.4, Jan. 29, 2020.
1662. *See* United States-Mexico-Canada Agreement, Section 28.5, Jan. 29, 2020.
1663. *See* United States-Mexico-Canada Agreement, Section 28.5, Jan. 29, 2020.
1664. *See* United States-Mexico-Canada Agreement, Section 28.6, Jan. 29, 2020.
1665. *See* United States-Mexico-Canada Agreement, Section 28.6, Jan. 29, 2020.
1666. *See* United States-Mexico-Canada Agreement, Section 28.6, Jan. 29, 2020.

§28.6 ARTICLE 28.7. DEDICATED WEBSITE

Parties must have one free and publicly available website that contains all information that it is required to publish for transparency purposes.[1667] Parties may only use more than one website if all of the information can be accessed, and submissions can be made from a single web portal with links.[1668]

§28.7 ARTICLE 28.8. USE OF PLAIN LANGUAGE

All regulations must be clear, concise, and easy for the public to understand—with an exception for those that require technical expertise.[1669]

§28.8 ARTICLE 28.9. TRANSPARENT DEVELOPMENT OF REGULATIONS

When a regulatory authority is developing a regulation, a Party must, under normal circumstances, publish: the text; any regulatory impact assessments; an explanation with objectives, rationale, and alternatives considered; explanation of the data and information that the regulatory authority relied on; and a contact point for inquiries.[1670] This information needs to be published before the regulation is finalized with enough time for written and electronic comments (usually four weeks).[1671] These comments must be made public to the extent practicable on a Party's Dedicated Website.[1672] Parties must consider reasonable requests to extend the comment period.[1673]

If a draft regulation is expected to have a significant impact on Trade, Parties should allow comments for at least sixty days after the necessary items are published—and perhaps even longer time periods for complex regulations.[1674]

§28.9 ARTICLE 28.10. EXPERT ADVISORY GROUPS

Expert Advisory Groups are established by a Party.[1675] They contain members who are not employees or contractors of the Party.[1676] They provide advice or recommendations to the regulatory authority of the Party.[1677] It does not include groups established to enhance intergovernmental coordination and give advice on international affairs.[1678]

1667. *See* United States-Mexico-Canada Agreement, Section 28.7, Jan. 29, 2020.
1668. *See* United States-Mexico-Canada Agreement, Section 28.7, Jan. 29, 2020.
1669. *See* United States-Mexico-Canada Agreement, Section 28.8, Jan. 29, 2020.
1670. *See* United States-Mexico-Canada Agreement, Section 28.9, Jan. 29, 2020.
1671. *See* United States-Mexico-Canada Agreement, Section 28.9, Jan. 29, 2020.
1672. *See* United States-Mexico-Canada Agreement, Section 28.9, Jan. 29, 2020.
1673. *See* United States-Mexico-Canada Agreement, Section 28.9, Jan. 29, 2020.
1674. *See* United States-Mexico-Canada Agreement, Section 28.9, Jan. 29, 2020.
1675. *See* United States-Mexico-Canada Agreement, Section 28.10, Jan. 29, 2020.
1676. *See* United States-Mexico-Canada Agreement, Section 28.10, Jan. 29, 2020.
1677. *See* United States-Mexico-Canada Agreement, Section 28.10, Jan. 29, 2020.
1678. *See* United States-Mexico-Canada Agreement, Section 28.10, Jan. 29, 2020.

Parties must publish the name of any Expert Advisory Group it creates or uses, the names of the members, and their affiliations.[1679] They must publish the group's mandate and functions, upcoming meeting agendas, and summaries of meeting outcomes.[1680] They must endeavor to make available documentation that is made available or is prepared for/by the Expert Advisory Group.[1681]

§28.10   ARTICLE 28.11. REGULATORY IMPACT ASSESSMENT

Parties should encourage the use of regulatory impact assessment to assess the impacts and anticipated costs of proposed regulations.[1682] These assessments must involve assessing: (a) the need for the regulation; (b) feasible and appropriate alternatives that would address the need; (c) cost and benefits of the proposed regulation and its alternatives, including the risks and distributional effects over time; and (d) the reason the proposed regulation is preferable.[1683]

Parties should consider adverse economic impacts on small enterprises and take steps to minimize those impacts.[1684]

§28.11   ARTICLE 28.12. FINAL PUBLICATION

Final publication must be promptly published on a free, publicly available website and include: (a) the date by which compliance is required; (b) an explanation of how the regulation achieves the Party's objectives, the rationale for material features of the regulation, and the nature and reasons for any significant revisions; (c) the regulatory body's view on substantive issues raised in comments; (d) major alternatives and rationale for why the final regulation was selected; and (e) relationship between the regulation and the information it considered in finalizing the regulation.[1685]

§28.12   ARTICLE 28.13. RETROSPECTIVE REVIEW

Parties must conduct a retrospective review of their respective regulations to determine whether modification or repeal is needed.[1686] They must consider a regulation's effectiveness in meeting its objectives, changed circumstances, availability of new information, new opportunities to reduce regulatory burden, ways to address regulatory differences, relevant public views, and impact on small enterprises.[1687] Parties are encouraged to publish these reviews.[1688]

1679. *See* United States-Mexico-Canada Agreement, Section 28.10, Jan. 29, 2020.
1680. *See* United States-Mexico-Canada Agreement, Section 28.10, Jan. 29, 2020.
1681. *See* United States-Mexico-Canada Agreement, Section 28.10, Jan. 29, 2020.
1682. *See* United States-Mexico-Canada Agreement, Section 28.11, Jan. 29, 2020.
1683. *See* United States-Mexico-Canada Agreement, Section 28.11, Jan. 29, 2020.
1684. *See* United States-Mexico-Canada Agreement, Section 28.11, Jan. 29, 2020.
1685. *See* United States-Mexico-Canada Agreement, Section 28.12, Jan. 29, 2020.
1686. *See* United States-Mexico-Canada Agreement, Section 28.13, Jan. 29, 2020.
1687. *See* United States-Mexico-Canada Agreement, Section 28.13, Jan. 29, 2020.
1688. *See* United States-Mexico-Canada Agreement, Section 28.13, Jan. 29, 2020.

§28.13   ARTICLE 28.14. SUGGESTIONS FOR IMPROVEMENT

Parties must allow the submission to any regulatory authority, written suggestions for the issuance, modification, or repeal of a regulation.[1689] These suggestions may be based on the view that the regulation is ineffective "at protecting health, welfare, or safety, has become more burdensome than necessary to achieve its objective...fails to take into account changed circumstances...or relies on incorrect or outdated information."[1690]

§28.14   ARTICLE 28.15. INFORMATION ABOUT REGULATORY PROCESSES

Parties must publish online descriptions of the regulatory mechanisms used to prepare, evaluate and review regulations.[1691] The descriptions must include applicable guidelines, rules and procedures. (*Id.*)

Parties must also publish a "description of the functions and organization of each of its regulatory authorities."[1692] They must publish procedural requirements or forms used by those authorities.[1693] Parties must publish the legal authority for regulatory authorities to verify, inspect, and implement compliance measures.[1694] They must publish the available judicial and administrative procedures for challenging regulations.[1695] They must publish any fees charged by a regulatory authority.[1696]

§28.15   ARTICLE 28.16. ANNUAL REPORT

Parties must prepare and make freely available an annual report on the estimated annual costs and benefits of economically significant regulations and any regulatory changes and proposals.[1697]

§28.16   ARTICLE 28.17. ENCOURAGEMENT OF REGULATORY COMPATIBILITY AND COOPERATION

Parties must encourage their regulatory authorities to cooperate with their relevant counterparts to achieve the goals of regulatory compatibility and the facilitation of trade and investment.[1698]

1689. *See* United States-Mexico-Canada Agreement, Section 28.14, Jan. 29, 2020.
1690. *See* United States-Mexico-Canada Agreement, Section 28.14, Jan. 29, 2020.
1691. *See* United States-Mexico-Canada Agreement, Section 28.15, Jan. 29, 2020.
1692. *See* United States-Mexico-Canada Agreement, Section 28.15, Jan. 29, 2020.
1693. *See* United States-Mexico-Canada Agreement, Section 28.15, Jan. 29, 2020.
1694. *See* United States-Mexico-Canada Agreement, Section 28.15, Jan. 29, 2020.
1695. *See* United States-Mexico-Canada Agreement, Section 28.15, Jan. 29, 2020.
1696. *See* United States-Mexico-Canada Agreement, Section 28.15, Jan. 29, 2020.
1697. *See* United States-Mexico-Canada Agreement, Section 28.16, Jan. 29, 2020.
1698. *See* United States-Mexico-Canada Agreement, Section 28.17, Jan. 29, 2020.

§28.17   ARTICLE 28.18. COMMITTEE ON GOOD REGULATORY PRACTICES

It establishes the Committee on Good Regulatory Practices (GRP Committee) that will enhance efforts to improve regulatory compatibility and cooperation between Parties in a manner that facilitates trades.[1699]

§28.18   ARTICLE 28.19. CONTACT POINTS

Parties must maintain contact points for regulatory matters that arise under the USMCA.[1700]

§28.19   ARTICLE 28.20. APPLICATION OF DISPUTE SETTLEMENT

Parties must exercise their judgment as to whether Chapter 31 (Dispute Settlement) will be useful and may only use Chapter 31 to "address a sustained or recurring course of action or inaction that is inconsistent with a provision of this Chapter."[1701] Chapter 31 will apply to a responding Party beginning one year after USMCA's effective dates.[1702]

Annex 28-A: Additional Provisions Concerning the Scope of "Regulations" and "Regulatory Authorities"

General policy statements that do not prescribe legally enforceable requirements are not regulations for the purposes of this chapter.[1703] The Annex further defines measures specific to each country that are not considered regulations for the purposes of this chapter.[1704] The President of the United States and the Governor in Council are not regulatory authorities for the purposes of this chapter.[1705]

1699. *See* United States-Mexico-Canada Agreement, Section 28.18, Jan. 29, 2020.
1700. *See* United States-Mexico-Canada Agreement, Section 28.19, Jan. 29, 2020.
1701. *See* United States-Mexico-Canada Agreement, Section 28.20, Jan. 29, 2020.
1702. *See* United States-Mexico-Canada Agreement, Section 28.20, Jan. 29, 2020.
1703. *See* United States-Mexico-Canada Agreement, Annex 28-A, Jan. 29, 2020.
1704. *See* United States-Mexico-Canada Agreement, Annex 28-A, Jan. 29, 2020.
1705. *See* United States-Mexico-Canada Agreement, Annex 28-A, Jan. 29, 2020.

CHAPTER 29

Publication and Administration

All laws, regulations, procedures and administrative rulings (measures) that relate to matters covered by the USMCA must be promptly published or otherwise made available. Parties must publish its laws and regulations that regard the central level of government on a free and public website that has a search function. When initiating an administrative proceeding, a Person of another Party must be reasonably notified in a manner that describes the nature of the proceeding, the legal authority, and the issue at hand. Parties must maintain judicial or administrative tribunals for review and possible correction of a final administrative action regarding a matter covered by the USMCA. The tribunals must be impartial and independent of the authority that has issued the final ruling. Parties agree to facilitate high-quality health care and improve public health. If a Party's national health care authority has procedures for listing new medical devices or pharmaceutical products or medical devices for reimbursement or procedures for setting the reimbursement amount, that Party must ensure that all proposals for these listings are completed within a specified time period. They must disclose rules, methodology, principles and guidelines with which they will assess the proposals and give the applicants time to comment during the decision-making process. As their respective laws permit, Parties must allow drug manufacturers to inform health professionals and consumers of truthful information regarding its product that is approved for marketing in a Party's territory.

§29.1   SECTION A: PUBLICATION AND ADMINISTRATION

[A]   Article 29.2. Publication

All laws, regulations, procedures and administrative rulings (measures) that relate to matters covered by the USMCA must be promptly published or otherwise made available.[1706] When possible, Parties must publish proposed measures and provide a

---

1706. *See* United States-Mexico-Canada Agreement, Section 29.2, Jan. 29, 2020.

reasonable time for comments.[1707] Parties must publish its laws and regulations that regard the central level of government on a free and public website that has a search function.[1708]

[B]   Article 29.3. Administrative Proceedings

When initiating an administrative proceeding, a Person of another Party must be reasonably notified in a manner that describes the nature of the proceeding, the legal authority, and the issue at hand.[1709] The person affected by the proceeding must be able to support its position prior to any final administrative action.[1710]

[C]   Article 29.4. Review and Appeal

Parties must maintain judicial or administrative tribunals for review and possible correction of a final administrative action regarding a matter covered by the USMCA.[1711] The tribunals must be impartial and independent of the authority who issued the final ruling.[1712] They must give the Parties "a reasonable opportunity to support or defend their respective positions" and base their decisions on evidence in the record."[1713] Once a decision is made, and no other appeal is sought/allowed, the final decision must be implemented and precedential.[1714]

§29.2   SECTION B: TRANSPARENCY AND PROCEDURAL FAIRNESS FOR PHARMACEUTICAL PRODUCTS AND MEDICAL DEVICES

[A]   Article 29.6. Principles

Parties agree to facilitate high-quality health care and improve public health.[1715]

[B]   Article 29.7. Procedural Fairness

If a Party's national health care authority has procedures for listing new medical devices or pharmaceutical products or medical devices for reimbursement or

---

1707. *See* United States-Mexico-Canada Agreement, Section 29.2, Jan. 29, 2020.
1708. *See* United States-Mexico-Canada Agreement, Section 29.2, Jan. 29, 2020.
1709. *See* United States-Mexico-Canada Agreement, Section 29.3, Jan. 29, 2020.
1710. *See* United States-Mexico-Canada Agreement, Section 29.3, Jan. 29, 2020.
1711. *See* United States-Mexico-Canada Agreement, Section 29.4, Jan. 29, 2020.
1712. *See* United States-Mexico-Canada Agreement, Section 29.4, Jan. 29, 2020.
1713. *See* United States-Mexico-Canada Agreement, Section 29.4, Jan. 29, 2020.
1714. *See* United States-Mexico-Canada Agreement, Section 29.4, Jan. 29, 2020.
1715. *See* United States-Mexico-Canada Agreement, Section 29.6, Jan. 29, 2020.

procedures for setting the reimbursement amount, that Party must ensure that all proposals for these listings are completed within a specified time period.[1716] They must disclose rules, methodology, principles and guidelines with which they will assess the proposals and give the applicants time to comment during the decision-making process.[1717] They must give a written explanation of the basis of their decisions.[1718] Parties must allow independent review or internal review (provided the internal review substantively reconsiders the application).[1719]

[C]   Article 29.8. Dissemination of Information to Health Professionals and Consumers

As their respective laws permit, Parties must allow drug manufacturers to inform health professionals and consumers of truthful information regarding its product that is approved for marketing in a Party's territory.[1720] Parties can require that the marketing indicate which authority approved the product (e.g., FDA) and include information regarding the risks.[1721]

[D]   Article 29.9. Consultations

Parties must consider and allow consultations on matters related to this chapter.[1722] Consultations must take place within three months of the request's delivery and must involve national health care authority or officials.[1723]

[E]   Article 29.10. Non-Application of Dispute Settlement

Chapter 31 (Dispute Settlement) is not available for matters arising under this section.[1724]

Annex 29-A: Publication of Laws and Regulations of General Application

This Annex lists the websites where the laws and regulations of the general application of each Party are published.[1725]

1716. *See* United States-Mexico-Canada Agreement, Section 29.7, Jan. 29, 2020.
1717. *See* United States-Mexico-Canada Agreement, Section 29.7, Jan. 29, 2020.
1718. *See* United States-Mexico-Canada Agreement, Section 29.7, Jan. 29, 2020.
1719. *See* United States-Mexico-Canada Agreement, Section 29.7, Jan. 29, 2020.
1720. *See* United States-Mexico-Canada Agreement, Section 29.8, Jan. 29, 2020.
1721. *See* United States-Mexico-Canada Agreement, Section 29.8, Jan. 29, 2020.
1722. *See* United States-Mexico-Canada Agreement, Section 29.9, Jan. 29, 2020.
1723. *See* United States-Mexico-Canada Agreement, Section 29.9, Jan. 29, 2020.
1724. *See* United States-Mexico-Canada Agreement, Section 29.10, Jan. 29, 2020.
1725. *See* United States-Mexico-Canada Agreement, Annex 29-A, Jan. 29, 2020.

Annex 29-B: Party-Specific Definitions

Canada's national health care authority is the Federal Drug Benefits Committee.[1726]

The United States' national health care authority is the Centers for Medicare & Medicaid Services (CMS), "with respect to CMS's role in making Medicare national coverage determinations."[1727]

1726. *See* United States-Mexico-Canada Agreement, Annex 29-B, Jan. 29, 2020.
1727. *See* United States-Mexico-Canada Agreement, Annex 29-B, Jan. 29, 2020.

CHAPTER 30

Administrative and Institutional Provisions

This article establishes the Commission comprising government representatives of each Party at the level of Ministers or their designees. The Commission must consider matters and proposals related to the USMCA: supervise committees, working groups and other similar USMCA bodies. They must consider ways to enhance trade between Parties, maintain and update procedural rules and dispute settlement proceedings. Decisions made by the committee must be made by consensus unless otherwise provided for in the USMCA or decided by the Parties. Consensus occurs when all Parties are present at a meeting and no objections are made to the proposed decisions. The Commission must meet within one year of the USMCA's effective date and then as Parties decide. The Party who leads the meeting must provide administrative support, and the Commission and other USMCA may work via email or videoconferencing and they may establish their own rules of procedure. Each Party must have an agreement coordinator who communicates with their counterparts as well as other USMCA contact points. This communication must be done and the other Parties must be notified within 60 of the implementation of the USMCA. If a Party decides to change its contact point or agreement coordinator, all other Parties must be notified. Each Party must have a Secretariat broken down into national Sections which have permanent offices and individual secretaries who are responsible for administration and management. The main goal of the Secretariat is to assist the Commission, panels, and committees.

§30.1 ARTICLE 30.1. ESTABLISHMENT OF THE FREE TRADE COMMISSION (COMMISSION)

This article establishes the Commission comprising "government representatives of each Party at the level of Ministers or their designees."[1728]

1728. *See* United States-Mexico-Canada Agreement, Section 30.1, Jan. 29, 2020.

219

§30.2   ARTICLES 30.2. FUNCTIONS OF THE COMMISSION

The Commission must consider matters and proposals related to the USMCA; supervise committees, working groups and other similar USMCA bodies; consider ways to enhance trade between Parties, maintain and update procedural rules and dispute settlement proceedings.[1729]

They may take on matters raised by other USMCA bodies, merge or dissolve these groups. They may eliminate tariffs in Annex 2-B; adjust Chapter 6 Tariff Preferential levels; modify the rules of origin in Annex 4-B; modify minimum data requirements for certificates of origin; modify the USMCA to better conform with Harmonized System changes; and modify the entities, goods/services, and thresholds listed in the Chapter 13 Government Procurement provisions.[1730] They can issue interpretations of the USMCA or design ways to implement it. (*Id.*) They may seek advice from non-governmental groups or people and modify regulations when they agree jointly.[1731]

§30.3   ARTICLE 30.3. DECISION-MAKING

Decisions must be made by consensus unless otherwise provided for in the USMCA or decided by the Parties.[1732] Consensus occurs when all Parties are present at a meeting and no objections are made to the proposed decision.[1733]

§30.4   ARTICLE 30.4. RULES OF PROCEDURE OF THE COMMISSION
AND SUBSIDIARY BODIES

The Commission must meet within one year of the USMCA's effective date and then as Parties decide.[1734] The Party who leads the meeting must provide administrative support.[1735] The Commission and other USMCA may work via email or videoconferencing and they may establish their own rules of procedure.[1736]

§30.5   ARTICLE 30.5. AGREEMENT COORDINATOR AND CONTACT
POINTS

Parties must each have an agreement coordinator who communicates with their counterparts as well as other USMCA contact points.[1737] This must be done, and notification must be made to other parties within sixty days of the USMCA effective

---

1729. *See* United States-Mexico-Canada Agreement, Section 30.2, Jan. 29, 2020.
1730. *See* United States-Mexico-Canada Agreement, Section 30.2, Jan. 29, 2020.
1731. *See* United States-Mexico-Canada Agreement, Section 30.2, Jan. 29, 2020.
1732. *See* United States-Mexico-Canada Agreement, Section 30.3, Jan. 29, 2020.
1733. *See* United States-Mexico-Canada Agreement, Section 30.3, Jan. 29, 2020.
1734. *See* United States-Mexico-Canada Agreement, Section 30.4, Jan. 29, 2020.
1735. *See* United States-Mexico-Canada Agreement, Section 30.4, Jan. 29, 2020.
1736. *See* United States-Mexico-Canada Agreement, Section 30.4, Jan. 29, 2020.
1737. *See* United States-Mexico-Canada Agreement, Section 30.5, Jan. 29, 2020.

date.[1738] If a Party's contact point or agreement coordinator changes, they must promptly notify the others.[1739]

§30.6   ARTICLE 30.6. THE SECRETARIAT

Parties must have a Secretariat broken down into national Sections which have permanent offices and individual secretaries who are responsible for administration and management.[1740]

The Secretariat, at large, must assist the Commission, panels, and committees.[1741] They are responsible for paying panelists, assistants, and experts involved in dispute resolution.[1742]

1738. *See* United States-Mexico-Canada Agreement, Section 30.5, Jan. 29, 2020.
1739. *See* United States-Mexico-Canada Agreement, Section 30.5, Jan. 29, 2020.
1740. *See* United States-Mexico-Canada Agreement, Section 30.6, Jan. 29, 2020.
1741. *See* United States-Mexico-Canada Agreement, Section 30.6, Jan. 29, 2020.
1742. *See* United States-Mexico-Canada Agreement, Section 30.6, Jan. 29, 2020.

CHAPTER 31

Dispute Settlement

Parties must try to agree on the interpretation and application of the USMCA and consult to resolve any disagreement. As expressed in Article 31.3: Choice of Forum, if the dispute arises under the USMCA and another international agreement that Parties are party to, the complainant may select the forum, and the forum must be exclusively used. If consultations do not work, a consulting Party may request a meeting of the Commission; they must convene within ten days of the request. If the Commission does not resolve the matter within thirty days, a consulting Party may request a panel. Terms of reference must be to examine the matter under the USMCA and make determinations and recommendations with reasoning. Before the USMCA becomes effective, Parties must agree to a roster of up to 30 people willing to serve as panelists. For disputes between two Parties the panel must include five individuals, and the chair must be chosen within fifteen days of the panel request. The time frames applicable to panel proceedings freeze when a panelist needs to be replaced. Disputing Parties must be able to provide oral arguments at least once and the hearings should be open to the public unless decided otherwise. All dispute-related documents must be e-filed through a Party's Section of the Secretariat. Panels are to issue reports containing findings of fact, determinations regarding inconsistencies or failure to carry out USMCA obligations. Parties agree to encourage and promote alternative dispute resolution for international commercial disputes in the free trade area.

§31.1   SECTION A: DISPUTE SETTLEMENT

[A]   Article 31.1. Cooperation

Parties must try to agree on the interpretation and application of the USMCA and consult to resolve any disagreement.[1743]

1743. *See* United States-Mexico-Canada Agreement, Section 31.1, Jan. 29, 2020.

[B]   Article 31.2. Scope

With the exceptions mentioned in the USMCA, Chapter 31 Dispute Settlement applies to:

> interpreting or applying the USMCA; allegations that a measure of another Party is or would be inconsistent with the USMCA or that a Party has failed to carry out its USMCA obligations; and allegations that a Party's benefit is being nullified or impaired by a measure of another party that is consistent with the USMCA.[1744]

[C]   Article 31.3. Choice of Forum

If the dispute arises under the USMCA and another international agreement that Parties are party to, the complainant may select the forum.[1745] Once a Party has established a panel or tribunal under the USMCA, the forum selected must be used exclusively.[1746]

[D]   Article 31.4. Consultations

Parties may request consultations with each other regarding anything covered by the scope of this chapter (Article 31.2).[1747] Consultations must be made in writing, including reasoning, legal basis, and identify the specific measure at issue.[1748] Requests must be delivered to the respected Sections of the Secretariat.[1749] A third party that has a substantial interest in the matter may participate in consultations by similar notification but must explain its substantial interest.[1750] The latest Parties may begin consultations is thirty days after the requester's delivery, and it may be in-person or electronically.[1751]

[E]   Article 31.5. Commission, Good Offices, Conciliation, and Mediation

If consultations do not work, a consulting Party may request a meeting of the Commission by stating, in writing, the measure complained of and the relevant USMCA provisions.[1752] The Commission must convene within ten days of the request's delivery unless they decide otherwise.[1753] They may use technical advisors, experts, or working

---

1744. *See* United States-Mexico-Canada Agreement, Section 31.2, Jan. 29, 2020.
1745. *See* United States-Mexico-Canada Agreement, Section 31.3, Jan. 29, 2020.
1746. *See* United States-Mexico-Canada Agreement, Section 31.3, Jan. 29, 2020.
1747. *See* United States-Mexico-Canada Agreement, Section 31.4, Jan. 29, 2020.
1748. *See* United States-Mexico-Canada Agreement, Section 31.4, Jan. 29, 2020.
1749. *See* United States-Mexico-Canada Agreement, Section 31.4, Jan. 29, 2020.
1750. *See* United States-Mexico-Canada Agreement, Section 31.4, Jan. 29, 2020.
1751. *See* United States-Mexico-Canada Agreement, Section 31.4, Jan. 29, 2020.
1752. *See* United States-Mexico-Canada Agreement, Section 31.5, Jan. 29, 2020.
1753. *See* United States-Mexico-Canada Agreement, Section 31.5, Jan. 29, 2020.

groups.[1754] They can make recommendations or have recourse to good office, mediation, or other alternative dispute resolution procedures.[1755]

If two or more proceedings regard the same measure, the Commission may consolidate them.[1756]

Parties at any time can undertake alternative dispute resolution and/or suspend or terminate those proceedings.[1757]

[F]   Article 31.6. Establishment of a Panel

If the Commission does not resolve the matter within thirty days (or another time period that consulting Parties decided), a consulting Party may request a panel by giving notice to the Secretariat of the responding Party.[1758] A third party may join as a complaining part by notifying the disputing Parties no later than seven days after the original panel request.[1759] Panels may be consolidated when two panels regard the same matter.[1760]

[G]   Article 31.7. Terms of Reference

Terms of reference must be to examine the matter under the USMCA and make determinations and recommendations with reasoning.[1761] If the original panel request claims that a benefit is nullified or impaired, the terms of reference must say that.[1762] If a Party wants the panel to make findings on adverse trade effects, they must indicate that in terms of reference.[1763]

[H]   Article 31.8. Roster and Qualifications of Panelists

Before the USMCA becomes effective, Parties must agree to a roster of up to 30 people willing to serve as panelists.[1764] The roster will be effective for at least three years or until a new roster is agreed upon.[1765] Reappointments are allowed.[1766]

Panelists must have expertise in international trade, international law, or matters covered by the USMCA.[1767] They must be selected objectively and with sound

---

1754. *See* United States-Mexico-Canada Agreement, Section 31.5, Jan. 29, 2020.
1755. *See* United States-Mexico-Canada Agreement, Section 31.5, Jan. 29, 2020.
1756. *See* United States-Mexico-Canada Agreement, Section 31.5, Jan. 29, 2020.
1757. *See* United States-Mexico-Canada Agreement, Section 31.5, Jan. 29, 2020.
1758. *See* United States-Mexico-Canada Agreement, Section 31.6, Jan. 29, 2020.
1759. *See* United States-Mexico-Canada Agreement, Section 31.6, Jan. 29, 2020.
1760. *See* United States-Mexico-Canada Agreement, Section 31.6, Jan. 29, 2020.
1761. *See* United States-Mexico-Canada Agreement, Section 31.7, Jan. 29, 2020.
1762. *See* United States-Mexico-Canada Agreement, Section 31.7, Jan. 29, 2020.
1763. *See* United States-Mexico-Canada Agreement, Section 31.7, Jan. 29, 2020.
1764. *See* United States-Mexico-Canada Agreement, Section 31.8, Jan. 29, 2020.
1765. *See* United States-Mexico-Canada Agreement, Section 31.8, Jan. 29, 2020.
1766. *See* United States-Mexico-Canada Agreement, Section 31.8, Jan. 29, 2020.
1767. *See* United States-Mexico-Canada Agreement, Section 31.8, Jan. 29, 2020.

judgment.[1768] They must be independent of each Party and comply with the Commission's Code of Conduct.[1769]

For environmental disputes, panelists must have expertise or experience in environmental law or practice—with the exception of the panel chair.[1770] For labor disputes, panelists must have expertise or experience in labor law or practice—with the exception of the panel chair.[1771] The same goes for other specialized areas of law; the panel must consist of individuals with expertise in those particular areas.[1772]

Individuals who have participated in consultations, commission, good offices, conciliation or mediation cannot serve on a panel for the same dispute.[1773]

[I]   Article 31.9. Panel Composition

For disputes between two Parties, the panel must include five individuals, and the chair must be chosen within fifteen days of the panel request.[1774] If Parties cannot decide on a chair within this time frame, a Party will be chosen by lot to pick the chair—who cannot be a citizen of the chosen Party.[1775] Then, the Parties must choose two panelists who are citizens of the other Party within fifteen days.[1776] If a Party fails to choose within the timeframe, those panelists are randomly selected from the roster members who are citizens of the other Party.[1777]

For disputes between more than two Parties, the panel also includes 5 members to be chosen within fifteen days.[1778] If there is disagreement on the chair, a Party/Parties on one side of the dispute will be chosen by lot and select a chair that is a non-citizen to the Party/Parties chosen.[1779] Then, the responding Parties must select two panelists from two distinct complaining Parties.[1780] The complaining Parties select two panelists from the responding Party.[1781] If a Party fails to choose within the timeframe, those panelists are randomly selected from the roster members who are citizens of the other Party.[1782]

Panelists should normally be selected from the roster, and Parties may raise peremptory challenges against someone not on the roster within fifteen days after that person has been proposed unless the roster member has the necessary specialized expertise.[1783] Where a proposed panelist does not have the necessary expertise, a Party

---

1768. *See* United States-Mexico-Canada Agreement, Section 31.8, Jan. 29, 2020.
1769. *See* United States-Mexico-Canada Agreement, Section 31.8, Jan. 29, 2020.
1770. *See* United States-Mexico-Canada Agreement, Section 31.8, Jan. 29, 2020.
1771. *See* United States-Mexico-Canada Agreement, Section 31.8, Jan. 29, 2020.
1772. *See* United States-Mexico-Canada Agreement, Section 31.8, Jan. 29, 2020.
1773. *See* United States-Mexico-Canada Agreement, Section 31.8, Jan. 29, 2020.
1774. *See* United States-Mexico-Canada Agreement, Section 31.9, Jan. 29, 2020.
1775. *See* United States-Mexico-Canada Agreement, Section 31.9, Jan. 29, 2020.
1776. *See* United States-Mexico-Canada Agreement, Section 31.9, Jan. 29, 2020.
1777. *See* United States-Mexico-Canada Agreement, Section 31.9, Jan. 29, 2020.
1778. *See* United States-Mexico-Canada Agreement, Section 31.9, Jan. 29, 2020.
1779. *See* United States-Mexico-Canada Agreement, Section 31.9, Jan. 29, 2020.
1780. *See* United States-Mexico-Canada Agreement, Section 31.9, Jan. 29, 2020.
1781. *See* United States-Mexico-Canada Agreement, Section 31.9, Jan. 29, 2020.
1782. *See* United States-Mexico-Canada Agreement, Section 31.9, Jan. 29, 2020.
1783. *See* United States-Mexico-Canada Agreement, Section 31.9, Jan. 29, 2020.

may not use a peremptory challenge but may raise concerns that the proposed panelist does not meet panel qualifications.[1784]

If a Party alleges a panelist is in violation of the Code of Conduct, the disputing Parties must consult and may remove and replace the panelist.[1785]

[J]   Article 31.10. Replacement of Panelists

The time frames applicable to panel proceedings freeze when a panelist needs to be replaced due to resignation, removal, or inability to serve.[1786] However, the replacement must be appointed within fifteen days under the same method as initial appointments.[1787]

[K]   Article 31.11. Rules of Procedure for Panels

Disputing Parties must be able to provide oral arguments at least once and the hearings should be open to the public unless decided otherwise.[1788] The disputing Parties must be able to submit an initial motion and a rebuttal.[1789] Any written submissions must be available to the public as soon as possible, with the exception of confidential information.[1790] The Panel must consider written views from non-governmental entities that may assist the panel in evaluating the disputing Parties' positions.[1791] Unless otherwise decided, the hearings will be held in the capital of the responding party.[1792]

[L]   Article 31.12. Electronic Document Filing

All dispute-related documents must be e-filed through a Party's Section of the Secretariat.[1793]

[M]   Article 31.13. Function of Panels

Panels are to issue reports containing findings of fact, determinations regarding inconsistencies or failure to carry out USMCA obligations, recommendations, and reasoning for the aforementioned.[1794]

1784. *See* United States-Mexico-Canada Agreement, Section 31.9, Jan. 29, 2020.
1785. *See* United States-Mexico-Canada Agreement, Section 31.9, Jan. 29, 2020.
1786. *See* United States-Mexico-Canada Agreement, Section 31.10, Jan. 29, 2020.
1787. *See* United States-Mexico-Canada Agreement, Section 31.10, Jan. 29, 2020.
1788. *See* United States-Mexico-Canada Agreement, Section 31.11, Jan. 29, 2020.
1789. *See* United States-Mexico-Canada Agreement, Section 31.11, Jan. 29, 2020.
1790. *See* United States-Mexico-Canada Agreement, Section 31.11, Jan. 29, 2020.
1791. *See* United States-Mexico-Canada Agreement, Section 31.11, Jan. 29, 2020.
1792. *See* United States-Mexico-Canada Agreement, Section 31.11, Jan. 29, 2020.
1793. *See* United States-Mexico-Canada Agreement, Section 31.12, Jan. 29, 2020.
1794. *See* United States-Mexico-Canada Agreement, Section 31.13, Jan. 29, 2020.

The USMCA should be interpreted according to customary interpretation, as reflected in Articles 31 and 32 of the *Vienna Convention on the Law of Treaties*, done at Vienna on May 23, 1969.[1795]

Decisions must be made by consensus or majority vote.[1796] Reports must be based on relevant USMCA revisions, expert advice, and the materials submitted by disputing Parties.[1797] They cannot be drafted in the presence of any Party.[1798] Panelists may present concurrences or dissents but should not disclose which panelists are associated with majority or minority views.[1799]

[N]   Article 31.14. Third-Party Participation

Non-disputing Parties are entitled to attend hearings and make and receive submissions provided that they give notice to the disputing Parties no longer than ten days after the Panel is established.[1800]

[O]   Article 31.15. Role of Experts

Subject to an agreement and subject to terms and conditions imposed by disputing Parties, a panel may seek information or technical advice from those it deems appropriate.[1801] Parties must be able to comment on this information or advice.[1802]

[P]   Article 31.16. Suspension or Termination of Proceedings

If a complaining Party requests suspension, the panel may suspend its work for up to twelve consecutive months.[1803] If all disputing Parties request suspension, the panel must suspend its work.[1804] Any dispute settlement timeframe must be extended as well.[1805] If a panel is suspended for longer than twelve consecutive months, the proceedings lapse unless the disputing Parties decide otherwise.[1806]

A panel must terminate its proceedings at the disputing Parties' request.[1807]

1795. *See* United States-Mexico-Canada Agreement, Section 31.13, Jan. 29, 2020.
1796. *See* United States-Mexico-Canada Agreement, Section 31.13, Jan. 29, 2020.
1797. *See* United States-Mexico-Canada Agreement, Section 31.13, Jan. 29, 2020.
1798. *See* United States-Mexico-Canada Agreement, Section 31.13, Jan. 29, 2020.
1799. *See* United States-Mexico-Canada Agreement, Section 31.13, Jan. 29, 2020.
1800. *See* United States-Mexico-Canada Agreement, Section 31.14, Jan. 29, 2020.
1801. *See* United States-Mexico-Canada Agreement, Section 31.15, Jan. 29, 2020.
1802. *See* United States-Mexico-Canada Agreement, Section 31.15, Jan. 29, 2020.
1803. *See* United States-Mexico-Canada Agreement, Section 31.16, Jan. 29, 2020.
1804. *See* United States-Mexico-Canada Agreement, Section 31.16, Jan. 29, 2020.
1805. *See* United States-Mexico-Canada Agreement, Section 31.16, Jan. 29, 2020.
1806. *See* United States-Mexico-Canada Agreement, Section 31.16, Jan. 29, 2020.
1807. *See* United States-Mexico-Canada Agreement, Section 31.16, Jan. 29, 2020.

[Q]   Article 31.17. Panel Report

Once the last panelist is appointed, the Panel has 150 days to present an initial report to Parties—for perishable goods, this time should is reduced to 120 days—as feasible.[1808] If the panel cannot release the initial report within this timeframe, it must tell the disputing Parties why and give an estimate of the report's release.[1809] A delay must not exceed thirty more days unless the disputing Parties agree otherwise.[1810]

Disputing Parties may submit written comments on the initial report within fifteen days of its presentation, and in response to the comments, a panel may request more information from a Party, reconsider its report, or make further examinations.[1811] The final report must be issued within thirty days of the initial report unless the disputing Parties agree otherwise.[1812] While protecting confidential information, the disputing Parties must make the final report public within fifteen days of its release.[1813]

[R]   Article 31.18. Implementation of Final Report

Disputing Parties must endeavor to agree on a dispute resolution within forty-five days of receiving a final report that confirms a Party took an inconsistent measure to the USMCA, did not carry out its USMCA obligations, or nullified or impaired a benefit for a Party under the USMCA.[1814] This can include eliminating non-conformity/nullification/impairment, compensation, or any other agreed-upon remedy.[1815]

[S]   Article 31.19. Non-Implementation—Suspension of Benefits

If Parties are unable to resolve the dispute within forty-five days of the final report, the complaining Party may suspend measures giving the equivalent effect to the non-conformity, nullification, or impairment until the dispute is agreed upon.[1816] A complaining Party must look to the same sector that was subject to the dispute before suspending benefits in other sectors.[1817]

If the responding Party believes it has eliminated the issue at dispute or the proposed suspension is "manifestly excessive," they may request the panel reconvene.[1818]

1808. *See* United States-Mexico-Canada Agreement, Section 31.17, Jan. 29, 2020.
1809. *See* United States-Mexico-Canada Agreement, Section 31.17, Jan. 29, 2020.
1810. *See* United States-Mexico-Canada Agreement, Section 31.17, Jan. 29, 2020.
1811. *See* United States-Mexico-Canada Agreement, Section 31.17, Jan. 29, 2020.
1812. *See* United States-Mexico-Canada Agreement, Section 31.17, Jan. 29, 2020.
1813. *See* United States-Mexico-Canada Agreement, Section 31.17, Jan. 29, 2020.
1814. *See* United States-Mexico-Canada Agreement, Section 31.18, Jan. 29, 2020.
1815. *See* United States-Mexico-Canada Agreement, Section 31.18, Jan. 29, 2020.
1816. *See* United States-Mexico-Canada Agreement, Section 31.19, Jan. 29, 2020.
1817. *See* United States-Mexico-Canada Agreement, Section 31.19, Jan. 29, 2020.
1818. *See* United States-Mexico-Canada Agreement, Section 31.19, Jan. 29, 2020.

§31.2 SECTION B. DOMESTIC PROCEEDINGS AND PRIVATE COMMERCIAL DISPUTE SETTLEMENT

[A] Article 31.20. Referrals of Matters from Judicial or Administrative Proceedings

If interpretation or application of the USMCA arises in a domestic proceeding in a Party's territory, or if a court or administrative bodies solicits the view of a Party, that Party must notify the other Parties, and the Commission should agree on a response as soon as possible.[1819] The Party whose territory the court or administrative body is in must submit this Commission's response to the court or administrative body.[1820] If the Commission is unable to agree, the Party may submit its own views.[1821]

[B] Article 31.21. Private Rights

"Taking measures inconsistent with the USMCA" may not give rise to a cause of action against another Party under a Party's law.[1822]

[C] Article 31.22. Alternative Dispute Resolution

Parties agree to encourage and promote alternative dispute resolution for international commercial disputes in the free trade area.[1823] Parties who are in compliance with the *Convention on the Recognition and Enforcement of Foreign Arbitral Awards*, done at New York on June 10, 1958, or the *Inter-American Convention on International Commercial Arbitration*, done at Panama on January 30, 1975, are deemed to have taken appropriate procedures related to alternative dispute resolution.[1824]

The Commission must form and maintain an Advisory Committee on Private Commercial Disputes to further the use of alternative dispute resolution.[1825]

1819. *See* United States-Mexico-Canada Agreement, Section 31.20, Jan. 29, 2020.
1820. *See* United States-Mexico-Canada Agreement, Section 31.20, Jan. 29, 2020.
1821. *See* United States-Mexico-Canada Agreement, Section 31.20, Jan. 29, 2020.
1822. *See* United States-Mexico-Canada Agreement, Section 31.21, Jan. 29, 2020.
1823. *See* United States-Mexico-Canada Agreement, Section 31.22, Jan. 29, 2020.
1824. *See* United States-Mexico-Canada Agreement, Section 31.22, Jan. 29, 2020.
1825. *See* United States-Mexico-Canada Agreement, Section 31.22, Jan. 29, 2020.

CHAPTER 32

Exceptions and General Provisions

Parties do not necessarily have to allow access to essential secured information. If a tax agreement between Parties is inconsistent with the USMCA, the issue should be referred to the Parties' designated authorities to discuss the inconsistency, and a panel or tribunal can meet to discuss the issue. This applies to export duties, income tax, capital gains tax, and corporate capital tax that relate to the purchase or consumption of particular services. However, this does not apply to non-conforming tax measures in existence when NAFTA 1994 entered into force on January 1, 1994, nor does it apply to new measures aimed at ensuring the equitable or effective administration of taxes. If a Party has serious financial difficulties, they may adopt restrictive measures regarding payments or transfers for current accounts or the movement of capital. The USMCA does not prevent Parties from providing measures that fulfill its legal obligations to indigenous people, as long as measures are not discriminatory or restrict trade. For the most part, the USMCA does not apply to Canada with respect to a cultural industry (e.g., motion pictures). In return, the U.S. and Mexico may provide similar measures with respect to Canadian goods and services. Parties in the USMCA are not required to disclose any information that contradicts laws or impedes law enforcement and must legally protect information of people. For transparency, Parties must allow access to their records. In order to trade with Non-Market FTA countries, agreements must be worked out around thirty days in advance.

§32.1   SECTION A: EXCEPTIONS

[A]   Article 32.2. Essential Security

Parties need not furnish or allow access to essential secured information.[1826] Parties can adopt measures necessary to maintain or restore international or domestic peace or security.[1827]

1826. *See* United States-Mexico-Canada Agreement, Section 32.2, Jan. 29, 2020.
1827. *See* United States-Mexico-Canada Agreement, Section 32.2, Jan. 29, 2020.

[B]   Article 32.3. Taxation Measures

Except for provided in this article, the USMCA does not apply to taxation measures.[1828] If a tax convention between or more Parties is inconsistent with the USMCA, the issue should be referred to the Parties' designated authorities to discuss the inconsistency, and a panel or tribunal can meet to discuss the issue.[1829]

National Treatments (§ 2.3) and Export Duties, Taxes, or other Charges (§ 2.15) apply to taxation measures.[1830]

National Treatment provisions (§ 15.3 and § 17.3) apply to income tax, capital gains tax, and corporate capital tax that relate to the purchase or consumption of particular services.[1831]

Certain National Treatment (§ 14.4; § 15.3; § 17.3), Most-Favored-Nation Treatment (§ 14.5; § 17.4), and Nondiscriminatory Treatment (§ 19.4) provisions apply to taxation measures (except for taxes on income, capital gains, taxable corporation capital, estates, inheritances, gifts, and generation-skipping transfers).[1832]

Nondiscriminatory Treatment of Digital Products (§ 19.4) applies to income tax, capital gains tax, and corporate capital tax that relate to the purchase or consumption of particular digital products.[1833]

However, none of the above, § 32.3.6(a)-(c), apply to an MFN obligation with respect to an advantage given by a Party pursuant to a tax measure.[1834] They do not apply to non-conforming tax measures in existence when NAFTA 1994 entered into force on January 1, 1994, or the continuation, renewal, or amendment of such measure (provided the amendment does not decrease conformity.[1835]

The above-listed, § 32.3.6(a)-(c), do not apply to new measures aimed at ensuring the equitable or effective administration of taxes, including a measure that differentiates between persons based on their residence, provided that discrimination is not arbitrary (§ 32.3.6(h)).[1836] Those provisions do not apply to an advantage conditional on receiving income from or contributing to a pension plan if a Party maintains regulation over the plan.[1837] They do not apply to excise duties on insurance premiums given that if they were levied by another Party, they would be covered under § 32.3.6(e), (f), or (g).[1838]

Performance Requirements (§ 14.10.2; § 14.10.3; § 14.10.4) apply to tax measures.[1839]

1828. *See* United States-Mexico-Canada Agreement, Section 32.3, Jan. 29, 2020.
1829. *See* United States-Mexico-Canada Agreement, Section 32.3, Jan. 29, 2020.
1830. *See* United States-Mexico-Canada Agreement, Section 32.3, Jan. 29, 2020.
1831. *See* United States-Mexico-Canada Agreement, Section 32.3, Jan. 29, 2020.
1832. *See* United States-Mexico-Canada Agreement, Section 32.3, Jan. 29, 2020.
1833. *See* United States-Mexico-Canada Agreement, Section 32.3, Jan. 29, 2020.
1834. *See* United States-Mexico-Canada Agreement, Section 32.3, Jan. 29, 2020.
1835. *See* United States-Mexico-Canada Agreement, Section 32.3, Jan. 29, 2020; *see also* North American Free Trade Agreement, Jan. 1, 1994.
1836. *See* United States-Mexico-Canada Agreement, Section 32.3, Jan. 29, 2020.
1837. *See* United States-Mexico-Canada Agreement, Section 32.3, Jan. 29, 2020.
1838. *See* United States-Mexico-Canada Agreement, Section 32.3, Jan. 29, 2020.
1839. *See* United States-Mexico-Canada Agreement, Section 32.3, Jan. 29, 2020.

Expropriation and Compensation (§ 14.8) apply to tax measures. However, between the U.S. and Mexico, if this paragraph has allowed a determination that a measure is not an expropriation, no investor can invoke § 14.8 as the basis for a claim.[1840] If an investor seeks to invoke § 14.8, they must refer the issue of whether a tax measure is an expropriation to the designated authorities of the Parties at the time it gives notice of the intent to submit a claim to arbitration.[1841]

[C] Article 32.4. Temporary Safeguards Measures

If a Party has serious payment balances and external financial difficulties, or threats thereof, they may adopt restrictive measures regarding payments or transfers for current accounts or the movement of capital.[1842] In exceptional circumstances, a Party can maintain restricted measures relating to capital movement it causes or threatens to cause serious macroeconomic management problems.[1843] However, none of these measures may apply to payments or transfers related to foreign direct investment.[1844]

Any restrictive measure must be consistent with certain National Treatment (§ 14.4; § 15.3; § 17.3) and Most-Favored-Nation Treatment (§ 15.4; § 17.4) provisions and the IMF Articles of Agreement.[1845] The measure must avoid unnecessary damage to the interests of another Party and not exceed the extent necessary to deal with the circumstances.[1846] The restrictive measure must be temporary, phased out, and for a period of time less than twelve months, or with notification at the end of the first year, twenty-four months.[1847] The restrictive measure must be consistent with the USMCA's Expropriation and Compensation provisions (§ 14.8).[1848] For capital outflow restrictions, the measure must not interfere with an investor's ability to earn a market rate of return in the territory.[1849] The temporary safeguard cannot be used to avoid necessary macroeconomic adjustment.[1850]

When a Party takes a temporary safeguard measure, they must submit the restrictions to the IMF, as soon as practicable.[1851] Then, the Party must wait for the approval and consult in good faith on measures to remove the restrictions and adopt measures consistent with the consultations.[1852]

Any measure taken should be priced-passed or explain the rationale for using quantitative restrictions in its notification. § 32.4.7. The Party must notify the other Parties within thirty days of any measure's adoption, present a time schedule or

---

1840. *See* United States-Mexico-Canada Agreement, Section 32.3, Jan. 29, 2020.
1841. *See* United States-Mexico-Canada Agreement, Section 32.3, Jan. 29, 2020.
1842. *See* United States-Mexico-Canada Agreement, Section 32.4, Jan. 29, 2020.
1843. *See* United States-Mexico-Canada Agreement, Section 32.4, Jan. 29, 2020.
1844. *See* United States-Mexico-Canada Agreement, Section 32.4, Jan. 29, 2020.
1845. *See* United States-Mexico-Canada Agreement, Section 32.4, Jan. 29, 2020.
1846. *See* United States-Mexico-Canada Agreement, Section 32.4, Jan. 29, 2020.
1847. *See* United States-Mexico-Canada Agreement, Section 32.4, Jan. 29, 2020.
1848. *See* United States-Mexico-Canada Agreement, Section 32.4, Jan. 29, 2020.
1849. *See* United States-Mexico-Canada Agreement, Section 32.4, Jan. 29, 2020.
1850. *See* United States-Mexico-Canada Agreement, Section 32.4, Jan. 29, 2020.
1851. *See* United States-Mexico-Canada Agreement, Section 32.4, Jan. 29, 2020.
1852. *See* United States-Mexico-Canada Agreement, Section 32.4, Jan. 29, 2020.

conditions for removal, publish the measure, and begin consulting with the other Parties to review the measure:[1853]

> In the case of trade in goods, Article XII of GATT 1994 and the *Understanding on the Balance of Payments Provisions of the GATT 1994*, set out in Annex 1A to the WTO Agreement, are incorporated into and made part of this Agreement, *mutatis mutandis*. Any measure it adopts or maintains under this paragraph shall not impair the relative benefits accorded to another Party under this Agreement as compared to the treatment of a non-Party.[1854]

[D]   Article 32.5. Indigenous Peoples Rights

The USMCA does not prevent Parties from providing measures that fulfill its legal obligations to indigenous people—provided the measures are not used for arbitrary discrimination or restriction on trade.[1855]

[E]   Article 32.6. Cultural Industries

Cultural industry includes special industries, such as the print/publishing industry, the filmmaking industry, the music industry, and the radio/television/cable broadcasting industry.[1856] With the exception of the Treatment of Customs Duties (§ 2.4) and Programming Services (Annex 15-D), the USMCA does not apply to Canada with respect to a cultural industry.[1857] In return, the U.S. and Mexico may provide similar measures with respect to Canadian goods and services, provided that, if the measure were adopted by Canada, it would have been inconsistent with the USMCA if not for § 32.6.2.[1858] The USMCA further states that Parties may take a measure with equivalent commercial effect in response to any of the actions taken under §§ 32.6.2-32.6.3, provided the measure is consistent with the rest of the USMCA.[1859]

Disputes relating to measures taken under § 32.6.4 must be settled exclusively under the USMCA unless a Party has been unable to establish a panel within ninety days of delivering a request for consultations.[1860] If a panel is established, they may only make findings regarding whether a measure properly relates to a cultural industry and whether the responsive action is of "equivalent commercial effect."[1861]

1853. *See* United States-Mexico-Canada Agreement, Section 32.4, Jan. 29, 2020.
1854. *See* United States-Mexico-Canada Agreement, Section 32.4, Jan. 29, 2020.
1855. *See* United States-Mexico-Canada Agreement, Section 32.5, Jan. 29, 2020.
1856. *See* United States-Mexico-Canada Agreement, Section 32.6, Jan. 29, 2020.
1857. *See* United States-Mexico-Canada Agreement, Section 32.6, Jan. 29, 2020.
1858. *See* United States-Mexico-Canada Agreement, Section 32.6, Jan. 29, 2020.
1859. *See* United States-Mexico-Canada Agreement, Section 32.6, Jan. 29, 2020.
1860. *See* United States-Mexico-Canada Agreement, Section 32.6, Jan. 29, 2020.
1861. *See* United States-Mexico-Canada Agreement, Section 32.6, Jan. 29, 2020.

§32.2   SECTION B: GENERAL PROVISIONS

[A]   Article 32.7. Disclosure of Information

Under the USMCA, Parties are not required to disclose information that would be contrary to their laws, impede law enforcement, be contrary to public interest, or prejudice a particular enterprise's legitimate commercial interests.[1862]

[B]   Article 32.8. Personal Information Protection

Parties must legally protect personal information ("information [and]…data about an identified or identifiable natural person") by taking account of international guidelines, such as the *APEC Privacy Framework* and the *OECD Recommendation of the Council concerning Guidelines governing the Protection of Privacy and Transborder Flows of Personal Data (2013)*.[1863] Parties must publish information about their method of protection, including remedies available and compliance guidelines.[1864] Parties should encourage compatibility between their privacy regimes and foster cooperation to assist those in making cross-border information transfers and complaints.[1865]

[C]   Article 32.9. Access to Information

Parties must allow natural persons in its territory and the territory of other Parties to access records held by the central level of government (e.g., agencies), subject to reasonable and equally favorable limitations.[1866]

[D]   Article 32.10. Non-Market Country FTA

A non-market country is a country that does not have a free trade agreement ("FTA") with any Party, and on the date of signing the USMCA, a Party has determined that country to be a non-market economy for trade remedy purposes.[1867]

    If a Party wishes to begin FTA negotiations with a non-market country, it must notify the other Parties at least three months prior and, upon request, should provide as much information as possible on the objectives for the FTA negotiations.[1868]

    At least thirty days before signing an FTA with a non-market country, a Party must allow the other Parties to review the full text of the FTA.[1869]

1862. *See* United States-Mexico-Canada Agreement, Section 32.7, Jan. 29, 2020.
1863. *See* United States-Mexico-Canada Agreement, Section 32.8, Jan. 29, 2020.
1864. *See* United States-Mexico-Canada Agreement, Section 32.8, Jan. 29, 2020.
1865. *See* United States-Mexico-Canada Agreement, Section 32.8, Jan. 29, 2020.
1866. *See* United States-Mexico-Canada Agreement, Section 32.9, Jan. 29, 2020.
1867. *See* United States-Mexico-Canada Agreement, Section 32.10, Jan. 29, 2020.
1868. *See* United States-Mexico-Canada Agreement, Section 32.10, Jan. 29, 2020.
1869. *See* United States-Mexico-Canada Agreement, Section 32.10, Jan. 29, 2020.

If a Party enters into an FTA with a non-market economy, the other Parties can terminate the USMCA with six months' notice and replace it with a bilateral agreement identical to the USMCA with exception to provisions that are inapplicable to the remaining Parties.[1870] Parties should use the six months to determine whether any provisions need to be amended.[1871]

The agreement enters into force sixty days after the last Party to the new bilateral agreement has notified the other that it has completed the necessary legal procedures.[1872]

[E]   Article 32.11. Specific Provision on Cross-Border Trade in Services, Investment, and State-Owned Enterprises and Designated Monopolies for Mexico

To the extent the measures are consistent with the least restrictive measures that Mexico may take under parallel trade and investment agreements, Mexico may take measures with respect to a sector or subsector that it did not make a reservation to in Schedules to USMCA Annexes I, II, and IV.[1873]

[F]   Article 32.12. Exclusion from Dispute Settlement

Chapter 31 (Dispute Settlement) does not apply to a decision by Canada following a review under the *Investment Canada Act*, R.S.C. 1985, c.28 (1st Supp.), with respect to whether or not to permit an investment.[1874]

1870. *See* United States-Mexico-Canada Agreement, Section 32.10, Jan. 29, 2020.
1871. *See* United States-Mexico-Canada Agreement, Section 32.10, Jan. 29, 2020.
1872. *See* United States-Mexico-Canada Agreement, Section 32.10, Jan. 29, 2020.
1873. *See* United States-Mexico-Canada Agreement, Section 32.11, Jan. 29, 2020.
1874. *See* United States-Mexico-Canada Agreement, Section 32.12, Jan. 29, 2020.

CHAPTER 33

Macroeconomic Policies and Exchange Rate Matters

Under the USMCA, Parties agree to pursue policies that strengthen economic fundamentals, foster macroeconomic growth and transparency, and avoid unsustainable imbalances. Under the USMCA, Parties must make monthly disclosures that include (a) monthly foreign exchange reserves data and forward positions, no later than thirty days after the end of each month and (b) monthly interventions in spot and forward foreign exchange markets, no later than seven days after the end of each month. They must also make quarterly disclosures that include (c) quarterly balance of payments portfolio capital flows and (d) quarterly exports and imports, no later than ninety days at the end of each quarter. The USMCA establishes a Macroeconomic Committee to, amongst other things, consider exchange rate policies, increase transparency, and monitor the implementation of this Chapter. A Party's principal representative may request expedited bilateral consultations with their counterpart in another Party regarding competitive devaluation, the targeting of exchange rates for competitive purpose, or transparency and reporting compliance. If the consultations are regarding transparency, Parties must consider the circumstances that affect the practicability of disclosure. If Parties cannot agree to a solution, Parties may request that the IMF conduct surveillance of the macroeconomic, exchange rate, data transparency, and reporting policies of the requested Party or initiate formal consultations. If the consultations are determined to be a failure, a Party may suspend benefits.

Under the USMCA, Parties agree to pursue policies that strengthen economic fundamentals, foster macroeconomic growth and transparency, and avoid unsustainable imbalances.[1875] The provisions in this chapter are very similar to the Joint Declaration of the Macroeconomic Policy Authorities of the Transpacific Partnership Countries.[1876] However, the key difference is that the USMCA incorporates the macroeconomic

---

1875. *See* United States-Mexico-Canada Agreement, Section 33.1, Jan. 29, 2020.
1876. This Joint Declaration is a side agreement that was released and took effect when the TPP entered into force. *See* Stephanie Segal, USMCA Currency Provisions Set a New Precedent, Center for Strategic & International Studies (Oct. 5, 2018), https://www.csis.org/analysis/usmca-currency-provisions-set-new-precedent.

provisions in its text, which means that these commitments are legally enforceable.[1877] On the contrary, TPP's Joint Declaration omitted reference to the TPP enforcement framework and was even set aside during talks regarding the Comprehensive and Progressive Agreement for Transpacific Partnership ("CPTPP"), TPP's successor.[1878] Furthermore, its participation in the USMCA will be the first time the United States has been party to a trade agreement that explicitly covers macroeconomic and exchange rate policy.[1879] Some have suggested that the inclusion of macroeconomic and exchange rate provisions in the USMCA will lead the United States to insist on similar commitments in future trade agreements, such as those being renegotiated with South Korea and Japan[1880] (countries which the U.S. has accused of currency manipulation).[1881] Chapter 33 does not interfere with the regulation, supervision, monetary policy, credit policy, and related conduct of exchange rates, fiscal authority or monetary authority of a Party (e.g., a central bank).[1882]

§33.1   CURRENCY AND EXCHANGE RATES

Under the USMCA, the Parties confirm their commitment to the IMF Articles of Agreement. Under the IMF, Parties cannot manipulate exchange rates or the international monetary system in order to gain an unfair competitive advantage or prevent effective balance adjustments.[1883] Thus, Parties should use a market-determined exchange rate, refrain from competitive devaluation, and strengthen underlying economic fundamentals.[1884] The United States, Mexico, and Canada already maintain a floating exchange rate system in accordance with Chapter 33.[1885]

1877. *See* Stephanie Segal, USMCA Currency Provisions Set a New Precedent, Center for Strategic & International Studies (Oct. 5, 2018), https://www.csis.org/analysis/usmca-currency-provisions-set-new-precedent.

1878. *See* Stephanie Segal, USMCA Currency Provisions Set a New Precedent, Center for Strategic & International Studies (Oct. 5, 2018), https://www.csis.org/analysis/usmca-currency-provisions-set-new-precedent.

1879. *See* Stephanie Segal, USMCA Currency Provisions Set a New Precedent, Center for Strategic & International Studies (Oct. 5, 2018), https://www.csis.org/analysis/usmca-currency-provisions-set-new-precedent ("Previous U.S. administrations have resisted this linkage in order to avoid any threat to macroeconomic and exchange rate policy independence.").

1880. *See* Stephanie Segal, USMCA Currency Provisions Set a New Precedent, Center for Strategic & International Studies (Oct. 5, 2018), https://www.csis.org/analysis/usmca-currency-provisions-set-new-precedent.

1881. *See* Noah Smith, Trump Isn't All Wrong about Currency Manipulation, Bloomberg (Feb. 6, 2017) (quoting President Trump "You look at what China's doing, you look at what Japan has done over the years. They play the money market, they play the devaluation market and we sit there like a bunch of dummies.").

1882. *See* United States-Mexico-Canada Agreement, Section 33.2, Jan. 29, 2020.

1883. *See* United States-Mexico-Canada Agreement, Section 33.4, Jan. 29, 2020.

1884. *See* United States-Mexico-Canada Agreement, Section 33.4, Jan. 29, 2020.

1885. *See* Stephanie Segal, USMCA Currency Provisions Set a New Precedent, Center for Strategic & International Studies (Oct. 5, 2018), https://www.csis.org/analysis/usmca-currency-provisions-set-new-precedent.

§33.2 TRANSPARENCY AND REPORTING

Under the USMCA, Parties must make monthly disclosures that include: (a) monthly foreign exchange reserves data and forward positions, no later than thirty days after the end of each month; and (b) monthly interventions in spot and forward foreign exchange markets, no later than seven days after the end of each month.[1886] They must also make quarterly disclosures that include: (c) quarterly balance of payments portfolio capital flows; and (d) quarterly exports and imports no later than ninety days at the end of each quarter.[1887] The USMCA transparency and reporting requirements are currently met by the United States, Mexico, and Canada; as a result, this provision will have a limited impact on how the Parties interact.[1888]

In addition, Parties must allow the IMF to disclose Staff Reports on the Party within four weeks of the IMF Executive Board discussion and confirmation of the Party's participation in the IMF Currency Composition of Official Foreign Exchange Reserves (COFER) database.[1889] If the IMF does not publicly disclose either of these, a Party must request they do so.[1890]

§33.3 MACROECONOMIC COMMITTEE

The USMCA establishes a Macroeconomic Committee to, among other things, consider exchange rate policies, increases transparency, and monitor the implementation of this chapter.[1891] By a consensus of the Macroeconomic Committee, Parties may amend the scope of Chapter 33.[1892] The TPP's Joint Declaration also established a macroeconomic committee that met annually and allowed the IMF to be an independent arbiter.[1893]

§33.4 PRINCIPAL REPRESENTATIVE CONSULTATIONS AND DISPUTE RESOLUTION

A Party's principal representative may request expedited bilateral consultations with their counterpart in another Party regarding competitive devaluation, the targeting of exchange rates for competitive purpose, or transparency and reporting compliance.[1894] A Party may invite the non-engaged Party to provide input.[1895] This meeting should

---

1886. *See* United States-Mexico-Canada Agreement, Section 33.5, Jan. 29, 2020.
1887. *See* United States-Mexico-Canada Agreement, Section 33.5, Jan. 29, 2020.
1888. *See* Stephanie Segal, USMCA Currency Provisions Set a New Precedent, Center for Strategic & International Studies (Oct. 5, 2018), https://www.csis.org/analysis/usmca-currency-provisions-set-new-precedent.
1889. *See* United States-Mexico-Canada Agreement, Section 33.5, Jan. 29, 2020.
1890. *See* United States-Mexico-Canada Agreement, Section 33.5, Jan. 29, 2020.
1891. *See* United States-Mexico-Canada Agreement, Section 33.6, Jan. 29, 2020.
1892. *See* United States-Mexico-Canada Agreement, Section 33.6, Jan. 29, 2020.
1893. *See* Stephanie Segal, USMCA Currency Provisions Set a New Precedent, Center for Strategic & International Studies (Oct. 5, 2018), https://www.csis.org/analysis/usmca-currency-provisions-set-new-precedent.
1894. *See* United States-Mexico-Canada Agreement, Section 33.7, Jan. 29, 2020.
1895. *See* United States-Mexico-Canada Agreement, Section 33.7, Jan. 29, 2020.

take place within thirty days of the request, and the matter should be resolved within sixty days of the first meeting.[1896]

If the consultations are regarding transparency, Parties must consider the circumstances that affect the practicability of disclosure.[1897] If Parties cannot agree to a solution, Parties may request that the IMF conduct surveillance of the macroeconomic, exchange rate, data transparency, and reporting policies of the requested Party or initiate formal consultations.[1898]

Chapter 31 (Dispute Settlement) is available for claims that a Party consistently failed to carry out the USMCA transparency and reporting obligations, and the issue was not resolved during consultations.[1899] Panelists must meet the requirements of (2)(b) through (2)(d) of Article 31.8 (Roster and Qualification of Panelists), and they must be an IMF senior official or a senior official of an exchange rate, monetary, or fiscal authority.[1900] Panelists may use Article 31.15 (Role of Experts) to seek the views of the IMF in determining whether a Party failed its transparency and reporting obligations and that Party has not remediated the failure.[1901] When there is a determination of failure, a Party may suspend benefits—provided they do not exceed benefits equivalent to the effect of the other Party's failure.[1902]

1896. *See* United States-Mexico-Canada Agreement, Section 33.7, Jan. 29, 2020.
1897. *See* United States-Mexico-Canada Agreement, Section 33.7, Jan. 29, 2020.
1898. *See* United States-Mexico-Canada Agreement, Section 33.7, Jan. 29, 2020.
1899. *See* United States-Mexico-Canada Agreement, Section 33.8, Jan. 29, 2020.
1900. *See* United States-Mexico-Canada Agreement, Section 33.8, Jan. 29, 2020.
1901. *See* United States-Mexico-Canada Agreement, Section 33.8, Jan. 29, 2020.
1902. *See* United States-Mexico-Canada Agreement, Section 33.8, Jan. 29, 2020.

CHAPTER 34

Final Provisions

All Parties intend to smoothly transition from NAFTA to the USMCA. Anything under review by NAFTA will be continued under the USMCA. In regards to changing the agreement, the USMCA is amendable and amendments are effective sixty days after the last Party has given its written notice of its approval of the amendment or any agreed upon date. With regards to the WTO, if a WTO Agreement amends a provision that the Parties have incorporated into the USMCA, the Parties shall, unless otherwise provided in the USMCA, consult on whether to amend this USMCA. The USMCA enters into force in accordance with paragraph 2 of the Protocol. Replacing the NAFTA with the Agreement between the United States of America, the United Mexican States, and Canada which States that all Parties must notify the other Parties, in writing, once they have completed their internal obligations and are ready to enter the protocol. If a Party wishes to exit the USMCA, they must notify the other Parties in writing, and it will take six months for the withdrawal to take place.

Unless the agreement gets renewed, it will expire sixteen years after going into effect. A joint review will take place on the sixth anniversary of the USMCA going into effect. During the review, Parties will decide whether or not to extend for another sixteen years. If no Parties do not wish to extend, a joint review will be held every year until the agreement expires. In contrast, NAFTA had no expiration date. Some, like U.S. Senator Pat Toomey, objected to this as creating unnecessary uncertainty.

§34.1   ARTICLE 34.1. TRANSITIONAL PROVISION FROM NAFTA 1994

Parties intend to smoothly transition from NAFTA to the USMCA.[1903] To that end, any issues under consideration by a NAFTA body may be continued under the USMCA.[1904] Alternative Dispute Resolution Committee members under NAFTA may be maintained for USMCA's Alternative Dispute Resolution Committee.[1905] For binational panel reviews related to final determinations published before the USMCA is effective,

---

1903. *See* United States-Mexico-Canada Agreement, Section 34.1, Jan. 29, 2020.
1904. *See* United States-Mexico-Canada Agreement, Section 34.1, Jan. 29, 2020.
1905. *See* United States-Mexico-Canada Agreement, Section 34.1, Jan. 29, 2020.

Chapter 19 of NAFTA applies.[1906] The USMCA Secretariat must perform the functions that were assigned to the NAFTA Secretariat under Chapter 19 and use the procedures adopted under Chapter 19 until the binational panel has made a decision and given a Notice of Completion pursuant to Rules of Procedure for Article 1904 Binational Panel Reviews.[1907] For claims for preferential tariff treatment made under NAFTA, Parties must grant these claims, as appropriate, in accordance with NAFTA after the USMCA is effective.[1908] When this happens, NAFTA customs procedures apply to the goods with preferential tariff treatment that were claimed in accordance with NAFTA and last for the period mentioned in NAFTA Article 505 (Records).[1909]

§34.2   ARTICLE 34.2. ANNEXES, APPENDICES, AND FOOTNOTES

USMCA's annexes, appendices, and footnotes are integral to the Agreement.[1910]

§34.3   ARTICLE 34.3. AMENDMENTS

The USMCA is amendable and amendments are effective sixty days after the last Party has given written notice of its approval of the amendment or any agreed upon date.

§34.4   ARTICLE 34.4. AMENDMENT OF THE WTO AGREEMENT

If a WTO Agreement amends a provision that the Parties have incorporated into the USMCA, the Parties shall, unless otherwise provided in the USMCA, consult on whether to amend this USMCA.[1911]

§34.5   ARTICLE 34.5. ENTRY INTO FORCE

The USMCA enters into force in accordance with paragraph 2 of the Protocol Replacing the NAFTA with the Agreement between the United States of America, the United Mexican States, and Canada, which States that "[e]ach Party shall notify the other Parties, in writing, once it has completed the internal procedures required for the entry into force of this Protocol.[1912] This Protocol and its Annex shall enter into force on the first day of the third month following the last notification."[1913]

1906. *See* United States-Mexico-Canada Agreement, Section 34.1, Jan. 29, 2020.
1907. *See* United States-Mexico-Canada Agreement, Section 34.1, Jan. 29, 2020.
1908. *See* United States-Mexico-Canada Agreement, Section 34.1, Jan. 29, 2020.
1909. *See* United States-Mexico-Canada Agreement, Section 34.1, Jan. 29, 2020.
1910. *See* United States-Mexico-Canada Agreement, Section 34.2, Jan. 29, 2020.
1911. *See* United States-Mexico-Canada Agreement, Section 34.4, Jan. 29, 2020.
1912. *See* United States-Mexico-Canada Agreement, Section 34.5, Jan. 29, 2020.
1913. *See* United States-Mexico-Canada Agreement, Section 34.5, Jan. 29, 2020; *see also* Protocol Replacing the North American Free Trade Agreement with the Agreement between the United States of America, the United Mexican States, and Canada (Nov. 30, 2018).

§34.6   ARTICLE 34.6. WITHDRAWAL

Parties must give written notice in order to withdraw from the USMCA.[1914] The Party is effectively withdrawn six months thereafter.[1915] This provision is identical to NAFTA. Prior to and during the USMCA negotiations, the U.S. had threatened at various times to withdraw from NAFTA.

§34.7   ARTICLE 34.7. REVIEW AND TERM EXTENSION

Unless renewed for another sixteen-year term, the USMCA expires sixteen years after its effective date.[1916]

A joint review by the Commission must take place on the sixth anniversary of the USMCA's effective date, where the Commission will review and make decisions on recommendations for action submitted by each Party at least one month prior to the review.[1917] During the joint review, Parties must confirm in writing, through their heads of government, whether they wish to extend the USMCA for sixteen more years.[1918] If all Parties agree, the USMCA is extended, and another joint review must be conducted no later than the end of the next six-year period.[1919]

If a Party does not wish to extend the USMCA, the Commission must conduct joint reviews every year until the USMCA expires.[1920] Furthermore, after a joint review but before the USMCA expires, Parties may, at any time, confirm their desire to extend the Agreement, and if at that time all Parties have confirmed, the agreement is extended for another sixteen-year period.[1921] The cycle of mandatory joint reviews is six years after each extension continues.[1922]

1914. *See* United States-Mexico-Canada Agreement, Section 34.6, Jan. 29, 2020.
1915. *See* United States-Mexico-Canada Agreement, Section 34.6, Jan. 29, 2020.
1916. *See* United States-Mexico-Canada Agreement, Section 34.7, Jan. 29, 2020.
1917. *See* United States-Mexico-Canada Agreement, Section 34.7, Jan. 29, 2020.
1918. *See* United States-Mexico-Canada Agreement, Section 34.7, Jan. 29, 2020.
1919. *See* United States-Mexico-Canada Agreement, Section 34.7, Jan. 29, 2020.
1920. *See* United States-Mexico-Canada Agreement, Section 34.7, Jan. 29, 2020.
1921. *See* United States-Mexico-Canada Agreement, Section 34.7, Jan. 29, 2020.
1922. *See* United States-Mexico-Canada Agreement, Section 34.7, Jan. 29, 2020.

CHAPTER 35
Conclusion

As an attorney working in the international trade and customs field for over forty years, and having participated in the original NAFTA negotiation process over twenty-five years ago on behalf of private clients, the USMCA negotiations and passage have been an interesting, challenging and sometimes frustrating experience. For those in the U.S. that criticized NAFTA, it was a chance for a re-leveling of the playing field and promoting new rules more favorable to the United States interests. This was largely the official view of the Trump Administration. They avoided calling it NAFTA 2.0 as some commentators did and even omitted the word "trade" from the title. For the business community, most of which supported NAFTA, they had to be satisfied that the Trump Administration did not actually revoke NAFTA as it had threatened to do, and celebrate, although without using the term a "modernized NAFTA". Having worked with a number of national business organizations, I know they would have liked to have seen a stronger Investor-State Dispute provision. In fact, the U.S. companies that invested in Mexico benefited greatly from those provisions that secured their investment against direct or indirect state expropriation and largely freed them from the uncertainties of the Mexican legal system, which operates under the civil law system, inherited from the Napoleonic code much different than the U.S. common law system inherited from the British. Why the U.S. government sought not to pursue a stronger Investor-State Dispute provisions remains unclear. Many businesses would also have liked to have seen a significant strengthening of the Government Procurement chapters that were not a subject of much interest in the USMCA. Yet despite these shortcomings, most agree that the fact that any agreement was obtained at all was a considerable achievement. We had a Mexican President Lopez Obredor who was a populist and largely opposed NAFTA and USMCA before he was elected but surprisingly was mostly supportive of the new agreement with his Party in the majority, and was able to pass major reforms to the Mexican labor system. The U.S. President, Donald Trump, had openly campaigned against NAFTA and withdrew from the Transpacific Partnership just days from taking office, an agreement that included Mexico, Canada, and the U.S. Much of the credit must go to his trade representative, Robert Lighthizer, whose prior experience in government and diplomatic skills enabled him to be trusted by all sides, including an originally largely hostile House of Representatives. The Canadian Prime Minister, Justin Trudeau, faced opposition in Canada to the liberalization of agricultural trade, key to Canada's economy, and was considering skipping a summit of the leaders of the three countries held in Washington shortly after passage.

Yet, despite all of the challenges, the agreement was signed, ratified and implemented by all three countries. There are many complex and challenging provisions, such as the automotive rules of origin and labor value content rules that will require companies to work hard to understand them and comply with them. The impact on the U.S. economy is yet to be seen.

Appendix

Subject to Legal Review in English, Spanish and French for Accuracy, Clarity and Consistency

Subject to Authentication of English, Spanish and French Versions   June 3, 2020

UNIFORM REGULATIONS REGARDING THE INTERPRETATION, APPLICATION, AND ADMINISTRATION OF CHAPTER 4 (RULES OF ORIGIN) AND RELATED PROVISIONS IN CHAPTER 6 (TEXTILE AND APPAREL GOODS) OF THE AGREEMENT BETWEEN THE UNITED STATES OF AMERICA, THE UNITED MEXICAN STATES, AND CANADA.

PART I

SECTION 1. DEFINITIONS AND INTERPRETATIONS

(1) *Definitions.* The following definitions apply in these Regulations,

accessories, spare parts, tools, instructional or other information materials means goods that are delivered with a good, whether or not they are physically affixed to that good, and that are used for the transport, protection, maintenance or cleaning of the good, for instruction in the assembly, repair or use of that good, or as replacements for consumable or interchangeable parts of that good;

adjusted to exclude any costs incurred in the international shipment of the good means, with respect to the transaction value of a good, adjusted by

    (a) deducting the following costs if those costs are included in the transaction value of the good:

        (i) the costs of transporting the good after it is shipped from the point of direct shipment,

        (ii) the costs of unloading, loading, handling and insurance that are associated with that transportation, and

        (iii) the cost of packing materials and containers, and

    (b) if those costs are not included in the transaction value of the good, adding

        (i) the costs of transporting the good from the place of production to the point of direct shipment,

        (ii) the costs of loading, unloading, handling and insurance that are associated with that transportation, and

        (iii) the costs of loading the good for shipment at the point of direct shipment;

Agreement means the United States-Mexico-Canada Agreement;

applicable change in tariff classification means, with respect to a non-originating material used in the production of a good, a change in tariff classification specified in a rule established in Schedule I for the tariff provision under which the good is classified;

aquaculture means the farming of aquatic organisms, including fish, molluscs, crustaceans, other aquatic invertebrates and aquatic plants from seed stock such as eggs, fry, fingerlings, or larvae, by intervention in the rearing or growth processes to enhance production such as regular stocking, feeding, or protection from predators;

costs incurred in packing means, with respect to a good or material, the value of the packing materials and containers in which the good or material is packed for shipment and the labor costs incurred in packing it for shipment, but does not include the costs of preparing and packaging it for retail sale;

customs value means

    (a) in the case of Canada, value for duty as defined in the *Customs Act*, except that for the purpose of determining that value the reference in section 55 of that Act to "in accordance with the regulations made under the *Currency Act*" is to be read as a reference to "in accordance with subsection 2(1) of these *CUSMA Rules of Origin Regulations*",

    (b) in the case of Mexico, the *valor en aduana* as determined in accordance with the *Ley Aduanera*, converted, if such value is not expressed in Mexican currency, to Mexican currency at the rate of exchange determined in accordance with subsection 2(1), and

    (c) in the case of the United States, the value of imported merchandise as determined by the U.S. Customs and Border Protection in accordance with section 402 of the *Tariff Act of 1930*, as amended, converted, if that value is not expressed in United States currency, to United States currency at the rate of exchange determined in accordance with subsection 2(1);

days means calendar days, and includes Saturdays, Sundays and holidays;

direct labor costs means costs, including fringe benefits, that are associated with employees who are directly involved in the production of a good;

direct material costs means the value of materials, other than indirect materials and packing materials and containers, that are used in the production of a good;

direct overhead means costs, other than direct material costs and direct labor costs, that are directly associated with the production of a good;

enterprise means an entity constituted or organized under applicable law, whether or not for profit, and whether privately-owned or governmentally-owned or controlled, including a corporation, trust, partnership, sole proprietorship, joint venture, association or similar organization;

excluded costs means, with respect to net cost or total cost, sales promotion, marketing and after-sales service costs, royalties, shipping and packing costs and non-allowable interest costs;

fungible goods means goods that are interchangeable for commercial purposes with another good and the properties of which are essentially identical;

fungible materials means materials that are interchangeable with another material for commercial purposes and the properties of which are essentially identical;

Harmonized System means the *Harmonized Commodity Description and Coding System*, including its General Rules of Interpretation, Section Notes, Chapter Notes and Subheading Notes, as set out in

    (a) in the case of Canada, the *Customs Tariff*,

(b) in the case of Mexico, the *Tarifa de la Ley de los Impuestos Generales de Importación y de Exportación*, and

(c) in the case of the United States, the *Harmonized Tariff Schedule of the United States*;

identical goods means, with respect to a good, including the valuation of a good, goods that

(a) are the same in all respects as that good, including physical characteristics, quality and reputation but excluding minor differences in appearance,

(b) were produced in the same country as that good, and

(c) were produced
     (i) by the producer of that good, or
     (ii) by another producer, if no goods that satisfy the requirements of paragraphs (a) and (b) were produced by the producer of that good;

identical materials means, with respect to a material, including the valuation of a material, materials that

(a) are the same as that material in all respects, including physical characteristics, quality and reputation but excluding minor differences in appearance,

(b) were produced in the same country as that material, and

(c) were produced
     (i) by the producer of that material, or
     (ii) by another producer, if no materials that satisfy the requirements of paragraphs (a) and (b) were produced by the producer of that material;

incorporated means, with respect to the production of a good, a material that is physically incorporated into that good, and includes a material that is physically incorporated into another material before that material or any subsequently produced material is used in the production of the good;

indirect material means a material used or consumed in the production, testing or inspection of a good but not physically incorporated into the good, or a material used or consumed in the maintenance of buildings or the operation of equipment associated with the production of a good, including

(a) fuel and energy,

(b) tools, dies, and molds,

(c) spare parts and materials used or consumed in the maintenance of equipment and buildings,

(d) lubricants, greases, compounding materials and other materials used or consumed in production or used to operate equipment and buildings,

(e) gloves, glasses, footwear, clothing, safety equipment, and supplies,

(f) equipment, devices and supplies used or consumed for testing or inspecting the goods,

(g) catalysts and solvents, and

(h) any other material that is not incorporated into the good but if the use in the production of the good can reasonably be demonstrated to be part of that production;

interest costs means all costs paid or payable by a person to whom credit is, or is to be advanced, for the advancement of credit or the obligation to advance credit;

intermediate material means a material that is self-produced and used in the production of a good, and designated as an intermediate material under subsection 8(6);

location of the producer means,

(a) the place where the producer uses a material in the production of the good; or

249

(b) the warehouse or other receiving station where the producer receives materials for use in the production of the good, provided that it is located within a radius of 75 km (46.60 miles) from the production site.

material means a good that is used in the production of another good, and includes a part or ingredient;

month means a calendar month;

national means a natural person who is a citizen or permanent resident of a USMCA country, and includes

(a) with respect to Mexico, a national or citizen according to Articles 30 and 34, respectively, of the Mexican Constitution, and
(b) with respect to the United States, a "national of the United States" as defined in the *Immigration and Nationality Act* on the date of entry into force of the Agreement;

net cost means total cost minus sales promotion, marketing and after-sales service costs, royalties, shipping and packing costs, and non-allowable interest costs that are included in the total cost;

net cost of a good means the net cost that can be reasonably allocated to a good using one of the methods set out in subsection 7(3) (Regional Value Content);

net cost method means the method of calculating the regional value content of a good that is set out in subsection 7(3) (Regional Value Content);

non-allowable interest costs means interest costs incurred by a producer on the producer's debt obligations that are more than 700 basis points above the interest rate issued by the federal government for comparable maturities of the country in which the producer is located;

non-originating good means a good that does not qualify as originating under these Regulations;

non-originating material means a material that does not qualify as originating under these Regulations;

originating good means a good that qualifies as originating under these Regulations;

originating material means a material that qualifies as originating under these Regulations;

packaging materials and containers means materials and containers in which a good is packaged for retail sale;

packing materials and containers means materials and containers that are used to protect a good during transportation, but does not include packaging materials and containers;

payments means, with respect to royalties and sales promotion, marketing and after-sales service costs, the costs expensed on the books of a producer, whether or not an actual payment is made;

person means a natural person or an enterprise;

person of a USMCA country means a national, or an enterprise constituted or organized under the laws of a USMCA country;

point of direct shipment means the location from which a producer of a good normally ships that good to the buyer of the good;

producer means a person who engages in the production of a good;

production means growing, cultivating, raising, mining, harvesting, fishing, trapping, hunting, capturing, breeding, extracting, manufacturing, processing, or assembling a good, or aquaculture;

reasonably allocate means to apportion in a manner appropriate to the circumstances;

recovered material means a material in the form of one or more individual parts that results from:

(a) the disassembly of a used good into individual parts; and

(b) the cleaning, inspecting, testing or other processing of those parts as necessary for improvement to sound working condition;

related person means a person related to another person on the basis that

(a) they are officers or directors of one another's businesses,

(b) they are legally recognized partners in business,

(c) they are employer and employee,

(d) any person directly or indirectly owns, controls or holds 25 percent or more of the outstanding voting stock or shares of each of them,

(e) one of them directly or indirectly controls the other,

(f) both of them are directly or indirectly controlled by a third person, or

(g) they are members of the same family;

remanufactured good means a good classified in HS Chapters 84 through 90 or under heading 94.02 except goods classified under HS headings 84.18, 85.09, 85.10, and 85.16, 87.03 or subheadings 8414.51, 8450.11, 8450.12, 8508.11, and 8517.11, that is entirely or partially composed of recovered materials and:

(a) has a similar life expectancy and performs the same as or similar to such a good when new; and

(b) has a factory warranty similar to that applicable to such a good when new;

reusable scrap or by-product means waste and spoilage that is generated by the producer of a good and that is used in the production of a good or sold by that producer;

right to use, for the purposes of the definition of royalties, includes the right to sell or distribute a good;

royalties means payments of any kind, including payments under technical assistance or similar agreements, made as consideration for the use of, or right to use, a copyright, literary, artistic, or scientific work, patent, trademark, design, model, plan, or secret formula or process, excluding those payments under technical assistance or similar agreements that can be related to specific services such as

(a) personnel training, without regard to where the training is performed, or

(b) if performed in the territory of one or more of the USMCA countries, engineering, tooling, die- setting, software design and similar computer services, or other services;

sales promotion, marketing, and after-sales service costs means the following costs related to sales promotion, marketing and after-sales service:

(a) sales and marketing promotion; media advertising; advertising and market research; promotional and demonstration materials; exhibits; sales conferences, trade shows and conventions; banners; marketing displays; free samples; sales, marketing and after-sales service literature (product brochures, catalogs, technical literature, price lists, service manuals, or sales aid information); establishment and protection of logos and trademarks; sponsorships; wholesale and retail restocking charges; or entertainment;

(b) sales and marketing incentives; consumer, retailer or wholesaler rebates; or merchandise incentives;

(c) salaries and wages, sales commissions, bonuses, benefits (for example, medical, insurance, or pension), travelling and living expenses, or membership and professional fees for sales promotion, marketing and after-sales service personnel;

(d) recruiting and training of sales promotion, marketing and after-sales service personnel, and after- sales training of customers' employees, if those costs are identified separately for sales promotion, marketing and after-sales service of goods on the financial statements or cost accounts of the producer;

(e) product liability insurance;

(f) office supplies for sales promotion, marketing and after-sales service of goods, if those costs are identified separately for sales promotion, marketing, and after-sales service of goods on the financial statements or cost accounts of the producer;

(g) telephone, mail and other communications, if those costs are identified separately for sales promotion, marketing, and after-sales service of goods on the financial statements or cost accounts of the producer;

(h) rent and depreciation of sales promotion, marketing, and after-sales service offices and distribution centers;

(i) property insurance premiums, taxes, cost of utilities, and repair and maintenance of sales promotion, marketing, and after-sales service offices and distribution centers, if those costs are identified separately for sales promotion, marketing and after-sales service of goods on the financial statements or cost accounts of the producer; and

(j) payments by the producer to other persons for warranty repairs;

self-produced material means a material that is produced by the producer of a good and used in the production of that good;

shipping and packing costs means the costs incurred in packing a good for shipment and shipping the good from the point of direct shipment to the buyer, excluding the costs of preparing and packaging the good for retail sale;

similar goods means, with respect to a good, goods that

(a) although not alike in all respects to that good, have similar characteristics and component materials that enable the goods to perform the same functions and to be commercially interchangeable with that good,

(b) were produced in the same country as that good, and

(c) were produced
    (i) by the producer of that good, or
    (ii) by another producer, if no goods that satisfy the requirements of paragraphs (a) and (b) were produced by the producer of that good;

similar materials means, with respect to a material, materials that

(a) although not alike in all respects to that material, have similar characteristics and component materials that enable the materials to perform the same functions and to be commercially interchangeable with that material,

(b) were produced in the same country as that material, and

(c) were produced
    (i) by the producer of that material, or
    (ii) by another producer, if no materials that satisfy the requirements of paragraphs (a) and (b) were produced by the producer of that material;

subject to a regional value content requirement means, with respect to a good, that the provisions of these Regulations that are applied to determine whether the good is an originating good include a regional value content requirement;

tariff provision means a heading, subheading or tariff item;

territory means:

    (a) for Canada, the following zones or waters as determined by its domestic law and consistent with international law:

        (i) the land territory, air space, internal waters, and territorial sea of Canada,

        (ii) the exclusive economic zone of Canada, and

        (iii) the continental shelf of Canada;

    (b) for Mexico,

        (i) the land territory, including the states of the Federation and Mexico City,

        (ii) the air space, and

        (iii) the internal waters, territorial sea, and any areas beyond the territorial seas of Mexico within which Mexico may exercise sovereign rights and jurisdiction, as determined by its domestic law, consistent with the *United Nations Convention on the Law of the Sea*, done at Montego Bay on December 10, 1982; and

    (c) for the United States,

        (i) the customs territory of the United States, which includes the 50 states, the District of Columbia, and Puerto Rico,

        (ii) the foreign trade zones located in the United States and Puerto Rico, and

        (iii) the territorial sea and air space of the United States and any area beyond the territorial sea within which, in accordance with customary international law as reflected in the *United Nations Convention on the Law of the Sea*, the United States may exercise sovereign rights or jurisdiction.

total cost means all product costs, period costs, and other costs incurred in the territory of one or more of the USMCA countries, where:

    (a) product costs are costs that are associated with the production of a good and include the value of materials, direct labor costs, and direct overheads;

    (b) period costs are costs, other than product costs, that are expensed in the period in which they are incurred, such as selling expenses and general and administrative expenses; and

    (c) other costs are all costs recorded on the books of the producer that are not product costs or period costs, such as interest.

Total cost does not include profits that are earned by the producer, regardless of whether they are retained by the producer or paid out to other persons as dividends, or taxes paid on those profits, including capital gains taxes;

transaction value means the customs value as determined in accordance with the Customs Valuation Agreement, that is, the price actually paid or payable for a good or material with respect to a transaction of, except for the application of Articles 10.3(a) in the Appendix to Annex 4-B (Product-Specific Rules of Origin), the producer of the good, adjusted in accordance with the principles of Articles 8(1), 8(3), and 8(4) of the Customs Valuation Agreement, regardless of whether the good or material is sold for export;

transaction value method means the method of calculating the regional value content of a good that is set out in subsection 7(2) (Regional Value Content);

used means used or consumed in the production of a good;

USMCA country means a Party to the Agreement;

value means the value of a good or material for the purpose of calculating customs duties or for the purpose of applying these Regulations.

verification of origin means a verification of origin of goods under

    (a) in the case of Canada, paragraph 42.1(1)(a) or subsection 42.2(2) of the Customs Act,

(b) in the case of Mexico, Article 5.9 of the Agreement, and

(c) in the case of the United States, section 509 of the Tariff Act of 1930, as amended.

(2) *Interpretation: "similar goods" and "similar materials".* For the purposes of the definitions of **similar goods** and **similar materials**, the quality of the goods or materials, their reputation and the existence of a trademark are among the factors to be considered for the purpose of determining whether goods or materials are similar.

(3) *Other definitions.* For the purposes of these Regulations,

(a) **chapter**, unless otherwise indicated, refers to a chapter of the Harmonized System;

(b) **heading** refers to any four-digit number set out in the "Heading" column in the Harmonized System, or the first four digits of any tariff provision;

(c) **subheading** refers to any six-digit number, set out in the "H.S. Code" column in the Harmonized System or the first six digits of any tariff provision;

(d) **tariff item** refers to the first eight digits in the tariff classification number under the Harmonized System as implemented by each USMCA country;

(e) any reference to a tariff item in Chapter Four of the Agreement or these Regulations that includes letters is to be reflected as the appropriate eight-digit number in the Harmonized System as implemented in each USMCA country; and

(f) **books** refers to,

(i) with respect to the books of a person who is located in a USMCA country,

(A) books and other documents that support the recording of revenues, expenses, costs, assets and liabilities and that are maintained in accordance with Generally Accepted Accounting Principles set out in the publications listed in Schedule X with respect to the territory of the USMCA country in which the person is located, and

(B) financial statements, including note disclosures, that are prepared in accordance with Generally Accepted Accounting Principles set out in the publications listed in Schedule X with respect to the territory of the USMCA country in which the person is located, and

(ii) with respect to the books of a person who is located outside the territories of the USMCA countries,

(A) books and other documents that support the recording of revenues, expenses, costs, assets and liabilities and that are maintained in accordance with generally accepted accounting principles applied in that location or, if there are no such principles, in accordance with the International Accounting Standards, and

(B) financial statements, including note disclosures, that are prepared in accordance with generally accepted accounting principles applied in that location or, if there are no such principles, in accordance with the International Accounting Standards.

(4) *Use of examples.* If an example, referred to as an "Example", is set out in these Regulations, the example is for the purpose of illustrating the application of a provision, and if there is any inconsistency between the example and the provision, the provision prevails to the extent of the inconsistency.

(5) *References to domestic laws.* Except as otherwise provided, references in these Regulations to domestic laws of the USMCA countries apply to those laws as they are currently in effect and as they may be amended or superseded.

(6) *Calculation of Total Cost.* For the purposes of subsections 5(11), 7(11) and 8(8),

(a) total cost consists of all product costs, period costs and other costs that are recorded, except as otherwise provided in subparagraphs (b)(i) and (ii), on the books of the producer without regard to the location of the persons to whom payments with respect to those costs are made;

(b) in calculating total cost,

    (i) the value of materials, other than intermediate materials, indirect materials and packing materials and containers, is the value determined in accordance with subsections 8(1) and 8(2),

    (ii) the value of intermediate materials used in the production of the good or material with respect to which total cost is being calculated must be calculated in accordance with subsection 8(6),

    (iii) the value of indirect materials and the value of packing materials and containers is to be the costs that are recorded on the books of the producer for those materials, and

    (iv) product costs, period costs and other costs, other than costs referred to in subparagraphs (i) and (ii), is to be the costs thereof that are recorded on the books of the producer for those costs;

(c) total cost does not include profits that are earned by the producer, regardless of whether they are retained by the producer or paid out to other persons as dividends, or taxes paid on those profits, including capital gains taxes;

(d) gains related to currency conversion that are related to the production of the good must be deducted from total cost, and losses related to currency conversion that are related to the production of the good must be included in total cost;

(e) the value of materials with respect to which production is accumulated under section 9 must be determined in accordance with that section; and

(f) total cost includes the impact of inflation as recorded on the books of the producer, if recorded in accordance with the Generally Accepted Accounting Principles of the producer's country.

(7) *Period for the calculation of total cost.* For the purpose of calculating total cost under subsections 5(11) and 7(11) and 8(8),

(a) if the regional value content of the good is calculated on the basis of the net cost method and the producer has elected under subsection 7(15), 16(1) or (3) to calculate the regional value content over a period, the total cost must be calculated over that period; and

(b) in any other case, the producer may elect that the total cost be calculated over

    (i) a one-month period,

    (ii) any consecutive three-month or six-month period that falls within and is evenly divisible into the number of months of the producer's fiscal year remaining at the beginning of that period, or

    (iii) the producer's fiscal year.

(8) *Election not modifiable.* An election made under subsection (7) may not be rescinded or modified with respect to the good or material, or the period, with respect to which the election is made.

(9) *Election considered made with respect to period.* If a producer chooses a one, three or six-month period under subsection (7) with respect to a good or material, the producer is considered to have chosen under that subsection a period or periods of the same duration for the remainder of the producer's fiscal year with respect to that good or material.

(10) *Election considered made with respect to cost.* With respect to a good exported to a USMCA country, an election to average is considered to have been made

(a) in the case of an election referred to in subsection 16(1) or (3), if the election is received by the customs administration of that USMCA country; and

(b) in the case of an election referred to in subsection 1(7), 7(15) or 16(9), if the customs administration of that USMCA country is informed in writing during the course of a verification of origin of the good that the election has been made.

2 (1) *Conversion of currency.* If the value of a good or a material is expressed in a currency other than the currency of the country where the producer of the good is located, that value must be converted to the currency of the country in which that producer is located, based on the following rates of exchange:

(a) in the case of the sale of that good or the purchase of that material, the rate of exchange used by the producer for the purpose of recording that sale or purchase, or
(b) in the case of a material that is acquired by the producer other than by a purchase,
   (i) if the producer used a rate of exchange for the purpose of recording another transaction in that other currency that occurred within 30 days of the date on which the producer acquired the material, that rate, or
   (ii) in any other case,
      (A) with respect to a producer located in Canada, the rate of exchange referred to in section 5 of the *Currency Exchange for Customs Valuation Regulations* for the date on which the material was shipped directly to the producer,
      (B) with respect to a producer located in Mexico, the rate of exchange published by the *Banco de Mexico* in the *Diario Oficial de la Federacion*, under the title *"TIPO de cambio para solventar obligaciones denominadas en moneda extranjera pagaderas en la Republica Mexicana"*, for the date on which the material was shipped directly to the producer, and
      (C) with respect to a producer located in the United States, the rate of exchange referred to in 31 U.S.C. 5151 for the date on which the material was shipped directly to the producer.

(2) *Information in other currency in statement.* If a producer of a good has a statement referred to in section 9 that includes information in a currency other than the currency of the country in which that producer is located, the currency must be converted to the currency of the country in which the producer is located based on the following rates of exchange:

(a) if the material was purchased by the producer in the same currency as the currency in which the information in the statement is provided, the rate of exchange must be the rate used by the producer for the purpose of recording the purchase; or
(b) if the material was purchased by the producer in a currency other than the currency in which the information in the statement is provided,
   (i) and the producer used a rate of exchange for the purpose of recording a transaction in that other currency that occurred within 30 days of the date on which the producer acquired the material, the rate of exchange must be that rate, or
   (ii) in any other case,
      (A) with respect to a producer located in Canada, the rate of exchange is the rate referred to in section 5 of the *Currency Exchange for Customs Valuation Regulations* for the date on which the material was shipped directly to the producer,
      (B) with respect to a producer located in Mexico, the rate of exchange is the rate published by the *Banco de Mexico* in the *Diario Oficial de la Federacion*, under the title *"TIPO de cambio para solventar obligaciones denominadas en moneda extranjera pagaderas en la Republica Mexicana"*, for the date on which the material was shipped directly to the producer, and

        (C) with respect to a producer located in the United States, the rate of exchange is the rate referred to in 31 U.S.C. 5151 for the date on which the material was shipped directly to the producer; and

(c) if the material was acquired by the producer other than by a purchase,

      (i) if the producer used a rate of exchange for the purpose of recording a transaction in that other currency that occurred within 30 days of the date on which the producer acquired the material, the rate of exchange must be that rate, and

    (ii) in any other case,

        (A) with respect to a producer located in Canada, the rate of exchange must be the rate referred to in section 5 of the *Currency Exchange for Customs Valuation Regulations* for the date on which the material was shipped directly to the producer,

        (B) with respect to a producer located in Mexico, the rate of exchange must be the rate published by the *Banco de Mexico* in the *Diario Oficial de la Federacion*, under the title "*TIPO de cambio para solventar obligaciones denominadas en moneda extranjera pagaderas en la Republica Mexicana*", for the date on which the material was shipped directly to the producer, and

        (C) with respect to a producer located in the United States, the rate of exchange must be the rate referred to in 31 U.S.C. 5151 for the date on which the material was shipped directly to the producer.

PART II

SECTION 3. ORIGINATING GOODS

3(1) *Wholly obtained goods.* A good is originating in the territory of a USMCA country if the good satisfies all other applicable requirements of these Regulations and is:

(a) a mineral good or other naturally occurring substance extracted in or taken from the territory of one or more of the USMCA countries;

(b) a plant, plant good, vegetable, or fungus, grown, harvested, picked, or gathered in the territory of one or more of the USMCA countries;

(c) a live animal born and raised in the territory of one or more of the USMCA countries;

(d) a good obtained from a live animal in the territory of one or more of the USMCA countries;

(e) an animal obtained from hunting, trapping, fishing, gathering or capturing in the territory of one or more of the USMCA countries;

(f) a good obtained from aquaculture in the territory of one or more of the USMCA countries;

(g) fish, shellfish or other marine life taken from the sea, seabed or subsoil outside the territories of the USMCA countries and, under international law, outside the territorial sea of non- USMCA countries, by vessels that are registered, listed, or recorded with a USMCA country and entitled to fly the flag of that USMCA country;

(h) a good produced from goods referred to in paragraph (g) on board a factory ship where the factory ship is registered, listed, or recorded with a USMCA country and entitled to fly the flag of that USMCA country;

      (i) a good, other than fish, shellfish or other marine life, taken by a USMCA country or a person of a USMCA country from the seabed or subsoil outside the territories of the USMCA countries, if that USMCA country has the right to exploit that seabed or subsoil;

      (j) waste and scrap derived from:

          (i) production in the territory of one or more of the USMCA countries, or

          (ii) used goods collected in the territory of one or more of the USMCA countries, provided the goods are fit only for the recovery of raw materials; or

      (k) a good produced in the territory of one or more of the USMCA countries, exclusively from a good referred to in any of paragraphs (a) through (j), or from their derivatives, at any stage of production.

(2) *Goods produced from non-originating materials.* A good, produced entirely in the territory of one or more of the USMCA countries, is originating in the territory of a USMCA country if each of the non-originating materials used in the production of the good satisfies all applicable requirements of Schedule I, and the good satisfies all other applicable requirements of these Regulations.

(3) *Goods produced exclusively from originating materials.* A good is originating in the territory of a USMCA country if the good is produced entirely in the territory of one or more of the USMCA countries exclusively from originating materials and the good satisfies all other applicable requirements of these Regulations.

(4) *Exceptions to the change in tariff classification requirement.* Except in the case of a good of any of Chapters 61 through 63, a good is originating in the territory of a USMCA country if:

      (a) one or more of the non-originating materials used in the production of that good cannot satisfy the change in tariff classification requirements set out in Schedule I because both the good and its materials are classified in the same subheading or same heading that is not further subdivided into subheadings, and,

          (i) the good is produced entirely in the territory of one or more of the USMCA countries;

          (ii) the regional value content of the good, calculated in accordance with section 7 (Regional Value Content), is not less than 60 percent if the transaction value method is used, or not less than 50 percent if the net cost method is used; and

         (iii) the good satisfies all other applicable requirements of these Regulations; or

      (b) it was imported into the territory of a USMCA country in an unassembled or a disassembled form but classified as an assembled good in accordance with rule 2(a) of the General Rules of Interpretation for the Harmonized System, originates in the territory of a USMCA country and,

          (i) the good is produced entirely in the territory of one or more of the USMCA countries;

          (ii) the regional value content of the good, calculated in accordance with section 7 (Regional Value Content), is not less than 60 percent if the transaction value method is used, or not less than 50 percent if the net cost method is used; and

         (iii) the good satisfies all other applicable requirements of these Regulations.

(5) Interpretation of goods and parts of goods. For the purposes of paragraph (4)(a),

      (a) the determination of whether a heading or subheading provides for a good and its parts is to be made on the basis of the nomenclature of the heading or subheading and the relevant Section or Chapter Notes, in accordance with the General Rules for the Interpretation of the Harmonized System; and

(b) if, in accordance with the Harmonized System, a heading includes parts of goods by application of a Section Note or Chapter Note of the Harmonized System and the subheadings under that heading do not include a subheading designated "Parts", a subheading designated "Other" under that heading is to be considered to cover only the goods and parts of the goods that are themselves classified under that subheading.

(6) *Requirement to meet one rule.* For the purposes of subsection (2), if Schedule I sets out two or more alternative rules for the tariff provision under which a good is classified, if the good satisfies the requirements of one of those rules, it need not satisfy the requirements of another of the rules in order to qualify as an originating good.

(7) *Special rule for certain goods.* A good is originating in the territory of a USMCA country if the good is referred to in Schedule II and is imported from the territory of a USMCA country.

(8) *Self-produced material considered as a material.* For the purpose of determining whether non-originating materials undergo an applicable change in tariff classification, a self-produced material may, at the choice of the producer of that material, be considered as a material used in the production of a good into which the self-produced material is incorporated.

(9) Each of the following examples is an "Example" as referred to in subsection 1(4).

Example 1: Subsection 3(2) Regarding the 'component that determines the tariff classification' of a textile or apparel good)

Producer A, located in a USMCA country, produces women's wool overcoats of subheading 6202.11 from two different fabrics, one for the body and another for the sleeves. Both fabrics are produced using originating and non-originating materials. The overcoat's body is made of woven wool and silk fabric, and the sleeves are made of knit cotton fabric.

For the purpose of determining if the women's wool overcoats are originating goods, Producer A must take into account Note 2 of Chapter 62 of Schedule I, which indicates that the applicable rule will apply only to the component that determines the tariff classification of the good and that the component must satisfy the tariff change requirements set out in the rule for that good.

The woven fabric (80% wool and 20% silk) used for the body is the component of the women's wool overcoat that determines its tariff classification under subheading 6202.11, because it constitutes the predominant material by weight and makes up the largest surface area of the overcoat. This fabric is made by Producer A from originating wool yarn classified in heading 51.06 and non-originating silk yarn classified in heading 50.04.

Since the knit cotton fabric used in the sleeves is not the component that determines the tariff classification of the good, it does not need to meet the requirements set out in the rule for the good.

Producer A must determine whether the non-originating materials used in the production of the component that determines the tariff classification of the women's wool overcoats (the woven fabric) satisfy the requirements established in the product-specific rule of origin, which requires both a change in tariff classification from any other chapter, except from some headings and chapters under which certain yarns and fabrics are classified, and a requirement that the good be cut or knit to shape and sewn or otherwise assembled in the territory of one or more of the USMCA countries. The non-originating silk yarn of heading 50.04 used by Producer A satisfies the change in tariff classification requirement, since heading 50.04 is not excluded under the product-specific rule of origin. Additionally, the overcoats are cut and sewn in the territory of one of the USMCA countries, and therefore the women's wool overcoats would be considered to be originating goods.

Example 2: (subsection 3(2))

Producer A, located in a USMCA country, produces T-shirts of subheading 6109.10 from knit cotton and polyester fabric (60% cotton and 40% polyester), which is also produced by Producer A using originating cotton yarn of heading 52.05 and polyester yarn made of non-originating filaments of heading 54.02.

As the t-shirt is made of a single fabric and classified under GRI 1 in subheading 6109.10, this fabric is the component that determines tariff classification. Therefore, to be considered originating by application of the tariff-shift rule for subheading 6109.10, each of the non-originating materials used in the production of the t- shirt must undergo the required change in tariff classification.

In this case, the non-originating polyester filaments of heading 54.02 used in the production of the T-shirts do not satisfy the change in tariff classification set out in the product-specific rule of origin. In addition, the weight of the non-originating polyester is over the "de minimis" allowance. Therefore, the T-shirts do not qualify as originating goods.

Example 3: (subsection 3(2))—Note 2 contained in Section XI—Textiles and Textile Articles (Chapter 50-63)

Producer A, located in a USMCA country, produces fabrics of subheading 5211.42 from originating cotton and polyester yarns, and non-originating rayon filament. For the purpose of determining if the fabrics are originating goods, Producer A must consider Note 2 of Section XI of Schedule I, which indicates a good of Chapter 50 through 63 is considered as originating, regardless of whether the rayon filaments used in its production are non-originating materials, provided that the good meets the requirements of the applicable product-specific rule of origin.

With the exception of the rayon filaments of heading 54.03, that Note 2 of Section XI of Schedule I allows, all of the materials used in the production of the fabrics are originating materials, and since General Interpretative Note (d) of Schedule I provides that a change in tariff classification of a product-specific rule of origin applies only to non-originating materials, the fabrics are considered to be originating goods.

Example 4: subsection 3(2) Note 2 and 5 of Chapter 62 regarding the interpretation of the component that determines the tariff classification and the requirement for pockets.

Producer A, located in a USMCA country, produces men's suits classified in subheading 6203.12, which are made of three fabrics: a non-originating fabric of subheading 5407.61 used to make a visible lining, an originating fabric of 5514.41 used to make the outer part of the suit and a non-originating fabric of subheading 5513.21 used to make pocket bags.

For the purpose of determining if the men's suits are originating goods, Producer A should take into account Note 2 of Chapter 62 of Schedule I, which indicates that the applicable rule will only apply to the component that determines the tariff classification of the good and that the component must satisfy the tariff change requirements set out in the rule for that good.

The originating fabric used to make the outer part of the suit is the component of the suit that determines the tariff classification under subheading 6203.12, because it constitutes the predominant material by weight and is the largest surface area of the suit. The origin of the fabric used as visible lining is disregarded for the purpose of determining whether the suit is an originating good since that fabric is not considered the component that determines the tariff classification, and there are no Chapter notes related to visible lining for apparel goods.

Additionally, Producer A uses a non-originating fabric of subheading 5513.21 for the pocket bags of the suits, so it should take into account the second paragraph of Note 5 of Chapter 62 of Schedule I, which requires that the pocket bag fabric must be formed and finished in the territory of one or more USMCA countries from yarn wholly formed in one or more USMCA countries.

In this case, for the production of men's suits, Producer A uses non-originating fabric for the pockets, and such fabric was not formed and finished in the territory of one or more Parties, therefore the suits would be considered to be non-originating goods.

Example 5 (subsection 3(7)): A wholesaler located in USMCA Country A imports non-originating storage units provided for in subheading 8471.70 from outside the territory of the USMCA countries. The wholesaler resells the storage units to a buyer in USMCA Country B. While in the territory of Country A, the storage units do not undergo any production and therefore do not meet the rule in Schedule I for goods of subheading 8471.70 when imported into the territory of USMCA Country B.

Notwithstanding the rule in Schedule I, the storage units of subheading 8471.70 are considered originating goods when they are imported to the territory of USMCA Country B because they are referred to in Schedule II and were imported from the territory of another USMCA country.

The buyer in USMCA Country B subsequently uses the storage units provided for in subheading 8471.70 as a material in the production of another good. For the purpose of determining whether the other good originates, the buyer in USMCA Country B may treat the storage units of subheading 8471.70 as originating materials.

Example 6 subsection 3(8): Self-produced Materials as Materials for the purpose of Determining Whether Non- originating Materials Undergo an Applicable Change in Tariff Classification

Producer A, located in a USMCA country, produces Good A. In the production process, Producer A uses originating Material X and non-originating Material Y to produce Material Z. Material Z is a self-produced material that will be used to produce Good A.

The rule set out in Schedule I for the heading under which Good A is classified specifies a change in tariff classification from any other heading. In this case, both Good A and the non-originating Material Y are of the same heading. However, the self-produced Material Z is of a heading different than that of Good A.

For the purpose of determining whether the non-originating materials that are used in the production of Good A undergo the applicable change in tariff classification, Producer A has the option to consider the self- produced Material Z as the material that must undergo a change in tariff classification. As Material Z is of a heading different than that of Good A, Material Z satisfies the applicable change in tariff classification and Good A would qualify as an originating good.

SECTION 4. TREATMENT OF RECOVERED MATERIALS USED IN THE PRODUCTION OF A REMANUFACTURED GOOD

4(1) *Treatment of recovered materials used in the production of remanufactured goods.* A recovered material derived in the territory of one or more of the USMCA countries, will be treated as originating, provided that:
 (a) It is the result of a disassembly process of a used good into individual parts;
 (b) It has undergone certain processing, such as cleaning, inspection, testing or other improvement processing, to sound working condition; and
 (c) It is used in the production of, and incorporated into, a remanufactured good.

 (2) *Recovered material not used in remanufactured good.* In the case that the recovered material is not used or incorporated in the production of a remanufactured good, it is originating only if it satisfies the requirements established in Section 3 (Originating Goods) of these Regulations, and satisfies all other applicable requirements in these Regulations.

 (3) *Requirements of Schedule I.* A remanufactured good is originating in the territory of a USMCA country only if it satisfies the applicable requirements established in Schedule I, and satisfies all other applicable requirements in these Regulations.

 (4) Each of the following examples is an "Example" as referred to in subsection 1(4)

261

Example 1: (section 4)

In July 2023, Producer A located in a USMCA country manufactures water pumps of subheading 8413.30 for use in automotive engines. In addition to selling new water pumps, Producer A also sells water pumps that incorporate used parts.

To obtain the used parts, Producer A disassembles used water pumps in the USMCA territory and cleans, inspects, and tests the individual parts. Accordingly, these parts qualify as recovered materials.

The water pumps that Producer A manufactures incorporate the recovered materials, have the same life expectancy and performance as new water pumps, and are sold with a warranty that is similar to the warranty for new water pumps. The water pumps therefore qualify as remanufactured goods, and the recovered materials are treated as originating materials when determining whether the good qualifies as an originating good.

In this case, because the water pumps are for use in an automotive good, the provisions of Part VI apply. Because the water pump is a part listed in Table B, the RVC required is 70% under the net cost method or 80% under the transaction value method.

The producer chooses to calculate the RVC using net cost as follows:

> Water pump net cost = $ 1,000
> Value of recovered materials = $ 600
> Value other originating materials = $ 20
> Value of non-originating materials = $ 280
>
> $$RVC = (NC - VNM) / NC \times 100$$
> $$RVC = (1,000 - 280) / 1,000 \times 100 = 72\%$$

The remanufactured water pumps are originating goods because their regional value content exceeds the 70% requirement by net cost method.

Example 2: section 4

Producer A located in a USMCA country, uses recovered materials derived in the territory of a USMCA country in the production of self-propelled "bulldozers" classified in subheading 8429.11.

In the production of the bulldozers, Producer A uses recovered engines, classified in heading 84.07. The engines are recovered materials because they are disassembled from used bulldozers in a USMCA country and then subject to cleaning, inspecting and technical tests to verify their sound working condition.

In addition to the recovered materials, other non-originating materials, classified in subheading 8413.91, are also used in the production of the bulldozers.

Producer A's bulldozers are considered a "remanufactured good" because they are classified in a tariff provision set out in the definition of a remanufactured good, are partially composed of recovered materials, have a similar life expectancy and perform the same as or similar to new self-propelled bulldozers, and have a factory warranty similar to new self-propelled bulldozers.

Once the recovered engines are used in the production of, and incorporated into, the remanufactured bulldozers, the recovered engines would be treated considered as originating materials for the purpose of determining if the remanufactured bulldozers are originating.

The rule of origin set out in in Schedule I for subheading 8429.11 specifies a change in tariff classification from any other subheading.

In this case, because the recovered engines are treated as originating materials, and the non-originating materials, classified in subheading 8413.91, satisfy the requirements set out in Schedule I, the remanufactured bulldozers are originating goods.

SECTION 5. *DE MINIMIS*

5(1) *De minimis rule for non-originating materials.* Except as otherwise provided in subsection (3) (Exceptions), a good is originating in the territory of a USMCA country if

    (a) the value of all non-originating materials that are used in the production of the good and that do not undergo an applicable change in tariff classification as a result of production occurring entirely in the territory of one or more of the USMCA countries is not more than ten percent

        (i) of the transaction value of the good, determined in accordance with Schedule III (Value of Goods), and adjusted to exclude any costs incurred in the international shipment of the good, or

        (ii) of the total cost of the good;

    (b) if the good is also subject to a regional content requirement under the rule in which the applicable change in tariff classification is specified, the value of those non-originating materials is to be taken into account in calculating the regional value content of the good in accordance with the method set out for that good; and

    (c) the good satisfies all other applicable requirements of these Regulations.

(2) *Only one rule to satisfy.* If Schedule I sets out two or more alternative rules for the tariff provision under which the good is classified, and the good is considered an originating good under one of those rules in accordance with subsection (1), it need not satisfy the requirements of any alternative rule to be originating.

(3) *Exceptions.* Subsections (1) and (2) do not apply to:

    (a) a non-originating material of heading 04.01 through 04.06, or a non-originating material that is a dairy preparation containing over 10 percent by dry weight of milk solids of subheading 1901.90 or 2106.90, used in the production of a good of heading 04.01 through 04.06;

    (b) a non-originating material of heading 04.01 through 04.06, or a non-originating material that is a dairy preparation containing over 10 percent by dry weight of milk solids of subheading 1901.90 or 2106.90, used in the production of a good of:

        (i) infant preparations containing over 10 percent by dry weight of milk solids of subheading 1901.10,

        (ii) mixes and doughs, containing over 25 percent by dry weight of butterfat, not put up for retail sale of subheading 1901.20,

        (iii) dairy preparations containing over 10 percent by dry weight of milk solids of subheading 1901.90 or 2106.90,

        (iv) goods of heading 21.05,

        (v) beverages containing milk of subheading 2202.90, or

        (vi) animal feeds containing over 10 percent by dry weight of milk solids of subheading 2309.90;

    (c) a non-originating material of any of heading 08.05 and subheadings 2009.11 through 2009.39 that is used in the production of a good of any of subheadings 2009.11 through 2009.39 or a fruit or vegetable juice of any single fruit or vegetable, fortified with minerals or vitamins, concentrated or unconcentrated, of subheading 2106.90 or 2202.90;

    (d) a non-originating material of Chapter 9 that is used in the production of instant coffee, not flavored, of subheading 2101.11;

    (e) a non-originating material of Chapter 15 that is used in the production of a good of any of headings 15.01 through 15.08, 15.12, 15.14 or 15.15;

    (f) a non-originating material of heading 17.01 that is used in the production of a good of any of headings 17.01 through 17.03;

(g) a non-originating material of Chapter 17 or heading 18.05 that is used in the production of a good of subheading 1806.10;

(h) a non-originating material that is pears, peaches or apricots of Chapter 8 or 20 that is used in the production of a good of heading 20.08;

(i) a non-originating material that is a single juice ingredient of heading 20.09 that is used in the production of a good of any of subheading 2009.90, or tariff item 2106.90.92 or 2202.90.32;

(j) a non-originating material of heading 22.03 through 22.08 that used in the production of a good provided for in any of heading 22.07 or 22.08;

(k) a non-originating material that is used in the production of a good of any of Chapters 1 through 27, unless the non-originating material is of a different subheading than the good for which origin is being determined under this section; or

(l) a non-originating material that is used in the production of a good of any of Chapters 50 through 63.

(4) *De minimis rule for regional value content requirement.* A good that is subject to a regional value content requirement is originating in the territory of a USMCA country and is not required to satisfy that requirement if

(a) the value of all non-originating materials used in the production of the good is not more than ten per cent

(i) of the transaction value of the good, determined in accordance with Schedule III (Value of the Good), and adjusted to exclude any costs incurred in the international shipment of the good, or

(ii) of the total cost of the good, and

(b) the good satisfies all other applicable requirements of these Regulations.

(5) *Value of non-originating materials for subsections (1) and (4).* For the purposes of subsections (1) and (4), the value of non-originating materials is to be determined in accordance with subsections 8(1) through (6).

(6) *De minimis rule for textile goods.* A good of any of Chapters 50 through 60 or heading 96.19, that contains non-originating materials that do not satisfy the applicable change in tariff classification requirements, will be considered originating in the territory of a USMCA country if:

(a) the total weight of all those non-originating materials is not more than ten per cent of the total weight of the good, of which the total weight of elastomeric content may not exceed seven per cent of the total weight of the good; and

(b) the good satisfies all other applicable requirements of these Regulations.

(7) A good of any of Chapters 61 through 63, that contains non-originating fibers or yarns in the component of the good that determines the tariff classification that do not undergo the applicable change in tariff classification requirements, will be considered originating in the territory of a USMCA country if:

(a) the total weight of all those non-originating materials is not more than ten per cent of the total weight of that component, of which the elastomeric content may not exceed seven per cent; and

(b) the good satisfies all other applicable requirements of these Regulations.

(8) For purposes of subsection (6),

(a) the component of a good that determines the tariff classification of that good is identified in accordance with the first of the following General Rules for the Interpretation of the Harmonized System under which the identification can be determined, namely, Rule 3(b), Rule 3(c) and Rule 4; and

(b) if the component of the good that determines the tariff classification of the good is a blend of two or more yarns or fibers, all yarns and fibers used in the production of the component must be taken into account in determining the weight of fibers and yarns in that component.

(9) For the purpose of determining if a good of Chapter 61 through 63 is originating, the requirements set out in Schedule I only apply to the component that determines the tariff classification of the good. Materials that are not part of the component that determines the tariff classification of the good are disregarded when determining if a good is originating. Similarly, for the purposes of Section 5 as applicable to a good of Chapters 61 through 63, only the materials used in the component that determines the tariff classification are taken into account in the de minimis calculation.

(10) Subsection (6) does not apply to sewing thread, narrow elastic bands, and pocket bag fabric subject to the requirements set out in Chapter 61 Notes 2 through 4, Chapter 62 Notes 3 through 5 or for coated fabric as set out in Chapter 63 Note 2 of Schedule I.

(11) *Calculation of "Total Cost", choice of methods.* For the purposes of paragraph (1)(a)(ii) and subparagraph (4)(a)(ii), the total cost of a good is, at the choice of the producer of the good,

    (a) the total cost incurred with respect to all goods produced by the producer that can be reasonably allocated to that good in accordance with Schedule V; or

    (b) the aggregate of each cost that forms part of the total cost incurred with respect to that good that can be reasonably allocated to that good in accordance with Schedule V.

(12) *Calculation of total cost.* Total cost under subsection (9) consists of the costs referred to in subsection 1(6), and is calculated in accordance with that subsection and subsection 1(7).

(13) *Value of non-originating materials—other methods.* For the purpose of determining the value under subsection (1) of non-originating materials that do not undergo an applicable change in tariff classification, if an inventory management method either recognized in the Generally Accepted Accounting Principles (GAAP) of the USMCA country where the production was performed or a method set out in Schedule VIII, is not being used to determine the value of those non-originating materials, the following methods are to be used:

    (a) if the value of those non-originating materials is being determined as a percentage of the transaction value of the good and the producer chooses under subsection 7(10) to use one of the methods recognized in the GAAP of the USMCA country where the material was produced, or a method set out in Schedule VII to determine the value of those non-originating materials for the purpose of calculating the regional value content of the good, the value of those non-originating materials must be determined in accordance with that method;

    (b) if the following conditions are met and if the value of those non-originating materials is equal to the sum of the values of non-originating materials, determined in accordance with the election under subparagraph (iv), divided by the number of units of the goods with respect to which the election is made

        (i) the value of those non-originating materials is being determined as a percentage of the total cost of the good,

        (ii) under the rule in which the applicable change in tariff classification is specified, the good is also subject to a regional value content requirement and paragraph (5)(a) does not apply with respect to that good,

        (iii) the regional value content of the good is calculated on the basis of the net cost method, and

        (iv) the producer elects under subsection 7(15), 16(1) (3), (9) that the regional value content of the good be calculated over a period;

    (c) if the conditions below are met the value of those non-originating materials is the sum of the values of non-originating materials divided by the number of units produced during the period under subparagraph (iii):

>>> (i) the value of those non-originating materials is being determined as a percentage of the total cost of the good,
>>> (ii) under the rule in which the applicable change in tariff classification is specified, the good is not also subject to a regional value content requirement or paragraph (5)(a) applies with respect to that good, and
>>> (iii) the producer elects under paragraph 11(1)(b) that, for the purposes of subsection 5(11), the total cost of the good be calculated over a period; and

>> (d) in any other case, the value of those non-originating materials may, at the choice of the producer, be determined in accordance with an inventory management method recognized in the GAAP of the USMCA country where the production was performed or one of the methods set out in Schedule VII.

> (14) *Value of non-originating materials—production of the good.* For the purposes of subsection (4), the value of the non-originating materials used in the production of the good may, at the choice of the producer, be determined in accordance with an inventory management method recognized in the GAAP of the USMCA country where the production was performed or one of the methods set out in Schedule VII

> (15) *Examples illustrating de minimis rules.* Each of the following examples is an "Example" as referred to in subsection 1(4).

Example 1: subsection 5(1)

Producer A, located in a USMCA country, uses originating materials and non-originating materials in the production of aluminum powder of heading 76.03. The product-specific rule of origin set out in Schedule I for heading 76.03 specifies a change in tariff classification from any other chapter. There is no applicable regional value content requirement for this heading. Therefore, in order for the aluminum powder to qualify as an originating good under the rule set out in Schedule I, Producer A may not use any non-originating material of Chapter 76 in the production of the aluminum powder.

All of the materials used in the production of the aluminum powder are originating materials, with the exception of a small amount of aluminum scrap of heading 76.02, that is in the same chapter as the aluminum powder. Under subsection 5(1), if the value of the non-originating aluminum scrap does not exceed ten per cent of the transaction value of the aluminum powder or the total cost of the aluminum powder, whichever is applicable, the aluminum powder would be considered an originating good.

Example 2: subsection 5(2)

Producer A, located in a USMCA country, uses originating materials and non-originating materials in the production of fans of subheading 8414.59. There are two alternative rules set out in Schedule I for subheading 8414.59, one of which specifies a change in tariff classification from any other heading. The other rule specifies both a change in tariff classification from the subheading under which parts of the fans are classified and a regional value content requirement. In order for the fan to qualify as an originating good under the first of the alternative rules, all of the materials that are classified under the subheading for parts of fans and used in the production of the completed fan must be originating materials.

In this case, all of the non-originating materials used in the production of the fan satisfy the change in tariff classification set out in the rule that specifies a change in tariff classification from any other heading, with the exception of one non-originating material that is classified under the subheading for parts of fans. Under subsection 5(1), if the value of the non-originating material that does not satisfy the change in tariff classification specified in the first rule does not exceed ten per cent of the transaction value of the fan or the total cost of the fan, whichever is applicable, the fan would be considered an originating good. Therefore, under subsection 5(2), the fan would not be required to satisfy the alternative rule t h a t specifies both a change in tariff classification and a regional value content requirement.

Example 3: subsection 5(2)

Producer A, located in a USMCA country, uses originating materials and non-originating materials in the production of copper anodes of heading 74.02. The product-specific rule of origin set out in Schedule I for heading 74.02 specifies both a change in tariff classification from any other heading, except from heading 74.04, under which certain copper materials are classified, and a regional value content requirement. With respect to that part of the rule that specifies a change in tariff classification, in order for the copper anode to qualify as an originating good, any copper materials that are classified under heading 74.02 or 74.04 and that are used in the production of the copper anode must be originating materials.

In this case, all of the non-originating materials used in the production of the copper anode satisfy the specified change in tariff classification, with the exception of a small amount of copper materials classified under heading 74.04. Subsection 5(1) provides that the copper anode can be considered an originating good if the value of the non-originating copper materials that do not satisfy the specified change in tariff classification does not exceed ten per cent of the transaction value of the copper anode or the total cost of the copper anode, whichever is applicable. In this case, the value of those non-originating materials that do not satisfy the specified change in tariff classification does not exceed the ten per cent limit.

However, the rule set out in Schedule I for heading 74.02 specifies both a change in tariff classification and a regional value content requirement. Under paragraph 5(1)(c), in order to be considered an originating good, the copper anode must also, except as otherwise provided in subsection 5(5), satisfy the regional value content requirement specified in that rule. As provided in paragraph 5(1)(c), the value of the non-originating materials that do not satisfy the specified change in tariff classification, together with the value of all other non- originating materials used in the production of the copper anode, will be taken into account in calculating the regional value content of the copper anode.

Example 4: subsection 5(4)

Producer A, located in a USMCA country, primarily uses originating materials in the production of shoes of heading 64.05. The product-specific rule of origin set out in Schedule I for heading 64.05 specifies both a change in tariff classification from any heading other than headings 64.01 through 64.05 or subheading 6406.10 and a regional value content requirement.

With the exception of a small amount of materials of Chapter 39, all of the materials used in the production of the shoes are originating materials.

Under subsection 5(4), if the value of all of the non-originating materials used in the production of the shoes does not exceed ten per cent of the transaction value of the shoes or the total cost of the shoes, whichever is applicable, the shoes are not required to satisfy the regional value content requirement specified in the rule set out in Schedule I in order to be considered originating goods.

Example 5: subsection 5(4)

Producer A, located in a USMCA country, produces barbers' chairs of subheading 9402.10. The product- specific rule of origin set out in Schedule I for goods of subheading 9402.10 specifies a change in tariff classification from any other subheading. All of the materials used in the production of these chairs are originating materials, with the exception of a small quantity of non-originating materials that are classified as parts of barbers' chairs. These parts undergo no change in tariff classification because subheading 9402.10 provides for both barbers' chairs and their parts.

Although Producer A's barbers' chairs do not qualify as originating goods under the rule set out in Schedule I, paragraph 3(4)(a) provides, among other things, that, if there is no change in tariff classification from the non- originating materials to the goods because the subheading under which the goods are classified provides for both the goods and their parts, the goods will qualify as originating goods if they satisfy a specified regional value content requirement.

However, under subsection 5(4), if the value of the non-originating materials does not exceed ten per cent of the transaction value of the barbers' chairs or the total cost of the barbers' chairs, whichever is applicable, the barbers' chairs will be considered originating goods and are not required to satisfy the regional value content requirement set out in subparagraph 3(4)(a)(ii).

Example 6: Subsection 5(6):

Producer A, located in a USMCA country, manufactures an infant diaper, classified in heading 96.19, consisting of an outer shell of 94 percent nylon and 6 percent elastomeric fabric, by weight, and a terry knit cotton absorbent crotch. All materials used are produced in a USMCA country, except for the elastomeric fabric, which is from a non-USMCA country. The elastomeric fabric is only 6 percent of the total weight of the diaper. The product otherwise satisfies all other applicable requirements of these Regulations. Therefore, the product is considered originating from a USMCA country as per subsection (6).

Example 7: subsections 5(6) and (8)

Producer A, located in a USMCA country, produces cotton fabric of subheading 5209.11 from cotton yarn of subheading 5205.11. This cotton yarn is also produced by Producer A.

The product-specific rule of origin set out in Schedule I for subheading 5209.11, under which the fabric is classified, specifies a change in tariff classification from any other heading outside 52.08 through 52.12, except from certain headings under which certain yarns are classified, including cotton yarn of subheading 5205.11.

Therefore, with respect to that part of the rule that specifies a change in tariff classification, in order for the fabric to qualify as an originating good, the cotton yarn that is used by Producer A in the production of the fabric must be an originating material.

At one point Producer A uses a small quantity of non-originating cotton yarn in the production of the cotton fabric. Under subsection 5(6), if the total weight of the non-originating cotton yarn does not exceed ten per cent of the total weight of the cotton fabric, it would be considered an originating good.

Example 8: subsections 5(7) and (8)

Producer A, located in a USMCA country, produces women's dresses of subheading 6204.41 from fine wool fabric of heading 51.12. This fine wool fabric, also produced by Producer A, is the component of the dress that determines its tariff classification under subheading 6204.41.

The product-specific rule of origin set out in Schedule I for subheading 6204.41, under which the dress is classified, specifies both a change in tariff classification from any other chapter, except from those headings and chapters under which certain yarns and fabrics, including combed wool yarn and wool fabric, are classified, and a requirement that the good be cut and sewn or otherwise assembled in the territory of one or more of the USMCA countries. In addition, narrow elastics classified in subheading 5806.20 or heading 60.02 and sewing thread classified in heading 52.04, 54.01 or 55.08 or yarn classified in heading 54.02 that is used as sewing thread, must be formed and finished in the territory of one or more of the USMCA countries for the dress to be originating. Furthermore, if the dress has a pocket, the pocket bag fabric must be formed and finished in the territory of one or more of the USMCA countries for the dress to be originating.

Therefore, with respect to that part of the rule that specifies a change in tariff classification, in order for the dress to qualify as an originating good, the combed wool yarn and the fine wool fabric made therefrom that are used by Producer A in the production of the dress must be originating materials. In addition, the sewing thread, narrow elastics and pocket bags that are used by Producer A in the production of the dress must also be formed and finished in the territory of one or more of the USMCA countries.

At one point Producer A uses a small quantity of non-originating combed wool yarn in the production of the fine wool fabric. Under subsection 5(7), if the total weight of the non-originating combed wool yarn does not exceed ten per cent of the total weight of all the yarn used in the production of the component of the dress that determines its tariff classification, that is, the wool fabric, the dress would be considered an originating good.

Example 9: Subsection 5(7)

Producer A, located in a USMCA country, manufactures women's knit sweaters, which have knit bodies and woven sleeves. The knit body is composed of 95 percent polyester and 5 percent spandex, by weight. The sleeves are made of non-USMCA woven fabric that is 100 percent polyester. All materials of the knit body are from a USMCA country, except for the spandex, which is from a non-USMCA country. The sweater is cut and sewn in a USMCA country. Since the knit body gives the garment its essential character, the sweater is classified in subheading 6110.30. The product-specific rule of origin set out in Schedule I for subheading 6110.30 is that the product is both cut (or knit to shape) and sewn or otherwise assembled in the territory of one or more of the USMCA countries. The sleeves are disregarded in determining whether the sweater originates in a USMCA country because only the component that determines the tariff classification of the good must be originating and the de minimis provision is applied to that component. Moreover, the total weight of the spandex is less than 10 percent of the total weight of the knit body fabric, which is the component that determines the tariff classification of the sweater, and the spandex does not exceed seven percent of the total weight of good. Assuming that the women's knit sweater satisfies all other applicable requirements of these Regulations, the women's knit sweater is originating from the USMCA country.

Example 10: subsection 5(9)

A men's shirt of Chapter 61 is made using two different fabrics; one for the body and another for the sleeves. The component that determines the tariff classification of the men's shirt would be the fabric used for the body, as it constitutes the material that predominates by weight and makes up the largest surface area of the shirt's exterior. If this fabric is produced using non-originating fibers and yarns that do not satisfy a tariff change rule, the de minimis provision would be calculated on the basis of the total weight of the non-originating fibers or yarns used in the production of the fabric that makes up the body of the shirt. The weight of these non-originating fibers or yarns must be ten percent or less of the total weight of that fabric and any elastomeric content must be seven per cent of the total weight of that fabric.

Alternatively, if the shirt is made entirely of the same fabric, the component that determines the tariff classification of that shirt would be that fabric, as the shirt is made out of the same material throughout. Therefore, under this second scenario, the total weight of all non-originating fibers and yarns used in the production of the shirt that do not satisfy a tariff change rule, must be ten percent or less of the total weight of the shirt, and any elastomeric content must be seven per cent of the total weight of that shirt, for the shirt to be considered as an originating good.

Example 11: subsection 5(9)

Producer A, located in a USMCA country, produces women's blouses of subheading 6206.40 from a fabric also produced by Producer A using 90% by weight originating polyester yarns of subheading 5402.33, 3% by weight non-originating lyocell yarn of subheading 5403.49 and 7% by weight non-originating elastomeric filament yarn of subheading 5402.44. This fabric is the component of the women's blouses that determines its tariff classification under subheading 6206.40.

The product-specific rule of origin of Schedule I applicable to the women's blouses of subheading 6206.40 requires a change in tariff classification from any other chapter, except from those headings and chapters under which certain yarns and fabrics, including polyester, lyocell and elastomeric filament yarns, are classified and a requirement that the good is cut and sewn or otherwise assembled in the territory of one or more of the USMCA countries.

In this case, the non-originating lyocell yarns of subheading 5403.49 and the non-originating elastomeric filament yarn of subheading 5402.44 do not satisfy the change in tariff classification required by the product- specific rule of origin of Schedule I, because the product specific rule of origin for heading 62.06 excludes a change from Chapter 54 to heading 62.06."

However, according to subsection (7), a textile or apparel good classified in Chapters 61 through 63 of the Harmonized System that contains non-originating fibers or yarns in the component of the good that determines its tariff classification that do not satisfy the applicable change in tariff classification, will nonetheless be considered an originating good if the total weight of all those fibers or yarns is not more than 10 percent of the total weight of that component, of which the total weight of elastomeric content may not exceed 7 percent of the total weight of the component, and such good meets all the other applicable requirements of these Regulations.

Since the weight of the non-originating materials used by Producer A does not exceed 10 percent of the total weight of the component that determines the tariff classification of the women's blouses, and the weight of elastomeric content also does not exceed 7 percent of such total weight, the women's blouses qualify as originating goods.

Example 12: subsection 5(10)

A producer located in a USMCA country manufactures boys' swimwear of subheading 6211.11 from fabric that has been woven in a USMCA country from yarn spun in a USMCA country; however, the producer uses non- originating narrow elastic of heading 60.02 in the waist-band of the swimwear. As a result of the use of non- originating narrow elastic of heading 60.02 in the waistband, and provided the garment is imported into a USMCA country at least 18 months after the Agreement enters into force, the swimwear is considered non- originating because it does not satisfy the requirement set out in Note 3 of Chapter 62. In addition, subsection 5(7) is not applicable regarding the narrow elastic of 60.02 and the good is therefore a non-originating good.

Section 6 SETS OF GOODS, KITS OR COMPOSITE GOODS

6(1) This section applies to a good that is classified as a set as a result of the application of rule 3 of the General Rules for the Interpretation of the Harmonized Tariff Schedule.

(2) *Requirements.* Except as otherwise provided in Schedule I, a set is originating in the territory of one or more of the USMCA countries only if each good in the set is originating and both the set and the goods meet the other applicable requirements of these Regulations.

(3) *Exceptions.* Notwithstanding, paragraph 2, a set is only originating if the value of all the non-originating goods included in the set does not exceed 10 percent of the value of the set.

(4) *Value.* For the purposes of paragraph 3, the value of non-originating goods in the set and the value of the set is to be calculated in the same manner as the value of non-originating materials determined in accordance with section 8 and the value of the good determined in accordance with section 7.

(5) Examples. Each of the following examples is an "Example" as referred to in subsection 1(4).

Example 1 (paint set)

Producer A assembles a paint set for arts and crafts. The set includes tubes of paint, paint brushes, and paper all presented in a reusable wooden box. The paint set for arts and crafts is classified in subheading 3210.00 as a result of the application of Rule 3 of the General Rules for the Interpretation of the Harmonized System and, as a result, Section 6 will apply with respect to such set. The paint, paper and wooden box are all originating as they each undergo the changes required in the product-specific rules of origin in Schedule I. The paint brushes, which represent four percent of the value of the set, are produced in the territory of a non-USMCA country and are therefore non-originating. The set is nonetheless originating.

Example 2 Subsection 6(2)

Producer A, located in a USMCA country, uses originating materials and non-originating materials to assemble a manicure set of subheading 8214.20. The set includes a nail nipper, cuticle scissors, a nail clipper and a nail file with cardboard support, all presented in a plastic case with zipper. The items are not classified as a set as a result of the application of rule 3 of the General Rules for the Interpretation of the Harmonized System. The Harmonized System specifies that manicure sets are classified in subheading 8214.20. This means that the specific rule of origin set out in Schedule I is applied. This rule requires a change in tariff classification from any other chapter. In order for the manicure set to qualify as an originating good under the rule set out in Schedule I, Producer A may not use any non-originating material of Chapter 82 in the assembly of the manicure set.

In this case, Producer A, located in a USMCA country, produces the nail nipper, the cuticle scissors and the nail clipper included in the set, and all qualify as originating. Despite being classified in the same chapter as the manicure set (chapter 82), the originating nail nipper, the cuticle scissors and the nail clipper satisfy the change in tariff classification applicable to the manicure set. The nail file with cardboard support (6805.20) and the plastic case with zipper (4202.12) are imported from outside the territories of the USMCA countries; however, these items are not classified in chapter 82, so they satisfy the applicable change in tariff classification. Therefore, the manicure set is an originating good.

Example 3: Pants set Section 6(2)

Producer A makes a pants set, containing men's cotton denim trousers and a polyester belt, packed together for a retail sale. The trousers are made of cotton fabric formed and finished from yarn in a USMCA country. The sewing thread is formed and finished in a USMCA country. The pocket bag fabric is formed and finished in a USMCA country, of yarn wholly formed in a USMCA country. The trousers are cut and sewn in USMCA country A. A polyester webbing belt with a metal buckle is made in a non-USMCA country and shipped to USMCA country A, where it is threaded through the belt loops of the trousers. The value of the belt is 8% of the value of the trousers and belt combined.

The men's trousers are classified under subheading 6203.42. The rule of origin set out in Schedule I for subheading 6203.42 requires that the trousers be made from fabric produced in a USMCA country from yarn produced in a USMCA country. The trousers satisfy the product-specific rules provided in Schedule I and are considered originating. However, the belt does not satisfy the rules and would not be considered originating. The set is nonetheless an originating good if the belt value is 10% or less of the value of the set. Since the value of the belt is 8% of the value of the set, the men's trousers and belt set would be treated as an originating good under the USMCA.

Example 4: Shirt and Tie Set Section 6(2)

Producer A makes a boys' shirt and tie set in a USMCA country. The shirt is constructed from 55% cotton, 45% polyester, solid color, dyed, woven fabric, classified in subheading 5210.31. The fabric contains 73.2 total yarns per square centimeter and 76 metric yarns. The shirt is packaged in a retail polybag with a coordinating color, 100% polyester, woven fabric tie. The yarns used in the shirt fabric are spun in non-USMCA country and the fabric is woven and dyed in the same non-USMCA country. The shirt fabric is sent to the USMCA country where it is cut and sewn into finished garments. The coordinating tie is made in a non-USMCA country from fabric that is woven in that country from yarns that are spun in that country. The value of the coordinating tie is approximately 13% of the value of the set.

The shirt is classified under heading 62.05. The shirt satisfies the product-specific rule for subheading 62.05 set out in Schedule I and is considered originating because it is wholly made from fabric of heading 5210.31 (not of square construction, containing more than 70 warp ends and filling picks per square centimeter, of average yarn number exceeding 70 metric) and cut and sewn into finished garments in the USMCA country. On the other hand, the tie does not satisfy the product specific rule for heading 62.15 and would not be considered originating. For purposes of the sets rule, provided the tie is valued at 10% or less of the value of the set, the set will be treated as originating. However, since the value of the coordinating tie is approximately 13% of the value of the set, the shirt and tie set would not be treated as an originating good under the USMCA.

Example 5: Chef set Section 6(2)

Producer A, located in a USMCA country, produces a chef set for retail sale using originating and non-originating materials. This set includes an apron, cooking gloves and a chef hat. The chef set is classified in heading 62.11 as a result of the application of rule 3 of the General Rules for the Interpretation of the Harmonized System. For this reason, subsection (3) applies to this set. Both the apron and cooking gloves meet the product-specific rules of origin for their respective product categories and are therefore considered to be originating. The chef hat, which represents 9.7 percent of the value of the set, is produced in the territory of a non-USMCA country and is therefore non-originating. The set is nonetheless an originating good because less than ten percent of the value of the set is non-originating.

PART III

SECTION 7. REGIONAL VALUE CONTENT

7(1) *Calculation.* Except as otherwise provided in subsection (6), the regional value content of a good is to be calculated, at the choice of the importer, exporter or producer of the good, on the basis of either the transaction value method or the net cost method.

(2) *Transaction value method.* The transaction value method for calculating the regional value content of a good is as follows:

$$RVC = (TV - VNM)/TV * 100$$

Where

RVC is the regional value content of the good, expressed as a percentage;

TV is the transaction value of the good, determined in accordance with Schedule III with respect to the transaction in which the producer of the good sold the good, adjusted to exclude any costs incurred in the international shipment of the good; and

VNM is the value of non-originating materials used by the producer in the production of the good, determined in accordance with section 8.

(3) *Net cost method.* The net cost method for calculating the regional value content of a good is as follows: RVC = (NC – VNM)/NC*100

Where

RVC is the regional value content of the good, expressed as a percentage;

NC is the net cost of the good, calculated in accordance with subsection (11); and

VNM is the value of non-originating materials used by the producer in the production of the good, determined, except as otherwise provided in sections 14 and 15 and, in accordance with section 8.

(4) *Non-originating materials—values not included.* For the purpose of calculating the regional value content of a good under subsection (2) or (3), the value of non-originating materials used by a producer in the production of the good must not include

(a) the value of any non-originating materials used by another producer in the production of originating materials that are subsequently acquired and used by the producer of the good in the production of that good; or

(b) the value of any non-originating materials used by the producer in the production of a self-produced material that is an originating material and is designated as an intermediate material.

(5) *Self-produced material.* For the purposes of subsection (4),

(a) in the case of any self-produced material that is not designated as an intermediate material, only the value of any non-originating materials used in the production of the self-produced material is to be included in the value of non-originating materials used in the production of the good; and

(b) if a self-produced material that is designated as an intermediate material and is an originating material is used by the producer of the good with non-originating materials (whether or not those non- originating materials are produced by that producer) in the production of the good, the value of those non-originating materials is to be included in the value of non-originating materials.

(6) *Net cost method—when required.* The regional value content of a good is to be calculated only on the basis of the net cost method if the rule set in Schedule I (Product-Specific Rules of Origin) does not provide a rule based on the transaction value method;

(7) *Net cost method—when change permitted.* If the importer, exporter or producer of a good calculates the regional value content of the good on the basis of the transaction value method and the customs administration of a USMCA country subsequently notifies that importer, exporter or producer in writing, during the course of a verification of origin, that

(a) the transaction value of the good, as determined by the importer, exporter or producer, is required to be adjusted under section 4 of Schedule III, or

(b) the value of any material used in the production of the good, as determined by the importer, exporter or producer, is required to be adjusted under section 5 of Schedule VI,

the importer, exporter or producer may choose that the regional value content of the good be calculated on the basis of the net cost method, in which case the calculation must be made within 30 days after receiving the notification, or such longer period as that customs administration specifies.

(8) *Net cost method—no change permitted.* If the importer, exporter or producer of a good chooses that the regional value content of the good be calculated on the basis of the net cost method and the customs administration of a USMCA country subsequently notifies that importer, exporter or producer in writing, during the course of a verification of origin, that the good does not satisfy the applicable regional value content requirement, the importer, exporter or producer of the good may not recalculate the regional value content on the basis of the transaction value method.

(9) *Clarification.* Nothing in subsection (7) is to be construed as preventing any review and appeal under Article 5.15 of the Agreement, as implemented in each USMCA country, of an adjustment to or a rejection of

(a) the transaction value of the good; or

(b) the value of any material used in the production of the good.

(10) *Value of identical non-originating materials.* For the purposes of the transaction value method, if non- originating materials that are the same as one another in all respects, including physical characteristics, quality and reputation but excluding minor differences in appearance, are used in the production of a good, the value of those non-originating materials may, at the choice of the producer of the good, be determined in accordance with one of the methods set out in Schedule VII.

(11) *Calculating the net cost of a good.* For the purposes of subsection (3), the net cost of a good may be calculated, at the choice of the producer of the good, by

(a) calculating the total cost incurred with respect to all goods produced by that producer, subtracting any excluded costs that are included in that total cost, and reasonably allocating, in accordance with Schedule V, the remainder to the good;

(b) calculating the total cost incurred with respect to all goods produced by that producer, reasonably allocating, in accordance with Schedule V, that total cost to the good, and subtracting any excluded costs that are included in the amount allocated to that good; or

(c) reasonably allocating, in accordance with Schedule V, each cost that forms part of the total cost incurred with respect to the good so that the aggregate of those costs does not include any excluded costs.

(12) *Calculation of total cost.* Total cost under subsection (11) consists of the costs referred to in subsection 1(6), and is calculated in accordance with that subsection.

(13) *Calculation of net cost of a good.* For the purpose of calculating the net cost under subsection (11),

(a) excluded costs must be the excluded costs that are recorded on the books of the producer of the good;

(b) excluded costs that are included in the value of a material that is used in the production of the good must not be subtracted from or otherwise excluded from the total cost; and

(c) excluded costs do not include any amount paid for research and development services performed in the territory of a USMCA country.

(14) *Non-allowable interest.* For the purpose of calculating non-allowable interest costs, the determination of whether interest costs incurred by a producer are more than 700

basis points above the yield on debt obligations of comparable maturities issued by the federal government of the country in which the producer is located is to be made in accordance with Schedule I X.

(15) *Use of "averaging" over a period.* For the purposes of the net cost method, the regional value content of the good, other than a good with respect to which an election to average may be made under subsection 16(1), (3) or (9), may be calculated, if the producer elects to do so, by

(a) calculating the sum of the net costs incurred and the sum of the values of non-originating materials used by the producer of the good with respect to the good and identical goods or similar goods, or any combination thereof, produced in a single plant by the producer over

(i) a one-month period,

(ii) any consecutive three-month or six-month period that falls within and is evenly divisible into the number of months of the producer's fiscal year remaining at the beginning of that period, or

(iii) the producer's fiscal year; and

(b) using the sums referred to in paragraph (a) as the net cost and the value of non-originating materials, respectively.

(16) *Application.* The calculation made under subsection (15) applies with respect to all units of the good produced during the period chosen by the producer under paragraph (15)(a).

(17) *No change to the goods or period.* An election made under subsection (15) may not be rescinded or modified with respect to the goods or the period with respect to which the election is made.

(18) *Period considered to be chosen.* If a producer chooses a one, three or six-month period under subsection (15) with respect to a good, the producer will be considered to have chosen under that subsection a period or periods of the same duration for the remainder of the producer's fiscal year with respect to this good.

(19) *Method and period for remainder of fiscal year.* If the net cost method is required to be used or has been chosen and an election has been made under subsection (15), the regional value content of the good is to be calculated on the basis of the net cost method over the period chosen under that subsection and for the remainder of the producer's fiscal year.

(20) *Analysis of actual costs.* Except as otherwise provided in subsections 16(10), 12(11) and 13(10), if the producer of a good has calculated the regional value content of the good under the net cost method on the basis of estimated costs, including standard costs, budgeted forecasts or other similar estimating procedures, before or during the period chosen under paragraph (15)(a), the producer must conduct an analysis at the end of the producer's fiscal year of the actual costs incurred over the period with respect to the production of the good.

(21) *Option to treat any material as non-originating.* For the purpose of calculating the regional value content of a good, the producer of that good may choose to treat any material used in the production of that good as a non-originating material.

(22) *Examples.* Each of the following examples is an "Example" as referred to in subsection 1(4).

Example 1: example of point of direct shipment (with respect to adjusted to exclude any costs incurred in the international shipment of the good)

A producer has only one factory, at which the producer manufactures finished office chairs. Because the factory is located close to transportation facilities, all units of the finished good are stored in a factory warehouse 200 meters from the end of the production line. Goods are shipped worldwide from this warehouse. The point of direct shipment is the warehouse.

Example 2: examples of point of direct shipment (with respect to adjusted to exclude any costs incurred in the international shipment of the good)

A producer has six factories, all located within the territory of one of the USMCA countries, at which the producer produces garden tools of various types. These tools are shipped worldwide, and orders usually consist of bulk orders of various types of tools. Because different tools are manufactured at different factories, the producer decided to consolidate storage and shipping facilities and ships all finished products to a large warehouse located near the seaport, from which all orders are shipped. The distance from the factories to the warehouse varies from 3 km to 130 km. The point of direct shipment for each of the goods is the warehouse.

Example 3: examples of point of direct shipment (with respect to adjusted to exclude any costs incurred in the international shipment of the good)

A producer has only one factory, located near the center of one of the USMCA countries, at which the producer manufactures finished office chairs. The office chairs are shipped from that factory to three warehouses leased by the producer, one on the west coast, one near the factory and one on the east coast. The office chairs are shipped to buyers from these warehouses, the shipping location depending on the shipping distance from the buyer. Buyers closest to the west coast warehouse are normally supplied by the west coast warehouse, buyers closest to the east coast are normally supplied by the warehouse located on the east coast and buyers closest to the warehouse near the factory are normally supplied by that warehouse. In this case, the point of direct shipment is the location of the warehouse from which the office chairs are normally shipped to customers in the location in which the buyer is located.

Example 4: subsection 7(3), net cost method

A producer located in USMCA country A sells Good A that is subject to a regional value content requirement to a buyer located in USMCA country B. The producer of Good A chooses that the regional value content of that good be calculated using the net cost method. All applicable requirements of these Regulations, other than the regional value content requirement, have been met. The applicable regional value content requirement is 50 per cent.

    In order to calculate the regional value content of Good A, the producer first calculates the net cost of Good A. Under paragraph 6(11)(a), the net cost is the total cost of Good A (the aggregate of the product costs, period costs and other costs) per unit, minus the excluded costs (the aggregate of the sales promotion, marketing and after-sales service costs, royalties, shipping and packing costs and non-allowable interest costs) per unit. The producer uses the following figures to calculate the net cost:

Product costs:

Value of originating materials $1.00

Value of non-originating materials 40.00

Other product costs 20.00

Period costs 10.00

Other costs 0.00

Total cost of Good A, per unit $100.00

Excluded costs:

Sales promotion, marketing and after-sales service cost $5.00 Royalties 2.50

Shipping and packing costs 3.00 Non-allowable interest costs 1.50 Total excluded costs $12.00

The net cost is the total cost of Good A, per unit, minus the excluded costs. Total cost of Good A, per unit: $100.00

Excluded costs: - 12.00

Net cost of Good A, per unit: $ 88.00

The value for net cost ($88) and the value of non-originating materials ($40) are needed in order to calculate the regional value content. The producer calculates the regional value content of Good A under the net cost method in the following manner:

$$RVC = (NC - VNM)/NC*100 = (88-40)/88*100 = 54.5\%$$

Therefore, under the net cost method, Good A qualifies as an originating good, with a regional value content of 54.5 per cent.

Example 5: paragraph 6(11)(a)

A producer in a USMCA country produces Good A and Good B during the producer's fiscal year.

The producer uses the following figures, which are recorded on the producer's books and represent all of the costs incurred with respect to both Good A and Good B, to calculate the net cost of those goods:

Product costs:

Value of originating materials $2,000 Value of non-originating materials 1,000 Other product costs 2,400

Period costs: (including $1,200 in excluded costs) 3,200 Other costs: 400

Total cost of Good A and Good B: $9,000

The net cost is the total cost of Good A and Good B, minus the excluded costs incurred with respect to those goods.

Total cost of Good A and Good B: $9,000 Excluded costs: - 1,200

Net cost of Good A and Good B: $7,800

The net cost must then be reasonably allocated, in accordance with Schedule VII, to Good A and Good B.

Example 6: paragraph 6(11)(b))

A producer located in a USMCA country produces Good A and Good B during the producer's fiscal year. In order to calculate the regional value content of Good A and Good B, the producer uses the following figures that are recorded on the producer's books and incurred with respect to those goods:

Product costs:

Value of originating materials $2,000

Value of non-originating materials 1,000

Other product costs 2,400

Period costs: (including $1,200 in excluded costs) 3,200

Other costs: 400

Total cost of Good A and Good B: $9,000

Under paragraph 6(11)(b), the total cost of Good A and Good B is then reasonably allocated, in accordance with Schedule VII, to those goods. The costs are allocated in the following manner:

Allocated to Good A 5,220 Allocated to Good B 3,780

Total cost ($9,000 for both Good A and Good B)

The excluded costs ($1,200) that are included in total cost allocated to Good A and Good B, in accordance with Schedule VII, are subtracted from that amount.

Total Excluded costs:

Sales promotion, marketing and after-sale service costs 500 Royalties 200

Shipping and packing costs 500

Excluded Cost Allocated to Good A:

Sales promotion, marketing and after-sale service costs 290 Royalties 116

Shipping and packing costs 290

Net cost (total cost minus excluded costs): $4,524

Excluded Cost Allocated to Good B

Sales promotion, marketing and after-sale service costs 210 Royalties 84

Shipping and packing costs 210

Net cost (total cost minus excluded costs): $3,276

The net cost of Good A is thus $4,524, and the net cost of Good B is $3,276.

Example 7: paragraph 6(11)(c)

> *A producer located in a USMCA country produces Good C and Good D. The following costs are recorded on the producer's books for the months of January, February and March, and each cost that forms part of the total cost are reasonably allocated, in accordance with Schedule VII, to Good C and Good D.*
> *Total cost: Good C and Good D (in thousands of dollars) Product costs:*
> > *Value of originating materials 100*
> > *Value of non-originating materials 900*
> > *Other product costs 500*
> *Period costs: (including $420 in excluded costs) 5,679*
> *Minus Excluded costs 420*
> *Other costs: 0*
> *Total cost (aggregate of product costs, period costs and other costs): 6,759*
> *Allocated to Good C (in thousands of dollars) Product costs:*
> > *Value of originating materials 0*
> > *Value of non-originating materials 800*
> > *Other product costs 300*
> *Period costs: (including $420 in excluded costs) 3,036*
> *Minus Excluded costs 300*
> *Other costs: 0*
> *Total cost (aggregate of product costs, period costs and other costs): 3,836*
> *Allocated to Good D (in thousands of dollars)*
> *Product costs:*
> > *Value of originating materials 100*
> > *Value of non-originating materials 100*
> > *Other product costs 200*
> *Period costs: (including $420 in excluded costs) 2,643*
> *Minus Excluded costs 120*

Other costs: 0
Total cost (aggregate of product costs, period costs and other costs): 2,923

Example 8: subsection 7(12)

Producer A, located in a USMCA country, produces Good A that is subject to a regional value content requirement. The producer chooses that the regional value content of that good be calculated using the net cost method. Producer A buys Material X from Producer B, located in a USMCA country. Material X is a non-originating material and is used in the production of Good A. Producer A provides Producer B, at no charge, with molds to be used in the production of Material X. The cost of the molds that is recorded on the books of Producer A has been expensed in the current year. Pursuant to subparagraph 4(1)(b)(ii) of Schedule VI, the value of the molds is included in the value of Material X. Therefore, the cost of the molds that is recorded on the books of Producer A and that has been expensed in the current year cannot be included as a separate cost in the net cost of Good A because it has already been included in the value of Material X.

Example 9: subsection 7(12)

Producer A, located in a USMCA country, produces Good A that is subject to a regional value content requirement. The producer chooses that the regional value content of that good be calculated using the net cost method and averages the calculation over the producer's fiscal year under subsection 7(15). Producer A determines that during that fiscal year Producer A incurred a gain on foreign currency conversion of $10,000 and a loss on foreign currency conversion of $8,000, resulting in a net gain of $2,000. Producer A also determines that $7,000 of the gain on foreign currency conversion and $6,000 of the loss on foreign currency conversion is related to the purchase of non-originating materials used in the production of Good A, and $3,000 of the gain on foreign currency conversion and $2,000 of the loss on foreign currency conversion is not related to the production of Good A. The producer determines that the total cost of Good A is $45,000 before deducting the $1,000 net gain on foreign currency conversion related to the production of Good A. The total cost of Good A is therefore $44,000. That $1,000 net gain is not included in the value of non-originating materials under subsection 8(1).

Example 10: subsection 7(12)

Given the same facts as in example 10, except that Producer A determines that $6,000 of the gain on foreign currency conversion and $7,000 of the loss on foreign currency conversion is related to the purchase of non- originating materials used in the production of Good A. The total cost of Good A is $45,000, which includes the $1,000 net loss on foreign currency conversion related to the production of Good A. That $1,000 net loss is not included in the value of non-originating materials under subsection 8(1).

PART IV

SECTION 8. MATERIALS

8 (1) *Value of material used in production.* Except as otherwise provided for non-originating materials used in the production of a good referred to in section 14 or subsection 15(1), and except in the case of indirect materials, intermediate materials and packing materials and containers, for the purpose of calculating the regional value content of a good and for the purposes of subsection 5(1) and (4), the value of a material that is used in the production of the good is to be

(a) except as otherwise provided in subsection (4), if the material is imported by the producer of the good into the territory of the USMCA country in which the good is produced, the transaction value of the material at the time of importation, including the costs incurred in the international shipment of the material,

(b) if the material is acquired by the producer of the good from another person located in the territory of the USMCA country in which the good is produced

    (i) the price paid or payable by the producer in the USMCA country where the producer is located,

    (ii) the value as determined for an imported material in subparagraph (a), or

    (iii) the earliest ascertainable price paid or payable in the territory of the USMCA country where the good is produced, or

(c) for a material that is self-produced

    (i) all the costs incurred in the production of the material, which includes general expenses, and

    (ii) an amount equivalent to the profit added in the normal course of trade, or equal to the profit that is usually reflected in the sale of goods of the same class or kind as the self-produced material that is being valued provided that no self-produced material that has been used in its production has been valued including the amount equivalent or equal to the profit according to this paragraph.

(2) *Adjustments to the value of materials.* The following costs may be deducted from the value of a non- originating material or material of undetermined origin, if they are included under subsection (1):

(a) the costs of freight, insurance and packing and all other costs incurred in transporting the material to the location of the producer;

(b) duties and taxes paid or payable with respect to the material in the territory of one or more of the USMCA countries, other than duties and taxes that are waived, refunded, refundable or otherwise recoverable, including credit against duty or tax paid or payable,

(c) customs brokerage fees, including the cost of in-house customs brokerage services, incurred with respect to the material in the territory of one or more of the USMCA countries, and

(d) the cost of waste and spoilage resulting from the use of the material in the production of the good, minus the value of any reusable scrap or by-product.

(3) *Documentary evidence required.* If the cost or expense listed in subsection (2) is unknown or documentary evidence of the amount of the adjustment is not available, then no adjustment is allowed for that particular cost or expense.

(4) *Transaction value not acceptable.* For the purposes of paragraph (1)(a), if the transaction value of the material referred to in that paragraph is not acceptable or if there is no transaction value in accordance with Schedule IV (Unacceptable Transaction Value), the value of the material must be determined in accordance with Schedule VI (Value of Materials) and, if the costs referred to in subsection (2) are included in that value, those costs may be deducted from that value.

(5) *Costs recorded on books.* For the purposes of subsection (1), the costs referred to in paragraph (1)(c) are to be the costs referred to in those paragraphs that are recorded on the books of the producer of the good.

(6) *Designation of self-produced material as an intermediate material.* Except for the purpose of determining the value of a non-originating component identified in Table G of Part VI (Automotive Goods), for the purpose of calculating the regional value content of a good the

producer of the good may designate as an intermediate material any self-produced material that is used in the production of the good, provided that if an intermediate material is subject to a regional value content requirement, no other self-produced material that is subject to a regional value content requirement and is incorporated into that intermediate material is also designated by the producer as an intermediate material.

(7) *Particulars.* For the purposes of subsection (6),

(a) in order to qualify as an originating material, a self-produced material that is designated as an intermediate material must qualify as an originating material under these Regulations;

(b) the designation of a self-produced material as an intermediate material is to be made solely at the choice of the producer of that self-produced material; and

(c) except as otherwise provided in subsection 9(4), the proviso set out in subsection (6) does not apply with respect to an intermediate material used by another producer in the production of a material that is subsequently acquired and used in the production of a good by the producer referred to in subsection (6).

(8) *Value of an intermediate material.* The value of an intermediate material will be, at the choice of the producer of the good,

(a) the total cost incurred with respect to all goods produced by the producer that can be reasonably allocated to that intermediate material in accordance with Schedule V; or

(b) the aggregate of each cost that forms part of the total cost incurred with respect to that intermediate material that can be reasonably allocated to that intermediate material in accordance with Schedule V.

(9) *Calculation of total cost* Total cost under subsection (8) consists of the costs referred to in subsection 1(6), and is calculated in accordance with that subsection and subsection 1(7).

(10) *Rescission of a designation.* If a producer of a good designates a self-produced material as an intermediate material under subsection (6) and the customs administration of a USMCA country into which the good is imported determines during a verification of origin of the good that the intermediate material is a non- originating material and notifies the producer of this in writing before the written determination of whether the good qualifies as an originating good, the producer may rescind the designation, and the regional value content of the good must be calculated as though the self-produced material were not so designated.

(11) *Effect of a rescission.* A producer of a good who rescinds a designation under subsection (10) may, not later than 30 days after the customs administration referred to in subsection (10) notifies the producer in writing that the self-produced material referred to in paragraph (a) is a non-originating material, designate as an intermediate material another self-produced material that is incorporated into the good, subject to the provision set out in subsection (6).

(12) *Second rescission.* If a producer of a good designates another self-produced material as an intermediate material under subsection (6) and the customs administration referred to in subsection (10) determines during the verification of origin of the good that that self-produced material is a non-originating material,

(a) the producer may rescind the designation, and the regional value content of the good will be calculated as though the self-produced material were not so designated; and,

(b) the producer may not designate another self-produced material that is incorporated into the good as an intermediate material.

(13) *Indirect materials.* For the purpose of determining whether a good is an originating good, an indirect material that is used in the production of the good

(a) will be considered to be an originating material, regardless of where that indirect material is produced; and

(b) if the good is subject to a regional value content requirement, for the purpose of calculating the net cost under the net cost method, the value of the indirect material is to be the costs of that material that are recorded on the books of the producer of the good.

(14) *Packaging materials and containers.* Packaging materials and containers, if classified under the Harmonized System with the good that is packaged therein, will be disregarded for the purpose of

(a) determining whether all of the non-originating materials used in the production of the good undergo an applicable change in tariff classification;

(b) determining whether a good is wholly obtained or produced; and

(c) determining under subsection 5(1) the value of non-originating materials that do not undergo an applicable change in tariff classification.

(15) *Value of packaging materials and containers — cases where taken into account.* If packaging materials and containers in which a good is packaged for retail sale are classified under the Harmonized System with the good that is packaged therein and that good is subject to a regional value content requirement, the value of those packaging materials and containers will be taken into account as originating materials or non-originating materials, as the case may be, for the purpose of calculating the regional value content of the good.

(16) *Packaging materials and containers— self-produced.* For the purposes of subsection (15), if packaging materials and containers are self-produced materials, the producer may choose to designate those materials as intermediate materials under subsection (6).

(17) *Packing materials and containers.* For the purpose of determining whether a good is an originating good, packing materials and containers are disregarded.

(18) *Fungible materials and fungible goods.* A fungible material or good is originating if:

(a) when originating and non-originating fungible materials
   (i) are withdrawn from an inventory in one location and used in the production of the good, or
   (ii) are withdrawn from inventories in more than one location in the territory of one or more of the USMCA countries and used in the production of the good at the same production facility, the determination of whether the materials are originating is made on the basis of an inventory management method recognized in the Generally Accepted Accounting Principles of, or otherwise accepted by, the Party in which the production is performed or an inventory management method set out in Schedule VIII; or

(b) when originating and non-originating fungible goods are commingled and exported in the same form, the determination of whether the goods are originating is made on the basis of an inventory management method recognized in the Generally Accepted Accounting Principles of, or otherwise accepted by, the Party from which the good is exported or an inventory management method set out in Schedule VIII.

(19) The inventory management method selected under subsection 18 must be used throughout the fiscal year of the producer or the person that selected the inventory management method.

(20) An importer may claim that a fungible material or good is originating if the importer, producer, or exporter has physically segregated each fungible material or good as to allow their specific identification.

(21) *Choice of inventory management method.* If fungible materials referred to in paragraph (18)(a) and fungible goods referred to in paragraph (18)(b) are withdrawn from the same inventory, the inventory management method used for the materials must be the same as the inventory management method used for the goods, and if the averaging method is used, the respective averaging periods for fungible materials and fungible goods are to be used.

(22) *Written notice.* A choice of inventory management methods under subsection (18) will be considered to have been made when the customs administration of the USMCA country into which the good is imported is informed in writing of the choice during the course of a verification of origin of the good.

(23) *Accessories, spare parts, tools or instructional or other information materials.* For the purposes of subsections (24) through (27), "accessories, spare parts, tools, or instructional or other information materials" are covered when

(a) they are classified with, delivered with, but not invoiced separately from the good, and
(b) their type, quantity and value are customary for the good, within the industry that produces the good.

(24) *Exclusion.* Accessories, spare parts, tools, or instructional or other information materials are to be disregarded for the purpose of determining

(a) whether a good is wholly obtained;
(b) whether all the non-originating materials used in the production of the good satisfy a process or applicable change in tariff classification requirement established in Schedule I; or,
(c) under subsection 5(1), the value of non-originating materials that do not undergo an applicable change in tariff classification.

(25) *Value for regional value content requirement.* If a good is subject to a regional value content requirement, the value of accessories, spare parts, tools, or instructional or other information materials is to be taken into account as originating materials or non-originating materials, as the case may be, in calculating the regional value content of the good.

(26) *Designation.* For the purposes of subsection (25), if accessories, spare parts, tools, or instructional or other information materials are self-produced materials, the producer may choose to designate those materials as intermediate materials under subsection (4).

(27) *Originating status.* A good's accessories, spare parts, tools, or instructional or other information materials have the originating status of the good with which they are delivered.

(28) *Examples illustrating the provisions on materials.* Each of the following examples is an "Example" as referred to in subsection 1(4).

Example 1: subsection 7(4), Transaction Value not Determined in a Manner Consistent with Schedule VI

Producer A, located in USMCA country A, imports a bicycle chainring into USMCA country A. Producer A purchased material A from a middleman located in country B. The middleman purchased the chainring from a manufacturer located in country B. Under the laws in USMCA country A that implement the Agreement on Implementation of Article VII of the General Agreement on Tariffs and Trade, the customs value of material A was based on the price actually paid or payable by the middleman to the manufacturer. Producer A uses the chainring to produce a bicycle, and exports the bicycle to USMCA country D. The bicycle is subject to a regional value content requirement.

Under subsection 4(1) of Schedule VI (Value of Materials), the price actually paid or payable is the total payment made or to be made by the producer to or for the benefit of the seller of the material. Section 1 of that Schedule defines producer and seller for the purposes of the Schedule. A producer is the person who uses the material in the production of a good that is subject to a regional value content requirement. A seller is the person who sells the material being valued to the producer.

The transaction value of the chainring was not determined in a manner consistent with Schedule VI because it was based on the price actually paid or payable by the middleman to the manufacturer, rather than on the price actually paid or payable by Producer A to the middleman. Thus, subsection 8(4) applies and the chainring is valued in accordance with Schedule IV.

Example 2: subsection 8(7), Value of Intermediate Materials

A producer located in a USMCA country produces a bicycle, which is subject to a regional value content requirement under section 3(2). The producer also produces a chain ring, which is used in the production of the bicycle. Both originating materials and non-originating materials are used in the production of the chainring. The chainring is subject to a change in tariff classification requirement under section 3(2). The costs to produce the chainring are the following:

Product costs:

> *Value of originating materials $ 1.00*

> *Value of non-originating materials 7.50*

> *Other product costs 1.50*

Period costs (including $0.30 in royalties): 0.50

Other costs: 0.10

Total cost of the chainring: $10.60

The producer designates the chainring as an intermediate material and determines that, because all of the non- originating materials that are used in the production of the chainring undergo an applicable change in tariff classification set out in Schedule I, the chainring would, under section 3(2) qualify as an originating material. The cost of the non-originating materials used in the production of the chainring is therefore not included in the value of non-originating materials that are used in the production of the bicycle for the purpose of determining its regional value content of the bicycle. Because the chainring has been designated as an intermediate material, the total cost of the chainring, which is $10.60, is treated as the cost of originating materials for the purpose of calculating the regional value content of the bicycle. The total cost of the bicycle is determined in accordance with the following figures:

Product costs:

> *Value of originating materials*

> – *intermediate materials $10.60*
> – *other materials 3.00*

> *Value of non-originating materials 5.50*

Other product costs 6.50

Period costs: 2.50

Other costs: 0.10

Total cost of the bicycle: $28.20

Example 3: subsection 8(7), Effects of the Designation of Self-produced Materials on Net Cost

The ability to designate intermediate materials helps to put the vertically integrated producer who is self- producing materials that are used in the production of a good on par with a producer who is purchasing materials and valuing those materials in accordance with subsection 8(1). The following situations demonstrate how this is achieved:

Situation 1

A producer located in a USMCA country produces a bicycle, which is subject to a regional value content requirement of 50 per cent under the net cost method. The bicycle satisfies all other applicable requirements of these Regulations. The producer purchases a bicycle frame, which is used in the production of the bicycle, from a supplier located in a USMCA country. The value of the frame determined in accordance with subsection 8(1) is $11.00. The frame is an originating material. All other materials used in the production of the bicycle are non-originating materials. The net cost of the bicycle is determined as follows: Product costs:

> *Value of originating materials (bicycle frame) $11.00*
>
> *Value of non-originating materials 5.50*
>
> *Other product costs 6.50*

Period costs: (including $0.20 in excluded costs) 0.50

Other costs: 0.10

Total cost of the bicycle: $23.60

Excluded costs: (included in period costs) 0.20

Net cost of the bicycle: $23.40

The regional value content of the bicycle is calculated as follows:

$$RVC = (NC - VNM)/NC * 100$$
$$= (\$23.40 - \$5.50)/\$23.50 * 100$$
$$= 76.5\%$$

The regional value content of the bicycle is 76.5 per cent, and the bicycle, therefore, qualifies as an originating good.

Situation 2

A producer located in a USMCA country produces a bicycle, which is subject to a regional value content requirement of 50 per cent under the net cost method. The bicycle satisfies all other applicable requirements of these Regulations. The producer self-produces the bicycle frame which is used in the production of the bicycle. The costs to produce the frame are the following:

Product costs:

> *Value of originating materials $ 1.00*
>
> *Value of non-originating materials 7.50*
>
> *Other product costs 1.50*

Period costs: (including $0.20 in excluded costs) 0.50

Other costs: 0.10

Total cost of the bicycle frame: $10.60

Additional costs to produce the bicycle are the following:

Product costs:

    Value of originating materials $ 0.00

    Value of non-originating materials 5.50

    Other product costs 6.50

Period costs: (including $0.20 in excluded costs) 0.50

Other costs: 0.10

Total additional costs: $12.60

The producer does not designate the bicycle frame as an intermediate material under subsection 8(4). The net cost of the bicycle is calculated as follows:

	Costs of the bicycle frame (not designated as an intermediate	Additional Costs to Produce the bicycle	Total
Total Product costs:			
Value of originating materials	$1.00	$0.00	$1.00
Value of non-originating materials	7.50	5.50	13.00
Other product costs	1.50	6.50	8.00
Period costs (including $0.20 in excluded costs):			
Other costs	0.50	0.50	1.00
Total cost of the bicycle	0.10	0.10	0.20
Excluded costs (in period costs)	$10.60	$12.60	23.20
Net cost of the bicycle (total cost minus excluded costs):	0.20	0.20	0.40

The regional value content of the bicycle is calculated as follows:

$$RVC = (NC - VNM)/NC * 100$$
$$= (\$22.80 - \$13.00)/\$22.80 * 100$$
$$= 42.9\%$$

The regional value content of the bicycle is 42.9 per cent, and the bicycle, therefore, does not qualify as an originating good.

Situation 3

A producer located in a USMCA country produces the bicycle, which is subject to a regional value content requirement of 50 per cent under the net cost method. The bicycle satisfies all other applicable requirements of these Regulations. The producer self-produces the bicycle frame, which is used in the production of the bicycle. The costs to produce the frame are the following:

Product costs:

> Value of originating materials $ 1.00
> Value of non-originating materials 7.50
> Other product costs 1.50
> Period costs: (including $0.20 in excluded costs) 0.50
> Other costs: 0.10

Total cost of the bicycle frame: $10.60

Additional costs to produce the bicycle are the following: Product costs: 0.10

Product costs:

> Value of originating materials $ 0.00
> Value of non-originating materials 5.50
> Other product costs 6.50

Period costs: (including $0.20 in excluded costs) 0.50

Other costs: 0.10

Total additional costs: $12.60

The producer designates the frame as an intermediate material under subsection 8(6). The frame qualifies as an originating material under section 4(2). Therefore, the value of non originating materials used in the production of the frame is not included in the value of non-originating materials for the purpose of calculating the regional value content of the bicycle. The net cost of the bicycle is calculated as follows:

Product costs:	Costs of the bicycle frame (not designated as an intermediate material)	Additional Costs to Produce the bicycle	Total
Value of originating materials	$ 10.60	$ 0.00	$ 10.60
Value of non-originating materials		5.50	5.50
Other product costs		6.50	6.50
Period costs (including $0.20 in excluded costs):		0.50	0.50
Other costs		0.10	0.10

Appendix

Product costs:	Costs of the bicycle frame (not designated as an intermediate material)	Additional Costs to Produce the bicycle	Total
Total cost of the bicycle	$10.60	$12.60	$23.20
Excluded costs (in period costs)		0.20	0.20
Net cost of the bicycle (total cost minus excluded costs):			$23.00

The regional value content of the bicycle is calculated as follows:

$$RVC = (NC - VNM)/NC * 100$$
$$= (\$23.00 - \$5.50)/\$23.00 * 100$$
$$= 76.1\%$$

The regional value content of the bicycle is 76.1 per cent, and the bicycle, therefore, qualifies as an originating good.

Example 4: Originating Materials Acquired from a Producer Who Produced Them Using Intermediate Materials

Producer A, located in USMCA country A, produces switches. In order for the switches to qualify as originating goods, Producer A designates subassemblies of the switches as intermediate materials. The subassemblies are subject to a regional value content requirement. They satisfy that requirement, and qualify as originating materials. The switches are also subject to a regional value content requirement, and, with the subassemblies designated as intermediate materials, are determined to have a regional value content of 65 per cent.

    Producer A sells the switches to Producer B, located in USMCA country B, who uses them to produce switch assemblies that are used in the production of Good B. The switch assemblies are subject to a regional value content requirement. Producers A and B are not accumulating their production within the meaning of section 9. Producer B is therefore able, under subsection 8(4), to designate the switch assemblies as intermediate materials.

    If Producers A and B were accumulating their production within the meaning of section 14, Producer B would be unable to designate the switch assemblies as intermediate materials, because the production of both producers would be considered to be the production of one producer.

Example 5: Single Producer and Successive Designations of Materials Subject to a Regional Value Content Requirement as Intermediate Materials

Producer A, located in USMCA country, produces Material X and uses Material X in the production of Good B. Material X qualifies as an originating material because it satisfies the applicable regional value content requirement. Producer A designates Material X as an intermediate material.

    Producer A uses Material X in the production of Material Y, which is also used in the production of Good B. Material Y is also subject to a regional value content requirement. Under the proviso set out in subsection 8(6), Producer A cannot designate Material Y as an intermediate material, even if Material Y satisfies the applicable regional value content requirement, because Material X was already designated by Producer A as an intermediate material.

Example 6: Single Producer and Multiple Designations of Materials as Intermediate Materials

Producer X, who is located in USMCA country X, uses non-originating materials in the production of self- produced materials A, B and C. None of the self-produced materials are used in the production of any of the other self-produced materials.

Producer X uses the self-produced materials in the production of Good O, which is exported to USMCA country Y. Materials A, B and C qualify as originating materials because they satisfy the applicable regional value content requirements.

Because none of the self-produced materials are used in the production of any of the other self-produced materials, then even though each self-produced material is subject to a regional value content requirement, Producer X may, under subsection 8(4), designate all of the self-produced materials as intermediate materials. The proviso set out in subsection 8(4) only applies if self-produced materials are used in the production of other self-produced materials and both are subject to a regional value content requirement.

Example 7: subsection 7(22) Accessories, Spare Parts, Tools, Instruction or Other Information Materials

The following are examples of accessories, spare parts, tools, instructional or other information materials that are delivered with a good and form part of the good's standard accessories, spare parts, tools, instructional or other information materials:

(a) consumables that must be replaced at regular intervals, such as dust collectors for an air- conditioning system,
(b) a carrying case for equipment,
(c) a dust cover for a machine,
(d) an operational manual for a vehicle,
(e) brackets to attach equipment to a wall,
(f) a bicycle tool kit or a car jack,
(g) a set of wrenches to change the bit on a chuck,
(h) a brush or other tool to clean out a machine, and
(i) electrical cords and power bars for use with electronic goods.

Example 8: Value of Indirect Materials that are Assists

Producer A, located in a USMCA country, produces well-water pump that is subject to a regional value content requirement. The producer chooses that the regional value content of that good be calculated using the net cost method. Producer A buys a mold-injected plastic water flow sensor from Producer B, located in the same USMCA country, and uses it in the production of Good A. Producer A provides to Producer B, at no charge, molds to be used in the production of the water flow sensor. The molds have a value of $100 which is expensed in the current year by Producer A.

The water flow sensor is subject to a regional value content requirement which Producer B chooses to calculate using the net cost method. For the purpose of determining the value of non-originating materials in order to calculate the regional value content of the water flow sensor, the molds are considered to be an originating material because they are an indirect material. However, pursuant to subsection 8(13) they have a value of nil because the cost of the molds with respect to the water flow sensor is not recorded on the books of Producer B.

It is determined that the water flow sensor is a non-originating material. The cost of the molds that is recorded on the books of producer A is expensed in the current year. Pursuant to

289

section 5 of Schedule VI (Value of Materials), the value of the molds (see subparagraph 4(1)(b)(ii) of Schedule VI) must be included in the value of the water flow sensor by Producer A when calculating the regional value content of well-water pump. The cost of the molds, although recorded on the books of producer A, cannot be included as a separate cost in the net cost of well-water pump because it is already included in the value of the water flow sensor. The entire cost of Material X, which includes the cost of the molds, is included in the value of non-originating materials for the purposes of the regional value content of the well-water pump.

PART V GENERAL PROVISIONS SECTION 9. ACCUMULATION

(9) (1) Subject to subsections (2) through (5)

(a) a good is originating if the good is produced in the territory of one or more of the USMCA countries by one or more producers, provided that that the good satisfies the requirements of section 3 and all other applicable requirements of these Regulations;

(b) an originating good or material of one or more of the USMCA countries is considered as originating in the territory of another USMCA country when used as a material in the production of a good in the territory of another USMCA country; and

(c) production undertaken on a non-originating material in the territory of one or more of the USMCA countries may contribute toward the originating status of a good, regardless of whether that production was sufficient to confer originating status to the material itself.

(2) *Accumulation using the net cost method.* If a good is subject to a regional value content requirement based on the net cost method and an exporter or producer of the good has a statement signed by a producer of a material that is used in the production of the good that states

(a) the net cost incurred and the value of non-originating materials used by the producer of the material in the production of that material,

(i) net cost incurred by the producer of the good with respect to the material is to be the net cost incurred by the producer of the material plus, if not included in the net cost incurred by the producer of the material, the costs referred to in paragraphs 8(2)(a) through (c), and

(ii) the value of non-originating materials used by the producer of the good with respect to the material is to be the value of non-originating materials used by the producer of the material; or

(b) any amount, other than an amount that includes any of the value of non-originating materials, that is part of the net cost incurred by the producer of the material in the production of that material,

(i) the net cost incurred by the producer of the good with respect to the material is to be the value of the material, determined in accordance with subsection 8(1), and

(ii) the value of non-originating materials used by the producer of the good with respect to the material is to be the value of the material, determined in accordance with subsection 8(2), minus the amount stated in the statement.

(3) *Accumulation using the transaction value method.* If a good is subject to a regional value content requirement based on the transaction value method and an exporter or producer of the good has a statement signed by a producer of a material that is used in the production of the good that states the value of non- originating materials used by the producer of the material in the production of that material, the value of non- originating materials used by the producer of the good with respect to the material is the value of non- originating materials used by the producer of the material.

(4) *Averaging of costs—net cost method.* If a good is subject to a regional value content requirement based on the net cost method and an exporter or producer of the good does not have a statement described in subsection (2) but has a statement signed by a producer of a material that is used in the production of the good that

    (a) states the sum of the net costs incurred and the sum of the values of non-originating materials used by the producer of the material in the production of that material and identical materials or similar materials, or any combination thereof, produced in a single plant by the producer of the material over a month or any consecutive three, six or twelve month period that falls within the fiscal year of the producer of the good, divided by the number of units of materials with respect to which the statement is made,

        (i) the net cost incurred by the producer of the good with respect to the material is to be the sum of the net costs incurred by the producer of the material with respect to that material and the identical materials or similar materials, divided by the number of units of materials with respect to which the statement is made, plus, if not included in the net costs incurred by the producer of the material, the costs referred to in paragraphs 8(2)(a) through (c), and

        (ii) the value of non-originating materials used by the producer of the good with respect to the material is to be the sum of the values of non-originating materials used by the producer of the material with respect to that material and the identical materials or similar materials divided by the number of units of materials with respect to which the statement is made; or

    (b) states any amount, other than an amount that includes any of the values of non-originating materials, that is part of the sum of the net costs incurred by the producer of the material in the production of that material and identical materials or similar materials, or any combination thereof, produced in a single plant by the producer of the material over a month or any consecutive three, six or twelve month period that falls within the fiscal year of the producer of the good, divided by the number of units of materials with respect to which the statement is made,

        (i) the net cost incurred by the producer of the good with respect to the material is to be the value of the material, determined in accordance with subsection 8(1), and

        (ii) the value of non-originating materials used by the producer of the good with respect to the material is to be the value of the material, determined in accordance with subsection 7(1), minus the amount stated in the statement.

(5) *Averaging of costs—transaction value method.* If a good is subject to a regional value content requirement based on the transaction value method and an exporter or producer of the good does not have a statement described in subsection (3) but has a statement signed by a producer of a material that is used in the production of the good that states the sum of the values of non-originating materials used by the producer of the material in the production of that material and identical materials or similar materials, or any combination thereof, produced in a single plant by the producer of the material over a month or any consecutive three, six or twelve month period that falls within the fiscal year of the producer of the good, divided by the number of units of materials with respect to which the statement is made, the value of non-originating materials used by the producer of the good with respect to the material is the sum of the values of non-originating materials used by the producer of the material with respect to that material and the identical materials or similar materials divided by the number of units of materials with respect to which the statement is made.

(6) *Single producer.* For the purposes of subsection 8(4), if a producer of the good chooses to accumulate the production of materials under subsection (1), that production will be considered to be the production of the producer of the good.

(7) *Particulars.* For the purposes of this section,

    (a) in order to accumulate the production of a material,
        (i) if the good is subject to a regional value content requirement, the producer of the good must have a statement described in subsection (2) through (5) that is signed by the producer of the material, and
        (ii) if an applicable change in tariff classification is applied to determine whether the good is an originating good, the producer of the good must have a statement signed by the producer of the material that states the tariff classification of all non-originating materials used by that producer in the production of that material and that the production of the material took place entirely in the territory of one or more of the USMCA countries;
    (b) a producer of a good who chooses to accumulate is not required to accumulate the production of all materials that are incorporated into the good; and
    (c) any information set out in a statement referred to in subsection (2) through (5) that concerns the value of materials or costs is to be in the same currency as the currency of the country in which the person who provided the statement is located.

(8) Examples of accumulation of production.

Each of the following examples is an "Example" as referred to in subsection 1(4).

Example 1: subsection 9(1)

Producer A, located in USMCA country A, imports unfinished bearing rings provided for in subheading 8482.99 into USMCA country A from a non-USMCA territory. Producer A further processes the unfinished bearing rings into finished bearing rings, which are of the same subheading. The finished bearing rings of Producer A do not satisfy an applicable change in tariff classification and therefore do not qualify as originating goods.

    The net cost of the finished bearing rings (per unit) is calculated as follows:

Product Costs:	
Value of Originating materials	$0.15
Value of non-originating materials	0.75
Other Product costs	0.35
Period Costs: (including $0.05 in excluded costs)	0.15
Other costs:	0.05
Total cost of the finished bearing rings, per unit:	$1.45
Excluded costs: (included in period costs):	0.05
Net cost of the finished bearing rings, per unit:	$1.40

Producer A sells the finished bearing rings to Producer B who is located in USMCA country A for $1.50 each. Producer B further processes them into bearings, and intends to export the bearings to USMCA country B. Although the bearings satisfy the applicable change in tariff classification, the bearings are subject to a regional value content requirement.

Situation A:

Producer B does not choose to accumulate costs incurred by Producer A with respect to the bearing rings used in the production of the bearings. The net cost of the bearings (per unit) is calculated as follows:

Product Costs:	
Value of Originating materials	$0.45
Value of non-originating materials (value, per unit, of bargaining rings purchased from Producer A)	1.50
Other Product costs	0.75
Period Costs: (including $0.05 in excluded costs)	0.15
Other costs:	0.05
Total cost of the bearing rings, per unit:	$2.90
Excluded costs: (included in period costs):	0.05
Net cost of the bearing rings, per unit:	$2.485

Under the net cost method, the regional value content of the bearings is

$$RVC = ((NC - VNM)/NC) \times 100 = (($2.85 - $1.50)/$2.85) \times 100 = 47.4\%$$

Therefore, the bearings are non-originating goods.

Situation B:

Producer B chooses to accumulate costs incurred by Producer A with respect to the bearing rings used in the production of the bearings. Producer A provides a statement described in section 9(2)(a) to Producer B. The net cost of the bearings (per unit) is calculated as follows:

Product costs:	
Value of originating materials ($0.45 + 0.15)	$0.60
Value of non-originating materials (value, per unit, of the unfinished bearing rings imported by Producer A)	0.75
Other product costs ($0.45 + $0.15)	0.75
Period costs: (($0.15 + $0.15), including $0.10 in excluded costs)	0.30
Other costs: ($0.05 + $0.05)	0.10
Total cost of the bearings, per unit:	$2.85
Excluded costs: (included in period costs)	0.10
Net cost of the bearings, per unit:	$2.75

Under the net cost method, the regional value content of the bearings is

$$RVC = (NC - VNM/NC) \times 100 = (($2.75 - $0.75)/$2.75) \times 100 = 72.7\%$$

Therefore, the bearings are originating goods.

Appendix

Situation C:

Producer B chooses to accumulate costs incurred by Producer A with respect to the bearing rings used in the production of the bearings. Producer A provides to Producer B a statement described in section 9(2)(b) that specifies an amount equal to the net cost minus the value of non-originating materials used to produce the finished bearing rings ($1.40 – 0.75 = $0.65). The net cost of the bearings (per unit) is calculated as follows:

Product costs:	
Value of originating materials ($0.45 + 0.65)	$1.10
Value of non-originating materials ($1.50-0.65)	0.85
Other product costs	0.75
Period costs: (including $0.05 in excluded costs)	0.15
Other costs:	0.05
Total cost of the bearings, per unit:	$2.90
Excluded costs: (included in period costs)	0.05
Net cost of the bearings, per unit:	$2.85

Under the net cost method, the regional value content of the bearings is

$$RVC = ((NC - VNM)/NC) \times 100 = (($2.85\% - $0.85)/$2.85) \times 100$$

Therefore, the bearings are originating goods.

Situation D:

Producer B chooses to accumulate costs incurred by Producer A with respect to the bearing rings used in the production of the bearings. Producer A provides to Producer B a statement described in section 9(2)(b) that specifies an amount equal to the value of other product costs used in the production of the finished bearing rings ($0.35). The net cost of the bearings (per unit) is calculated as follows:

Product costs:	
Value of originating materials	$0.45
Value of non-originating materials ($1.50-0.35)	1.15
Other product costs ($0.75 + 0.35)	1.10
Period costs: (including $0.05 in excluded costs)	0.15
Other costs:	0.05
Total cost of the bearings, per unit:	$2.90
Excluded costs: (included in period costs)	0.05
Net cost of the bearings, per unit:	$2.85

Under the net cost method, the regional value content of the bearings is

$$RVC = ((NC - VNM)/NC) \times 100 = (($2.95 - $1.15)/$2.85) \times 100 = 59.7\%$$

Therefore, the bearings are originating goods.

294

Example 2: section 9(1)

Producer A, located in USMCA country A, imports non-originating cotton, carded or combed, provided for in heading 52.03 for use in the production of cotton yarn provided for in heading 52.05. Because the change from cotton, carded or combed, to cotton yarn is a change within the same chapter, the cotton does not satisfy the applicable change in tariff classification for heading 52.05, which is a change from any other chapter, with certain exceptions. Therefore, the cotton yarn that Producer A produces from non-originating cotton is a non- originating good.

Producer A then sells the non-originating cotton yarn to Producer B, also located in USMCA country A, who uses the cotton yarn in the production of woven fabric of cotton provided for in heading 52.08. The change from non-originating cotton yarn to woven fabric of cotton is insufficient to satisfy the applicable change in tariff classification for heading 52.08, which is a change from any heading outside headings 52.08 through 52.12, except from certain headings, under which various yarns, including cotton yarn provided for in heading 52.05, are classified. Therefore, the woven fabric of cotton that Producer B produces from non-originating cotton yarn produced by Producer A is a non-originating good.

However, Producer B can choose to accumulate the production of Producer A. The rule for heading 52.08, under which the cotton fabric is classified, does not exclude a change from heading 52.03, under which carded or combed cotton is classified. Therefore, under section 15(1), the change from carded or combed cotton provided for in heading 52.03 to the woven fabric of cotton provided for in heading 52.08 would satisfy the applicable change of tariff classification for heading 52.08. The woven fabric of cotton would be considered as an originating good.

Producer B, in order to choose to accumulate Producer A's production, must have a statement described in section 9(4)(a)(ii).

Situation E:

Producer B chooses to accumulate costs incurred by Producer A with respect to the bearing rings used in the production of the bearings. Producer A provides to Producer B a signed statement described in section 14(4)(a) that specifies the value of non-originating materials used in the production of the finished bearing rings ($0.75). Producer B chooses to calculate the regional value content of the bearings under the transaction value method. The regional value content of the bearings (per unit) is calculated as follows:

Transaction value of the bearings, per unit	$3.15
Costs incurred, per unit, in the international shipment of the good (included in transaction value of the bearings)	0.15
Transaction value, per unit, adjusted to exclude any costs incurred in the international shipment of the good	$3.00
Value of non-originating materials (value, per unit, of the unfinished bearing rings imported by Producer A)	$0.75

Under the transaction value method, the regional value content of the bearings is

$$RVC = (TV - VNM) / TV \times 100 = (\$3.00 - \$0.75) / \$3.00 \times 100 = 75\%$$

Therefore, because the bearings have a regional value content of at least 60 percent under transaction value method, the bearings are originating goods.

SECTION 10. TRANSSHIPMENT

10 (1) *Transport requirements to retain originating status.* If an originating good is transported outside the territories of the USMCA countries, the good retains its originating status if

- (a) the good remains under customs control outside the territories of the USMCA countries; and
- (b) the good does not undergo further production or any other operation outside the territories of the USMCA countries, other than unloading; reloading; separation from a bulk shipment; storing; labeling or other marking required by the importing USMCA country; or any other operation necessary to transport the good to the territory of the importing USMCA country or to preserve the good in good condition, including:
    - (i) inspection;
    - (ii) removal of dust that accumulates during shipment;
    - (iii) ventilation;
    - (iv) spreading out or drying;
    - (v) chilling;
    - (vi) replacing salt, sulphur dioxide or other aqueous solutions; or
    - (vii) replacing damaged packing materials and containers and removal of units of the good that are spoiled or damaged and present a danger to the remaining units of the good.

(2) *Good entirely non-originating.* A good that is a non-originating good by application of subsection (1) is considered to be entirely non-originating for the purposes of these Regulations.

(3) *Exceptions for certain goods.* Subsection (1) does not apply with respect to

- (a) a "smart card" of subheading 8523.52 containing a single integrated circuit, if any further production or other operation that that good undergoes outside the territories of the USMCA countries does not result in a change in the tariff classification of the good to any other subheading;
- (b) a good of any of subheadings 8541.10 through 8541.60 or 8542.31 through 8542.39, if any further production or other operation that that good undergoes outside the territories of the USMCA countries does not result in a change in the tariff classification of the good to a subheading outside of that group;
- (c) an electronic microassembly of subheading 8543.90, if any further production or other operation that that good undergoes outside the territories of the USMCA countries does not result in a change in the tariff classification of the good to any other subheading; or
- (d) an electronic microassembly of subheading 8548.90, if any further production or other operation that that good undergoes outside the territories of the USMCA countries does not result in a change in the tariff classification of the good to any other subheading.

SECTION 11. NON-QUALIFYING OPERATIONS

11 A good is not an originating good merely by reason of

- (a) mere dilution with water or another substance that does not materially alter the characteristics of the good; or
- (b) any production or pricing practice with respect to which it may be demonstrated, on the basis of a preponderance of evidence, that the object was to circumvent these Regulations.

PART VI AUTOMOTIVE GOODS

SECTION 12. DEFINITIONS AND INTERPRETATION

(1) For purposes of this part,

aftermarket part means a good that is not for use as original equipment in the production of passenger vehicles, light trucks or heavy trucks as defined in these Regulations;

all-terrain vehicle means a vehicle that does not meet United States federal safety and emissions standards permitting unrestricted on-road use or the equivalent Mexican and Canadian on-road standards;

annual purchase value (APV) means the sum of the values of high-wage materials purchased annually by a producer for use in the production of passenger vehicles, light trucks or heavy trucks in a plant located in the territory of a USMCA country;

average base hourly wage rate means the average hourly rate of pay based on all the hours performed on direct production work at a plant or facility, even if such workers performing that work are paid on a salary, piece-rate, or day-rate basis. This includes all hours performed by full-time, part time, temporary, and seasonal workers. The rate of pay does not include benefits, bonuses or shift-premiums, or premium pay for overtime, holidays or weekends. If a worker is paid by a third party, such as a temporary employment agency, only the wages received by the worker are included in the average base hourly wage rate calculation.

For direct production workers, the average base hourly wage rate of pay is calculated based on all their working hours. For other workers performing direct production work, the average base hourly rate is calculated based on the amount of hours performing direct production work. The rate also does not include any hours worked by interns, trainees, students, or any other worker that does not have an express or implied compensation agreement with the employer.

If any direct production worker or worker performing direct production work is compensated by a method other than hourly, such as a salary, piece-rate, or day-rate basis, the worker's hourly base wage rate is calculated by converting the salary, piece-rate, or day-rate to an hourly equivalent. This hourly equivalent is then multiplied by the number of hours worked in direct production for purposes of calculating the average base hourly base wage rate.

class of motor vehicles means one of the following categories of motor vehicles:

(a) road tractors for semi-trailers of subheading 8701.20, vehicles for the transport of 16 or more persons of subheading 8702.10 or 8702.90, motor vehicles for the transport of goods of subheading 8704.10, 8704.22, 8704.23, 8704.32 or 8704.90, special purpose motor vehicles of heading 87.05, or chassis fitted with engines of heading 87.06;

(b) tractors of subheading 8701.10 or 8701.30 through 8701.90;

(c) vehicles for the transport of 15 or fewer persons of subheading 8702.10 or 8702.90, or light trucks of subheading 8704.21 or 8704.31; or

(d) passenger vehicles of subheading 8703.21 through 8703.90;

complete motor vehicle assembly process means the production of a motor vehicle from separate constituent parts, including the following:

(a) a structural frame or unibody

(b) body panels

(c) an engine, a transmission and a drive train

(d) brake components

(e) steering and suspension components

(f) seating and internal trim

297

    (g) bumpers and external trim

    (h) wheels and

    (i) electrical and lighting components;

direct production work means work by any employee directly involved in the production of passenger vehicles, light trucks, heavy trucks, or parts used in the production of these vehicles in a USMCA country. It also includes work by an employee directly involved in the set-up, operation, or maintenance of tools or equipment used in the production of those vehicles or parts. Direct production work may take place on a production line, at a workstation, on the shop floor, or in another production area.

Direct production work also includes:

a) material handling of vehicles or parts;

b) inspection of vehicles or parts, including inspections that are normally catego-rized as quality control and, for heavy trucks, pre-sale inspections carried out at the place where the vehicle is produced;

c) work performed by skilled tradespeople, such as process or production engineers, mechanics, technicians and other employees responsible for maintaining and ensuring the operation of the production line or tools and equipment used in the production of vehicles or parts; and

d) on-the-job training regarding the execution of a specific production task.

Direct production work does not include any work by executive or management staff that have the authority to make final decisions to hire, fire, promote, transfer and discipline employees; workers engaged in research and development, or work by engineering or other personnel that are not responsible for maintaining and ensuring the operation of the produc-tion line or tools and equipment used in the production of vehicles or parts. It also does not include any work by interns, trainees, students, or any other worker that does not have an express or implied compensation agreement with the employer.

direct production worker means any worker whose primary responsibilities are direct production work, meaning at least 85% of the worker's time is spent performing direct production work.

first motor vehicle prototype means the first motor vehicle that

(a) is produced using tooling and processes intended for the production of motor vehicles to be offered for sale, and

(b) follows the complete motor vehicle assembly process in a manner not specifically designed for testing purposes;

floor pan of a motor vehicle means a component, comprising a single part or two or more parts joined together, with or without additional stiffening members, that forms the base of a motor vehicle, beginning at the fire-wall or bulkhead of the motor vehicle and ending:

(a) if there is a luggage floor panel in the motor vehicle, at the place where that luggage floor panel begins, or

(b) if there is no luggage floor panel in the motor vehicle, at the place where the passenger compartment of the motor vehicle ends;

heavy truck means a vehicle of subheading 8701.20, 8704.22, 8704.23, 8704.32 or 8704.90, or a chassis fitted with an engine of heading 87.06 that is for use in a vehicle of subheading 8701.20, 8704.22, 8704.23, 8704.32 or 8704.90, except for a vehicle that is solely or principally for off-road use;

high-wage assembly plant for passenger vehicle or light truck parts means a qualifying wage-rate production plant, operated by a corporate producer, or by a supplier with whom the producer has a contract of at least 3 years for the materials listed in sub-paragraphs (a) through (c), provided that the plant is located in the territory of a USMCA country and that it has a production capacity of:

(a) 100,000 or more engines of heading 84.07 or 84.08,
(b) 100,000 or more transmissions of subheading 8708.40, or
(c) 25,000 or more advanced battery packs;

For the purposes of this definition, such engines, transmissions, or advanced battery packs are not required to qualify as originating;

high-wage assembly plant for heavy truck parts means a qualifying wage rate production plant, operated by a corporate producer, or by a supplier with whom the producer has a contract of at least three years for the materials listed below, provided that the plant is located in the territory of a USMCA country and that it has a production capacity of:

(a) 20,000 or more engines of heading 84.07 or 84.08,
(b) 20,000 or more transmissions of subheading 8708.40, or
(c) 20,000 or more advanced battery packs;

For the purposes of this definition, such engines, transmissions, or advanced battery packs are not required to qualify as originating;

high-wage labor costs (HWLC) means the sum of wage expenditures, not including benefits, for workers who perform direct production work at a qualifying wage-rate vehicle assembly plant;

high-wage material (HWM) means a material that is produced in a qualifying wage-rate production plant;

high-wage technology expenditures means wage expenditures—expressed as a percentage of a passenger vehicle, light truck, or heavy truck producer's total production wage expenditures—at a corporate level in the territory of one or more of the USMCA countries on:

(a) research and development, including prototype development, design, engineering, or testing operations and any work undertaken by a producer for the purpose of creating new, or improving existing, materials, parts, vehicles or processes, including incremental improvements thereto, and
(b) information technology, including software development, technology integration, vehicle communications, or information technology support operations,

Expenditures on capital or other non-wage costs for R&D or IT are not included. For greater certainty, there is no minimum wage rate associated with high-wage technology expenditures;

high-wage transportation or related costs for shipping means costs incurred by a producer for transportation, logistics, or material handling associated with the movement of high-wage parts or materials within the territories of the USMCA countries, provided that the transportation, logistics, or material handling provider pays an average base hourly wage rate to direct production employees performing these services of at least:

(a) US$16 in the United States;
(b) CA$20.88 in Canada; and
(c) MXN$294.22 in Mexico;

High-wage transportation or related costs for shipping may be included in high wage material and manufacturing expenses if those costs are not otherwise included;

light truck means a vehicle of subheading 8704.21 or 8704.31, except for a vehicle that is solely or principally for off-road use;

marque means the trade name used by a separate marketing division of a motor vehicle assembler;

model line means a group of motor vehicles having the same platform or model name;

model name means the word, group of words, letter, number or similar designation assigned to a motor vehicle by a marketing division of a motor vehicle assembler to:

(a) differentiate the motor vehicle from other motor vehicles that use the same platform design,

(b) associate the motor vehicle with other motor vehicles that use different platform designs, or

(c) denote a platform design;

motorhome or entertainer coach means a vehicle of heading 87.02 or 87.03 built on a self-propelled motor vehicle chassis that is solely or principally designed as temporary living quarters for recreational, camping, entertainment, corporate or seasonal use;

motor vehicle assembler means a producer of motor vehicles and any related persons or joint ventures in which the producer participates;

new building means a new construction, including at least the pouring or construction of a new foundation and floor, the erection of a new structure and roof and installation of new plumbing, electrical and other utilities to house a complete vehicle assembly process;

passenger vehicle means a vehicle of subheading 8703.21 through 8703.90, except for:

(a) a vehicle with a compression-ignition engine classified in subheading 8703.31 through 8703.33 or a vehicle of subheading 8703.90 with both a compression-ignition engine and an electric motor for propulsion,

(b) a three- or four-wheeled motorcycle,

(c) an all-terrain vehicle,

(d) a motorhome or entertainer coach, or

(e) an ambulance, hearse or prison van;

plant means a building, or buildings in close proximity but not necessarily contiguous, machinery, apparatus and fixtures that are under the control of a producer and are used in the production of any of the following:

(a) passenger vehicles, light trucks or heavy trucks,

(b) a good listed in Table A.1, A.2, B, C, D, E, F or G;

platform means the primary load-bearing structural assembly of a motor vehicle that determines the basic size of the motor vehicle, and is the structural base that supports the driveline and links the suspension components of the motor vehicle for various types of frames, such as the body-on-frame or space-frame, and monocoques;

qualifying wage-rate production plant means a plant that produces materials for passenger vehicles, light trucks or heavy trucks located in a USMCA country, at which the average base hourly wage rate is at least:

(a) US$16 in the United States;

(b) CA$20.88 in Canada; and

(c) MXN$294.22 in Mexico;

qualifying wage-rate vehicle assembly plant means a passenger vehicle, light truck or heavy truck assembly plant located in a USMCA country, at which the average base hourly wage rate is at least:

(a) US$16 in the United States;
(b) CA$20.88 in Canada; and
(c) MXN$294.22 in Mexico;

refit means a plant closure, for purposes of plant conversion or retooling, that lasts at least three months;

size category, with respect to a light-duty vehicle, means that the total of the interior volume for passengers and the interior volume for luggage is

(a) 85 cubic feet (2.38 m3) or less,
(b) more than 85 cubic feet (2.38 m3) but less than 100 cubic feet (2.80 m3),
(c) 100 cubic feet (2.80 m3) or more but not more than 110 cubic feet (3.08 m3),
(d) more than 110 cubic feet (3.08 m3) but less than 120 cubic feet (3.36 m3), or
(e) 120 cubic feet (3.36 m3) or more;

super-core means the parts listed in the left column of Table A.2 of this Part, which are considered as a single part for the purpose of performing a Regional Value Content calculation in accordance with subsections 14(10), 14(11), 14(13) and 16(9);

total vehicle plant assembly annual purchase value (TAPV) means the sum of the values of all parts or materials purchased, on an annual basis, for use in the production of passenger vehicles, light trucks or heavy trucks in a plant located in the territory of a USMCA country;

underbody means a component, comprising a single part or two or more parts joined together, with or without additional stiffening members, that forms the base of a motor vehicle, beginning at the fire-wall or bulkhead of the motor vehicle and ending:

(a) if there is a luggage floor panel in the motor vehicle, at the place where that luggage floor panel begins, or
(b) if there is no luggage floor panel in the motor vehicle, at the place where the passenger compartment of the motor vehicle ends;

vehicle that is solely or principally for off-road use is defined as a vehicle that does not meet U.S. federal safety and emissions standards permitting unrestricted on-road use or the equivalent Mexican and Canadian on-road standards.

SECTION 13: PRODUCT-SPECIFIC RULES OF ORIGIN FOR VEHICLES AND CERTAIN AUTO PARTS

(1) Except as provided for in section 19 (Alternative Staging Regimes), the product-specific rule of origin for a good of heading 87.01 through 87.08 is:

8701.10	A change to a good of subheading 8701.10 from any other heading, provided there is a regional value content of not less than 60 percent under the net cost method.
8701.20	A change to a good of subheading 8701.20 from any other heading, provided there is a regional value content of not less than:

(c) 60 percent under the net cost method, beginning on July 1, 2020 until June 30, 2024;
(d) 64 percent under the net cost method, beginning on July 1, 2024 until June 30, 2027; or
(e) 70 percent under the net cost method, beginning on July 1, 2027, and thereafter.

8701.30 – 8701.90	A change to a good of subheading 8701.30 through 8701.90 from any other heading, provided there is a regional value content of not less than 60 percent under the net cost method.
8702.10 – 8702.90	(1) A change to a motor vehicle for the transport of 15 or fewer persons of subheading 8702.10 through 8702.90 from any other heading, provided there is a regional value content of not less than 62.5 percent under the net cost method; or
	(2) A change to a motor vehicle for the transport of 16 or more persons of subheading 8702.10 through 8702.90 from any other heading, provided there is a regional value content of not less than 60 percent under the net cost method.

8703.10 A change to subheading 8703.10 from any other heading, provided there is a regional value content of not less than:

    (a) 60 percent under the transaction value method, or
    (b) 50 percent under the net cost method.

8703.21 – 8703.90	(1) A change to a passenger vehicle of subheading 8703.21 through 8703.90 from any other heading, provided there is a regional value content of not less than:

    (a) 66 percent under the net cost method, beginning on July 1, 2020 until June 30, 2021;
    (b) 69 percent under the net cost method, beginning on July 1, 2021 until June 30, 2022;
    (c) 72 percent under the net cost method, beginning on July 1, 2022 until June 30, 2023;
    (d) 75 percent under the net cost method, beginning on July 1, 2023, and thereafter; or

(2) A change to any other good of subheading 8703.21 through 8703.90 from any other heading, provided there is a regional value content of not less than 62.5 percent under the net cost method.

8704.10 A change to a good of subheading 8704.10 from any other heading, provided there is a regional value content of not less than 60 percent under the net cost method.

8704.21	(1) A change to a light truck of subheading 8704.21 from any other heading, provided there
	(a) is a regional value content of not less than: 66 percent under the net cost method, beginning on July 1, 2020 until June 30, 2021;
	(b) 69 percent under the net cost method, beginning on July 1, 2021 until June 30, 2022;
	(c) 72 percent under the net cost method, beginning on July 1, 2022 until June 30, 2023;
	(d) 75 percent under the net cost method, beginning on July 1, 2023, and thereafter; or
	(2) A change to a vehicle that is solely or principally for off-road use subheading 8704.21 from any other heading, provided there is a regional value content of not less than 62.5 percent under the net cost method.

8704.22 – 8704.23	(1) A change to a heavy truck of subheading 8704.22 through 8704.23 from any other heading, provided there is a regional value content of not less than: (a) 60 percent under the net cost method, beginning on July 1, 2020 until June 30, 2024; (b) 64 percent under the net cost method, beginning on July 1, 2024 until June 30, 2027; (c) 70 percent under the net cost method, beginning on July 1, 2027, and thereafter; or (2) A change to a vehicle that is solely or principally for off-road use subheading 8704.22 through 8704.23 from any other heading, provided there is a regional value content of not less than 60 percent under the net cost method.
8704.31	(1) A change to a light truck of subheading 8704.31 from any other heading, provided there is a regional value content of not less than: (a) 66 percent under the net cost method, beginning on July 1, 2020 until June 30, 2021; (b) 69 percent under the net cost method, beginning on July 1, 2021 until June 30, 2022; (c) 72 percent under the net cost method, beginning on July 1, 2022 until June 30, 2023; (d) 75 percent under the net cost method, beginning on July 1, 2023, and thereafter; or (2) A change to a vehicle that is solely or principally for off-road use subheading 8704.31 from any other heading, provided there is a regional value content of not less than 62.5 percent under the net cost method.
8704.32 – 8704.90	(1) A change to a heavy truck of subheading 8704.32 through 8704.90 from any other heading, provided there is a regional value content of not less than: (a) 60 percent under the net cost method, beginning on July 1, 2020 until June 30, 2024; (b) 64 percent under the net cost method, beginning on July 1, 2024 until June 30, 2027; (c) 70 percent under the net cost method, beginning on July 1, 2027, and thereafter; or (2) A change to a vehicle that is solely or principally for off-road use of subheading 8704.32 through 8704.90 from any other heading, provided there is a regional value content of not less than 60 percent under the net cost method.
87.05	A change to heading 87.05 from any other heading, provided there is a regional value content of not less than 60 percent under the net cost method.

87.06	For a good of heading 87.06 for use as original equipment in a passenger vehicle or light truck:
	(1) No required change in tariff classification provided there is a regional value content of not less than:
	    (a) 66 percent under the net cost method, beginning on July 1, 2020 until June 30, 2021;
	    (b) 69 percent under the net cost method, beginning on July 1, 2021 until June 30, 2022;
	    (c) 72 percent under the net cost method, beginning on July 1, 2022 until June 30, 2023;
	    (d) 75 percent under the net cost method, beginning on July 1, 2023, and thereafter.
	For a good of heading 87.06 for use as original equipment in a heavy truck:
	(2) No required change in tariff classification provided there is a regional value content of not less than:
	    (a) 60 percent under the net cost method, beginning on July 1, 2020 until June 30, 2024;
	    (b) 64 percent under the net cost method, beginning on July 1, 2024 until June 30, 2027;
	    (c) 70 percent under the net cost method, beginning on July 1, 2027, and thereafter.
	For any other good of heading 87.06 for use as original equipment in any other vehicle, or as an aftermarket part:
	(3) No required change in tariff classification provided there is a regional value content of not less than 60 percent under the net cost method.

87.07	For a good of heading 87.07 for use as original equipment in a passenger vehicle or light truck:
	(1) No required change in tariff classification provided there is a regional value content of not less than:
	    (a) 66 percent under the net cost method, beginning on July 1, 2020 until June 30, 2021;
	    (b) 69 percent under the net cost method, beginning on July 1, 2021 until June 30, 2022;
	    (c) 72 percent under the net cost method, beginning on July 1, 2022 until June 30, 2023;
	    (d) 75 percent under the net cost method, beginning on July 1, 2023, and thereafter.
	For a good of heading 87.07 for use as original equipment in a heavy truck:
	(2) No required change in tariff classification provided there is a regional value content of not less than:
	    (a) 60 percent under the net cost method, beginning on July 1, 2020 until June 30, 2024;
	    (b) 64 percent under the net cost method, beginning on July 1, 2024 until June 30, 2027;
	    (c) 70 percent under the net cost method, beginning on July 1, 2027, and thereafter.

For any other good of heading 87.07 for use as original equipment in any other vehicle or as an aftermarket part:

(3) No required change in tariff classification provided there is a regional value content of not less than 60 percent under the net cost method.

8708.10   For a good of subheading 8708.10 for use as original equipment in a passenger vehicle or light truck:

(1) A change to subheading 8708.10 from any other heading; or

(2) A change to subheading 8708.10 from subheading 8708.99, whether or not there is also a change from any other heading, provided there is a regional value content of not less than:

    (a) 62.5 percent under the net cost method, beginning on July 1, 2020 until June 30, 2021;

    (b) 65 percent under the net cost method, beginning on July 1, 2021 until June 30, 2022;

    (c) 67.5 percent under the net cost method, beginning on July 1, 2022 until June 30, 2023;

    (d) 70 percent under the net cost method, beginning on July 1, 2023, and thereafter. For a good of subheading 8708.10 for use as original equipment in a heavy truck:

(3) A change to subheading 8708.10 from any other heading; or

(4) A change to subheading 8708.10 from subheading 8708.99, whether or not there is also a change from any other heading, provided there is a regional value content of not less than:

    (a) 60 percent under the net cost method, beginning on July 1, 2020 until June 30, 2024;

    (b) 64 percent under the net cost method, beginning on July 1, 2024 until June 30, 2027;

    (c) 70 percent under the net cost method, beginning on July 1, 2027, and thereafter.

For any other good of subheading 8708.10 for use as original equipment in any other vehicle or as an aftermarket part:

(5) A change to subheading 8708.10 from any other heading; or

(6) A change to subheading 8708.10 from subheading 8708.99, whether or not there is also a change from any other heading, provided there is a regional value content of not less than 50 percent under the net cost method.

8708.21   For a good of subheading 8708.21 for use as original equipment in a passenger vehicle or light truck:

(1) A change to subheading 8708.21 from any other heading; or

(2) A change to subheading 8708.21 from subheading 8708.99, whether or not there is also a change from any other heading, provided there is a regional value content of not less than:

    (a) 62.5 percent under the net cost method, beginning on July 1, 2020 until June 30, 2021;

    (b) 65 percent under the net cost method, beginning on July 1, 2021 until June 30, 2022;

    (c) 67.5 percent under the net cost method, beginning on July 1, 2022 until June 30, 2023;

    (d) 70 percent under the net cost method, beginning on July 1, 2023, and thereafter. For a good of subheading 8708.21 for use as original equipment in a heavy truck:

(3) A change to subheading 8708.21 from any other heading; or

(4) A change to subheading 8708.21 from subheading 8708.99, whether or not there is also a change from any other heading, provided there is a regional value content of not less than:

    (a) 60 percent under the net cost method, beginning on July 1, 2020 until June 30, 2024;

    (b) 64 percent under the net cost method, beginning on July 1, 2024 until June 30, 2027;

    (c) 70 percent under the net cost method, beginning on July 1, 2027, and thereafter.

For any other good of subheading 8708.21 for use as original equipment in any other vehicle or as an aftermarket part:

(5) A change to subheading 8708.10 from any other heading; or

(6) A change to subheading 8708.10 from subheading 8708.99, whether or not there is also a change from any other heading, provided there is a regional value content of not less than 50 percent under the net cost method.

8708.29 For a body stamping of subheading 8708.29 for use as original equipment in a passenger vehicle or light truck:

(1) No required change in tariff classification to a body stamping of subheading 8708.29, provided there is a regional value content of not less than:

    (a) 66 percent under the net cost method, beginning on July 1, 2020 until June 30, 2021;

    (b) 69 percent under the net cost method, beginning on July 1, 2021 until June 30, 2022;

    (c) 72 percent under the net cost method, beginning on July 1, 2022 until June 30, 2023;

    (d) 75 percent under the net cost method, beginning on July 1, 2023, and thereafter.

For any other good of subheading 8708.29 for use as original equipment in a passenger vehicle or light truck:

(2) A change to subheading 8708.29 from any other heading; or

(3) No required change in tariff classification to subheading 8708.29, provided there is a regional value content of not less than:

    (a) 62.5 percent under the net cost method, beginning on July 1, 2020 until June 30, 2021;

    (b) 65 percent under the net cost method, beginning on July 1, 2021 until June 30, 2022;

    (c) 67.5 percent under the net cost method, beginning on July 1, 2022 until June 30, 2023;

    (d) 70 percent under the net cost method, beginning on July 1, 2023, and thereafter. For a good of subheading 8708.29 for use as original equipment in a heavy truck:

(4) A change to subheading 8708.29 from any other heading; or

(5) No required change in tariff classification to subheading 8708.29, provided there is a regional value content of not less than:

    (a) 60 percent under the net cost method, beginning on July 1, 2020 until June 30, 2024;

    (b) 64 percent under the net cost method, beginning on July 1, 2024 until June 30, 2027;

    (c) 70 percent under the net cost method, beginning on July 1, 2027, and thereafter.

For any other good of subheading 8708.29 for use as original equipment in any other vehicle or as an aftermarket part:

(6) A change to subheading 8708.29 from any other heading; or

(7) No required change in tariff classification to subheading 8708.29, provided there is a regional value content of not less than 50 percent under the net cost method.

8708.30

For a good of subheading 8708.30 for use as original equipment in a passenger vehicle or light truck:

(1) A change to subheading 8708.30 from any other heading; or

(2) No required change in tariff classification to subheading 8708.30, provided there is a regional value content of not less than:

    (a) 62.5 percent under the net cost method, beginning on July 1, 2020 until June 30, 2021;

    (b) 65 percent under the net cost method, beginning on July 1, 2021 until June 30, 2022;

    (c) 67.5 percent under the net cost method, beginning on July 1, 2022 until June 30, 2023;

    (d) 70 percent under the net cost method, beginning on July 1, 2023, and thereafter. For a good of subheading 8708.30 for use as original equipment in a heavy truck:

(3) A change to subheading 8708.30 from any other heading; or

(4) No required change in tariff classification to subheading 8708.30, provided there is a regional value content of not less than:

    (a) 60 percent under the net cost method, beginning on July 1, 2020 until June 30, 2024;

    (b) 64 percent under the net cost method, beginning on July 1, 2024 until June 30, 2027;

    (c) 70 percent under the net cost method, beginning on July 1, 2027, and thereafter.

For any other good of subheading 8708.30 for use as original equipment in any other vehicle or as an aftermarket part:

(5) A change to mounted brake linings of subheading 8708.30 from any other heading; or

(6) A change to mounted brake linings of subheading 8708.30 from parts of mounted brake linings, brakes or servo-brakes of sub-heading 8708.30 or 8708.99, whether or not there is also a change from any other heading, provided there is a regional value content of not less than 50 percent under the net cost method;

(7) A change to any other good of subheading 8708.30 from any other heading; or

(8) A change to any other good of subheading 8708.30 from mounted brake linings or parts of brakes or servo-brakes of subheading 8708.30, or 8708.99, whether or not there is also a change from any other heading, provided there is a regional value content of not less than 50 percent under the net cost method.

8708.40   For a good of subheading 8708.40 for use as original equipment in a passenger vehicle or light truck:

(1) No required change in tariff classification to subheading 8708.40, provided there is a regional value content of not less than:

   (a) 66 percent under the net cost method, beginning on July 1, 2020 until June 30, 2021;

   (b) 69 percent under the net cost method, beginning on July 1, 2021 until June 30, 2022;

   (c) 72 percent under the net cost method, beginning on July 1, 2022 until June 30, 2023;

   (d) 75 percent under the net cost method, beginning on July 1, 2023, and thereafter. For a good of subheading 8708.40 for use as original equipment in a heavy truck:

(2) A change to subheading 8708.40 from any other heading; or

(3) No required change in tariff classification to subheading 8708.40, provided there is a regional value content of not less than:

   (a) 60 percent under the net cost method, beginning on July 1, 2020 until June 30, 2024;

   (b) 64 percent under the net cost method, beginning on July 1, 2024 until June 30, 2027;

   (c) 70 percent under the net cost method, beginning on July 1, 2027, and thereafter.

For a good of subheading 8708.40 for use as original equipment in any other vehicle or as an aftermarket part:

(4) A change to gear boxes of subheading 8708.40 from any other heading; or

(5) A change to gear boxes of subheading 8708.40 from any other good of subheading 8708.40 or 8708.99, whether or not there is also a change from any other heading, provided there is a regional value content of not less than 50 percent under the net cost method;

(6) A change to any other good of subheading 8708.40 from any other heading; or

(7) No required change in tariff classification to any other good of subheading 8708.40, provided there is a regional value content of not less than 50 percent under the net cost method.

8708.50   For a good of subheading 8708.50 for use as original equipment in a passenger vehicle or light truck:

(1) No required change in tariff classification to subheading 8708.50, provided there is a regional value content of not less than:
  (a) 66 percent under the net cost method, beginning on July 1, 2020 until June 30, 2021;
  (b) 69 percent under the net cost method, beginning on July 1, 2021 until June 30, 2022;
  (c) 72 percent under the net cost method, beginning on July 1, 2022 until June 30, 2023;
  (d) 75 percent under the net cost method, beginning on July 1, 2023, and thereafter. For a good of subheading 8708.50 for use as original equipment in a heavy truck:

(2) A change to drive-axles with differential, whether or not provided with other transmission components, for vehicles of heading 87.03, of subheading 8708.50 from any other heading, except from subheading 8482.10 through 8482.80; or

(3) A change to drive-axles with differential, whether or not provided with other transmission components, for vehicles of heading 87.03, of subheading 8708.50 from subheading 8482.10 through 8482.80 or parts of drive-axles of subheading 8708.50, whether or not there is also a change from any other heading, provided there is a regional value content of not less than:
  (a) 60 percent under the net cost method, beginning on July 1, 2020 until June 30, 2024;
  (b) 64 percent under the net cost method, beginning on July 1, 2024 until June 30, 2027;
  (c) 70 percent under the net cost method, beginning on July 1, 2027, and thereafter.

(4) A change to other drive-axles with differential, whether or not provided with other transmission components, of subheading 8708.50 from any other heading; or

(5) A change to other drive-axles with differential, whether or not provided with other transmission components, of subheading 8708.50 from subheading 8708.99, whether or not there is also a change from any other heading, provided there is a regional value content of not less than:
  (a) 60 percent under the net cost method, beginning on July 1, 2020 until June 30, 2024;
  (b) 64 percent under the net cost method, beginning on July 1, 2024 until June 30, 2027;
  (c) 70 percent under the net cost method, beginning on July 1, 2027, and thereafter.

(6) A change to non-driving axles and parts thereof, for vehicles of heading 87.03, of subheading 8708.50 from any other heading, except from subheading 8482.10 through 8482.80; or

(7) A change to non-driving axles and parts thereof, for vehicles of heading 87.03, of subheading 8708.50 from subheading 8482.10 through 8482.80 or 8708.99, whether or not there is also a change from any other heading, provided there is a regional value content of not less than:

    (a) 60 percent under the net cost method, beginning on July 1, 2020 until June 30, 2024;

    (b) 64 percent under the net cost method, beginning on July 1, 2024 until June 30, 2027;

    (c) 70 percent under the net cost method, beginning on July 1, 2027, and thereafter;

(8) A change to other non-driving axles and parts thereof of subheading 8708.50 from any other heading; or

(9) A change to other non-driving axles and parts thereof of subheading 8708.50 from subheading 8708.99, whether or not there is also a change from any other heading, provided there is a regional value content of not less than:

    (a) 60 percent under the net cost method, beginning July 1, 2020 until June 30, 2024;

    (b) 64 percent under the net cost method, beginning on July 1, 2024 until June 30, 2027;

    (c) 70 percent under the net cost method, beginning on July 1, 2027, and thereafter.

(10) A change to any other good of subheading 8708.50 from any other heading; or

(11) No required change in tariff classification to any other good of subheading 8708.50, provided there is a regional value content of not less than:

    (a) 60 percent under the net cost method, beginning on July 1, 2020 until June 30, 2024;

    (b) 64 percent under the net cost method, beginning on July 1, 2024 until June 30, 2027;

    (c) 70 percent under the net cost method, beginning on July 1, 2027, and thereafter.

For a good of subheading 8708.50 for use as original equipment in any other vehicle or as an aftermarket part:

(12) A change to drive-axles with differential, whether or not provided with other transmission components, for vehicles of heading 87.03, of subheading 8708.50 from any other heading, except from subheading 8482.10 through 8482.80; or

(13) A change to drive-axles with differential, whether or not provided with other transmission components, for vehicles of heading 87.03, of subheading 8708.50 from subheading 8482.10 through 8482.80 or parts of drive-axles of subheading 8708.50, whether or not there is also a change from any other heading, provided there is a regional value content of not less than 50 percent under the net cost method;

(14) A change to other drive-axles with differential, whether or not provided with other transmission components, of subheading 8708.50 from any other heading; or

(15) A change to other drive-axles with differential, whether or not provided with other transmission components, of subheading 8708.50 from subheading 8708.99, whether or not there is also a change from any other heading, provided there is a regional value content of not less than 50 percent under the net cost method;

(16) A change to non-driving axles and parts thereof, for vehicles of heading 87.03, of subheading 8708.50 from any other heading, except from subheading 8482.10 through 8482.80; or

(17) A change to non-driving axles and parts thereof, for vehicles of heading 87.03, of subheading 8708.50 from subheading 8482.10 through 8482.80 or 8708.99, whether or not there is also a change from any other heading, provided there is a regional value content of not less than 50 percent under the net cost method;

(18) A change to other non-driving axles and parts thereof of subheading 8708.50 from any other heading; or

(19) A change to other non-driving axles and parts thereof of subheading 8708.50 from subheading 8708.99, whether or not there is also a change from any other heading, provided there is a regional value content of not less than 50 percent under the net cost method;

(20) A change to any other good of subheading 8708.50 from any other heading; or

(21) No required change in tariff classification to any other good of subheading 8708.50, provided there is a regional value content of not less than 50 percent under the net cost method.

8708.70   For a good of subheading 8708.70 for use as original equipment in a passenger vehicle or light truck:

(1) A change to subheading 8708.70 from any other heading; or

(2) A change to subheading 8708.70 from subheading 8708.99, whether or not there is also a change from any other heading, provided there is a regional value content of not less than 50 percent under the net cost method.

(a) 62.5 percent under the net cost method, beginning on July 1, 2020 until June 30, 2021;

(b) 65 percent under the net cost method, beginning on July 1, 2021 until June 30, 2022;

(c) 67.5 percent under the net cost method, beginning on July 1, 2022 until June 30, 2023;

(d) 70 percent under the net cost method, beginning on July 1, 2023, and thereafter. For a good of subheading 8708.70 for use as original equipment in a heavy truck:

(3) A change to subheading 8708.70 from any other heading; or

(4) A change to subheading 8708.70 from subheading 8708.99, whether or not there is also a change from any other heading, provided there is a regional value content of not less than 50 percent under the net cost method.

(a) 60 percent under the net cost method, beginning on July 1, 2020 until June 30, 2024;

(b) 64 percent under the net cost method, beginning on July 1, 2024 until June 30, 2027;

(c) 70 percent under the net cost method, beginning on July 1, 2027, and thereafter.

For any other good of subheading 8708.70 for use as original equipment in any other vehicle or as an aftermarket part:

(5) A change to subheading 8708.70 from any other heading; or

(6) A change to subheading 8708.70 from subheading 8708.99, whether or not there is also a change from any other heading, provided there is a regional value content of not less than 50 percent under the net cost method.

8708.80   For a good of subheading 8708.80 for use as original equipment in a passenger vehicle or light truck:

(1) No required change in tariff classification to subheading 8708.80, provided there is a regional value content of not less than:

(a) 66 percent under the net cost method, beginning on July 1, 2020 until June 30, 2021;

(b) 69 percent under the net cost method, beginning on July 1, 2021 until June 30, 2022;

(c) 72 percent under the net cost method, beginning on July 1, 2022 until June 30, 2023;

(d) 75 percent under the net cost method, beginning on July 1, 2023, and thereafter. For a good of subheading 8708.80 for use as original equipment in a heavy truck:

(2) A change to McPherson struts of subheading 8708.80 from parts thereof of subheading 8708.80 or any other subheading, provided there is a regional value content of not less than 50 percent under the net cost method;

(3) A change to any other good of subheading 8708.80 from any other heading; or

(4) A change to suspension systems (including shock absorbers) of subheading 8708.80 from parts thereof of subheading 8708.80 or 8708.99, whether or not there is also a change from any other heading, provided there is a regional value content of not less than:

    (a) 60 percent under the net cost method, beginning on July 1, 2020 until June 30, 2024;

    (b) 64 percent under the net cost method, beginning on July 1, 2024 until June 30, 2027;

    (c) 70 percent under the net cost method, beginning on July 1, 2027, and thereafter; or

(5) No required change in tariff classification to parts of suspension systems (including shock absorbers) of subheading 8708.80, provided there is a regional value content of not less than:

    (a) 60 percent under the net cost method, beginning on July 1, 2020 until June 30, 2024;

    (b) 64 percent under the net cost method, beginning on July 1, 2024 until June 30, 2027;

    (c) 70 percent under the net cost method, beginning on July 1, 2027, and thereafter.

For any other good of subheading 8708.80 for use as original equipment in any other vehicle or as an aftermarket part:

(6) A change to McPherson struts of subheading 8708.80 from parts thereof of subheading 8708.80 or any other subheading, provided there is a regional value content of not less than 50 percent under the net cost method;

(7) A change to subheading 8708.80 from any other heading;

(8) A change to suspension systems (including shock absorbers) of subheading 8708.80 from parts thereof of subheading 8708.80 or 8708.99, whether or not there is also a change from any other heading, provided there is a regional value content of not less than 50 percent under the net cost method; or

(9) No required change in tariff classification to subheading 8708.80, provided there is a regional value content of not less than 50 percent under the net cost method.

8708.91   For a good of subheading 8708.91 for use as original equipment in a passenger vehicle or light truck:

(1) A change to radiators of subheading 8708.91 from any other heading;

(2) A change to radiators of subheading 8708.91 from any other good of subheading 8708.91, whether or not there is also a change from any other heading, provided there is a regional value content of not less than:

      (a) 62.5 percent under the net cost method, beginning on July 1, 2020 until June 30, 2021;

      (b) 65 percent under the net cost method, beginning on July 1, 2021 until June 30, 2022;

      (c) 67.5 percent under the net cost method, beginning on July 1, 2022 until June 30, 2023; or

      (d) 70 percent under the net cost method, beginning on July 1, 2023, and thereafter. For a good of subheading 8708.91 for use as original equipment in a heavy truck:

(3) A change to radiators of subheading 8708.91 from any other heading;

(4) A change to radiators of subheading 8708.91 from any other good of subheading 8708.91, whether or not there is also a change from any other heading, provided there is a regional value content of not less than:

(5) A change to radiators of subheading 8708.91 from any other heading;

(6) A change to radiators of subheading 8708.91 from any other good of subheading 8708.91, whether or not there is also a change from any other heading, provided there is a regional value content of not less than 50 percent under the net cost method; or

(7) No required change in tariff classification to any other good of subheading 8708.91, provided there is a regional value content of not less than 50 percent under the net cost method.

8708.92   For a good of subheading 8708.92 for use as original equipment in a passenger vehicle or light truck:

(1) A change to silencers (mufflers) of subheading 8708.92 from any other heading;

(2) A change to silencers (mufflers) of subheading 8708.92 from any other good of subheading 8708.92, whether or not there is also a change from any other heading, provided there is a regional value content of not less than; or

      (a) 62.5 percent under the net cost method, beginning on July 1, 2020 until June 30, 2021;

      (b) 65 percent under the net cost method, beginning on July 1, 2021 until June 30, 2022;

      (c) 67.5 percent under the net cost method, beginning on July 1, 2022 until June 30, 2023;

      (d) 70 percent under the net cost method, beginning on July 1, 2023, and thereafter.

For a good of subheading 8708.92 for use as original equipment in a heavy truck:

(3) A change to silencers (mufflers) of subheading 8708.92 from any other heading;

(4) A change to silencers (mufflers) of subheading 8708.92 from any other good of subheading 8708.92, whether or not there is also a change from any other heading, provided there is a regional value content of not less than; or

(c) 70 percent under the net cost method, beginning on July 1, 2027, and thereafter.

For any other good of subheading 8708.92 for use as original equipment in any other vehicle or as an aftermarket part:

(5) A change to silencers (mufflers) of subheading 8708.92 from any other heading;

(6) A change to silencers (mufflers) of subheading 8708.92 from any other good of subheading 8708.92, whether or not there is also a change from any other heading, provided there is a regional value content of not less than 50 percent under the net cost method; or

(7) No required change in tariff classification to any other good of subheading 8708.92, provided there is a regional value content of not less than 50 percent under the net cost method.

8708.93   For a good of subheading 8708.93 for use as original equipment in a passenger vehicle or light truck:

(1) A change to subheading 8708.92 from any other heading;

(2) A change to subheading 8708.92 from subheading 8708.99, whether or not there is also a change from any other heading, provided there is a regional value content of not less than 70 percent under the net cost method; or

(a) 62.5 percent under the net cost method, beginning on July 1, 2020 until June 30, 2021;

(b) 65 percent under the net cost method, beginning on July 1, 2021 until June 30, 2022;

(c) 67.5 percent under the net cost method, beginning on July 1, 2022 until June 30, 2023;

(d) 70 percent under the net cost method, beginning on July 1, 2023, and thereafter. For a good of subheading 8708.93 for use as original equipment in a heavy truck:

(3) A change to subheading 8708.92 from any other heading;

(4) A change to subheading 8708.92 from subheading 8708.99, whether or not there is also a change from any other heading, provided there is a regional value content of not less than 70 percent under the net cost method; or

(a) 60 percent under the net cost method, beginning on July 1, 2020 until June 30, 2024;

(b) 64 percent under the net cost method, beginning on July 1, 2024 until June 30, 2027;

(c) 70 percent under the net cost method, beginning on July 1, 2027, and thereafter.

For any other good of subheading 8708.93 for use as original equipment in any other vehicle or as an aftermarket part:

(5) A change to subheading 8708.93 from any other heading;

(6) A change to subheading 8708.93 from subheading 8708.99, whether or not there is also a change from any other heading, provided there is a regional value content of not less than 50 percent under the net cost method.

8708.94   For a good of subheading 8708.94 for use as original equipment in a passenger vehicle or light truck:

(1) No required change in tariff classification to subheading 8708.94, provided there is a regional value content of not less than:

    (a) 66 percent under the net cost method, beginning on July 1, 2020 until June 30, 2021;

    (b) 69 percent under the net cost method, beginning on July 1, 2021 until June 30, 2022;

    (c) 72 percent under the net cost method, beginning on July 1, 2022 until June 30, 2023;

    (d) 75 percent under the net cost method, beginning on July 1, 2023, and thereafter. For a good of subheading 8708.94 for use as original equipment in a heavy truck:

(2) A change to subheading 8708.94 from any other heading; or

(3) A change to steering wheels, steering columns or steering boxes of subheading 8708.94 from parts thereof of subheading 8708.94 or 8708.99, whether or not there is also a change from any other heading, provided there is a regional value content of not less than:

    (a) 60 percent under the net cost method, beginning on July 1, 2020 until June 30, 2024;

    (b) 64 percent under the net cost method, beginning on July 1, 2024 until June 30, 2027;

    (c) 70 percent under the net cost method, beginning on July 1, 2027, and thereafter;

(4) No required change in tariff classification to parts of steering wheels, steering columns or steering boxes of subheading 8708.94, provided there is a regional value content of not less than:

    (a) 60 percent under the net cost method, beginning on July 1, 2020 until June 30, 2024;

    (b) 64 percent under the net cost method, beginning on July 1, 2024 until June 30, 2027;

    (c) 70 percent under the net cost method, beginning on July 1, 2027, and thereafter.

For any other good of subheading 8708.94 for use as original equipment in any other vehicle or as an aftermarket part:

(5) A change to subheading 8708.94 from any other heading; or

(6) A change to steering wheels, steering columns or steering boxes of subheading 8708.94 from parts thereof of subheading 8708.94 or 8708.99, whether or not there is also a change from any other heading, provided there is a regional value content of not less than 50 percent under the net cost method;

(7) No required change in tariff classification to parts of steering wheels, steering columns or steering boxes of subheading 8708.94, provided there is a regional value content of not less than 50 percent under the net cost method.

8708.95   For a good of subheading 8708.95 for use as original equipment in a passenger vehicle or light truck:

(1) A change to subheading 8708.95 from any other heading; or

(2) No required change in tariff classification to subheading 8708.95, provided there is a regional value content of not less than:

(a) 62.5 percent under the net cost method, beginning on July 1, 2020 until June 30, 2021;

(b) 65 percent under the net cost method, beginning on July 1, 2021 until June 30, 2022;

(c) 67.5 percent under the net cost method, beginning on July 1, 2022 until June 30, 2023;

(d) 70 percent under the net cost method, beginning on July 1, 2023, and thereafter.

For a good of subheading 8708.95 for use as original equipment in a heavy truck:

(1) A change to subheading 8708.95 from any other heading; or

(2) No required change in tariff classification to subheading 8708.95, provided there is a regional value content of not less than:

(a) 60 percent under the net cost method, beginning on July 1, 2020 until June 30, 2024;

(b) 64 percent under the net cost method, beginning on July 1, 2024 until June 30, 2027;

(c) 70 percent under the net cost method, beginning on July 1, 2027, and thereafter.

For any other good of subheading 8708.95 for use as original equipment in any other vehicle or as an aftermarket part:

(3) A change to subheading 8708.95 from any other heading; or

(4) No required change in tariff classification to subheading 8708.95, provided there is a regional value content of not less than 50 percent under the net cost method.

8708.99	For a chassis frame of subheading 8708.99 for use as original equipment in a passenger vehicle or light truck:

(1) No required change in tariff classification to subheading 8708.99, provided there is a regional value content of not less than:

    (a) 66 percent under the net cost method, beginning on July 1, 2020 until June 30, 2021;

    (b) 69 percent under the net cost method, beginning on July 1, 2021 until June 30, 2022;

    (c) 72 percent under the net cost method, beginning on July 1, 2022 until June 30, 2023;

    (d) 75 percent under the net cost method, beginning on July 1, 2023, and thereafter. For a chassis of subheading 8708.99 for use as original equipment in a heavy truck:

(2) No required change in tariff classification to subheading 8708.99, provided there is a regional value content of not less than:

    (a) 60 percent under the net cost method, beginning on July 1, 2020 until June 30, 2024;

    (b) 64 percent under the net cost method, beginning on July 1, 2024 until June 30, 2027;

    (c) 70 percent under the net cost method, beginning on July 1, 2027, and thereafter.

For any other good of subheading 8708.99 for use as original equipment in a passenger vehicle or light truck:

8708.99.aa	A change to tariff item 8708.99.aa from any other subheading, provided there is a regional value content of not less than:

(a) 62.5 percent under the net cost method, beginning on July 1, 2020 until June 30, 2021;

(b) 65 percent under the net cost method, beginning on July 1, 2021 until June 30, 2022;

(c) 67.5 percent under the net cost method, beginning on July 1, 2022 until June 30, 2023;

(d) 70 percent under the net cost method, beginning on July 1, 2023, and thereafter. 8708.99.bb A change to tariff item 8708.99.bb from any other heading, except from subheading 8482.10 through 8482.80 or tariff item 8482.99.aa; or

A change to tariff item 8708.99.bb from subheadings 8482.10 through 8482.80 or tariff item 8482.99.aa, whether or not there is also a change from any other heading, provided there is a regional value content of not less than:

(a) 62.5 percent under the net cost method, beginning on July 1, 2020 until June 30, 2021;

(b) 65 percent under the net cost method, beginning on July 1, 2021 until June 30, 2022;

(c) 67.5 percent under the net cost method, beginning on July 1, 2022 until June 30, 2023;

(d) 70 percent under the net cost method, beginning on July 1, 2023, and thereafter. 8708.99 No required change in tariff classification to subheading 8708.99, provided there is a regional value content of not less than:

(a) 62.5 percent under the net cost method, beginning on July 1, 2020 until June 30, 2021;

(b) 65 percent under the net cost method, beginning on July 1, 2021 until June 30, 2022;

(c) 67.5 percent under the net cost method, beginning on July 1, 2022 until June 30, 2023;

(d) 70 percent under the net cost method, beginning on July 1, 2023, and thereafter.

For any other good of subheading 8708.99 for use as original equipment in a heavy truck:

8708.99.aa	A change to tariff item 8708.99.aa from any other subheading, provided there is a regional value content of not less than:

(a) 60 percent under the net cost method, beginning on July 1, 2020 until June 30, 2024;

(b) 64 percent under the net cost method, beginning on July 1, 2024 until June 30, 2027;

(c) 70 percent under the net cost method, beginning on July 1, 2027, and thereafter.

8708.99.bb	A change to tariff item 8708.99.bb from any other heading, except from subheading 8482.10 through 8482.80 or tariff item 8482.99.aa; or

A change to tariff item 8708.99.bb from subheadings 8482.10 through 8482.80 or tariff item 8482.99.aa, whether or not there is also a change from any other heading, provided there is a regional value content of not less than:

(a) 60 percent under the net cost method, beginning on July 1, 2020 until June 30, 2024;

(b) 64 percent under the net cost method, beginning on July 1, 2024 until June 30, 2027;

(c) 70 percent under the net cost method, beginning on July 1, 2027, and thereafter.

8708.99	No required change in tariff classification to subheading 8708.99, provided there is a regional value content of not less than:

(a) 60 percent under the net cost method, beginning on July 1, 2020 until June 30, 2024;

(b) 64 percent under the net cost method, beginning on July 1, 2024 until June 30, 2027;

(c) 70 percent under the net cost method, beginning on July 1, 2027, and thereafter.

For any other good of subheading 8708.99 for use as original equipment in any other vehicle or as an aftermarket part:

8708.99.aa	A change to tariff item 8708.99.aa from any other subheading, provided there is a regional value content of not less than 50 per cent under the net cost method.

8708.99.bb	A change to tariff item 8708.99.bb from any other heading, except from subheading 8482.10 through 8482.80 or tariff item 8482.99.aa; or
	A change to tariff item 8708.99.bb from subheadings 8482.10 through 8482.80 or tariff item 8482.99.aa, whether or not there is also a change from any other heading, provided there is a regional value content of not less than 50 per cent under the net cost method.
8708.99	A change to subheading 8708.99 from any other heading; or
	No required change in tariff classification to subheading 8708.99, provided there is a regional value content of not less than 50 percent under the net cost method.

SECTION 14: FURTHER REQUIREMENTS RELATED TO THE REGIONAL VALUE CONTENT FOR PASSENGER VEHICLES, LIGHT TRUCKS, AND PARTS THEREOF

ROLL-UP OF ORIGINATING MATERIALS

(1) The value of non-originating materials used by the producer in the production of a passenger vehicle, light truck and parts thereof must not, for the purpose of calculating the regional value content of the good, include the value of non-originating materials used to produce originating materials that are subsequently used in the production of the good. For greater certainty, if the production under-taken on non-originating materials results in the production of a good that qualifies as originating, no account is to be taken of the non-originating material contained therein if that good is used in the subsequent production of another good.

REQUIREMENTS RELATED TO CORE PARTS LISTED IN TABLE A.1

(2) A part listed in Table A.1 that is for use as original equipment in the production of a passenger vehicle or light truck, except for batteries of subheading 8507.60 that are used as the primary source of electrical power for the propulsion of an electric passenger vehicle or an electric light truck, is originating only if it satisfies the regional value content requirement in sections 13 or 14 or Schedule I (PSRO Annex).

(3) A battery of subheading 8507.60 that is used as the primary source of electrical power for the propulsion of an electric passenger vehicle or an electric light truck is originating if it meets the applicable requirements set out in section 14 or Schedule I (PSRO Annex).

PARTS LISTED IN COLUMN 1 OF TABLE A.2 MUST BE ORIGINATING FOR PASSENGER VEHICLE OR LIGHT TRUCK TO BE ORIGINATING

(4) In addition to other applicable requirements set out in these Regulations, a passenger vehicle or light truck is only originating if the parts listed in column 1 of Table A.2 of these Regulations used in its production are originating. The value of non-originating materials (VNM) for such parts must be calculated in accordance with subsections 14(7) through 14(8), or, at the choice of the vehicle producer or exporter, subsections 14(9) through 14(11). The net cost of a part must be calculated in accordance with section 7 (Regional Value Content), without regard to the VNM calculation method chosen.

*PARTS LISTED IN COLUMN 1 OF TABLE A.2 MUST MEET AN RVC REQUIREMENT; AD-
VANCED BATTERIES MAY MEET AN RVC OR TARIFF SHIFT REQUIREMENT*

(5) Except for an advanced battery of subheading 8507.60, a part listed in column 1 of
Table A.2, that is for use in a passenger vehicle or light truck, must meet the regional
value content requirement of section 13 or Schedule I (PSRO Annex) to be considered originating.

(6) An advanced battery of subheading 8507.60, that is for use in a passenger vehicle or
light truck, is originating if it meets the applicable change in tariff classification or
regional value content requirements set out in Schedule I (PSRO Annex).

*VNM FOR CORE PARTS MAY INCLUDE ALL NON-ORIGINATING MATERIALS, OR ONLY
MATERIALS LISTED IN COLUMN 2 OF TABLE A.2*

(7) For the purpose of satisfying the requirement specified in subsections (4) through
(6), the regional value content of a part listed in column 1 of Table A.2, the value of
non-originating materials (VNM) may be determined, at the choice of the vehicle
producer or exporter, taking into consideration:
 (a) the value of all non-originating materials used in the production of the part; or
 (b) the value of non-originating components that are listed in column 2 of Table A.2
  that are used in the production of the part.

(8) For the purposes of a regional value content calculation for a good listed in column
1 of Table A.2, based on paragraph (7)(b), any non-originating materials used in the
production of the good that are not listed in column 2 of Table A.2 may be
disregarded. For greater certainty, any non-originating parts listed in column 1 of
Table A.2 must be included in the VNM calculation. Any parts not listed in column
1 of Table A.2 or materials or components used to produce such parts should also not
be part of the VNM calculation.

(9) Subsections (7) and (8) do not apply when calculating the regional value content of
a part listed in Column 1 of Table A.2 traded on its own. The rules for such parts are
listed in section 13 of these regulations.

*PARTS LISTED IN COLUMN 1 OF TABLE A.2 MAY BE TREATED AS A SINGLE, SUPER-CORE
PART*

(10) For the purpose of satisfying the requirement specified in subsections (4) through (6)
and as an alternative to determining the VNM based on the method in subsection (7),
the regional value content of the parts listed in column 1 of Table A.2 of these
Regulations may be determined, at the choice of the vehicle producer or exporter, by
treating these parts as a single part, which may be referred to as a super-core part,
using the sum of the net cost of each part listed under column 1 of Table A.2 of these
Regulations, and when calculating the VNM taking into consideration:
 (a) the sum of the value of all non-originating materials used in the production of
  the parts listed under column 1 of table A.2; or
 (b) the sum of the value of the non-originating components that are listed in column
  2 of Table A.2 that are used in the production of the parts listed in column 1 of
  Table A.2.

(11) If a non-originating material used in the production of a component listed in column
2 of Table A.2 undergoes further production such that it satisfies the requirements of
these Regulations, the component is treated as originating when determining the
originating status of the subsequently produced part listed in column 1 of Table A.2,
regardless of whether that component was produced by the producer of the part.

(12) The regional value content requirement for the parts listed in the left hand column of Table A.2 may be averaged in accordance with the provisions in Section 16. Such an average may be calculated using the average regional value content for each individual parts category in the left hand column of Table A.2, or by calculating the average regional value content for all parts in the left hand column of Table A by treating them as a single part, defined as a super-core. Once this average, by either methodology, exceeds the required thresholds listed in paragraphs (12)(a) through (d), all parts used to calculate this average are considered originating.

RVC REQUIREMENTS RELATED TO PARTS LISTED IN TABLES A.1 AND A.2

(13) Further to subsections (2), (7) and (10), the following regional value content thresholds apply to parts for use as original equipment listed under Table A.1 and column 1 of Table A.2:
  (a) 66 percent under the net cost method or 76 percent under the transaction value method beginning on July 1, 2020 until June 30, 2021;
  (b) 69 percent under the net cost method or 79 percent under the transaction value method beginning on July 1, 2021 until June 30, 2022;
  (c) 72 percent under the net cost method or 82 percent under the transaction value method, beginning on July 1, 2022 until June 30, 2023; or
  (d) 75 percent under the net cost method or 85 percent under the transaction value method, beginning on July 1, 2023, and thereafter.

REQUIREMENTS RELATED TO PRINCIPAL AND COMPLEMENTARY PARTS LISTED IN TABLES B AND C

(14) Notwithstanding the regional value content requirements set out in Schedule I (PSRO Annex), a material listed in Table B is considered originating if it satisfies the applicable change in tariff classification requirement or the applicable regional value-content requirement provided in Schedule I (PSRO Annex).
(15) Further to subsection (14), the following regional value content thresholds apply to parts for use as original equipment listed under Table B:
  (a) 62.5 percent under the net cost method or 72.5 percent under the transaction value method beginning on July 1, 2020 until June 30, 2021;
  (b) 65 percent under the net cost method or 75 percent under the transaction value method beginning on July 1, 2021 until June 30, 2022;
  (c) 67.5 percent under the net cost method or 77.5 percent under the transaction value method, beginning on July 1, 2022 until June 30, 2023; or
  (d) 70 percent under the net cost method or 80 percent under the transaction value method, beginning on July 1, 2023, and thereafter.
(16) Notwithstanding the regional value content requirements set out in Schedule I (PSRO Annex), a material listed in Table C is originating if it meets the applicable change in tariff classification requirement or the applicable regional value-content requirement provided in Schedule I (PSRO Annex).
(17) Further to subsection (16), the following regional value content thresholds apply to parts for use as original equipment listed under Table C:
  (a) 62 percent under the net cost method or 72 percent under the transaction value method beginning on July 1, 2020 until June 30, 2021;
  (b) 63 percent under the net cost method or 73 percent under the transaction value method beginning on July 1, 2021 until June 30, 2022;
  (c) 64 percent under the net cost method or 74 percent under the transaction value method, beginning on July 1, 2022 until June 30, 2023; or

(d) 65 percent under the net cost method or 75 percent under the transaction value method, beginning on July 1, 2023, and thereafter.

(18) For greater certainty, subsections (13), (15) or (17) do not apply to aftermarket parts.

SECTION 15: FURTHER REQUIREMENTS RELATED TO THE REGIONAL VALUE CONTENT FOR HEAVY TRUCKS AND PARTS THEREOF

(1) The value of non-originating materials used by the producer in the production of a heavy truck and parts thereof must not, for the purpose of calculating the regional value content of the good, include the value of non- originating materials used to produce originating materials that are subsequently used in the production of the good.

(2) Notwithstanding the Product-Specific Rules of Origin in Schedule I (PSRO Annex), the regional value content requirement for a part listed in Table D that is for use in a heavy truck is:

(a) 60 percent under the net cost method or 70 percent under the transaction value method, if the corresponding rule includes a transaction value method, beginning on July 1, 2020 until June 30, 2024;

(b) 64 percent under the net cost method or 74 percent under the transaction value method, if the corresponding rule includes a transaction value method beginning on July 1, 2024 until June 30, 2027; or

(c) 70 percent under the net cost method or 80 percent under the transaction value method, if the corresponding rule includes a transaction value method, beginning on July 1, 2027, and thereafter.

(3) Notwithstanding the Product-Specific Rules of Origin in Schedule I (PSRO Annex), the regional value content requirement for a part listed in Table E that is for use in a heavy truck is:

(a) 50 percent under the net cost method or 60 percent under the transaction value method, if the corresponding rule includes a transaction value method, beginning on July 1, 2024 until June 30, 2027; or

(b) 54 percent under the net cost method or 64 percent under the transaction value method, if the corresponding rule includes a transaction value method beginning on July 1, 2024 until June 30, 2027; or

(c) 60 percent under the net cost method or 70 percent under the transaction value method, if the corresponding rule includes a transaction value method, beginning on July 1, 2027, and thereafter.

(4) Notwithstanding section 13 (Product-Specific Rules of Origin for Vehicles) or Schedule I (PSRO Annex), an engine of heading 84.07 or 84.08, or a gear box (transmission) of subheading 8708.40, or a chassis classified in 8708.99, that is for use in a heavy truck, is originating only if it satisfies the applicable regional value content requirement in subsection (2).

SECTION 16: AVERAGING FOR PASSENGER VEHICLES, LIGHT TRUCKS AND HEAVY TRUCKS

(1) For the purpose of calculating the regional value content of a passenger vehicle, light truck, or heavy truck, the calculation may be averaged over the producer's fiscal year, using any one of the following categories, on the basis of either all motor vehicles in the category or only those motor vehicles in the category that are exported to the territory of one or more of the other USMCA countries:

(a) the same model line of motor vehicles in the same class of vehicles produced in the same plant in the territory of a USMCA country;

(b) the same class of motor vehicles produced in the same plant in the territory of a USMCA country;

(c) the same model line or same class of motor vehicles produced in the territory of a USMCA country;

(d) all vehicles produced in one or more plants in the territory of a Party that are exported to the territory of one or more of the other USMCA countries: or

(e) any other category as the USMCA countries may decide.

(2) For the purposes of paragraph (1)(c), vehicles within the same model line or class may be averaged separately if such vehicles are subject to different regional value content requirements.

(3) If a producer chooses to use averaging for the purpose of calculating regional value content, the producer must state the category it has chosen, and:

(a) if the category referred to in paragraph (1)(a) is chosen, state the model line, model name, class of passenger vehicle, light truck, or heavy truck and tariff classification of the motor vehicles in that category, and the location of the plant at which the motor vehicles are produced,

(b) if the category referred to in paragraph (1)(b) is chosen, state the model name, class of passenger vehicle, light truck, or heavy truck and tariff classification of the motor vehicles in that category, and the location of the plant at which the motor vehicles are produced,

(c) if the category referred to in paragraph (1)(c) is chosen, state the model line, model name, class of motor vehicle and tariff classification of the passenger vehicle, light truck, or heavy truck in that category, and the locations of the plants at which the motor vehicles are produced,

(d) if the category referred to in paragraph (1)(d) is chosen, state the model lines, model names, classes of motor vehicles and tariff classifications of the passenger vehicles, light trucks, or heavy trucks, and the location of the plants at which the motor vehicles are produced, or

(e) if the category referred to in paragraph (1)(e) is chosen, state the model lines, model names, classes of motor vehicles and tariff classifications of the passenger vehicles, light trucks, or heavy trucks, the location of the plants at which the motor vehicles are produced and the party or parties to which the vehicles are exported;

AVERAGING PERIOD

(4) If the fiscal year of a producer begins after July 1, 2020, but before July 1, 2021, the producer may calculate its regional value content for passenger vehicles, light trucks, heavy trucks, other vehicles, core parts listed in Table A2 used in the production of passenger vehicles, light trucks or heavy trucks, an automotive good listed in Tables A.1, B, C, D or E, steel and aluminum purchasing requirement and labor value content, for the period beginning on July 1, 2020 and ending at the end of the following fiscal year.

TIMELY FILING OF CHOICE TO AVERAGE

(5) If a producer chooses to average its regional value content calculations the producer must notify the customs administration of the USMCA country to which passenger vehicles, light trucks, or heavy trucks are to be exported, by July 31, 2020 and subsequently at least 10 days before the first day of the producer's fiscal year during which the vehicles will be exported, or such shorter period as the customs administration may accept.

CHOICE TO AVERAGE MAY NOT BE RESCINDED

(6) The producer may not modify or rescind the category of passenger vehicles, light trucks, or heavy trucks or the period that they have notified the customs authority they intend to use for their averaged regional value calculation.

AVERAGED NET COST AND VNM INCLUDED IN CALCULATION OF RVC ON THE BASIS OF PRODUCER'S OPTION TO INCLUDE ALL VEHICLES OF CATEGORY OR ONLY CERTAIN EXPORTED VEHICLES OF CATEGORY

(7) For purposes of sections 13 through 15, if a producer chooses to average its net cost calculation, the net costs incurred and the values of non-originating materials used by the producer, with respect to
  (a) all passenger vehicles, light trucks, or heavy trucks that fall within the category chosen by the producer and that are produced during the fiscal year, or partial fiscal year if the producer's fiscal year begins after the date of the entry into force of this agreement, or
  (b) those passenger vehicles, light trucks, or heavy trucks to be exported to the territory of one or more of the USMCA countries that fall within the category chosen by the producer and that are produced during the fiscal year or, or partial fiscal year if the producer's fiscal year begins after the date of the entry into force of this agreement, must be included in the calculation of the regional value content under any of the categories set out in subsection (1).

YEAR-END ANALYSIS REQUIRED IF AVERAGING BASED OF ESTIMATED COSTS; OBLIGA-TION TO NOTIFY OF CHANGE IN STATUS

(8) If the producer of a passenger vehicle, light truck, or heavy truck has calculated the regional value content of the motor vehicle on the basis of estimated costs, including standard costs, budgeted forecasts or other similar estimating procedures, before or during the producer's fiscal year, the producer must conduct an analysis at the end of the producer's fiscal year of the actual costs incurred over the period with respect to the production of the motor vehicle, and, if the passenger vehicle, light truck, or heavy truck does not satisfy the regional value content requirement on the basis of the actual costs, immediately inform any person to whom the producer has provided a Certificate of Origin for the motor vehicle, or a written statement that the motor vehicle is an originating good, that the motor vehicle is a non-originating good.

(9) For the purpose of calculating the regional value content for an automotive good listed in Tables A.1, B, C, D, or E, produced in the same plant, a core part listed in Table A.2, or when treating the parts listed in column 1 of Table A.2 as a super-core, for use in a passenger vehicle or light truck, the calculation may be averaged:
  (a) over the fiscal year of the motor vehicle producer to whom the good is sold;
  (b) over any quarter or month;
  (c) over the fiscal year of the producer of the automotive material; or
  (d) over any of the categories in paragraph (1)(a) through (f), provided that the good was produced during the fiscal year, quarter, or month forming the basis for the calculation, in which:
    (i) the average in paragraph (9)(a) is calculated separately for those goods sold to one or more passenger vehicle, light truck, or heavy truck producer, or
    (ii) the average in paragraph (9)(a) or (d) is calculated separately for those goods that are exported to the territory of another USMCA country.

EXAMPLE RELATING TO THE FISCAL YEAR OF A PRODUCER NOT COINCIDING WITH THE ENTRY INTO FORCE OF THE AGREEMENT

(10) The following example is an "Example" as referred to in subsection 1(4).

Example: subsection (4)

The agreement enters into force on July 1, 2020. A producer's fiscal year begins on January 1, 2021. The producer may calculate their regional value content over the 18-month period beginning on July 1, 2020 and ending on December 31, 2021.

SECTION 17: STEEL AND ALUMINUM

(1) In addition to meeting the requirements of sections 13 through 16 or Schedule I (PSRO Annex), a passenger vehicle, light truck, or heavy truck is originating only if, during a time period provided for in subsection (2), at least 70 percent, by value, of the vehicle producer's purchases at the corporate level in the territories of one or more of the USMCA countries of:
(a) steel listed in Table S; and
(b) aluminum listed in Table S; are of originating goods.

(2) For the purposes of subsection (1), only the value of the steel or aluminum listed in Table S that is used in the production of the part will be taken into consideration for a part of subheading 8708.29 or 8708.99 listed in Table S.

(3) The requirement set out in subsection (1) applies to steel and aluminum purchases made by the producer of passenger vehicles, light trucks or heavy trucks, including purchases made directly by the vehicle producer from a steel producer, purchases by the vehicle producer from a steel service center or a steel distributor. Subsection (1) also applies to steel or aluminum covered by a contractual arrangement in which a producer of passenger vehicles, light trucks, or heavy trucks negotiates the terms under which steel or aluminum will be supplied to a parts producer by a steel producer or supplier selected by the vehicle producer, for use in the production of parts that are supplied by the parts producer to a producer of passenger vehicles, light trucks, or heavy trucks. Such purchases must also include steel and aluminum purchases for major stampings that form the "body in white" or chassis frame, regardless of the producer that makes such purchases.

(4) The requirement set out in subsection (1) applies to steel and aluminum purchased for use in the production of passenger vehicles, light trucks or heavy trucks. Subsection (1) does not apply to steel and aluminum purchased by a producer for other uses, such as the production of other vehicles, tools, dies or molds.

(5) For the purpose subsection (1), as it applies to a steel good set out in Table S, a good is originating if:
(a) beginning on July 1, 2020 until June 30, 2027 the good satisfies the applicable requirements established in Schedule I (PSRO Annex) or section 13 and all other applicable requirements of these Regulations; or
(b) beginning on July 1, 2027 the good satisfies all other applicable requirements of these Regulations, and provided that all steel manufacturing processes occur in one or more of the USMCA countries, except for metallurgical processes involving the refinement of steel additives. Such steel manufacturing processes include the initial melting and mixing and continues through the coating stage. This requirement does not apply to raw materials of used in the steel manufacturing process, including iron ore or reduced, processed, or pelletized iron ore of heading 26.01, pig iron of heading 72.01, raw alloys of heading 72.02 or steel scrap of heading 72.04.

(6) The vehicle producer may calculate the value of steel and aluminum purchases in subsection (1) by the following methods:

    (a) for steel or aluminum imported or acquired in the territory of a USMCA country:

        (i) the price paid or payable by the producer in the USMCA country where the producer is located;

        (ii) the net cost of the material at the time of importation; or

        (iii) the transaction value of the material at the time of importation.

    (b) for steel or aluminum that is self-produced:

        (i) all costs incurred in the production of materials, which includes general expenses, and

        (ii) an amount equivalent to the profit added in the normal course of trade, or equal to the profit that is usually reflected in the sale of goods of the same class or kind as the self-produced material that is being valued.

(7) For the purpose of determining the vehicle producer's purchases of steel or aluminum in subsection 17(1), the producer may calculate the purchases:

    (a) over the previous fiscal year of the producer;

    (b) over the previous calendar year;

    (c) over the quarter or month to date in which the vehicle is exported;

    (d) over the producer's fiscal year to date in which the vehicle is exported; or

    (e) over the calendar year to date in which the vehicle is exported.

(8) If the producer chooses to base a steel or aluminum calculation on paragraph (7)(c), (d) or (e), that calculation may be based on the producer's estimated purchases for the applicable period.

(9) For the purpose of determining the vehicle producer's purchases of steel or aluminum in subsection (1), the producer may calculate the purchases on the basis of:

    (a) all motor vehicles produced in one or more plants in the territory of one or more USMCA countries;

    (b) all motor vehicles exported to the territory of one or more USMCA countries;

    (c) all motor vehicles in a category set out in subsection 16(1) that are produced in one or more plants in the territory of one or more USMCA countries; or,

    (d) all motor vehicles in a category set out in subsection 16(1) exported to the territory of one or more USMCA countries.

(10) The producer may choose different periods for the purpose of its steel and aluminum calculations.

(11) If the producer of a passenger vehicle, light truck, or heavy truck has calculated steel or aluminum purchases on the basis of estimates before or during the applicable period, the producer must conduct an analysis at the end of the producer's fiscal year of the actual purchases made over the period with respect to the production of the vehicle, and, if the passenger vehicle, light truck, or heavy truck does not satisfy the steel or aluminum requirement on the basis of the actual purchases, immediately inform any person to whom the producer has provided a certification of origin for the vehicle, or a written statement that the vehicle is an originating good, that the vehicle is a non-originating good.

SECTION 18: LABOR VALUE CONTENT

LABOR VALUE CONTENT REQUIREMENTS FOR PASSENGER VEHICLES

(1) In addition to the requirements in sections 13 through 17 and Schedule I (PSRO Annex), a passenger vehicle is originating only if the vehicle producer certifies that the passenger vehicle meets a Labor Value Content (LVC) requirement of:

(a) 30 percent, consisting of at least 15 percentage points of high-wage material and labor expenditures, no more than 10 percentage points of technology expenditures, and no more than 5 percentage points of high-wage assembly expenditures, beginning on July 1, 2020 until June 30, 2021;

(b) 33 percent, consisting of at least 18 percentage points of high-wage material and labor expenditures, no more than 10 percentage points of technology expenditures, and no more than 5 percentage points of high-wage assembly expenditures, beginning on July 1, 2021 until June 30, 2022;

(c) 36 percent, consisting of at least 21 percentage points of high-wage material and labor expenditures, no more than 10 percentage points of technology expenditures, and no more than 5 percentage points of high-wage assembly expenditures, beginning on July 1, 2022 until June 30, 2023; or

(d) 40 percent, consisting of at least 25 percentage points of high-wage material and labor expenditures, no more than 10 percentage points of technology expenditures, and no more than 5 percentage points of high-wage assembly expenditures, beginning on July 1, 2023, and thereafter.

LVC REQUIREMENT RELATED TO LIGHT TRUCKS OR HEAVY TRUCKS

(2) In addition to the requirements set out in sections 13 through 17 and Schedule I (PSRO Annex), a light truck or heavy truck is originating only if the vehicle producer certifies that the truck meets an LVC requirement of 45 percent, consisting of at least 30 percentage points based on high-wage material and labor expenditures, no more than 10 percentage points based on technology expenditures, and no more than 5 percentage points based on high-wage assembly expenditures.

CALCULATION OF LVC REQUIREMENT

(3) For purposes of an LVC calculation for a passenger vehicle, light truck or heavy truck, a producer may include:
  (a) an amount for high-wage materials used in production;
  (b) an amount for high-wage labor costs incurred in the assembly of the vehicle;
  (c) an amount for high-wage transportation or related costs for shipping materials to the location of the vehicle producer, if not included in the amount for high-wage materials;
  (d) a credit for technology expenditures; and
  (e) a credit for high-wage assembly expenditures.

(4) *High wage materials.* The amount that may be included for high-wage materials used in production is the net cost or the annual purchase value of materials that undergo production in a qualifying-wage-rate production plant and that are used in the production of passenger vehicles, light trucks or heavy trucks in a plant located in the territory of a USMCA country.

(5) A plant engaged in the production of vehicles or parts may be certified as a qualifying wage-rate vehicle assembly plant or a qualifying-wage-rate production plant based on the average wage paid to direct production workers at the plant for July 1 to December 31, 2020, or for July 1 to June 30, 2021. In subsequent periods, the certification of a qualifying-wage-rate production plant based on period less than 12 months is valid for the following period of the same length. The certification of a qualifying-wage-rate production plant based on a 12- month period is valid for the following 12 months.

(6) For the purpose of meeting the Labor Value Content requirement a producer may use one of the following formulas:

(a) Formula based on net cost

$$LVC = (((HWLC + HWM)/NC) \times 100)/ + HWTC + HWAC$$

(b) Formula based on total annual purchase value

$$LVC = ((APV + HWLC^*) \times 100) + HWTC + HWAC (TAPV + HWLC^*)$$

* HWLC is included in the numerator at the choice of the producer and, if included, must also be included in the denominator

Where:

APV is the annual purchase value of high-wage material expenditures HWAC is the credit for high-wage assembly expenditures;

HWLC is the sum of the high-wage labor costs incurred in the assembly of the vehicle; HWM is the sum or the high-wage material expenditures used in production;

HWTC is the credit for high-wage technology expenditures;

HWT is the high-wage transportation or related costs for shipping materials used in production, if not included in the amount for HWM;

NC is the net cost of the vehicle and,

TAPV is the total vehicle plant assembly annual purchase value of parts and materials for use in the production of the vehicle

HIGH WAGE MATERIAL EXPENDITURES

(7) The high wage material expenditures may be calculated as sum of the following values:
  (a) the annual purchase value (APV) or net cost, depending on the formula used, of a self-produced high- wage material used in the production of a vehicle;
  (b) the APV or net cost, depending on the formula used, of an imported or acquired high-wage material used in the production of a vehicle;
  (c) the APV or net cost, depending on the formula used, of a high-wage material used in the production of a part or material that is used in the production of an intermediate or self-produced part that is subsequently used in the production of a vehicle; and
  (d) the APV or net cost depending on the formula used of a high wage material used in the production of a part or material that is subsequently used in the production of a vehicle.
(8) It is suggested, but not required, that the vehicle producer calculate the high-wage material and labor expenditures in the order describe in paragraph (2). A vehicle producer need not calculate the elements in paragraph 2(b) or in 2(c) if the previous element or elements is sufficient to meet the LVC requirement.

HIGH-WAGE TECHNOLOGY EXPENDITURES CREDIT

(9) The high-wage technology expenditures credit (HWTC) is based on annual vehicle producer expenditures at the corporate level in one or more USMCA countries on wages paid by the producer for research and development (R&D) or information technology (IT), calculated as a percentage of total annual vehicle producer expenditures on wages paid to direct production workers in one or more USMCA countries. Expenditures on capital or other non-wage costs for R&D or IT should not be included.

(10) To determine the high-wage technology expenditures credit (HWTC), the following formula may be used: HWTC = (Annual producer expenditures for R&D or IT/Total annual vehicle production expenditures) × 100

Where

HWTC is the credit for high-wage technology expenditures, expressed as a percentage;

(11) For the purposes of subsection 14(10), expenditures on wages for R&D include wage expenditures on research and development including prototype development, design, engineering, testing, or certifying operations.

HIGH-WAGE ASSEMBLY CREDIT

(12) A high-wage assembly credit of five percentage points may be included in the LVC for passenger vehicles or light trucks produced by a producer that operates a high-wage assembly plant for passenger vehicle or light truck parts or has a long-term supply contract for those parts (i.e. a contract with a minimum of three years) with such a plant.

(13) A high-wage assembly credit of five percentage points may be included in the LVC for heavy trucks produced by a producer that operates a high-wage assembly plant for heavy truck parts or has a long-term supply contract (i.e. a contract with a minimum of three years) for those parts with such a plant.

(14) A high-wage assembly plant for passenger vehicle, light truck, or heavy truck parts need only have the capacity to produce the minimum amount of originating parts specified in the definition. There is no need to maintain or provide records or other documents that certify such parts are originating, as long as information demonstrating the capacity to produce these minimum amounts is maintained and can be provided.

AVERAGING FOR LVC REQUIREMENT

(15) For the purpose of calculating the LVC of a passenger vehicle, light truck or heavy truck, the producer may elect to average the calculation using any one of the following categories, on the basis of either all vehicles in the category or only those vehicles in the category that are exported to the territory of one or more of the other USMCA countries:

(a) the same model line of vehicles in the same class of vehicles produced in the same plant in the territory of a USMCA country;

(b) the same class of vehicles produced in the same plant in the territory of a USMCA country;

(c) the same model line of vehicles or same class of vehicles produced in the territory of a USMCA country;

(d) any other category as the USMCA countries may decide.

(16) An election made under subsection (15) must

a. state the category chosen by the producer, and

i. if the category referred to in paragraph (15)(a) is chosen, state the model line, model name, class of vehicle and tariff classification of the vehicles in that category, and the location of the plant at which the vehicles are produced,

ii. if the category referred to in paragraph (15)(b) is chosen, state the model name, class of vehicle and tariff classification of the vehicles in that category, and the location of the plant at which the vehicles are produced, and

   iii. if the category referred to in paragraph (15)(c) is chosen, state the model line, model name, class of vehicle and tariff classification of the vehicles in that category, and the locations of the plants at which the vehicles are produced;
  b. state whether the basis of the calculation is all vehicles in the category or only those vehicles in the category that are exported to the territory of one or more of the other USMCA countries;
  c. state the producer's name and address;
  d. state the period with respect to which the election is made, including the starting and ending dates;
  e. state the estimated labor value content of vehicles in the category on the basis stated under paragraph (b);
  f. be dated and signed by an authorized officer of the producer; and
  g. be filed with the customs administration of each USMCA country to which vehicles in that category are to be exported during the period covered by the election, by July 31, 2020, and subsequently at least 10 days before the first day of the producer's fiscal year, or such shorter period as that customs administration may accept.

(17) An election filed for the vehicles referred to in subsection (16) may not be
  a. rescinded; or
  b. modified with respect to the category or basis of calculation.

(18) For purposes of this section, if a producer files an election under paragraph (16)(a), it must include the labor value content and the net cost of the producer's passenger vehicles, light trucks or heavy trucks, calculated under one of the categories set out in subsection (15), with respect to
  a. all vehicles that fall within the category chosen by the producer, or
  b. those vehicles to be exported to the territory of one or more of the USMCA countries that fall within the category chosen by the producer.

LVC PERIODS

(19) For the purposes of determining the LVC in this section, the producer may base the calculation on the following periods:
  (a) the previous fiscal year of the producer;
  (b) the previous calendar year;
  (c) the quarter or month to date in which the vehicle is produced or exported;
  (d) the producer's fiscal year to date in which the vehicle is produced or exported; or
  (e) the calendar year to date in which the vehicle is produced or exported.

TRANSPORTATION AND RELATED COSTS

(20) High-wage transportation or related costs for shipping may be included in a producer's LVC calculation, if not included in the amount for high-wage materials. Alternatively, a producer may aggregate such costs within the territories of one or more of the USMCA countries. Based on this aggregate amount, the producer may attribute an amount for transportation or related costs for shipping for purposes of the LVC calculation. Transportation or related costs for shipping incurred in transporting a material from outside the territories of the USMCA countries to the territory of a USMCA country are not included in this calculation.

VALUE OF MATERIALS FOR LVC PURPOSES

(21) The value of both originating and non-originating materials must be taken into account for the purpose of calculating the labor value content of a good. For greater certainty, the full value of a non-originating material that has undergone production in a qualifying-wage-rate production plant may be included in the HWM described in subsection 6.

EXCESS LVC MAY BE USED TOWARDS RVC REQUIREMENT FOR HEAVY TRUCKS

(22) For the period ending seven years after entry into force of the Agreement July 1, 2027, if a producer certifies a Labor Value Content for a heavy truck that is higher than 45 percent by increasing the amount of high wage material and manufacturing expenditures above 30 percentage points, the producer may use the points above 30 percentage points as a credit towards the regional value content percentages under section 13, provided that the regional value content percentage is not below 60 percent.

SECTION 19: ALTERNATIVE STAGING REGIME

(1) For the purposes of this section, eligible vehicles means passenger vehicles or light trucks for which an alternative staging regime has been approved by the USMCA countries.
(2) Notwithstanding sections 13 through 18, eligible vehicles are subject to the requirements set forth in subsection (4) from July 1, 2020 to June 30, 2025, or any other period provided for in the producer's approved alternative staging regime. Eligible vehicles are also subject to any other applicable requirements established in these Regulations.
(3) Passenger vehicles or light trucks that are not eligible vehicles may qualify as originating under the rules of origin established in sections 13 through 18, and any other applicable requirements established in these Regulations.
(4) Eligible vehicles are considered originating if they meet the following requirements:
    a. a regional value content of not less than 62.5 percent, under the net cost method;
    b. for parts listed in Table A.1, except lithium ion batteries of subheading 8507.60, a regional value content of not less than:
        i. 62.5 percent where the net cost method is used; or
        ii. 72.5 percent where the transaction value method is used if the corresponding rule includes a transaction value method; and
        iii. for lithium-ion batteries of 8507.60, a change from within subheading 8507.60 or from any other subheading for lithium-ion batteries of 8507.60
    c. at least 70 percent of a vehicle producer's purchases of steel and at least 70 percent of a vehicle producer's purchases of aluminum, by value, must qualify as originating under the rules of origin established in Schedule I. This requirement will not apply to vehicle producers that have an exemption under an approved alternative staging regime from having to satisfy this requirement; and
    d. a labor value content of at least 25 percent, consisting of at least ten percentage points of high- wage material and manufacturing expenditures, no more than ten percentage points of high- wage technology expenditures, and no more than five percentage points of high-wage assembly expenditures.
(5) Eligible vehicles are exempt from the core parts requirement set out in section 14.
(6) All methods and calculations for the requirements applicable to eligible vehicles must be based on the applicable provisions in these Regulations.

(7) Vehicles that are presently covered under the alternative staging regime described in Article 403.6 of the NAFTA Agreement as of November 30, 2019, may continue to use this regime, including any regulations that were effect prior to entry into force of the USMCA Agreement, according to each Party's approval process for use of the alternative staging regime. After the expiration of the period under the Article 403.6 alternative staging period, such vehicles will be eligible for preferential treatment under the requirements described in subsection (5), until the end of the USMCA alternative staging period described in subsection (1). For greater certainty, such vehicles will also be eligible for preferential tariff treatment under the other rules of origin set forth in the Agreement and these regulations.

SECTION 20: REGIONAL VALUE CONTENT FOR OTHER VEHICLES

(1) The value of non-originating materials used by the producer in the production of other vehicles and parts thereof must not, for the purpose of calculating the regional value content of the good, include the value of non- originating materials used to produce originating materials that are subsequently used in the production of the good.

(2) Notwithstanding the Product-Specific Rules of Origin in section 13 and Schedule I (PSRO Annex), the regional value content requirement is 62.5 percent under the net cost method for:
   (a) a motor vehicle for the transport of 15 or fewer persons of subheading 8702.10 or 8702.90;
   (b) a passenger vehicle with a compression-ignition engine as the primary motor of propulsion of subheading 8703.21 through 8703.90,
   (c) a three or four-wheeled motorcycle of subheading 8703.21 through 8703.90,
   (d) a motorhome or entertainer coach of subheading 8703.21 through 8703.90;
   (e) an ambulance, a hearse, a prison van of subheading 8703.21 through 8703.90;
   (f) a vehicle solely principally for off road use of subheading 8703.21 through 8703.90; or
   (g) a vehicle of subheading 8704.21 or 8704.31 that is solely or principally for off-road use; and
   (h) a good of heading 84.07 or 84.08, or subheading 8708.40, that is for use in a motor vehicle in paragraphs (a) through (g).

(3) Notwithstanding the Product-Specific Rules of Origin in section 13 and Schedule I (PSRO Annex), the regional value content requirement is 60 percent under the net cost method for:
   (a) a good that is:
      (i) a motor vehicle of heading 87.01, except for subheading 8701.20;
      (ii) a motor vehicle for the transport of 16 or more persons of subheading 8702.10 or 8702.90;
      (iii) a motor vehicle of subheading 8704.10;
      (iv) a motor vehicle of subheading 8704.22, 8704.23, 8704.32, or 8704.90 that is solely or principally for off-road use;
      (v) a motor vehicle of heading 87.05; or,
      (vi) a good of heading 87.06 that is not for use in a passenger vehicle, light truck, or heavy truck;
   (b) a good of heading 84.07 or 84.08, or subheading 8708.40, that is for use in a motor vehicle in paragraph (3)(a); or
   (c) except for a good in paragraph (3)(b) or of subheading 8482.10 through 8482.80, 8483.20, or 8483.30, a good in Table F that is subject to a regional value content requirement and that is for use in a motor vehicle in paragraphs (2)(a) through (g) or (3)(a).

(4) For the purpose of calculating the regional value content under the net cost method for a good that is a motor vehicle provided for in paragraphs (2)(a) through (g) or (3)(a), a good listed in Table F for use as original equipment in the production of a good in paragraphs (2)(a) through (g), or a component listed in Table G for use as original equipment in the production of the motor vehicle in paragraph (3)(a), the value of non-originating materials used by the producer in the production of the good must be the sum of:

   (a) for each material used by the producer listed in Table F or Table G, whether or not produced by the producer, at the choice of the producer and determined in accordance with Part III (Regional Value Content), either

      (i) the value of such material that is non-originating, or

      (ii) the value of non-originating materials used in the production of such material; and

   (b) the value of any other non-originating material used by the producer that is not listed in Table F or Table G, determined in accordance with Part III (Regional Value Content).

(5) For greater certainty, notwithstanding subsection (5), for purposes of a good that is a motor vehicle provided for in paragraphs (2)(a) through (g) or (3)(a), the value of non-originating materials is the sum of the values of all non-originating materials used by the producer in the production of the vehicle.

(6) for the purpose of calculating the regional value content of a motor vehicle covered by subsections (2) or (3), the producer may average its calculation over its fiscal year, using any one of the following categories, on the basis of either all motor vehicles in the category or only those motor vehicles in the category that are exported to the territory of one or more of the other USMCA countries:

   (a) the same model line of motor vehicles in the same class of vehicles produced in the same plant in the territory of a USMCA country;

   (b) the same class of motor vehicles produced in the same plant in the territory of a USMCA country; or

   (c) the same model line of motor vehicles produced in the territory of a USMCA country.

(7) For the purpose of calculating the regional value content for a good listed in Table F, or a component or material listed in Table G, produced in the same plant, the producer of the good may:

   (a) average its calculation:

      (i) over the fiscal year of the motor vehicle producer to whom the good is sold,

      (ii) over any quarter or month, or

      (iii) over its fiscal year, if the good is sold as an aftermarket part;

   (b) calculate the average referred to in paragraph (a) separately for a good sold to one or more motor vehicle producers; or

   (c) with respect to any calculation under this subsection, calculate the average separately for goods that are exported to the territory of one or more of the USMCA countries.

(8) The regional value content requirement for a motor vehicle identified in subsection (2) or (3) is:

   (a) 50 percent for five years after the date on which the first motor vehicle prototype is produced in a plant by a motor vehicle assembler, if:

      (i) it is a motor vehicle of a class, or marque, or, except for a motor vehicle identified in subsection (3), size category and underbody, not previously produced by the motor vehicle assembler in the territory of any of the USMCA countries,

(ii) the plant consists of a new building in which the motor vehicle is assembled, and

(iii) the plant contains substantially all new machinery that is used in the assembly of the motor vehicle; or

(b) 50 percent for two years after the date on which the first motor vehicle prototype is produced at a plant following a refit, if it is a different motor vehicle of a class, or marque, or, except for a motor vehicle identified in subsection (3), size category and underbody, that was assembled by the motor vehicle assembler in the plant before the refit.

CORE PARTS FOR PASSENGER VEHICLES AND LIGHT TRUCKS

Note: The Regional Value Content requirements set out in sections 13 or 14 or Schedule I (PSRO Annex) apply to a good for use as original equipment in the production of a passenger vehicle or light truck. For an aftermarket part, the applicable product-specific rule of origin set out in section 13 or 14 or Schedule I (PSRO Annex) is the alternative that includes the phrase "for any other good."

HS 2012	DESCRIPTION
8407.31	Reciprocating piston engines of a kind used for the propulsion of passenger vehicles of Chapter 87, of a cylinder capacity not exceeding 50 cc
8407.32	Reciprocating piston engines of a kind used for the propulsion of vehicles of Chapter 87, of a cylinder capacity exceeding 50 cc but not exceeding 250 cc
8407.33	Reciprocating piston engines of a kind used for the propulsion of vehicles of Chapter 87, of a cylinder capacity exceeding 250 cc but not exceeding 1,000 cc
8407.34	Reciprocating piston engines of a kind used for the propulsion of vehicles of Chapter 87, of a cylinder capacity exceeding 1,000 cc
Ex 8408.20	Compression-ignition internal combustion piston engines of a kind used for the propulsion of vehicles of subheading 8704.21 or 8704.31
8409.91	Parts suitable for use solely or principally with the engines of heading 84.07 or 84.08, suitable for use solely or principally with spark-ignition internal combustion piston engines
8409.99	Parts suitable for use solely or principally with the engines of heading 84.07 or 84.08, other 8507.60 Lithium-ion batteries that are used as the primary source of electrical power for the propulsion of an electric passenger vehicle or electric light truck
8706.00	Chassis fitted with engines, for the motor vehicles of heading 87.03 or subheading 8704.21 or 8704.31
8707.10	Bodies for the vehicles of heading 87.03
8707.90	Bodies for the vehicles of subheading 8704.21 or 8704.31
Ex 8708.29	Body stampings
8708.40	Gear boxes and parts thereof

HS 2012	DESCRIPTION
8708.50	Drive axles with differential, whether or not provided with other transmission components, and non-driving axles; parts thereof
8708.80	Suspension systems and parts thereof (including shock absorbers)
8708.94	Steering wheels, steering columns, and steering boxes; parts thereof
Ex 8708.99	Chassis frames

TABLE A.2

PARTS AND COMPONENTS FOR DETERMINING THE ORIGIN OF PASSENGER VEHICLES AND LIGHT TRUCKS UNDER SECTIONS 13 OR 14 OR SCHEDULE I (PSRO ANNEX)

The following table sets out the parts and components applicable to Table A.2 and their related tariff provisions, to facilitate implementation of the core parts requirement pursuant to Article 3.7 of the Appendix to the Annex 4-B of the Agreement.

These parts, and components used to produce such parts, are for the production of a passenger vehicle or light truck in order to meet the requirements under Section 14. The prefix "ex" is used to indicate that only the parts described in the components column and used in the production of parts for use as original equipment in a passenger vehicle or light truck are taken into consideration when performing the calculation.

COLUMN 1 *(the parts listed in this column may be referred to collectively as a super-core part)*	COLUMN 2	
PARTS	**COMPONENTS**	**6-DIGIT HS SUBHEADING**
ENGINES	Spark-ignition reciprocating or rotary internal combustion piston engines and Compression-ignition internal combustion piston engines (diesel or semi-diesel engines)	ex 8407.33 ex 8407.34 ex 8408.20
	Heads	ex 8409.91 ex 8409.99
	Blocks	ex 8409.91 ex 8409.99
	Crankshafts	ex 8483.10
	Crankcases	ex 8409.91 ex 8409.99
	Pistons	ex 8409.91
	Rods	ex 8409.91 ex 8409.99
	Head subassembly	ex 8409.91 ex 8409.99

COLUMN 1 *(the parts listed in this column may be referred to collectively as a super-core part)*	COLUMN 2	
PARTS	**COMPONENTS**	**6-DIGIT HS SUBHEADING**
TRANSMISSIONS	Gear boxes	ex 8708.40
	Transmission cases	ex 8708.40
	Torque converters	ex 8708.40 ex 8483.90
	Torque converter housings	ex 8708.40 ex 8483.90
	Gears and gear blanks	ex 8708.40 ex 8483.90
	Clutches, including continuously variable transmissions, but not parts thereof	ex 8708.93
	Valve body assembly	ex 8481.90 ex 8708.40
BODY AND CHASSIS	Major stampings that form the "body in white" or chassis frame	ex 8707.10 ex 8707.90 ex 8708.29 ex 8708.99
	Major body panel stampings	ex 8708.10 ex 8708.29
	Secondary panel stampings	ex 8708.29
	Structural panel stampings	ex 8708.29 ex 8708.99
	Stamped Frame components	ex 8708.29 ex 8708.99
AXLES	Drive-axles with differential, whether or not provided with other transmission components, and non- driving axles	ex 8708.50
	Axle shafts	ex 8708.50
	Axle housings	ex 8708.50
	Axle hubs	ex 8482.10 ex 8482.20 ex 8708.50 ex 8708.99 ex 8708.50
	Carriers	ex 8708.50

337

COLUMN 1		COLUMN 2
(the parts listed in this column may be referred to collectively as a super-core part)		
PARTS	**COMPONENTS**	**6-DIGIT HS SUBHEADING**
	Differentials	ex 8708.50
SUSPEN- SION SYSTEMS	Suspension systems (including shock absorbers)	ex 8708.80
	Shock absorbers	ex 8708.80
	Struts	ex 8708.80
	Control arms	ex 8708.80
	Sway bars	ex 8708.80
	Knuckles	ex 8708.80
	Coil springs	ex 7320.20
	Leaf springs	ex 7320.10
STEERING SYSTEMS	Steering wheels, steering columns and steering boxes	ex 8708.94
	Steering columns	ex 8708.94
	Steering gears/racks	ex 8708.94
	Control units	ex 8537.10 ex 8537.90 ex 8543.70
ADVANCED BATTERIES	Batteries of a kind used as the primary source for the propulsion of electrical power for electrically powered vehicles for passenger vehicles and light trucks	ex 8507.60 ex 8507.80
For	Cells	ex 8507.60 ex 8507.80 ex 8507.90
	Modules/arrays	ex 8507.60 ex 8507.80 ex 8507.90
	Assembled packs	ex 8507.60 ex 8507.80

TABLE B

PRINCIPAL PARTS FOR PASSENGER VEHICLES AND LIGHT TRUCKS

Note: The Regional Value Content requirements set out in section 13 or 14 or Schedule I (PSRO Annex) apply to a good for use as original equipment in the production of a passenger vehicle or light truck.

For an aftermarket part, the applicable product-specific rule of origin set out in section 13 or 14 or Schedule I (PSRO Annex) is the alternative that includes the phrase "for any other good."

HS 2012	DESCRIPTION
8413.30	Fuel, lubricating or cooling medium pumps for internal combustion piston engines
8413.50	Other reciprocating positive displacement pumps
8414.59	Other fans
8414.80	Other air or gas pumps, compressors and fans
8415.20	Air conditioning machines, comprising a motor-driven fan and elements for changing the temperature and humidity, including those machines in which humidity cannot be separately regulated, of a kind used for persons, in motor vehicles
Ex 8479.89	Electronic brake systems, including ABS and ESC systems
8482.10	Ball bearings
8482.20	Tapered roller bearings, including cone and tapered roller assemblies
8482.30	Spherical roller bearings
8482.40	Needle roller bearings
8482.50	Other cylindrical roller bearings
8482.80	Other ball or roller bearings, including combined ball/roller bearings
8483.10	Transmission shafts (including cam shafts and crank shafts) and cranks
8483.20	Bearing housings, incorporating ball or roller bearings
8483.30	Bearing housings, not incorporating ball or roller bearings; plain shaft bearings
8483.40	Gears and gearing, other than toothed wheels, chain sprockets and other transmission elements presented separately; ball or roller screws; gear boxes and other speed changers, including torque converters
8483.50	Flywheels and pulleys, including pulley blocks
8483.60	Clutches and shaft couplings (including universal joints)
8501.32	Other DC motors and generators of an output exceeding 750W but not exceeding 75 kW
8501.33	Other DC motors and generators of an output exceeding 75 kW but not exceeding 375 kW
8505.20	Electro-magnetic couplings, clutches and brakes

HS 2012	DESCRIPTION
8505.90	Other electro-magnets; electro-magnetic or permanent magnet chucks, clamps and similar holding devices; electro-magnetic lifting heads; including parts
8511.40	Starter motors and dual purpose starter-generators of a kind used for spark-ignition or compression-ignition internal combustion engines
8511.50	Other generators
8511.80	Other electrical ignition or starting equipment of a kind used for spark-ignition or compression- ignition internal combustion engines
Ex 8511.90	Parts of electrical ignition or starting equipment of a kind used for spark-ignition or compression-ignition internal combustion engines
8537.10	Electric controls for a voltage not exceeding 1,000 V
8708.10	Bumpers and parts thereof
8708.21	Safety seat belts
Ex 8708.29	Other parts and accessories of bodies (including cabs) of motor vehicles (excluding body stampings)
8708.30	Brakes and servo-brakes; parts thereof
8708.70	Road wheels and parts and accessories thereof
8708.91	Radiators and parts thereof
8708.92	Silencers (mufflers) and exhaust pipes; parts thereof
8708.93	Clutches and parts thereof
8708.95	Safety airbags with inflator system; parts thereof
Ex 8708.99	Other parts and accessories of motor vehicles of headings 87.01 to 87.05 (excluding chassis frames)
9401.20	Seats of a kind used for motor vehicles

COMPLEMENTARY PARTS FOR PASSENGER VEHICLES AND LIGHT TRUCKS

Note: The Regional Value Content requirements set out in sections 13 or 14 or Schedule I (PSRO Annex) apply to a good for use as original equipment in the production of a passenger vehicle or light truck. For an aftermarket part, the applicable product-specific rule of origin set out in section 13 or 14 or Schedule I (PSRO Annex) is the alternative that includes the phrase "for any other good."

HS 2012	DESCRIPTION
4009.12	Tubes, pipes and hoses of vulcanised rubber other than hard rubber, not reinforced or otherwise combined with other materials, with fittings
4009.22	Tubes, pipes and hoses of vulcanised rubber other than hard rubber, reinforced or otherwise combined only with metal, with fittings

HS 2012	DESCRIPTION
4009.32	Tubes, pipes and hoses of vulcanised rubber other than hard rubber, reinforced or otherwise combined only with textile materials, with fittings
4009.42	Tubes, pipes and hoses of vulcanised rubber other than hard rubber, reinforced or otherwise combined with other materials, with fittings
8301.20	Locks of a kind used for motor vehicles
Ex 8421.39	Catalytic converters
8481.20	Valves for oleohydraulic or pneumatic transmissions
8481.30	Check (nonreturn) valves
8481.80	Other taps, cocks, valves and similar appliances, including pressure-reducing valves and thermostatically controlled valves
8501.10	Electric motors of an output not exceeding 37.5 W
8501.20	Universal AC/DC motors of an output exceeding 37.5 W
8501.31	Other DC motors and generators of an output not exceeding 750 W
Ex 8507.20	Other lead-acid batteries of a kind used for the propulsion of motor vehicles of Chapter 87
Ex 8507.30	Nickel-cadmium batteries of a kind used for the propulsion of motor vehicles of Chapter 87
Ex 8507.40	Nickel-iron batteries of a kind used for the propulsion of motor vehicles of Chapter 87
Ex 8507.80	Other batteries of a kind used for the propulsion of motor vehicles of Chapter 87
8511.30	Distributors; ignition coils
8512.20	Other lighting or visual signalling equipment
8512.40	Windshield wipers, defrosters and demisters Ex 8519.81 Cassette decks
8536.50	Other electrical switches, for a voltage not exceeding 1,000 V
Ex 8536.90	Junction boxes
8539.10	Sealed beam lamp units
8539.21	Tungsten halogen filament lamp
8544.30	Ignition wiring sets and other wiring sets of a kind used in motor vehicles
9031.80	Other measuring and checking instruments, appliances & machines
9032.89	Other automatic regulating or controlling instruments and apparatus

TABLE D

PRINCIPAL PARTS FOR HEAVY TRUCKS

Note: The Regional Value Content requirements set out in sections 13 or 15 or Schedule I (PSRO Annex) apply to a good for use as original equipment in the production of a heavy truck. For an aftermarket part, the applicable product-specific rule of origin set out in section 13 or Schedule I (PSRO Annex) is the alternative that includes the phrase "for any other good."

8407.31	Reciprocating piston engines of a kind used for the propulsion of passenger vehicles of Chapter 87, of a cylinder capacity not exceeding 50 cc
8407.32	Reciprocating piston engines of a kind used for the propulsion of vehicles of Chapter 87, of a cylinder capacity exceeding 50 cc but not exceeding 250 cc
8407.33	Reciprocating piston engines of a kind used for the propulsion of vehicles of Chapter 87, of a cylinder capacity exceeding 250 cc but not exceeding 1,000 cc
8407.34	Reciprocating piston engines of a kind used for the propulsion of vehicles of Chapter 87, of a cylinder capacity exceeding 1,000 cc
8408.20	Compression-ignition internal combustion piston engines of a kind used for the propulsion of vehicles of Chapter 87
8409.91	Parts suitable for use solely or principally with the engines of heading 84.07 or 84.08, suitable for use solely or principally with spark-ignition internal combustion piston engines
8409.99	Parts suitable for use solely or principally with the engines of heading 84.07 or 84.08, other
8413.30	Fuel, lubricating or cooling medium pumps for internal combustion piston engines
Ex 8414.59	Turbochargers and superchargers
8414.80	Other air or gas pumps, compressors and fans
8415.20	Air conditioning machines, comprising a motor-driven fan and elements for changing the temperature and humidity, including those machines in which humidity cannot be separately regulated, of a kind used for persons, in motor vehicles
8483.10	Transmission shafts (including cam shafts and crank shafts) and cranks
8483.40	Gears and gearing, other than toothed wheels, chain sprockets and other transmission elements presented separately; ball or roller screws; gear boxes and other speed changers, including torque converters
8483.50	Flywheels and pulleys, including pulley blocks
Ex 8501.32	Other DC motors and generators of an output exceeding 750W but not exceeding 75 kW, of a kind used for the propulsion of motor vehicles of Chapter 87
8511.40	Starter motors and dual purpose starter-generators of a kind used for spark-ignition or compression-ignition internal combustion engines
8511.50	Other generators
8537.10	Electric controls for a voltage not exceeding 1,000 V
8706.00	Chassis fitted with engines, for the motor vehicles of heading 87.01 through 87.05
8707.90	Bodies for the vehicles of heading 87.01, 87.02, 87.04 or 87.05
8708.10	Bumpers and parts thereof
8708.21	Safety seat belts
8708.29	Other parts and accessories of bodies (including cabs) of motor vehicles

8708.30	Brakes and servo-brakes; parts thereof
8708.40	Gear boxes and parts thereof
8708.50	Drive axles with differential, whether or not provided with other transmission components, and non-driving axles; and parts thereof
8708.70	Road wheels and parts and accessories thereof
8708.80	Suspension systems and parts thereof (including shock absorbers)
8708.91	Radiators and parts thereof
8708.92	Silencers (mufflers) and exhaust pipes; parts thereof
8708.93	Clutches and parts thereof
8708.94	Steering wheels, steering columns and steering boxes; parts thereof
8708.95	Safety airbags with inflator system; parts thereof
8708.99	Other parts and accessories of motor vehicles of headings 87.01 to 87.05
9401.20	Seats of a kind used for motor vehicles

TABLE E COMPLEMENTARY PARTS FOR HEAVY TRUCKS

Note: The Regional Value Content requirements set out in sections 13 or 15 or Schedule I (PSRO Annex) apply to a good for use as original equipment in the production of a heavy truck. For an aftermarket part, the applicable product-specific rule of origin set out in section 13 or Schedule I (PSRO Annex) is the alternative that includes the phrase "for any other good."

8413.50	Other reciprocating positive displacement pumps
Ex 8479.89	Electronic brake systems, including ABS and ESC systems
8482.10	Ball bearings
8482.20	Tapered roller bearings, including cone and tapered roller assemblies
8482.30	Spherical roller bearings
8482.40	Needle roller bearings
8482.50	Other cylindrical roller bearings
8483.20	Bearing housings, incorporating ball or roller bearings
8483.30	Bearing housings, not incorporating ball or roller bearings; plain shaft bearings
8483.60	Clutches and shaft couplings (including universal joints)
8505.20	Electro-magnetic couplings, clutches and brakes
8505.90	Other electro-magnets; electro-magnetic or permanent magnet chucks, clamps and similar holding devices; electro-magnetic lifting heads; including parts
8507.60	Lithium-ion batteries
8511.80	Other electrical ignition or starting equipment of a kind used for spark-ignition or compression- ignition internal combustion engines
8511.90	Parts of electrical ignition or starting equipment of a kind used for spark-ignition or compression-ignition internal combustion engines or generators and cut-outs of a kind used in conjunction with such engines

TABLE F

PARTS FOR OTHER VEHICLES

Note: The Regional Value Content requirements set out in section 20 or Schedule I (PSRO Annex) apply to a good for use in a vehicle specified in subsections 20(2) and 20(3).

HS 2012	Description
40.09	Tubes, pipes and hoses
4010.31	Endless transmission belts (V-belts), V-ribbed, of an outside circumference exceeding 60 cm but not exceeding 180 cm
4010.32	Endless transmission belts (V-belts), other than V-ribbed, of an outside circumference exceeding 60 cm but not exceeding 180 cm
4010.33	Endless transmission belts (V-belts), V-ribbed, of an outside circumference exceeding 180 cm but not exceeding 240 cm
4010.34	Endless transmission belts (V-belts), other than V-ribbed, of an outside circumference exceeding 180 cm but not exceeding 240 cm
4010.39.aa	Other endless transmission belts (V-belts)
40.11	New pneumatic tires, of rubber
4016.93.aa	Gaskets, washers and other seals of vulcanised rubber other than hard rubber
4016.99.aa	Vibration control goods
7007.11	Toughened (tempered) safety glass of a size and shape suitable for incorporation in vehicles
7007.21	Laminated safety glass of a size and shape suitable for incorporation in vehicles
7009.10	Rearview mirrors for vehicles
8301.20	Locks of a kind used for motor vehicles
8407.31	Reciprocating piston engines of a kind used for the propulsion of passenger vehicles of Chapter 87, of a cylinder capacity not exceeding 50 cc
8407.32	Reciprocating piston engines of a kind used for the propulsion of vehicles of Chapter 87, of a cylinder capacity exceeding 50 cc but not exceeding 250 cc
8407.33	Reciprocating piston engines of a kind used for the propulsion of vehicles of Chapter 87, of a cylinder capacity exceeding 250 cc but not exceeding 1,000 cc
8407.34.aa	Reciprocating piston engines of a kind used for the propulsion of vehicles of Chapter 87, of a cylinder capacity exceeding 1,000 cc but not exceeding 2,000cc
8407.34.bb	Reciprocating piston engines of a kind used for the propulsion of vehicles of Chapter 87, of a cylinder capacity exceeding 2,000 cc
8408.20	Compression-ignition internal combustion piston engines of a kind used for the propulsion of vehicles of Chapter 87
84.09	Parts suitable for use solely or principally with spark-ignition internal combustion piston engines

8413.30	Fuel, lubricating or cooling medium pumps for internal combustion piston engines
8414.80.aa	Other air or gas pumps, compressors and fans (turbochargers and superchargers for motor vehicles, where not provided for under subheading 8414.59)
8414.59.aa	Other fans (turbochargers and superchargers for motor vehicles, where not provided for under subheading 8414.80)
8415.20	Air conditioning machines, comprising a motor-driven fan and elements for changing the temperature and humidity, including those machines in which humidity cannot be separately regulated, of a kind used for persons, in motor vehicles
8421.39.aa	Catalytic converters
8481.20	Valves for oleohydraulic or pneumatic transmissions
8481.30	Check (nonreturn) valves
8481.80	Other taps, cocks, valves and similar appliances, including pressure-reducing valves and thermostatically controlled valves
8482.10 through 8482.80	Ball or roller bearings
8483.10	Transmission shafts (including cam shafts and crank shafts) and cranks
8483.20	Bearing housings, incorporating ball or roller bearings
8483.30	Bearing housings; not incorporating ball or roller bearings; plain shaft bearings
8483.40	Gears and gearing, other than toothed wheels, chain sprockets and other transmission elements presented separately; ball or roller screws; gear boxes and other speed changes, including torque converters
8483.50	Flywheels and pulleys, including pulley blocks
8501.10	Electric motors and generators of an output not exceeding 37.5 W
8501.20	Universal AC/DC motors of an output exceeding 37.5 W
8501.31	Other DC motors and generators of an output not exceeding 750 W
8501.32.aa	Other DC motors and generators of an output exceeding 750W but not exceeding 75 kW of a kind used for the propulsion of vehicles of Chapter 87
8507.20.aa, 8507.30.aa, 8507.40.aa and 8507.80.aa	Batteries that provide primary source for electric cars
8511.30	Distributors; ignition coils
8511.40	Starter motors and dual purpose starter-generators of a kind used for spark-ignition or compressing-ignition internal combustion engines
8511.50	Other generators
8512.20	Other lighting or visual signalling equipment
8512.40	Windshield wipers, defrosters and demisters
ex 8519.81	Cassette decks

8527.21	Radios combined with cassette players
8527.29	Radios
8536.50	Other electrical switches, for a voltage not exceeding 1,000 V
8536.90	Junction boxes
8537.10.bb	Motor control centers
8539.10	Sealed beam lamp units
8539.21	Tungsten halogen filament lamp
8544.30	Ignition wiring sets and other wiring sets of a kind used in vehicles
87.06	Chassis fitted with engines, for the motor vehicles of heading 87.01 through 87.05
87.07	Bodies (including cabs) for the motor vehicles of headings 87.01 to 87.05
8708.10.aa	Bumpers (but not parts thereof)
8708.21	Safety seat belts
8708.29.aa	Body stampings
8708.29.cc	Door assemblies
8708.30	Brakes and servo-brakes; parts thereof
8708.40	Gear boxes and parts thereof
8708.50	Drive axles with differential, whether or not provided with other transmission components, and non-driving axles
8708.70.aa	Road wheels, but not parts or accessories thereof
8708.80	Suspension systems and parts thereof (including shock absorbers)
8708.91	Radiators and parts thereof
8708.92	Silencers (mufflers) and exhaust pipes; parts thereof
8708.93.aa	Clutches (but not parts thereof)
8708.94	Steering wheels, steering columns and steering boxes; parts thereof
8708.95	Safety airbags with inflator systems, and parts thereof
8708.99.aa	Vibration control goods containing rubber
8708.99.bb	Double flanged wheel hub units incorporating ball bearings
8708.99.ee	Other parts for powertrains
8708.99.hh	Other parts and accessories not provided for elsewhere in subheading 8708.99
9031.80	Other measuring and checking instruments, appliances & machines
9032.89	Other automatic regulating or controlling instruments and apparatus
9401.20	Seats of a kind used for motor vehicles

TABLE G

LIST OF COMPONENTS AND MATERIALS FOR OTHER VEHICLES

1. Component: Engines provided for in heading 84.07 or 84.08
   Materials: cast block, cast head, fuel nozzle, fuel injector pumps, glow plugs, turbochargers and superchargers, electronic engine controls, intake manifold,

exhaust manifold, intake/exhaust valves, crankshaft/camshaft, alternator, starter, air cleaner assembly, pistons, connecting rods and assemblies made therefrom (or rotor assemblies for rotary engines), flywheel (for manual transmissions), flexplate (for automatic transmissions), oil pan, oil pump and pressure regulator, water pump, crankshaft and camshaft gears, and radiator assemblies or charge-air coolers.

2. Component: Gear boxes (transmissions) provided for in subheading 8708.40

Materials: (a) for manual transmissions—transmission case and clutch housing; clutch; internal shifting mechanism; gear sets, synchronizers and shafts; and (b) for torque convertor type transmissions—transmission case and convertor housing; torque convertor assembly; gear sets and clutches; and electronic transmission controls.

TABLE S

Steel and Aluminum

The following table lists the HS subheadings for steel and aluminum subject to the USMCA steel and aluminum purchasing requirements set out in Section 17 to facilitate implementation of the steel and aluminum purchasing requirement, pursuant to Article 6.3 of the Appendix to Annex 4-B of the Agreement.

The prefix "ex" is used to indicate that only goods described in the "Description" column are taken into consideration when performing the calculation.

These descriptions cover structural steel or aluminum purchases by vehicle producers used in the production of passenger vehicles, light trucks, or heavy trucks, including all steel or aluminum purchases used for the production of major stampings that form the "body in white" or chassis frame as defined in Table A.2 (Parts and Components for Passenger Vehicles and Light Trucks). The descriptions do not cover structural steel or aluminum purchased by parts producers or suppliers used in the production of other automotive parts.

DESCRIPTION	6-DIGIT HS SUBHEADING(S)
STEEL	
Flat-rolled products of iron or non-alloy steel, of a width of 600 mm or more, hot-rolled, not clad, plated or coated:	
Other, in coils, not further worked than hot-rolled,	7208.25
Pickled	7208.26
	7208.27
Other, in coils, not further worked than hot-rolled	7208.36
	7208.37
	7208.38
	7208.39
Other, not in coils, not further worked than hot-rolled	7208.51
	7208.52
	7208.53

DESCRIPTION	6-DIGIT HS SUBHEADING(S)
	7208.54
Flat-rolled products of iron or non-alloy steel, of a width of 600 mm or more, cold-rolled (cold-reduced), not clad, plated or coated:	
In coils, not further worked than cold-rolled (cold-reduced):	7209.15
	7209.16
	7209.17
	7209.18
Not in coils, not further worked than cold-rolled (cold-reduced):	7209.25
	7209.26
	7209.27
	7209.28
	7209.90
Flat-rolled products of iron or non-alloy steel, of a width of 600 mm or more, clad, plated or coated:	
Electrolytically plated or coated with zinc	7210.30
Otherwise plated or coated with zinc, Other (Not Corrugated)	7210.49
Other plated or coated with aluminum	7210.69
Other: Clad; Other: Electrolytically coated or plated with base metal, Other	7210.90
Flat-rolled products of iron or non-alloy steel, of a width of less than 600 mm, not clad, plated or coated:	
Other, of a thickness of 4.75 mm or more	7211.14
Other:	7211.19
Not further worked than cold-rolled (cold-reduced), Containing by weight less than 0.25 percent of carbon:	7211.23
Flat-rolled products of iron or non-alloy steel, of a width of less than 600 mm, clad, plated or coated:	
Electrolytically plated or coated with zinc	7212.20
Otherwise plated or coated with zinc	7212.30
Bars and rods, hot-rolled, in irregularly wound coils, of iron or non-alloy steel	
Other, of free-cutting steel	7213.20
Other: Other	7213.99
Other bars and rods of iron or non-alloy steel, not further worked than forged, hot-rolled, hot-drawn or hot-extruded, but including those twisted after rolling	

DESCRIPTION	6-DIGIT HS SUBHEADING(S)
Other, of free-cutting steel	7214.30
Of rectangular (other than square) cross-section	7214.91
Other: Other	7214.99
Flat-rolled products of other alloy steel, of a width of 600 mm or more	
Other, not further worked than hot-rolled, in coils:	7225.30
Other, not further worked than hot-rolled, not in coils:	7225.40
Other, not further worked than cold-rolled (cold-reduced):	7225.50
Electrolytically plated or coated with zinc	7225.91
Other: Otherwise plated or coated with zinc	7225.92
Other: Other	7225.99
Flat-rolled products of other alloy steel, of a width of less than 600 mm:	
Other: Not further worked than hot-rolled: Of tool steel (other than high-speed steel):	7226.91
Not further worked than cold-rolled (cold-reduced):	7226.92
Other:	7226.99
Bars and rods, hot-rolled, in irregularly wound coils, of other alloy steel	
Of silico-manganese steel	7227.20
Other	7227.90
Other bars and rods of other alloy steel; angles, shapes	
and sections, of other alloy steel; hollow drill bars and rods, of alloy or non-alloy steel	
Bars and rods, of high speed steel	7228.10
Bars and rods, of silico-manganese steel	7228.20
Other bars and rods, not further worked than hot-rolled, hot-drawn or extruded	7228.30
Other bars and rods	7228.60
Other tubes, pipes and hollow profiles (for example, open seamed or welded, riveted or similarly closed), of iron or steel:	
Other, welded, of circular cross section, of iron or nonalloy steel:	7306.30
Other, welded, of circular cross section, of other alloy steel:	7306.50

DESCRIPTION	6-DIGIT HS SUBHEADING(S)
Other, welded, of noncircular cross section:	7306.61
	7306.69
	7306.90
Parts and accessories of the motor vehicles of headings 8701 to 8705:	
Major, secondary, and structural body panel stampings, that form the "body in white"	ex 8708.29
Stamped frame components that form the chassis frame	ex 8708.99

DESCRIPTIONS	HS HEADING OR SUBHEADING
ALUMINUM	
Unwrought aluminum	76.01
Aluminum waste and scrap	76.02
Aluminum bars, rods and profiles	76.04
Aluminum wire	76.05
Aluminum plates, sheets and strip, of a thickness exceeding 0.2 mm:	76.06
Aluminum tubes and pipes	76.08
Parts and accessories of the motor vehicles of headings 8701 to 8705:	
Major, secondary, and structural body panel stampings, that form the "body in white"	ex 8708.29
Stamped frame components that form the chassis frame	ex 8708.99

Schedule I (Specific Rules of Origin)

1. This schedule is deemed to be the contents of Sections A, B and C of Annex 4-B of the Agreement, as implemented by each USMCA country, except that the following rules of interpretation apply:

(a) for the purpose of Chapter 61, Note 2 or Chapter 62, Note 3 of Annex 4–B, a fabric of subheading 5806.20 or heading 60.02 is considered formed from yarn and finished, or formed and finished from yarn, in the territory of one or more Parties if all production processes and finishing operations, starting with the weaving, knitting, needling, tufting, or other process, and ending with the fabric ready for cutting or assembly without further processing, took place in the territories of one or more of the USMCA countries, even if non-originating yarn is used in the production of the fabric of subheading 5806.20 or heading 60.02;

(b) for the purposes of Chapter 61, Note 3 and Chapter 62, Note 4 of Annex 4–B, sewing thread is considered formed and finished in the territory of one or more Parties if all production processes and finishing operations, starting with the extrusion of filaments, strips, film or sheet, and including slitting a film or sheet into strip, or the spinning of all fibers into yarn, or both, and ending with the finished single or plied thread ready for use for sewing without further processing, took place in the territories of one or more of the USMCA countries even if non-originating fibre is used in the production of sewing thread of heading 52.04, 54.01 or 55.08, or yarn of heading 54.02 used as sewing thread referred to in the Notes;

(c) for the purpose of Chapter 61, Note 4 or Chapter 62, Note 5 of Annex 4–B, pocket bag fabric is considered formed and finished in the territory of one or more of the Parties if all production processes and finishing operations, starting with the weaving, knitting, needling, tufting, felting, entangling, or other process, and ending with the fabric ready for cutting or assembly without further processing, took place in the territories of one or more of the USMCA countries, even if non-originating fiber is used in the production of the yarn used to produce the pocket bag fabric;

(d) for the purpose of Chapter 61, Note 4 or Chapter 62, Note 5 of Annex 4–B, pocket bag fabric is considered a pocket or pockets if the pockets in which fabric is shaped to form a bag is not visible as the pocket is in the interior of the garment (i.e. pockets consisting of "bags" in the interior of the garment). Visible pockets such as patch pockets, cargo pockets, or typical shirt pockets are not subject to the chapter rule;

(e) for the purpose of Chapter 61, Note 4 or Chapter 62, Note 5 of Annex 4–B, yarn is considered wholly formed in the territory of one or more Parties if all the production processes and finishing operations, starting with the extrusion of filaments, strips, film, or sheet, and including slitting a film or sheet into strip, or the spinning of all fibers into yarn, or both, and ending with a finished single or plied yarn, took place in the territory of one or more of the USMCA countries, even if non-originating fiber is used in the production of the yarn used to produce the pocket bag fabric; and,

(f) for the purpose of Chapter 63, Note 2 of Annex 4–B, a fabric of heading 59.03 is considered formed and finished in the territory of one or more Parties if all production processes and finishing operations, starting with the weaving, knitting, needling, tufting, felting, entangling, or other process, including coating, covering, laminating, or impregnating, and ending with the fabric ready for cutting or assembly without further processing, took place in the territories of one or more of the USMCA countries, even if non-originating fiber or yarn is used in the production of the fabric of heading 59.03;

Schedule II (Most-Favored-Nation Rates of Duty on Certain Goods set out in Table 2.10.1 of the Agreement)

A. Automatic Data Processing Machines (ADP)

8471.30

8471.41

8471.49

B. Digital Processing Units

8471.50

C. Input or Output Units

Combined Input/Output Units

Canada	8471.60.00
Mexico	8471.60.02
United States	8471.60.10

Display Units

Canada	8528.42.00
	8528.52.00
	8528.62.00
Mexico	8528.41.99
	8528.51.01
	8528.51.99
	8528.61.01
United States	8528.42.00
	8528.52.00
	8528.62.00

Other Input or Output Units

Canada	8471.60.00
Mexico	8471.60.03
	8471.60.99
United States	8471.60.20
	8471.60.70
	8471.60.80
	8471.60.90

D. Storage Units

8471.70

E. Other Units of Automatic Data Processing Machines

8471.80

F. Parts of Computers

	8443.99	parts of machines of subheading 8443.31 and 8443.32, excluding facsimile machines and teleprinters
	8473.30	parts of ADP machines and units thereof
	8517.70	parts of LAN equipment of subheading 8517.62
Canada	8529.90.19	parts of monitors and projectors of subheading 8528.42, 8528.52, and 8528.62
	8529.90.50	
	8529.90.90	
Mexico	8529.90.01	parts of monitors or projectors of subheadings 8528.41, 8528.51, and 8528.61
	8529.90.06	

United States	8529.90.22	parts of monitors and projectors of
	8529.90.75	subheading 8528.42, 8528.52, and
	8529.90.99	8528.62

G. Computer Power Supplies

Canada	8504.40.30	
	8504.40.90	
	8504.90.10	
	8504.90.20	
	8504.90.90	
Mexico	8504.40.12	parts of goods classified in tariff
	8504.40.14	item 8504.40.12
	8504.90.02	
	8504.90.07	
	8504.90.08	
United States	8504.40.60	
	8504.40.70	
	8504.90.20	
	8504.90.41	

Schedule III (Value of Goods)

1 Unless otherwise stated, the following definitions apply in this Schedule.

buyer refers to a person who purchases a good from the producer;

buying commissions means fees paid by a buyer to that buyer's agent for the agent's services in representing the buyer in the purchase of a good;

producer refers to the producer of the good being valued.

2 For purposes of subsection 7(2) of these Regulations, the transaction value of a good is the price actually paid or payable for the good, determined in accordance with section 3 and adjusted in accordance with section 4.

3(1) The price actually paid or payable is the total payment made or to be made by the buyer to or for the benefit of the producer. The payment need not necessarily take the form of a transfer of money. It may be made by letters of credit or negotiable instruments. The payment may be made directly or indirectly to the producer. For an illustration of this, the settlement by the buyer, whether in whole or in part, of a debt owed by the producer is an indirect payment.

(2) Activities undertaken by the buyer on the buyer's own account, other than those for which an adjustment is provided in section 4, must not be considered to be an indirect payment, even though the activities may be regarded as being for the benefit of the producer. For an illustration of this, the buyer, by agreement with the producer, undertakes activities relating to the marketing of the good. The costs of such activities must not be added to the price actually paid or payable.

(3) The transaction value must not include the following charges or costs, provided that they are distinguished from the price actually paid or payable:

(a) charges for construction, erection, assembly, maintenance or technical assistance related to the good undertaken after the good is sold to the buyer; or

    (b) duties and taxes paid in the country in which the buyer is located with respect to the good.

(4) The flow of dividends or other payments from the buyer to the producer that do not relate to the purchase of the good are not part of the transaction value.

4(1) In determining the transaction value of a good, the following must be added to the price actually paid or payable:

    (a) to the extent that they are incurred by the buyer, or by a related person on behalf of the buyer, with respect to the good being valued and are not included in the price actually paid or payable

        (i) commissions and brokerage fees, except buying commissions,

        (ii) the costs of transporting the good to the producer's point of direct shipment and the costs of loading, unloading, handling and insurance that are associated with that transportation, and

        (iii) where the packaging materials and containers are classified with the good under the Harmonized System, the value of the packaging materials and containers;

    (b) the value, reasonably allocated in accordance with subsection (13), of the following elements if they are supplied directly or indirectly to the producer by the buyer, free of charge or at reduced cost for use in connection with the production and sale of the good, to the extent that the value is not included in the price actually paid or payable:

        (i) a material, other than an indirect material, used in the production of the good,

        (ii) tools, dies, molds and similar indirect materials used in the production of the good,

        (iii) an indirect material, other than those referred to in subparagraph (ii) or in paragraphs (c), (e) or (f) of the definition indirect material set out in subsection 1(1) of these Regulations, used in the production of the good, and

        (iv) engineering, development, artwork, design work, and plans and sketches necessary for the production of the good, regardless of where performed;

    (c) the royalties related to the good, other than charges with respect to the right to reproduce the good in the territory of one or more of the USMCA countries, that the buyer must pay directly or indirectly as a condition of sale of the good, to the extent that such royalties are not included in the price actually paid or payable; and

    (d) the value of any part of the proceeds of any subsequent resale, disposal or use of the good that accrues directly or indirectly to the producer.

(2) The additions referred to in subsection (1) must be made to the price actually paid or payable under this section only on the basis of objective and quantifiable data.

(3) If objective and quantifiable data do not exist with regard to the additions required to be made to the price actually paid or payable under subsection (1), the transaction value cannot be determined under section 2.

(4) Additions must not be made to the price actually paid or payable for the purpose of determining the transaction value except as provided in this section.

(5) The amounts to be added under subparagraphs (1)(a)(i) and (ii) are:

    (a) those amounts that are recorded on the books of the buyer; or

    (b) if those amounts are costs incurred by a related person on behalf of the buyer and are not recorded on the books of the buyer, those amounts that are recorded on the books of that related person.

(6) The value of the packaging materials and containers referred to in subparagraph (1)(a)(iii) and the value of the elements referred to in subparagraph (1)(b)(i) are

(a) if the packaging materials and containers or the elements are imported from outside the territory of the USMCA country in which the producer is located, the customs value of the packaging materials and containers or the elements,

(b) if the buyer, or a related person on behalf of the buyer, purchases the packaging materials and containers or the elements from a person who is not a related person in the territory of the USMCA country in which the producer is located, the price actually paid or payable for the packaging materials and containers or the elements,

(c) if the buyer, or a related person on behalf of the buyer, acquires the packaging materials and containers or the elements from a person who is not a related person in the territory of the USMCA country in which the producer is located other than through a purchase, the value of the consideration related to the acquisition of the packaging materials and containers or the elements, based on the cost of the consideration that is recorded on the books of the buyer or the related person, or

(d) if the packaging materials and containers or the elements are produced by the buyer, or by a related person, in the territory of the USMCA country in which the producer is located, the total cost of the packaging materials and containers or the elements, determined in accordance with subsection (8),

(7) The value referred to in subsection (6), to the extent that such costs are not included under paragraphs 6(a) through (d), must include the following costs that are recorded on the books of the buyer or the related person supplying the packaging materials and containers or the elements on behalf of the buyer:

(a) the costs of freight, insurance, packing, and all other costs incurred in transporting the packaging materials and containers or the elements to the location of the producer,

(b) duties and taxes paid or payable with respect to the packaging materials and containers or the elements, other than duties and taxes that are waived, refunded, refundable or otherwise recoverable, including credit against duty or tax paid or payable,

(c) customs brokerage fees, including the cost of in-house customs brokerage services, incurred with respect to the packaging materials and containers or the elements, and

(d) the cost of waste and spoilage resulting from the use of the packaging materials and containers or the elements in the production of the good, less the value of renewable scrap or by-product.

(8) For purposes of paragraph (6)(d), the total cost of the packaging materials and containers referred to in subparagraph (1)(a)(iii) or the elements referred to in subparagraph (1)(b)(i) are

(a) if the packaging materials and containers or the elements are produced by the buyer, at the choice of the buyer:

(i) the total cost incurred with respect to all goods produced by the buyer, calculated on the basis of the costs that are recorded on the books of the buyer, that can be reasonably allocated to the packaging materials and containers or the elements in accordance with Schedule V, or

(ii) the aggregate of each cost incurred by the buyer that forms part of the total cost incurred with respect to the packaging materials and containers or the elements, calculated on the basis of the costs that are recorded on the books of the buyer, that can be reasonably allocated to the packaging materials and containers or the elements in accordance with Schedule V; and

(b) if the packaging materials and containers or the elements are produced by a person who is related to the buyer, at the choice of the buyer:

    (i) the total cost incurred with respect to all goods produced by that related person, calculated on the basis of the costs that are recorded on the books of that person, that can be reasonably allocated to the packaging materials and containers or the elements in accordance with Schedule V, or

   (ii) the aggregate of each cost incurred by that related person that forms part of the total cost incurred with respect to the packaging materials and containers or the elements, calculated on the basis of the costs that are recorded on the books of that person, that can be reasonably allocated to the packaging materials and containers or the elements in accordance with Schedule V.

 (9) Except as provided in subsections (11) and (12), the value of the elements referred to in subparagraphs (1)(b)(ii) through (iv) are

    (a) the cost of those elements that is recorded on the books of the buyer; or

    (b) if such elements are provided by another person on behalf of the buyer and the cost is not recorded on the books of the buyer, the cost of those elements that is recorded on the books of that other person.

(10) If the elements referred to in subparagraphs (1)(b)(ii) through (iv) were previously used by or on behalf of the buyer, the value of the elements must be adjusted downward to reflect that use.

(11) Where the elements referred to in subparagraphs (1)(b)(ii) and (iii) were leased by the buyer or a person related to the buyer, the value of the elements are the cost of the lease as recorded on the books of the buyer or that related person.

(12) An addition must not be made to the price actually paid or payable for the elements referred to in subparagraph (1)(b)(iv) that are available in the public domain, other than the cost of obtaining copies of them.

(13) The producer must choose the method of allocating to the good the value of the elements referred to in subparagraphs (1)(b)(ii) through (iv), provided that the value is reasonably allocated to the good. The methods the producer may choose to allocate the value include allocating the value over the number of units produced up to the time of the first shipment or allocating the value over the entire anticipated production where contracts or firm commitments exist for that production. For an illustration of this, a buyer provides the producer with a mold to be used in the production of the good and contracts with the producer to buy 10,000 units of that good. By the time the first shipment of 1,000 units arrives, the producer has already produced 4,000 units. In these circumstances, the producer may choose to allocate the value of the mold over 4,000 units or 10,000 units but must not choose to allocate the value of the elements to the first shipment of 1,000 units. The producer may choose to allocate the entire value of the elements to a single shipment of a good only if that single shipment comprises all of the units of the good acquired by the buyer under the contract or commitment for that number of units of the good between the producer and the buyer.

(14) The addition for the royalties referred to in paragraph (1)(c) is the payment for the royalties that is recorded on the books of the buyer, or if the payment for the royalties is recorded on the books of another person, the payment for the royalties that is recorded on the books of that other person.

(15) The value of the proceeds referred to in paragraph (1)(d) is the amount that is recorded for such proceeds on the books of the buyer or the producer.

SCHEDULE IV Unacceptable Transaction Value

1 Unless otherwise stated, the following definitions apply in this Schedule.

buyer refers to a person who purchases a good from the producer;

customs administration refers to the customs administration of the USMCA country into whose territory the good being valued is imported;

producer refers to the producer of the good being valued.

2(1)   There is no transaction value for a good if the good is not the subject of a sale.

(2)   The transaction value of a good is unacceptable if:

(a)   there are restrictions on the disposition or use of the good by the buyer, other than restrictions that

(i)   are imposed or required by law or by the public authorities in the territory of the USMCA country in which the buyer is located,

(ii)   limit the geographical area in which the good may be resold, or

(iii)   do not substantially affect the value of the good;

(b)   the sale or price actually paid or payable is subject to a condition or consideration for which a value cannot be determined with respect to the good;

(c)   part of the proceeds of any subsequent resale, disposal or use of the good by the buyer will accrue directly or indirectly to the producer, and an appropriate addition to the price actually paid or payable cannot be made in accordance with paragraph 4(1)(d) of Schedule III; or

(d)   except as provided in section 3, the producer and the buyer are related persons and the relationship between them influenced the price actually paid or payable for the good.

(3)   The cases or considerations referred to in paragraph (2)(b) include the following:

(a)   the producer establishes the price actually paid or payable for the good on condition that the buyer will also buy other goods in specified quantities;

(b)   the price actually paid or payable for the good is dependent on the price or prices at which the buyer sells other goods to the producer of the good; and

(c)   the price actually paid or payable is established on the basis of a form of payment extraneous to the good, such as where the good is a semi-finished good that is provided by the producer to the buyer on condition that the producer will receive a specified quantity of the finished good from the buyer.

(4)   For purposes of paragraph (2)(b), conditions or considerations relating to the production or marketing of the good must not render the transaction value unacceptable, such as if the buyer undertakes on the buyer's own account, even though by agreement with the producer, activities relating to the marketing of the good.

(5)   If objective and quantifiable data do not exist with regard to the additions required to be made to the price actually paid or payable under subsection 4(1) of Schedule III, the transaction value cannot be determined under the provisions of section 2 of that Schedule. For an illustration of this, a royalty is paid on the basis of the price actually paid or payable in a sale of a litre of a particular good that was purchased by the kilogram and made up into a solution. If the royalty is based partially on the purchased good and partially on other factors that have nothing to do with that good, such as when the purchased good is mixed with other ingredients and is no longer separately identifiable, or when the royalty cannot be distinguished from special financial arrangements between the producer and the buyer, it would be inappropriate to add the royalty and the transaction value of the good could not be determined. However, if the amount of the royalty is based only on the purchased good and can be readily quantified, an addition to the price actually paid or payable can be made and the transaction value can be determined.

SCHEDULE V (Reasonable Allocation of Costs)

Definitions and Interpretation

1 of the following definitions apply in this Schedule,

costs means any costs that are included in total cost and that can or need to be allocated in a reasonable manner under to subsections 5(11), 7(11) and 8(8) of these Regulations, subsection 4(8) of Schedule III and subsections 4(8) and 9(3) of Schedule VI;

discontinued operation, in the case of a producer located in a USMCA country, has the meaning set out in that USMCA country's Generally Accepted Accounting Principles;

indirect overhead means period costs and other costs;

internal management purpose means any purpose relating to tax reporting, financial reporting, financial planning, decision-making, pricing, cost recovery, cost control management or performance measurement;

overhead means costs, other than direct material costs and direct labor costs.

2(1) In this Schedule, reference to "producer", for purposes of subsection 4(8) of Schedule III, is to be read as a reference to "buyer".

(2) In this Schedule, a reference to "good",
  (a) for purposes of subsection 7(15) of these Regulations, is to be read as a reference to "identical goods or similar goods, or any combination thereof";
  (b) for purposes of subsection 8(8) of these Regulations, is to be read as a reference to "intermediate material";
  (c) for purposes of section 16 of these Regulations, is to be read as a reference to "category of vehicles that is chosen pursuant to subsection 16(1) of these Regulations";
  (d) for purposes of section 16 of these Regulations, be read as a reference to "category of vehicles chosen pursuant to subsection 16(9) of these Regulations";
  (e) for purposes of subsection 4(8) of Schedule III, be read as a reference to "packaging materials and containers or the elements"; and
  (f) for purposes of subsection 4(8) of Schedule VI, be read as a reference to "elements".

Methods to Reasonably Allocate Costs

3(1) If a producer of a good is using, for an internal management purpose, a cost allocation method to allocate to the good direct material costs, or part thereof, and that method reasonably reflects the direct material used in the production of the good based on the criterion of benefit, cause or ability to bear, that method must be used to reasonably allocate the costs to the good.

(2) If a producer of a good is using, for an internal management purpose, a cost allocation method to allocate to the good direct labor costs, or part thereof, and that method reasonably reflects the direct labor used in the production of the good based on the criterion of benefit, cause or ability to bear, that method must be used to reasonably allocate the costs to the good.

(3) If a producer of a good is using, for an internal management purpose, a cost allocation method to allocate to the good overhead, or part thereof, and that method is based on the criterion of benefit, cause or ability to bear, that method must be used to reasonably allocate the costs to the good.

4 If costs are not reasonably allocated to a good under section 3, those costs are reasonably allocated to the good if they are allocated,

(a) with respect to direct material costs, on the basis of any method that reasonably reflects the direct material used in the production of the good based on the criterion of benefit, cause or ability to bear;

(b) with respect to direct labor costs, on the basis of any method that reasonably reflects the direct labor used in the production of the good based on the criterion of benefit, cause or ability to bear; and

(c) with respect to overhead, on the basis of any of the following methods:

   (i) the method set out in Appendix A, B or C,

   (ii) a method based on a combination of the methods set out in Appendices A and B or Appendices A and C, and

   (iii) a cost allocation method based on the criterion of benefit, cause or ability to bear.

5 Notwithstanding sections 3 and 8, if a producer allocates, for an internal management purpose, costs to a good that is not produced in the period in which the costs are expensed on the books of the producer (such as costs with respect to research and development, and obsolete materials), those costs must be considered reasonably allocated if

(a) for purposes of subsection 7(11) of these Regulations, they are allocated to a good that is produced in the period in which the costs are expensed, and

(b) the good produced in that period is within a group or range of goods, including identical goods or similar goods, that is produced by the same industry or industry sector as the goods to which the costs are expensed.

6 Any cost allocation method referred to in section 3, 4 or 5 that is used by a producer for the purposes of these Regulations must be used throughout the producer's fiscal year. Costs Not Reasonably Allocated

7 The allocation to a good of any of the following is considered not to be reasonably allocated to the good:

(a) costs of a service provided by a producer of a good to another person where the service is not related to the good;

(b) gains or losses resulting from the disposition of a discontinued operation, except gains or losses related to the production of the good;

(c) cumulative effects of accounting changes reported in accordance with a specific requirement of the applicable Generally Accepted Accounting Principles; and

(d) gains or losses resulting from the sale of a capital asset of the producer.

8 Any costs allocated under section 3 on the basis of a cost allocation method that is used for an internal management purpose that is solely for the purpose of qualifying a good as an originating good are considered not to be reasonably allocated.

APPENDIX A—Cost Ratio Method

Calculation of Cost Ratio

For the overhead to be allocated, the producer may choose one or more allocation bases that reflect a relationship between the overhead and the good based on the criterion of benefit, cause or ability to bear.

With respect to each allocation base that is chosen by the producer for allocating overhead, a cost ratio is calculated for each good produced by the producer as determined by the formula:

$$CR = AB \div TAB$$

where

CR is the cost ratio with respect to the good;

AB is the allocation base for the good; and

TAB is the total allocation base for all the goods produced by the producer.

Allocation to a Good of Costs included in Overhead

The costs with respect to which an allocation base is chosen are allocated to a good in accordance with the following formula:

$$CAG = CA \times CR$$

where

CAG is the costs allocated to the good;

CA is the costs to be allocated; and

CR is the cost ratio with respect to the good.

Excluded Costs

Under paragraph 7(11)(b) of these Regulations, where excluded costs are included in costs to be allocated to a good, the cost ratio used to allocate that cost to the good is used to determine the amount of excluded costs to be subtracted from the costs allocated to the good.

Allocation Bases for Costs

The following is a non-exhaustive list of allocation bases that may be used by the producer to calculate cost ratios:

- Direct labor hours
- Direct labor costs
- Units produced
- Machine-hours
- Sales dollars or pesos
- Floor space

"Examples"

The following examples illustrate the application of the cost ratio method to costs included in overhead.

Example 1: Direct Labor Hours

A producer who produces Good A and Good B may allocate overhead on the basis of direct labor hours spent to produce Good A and Good B. A total of 8,000 direct labor hours have been spent to produce Good A and Good B: 5,000 hours with respect to Good A and 3,000 hours with respect to Good B. The amount of overhead to be allocated is $6,000,000.

    Calculation of the ratios:

        Good A: 5,000 hours/8,000 hours = .625 Good B: 3,000 hours/8,000 hours = .375
        Allocation of overhead to Good A and Good B:
        Good A: $6,000,000 × .625 = $3,750,000 Good B: $6,000,000 × .375 = $2,250,000

Example 2: Direct Labor Costs

A producer who produces Good A and Good B may allocate overhead on the basis of direct labour costs incurred in the production of Good A and Good B. The total direct labor costs incurred in the production of Good A and Good B is $60,000: $50,000 with respect to Good A and $10,000 with respect to Good B. The amount of overhead to be allocated is $6,000,000.

   Calculation of the ratios:

   Good A: $50,000/$60,000 = .833 Good B: $10,000/$60,000 = .167
   Allocation of Overhead to Good A and Good B: Good A: $6,000,000 × .833 = $4,998,000 Good B: $6,000,000 × .167 = $1,002,000

Example 3: Units Produced

A producer of Good A and Good B may allocate overhead on the basis of units produced. The total units of Good A and Good B produced is 150,000: 100,000 units of Good A and 50,000 units of Good B. The amount of overhead to be allocated is $6,000,000.

   Calculation of the ratios:

   Good A: 100,000 units/150,000 units = .667 Good B: 50,000 units/150,000 units = .333
   Allocation of Overhead to Good A and Good B: Good A: $6,000,000 × .667 = $4,002,000 Good B: $6,000,000 × .333 = $1,998,000

Example 4: Machine-hours

A producer who produces Good A and Good B may allocate machine-related overhead on the basis of machine-hours utilized in the production of Good A and Good B. The total machine-hours utilized for the production of Good A and Good B is 3,000 hours: 1,200 hours with respect to Good A and 1,800 hours with respect to Good B. The amount of machine-related overhead to be allocated is $6,000,000.

   Calculation of the ratios:

   Good A: 1,200 machine-hours/3,000 machine-hours = .40 Good B: 1,800 machine-hours/3,000 machine-hours = .60
   Allocation of machine-related overhead to Good A and Good B: Good A: $6,000,000 × .40 = $2,400,000
   Good B: $6,000,000 × .60 = $3,600,000

Example 5: Sales Dollars or Pesos

A producer who produces Good A and Good B may allocate overhead on the basis of sales dollars. The producer sold 2,000 units of Good A at $4,000 and 200 units of Good B at $3,000. The amount of overhead to be allocated is $6,000,000.

   Total sales dollars for Good A and Good B: Good A: $4,000 × 2,000 units = $8,000,000
   Good B: $3,000 × 200 units = $600,000
   Total sales dollars: $8,000,000 + $600,000 = $8,600,000 Calculation of the ratios:
   Good A: $8,000,000/$8,600,000 = .93 Good B: $600,000/$8,600,000 = .07
   Allocation of Overhead to Good A and Good B: Good A: $6,000,000 × .93 = $5,580,000 Good B: $6,000,000 × .07 = $420,000

Example 6: Floor Space

A producer who produces Good A and Good B may allocate overhead relating to utilities (heat, water and electricity) on the basis of floor space used in the production and storage of Good A and Good B. The total floor space used in the production and storage of Good A and Good B is 100,000 square feet: 40,000 square feet with respect to Good A and 60,000 square feet with respect to Good B. The amount of overhead to be allocated is $6,000,000.

   Calculation of the Ratios:

   Good A: 40,000 square feet/100,000 square feet = .40 Good B: 60,000 square feet/100,000 square feet = .60
   Allocation of overhead (utilities) to Good A and Good B: Good A: $6,000,000 × .40 = $2,400,000
   Good B: $6,000,000 × .60 = $3,600,000

APPENDIX B—Direct Labor and Direct Material Ratio Method

Calculation of Direct Labor and Direct Material Ratio

For each good produced by the producer, a direct labor and direct material ratio is calculated by the formula:

$$DLDMR = (DLC + DMC) \div (TDLC + TDMC)$$

where

DLDMR is the direct labor and direct material ratio for the good;

DLC is the direct labor costs of the good;

DMC is the direct material costs of the good;

TDLC is the total direct labor costs of all goods produced by the producer; and

TDMC is the total direct material costs of all goods produced by the producer.

Allocation of Overhead to a Good

Overhead is allocated to a good by the formula:

$$OAG = O \times DLDMR$$

where

OAG is the overhead allocated to the good;

O is the overhead to be allocated; and

DLDMR is the direct labor and direct material ratio for the good.

Excluded Costs

Under paragraph 7(11)(b) of these Regulations, if excluded costs are included in overhead to be allocated to a good, the direct labor and direct material ratio used to allocate overhead to the good is used to determine the amount of excluded costs to be subtracted from the overhead allocated to the good.

"Examples"

Example 1

The following example illustrates the application of the direct labor and direct material ratio method used by a producer of a good to allocate overhead where the producer chooses to calculate the net cost of the good in accordance with paragraph 7(11)(a) of these Regulations.

  A producer produces Good A and Good B. Overhead (O) minus excluded costs (EC) is $30 and the other relevant costs are set out in the following table:

	Good A	Good B	Total
	($)	($)	($)
Direct labor costs (DLC)	5	5	10
Direct material costs (DMC)	10	5	15
Total	15	10	25

Overhead Allocated to Good A

OAG (Good A) = O ($30) × DLDMR ($15/$25) OAG (Good A) = $18.00

Overhead Allocated to Good B

OAG (Good B) = O ($30) × DLDMR ($10/$25) OAG (Good B) = $12.00

Example 2

The following example illustrates the application of the direct labor and direct material ratio method used by a producer of a good to allocate overhead where the producer chooses to calculate the net cost of the good in accordance with paragraph 7(11)(b) of these Regulations and where excluded costs are included in overhead.

  A producer produces Good A and Good B. Overhead (O) is $50 (including excluded costs (EC) of $20). The other relevant costs are set out in the table to Example 1.

Overhead Allocated to Good A

OAG (Good A) = [O ($50) × DLDMR ($15/$25)] – [EC ($20) × DLDMR ($15/$25)] OAG (Good A) = $18.00

Overhead Allocated to Good B

OAG (Good B) = [O ($50) × DLDMR ($10/$25)] – [EC ($20) × DLDMR ($10/$25)] OAG (Good B) = $12.00

APPENDIX C—Direct Cost Ratio Method

Direct Overhead

Direct overhead is allocated to a good on the basis of a method based on the criterion of benefit, cause or ability to bear.

Indirect Overhead

Indirect overhead is allocated on the basis of a direct cost ratio.

Calculation of Direct Cost Ratio

For each good produced by the producer, a direct cost ratio is calculated by the formula:

$$DCR = (DLC + DMC + DO) \div (TDLC + TDMC + TDO)$$

where

DCR is the direct cost ratio for the good;

DLC is the direct labor costs of the good;

DMC is the direct material costs of the good;

DO is the direct overhead of the good;

TDLC is the total direct labor costs of all goods produced by the producer;

TDMC is the total direct material costs of all goods produced by the producer; and

TDO is the total direct overhead of all goods produced by the producer.

Allocation of Indirect Overhead to a Good

Indirect overhead is allocated to a good by the formula:

$$IOAG = IO \times DCR$$

where

IOAG is the indirect overhead allocated to the good;

IO is the indirect overhead of all goods produced by the producer; and

DCR is the direct cost ratio of the good.

Excluded Costs

Under paragraph 7(11)(b) of these Regulations, if excluded costs are included in

    (a) *direct overhead to be allocated to a good, those excluded costs are subtracted from the direct overhead allocated to the good; and*

    (b) *indirect overhead to be allocated to a good, the direct cost ratio used to allocate indirect overhead to the good is used to determine the amount of excluded costs to be subtracted from the indirect overhead allocated to the good.*

"Examples"

Example 1

The following example illustrates the application of the direct cost ratio method used by a producer of a good to allocate indirect overhead where the producer chooses to calculate the net cost of the good in accordance with paragraph 7(11)(a) of these Regulations.

    A producer produces Good A and Good B. Indirect overhead (IO) minus excluded costs (EC) is $30. The other relevant costs are set out in the following table:

	Good A ($)	Good B ($)	Total ($)
Direct labor costs (DLC)	5	5	10
Direct material costs (DMC)	10	5	15
Direct overhead (DO)	8	2	10
Totals	23	12	35

Indirect Overhead Allocated to Good A

IOAG (Good A) = IO ($30) × DCR ($23/$35) IOAG (Good A) = $19.71

Indirect Overhead Allocated to Good B

IOAG (Good B) = IO ($30) × DCR ($12/$35) IOAG (Good B) = $10.29

Example 2

The following example illustrates the application of the direct cost ratio method used by a producer of a good to allocate indirect overhead if the producer has chosen to calculate the net cost of the good in accordance with paragraph 7(11)(b) of these Regulations and where excluded costs are included in indirect overhead.

A producer produces Good A and Good B. The indirect overhead (IO) is $50 (including excluded costs (EC) of $20). The other relevant costs are set out in the table to Example 1.

Indirect Overhead Allocated to Good A

IOAG (Good A) = [IO ($50) × DCR ($23/$35)] – [EC ($20) × DCR ($23/$35)] IOAG (Good A) = $19.72

Indirect Overhead Allocated to Good B

IOAG (Good B) = [IO ($50) × DCR ($12/$35)] – [EC ($20) × DCR ($12/$35)] IOAG (Good B) = $10.28

Schedule VI Value of Materials

1 (1) Unless otherwise stated, the following definitions apply in this Schedule.

buying commissions means fees paid by a producer to that producer's agent for the agent's services in representing the producer in the purchase of a material;

customs administration refers to the customs administration of the USMCA country into whose territory the good, in the production of which the material being valued is used, is imported;

materials of the same class or kind means, with respect to materials being valued, materials that are within a group or range of materials that

(a) is produced by a particular industry or industry sector, and

(b) includes identical materials or similar materials;

producer refers to the producer who used the material in the production of a good that is subject to a regional value-content requirement;

seller refers to a person who sells the material being valued to the producer.

2(1) Except as provided under subsections (2), the transaction value of a material under paragraph 8(1)(b) of these Regulations is the price actually paid or payable for the material determined in accordance with section 3 and adjusted in accordance with section 4.

(2) There is no transaction value for a material if the material is not the subject of a sale.

(3) The transaction value of a material is unacceptable if:
  (a) there are restrictions on the disposition or use of the material by the producer, other than restrictions that
    (i) are imposed or required by law or by the public authorities in the territory of the USMCA country in which the producer of the good or the seller of the material is located,
    (ii) limit the geographical area in which the material may be used, or
    (iii) do not substantially affect the value of the material;
  (b) the sale or price actually paid or payable is subject to a condition or consideration for which a value cannot be determined with respect to the material;
  (c) part of the proceeds of any subsequent disposal or use of the material by the producer will accrue directly or indirectly to the seller, and an appropriate addition to the price actually paid or payable cannot be made in accordance with paragraph 4(1)(d); or
  (d) except as provided in section 3, the producer and the seller are related persons and the relationship between them influenced the price actually paid or payable for the material.

(4) The cases or considerations referred to in paragraph (3)(b) include the following:
  (a) the seller establishes the price actually paid or payable for the material on condition that the producer will also buy other materials or goods in specified quantities;
  (b) the price actually paid or payable for the material is dependent on the price or prices at which the producer sells other materials or goods to the seller of the material; and
  (c) the price actually paid or payable is established on the basis of a form of payment extraneous to the material, such as where the material is a semi-finished material that is provided by the seller to the producer on condition that the seller will receive a specified quantity of the finished material from the producer.

(5) For purposes of paragraph (3)(b), conditions or considerations relating to the use of the material will not render the transaction value unacceptable, such as where the producer undertakes on the producer's own account, even though by agreement with the seller, activities relating to the warranty of the material used in the production of a good.

(6) If objective and quantifiable data do not exist with regard to the additions required to be made to the price actually paid or payable under subsection 4(1), the transaction value cannot be determined under the provisions of subsection 2(1). For an illustration of this, a royalty is paid on the basis of the price actually paid or payable in a sale of a litre of a particular good that is produced by using a material that was purchased by the kilogram and made up into a solution. If the royalty is based partially on the purchased material and partially on other factors that have

nothing to do with that material, such as when the purchased material is mixed with other ingredients and is no longer separately identifiable, or when the royalty cannot be distinguished from special financial arrangements between the seller and the producer, it would be inappropriate to add the royalty and the transaction value of the material could not be determined. However, if the amount of the royalty is based only on the purchased material and can be readily quantified, an addition to the price actually paid or payable can be made and the transaction value can be determined.

3(1) The price actually paid or payable is the total payment made or to be made by the producer to or for the benefit of the seller of the material. The payment need not necessarily take the form of a transfer of money. It may be made by letters of credit or negotiable instruments. Payment may be made directly or indirectly to the seller. For an illustration of this, the settlement by the producer, whether in whole or in part, of a debt owed by the seller, is an indirect payment.

(2) Activities undertaken by the producer on the producer's own account, other than those for which an adjustment is provided in section 4, must not be considered to be an indirect payment, even though the activities might be regarded as being for the benefit of the seller.

(3) The transaction value must not include charges for construction, erection, assembly, maintenance or technical assistance related to the use of the material by the producer, provided that they are distinguished from the price actually paid or payable.

(4) The flow of dividends or other payments from the producer to the seller that do not relate to the purchase of the material are not part of the transaction value.

4(1) In determining the transaction value of the material, the following must be added to the price actually paid or payable:

(a) to the extent that they are incurred by the producer with respect to the material being valued and are not included in the price actually paid or payable,
   (i) commissions and brokerage fees, except buying commissions, and
   (ii) the costs of containers which, for customs purposes, are classified with the material under the Harmonized System;

(b) the value, reasonably allocated in accordance with subsection (13), of the following elements if they are supplied directly or indirectly to the seller by the producer free of charge or at reduced cost for use in connection with the production and sale of the material, to the extent that the value is not included in the price actually paid or payable:
   (i) a material, other than an indirect material, used in the production of the material being valued,
   (ii) tools, dies, mold and similar indirect materials used in the production of the material being valued,
   (iii) an indirect material, other than those referred to in subparagraph (ii) or in paragraphs (c), (e) or (f) of the definition *indirect material* in subsection 1(1) of these Regulations, used in the production of the material being valued, and
   (iv) engineering, development, artwork, design work, and plans and sketches made outside the territory of the USMCA country in which the producer is located that are necessary for the production of the material being valued;

(c) the royalties related to the material, other than charges with respect to the right to reproduce the material in the territory of the USMCA country in which the producer is located that the producer must pay directly or indirectly as a condition of sale of the material, to the extent that such royalties are not included in the price actually paid or payable; and

(d) the value of any part of the proceeds of any subsequent disposal or use of the material that accrues directly or indirectly to the seller.

(2) The additions referred to in subsection (1) must be made to the price actually paid or payable under this section only on the basis of objective and quantifiable data.

(3) If objective and quantifiable data do not exist with regard to the additions required to be made to the price actually paid or payable under subsection (1), the transaction value cannot be determined under subsection 2(1).

(4) Additions must not be made to the price actually paid or payable for the purpose of determining the transaction value except as provided in this section.

(5) The amounts to be added under paragraph (1)(a) must be those amounts that are recorded on the books of the producer.

(6) The value of the elements referred to in subparagraph (1)(b)(i) must be:
   (a) where the elements are imported from outside the territory of the USMCA country in which the seller is located, the customs value of the elements,
   (b) where the producer, or a related person on behalf of the producer, purchases the elements from an unrelated person in the territory of the USMCA country in which the seller is located, the price actually paid or payable for the elements,
   (c) where the producer, or a related person on behalf of the producer, acquires the elements from an unrelated person in the territory of the USMCA country in which the seller is located other than through a purchase, the value of the consideration related to the acquisition of the elements, based on the cost of the consideration that is recorded on the books of the producer or the related person, or
   (d) where the elements are produced by the producer, or by a related person, in the territory of the USMCA country in which the seller is located, the total cost of the elements, determined in accordance with subsection (8),

(7) Those elements must include the following costs, that are recorded on the books of the producer or the related person supplying the elements on behalf of the producer, to the extent that such costs are not included under paragraphs (6)(a) through (d):
   (a) the costs of freight, insurance, packing, and all other costs incurred in transporting the elements to the location of the seller,
   (b) duties and taxes paid or payable with respect to the elements, other than duties and taxes that are waived, refunded, refundable or otherwise recoverable, including credit against duty or tax paid or payable,
   (c) customs brokerage fees, including the cost of in-house customs brokerage services, incurred with respect to the elements, and
   (d) the cost of waste and spoilage resulting from the use of the elements in the production of the material, minus the value of reusable scrap or by-product.

(8) For the purposes of paragraph (6)(d), the total cost of the elements referred to in subparagraph (1)(b)(i) are:
   (a) where the elements are produced by the producer, at the choice of the producer,
      (i) the total cost incurred with respect to all goods produced by the producer, calculated on the basis of the costs that are recorded on the books of the producer, that can be reasonably allocated to the elements in accordance with Schedule V, or
      (ii) the aggregate of each cost incurred by the producer that forms part of the total cost incurred with respect to the elements, calculated on the basis of the costs that are recorded on the books of the producer, that can be reasonably allocated to the elements in accordance with Schedule V; and
   (b) if the elements are produced by a person who is related to the producer, at the choice of the producer:
      (i) the total cost incurred with respect to all goods produced by that related person, calculated on the basis of the costs that are recorded on the books of that person, that can be reasonably allocated to the elements in accordance with Schedule V, or

(ii) the aggregate of each cost incurred by that related person that forms part of the total cost incurred with respect to the elements, calculated on the basis of the costs that are recorded on the books of that person, that can be reasonably allocated to the elements in accordance with Schedule V.

(9) Except as provided in subsections (11) and (12), the value of the elements referred to in subparagraphs (1)(b)(ii) through (iv) are:

(a) the cost of those elements that is recorded on the books of the producer; or

(b) if such elements are provided by another person on behalf of the producer and the cost is not recorded on the books of the producer, the cost of those elements that is recorded on the books of that other person.

(10) If the elements referred to in subparagraphs (1)(b)(ii) through (iv) were previously used by or on behalf of the producer, the value of the elements must be adjusted downward to reflect that use.

(11) If the elements referred to in subparagraphs (1)(b)(ii) and (iii) were leased by the producer or a person related to the producer, the value of the elements are the cost of the lease that is recorded on the books of the producer or that related person.

(12) An addition must not be made to the price actually paid or payable for the elements referred to in subparagraph (1)(b)(iv) that are available in the public domain, other than the cost of obtaining copies of them.

(13) The producer must choose the method of allocating to the material the value of the elements referred to in subparagraphs (1)(b)(ii) through (iv), provided that the value is reasonably allocated. The methods the producer may choose to allocate the value include allocating the value over the number of units produced up to the time of the first shipment or allocating the value over the entire anticipated production where contracts or firm commitments exist for that production. For an illustration of this, a producer provides the seller with a mold to be used in the production of the material and contracts with the seller to buy 10,000 units of that material. By the time the first shipment of 1,000 units arrives, the seller has already produced 4,000 units. In these circumstances, the producer may choose to allocate the value of the mold over 4,000 units or 10,000 units but must not choose to allocate the value of the elements to the first shipment of 1,000 units. The producer may choose to allocate the entire value of the elements to a single shipment of material only where that single shipment comprises all of the units of the material acquired by the producer under the contract or commitment for that number of units of the material between the seller and the producer.

(14) The addition for the royalties referred to in paragraph (1)(c) is the payment for the royalties that is recorded on the books of the producer, or where the payment for the royalties is recorded on the books of another person, the payment for the royalties that is recorded on the books of that other person.

(15) The value of the proceeds referred to in paragraph (1)(d) is the amount that is recorded for those proceeds on the books of the producer or the seller.

5(1) If there is no transaction value under subsection 2(2) or the transaction value is unacceptable under subsection 2(3), the value of the material, referred to in subparagraph 8(1)(b)(ii) of Part IV of these Regulations, is the transaction value of identical materials sold, at or about the same time as the material being valued was shipped to the producer, to a buyer located in the same country as the producer.

(2) In applying this section, the transaction value of identical materials in a sale at the same commercial level and in substantially the same quantity of materials as the material being valued shall be used to determine the value of the material. If no such sale is found, the transaction value of identical materials sold at a different commercial level or in different quantities, adjusted to take into account the differences attributable to the commercial level or quantity, must be used, provided that such adjustments can be made on the basis of evidence that clearly establishes

that the adjustment is reasonable and accurate, whether the adjustment leads to an increase or a decrease in the value.

(3) A condition for adjustment under subsection (2) because of different commercial levels or different quantities is that such adjustment be made only on the basis of evidence that clearly establishes that an adjustment is reasonable and accurate. For an illustration of this, a bona fide price list contains prices for different quantities. If the material being valued consists of a shipment of 10 units and the only identical materials for which a transaction value exists involved a sale of 500 units, and it is recognized that the seller grants quantity discounts, the required adjustment may be accomplished by resorting to the seller's bona fide price list and using the price applicable to a sale of 10 units. This does not require that sales had to have been made in quantities of 10 as long as the price list has been established as being bona fide through sales at other quantities. In the absence of such an objective measure, however, the determination of a value under this section is not appropriate.

(4) If more than one transaction value of identical materials is found, the lowest such value must be used to determine the value of the material under this section.

6(1) If there is no transaction value under subsection 2(2) or the transaction value is unacceptable under section 2(3), and the value of the material cannot be determined under section 5, the value of the material, referred to in subparagraph 8(1)(b)(ii) of Part IV of these Regulations, is the transaction value of similar materials sold, at or about the same time as the material being valued was shipped to the producer, to a buyer located in the same country as the producer.

(2) In applying this section, the transaction value of similar materials in a sale at the same commercial level and in substantially the same quantity of materials as the material being valued must be used to determine the value of the material. Where no such sale is found, the transaction value of similar materials sold at a different commercial level or in different quantities, adjusted to take into account the differences attributable to the commercial level or quantity, must be used, provided that such adjustments can be made on the basis of evidence that clearly establishes that the adjustment is reasonable and accurate, whether the adjustment leads to an increase or a decrease in the value.

(3) A condition for adjustment under subsection (2) because of different commercial levels or different quantities is that such adjustment be made only on the basis of evidence that clearly establishes that an adjustment is reasonable and accurate. For an illustration of this, a bona fide price list contains prices for different quantities. If the material being valued consists of a shipment of 10 units and the only similar materials for which a transaction value exists involved a sale of 500 units, and it is recognized that the seller grants quantity discounts, the required adjustment may be accomplished by resorting to the seller's bona fide price list and using the price applicable to a sale of 10 units. This does not require that sales had to have been made in quantities of 10 as long as the price list has been established as being bona fide through sales at other quantities. In the absence of such an objective measure, however, the determination of a value under this section is not appropriate.

(4) If more than one transaction value of similar materials is found, the lowest of those values must be used to determine the value of the material under this section.

7 If there is no transaction value under subsection 2(2) or the transaction value is unacceptable under subsection 2(3), and the value of the material cannot be determined under section 5 or 6, the value of the material, referred to in subparagraph 8(1)(b)(ii) of Part IV of these Regulations, must be determined under section 8 or, when the value cannot be determined under that section, under section 9 except that, at the request of the producer, the order of application of sections 8 and 9 must be reversed.

8(1) Under this section, if identical materials or similar materials are sold in the territory of the USMCA country in which the producer is located, in the same condition as the material was in when received by the producer, the value of the material, referred to in subparagraph 8(1)(b)(ii) of Part IV of these Regulations, must be based on the unit price at which those identical materials or similar materials are sold, in the greatest aggregate quantity by the producer or, where the producer does not sell those identical materials or similar materials, by a person at the same trade level as the producer, at or about the same time as the material being valued is received by the producer, to persons located in that territory who are not related to the seller, subject to deductions for the following:

(a) either the amount of commissions usually earned or the amount generally reflected for profit and general expenses, in connection with sales, in the territory of that USMCA country, of materials of the same class or kind as the material being valued; and

(b) taxes, if included in the unit price, payable in the territory of that USMCA country, which are either waived, refunded or recoverable by way of credit against taxes actually paid or payable.

(2) If neither identical materials nor similar materials are sold at or about the same time the material being valued is received by the producer, the value must, subject to the deductions provided for under subsection (1), be based on the unit price at which identical materials or similar materials are sold in the territory of the USMCA country in which the producer is located, in the same condition as the material was in when received by the producer, at the earliest date within 90 days after the day on which the material being valued was received by the producer.

(3) The expression "unit price at which those identical materials or similar materials are sold, in the greatest aggregate quantity" in subsection (1) means the price at which the greatest number of units is sold in sales between persons who are not related persons. For an illustration of this, materials are sold from a price list which grants favourable unit prices for purchases made in larger quantities.

Sale Quantity	Unit Price	Number of Sales	Total Quantity Sold at Each Price
1-10 units	100	10 sales of 5 units	65
		5 sales of 3 units	
11-25 units	95	5 sales of 11 units	55
Over 25 units	90	1 sale of 30 units	80
		1 sale of 50 units	

(3) The greatest number of units sold at a particular price is 80; therefore, the unit price in the greatest aggregate quantity is 90.

As another illustration of this, two sales occur. In the first sale 500 units are sold at a price of 95 currency units each. In the second sale 400 units are sold at a price of 90 currency units each. In this illustration, the greatest number of units sold at a particular price is 500; therefore, the unit price in the greatest aggregate quantity is 95.

(4) Any sale to a person who supplies, directly or indirectly, free of charge or at reduced cost for use in connection with the production of the material, any of the elements specified in paragraph 4(1)(b), must not be taken into account in establishing the unit price for the purposes of this section.

(5) The amount generally reflected for profit and general expenses referred to in paragraph (1)(a) must be taken as a whole. The figure for the purpose of deducting

371

an amount for profit and general expenses must be determined on the basis of information supplied by or on behalf of the producer unless the figures provided by the producer are inconsistent with those usually reflected in sales, in the country in which the producer is located, of materials of the same class or kind as the material being valued. If the figures provided by the producer are inconsistent with those figures, the amount for profit and general expenses must be based on relevant information other than that supplied by or on behalf of the producer.

(6) For the purposes of this section, general expenses are the direct and indirect costs of marketing the material in question.

(7) In determining either the commissions usually earned or the amount generally reflected for profit and general expenses under this section, the question as to whether certain materials are materials of the same class or kind as the material being valued must be determined on a case-by-case basis with reference to the circumstances involved. Sales in the country in which the producer is located of the narrowest group or range of materials of the same class or kind as the material being valued, for which the necessary information can be provided, must be examined. For the purposes of this section, "materials of the same class or kind" includes materials imported from the same country as the material being valued as well as materials imported from other countries or acquired within the territory of the USMCA country in which the producer is located.

(8) For the purposes of subsection (2), the earliest date is the date by which sales of identical materials or similar materials are made, in sufficient quantity to establish the unit price, to other persons in the territory of the USMCA country in which the producer is located.

9(1) Under this section, the value of a material, referred to in subparagraph 8(1)(b)(ii) of Part IV of these Regulations, is the sum of:

    (a) the cost or value of the materials used in the production of the material being valued, as determined on the basis of the costs that are recorded on the books of the producer of the material,

    (b) the cost of producing the material being valued, as determined on the basis of the costs that are recorded on the books of the producer of the material, and

    (c) an amount for profit and general expenses equal to that usually reflected in sales

        (i) where the material being valued is imported by the producer into the territory of the USMCA country in which the producer is located, to persons located in the territory of the USMCA country in which the producer is located by producers of materials of the same class or kind as the material being valued who are located in the country in which the material is produced, and

        (ii) where the material being valued is acquired by the producer from another person located in the territory of the USMCA country in which the producer is located, to persons located in the territory of the USMCA country in which the producer is located by producers of materials of the same class or kind as the material being valued who are located in the country in which the producer is located,

(2) This value of a material, to the extent it is not are not already included under paragraph (a) or (b) must include the following costs and where the elements are supplied directly or indirectly to the producer of the material being valued by the producer free of charge or at a reduced cost for use in the production of that material,

    (a) the value of elements referred to in subparagraph 4(1)(b)(i), determined in accordance with subsections 4(6) and (7), and

    (b) the value of elements referred to in subparagraphs 4(1)(b)(ii) through (iv), determined in accordance with subsection 4(8) and reasonably allocated to the material in accordance with subsection 4(12).

(3) For purposes of paragraphs (1)(a) and (b), if the costs recorded on the books of the producer of the material relate to the production of other goods and materials as well as to the production of the material being valued, the costs referred to in paragraphs (1)(a) and (b) with respect to the material being valued must be those costs recorded on the books of the producer of the material that can be reasonably allocated to that material in accordance with Schedule V.

(4) The amount for profit and general expenses referred to in paragraph (1)(c) must be determined on the basis of information supplied by or on behalf of the producer of the material being valued unless the profit and general expenses figures that are supplied with that information are inconsistent with those usually reflected in sales by producers of materials of the same class or kind as the material being valued who are located in the country in which the material is produced or the producer is located, as the case may be. The information supplied must be prepared in a manner consistent with generally accepted accounting principles of the country in which the material being valued is produced. If the material is produced in the territory of a USMCA country, the information must be prepared in accordance with the Generally Accepted Accounting Principles set out in the authorities listed for that USMCA country in Schedule X.

(5) For purposes of paragraph (1)(c) and subsection (4), general expenses means the direct and indirect costs of producing and selling the material that are not included under paragraphs (1)(a) and (b).

(6) For purposes of subsection (4), the amount for profit and general expenses must be taken as a whole. If, in the information supplied by or on behalf of the producer of a material, the profit figure is low and the general expenses figure is high, the profit and general expense figures taken together may nevertheless be consistent with those usually reflected in sales of materials of the same class or kind as the material being valued. If the producer of a material can demonstrate that it is taking a nil or low profit on its sales of the material because of particular commercial circumstances, its actual profit and general expense figures must be taken into account, provided that the producer of the material has valid commercial reasons to justify them and its pricing policy reflects usual pricing policies in the branch of industry concerned. For an illustration of this, such a situation might occur if producers have been forced to lower prices temporarily because of an unforeseeable drop in demand, or if the producers sell the material to complement a range of materials and goods being produced in the country in which the material is sold and accept a low profit to maintain competitiveness. A further illustration is if a material was being launched and the producer accepted a nil or low profit to offset high general expenses associated with the launch.

(7) If the figures for the profit and general expenses supplied by or on behalf of the producer of the material are not consistent with those usually reflected in sales of materials of the same class or kind as the material being valued that are made by other producers in the country in which that material is sold, the amount for profit and general expenses may be based on relevant information other than that supplied by or on behalf of the producer of the material.

(8) Whether certain materials are of the same class or kind as the material being valued will be determined on a case-by-case basis with reference to the circumstances involved. For purposes of determining the amount for profit and general expenses usually reflected under the provisions of this section, sales of the narrowest group or range of materials of the same class or kind, which includes the material being valued, for which the necessary information can be provided, shall be examined. For the purposes of this section, the materials of the same class or kind must be from the same country as the material being valued.

10(1) If there is no transaction value under subsection 2(2) or the transaction value is unacceptable under subsection 2(3), and the value of the material cannot be determined under sections 5 through 9, the value of the material, referred to in subparagraph 8(1)(b)(ii) of Part IV of these Regulations, must be determined under this section using reasonable means consistent with the principles and general provisions of this Schedule and on the basis of data available in the country in which the producer is located.

(2) The value of the material determined under this section must not be determined on the basis of

(a) a valuation system which provides for the acceptance of the higher of two alternative values;

(b) a cost of production other than the value determined in accordance with section 10;

(c) minimum values;

(d) arbitrary or fictitious values;

(e) if the material is produced in the territory of the USMCA country in which the producer is located, the price of the material for export from that territory; or

(f) if the material is imported, the price of the material for export to a country other than to the territory of the USMCA country in which the producer is located.

(3) To the greatest extent possible, the value of the material determined under this section must be based on the methods of valuation set out in sections 2 through 9, but a reasonable flexibility in the application of such methods would be in conformity with the aims and provisions of this section. For an illustration of this, under section 5, the requirement that the identical materials should be sold at or about the same time as the time the material being valued is shipped to the producer could be flexibly interpreted. Similarly, identical materials produced in a country other than the country in which the material is produced could be the basis for determining the value of the material, or the value of identical materials already determined under section 8 could be used. For another illustration, under section 6, the requirement that the similar materials should be sold at or about the same time as the material being valued are shipped to the producer could be flexibly interpreted. Likewise, similar materials produced in a country other than the country in which the material is produced could be the basis for determining the value of the material, or the value of similar materials already determined under the provisions of section 8 could be used. For a further illustration, under section 9, the ninety days requirement could be administered flexibly.

SCHEDULE VII (Methods for Determining the Value of Non-Originating Materials that are Identical Materials and that are used in the Production of a Good)

Definitions

1 The following definitions apply in this Schedule.

FIFO method means the method by which the value of non-originating materials first received in materials inventory, determined in accordance with section 8 of these Regulations, is considered to be the value of non-originating materials used in the production of the good first shipped to the buyer of the good;

identical materials means, with respect to a material, materials that are the same as that material in all respects, including physical characteristics, quality and reputation but excluding minor differences in appearance;

LIFO method means the method by which the value of non-originating materials last received in materials inventory, determined in accordance with section 8 of these Regulations, is considered to be the value of non-originating materials used in the production of the good first shipped to the buyer of the good;

materials inventory means, with respect to a single plant of the producer of a good, an inventory of non-originating materials that are identical materials and that are used in the production of the good;

rolling average method means the method by which the value of non-originating materials used in the production of a good that is shipped to the buyer of the good is based on the average value, calculated in accordance with section 4, of the non-originating materials in materials inventory.

General

2 For purposes of subsections 5(13) and (14) and 7(10) of these Regulations, the following are the methods for determining the value of non-originating materials that are identical materials and are used in the production of a good:
(a) FIFO method;
(b) LIFO method; and
(c) rolling average method.

3(1) If a producer of a good chooses, with respect to non-originating materials that are identical materials, any of the methods referred to in section 2, the producer may not use another of those methods with respect to any other non-originating materials that are identical materials and that are used in the production of that good or in the production of any other good.

(2) If a producer of a good produces the good in more than one plant, the method chosen by the producer must be used with respect to all plants of the producer in which the good is produced.

(3) The method chosen by the producer to determine the value of non-originating materials may be chosen at any time during the producer's fiscal year and may not be changed during that fiscal year.

Average Value for Rolling Average Method

4(1) The average value of non-originating materials that are identical materials and that are used in the production of a good that is shipped to the buyer of the good is calculated by dividing:
(a) the total value of non-originating materials that are identical materials in materials inventory prior to the shipment of the good, determined in accordance with section 8 of these Regulations,
by
(b) the total units of those non-originating materials in materials inventory prior to the shipment of the good.

(2) The average value calculated under subsection (1) is applied to the remaining units of non- originating materials in materials inventory.

APPENDIX "Examples" Illustrating the Application of the Methods for Determining the Value of Non-Originating Materials That Are Identical Materials and That Are Used in the Production of a Good

The following examples are based on the figures set out in the table below and on the following assumptions:

(a) Materials A are non-originating materials that are identical materials that are used in the production of Good A;

(b) one unit of Materials A is used to produce one unit of Good A;

(c) all other materials used in the production of Good A are originating materials; and

(d) Good A is produced in a single plant.

MATERIALS INVENTORY			SALES
(RECEIPTS OF MATERIALS A)			(SHIPMENTS OF GOOD A)
DATE	QUANTITY		
(M/D/Y)	(UNITS)	UNIT COST ($)*	QUANTITY (UNITS)
01/01/21	200	1.05	
01/03/21	1,000	1.00	
01/05/21	1,000	1.10	
01/08/21			500
01/09/21			500
01/10/21	1,000	1.05	
01/14/21			1,500
01/16/21	2,000	1.10	
01/18/21			1,500

* Unit cost is determined in accordance with section 8 of these Regulations

Example 1: FIFO method

By applying the FIFO method:

(1) *the 200 units of Materials A received on 01/01/921and valued at $1.05 per unit and 300 units of the 1,000 units of Material A received on 01/03/21 and valued at $1.00 per unit are considered to have been used in the production of the 500 units of Good A shipped on 01/08/21; therefore, the value of the non-originating materials used in the production of those goods is considered to be $510 [(200 units × $1.05) + (300 units × $1.00)];*

(2) *500 units of the remaining 700 units of Materials A received on 01/03/21 and valued at $1.00 per unit are considered to have been used in the production of the 500 units of Good A shipped on 01/09/21; therefore, the value of the non-originating materials used in the production of those goods is considered to be $500 (500 units × $1.00);*

(3) *the remaining 200 units of the 1,000 units of Materials A received on 01/03/21 and valued at $1.00 per unit, the 1,000 units of Materials A received on 01/05/21 and valued at $1.10 per unit, and 300 units of the 1,000 units of Materials A received on 01/10/21 and valued at $1.05 per unit are considered to have been used in the production of the 1,500 units of Good A shipped on 01/14/21; therefore, the value of*

non-originating materials used in the production of those goods is considered to be $1,615 [(200 units × $1.00) + (1,000 units × $1.10) + (300 units x $1.05)]; and

(4) *the remaining 700 units of the 1,000 units of Materials A received on 01/10/21 and valued at $1.05 per unit and 800 units of the 2,000 units of Materials A received on 01/16/21 and valued at $1.10 per unit are considered to have been used in the production of the 1,500 units of Good A shipped on 01/18/21; therefore, the value of non-originating materials used in the production of those goods is considered to be $1,615 [(700 units × $1.05) + (800 units x $1.10)].*

Example 2: LIFO method

By applying the LIFO method:

(1) *500 units of the 1,000 units of Materials A received on 01/05/21 and valued at $1.10 per unit are considered to have been used in the production of the 500 units of Good A shipped on 01/08/21; therefore, the value of the non-originating materials used in the production of those goods is considered to be $550 (500 units × $1.10);*

(2) *the remaining 500 units of the 1,000 units of Materials A received on 01/05/21 and valued at $1.10 per unit are considered to have been used in the production of the 500 units of Good A shipped on 01/09/21; therefore, the value of non-originating materials used in the production of those goods is considered to be $550 (500 units × $1.10);*

(3) *the 1,000 units of Materials A received on 01/10/21 and valued at $1.05 per unit and 500 units of the 1,000 units of Material A received on 01/03/21 and valued at $1.00 per unit are considered to have been used in the production of the 1,500 units of Good A shipped on 01/14/21; therefore, the value of non-originating materials used in the production of those goods is considered to be $1,550 [(1,000 units × $1.05) + (500 units × $1.00)]; and*

(4) *1,500 units of the 2,000 units of Materials A received on 01/16/21 and valued at $1.10 per unit are considered to have been used in the production of the 1,500 units of Good A shipped on 01/18/21; therefore, the value of non-originating materials used in the production of those goods is considered to be $1,650 (1,500 units × $1.10).*

Example 3: Rolling average method

The following table identifies the average value of non-originating Materials A as determined under the rolling average method. For purposes of this example, a new average value of non-originating Materials A is calculated after each receipt.

MATERIALS INVENTORY	DATE (M/D/Y)	QUANTITY	UNIT COST*	TOTAL VALUE
		(UNITS)	*($)*	*($)*
Beginning Inventory	01/01/21	200	1.05	210
Receipt	01/03/21	1,000	1.00	1,000
AVERAGE VALUE		1,200	1.008	1,210
Receipt	01/05/21	1,000	1.10	1,100
AVERAGE VALUE		2,200	1.05	2,310

377

Appendix

MATERIALS INVENTORY	DATE (M/D/Y)	QUANTITY	UNIT COST*	TOTAL VALUE
		(UNITS)	($)	($)
Shipment	01/08/21	500	1.05	525
AVERAGE VALUE		1,700	1.05	1,785
Shipment	01/09/21	500	1.05	525
AVERAGE VALUE		1,200	1.05	1,260
Receipt	01/16/21	2,000	1.10	2,200
AVERAGE VALUE		3,200	1.08	3,460

* unit cost is determined in accordance with section 8 of these Regulations By applying the rolling average method:

(1) the value of non-originating materials used in the production of the 500 units of Good A shipped on 01/08/21 is considered to be $525 (500 units × $1.05); and

(2) the value of non-originating materials used in the production of the 500 units of Good A shipped on 01/09/21 is considered to be $525 (500 units × $1.05).

SCHEDULE VIII (Inventory Management Methods) PART I Fungible Materials

Definitions

1 The following definitions apply in this Part,

average method means the method by which the origin of fungible materials withdrawn from materials inventory is based on the ratio, calculated under section 5, of originating materials and non-originating materials in materials inventory;

FIFO method means the method by which the origin of fungible materials first received in materials inventory is considered to be the origin of fungible materials first withdrawn from materials inventory;

LIFO method means the method by which the origin of fungible materials last received in materials inventory is considered to be the origin of fungible materials first withdrawn from materials inventory;

materials inventory means,

    (a) with respect to a producer of a good, an inventory of fungible materials that are used in the production of the good, and

    (b) with respect to a person from whom the producer of the good acquired those fungible materials, an inventory from which fungible materials are sold or otherwise transferred to the producer of the good;

opening inventory means the materials inventory at the time an inventory management method is chosen;

origin identifier means any mark that identifies fungible materials as originating materials or non-originating materials.

378

General

2 The following inventory management methods may be used for determining whether fungible materials referred to in paragraph 8(18)(a) of these Regulations:

    (a) specific identification method;
    (b) FIFO method;
    (c) LIFO method; and
    (d) average method.

3 A producer of a good, or a person from whom the producer acquired the fungible materials that are used in the production of the good, may choose only one of the inventory management methods referred to in section 2, and, if the averaging method is chosen, only one averaging period in each fiscal year of that producer or person for the materials inventory.

Specific Identification Method

4(1) Except as otherwise provided under subsection (2), if the producer or person referred to in section 3 chooses the specific identification method, the producer or person must physically segregate, in materials inventory, originating materials that are fungible materials from non-originating materials that are fungible materials.

  (2) If originating materials or non-originating materials that are fungible materials are marked with an origin identifier, the producer or person need not physically segregate those materials under subsection (1) if the origin identifier remains visible throughout the production of the good.

Average Method

   5 If the producer or person referred to in section 3 chooses the average method, the origin of fungible materials withdrawn from materials inventory is determined on the basis of the ratio of originating materials and non-originating materials in materials inventory that is calculated under sections 6 through 8.

6(1) Except as otherwise provided in sections 7 and 8, the ratio is calculated with respect to a month or three-month period, at the choice of the producer or person, by dividing

    (a) the sum of
        (i) the total units of originating materials or non-originating materials that are fungible materials and that were in materials inventory at the beginning of the preceding one-month or three-month period, and
        (ii) the total units of originating materials or non-originating materials that are fungible materials and that were received in materials inventory during that preceding one-month or three-month period,

    by

    (b) the sum of
        (i) the total units of originating materials and non-originating materials that are fungible materials and that were in materials inventory at the beginning of the preceding one-month or three-month period, and
        (ii) the total units of originating materials and non-originating materials that are fungible materials and that were received in materials inventory during that preceding one-month or three-month period.

  (2) The ratio calculated with respect to a preceding month or three-month period under subsection (1) is applied to the fungible materials remaining in materials inventory at the end of the preceding month or three-month period.

7(1) If the good is subject to a regional value-content requirement and the regional value content is calculated under the net cost method and the producer or person chooses to average over a period under subsections 7(15), 16(1), (3) or (9) of these Regulations, the ratio is calculated with respect to that period by dividing
  (a) the sum of
      (i) the total units of originating materials or non-originating materials that are fungible materials and that were in materials inventory at the beginning of the period, and
      (ii) the total units of originating materials or non-originating materials that are fungible materials and that were received in materials inventory during that period,

  by
  (b) the sum of
      (i) the total units of originating materials and non-originating materials that are fungible materials and that were in materials inventory at the beginning of the period, and
      (ii) the total units of originating materials and non-originating materials that are fungible materials and that were received in materials inventory during that period.
  (2) The ratio calculated with respect to a period under subsection (1) is applied to the fungible materials remaining in materials inventory at the end of the period.
8(1) If the good is subject to a regional value-content requirement and the regional value content of that good is calculated under the transaction value method or the net cost method, the ratio is calculated with respect to each shipment of the good by dividing
  (a) the total units of originating materials or non-originating materials that are fungible materials and that were in materials inventory prior to the shipment,

  by
  (b) the total units of originating materials and non-originating materials that are fungible materials and that were in materials inventory prior to the shipment.
  (2) The ratio calculated with respect to a shipment of a good under subsection (1) is applied to the fungible materials remaining in materials inventory after the shipment.

Manner of Dealing with Opening Inventory

9(1) Except as otherwise provided under subsections (2) and (3), if the producer or person referred to in section 3 has fungible materials in opening inventory, the origin of those fungible materials is determined by
  (a) identifying, in the books of the producer or person, the latest receipts of fungible materials that add up to the amount of fungible materials in opening inventory;
  (b) determining the origin of the fungible materials that make up those receipts; and
  (c) considering the origin of those fungible materials to be the origin of the fungible materials in opening inventory.
  (2) If the producer or person chooses the specific identification method and has, in opening inventory, originating materials or non-originating materials that are fungible materials and that are marked with an origin identifier, the origin of those fungible materials is determined on the basis of the origin identifier.
  (3) The producer or person may consider all fungible materials in opening inventory to be non- originating materials.

PART II Fungible Goods

Definitions

10 The following definitions apply in this Part,

average method means the method by which the origin of fungible goods withdrawn from finished goods inventory is based on the ratio, calculated under section 14, of originating goods and non-originating goods in finished goods inventory;

FIFO method means the method by which the origin of fungible goods first received in finished goods inventory is considered to be the origin of fungible goods first withdrawn from finished goods inventory;

finished goods inventory means an inventory from which fungible goods are sold or otherwise transferred to another person;

LIFO method means the method by which the origin of fungible goods last received in finished goods inventory is considered to be the origin of fungible goods first withdrawn from finished goods inventory;

opening inventory means the finished goods inventory at the time an inventory management method is chosen;

origin identifier means any mark that identifies fungible goods as originating goods or non-originating goods.

General

11 The following inventory management methods may be used for determining whether fungible goods referred to in paragraph 8(18)(b) of these Regulations are originating goods:

      (a) specific identification method;
      (b) FIFO method;
      (c) LIFO method; and
      (d) average method.

12 An exporter of a good, or a person from whom the exporter acquired the fungible good, may choose only one of the inventory management methods referred to in section 11, including only one averaging period in the case of the average method, in each fiscal year of that exporter or person for each finished goods inventory of the exporter or person.

Specific Identification Method

    13(1) Except as provided under subsection (2), if the exporter or person referred to in section 12 chooses the specific identification method, the exporter or person must physically segregate, in finished goods inventory, originating goods that are fungible goods from non-originating goods that are fungible goods.
       (2) If originating goods or non-originating goods that are fungible goods are marked with an origin identifier, the exporter or person need not physically segregate those goods under subsection (1) if the origin identifier is visible on the fungible goods.

Average Method

14(1) If the exporter or person referred to in section 12 chooses the average method, the origin of each shipment of fungible goods withdrawn from finished goods inventory during a month or three-month period, at the choice of the exporter or person, is determined on the basis of the ratio of originating goods and non-originating goods in finished goods inventory for the preceding one-month or three-month period that is calculated by dividing
(a) the sum of
(i) the total units of originating goods or non-originating goods that are fungible goods and that were in finished goods inventory at the beginning of the preceding one-month or three-month period, and
(ii) the total units of originating goods or non-originating goods that are fungible goods and that were received in finished goods inventory during that preceding one-month or three-month period,

by
(b) the sum of
(i) the total units of originating goods and non-originating goods that are fungible goods and that were in finished goods inventory at the beginning of the preceding one-month or three-month period, and
(ii) the total units of originating goods and non-originating goods that are fungible goods and that were received in finished goods inventory during that preceding one-month or three-month period.
(2) The ratio calculated with respect to a preceding month or three-month period under subsection (1) is applied to the fungible goods remaining in finished goods inventory at the end of the preceding month or three-month period.

Manner of Dealing with Opening Inventory

15(1) Except as otherwise provided under subsections (2) and (3), if the exporter or person referred to in section 12 has fungible goods in opening inventory, the origin of those fungible goods is determined by
(a) identifying, in the books of the exporter or person, the latest receipts of fungible goods that add up to the amount of fungible goods in opening inventory;
(b) determining the origin of the fungible goods that make up those receipts; and
(c) considering the origin of those fungible goods to be the origin of the fungible goods in opening inventory.
(2) If the exporter or person chooses the specific identification method and has, in opening inventory, originating goods or non-originating goods that are fungible goods and that are marked with an origin identifier, the origin of those fungible goods is determined on the basis of the origin identifier.
(3) The exporter or person may consider all fungible goods in opening inventory to be non- originating goods.

APPENDIX A

"Examples" Illustrating the Application of the Inventory Management Methods to Determine the Origin of Fungible Materials

The following examples are based on the figures set out in the table below and on the following assumptions:

(a) *originating Material A and non-originating Material A that are fungible materials are used in the production of Good A;*
(b) *one unit of Material A is used to produce one unit of Good A;*
(c) *Material A is only used in the production of Good A;*
(d) *all other materials used in the production of Good A are originating materials; and*
(e) *the producer of Good A exports all shipments of Good A to the territory of a USMCA country.*

| | MATERIALS INVENTORY | | | SALES |
| | (RECEIPTS OF MATERIAL A) | | | (SHIPMENTS OF GOOD A) |
DATE (M/D/Y)	QUANTITY (UNITS)	UNIT COST*	TOTAL VALUE	QUANTITY (UNITS)
12/18/20	100 (O1)	$1.00	$ 100	
12/27/20	100 (N2)	1.10	110	
01/01/21	200 (OI3)			
01/01/21	1,000 (O)	1.00	1,000	
01/05/21	1,000 (N)	1.10	1,100	
01/10/21				100
01/10/21	1,000 (O)	1.05	1,050	
01/15/21				700
01/16/21	2,000 (N)	1.10	2,200	
01/20/21				1,000
01/23/21				900

* unit cost is determined in accordance with section 8 of these Regulations

1 "O" denotes originating materials

2 "N" denotes non-originating materials

3 "OI" denotes opening inventory

Example 1: FIFO method

Good A is subject to a regional value-content requirement. Producer A is using the transaction value method to determine the regional value content of Good A.

By applying the FIFO method:

(1) the 100 units of originating Material A in opening inventory that were received in materials inventory on 12/18/20 are considered to have been used in the production of the 100 units of Good A shipped on 01/10/21; therefore, the value of non-originating materials used in the production of those goods is considered to be $0;
(2) the 100 units of non-originating Material A in opening inventory that were received in materials inventory on 12/27/20 and 600 units of the 1,000 units of originating Material A that were received in materials inventory on 01/01/21 are considered to have been used in the production of the 700 units of Good A shipped on 01/15/21;

therefore, the value of non-originating materials used in the production of those goods is considered to be $110 (100 units × $1.10);

(3) the remaining 400 units of the 1,000 units of originating Material A that were received in materials inventory on 01/01/21 and 600 units of the 1,000 units of non-originating Material A that were received in materials inventory on 01/05/21 are considered to have been used in the production of the 1,000 units of Good A shipped on 01/20/21; therefore, the value of non-originating materials used in the production of those goods is considered to be $660 (600 units × $1.10); and

(4) the remaining 400 units of the 1,000 units of non-originating Material A that were received in materials inventory on 01/05/21 and 500 units of the 1,000 units of originating Material A that were received in materials inventory on 01/10/21 are considered to have been used in the production of the 900 units of Good A shipped on 01/23/21; therefore, the value of non- originating materials used in the production of those goods is considered to be $440 (400 units × $1.10).

Example 2: LIFO method

Good A is subject to a change in tariff classification requirement and the non-originating Material A used in the production of Good A does not undergo the applicable change in tariff classification. Therefore, if originating Material A is used in the production of Good A, Good A is an originating good and, if non-originating Material A is used in the production of Good A, Good A is a non-originating good.

By applying the LIFO method:

(1) *100 units of the 1,000 units of non-originating Material A that were received in materials inventory on 01/05/21 are considered to have been used in the production of the 100 units of Good A shipped on 01/10/21;*

(2) *700 units of the 1,000 units of originating Material A that were received in materials inventory on 01/10/21 are considered to have been used in the production of the 700 units of Good A shipped on 01/15/21;*

(3) *1,000 units of the 2,000 units of non-originating Material A that were received in materials inventory on 01/16/21 are considered to have been used in the production of the 1,000 units of Good A shipped on 01/20/21; and*

(4) *900 units of the remaining 1,000 units of non-originating Material A that were received in materials inventory on 01/16/21 are considered to have been used in the production of the 900 units of Good A shipped on 01/23/21.*

Example 3: Average method

Good A is subject to an applicable regional value-content requirement. Producer A is using the transaction value method to determine the regional value content of Good A. Producer A determines the average value of non-originating Material A and the ratio of originating Material A to total value of originating Material A and non-originating Material A in the following table.

	DATE (M/D/Y)	MATERIAL INVENTORY (RECEIPTS OF MATERIAL A) QUANTITY (UNITS)	TOTAL VALUE	UNIT COST*	(NON-ORIGINATING MATERIAL) QUANTITY (UNITS)	TOTAL VALUE	RATIO	SALES (SHIPMENTS OF GOOD A) QUANTITY (UNITS)
Receipt	12/18/20	100 (O1)	$ 100	$1.00				
Receipt	12/27/20	100 (N2)	110	1.10	100	$ 110.00		
NEW AVG INV VALUE		200 (OI3)	210	1.05	100	105.00	0.50	
Receipt	01/01/21	1,000 (O)	1,000	1.00				
NEW AVG INV VALUE		1,200	1,210	1.01	100	101.00	0.08	
Receipt	01/05/21	1,000 (N)	1,100	1.10	1,000	1,100.00		
NEW AVG INV VALUE		2,200	2,310	1.05	1,100	1,155.00	0.50	
Shipment	01/10/21	(100)	(105)	1.05	(50)	(52.50)		100
Receipt	01/10/21	1,000 (O)	1,050	1.05				
NEW AVG INV VALUE		3,100	3,255	1.05	1,050	1,102.50	0.34	
Shipment	01/15/21	(700)	(735)	1.05	(238)	(249.90)		700
Receipt	01/16/21	2,000 (N)	2,200	1.10	2,000	2,200.00		
NEW AVG INV VALUE		4,400	4,720	1.07	2,812	3,008.84	0.64	
Shipment	01/20/21	(1,000)	(1,070)	1.07	(640)	(684.80)		1,000
Shipment	01/23/21	(900)	(963)	1.07	(576)	(616.32)		900
NEW AVG INV VALUE		2,500	2,687	1.07	1,596	1,707.24	0.64	

* unit cost is determined in accordance with section 8 of these Regulations
1 "O" denotes originating materials
2 "N" denotes non-originating materials
3 "OI" denotes opening inventory

Appendix

By applying the average method:

(1) *before the shipment of the 100 units of Material A on 01/10/21, the ratio of units of originating Material A to total units of Material A in materials inventory was .50 (1,100 units/2,200 units) and the ratio of units of non-originating Material A to total units of Material A in materials inventory was .50 (1,100 units/2,200 units);*

based on those ratios, 50 units (100 units × .50) of originating Material A and 50 units (100 units × .50) of non-originating Material A are considered to have been used in the production of the 100 units of Good A shipped on 01/10/21; therefore, the value of non-originating Material A used in the production of those goods is considered to be $52.50 [100 units × $1.05 (average unit value) × .50];

the ratios are applied to the units of Material A remaining in materials inventory after the shipment: 1,050 units (2,100 units × .50) are considered to be originating materials and 1,050 units (2,100 units × .50) are considered to be non-originating materials;

(2) *before the shipment of the 700 units of Good A on 01/15/21, the ratio of units of originating Material A to total units of Material A in materials inventory was 66% (2,050 units/3,100 units) and the ratio of units of non-originating Material A to total units of Material A in materials inventory was 34% (1,050 units/3,100 units);*

based on those ratios, 462 units (700 units × .66) of originating Material A and 238 units (700 units × .34) of non-originating Material A are considered to have been used in the production of the 700 units of Good A shipped on 01/15/21; therefore, the value of non-originating Material A used in the production of those goods is considered to be $249.90 [700 units × $1.05 (average unit value) × 34%];

the ratios are applied to the units of Material A remaining in materials inventory after the shipment: 1,584 units (2,400 units × .66) are considered to be originating materials and 816 units (2,400 units × .34) are considered to be non-originating materials;

(3) *before the shipment of the 1,000 units of Material A on 01/20/21, the ratio of units of originating Material A to total units of Material A in materials inventory was 36% (1,584 units/4,400 units) and the ratio of units of non-originating Material A to total units of Material A in materials inventory was 64% (2,816 units/4,400 units);*

based on those ratios, 360 units (1,000 units × .36) of originating Material A and 640 units (1,000 units × .64) of non-originating Material A are considered to have been used in the production of the 1,000 units of Good A shipped on 01/20/21; therefore, the value of non- originating Material A used in the production of those goods is considered to be $684.80 [1,000 units × $1.07 (average unit value) × 64%];

those ratios are applied to the units of Material A remaining in materials inventory after the shipment: 1,224 units (3,400 units × .36) are considered to be originating materials and 2,176 units (3,400 units × .64) are considered to be non-originating materials;

(4) *before the shipment of the 900 units of Good A on 01/23/21, the ratio of units of originating Material A to total units of Material A in materials inventory was 36% (1,224 units/3,400 units) and the ratio of units of non-originating Material A to total units of Material A in materials inventory was 64% (2,176 units/3,400 units);*

based on those ratios, 324 units (900 units × .36) of originating Material A and 576 units (900 units × .64) of non-originating Material A are considered to have been used in the production of the 900 units of Good A shipped on 01/23/21; therefore, the value of non-originating Material A used in the production of those goods is considered to be $616.32 [900 units × $1.07 (average unit value) × 64%];

those ratios are applied to the units of Material A remaining in materials inventory after the shipment: 900 units (2,500 units × .36) are considered to be originating materials and 1,600 units (2,500 units × .64) are considered to be non-originating materials.

Example 4: Average method

Good A is subject to an applicable regional value-content requirement. Producer A is using the net cost method and is averaging over a period of one month under paragraph 7(15)(a) of these Regulations to determine the regional value content of Good A.

By applying the average method:

the ratio of units of originating Material A to total units of Material A in materials inventory for January 2021 is 40.4% (2,100 units/5,200 units);

based on that ratio, 1,091 units (2,700 units × .404) of originating Material A and 1,609 units (2,700 units – 1,091 units) of non-originating Material A are considered to have been used in the production of the 2,700 units of Good A shipped in January 2021; therefore, the value of non- originating materials used in the production of those goods is considered to be $0.64 per unit [$5,560 (total value of Material A in materials inventory)/5,200 (units of Material A in materials inventory) = $1.07 (average unit value) × (1 – .404)] or $1,728 ($0.64 × 2,700 units); and

that ratio is applied to the units of Material A remaining in materials inventory on January 31, 2021: 1,010 units (2,500 units × .404) are considered to be originating materials and 1,490 units (2,500 units – 1,010 units) are considered to be non-originating materials.

APPENDIX B

"Examples" Illustrating the Application of the Inventory Management Methods to Determine the Origin of Fungible Goods

The following examples are based on the figures set out in the table below and on the assumption that Exporter A acquires originating Good A and non-originating Good A that are fungible goods and physically combines or mixes Good A before exporting those goods to the buyer of those goods.

FINISHED GOODS INVENTORY		SALES
(RECEIPTS OF GOOD A)		(SHIPMENTS OF GOOD A)
DATE	QUANTITY	QUANTITY
(M/D/Y)	*(UNITS)*	*(UNITS)*
12/18/20	*100 (O1)*	
12/27/20	*100 (N2)*	
01/01/21	*200 (OI3)*	
01/01/21	*1,000 (O)*	
01/05/21	*1,000 (N)*	
01/10/21		*100*
01/10/21	*1,000 (O)*	
01/15/21		*700*
01/16/21	*2,000 (N)*	
01/20/21		*1,000*

FINISHED GOODS INVENTORY		SALES
(RECEIPTS OF GOOD A)		(SHIPMENTS OF GOOD A)
DATE	QUANTITY	QUANTITY
(M/D/Y)	*(UNITS)*	*(UNITS)*
01/23/21		*900*

1 "O" denotes originating goods

2 "N" denotes non-originating goods

3 "OI" denotes opening inventory

Example 1: FIFO method

By applying the FIFO method:

(1) *the 100 units of originating Good A in opening inventory that were received in finished goods inventory on 12/18/20 are considered to be the 100 units of Good A shipped on 01/10/21;*

(2) *the 100 units of non-originating Good A in opening inventory that were received in finished goods inventory on 12/27/20 and 600 units of the 1,000 units of originating Good A that were received in finished goods inventory on 01/01/21 are considered to be the 700 units of Good A shipped on 01/15/21;*

(3) *the remaining 400 units of the 1,000 units of originating Good A that were received in finished goods inventory on 01/01/21 and 600 units of the 1,000 units of non-originating Good A that were received in finished goods inventory on 01/05/21 are considered to be the 1,000 units of Good A shipped on 01/20/21; and*

(4) *the remaining 400 units of the 1,000 units of non-originating Good A that were received in finished goods inventory on 01/05/21 and 500 units of the 1,000 units of originating Good A that were received in finished goods inventory on 01/10/21 are considered to be the 900 units of Good A shipped on 01/23/21.*

Example 2: LIFO method

By applying the LIFO method:

(1) *100 units of the 1,000 units of non-originating Good A that were received in finished goods inventory on 01/05/21 are considered to be the 100 units of Good A shipped on 01/10/21;*

(2) *700 units of the 1,000 units of originating Good A that were received in finished goods inventory on 01/10/21 are considered to be the 700 units of Good A shipped on 01/15/21;*

(3) *1,000 units of the 2,000 units of non-originating Good A that were received in finished goods inventory on 01/16/21 are considered to be the 1,000 units of Good A shipped on 01/20/21; and*

(4) *900 units of the remaining 1,000 units of non-originating Good A that were received in finished goods inventory on 01/16/21 are considered to be the 900 units of Good A shipped on 01/23/21.*

Example 3: Average method

Exporter A chooses to determine the origin of Good A on a monthly basis. Exporter A exported 3,000 units of Good A during the month of February 2021. The origin of the units of Good A exported during that month is determined on the basis of the preceding month, that is January 2021.

> *By applying the average method:*

>> *the ratio of originating goods to all goods in finished goods inventory for the month of January 2021 is 40.4% (2,100 units/5,200 units);*
>> *based on that ratio, 1,212 units (3,000 units × .404) of Good A shipped in February 2021 are considered to be originating goods and 1,788 units (3,000 units − 1,212 units) of Good A are considered to be non-originating goods; and*
>> *that ratio is applied to the units of Good A remaining in finished goods inventory on January 31, 2021: 1,010 units (2,500 units × .404) are considered to be originating goods and 1,490 units (2,500 units − 1,010 units) are considered to be non-originating goods.*

SCHEDULE IX (Method for Calculating Non-Allowable Interest Costs)

Definitions and Interpretation

1 For purposes of this Schedule,

fixed-rate contract means a loan contract, instalment purchase contract or other financing agreement in which the interest rate remains constant throughout the life of the contract or agreement;

linear interpolation means, with respect to the yield on federal government debt obligations, the application of the following mathematical formula:

$$A + [((B - A) \times (E - D)) / (C - D)]$$

where

A is the yield on federal government debt obligations that are nearest in maturity but of shorter maturity than the weighted average principal maturity of the payment schedule under the fixed- rate contract or variable-rate contract to which they are being compared,

B is the yield on federal government debt obligations that are nearest in maturity but of greater maturity than the weighted average principal maturity of that payment schedule,

C is the maturity of federal government debt obligations that are nearest in maturity but of greater maturity than the weighted average principal maturity of that payment schedule,

D is the maturity of federal government debt obligations that are nearest in maturity but of shorter maturity than the weighted average principal maturity of that payment schedule, and

E is the weighted average principal maturity of that payment schedule;

payment schedule means the schedule of payments, whether on a weekly, bi-weekly, monthly, yearly or other basis, of principal and interest, or any combination thereof, made by a producer to a lender in accordance with the terms of a fixed-rate contract or variable-rate contract;

variable-rate contract means a loan contract, instalment purchase contract or other financing agreement in which the interest rate is adjusted at intervals during the life of the contract or agreement in accordance with its terms;

weighted average principal maturity means, with respect to fixed-rate contracts and variable-rate contracts, the numbers of years, or portion thereof, that is equal to the number obtained by

(a) dividing the sum of the weighted principal payments,
  (i) in the case of a fixed-rate contract, by the original amount of the loan, and
  (ii) in the case of a variable-rate contract, by the principal balance at the beginning of the interest rate period for which the weighted principal payments were calculated, and
(b) rounding the amount determined under paragraph (a) to the nearest single decimal place and, if that amount is the midpoint between two such numbers, to the greater of those two numbers;

weighted principal payment means,

(a) with respect to fixed-rate contracts, the amount determined by multiplying each principal payment under the contract by the number of years, or portion thereof, between the date the producer entered into the contract and the date of that principal payment, and
(b) with respect to variable-rate contracts
  (i) the amount determined by multiplying each principal payment made during the current interest rate period by the number of years, or portion thereof, between the beginning of that interest rate period and the date of that payment, and
  (ii) the amount equal to the outstanding principal owing, but not necessarily due, at the end of the current interest rate period, multiplied by the number of years, or portion thereof, between the beginning and the end of that interest rate period;

yield on federal government debt obligations means

(a) in the case of a producer located in Canada, the yield for federal government debt obligations set out in the Bank of Canada's *Daily Digest*
  (i) if the interest rate is adjusted at intervals of less than one year, under the title "Treasury Bills—1 Month", and
  (ii) in any other case, under the title "Government of Canada benchmark bond yields—3 Year", for the week that the producer entered into the contract or the week of the most recent interest rate adjustment date, if any, under the contract,
(b) in the case of a producer located in Mexico, the yield for federal government debt obligations set out in *La Seccion de Indicadores Monetarios, Financieros, y de Finanzas Publicas, de los Indicadores Economicos*, published by the Banco de Mexico under the title *"Certificados de la Tesoreria de la Federacion"* for the week that the producer entered into the contract or the week of the most recent interest rate adjustment date, if any, under the contract, and
(c) in the case of a producer located in the United States, the yield for federal government debt obligations set out in the Federal Reserve statistical release (H.15) *Selected Interest Rates*
  (i) if the interest rate is adjusted at intervals of less than one year, under the title "U.S. government securities, Treasury bills, Secondary market", and
  (ii) in any other case, under the title "U.S. Government Securities, Treasury constant maturities", for the week that the producer entered into the contract or the week of the most recent interest rate adjustment date, if any, under the contract.

General

2 For purposes of calculating non-allowable interest costs

(a) with respect to a fixed-rate contract, the interest rate under that contract must be compared with the yield on federal government debt obligations that have maturities of the same length as the weighted average principal maturity of the payment schedule under the contract (that yield determined by linear interpolation, if necessary);

(b) with respect to a variable-rate contract

(i) in which the interest rate is adjusted at intervals of less than or equal to one year, the interest rate under that contract must be compared with the yield on federal government debt obligations that have maturities closest in length to the interest rate adjustment period of the contract, and

(ii) in which the interest rate is adjusted at intervals of greater than one year, the interest rate under the contract must be compared with the yield on federal government debt obligations that have maturities of the same length as the weighted average principal maturity of the payment schedule under the contract (that yield determined by linear interpolation, if necessary); and

(c) with respect to a fixed-rate or variable-rate contract in which the weighted average principal maturity of the payment schedule under the contract is greater than the maturities offered on federal government debt obligations, the interest rate under the contract must be compared to the yield on federal government debt obligations that have maturities closest in length to the weighted average principal maturity of the payment schedule under the contract.

APPENDIX "Example" Illustrating the Application of the Method for Calculating Non-Allowable Interest Costs in the Case of a Fixed-Rate Contract

The following example is based on the figures set out in the table below and on the following assumptions:

(a) *a producer in a USMCA country borrows $1,000,000 from a person of the same USMCA country under a fixed-rate contract;*

(b) *under the terms of the contract, the loan is payable in 10 years with interest paid at the rate of 6 per cent per year on the declining principal balance;*

(c) *the payment schedule calculated by the lender based on the terms of the contract requires the producer to make annual payments of principal and interest of $135,867.36 over the life of the contract;*

(d) *there are no federal government debt obligations that have maturities equal to the 6-year weighted average principal maturity of the contract; and*

(e) *the federal government debt obligations that are nearest in maturity to the weighted average principal maturity of the contract are of 5- and 7-year maturities, and the yields on them are 4.7 per cent and 5.0 per cent, respectively.*

391

Appendix

Years of Loan	Principal Balance[1]	Interest Payment[2]	Principal Payment[3]	Payment Schedule	Weighted Principal Payment[4]
1	$924,132.04	$60,000.00	$ 75,867.96	$135,867.96	$ 75,867.96
2	843,712.00	55,447.92	80,420.04	135,867.96	160,840.08
3	758,466.76	50,622.72	85,245.24	135,867.96	255,735.72
4	668,106.81	45,508.01	90,359.95	135,867.96	361,439.82
5	572,325.26	40,086.41	95,781.55	135,867.96	478,907.76
6	470,796.81	34,339.52	101,528.44	135,867.96	609,170.67
7	363,176.66	28,247.81	107,620.15	135,867.96	753,341.06
8	249,099.30	21,790.60	114,077.36	135,867.96	912,618.88
9	128,177.30	14,945.96	120,922.00	135,867.96	1,088,298.02
10	(0.00)	7,690.66	128,177.32	135.867.96	1,281,773.22
					$5,977,993.19

[1] the principal balance represents the loan balance at the end of each full year the loan is in effect and is calculated by subtracting the current year's principal payment from the prior year's ending loan balance

[2] interest payments are calculated by multiplying the prior year's ending loan balance by the contract interest rate of 6 per cent

[3] principal payments are calculated by subtracting the current year's interest payments from the annual payment schedule amount

[4] the weighted principal payment is determined by, for each year of the loan, multiplying that year's principal payment by the number of years the loan had been in effect at the end of that year

[5] the weighted average principal maturity of the contract is calculated by dividing the sum of the weighted principal payments by the original loan amount and rounding the amount determined to the nearest decimal place

Weighted Average Principal Maturity

$5,977,993.19 / $1,000,000 = 5.977993 or 6 years5

By applying the above method,

(1) the weighted average principal maturity of the payment schedule under the 6 per cent contract is 6 years;

(2) the yields on the closest maturities for comparable federal government debt obligations of 5 years and 7 years are 4.7 per cent and 5.0 per cent, respectively; therefore, using linear interpolation, the yield on a federal government debt obligation that has a maturity equal to the weighted average principal maturity of the contract is 4.85 per cent. This number is calculated as follows:

$$4.7 + [((5.0 - 4.7) \times (6 - 5)) / (7 - 5)]$$
$$= 4.7 + 0.15$$
$$= 4.85\%; and$$

(3) *the producer's contract interest rate of 6 per cent is within 700 basis points of the 4.85 per cent yield on the comparable federal government debt obligation; therefore, none of the producer's interest costs are considered to be non-allowable interest costs for purposes of the definition* **non-allowable interest costs** *in subsection 1(1) of these Regulations.*

"Example" Illustrating the Application of the Method for Calculating Non-allowable Interest Costs in the Case of a Variable-rate Contract

The following example is based on the figures set out in the tables below and on the following assumptions:

(a) a producer in a USMCA country borrows $1,000,000 from a person of the same USMCA country under a variable-rate contract;

(b) under the terms of the contract, the loan is payable in 10 years with interest paid at the rate of 6 per cent per year for the first two years and 8 per cent per year for the next two years on the principal balance, with rates adjusted each two years after that;

(c) the payment schedule calculated by the lender based on the terms of the contract requires the producer to make annual payments of principal and interest of $135,867.96 for the first two years of the loan, and of $146,818.34 for the next two years of the loan;

(d) there are no federal government debt obligations that have maturities equal to the 1.9-year weighted average principal maturity of the first two years of the contract;

(e) there are no federal government debt obligations that have maturities equal to the 1.9-year weighted average principal maturity of the third and fourth years of the contract; and

(f) the federal government debt obligations that are nearest in maturity to the weighted average principal maturity of the contract are 1- and 2-year maturities, and the yields on them are 3.0 per cent and 3.5 per cent respectively.

Beginning of Year	Principal Balance	Interest Rate (%)	Interest Payment	Principal Payment	Payment Schedule	Weighted Principal Payment
1	$1,000,000.00	6.00	$60,000.00	$75,867.96	$135,867.96	$75,867.96
2	924,132.04	6.00	55,447.92	80,420.04	135,867.96	1,848,264.08
						$1,924,132.04

Weighted Average Principal Maturity

$1,924,132.04 / $1,000,000 = 1.92413204 or 1.9 years

By applying the above method:

(1) *the weighted average principal maturity of the payment schedule of the first two years of the contract is 1.9 years;*

(2) *the yield on the closest maturities of federal government debt obligations of 1 year and 2 years are 3.0 and 3.5 per cent, respectively; therefore, using linear interpolation, the yield on a federal government debt obligation that has a maturity equal to the*

weighted average principal maturity of the payment schedule of the first two years of the contract is 3.45 per cent. This amount is calculated as follows:

3.0 + [((3.5 – 3.0) × (1.9 – 1.0)) / (2.0 – 1.0)];
= 3.0 + 0.45
= 3.45%; and

(3) the producer's contract rate of 6 per cent for the first two years of the loan is within 700 basis points of the 3.45 per cent yield on federal government debt obligations that have maturities equal to the 1.9-year weighted average principal maturity of the payment schedule of the first two years of the producer's loan contract; therefore, none of the producer's interest costs are considered to be non-allowable interest costs for purposes of the definition **non- allowable interest costs** in subsection 1(1) of these Regulations.

Beginning of Year	Principal Balance	Interest Rate (%)	Interest Payment	Principal Payment	Payment Schedule	Weighted Principal Payment
1	$1,000,000.00	6.00	$60,000.00	$75,867.96	$135,867.96	
2	924,132.04	6.00	55,447.92	80,420.04	135,867.96	
3	843,712.01	8.00	67,496.96	79,321.38	146,818.34	$79,321.38
4	764,390.62	8.00	61,151.25	85,667.09	146,818.34	1,528,781.24
						$1,608,102.62

Weighted Average Principal Maturity

$1,608,102.62 / $843,712.01 = 1.905985 or 1.9 years

By applying the above method:

(1) the weighted average principal maturity of the payment schedule under the first two years of the contract is 1.9 years;
(2) the federal government debt obligations that are nearest in maturities to the weighted average principal maturity of the contract are 1- and 2-year maturities, and the yields on them are 3.0 and 3.5 per cent, respectively; therefore, using linear interpolation, the yield on a federal government debt obligation that has a maturity equal to the weighted average principal maturity of the payment schedule of the first two years of the contract is 3.45 per cent. This amount is calculated as follows:

3.0 + [((3.5 – 3.0) × (1.9 – 1.0)) / (2.0 – 1.0)];
= 3.0 + 0.45
= 3.45%

(3) the producer's contract interest rate, for the third and fourth years of the loan, of 8 per cent is within 700 basis points of the 3.45 per cent yield on federal government debt obligations that have maturities equal to the 1.9-year weighted average principal maturity of the payment schedule under the third and fourth years of the producer's loan contract; therefore, none of the producer's interest costs are considered to be non-allowable interest costs for purposes of the definition **non-allowable interest costs** in subsection 1(1) of these Regulations.

Schedule X (Generally Accepted Accounting Principles)

1 Generally Accepted Accounting Principles means the recognized consensus or substantial authoritative support in the territory of a USMCA country with respect to the recording of revenues, expenses, costs, assets and liabilities, disclosure of information and preparation of financial statements. These standards may be broad guidelines of general application as well as detailed standards, practices and procedures.

2 For purposes of Generally Accepted Accounting Principles, the recognized consensus or authoritative support are referred to or set out in the following publications:

(a) with respect to the territory of Canada, *The Chartered Professional Accountants of Canada Handbook*, as updated from time to time;

(b) with respect to the territory of Mexico, *Los Principios de Contabilidad Generalmente Aceptados*, issued by the *Instituto Mexicano de Contadores Públicos A.C. (IMCP)*, including the *boletines complementarios*, as updated from time to time; and

(c) *with respect to the territory of the United States, Financial Accounting Standards Board (FASB) Accounting Standards Codification and any interpretive guidance recognized by the American Institute of Certified Public Accountants (AICPA).*